CONNECTING ELITES AND REGIONS

Sidestone Press

CONNECTING ELITES AND REGIONS

Perspectives on contacts, relations and differentiation during the Early Iron Age Hallstatt C period in Northwest and Central Europe

edited by
Robert Schumann &
Sasja van der Vaart-Verschoof

A publication of the Institute for Pre- and Protohistoric Archaeology (Institut für Vor- und Frühgeschichtliche Archäologie) of the University of Hamburg and the Department for European Prehistory of the Faculty of Archaeology of Leiden University

Published by Sidestone Press, Leiden
www.sidestone.com

Lay-out & cover design: Sidestone Press
Illustration cover: Photograph of burial X/2 of Mitterkirchen: M. Pertlwieser, Upper Austrian State Museum, with kind permission of J. Leskovar. Photograph of Wijchen linchpin by J. van Donkersgoed.

ISBN 978-90-8890-442-4 (softcover)
ISBN 978-90-8890-443-1 (hardcover)
ISBN 978-90-8890-444-8 (PDF e-book)

Published with financial support of the Hamburg Scientific Foundation (Hamburgische Wissenschaftliche Stiftung), the Department for European Prehistory of the Faculty of Archaeology, Leiden University and a PhD in the Humanities (PGW-12-07) grant awarded to the second editor by the Netherlands Organisation for Scientific Research (NWO)

Contents

Preface

The Early Iron Age Hallstatt C period in Northwest and Central Europe is marked by the emergence of monumental tumuli with lavish burials, some of which are known as chieftains' or princely graves. This new burial rite reflects the beginning of one of the most noteworthy developments in Early Iron Age Europe: the rise of a new and elaborate way of elite representation north of the Alps. These sumptuous burials contain beautiful weaponry, bronze vessels and extravagantly decorated wagons and horse-gear. They reflect long-distance connections in material culture and elite (burial) practices across vast parts of Europe. Research into this period, however, tends to be regionally focused and poorly accessible to scholars from other areas – language barriers in particular are a hindering factor.

In an attempt to start to overcome this, we organized an international workshop at Leiden University on the 19-20 November 2015 as a joint project of the Faculty of Archaeology of Leiden University and the Institute for Pre- and Protohistoric Archaeology of the University of Hamburg. Some 40 archaeologists from ten nations gathered for two days to discuss 22 presented papers. This volume is the next step in our attempt to connect scholars and different regions of the early Hallstatt period, to discuss similarities and differences, to present current research and debates in parts of Europe and to re-emphasize the discussion on large-scale interdependencies and social differentiation during the Ha C period throughout Europe.

Connecting Elites and Regions brings together scholars from several research traditions and nations who present regional overviews and discussions of elite burials and material culture from all over Northwest and Central Europe. Most contributions in this volume take a classic approach with a clear focus on burial archaeology, which reflects the state of research into the period. In many cases these are the first overviews available in English and together they make regional research accessible to a wider audience. As such this volume contributes to and hopes to stimulate research on the Early Iron Age Hallstatt C period on a European scale. The chronological perspective in this volume is, of course, not solely on what is discussed as being Ha C or the 8th and first half of the 7th century BC in absolute terms. Some papers look into the preceding Late Bronze Age and others into the following later Hallstatt period as well. Especially the phase Ha D1 can, in many regions, not be separated from Ha C and is also discussed in several papers. The majority of the contributions presented here were papers held at the workshop in Leiden, to which we added some contributions. While the current volume does not claim to be an exhaustive study of this period and may have some geographical, methodological and thematical gaps, we hope that the mix of mostly regional studies can contribute to reemphasize discussions about Ha C on a supra-regional level and serve as a stimulus for further research.

Our efforts to organize the workshop and publish this volume as well as our general archaeological works were in every stage supported by our supervisors, David Fontijn and Harry Fokkens (Leiden) and Carola Metzner-Nebelsick (Munich), and we are grateful for their never-wavering encouragement and support. We also wish to thank the Department for Prehistory of the Faculty of Archaeology, the Hamburgische Wissenschaftliche Stiftung and the NWO for their financial support of both the workshop and the current publication. Our gratitude goes to all participants of the workshop and especially the speakers for creating a really stimulating atmosphere at and contributing to our discussions and understanding of the 8th and 7th centuries BC throughout Europe. We thank the authors who contributed to this volume as well as the publishing house for their work and patience during the editing process. Lastly, the editing of this volume was done while both editors became parents, and we thank our families for their understanding, support, patience and love.

Hamburg and Leiden, Spring 2017

Robert Schumann and Sasja van der Vaart-Verschoof

Differentiation and globalization in Early Iron Age Europe

Reintegrating the early Hallstatt period (Ha C) into the debate

Sasja van der Vaart-Verschoof

and Robert Schumann

Abstract

This paper discusses aspects of social structures of Early Iron Age societies and large-scale interaction in the early Hallstatt period between the Low Countries and the Hallstatt culture. In contrast to the later Hallstatt period and the Late Bronze Age, such contacts and societal differentiation are seldom discussed for the early Hallstatt period. Even though this period may have been organized on a more regional level in terms of culture groups and archaeologically traceable remnants of social interaction, underlying large-scale interactions are still visible as is evidence of social differentiation, especially in the burial practice. The burials of Oss in the Netherlands are the starting point to illustrate such interactions throughout Europe using the well-known Hallstatt imports in these burials as the first indicator of large-scale interactions. Furthermore, current research on burials both in the Low Countries and Central Europe allow more detailed insights into these burials and a comparison of the burial practices in these regions shows – among expected differences due to the regional embedment of burial rites – clear similarities in these, e.g. in the reuse of burial mounds, pars pro toto depositions and the wrapping of grave goods. These similarities indicate that it is more than just the objects that were traded throughout Europe and that there were shared underlying ideas of how these people were to be buried.

Zusammenfassung

In diesem Beitrag werden Aspekte der sozialen Strukturierung ältereisenzeitlicher Gesellschaften angesprochen und die älterhallstattzeitlichen Kontakte zwischen den Benelux-Ländern und der Hallstattkultur in Zentraleuropa thematisiert. Im Gegensatz zur jüngeren Hallstattzeit und zur späten Bronzezeit werden großräumige Kontakte und soziale Differenzierung für die ältere Hallstattzeit (Ha C) nur selten diskutiert. Auch wenn die ältere Hallstattzeit im Hinblick auf kulturelle Gruppierungen und archäologisch nachweisbare Interaktionen sozialer Gruppen deutlich regionaler organisiert sein dürfte, zeigen sich großräumige Interaktionen ebenso wie Nachweise sozialer Differenzierung, insbesondere in den Bestattungssitten. Die Bestattungen von Oss in den Niederlanden werden dabei als Ausgangspunkt genommen, derartige Kontakte in Europa zu thematisieren, wobei die bekannten wohl aus der Hallstattkultur importierten Grabbeigaben den ersten Hinweis auf entsprechende Interaktionen darstellen. Zudem erlauben aktuelle Forschungen zu ältereisenzeitlichen Bestattungen in den Benelux-Ländern ebenso wie in Zentraleuropa deutlich intensivere Einblicke in das Bestattungswesen und der Vergleich der Bestattungssitten zwischen diesen Regionen zeigt – neben den zu erwartenden Unterschieden aufgrund der regionalen Einbindung der jeweiligen Bestattungssitten – deutliche Gemeinsamkeiten. Diese offenbaren sich beispielsweise in der Nachnutzung von älteren Grabhügeln, pars pro toto-Beigaben oder dem Verhüllen und Einwickeln von Grabbeigaben in Textil. Diese Gemeinsamkeiten deuten darauf hin, dass in der älteren Hallstattzeit nicht nur die Objekte durch Europa verhandelt wurden, sondern dass diesen Bestattungen gemeinsame Ideen zugrunde liegen, wie derartige Personen bestattet werden sollten.

Social differentiation in the Early Iron Age

The Early Iron Age of southern Central Europe is one of the best-known prehistoric periods in Europe when it comes to the themes of social differentiation and large-scale contacts. This is mostly due to the prominent position the princely seats and elite burials of the Later Hallstatt period (Ha D) take in research on later Prehistory in temperate Europe. The residents and assumed leaders of the communities of those princely seats – *i.e.* the people buried in the ostentatious graves – are seen as elites representing social differentiation on a scale unknown in earlier times (Brun 1987; Krausse 2006).

Concepts of inherited status and early dynastic systems are frequently discussed for the later 7th to the 5th centuries BC. These reconstructions of social systems, however, have been debated and criticized and a consensus on the nature of Hallstatt societies seems out of reach (see Schier 2010). The ideas presented in this paper – and mostly throughout this volume – are based on the assumption that certain differences in the burial ritual and especially in the composition of grave goods can indicate social distinction and can therefore be a starting point for reconstructions of social differentiation. For the later Hallstatt period the increasing contact with the Mediterranean plays a key role in the debate on large-scale communication. The foundation of the Greek colony of Massalia marks a starting point for an increasing distribution of associated finds in the western Hallstatt culture. In the research tradition of the second half of the 20th century this contact was seen as a major catalyst for increasing social differentiation in Early Iron Age communities north of the Alps (*e.g.* Kimmig 1983), although this interpretation has been debated in the last few decades (*e.g.* Eggert 1991). Nowadays indigenous developments are emphasized, rather than the importance of contact with the Mediterranean (Krausse 2006). In short, the Later Hallstatt period is a well-known example of social differentiation and large-scale contacts in European Prehistory.

This, however, does not hold true for the early Hallstatt period (Ha C), roughly the 8th and the first half of the 7th centuries BC. The early Hallstatt period is often only seen as the phase leading up the Later Hallstatt period and is rarely analyzed on its own. Large-scale contacts and social differentiation in southern Central Europe during this time in particular are seldom discussed (see *e.g.* Schußmann 2012; Schumann 2015 for exceptions). In those instances where research into this period is conducted, it is done so mostly on a regional level, dominated by single site analyses and other regionally focused projects. A number of factors may explain the difference, such as the less developed contacts with the Mediterranean world or the nature of the burial rituals – including the composition of the grave goods – during the early Hallstatt period that make social analyses far more difficult than during the Later Hallstatt period. The poor state of research on settlements from the Ha C period, which never seem to match the later so-called princely seats in terms of size and structures, likely also plays a role. Nevertheless, social differentiation can be observed in the burials, finds and settlements (*e.g.*

Parzinger 1992; Schußmann 2012) and shows a clear continuity throughout the Hallstatt period in the western Hallstatt circle, especially in the burial sphere. These were recently interpreted as continuities in the system of status symbols and social organization (Schumann 2015). So if the nature of the burial data is used for concepts of social distinction and differentiation in the later Hallstatt period in the western Hallstatt circle, then shared aspects in the burial rituals from the Early to the Late Hallstatt period – like the use of wagons, weapons and drinking vessels as grave goods – justify the argument that early Hallstatt communities were differentiated in similar ways as well. Still the settlement structures in the later Hallstatt period with the princely seats indicate a far more distinct social differentiation than in the early Hallstatt period. So the depth of the differentiation might be up for discussion, but we still find shared concepts of social distinction in the burials that indicate shared ideas of social systems.

If we look further to the east, urbanization processes and high social hierarchies can be observed in the eastern parts of the early Hallstatt culture, especially in the Dolenjska region in Slovenia, testified by large hillforts and burial mounds with ostentatious burials like in Stična (see Teržan 2008 for several aspects of Early Iron Age Stična). Interestingly, similar concepts of social differentiation are discussed here as in the later western Hallstatt culture (see Dular/Tecco Hvala 2007 for an opposing view to Teržan 2008), so again one must discuss the nature of early Hallstatt societies here.

Yet still the earlier Hallstatt period plays only a minor role in discussions on social differentiation and large-scale contacts throughout Europe. In this paper we aim to reemphasize and refocus the debate on these topics in the 8th and 7th centuries BC by considering concepts of distinction and ancient globalization as exemplified by ostentatious burials from the Low Countries (see also Bourgeois/ Van der Vaart-Verschoof, De Mulder, Jansen/Van der Vaart-Verschoof and Warmenbol, all in this volume) to southern Germany (see also Fernandez-Götz/ Arnold in this volume), Austria (see also Egg in this volume) and Bohemia (see also Trefný in this volume). The case study presented exemplifies the need for a focused debate on early Hallstatt societies, but the themes discussed and arguments given can also be applied on a larger scale and to other areas of Early Iron Age Europe (as is also done in the course of this volume).

In the following we argue that these graves indicate shared concepts and meanings underlying the material culture that connect them. For it is our opinion that the reintegration of the early Hallstatt period into the debate on social distinction and large-scale contacts will not only lead to a better understanding of the early Hallstatt period itself but also advance our understanding of long-term developments in the Late Bronze and Early Iron Ages.

Large-scale contacts as ancient globalization

In archaeology large-scale contacts are generally and most frequently recognized by a shared material culture and through the identification of imports from far-flung reaches. While researchers may speculate whether such communities shared more than material culture or whether there were common customs, practices and ideas over large parts of Europe, it is notoriously difficult to empirically establish such things. Elsewhere one of us argued that globalization theory could offer insights into how one may tackle this problem.

D. Fontijn and S. van der Vaart-Verschoof (2016) argue that if it can be established that there is coherence in the treatment of objects between distant communities that this could help determine whether elite identities (believed to be represented in the elaborate Ha C burials) were globalized. Within the globalization debate it is 'networks of practices' (Brown/Duguid 2000) rather than 'networks of objects' that matter. Determining whether there were shared practices would be an empirically verifiable method to recognize the 'shared codes of conduct' that J. Jennings (2016) for example recently recognized as one of the characteristics of globalized behavior.

Connected communities must have a cultural conceptualization of the non-local other and an awareness of the distant people and communities that they have affinities with in order to be considered 'globalized' (*cf.* Steger 2003, 13). For as M. Helms (1993, 13-27) argued, 'distance' is primarily a 'cultural creation'. She furthermore demonstrates how conceptualizations of the foreign sometimes can be traced back to narratives and cosmologies based on or influenced by the travels of real people (Helms 1993, 28-51), although she also notes that imported objects can form the basis for the perception of the far-off societies (Helms 1993, 114). Objects 'do things' to people through their material and visual characteristics (Garrow/Gosden 2012, 25) and have, to a certain extent, agency within society (Gell 1992, 43).

However, it is not only what objects 'were made to be' that is important, it is also 'what they have become' (Thomas 1991, 84; also Diepeveen-Jansen 2001, 12). The cultural valuation of objects is not solely based on their physical and visual qualities. The way they are treated is also of importance as value and meaning "emerge in action" (Graeber 2001, 45). The manner in which people treat and interact with objects is important and may be fundamental to how they came to understand them (*cf.* Schatzki 1996). For this reason we discuss the similarities both in grave goods and the treatment of them and the dead in a number of distant, but in our opinion connected, elite burials.

From Oss to Otzing: connecting early Hallstatt ostentatious burials

When it comes to social differentiation and large-scale contacts during the early Hallstatt period several sites and regions can be discussed (and many are in the following chapters). Apart from the sites in the southeastern Alpine area already mentioned, like the Dolenjska region or Carinthia, Hallstatt itself is of course a major site offering insights into large-scale contacts during the early Hallstatt period and into social differentiation of a burial community (see also Glunz-Hüsken in this volume). O. Dörrer (2002), for example, discussed possible connections to the northeastern Alpine region based on observations of a burial inventory in Hallstatt that point towards the organization of the prehistoric salt trade from Hallstatt. Several distribution maps of distinctive finds also hint at such things, as clearly illustrated for example by the distribution of early Hallstatt helmets in the eastern Hallstatt regions (Egg *et al.* 1998). New integrated research approaches will add further nuance to the picture we can draw in Hallstatt on the topics mentioned here and will clearly reemphasize the role of Hallstatt in the debate.

In the following we focus on a number of elite burials of the early Hallstatt period covering a large geographical area from the Low Countries to Central Europe, where we focus primarily on southern Germany, but also consider finds from the Czech Republic and Austria. Thereby we want to show the interactions between these burials and regions by considering both the grave goods and the burial rituals. The graves of the Low Countries make a good starting point and case study in this respect for they are seldom discussed in large-scale interactions in Iron Age Europe at least from a Central European perspective, despite the clear connection that the burial goods represent.

This concentration of graves with Hallstatt culture imports in the Low Countries are not only an interesting case study in their own right (see Bourgeois/ Van der Vaart-Verschoof in this volume; Jansen/Van der Vaart-Verschoof in this volume; Van der Vaart-Verschoof forthcoming), they also offer a unique research opportunity with regard to considerations of large-scale contact and social differentiation in the Hallstatt C period. For these burials form a distinct concentration of elite graves that not only contain grave goods imported from the Hallstatt culture, we argue that they also appear to share some customs and practices with Hallstatt culture elite burials found in the regions north of the Alps. We primarily focus on the Chieftain's burial of Oss due to its outstanding role in the Early Iron Age of the Low Countries (see also Jansen/Van der Vaart-Verschoof this volume), and as it is the best suited to discuss large-scale interactions in comparison to two burials in southern Germany both in respect to the objects themselves as well as for the practices. As discussed above, this implies that more than objects were traveling to the Low Countries, and that we may be dealing with 'globalized' communities. Importantly, the lack of Hallstatt culture finds in the area between the Low Countries and the Hallstatt culture region implies there was likely direct contact between these regions, rather than down-the-line exchange (Van der Vaart-Verschoof forthcoming). Figure 1 shows the (burial) sites discussed in this paper.

Oss

The Chieftain's burial of Oss is an iconic archaeological find from the Prehistory of the Netherlands and one of the most elaborate burials with Hallstatt culture imports in the Low Countries. Not only has it repeatedly triggered archaeological investigations in the 80 years since its discovery (Fokkens/Jansen 2004; Holwerda 1934; Jansen/Fokkens 2007; Modderman 1964; Fokkens *et al.* 2012; Van der Vaart-Verschoof forthcoming), it remains a site (known as Oss-Vorstengraf) of local significance to both the Dutch people and residents of the Oss area in particular. Recent art projects, such as the creation of a sand sculpture of the Chieftain at a sand sculpture festival or a recreation of the Chieftain's burial by local D. Beelen in Lego (available on YouTube) testify to the significance this find still holds (Fig. 2).

The Chieftain of Oss was a man in his 30s or 40s when he died. His remains were cremated and placed in a bronze situla together with the dismantled bronze and iron remains of a yoke, two bridles with iron horse-bits and bronze trappings, an iron knife and axe, dress pins, a ribbed wooden bowl, two razors, precious textiles, animal bones from food offerings and a Mindelheim sword with gold-inlayed hilt that was intentionally bent round (Fig. 3). The cinerary urn thus

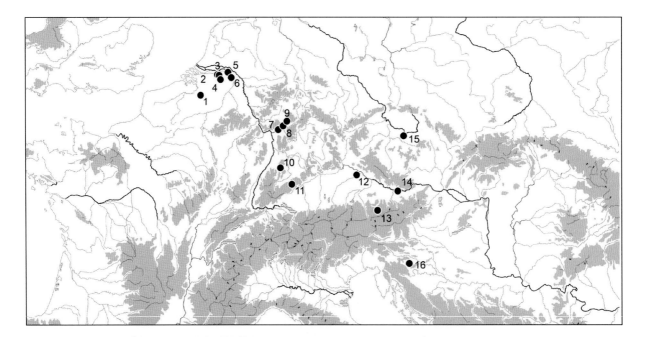

created was buried in a Bronze Age barrow in an existing cemetery (see fig. 2 in Jansen/Van der Vaart-Verschoof in this volume) and covered with the largest barrow in this part of Europe, some 53 m in diameter (see Van der Vaart-Verschoof forthcoming for more details).

While some of the Chieftain's grave goods were likely locally created, such as the axe and dress pins, others are interpreted as imports from the Hallstatt culture area. The famous sword, for example, has its closest parallels in the swords found at Gomadingen (Baden-Württemberg, Germany; see also Fernandez-Götz/Arnold this volume) and one of the swords from Hallstatt grave 573 (Upper Austria; Kromer 1959). They may even all have been made by the same master smith or workshop which was likely located in southern Germany or Upper Austria (Van der Vaart-Verschoof forthcoming). The situla and ribbed bowl have close parallels in finds from Frankfurt-Stadtwald discussed below. The extraordinary textiles that were used both to wrap grave goods and were also deposited as a grave good in their own right have close parallels in textiles from Central Europe and Italy and are likely imports from one of these regions (see Grömer in this volume and Grömer in Van der Vaart-Verschoof forthcoming). The horse-gear and yoke components would not look out of place in any Hallstatt culture grave.

The Chieftain of Oss, however, is not the only elite individual to be buried at Oss. A second Ha C elite burial was found not 500 m away in Mound 7 of Oss-Zevenbergen. Here a young man was cremated on top of a rounded dune. This natural mound was located in an existing barrow row and may have been interpreted as an ancestral barrow by the Early Iron Age mourners (see fig. 3 in Jansen/Van der Vaart-Verschoof in this volume). A dismantled bronze-studded yoke lay by the pyre as it burned. Following cremation, the burned out pyre was searched through. The majority of the man's cremated remains were collected and buried in an urn by the pyre, with some cremation remains being intentionally left behind in the pyre. The leather yoke panels with bronze decorations were pushed to one side and left there. At least one bronze ring, likely from the yoke, was broken and one fragment placed back among the burned out pyre, while the

Fig. 1. Hallstatt period sites discussed in this paper.
1: Court-St.-Etienne. –
2: Oss-Vorstengraf. –
3: Oss-Zevenbergen. –
4: Uden-Slabroek. –
5: Wijchen. – 6: Haps. –
7: Frankfurt-Stadtwald. –
8: Nidderau. – 9: Glauberg. –
10: Hochdorf. –
11: Gomadingen. –
12: Otzing. – 13: Hallstatt. –
14: Mitterkirchen. –
15: Hradenín. – 16: Stična.

Fig. 2. Sand sculpture created in Oss (photograph by S. van der Vaart-Verschoof).

Fig. 3. (Most of) the grave goods from the Chieftain's burial of Oss (photograph kindly provided by the National Museum of Antiquities, Leiden).

Fig. 4. The horse-gear and yoke from the Oss burials in (a romantic) reconstruction. Note that the stud-decorated chest-strap was found in Oss-Zevenbergen Mound 7 while the other metal components were found in the Chieftain's burial at Oss-Vorstengraf (drawing by I. Gelman).

other was removed (Fig. 4; see also fig. 3 in Jansen/Van der Vaart-Verschoof in this volume). The whole assemblage was then covered with a large barrow, 36 m in diameter (see Fontijn *et al.* 2013 for more details).

The bronze studs recovered here once decorated a wooden yoke and leather yoke panels that would have looked extremely similar to yokes in Hallstatt culture burials. In fact, it was viewing the yokes from Frankfurt-Stadtwald and Otzing that helped confirm the interpretation of the Zevenbergen Mound 7 bronze studs as the remains of a yoke (Fontijn/Van der Vaart 2013; see also Fernandez-Götz/ Arnold in this volume).

At present the finds from both burials can be viewed in the National Museum of Antiquities in Leiden where they take center-stage in the permanent exhibition on the Archaeology of the Netherlands.

Frankfurt-Stadtwald

The well-known *Fürstengrab* of Frankfurt-Stadtwald is not only geographically one of the closest Ha C elite burials to the Oss graves, it is also one of the closest parallels in terms of grave goods. This early Hallstatt ostentatious burial was excavated in the 1960s and became famous in the archaeology of the Early Iron Age due to its outstanding grave goods and good preservation (Fischer 1979;

Willms 2002). The deceased was buried in a Bronze Age burial mound that was enlarged to 36 m in diameter in the course of the Early Iron Age burial (Fischer 1979, 45). The inhumed individual was given a large set of exceptional grave goods, including a large bronze Mindelheim sword with a chape, bronze and pottery vessels (including a bronze ribbed bowl), a richly decorated yoke and horse-gear for two horses, animal bones as the remnants of food along with a large knife, clothing pins and a set of toiletry items in a leather pouch with an amber bead (Fig. 5).

As discussed above, this burial has many similarities to the Chieftain's burial of Oss. They both yielded bronze situlae, ribbed drinking bowls, Mindelheim swords, butchering knives, animal bones from food offerings, similar horse-gear and yokes, as well as textile. The yokes from Frankfurt-Stadtwald and Oss-Zevenbergen were both decorated with bronze studs (though of a different type). Moreover, a similar toilet kit and amber bead and dress pin with ring was found in the Dutch burial of Uden-Slabroek (Jansen *et al.* 2011; Bourgeois/Van der Vaart-Verschoof and Jansen/Van der Vaart-Verschoof, both in this volume). The chape from Frankfurt-Stadtwald matches a fragment found at Court-St-Etienne in Belgium. So overall there are many similarities in grave goods between this *Fürstengrab* and the burials of the Low Countries.

Otzing

A recently excavated burial located even further into Hallstatt culture territory is our last example. The burial of Otzing in Lower Bavaria was investigated in rescue excavations in 2010. In the course of the excavation it became evident that the burial was exceptional in several regards and a block lifting was conducted by the Archaeological State Collection Munich (*Archäologische Staatssammlung München*) in 2011 (Claßen *et al.* 2013; Gebhard *et al.* 2015). The burial block (Fig. 6) has been under investigation in the Museum laboratories in Munich ever since. This work has revealed a truly astonishing early Hallstatt period ensemble that will not only stimulate research on Ha C burials but will also form an important exhibition piece for the museum.

In the burial chamber (ca. 3.6 x 3.6 m) the inhumated remains of a man were found lying on a wooden furniture richly decorated with bronze studs (probably a wagon box). His other grave goods included a large set of pottery, one bronze vessel, a yoke and leather horse-gear panels all decorated with bronze studs and plaques, an iron dagger with decorated sheath and belt, two iron spearheads, animal bones, several tools and pins as parts of the costume.

Again the burial of Otzing can be seen in a large regional context concerning the analyses of the finds. The furniture finds its best comparison in a similar find from Mitterkirchen in Upper Austria (Pertlwieser 1987, 60). The weaponry already resembles typical weapon sets of the Later Hallstatt period in the western Hallstatt circle and beyond, with a similar dagger for example being found in the Dutch burial of Haps. And again, of course, the yoke warrants discussion in the context of other ostentatious burials of the earlier Hallstatt period. Besides the already mentioned burial of Frankfurt-Stadtwald and Oss-Zevenbergen, the best parallels come from Bohemia. Here, several well-known graves of the Bylany group were excavated in the early 20th century (Dvořák 1938), some of which yielded yokes with bronze studs and plates in geometrical patterns. Especially the

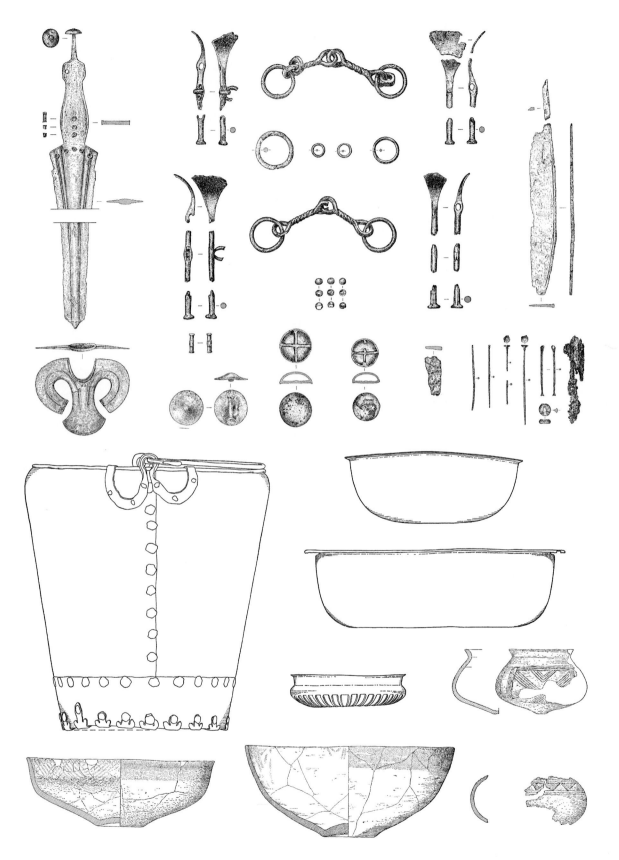

Fig. 5. The grave goods of the Fürstengrab of Frankfurt-Stadtwald (after Fischer 1979, pl. 7-12; Archäologisches Museum Frankfurt).

decorated leather straps of Otzing match the finds of those sites, of which the slightly later Hradenín is probably the best known (Fig. 7).

Similarities in grave goods

The similarities in grave goods between the burials of Oss, Frankfurt-Stadtwald and Otzing discussed above are striking, and they are only the tip of the iceberg. They all (as well as many other burials both in the Low Countries and the Hallstatt culture area) yielded drinking and feasting vessels, weaponry, horse-gear and wagons (or components thereof), tools, ornaments and toiletries, with a number of objects appearing virtually identical. The situlae from Oss and Frankfurt-Stadtwald, for example, are very similar and both were accompanied by ribbed bowls. Both graves also contained Mindelheim type swords. The decoration on the Otzing and Oss yokes is also extremely similar.

Fig. 6. The Otzing burial (St. Friedrich, Archäologische Staatssammlung München).

The similarity in horse-gear and yokes in particular has long since been recognized, as indicated by their presence on distribution maps of wagon, yoke and horse-gear components (Koch 2006; Pare 1992; Trachsel 2004). Their presence testifies to an area of communication mostly between Bohemia and Southern Germany in Ha C/D1, sometimes extending into remote areas such as the Low Countries. This area of communication is naturally situated in other, partly overlapping communication axes and the finds from the Low Countries illustrate this.

Fig. 7. The yokes from Hradenín (after Dvořák 1938, 23 fig. 20-21).

More than objects: similarities (and differences) in burial practice

Whereas the similarities in the objects have been long documented in different distribution maps and typological analyses, discussions of the burial rituals through which these burials were created offer interesting insights, for among several differences, there are also similarities in practice.

Firstly, for example, both the Chieftain of Oss and the deceased of Frankfurt were buried in older barrows with new mound phases added (and it is possible the mourners at Oss-Zevenbergen Mound 7 thought they were doing the same thing). Even though the reuse of ancient tumuli is a well-known habit in the Early Iron Age (see *e.g.* Müller-Scheeßel 2013 for Southern Germany), the similarity between Oss and Frankfurt-Stadtwald in this respect may not be a pure coincidence (as already noted by Roymans 1991, 57). In every case an ancient mound was reused to bury the elite dead and create impressive new Early Iron Age barrows (36-53 m in diameter).

Another similarity in practice is the placing of a toilet kit in some kind of pouch on the chest of the deceased. This was the case at the Dutch burial of Slabroek (Jansen *et al.* 2011; Bourgeois/Van der Vaart-Verschoof and Jansen/ Van der Vaart-Verschoof both in this volume), Frankfurt, Otzing and the later example of Hochdorf. In the case of Frankfurt, Slabroek and Otzing the toilet kits all appear to have been located in pouches that closed with an amber bead.

The use of textile during the burial ritual is also a shared practice. In the Chieftain's burial of Oss a number of objects were wrapped in high quality cloths (that themselves were most likely imports from Central Europe) during the burial ritual, like the sword, some horse-gear and the knife (Grömer in Van der Vaart-Verschoof forthcoming; see also Grömer in this volume). The use of textile to wrap grave goods is a known feature of Hallstatt culture burials, with wrapped swords for example known from early Hallstatt burials in Southern Germany; of which a find from Nidderau, where the sword was wrapped in at least three layers of textile, is probably the best example (Riedel 2012, 174-176; see Ney in this volume on the sword burials of Nidderau). The best-known example of this burial custom of wrapping the dead and grave goods in textile is probably the *Fürstengrab* of Hochdorf (though it dates later; Banck-Burgess 2014). The same custom is known from the Early La Tène princely burial from the Glauberg (Bartel *et al.* 2002, 163-166). The evidence of this practice in the burial of Oss and the mentioned wrapping of a sword in Nidderau (and other swords from Hallstatt culture burials) adds a diachronic perspective to that phenomenon and connects this burial of the Low Countries to Southern Germany in another respect. Due to the state of research and the burial customs in the early Hallstatt period in Southern Germany this custom is hardly known from Ha C. In the burial of Otzing fragments of textile were recorded (Claßen *et al.* 2013, 207-209) that might hint in this direction, though more research is needed. So again we see aspects of shared burial rites between the burials of the Hallstatt culture and the Low Countries.

There are, however, also differences in practice that demonstrate that the burials were also embedded within the local funerary practices. In the Low Countries the imported grave goods appear to have been re-contextualized in a regionally specific manner through a destructive burial practice that involved the transformation of both the dead and their grave goods through fire, manipulation and fragmentation, as well as placing a greater emphasis on *pars pro toto* depositions (see also Bourgeois/Van der Vaart-Verschoof in this volume). Not only were swords broken, a habit known in early Hallstatt culture burials that can be traced back to the Urnfield period (see *e.g.* Von Quillfeldt 1995, 19; Trachsel 2005, 67-69), they were frequently also bent and folded. In the Low Countries also other objects, like horse-gear, wagon components, tools, ornaments and vessels were intentionally bent and broken, and often burned as well.

The Dutch and Belgian graves also emphasize *pars pro toto* depositions to a much greater degree. While Ch. Pare (1992, 122-123) already noted that linchpins were interred as a *pars pro toto* depositions in several graves in the Hallstatt culture area as well as only parts of wagons being interred, in the Low Countries the dismantled wagon components were frequently bent and broken as well, with only some fragments being interred (and also deliberately keeping certain fragments out of the grave). This is the case also for the other grave goods categories. Fragments from all the important grave goods were selected for burial, while fragments were also frequently taken away.

These differences in treating the objects between the burials in the Low Countries and the Hallstatt culture still show some similarities. While swords were bent and folded in the Low Countries and broken in the Hallstatt culture, the objects in both regions were still intentionally changed and made unusable for the living. The same can be taken into account for the *pars pro toto* depositions. While they differ strongly in the degree of the *pars pro toto* and the execution of this practice, we still can observe the idea of substituting a part for a whole in both regions. So despite the differences in the practices, fragmentation, manipulation and *pars pro toto* still indicate similarities in the burial rituals, even though they were executed in a regional way. It is the similarities in practices that indicate that it was not only objects that moved and were traded between the Hallstatt culture and the Low Countries in the Early Iron Age. The similarities in practices show interactions on a larger scale, which might indicate shared ideas, a knowing of how objects were to be treated in the burial ritual as well as a shared identity of the burying communities and the buried in the mentioned burials.

Outlook

The case studies presented in this paper are some of the most striking examples of large-scale interactions in Ha C Europe from the Low Countries to the northern fringes of the Alps, though there are numerous other groups of finds, parts of the burial rituals or sites that could be discussed. The burials of Oss, Frankfurt, Otzing and Hradenín illustrate large-scale interactions throughout temperate Europe and beyond. We discussed similarities in the finds themselves, such as the comparable decoration of the yokes or the swords, and looked at aspects of the burial practice to show that while the burial rituals are rooted in local traditions, there are also clear similarities. These include the reuse of ancient monuments as the burial site, the wrapping of the grave goods in textiles, the custom of laying toiletries in a bag closed by an amber bead on the chest of the deceased and *pars pro toto* deposition of grave goods.

The scope could easily be widened by looking at other axes of interaction and other regions. This is clearly illustrated by Mediterranean influences in the regions north of the Alps as testified among other finds by the linchpins of Wijchen with Etruscan-style protomes (Pare 1992, 170-171) or the spit from a burial in Beilngries (Torbrügge 1965; Schußmann 2012, 202). The burial practices of the early Hallstatt period also offer insights into several aspects of social distinction that can be interpreted as expressions of social differentiation. As those aspects clearly resemble the distinction in the burials of the later Hallstatt period, we might see hierarchically structured societies in the earlier Hallstatt period as well (Schumann 2015).

All these aspects illustrate that it was not only objects that were distributed over widespread regions throughout Europe but that ideas associated with such items were shared as well. These ideas were fossilized in the burial rituals and indicate some ancient globalization in the definition given above, by which communities from the Low Countries to the circumalpine region shared ideas of ritual behavior, the manner of social distinction and probably a similar self-awareness and identity as elites (see also Fontijn/Van der Vaart-Verschoof 2016).

Therefore a fruitful debate on social differentiation and large-scale interactions seems warranted and desirable. Between the well-known Late Bronze Age, in which contacts on a European scale have stimulated research ever since, and the Late Hallstatt period, in which the so-called princely seats as symbols for increasing urbanization and differentiation and the increasing contacts with the Mediterranean testify large-scale connections throughout Europe, the early Hallstatt period lived a shadowy existence in the archaeological community. But both in terms of a *longue durée* in later Prehistory and for the sake of Ha C itself, it seems warranted to reintegrate the earlier Hallstatt period into the debate about differentiation and globalization. The mentioned sites testify the eligibility of approaches as presented in this volume.

Acknowledgements

This article was made possible by a NWO "PhDs in the Humanities" grant (no. 322-60-004) awarded to the first author for the project "Constructing powerful identities. The conception and meaning of 'rich' Hallstatt burials in the Low Countries (800-500 BC)".

Bibliography

Banck-Burgess 2014: J. Banck-Burgess, Wrapping as an Element of Early Celtic Burial Customs. In: S. Harris/L. Douny (eds.), Wrapping and unwrapping material culture. Archaeological and anthropological perpectives. Publications of the Institute of Archaeology, University College London (Walnut Creek 2014) 147-156.

Bartel *et al.* 2002: A. Bartel/F. Bodis/M. Bosinski/Th. Flügen/R. Frölich/S. Geilenkeusen/F. Herzig/S. Martins/A. Ulbrich/J. Warnke/P. Will, Bergung, Freilegung und Restaurierung. In: Glaube – Mythos – Wirklichkeit. Das Rätsel der Kelten vom Glauberg (Stuttgart 2002) 132-169.

Brown/Duguid 2000: J. Brown/P. Duguid, Knowledge and organization: A social-practice perspective. Organization Science 2,2, 2000, 198-213.

Brun 1987: P. Brun, Princes et princesses de la celtique. Le premier âge du Fer en Europe 850-450 av. J.-C. (Paris 1987).

Claßen *et al.* 2013: E. Claßen/St. Gussmann/G. von Looz, Regulär und doch außergewöhnlich. Eine hallstattzeitliche Bestattung mit Zuggeschirr von Otzing, Lkr. Deggendorf. In: L. Husty/K. Schmotz (eds.), Vorträge des 31. Niederbayerischen Archäologentages (Rahden/Westf. 2013) 191-214.

Diepeveen-Jansen 2001: M. Diepveen-Jansen, People, ideas and goods. New perspectives on 'celtic barbarians' in Western and Central Europe (500-250 BC). Amsterdam Archaeological Studies 7 (Amsterdam 2001).

Dörrer 2002: O. Dörrer, Das Grab eines nordostalpinen Kriegers in Hallstatt. Zur Rolle von Fremdpersonen in der alpinen Salznekropole. Archaeologia Austriaca 86, 2002, 55-81.

Dular/Tecco Hvala 2007: J. Dular/S. Tecco Hvala, South-Eastern Slovenia in the Early Iron Age. Jugovzhodna Slovenija v starejši železni dobi. Opera Instituti Archaeologici Sloveniae 12 (Ljubljana 2007).

Dvořák 1938: F. Dvořák, Knížecí pohřby na vozech ze starší doby železné. Wagengräber der älteren Eisenzeit in Böhmen. Praehistorica 1 (Prag 1938).

Egg *et al.* 1998: M. Egg/U. Neuhäuser/Ž. Škoberne, Ein Grab mit Schüsselhelm aus Budinjak in Kroatien. Jahrbuch des Römisch-Germanischen Zentralmuseums 45, 1998, 435-472.

Eggert 1991: M. Eggert, Prestigegüter und Sozialstruktur in der Späthallstattzeit: Eine kulturanthropologische Perspektive. In: Urgeschichte als Kulturanthropologie. Beiträge zum 70. Geburtstag von Karl J. Narr. Saeculum 42, 1991, 1-28.

Fernández-Götz/Krausse 2013: M. Fernández-Götz/D. Krausse, Rethinking Early Iron Age urbanisation in Central Europe. The Heuneburg site and its archaeological environment. Antiquity 87,336, 2013, 473-487.

Fischer 1979: U. Fischer, Ein Grabhügel der Bronze- und Eisenzeit im Frankfurter Stadtwald. Mit einem Frankfurter Museumsbericht 1961-1978. Schriften des Frankfurter Museums für Vor- und Frühgeschichte 4 (Frankfurt 1979).

Fokkens/Jansen 2004: H. Fokkens/R. Jansen, Het vorstengraf van Oss. Speurtocht naar een prehistorisch grafveld (Utrecht 2004).

Fokkens et al. 2009:H. Fokkens/R. Jansen/I. van Wijk, Oss-Zevenbergen: de lange termijn-geschiedenis van een prehistorisch grafveld (Alblasserdam 2009).

Fokkens et al. 2012: H. Fokkens/S. Van der Vaart/D. Fontijn/S. Lemmers/R. Jansen/I. Van Wijk/P. Valentijn, Hallstatt burials of Oss in context. In: C. Bakels/H. Kamermans (eds.), The end of our fifth decade. Analecta Praehistorica Leidensia 43/44 (Leiden 2012) 183-204.

Fontijn/Van der Vaart 2013: D. Fontijn/S. van der Vaart, Dismantled, transformed, and deposited – prehistoric bronze from the centre of mound 7. In: D. Fontijn/S. van der Vaart/R. Jansen (eds), Transformation through destruction. A monumental and extraordinary Early Iron Age Hallstatt C barrow from the ritual landscape of Oss-Zevenbergen (Leiden 2013) 151-194.

Fontijn/Van der Vaart-Verschoof 2016: D. Fontijn/S. van der Vaart-Verschoof, Local elites globalized in death: A practice approach to Early Iron Age Hallstatt C/D chieftains' burials in northwest Europe. In: T. Hodos (ed.), The Routledge Handbook of Archaeology and Globalization (London 2016) 522-536.

Fontijn et al. 2013: D. Fontijn/S. van der Vaart/R. Jansen (eds.), Transformation through destruction. A monumental and extraordinary Early Iron Age Hallstatt C barrow from the ritual landscape of Oss-Zevenbergen (Leiden 2013).

Garrow/Gosden 2012: D. Garrow/Ch. Gosden, Technologies of enchantment? Exploring Celtic art: 400 BC to AD 100 (Oxford 2012).

Gebhard et al. 2016: R. Gebhard/C. Metzner-Nebelsick/R. Schumann, Excavating an extraordinary burial of the Early Hallstatt Period from Otzing in Eastern Bavaria in the museum laboratories. PAST 82, 2016, 1-3.

Gell 1992: A. Gell, The technology of enchantment and the enchantment of ,technology'. In: J. Coote/A. Shelton (eds), Anthropology, arts and aesthetics (Oxford 1992) 40-63.

Graeber 2001: D. Graeber, Toward an anthropological theory of value: the false coin of our own dreams (New York 2001).

Grömer in Van der Vaart-Verschoof forthcoming: K. Grömer, Hallstatt period Textile Finds from the Netherlands. In: S. van der Vaart-Verschoof, Fragmenting the Chieftain. A practice-based study of Early Iron Age Hallstatt C elite burials of the Low Countries and their relation to the Hallstatt Culture of Central Europe (forthcoming).

Helms 1993: M. Helms, Craft and the kingly ideal: Art, trade, and power (Austin 1993).

Holwerda 1934: J. Holwerda, Een vroeg Gallish vorstengraf bij Oss (N.B). Oudheidkundige Mededelingen Rijksmuseum van Oudheden Leiden 15, 1934, 39-53.

Jansen/Fokkens 2007: R. Jansen/H. Fokkens, Het vorstengraf van Oss re-reconsidered. Archeologisch onderzoek Oss-Vorstengrafdonk 1997-2005 (Utrecht 2007).

Jansen et al. 2011: R. Jansen/Q. Bourgeois/A. Louwen/C. Van der Linde/I. Van Wijk, Opgraving van het grafveld Slabroekse Heide. In: R. Jansen/K. Van der Laan (eds.) Verleden van een bewogen landschap – Landschaps en bewoningsgeschiedenis van de Maashorst (Utrecht 2011) 104-119.

Jennings 2016: J. Jennings. Distinguishing Past Globalizations. In: T. Hodos (ed.), The Routledge Handbook of Archaeology and Globalization (London 2016) 12-28.

Kimmig 1983: W. Kimmig, Die griechische Kolonisation im westlichen Mittelmeergebiet und ihre Wirkung auf die Landschaften des westlichen Mitteleuropas. Jahrbuch des Römisch-Germanischen Zentralmuseums 30, 1983, 3-80.

Koch 2006: J. Koch, Hochdorf VI. Der Wagen und das Pferdegeschirr aus dem späthallstattzeitlichen Fürstengrab von Eberdingen-Hochdorf (Kr. Ludwigsburg). Forschungen und Berichte zur Vor- und Frühgeschichte in Baden-Württemberg 89 (Stuttgart 2006).

Krausse 2006: D. Krausse, Prunkgräber der nordwestalpinen Späthallstattkultur. Neue Fragestellungen und Untersuchungen zu ihrer sozialhistorischen Deutung. In: C. von Carnap-Bornheim/D. Krausse/A. Wesse (eds.), Herrschaft – Tod – Bestattung. Zu den vor- und frühgeschichtlichen Prunkgräbern als archäologisch-historische Quelle. Internationale Fachkonferenz Kiel, 16.-19. Oktober 2013. Universitätsforschungen zur prähistorischen Archäologie 139 (Bonn 2006) 61-80.

Kromer 1959: K. Kromer, Das Gräberfeld von Hallstatt (Firenze 1959).

Modderman 1964: P. Modderman, The Chieftain's grave of Oss reconsidered. Bulletin van de vereniging tot bevordering der kennis van de antieke beschaving 39, 1964, 57-62.

Müller-Scheeßel 2013: N. Müller-Scheeßel, Untersuchungen zum Wandel hallstattzeitlicher Bestattungssitten in Süd- und Südwestdeutschland. Universitätsforschungen zur prähistorischen Archäologie 245 (Bonn 2013).

Pare 1992: C. Pare, Wagons and wagon-graves of the Early Iron Age in Central Europe. Oxford University Committee for Archaeology, Monographs 35 (Oxford 1992).

Parzinger 1992: H. Parzinger, Zwischen „Fürsten" und „Bauern" – Bemerkungen zu Siedlungsform und Sozialstruktur unter besonderer Berücksichtigung der älteren Eisenzeit. Mitteilungen der Berliner Gesellschaft für Anthropologie, Ethnologie und Urgeschichte 13, 1992, 77-89.

Pertlwieser 1987: M. Pertlwieser, Prunkwagen und Hügelgrab. Frühhallstattzeitliche Wagenbestattungen in Mitterkirchen. Kultur der frühen Eisenzeit von Hallstatt bis Mitterkirchen. Kataloge des Oberösterreichischen Landesmuseums N. F. 13 (Linz 1987).

Von Quillfeldt 1995: I. von Quillfeldt, Die Vollgriffschwerter in Süddeutschland. Prähistorische Bronzefunde IV,11 (Stuttgart 1995).

Riedel 2012: C. Riedel, Ein Schwertträgergrab aus Nidderau-Windecke, Neubaugebiet „Allee Süd IV" – Bericht der Fundrestaurierung eines hallstattzeitlichen Grabinventars. In: B. Ramminger/H. Lasch (eds.), Hunde – Menschen – Artefakte. Gedenkschrift für Gretel Gallay. Internationale Archäologie, Studia honoraria 32 (Rahden/Westf. 2012) 171-179.

Roymans 1991: N. Roymans, Late urnfield societies in the northwest European plain and the expanding networks of central European Hallstatt groups. In: N. Roymans/F. Theuws (eds.), Images of the past: Studies on ancient societies in northwestern Europe (Amsterdam 1991) 9-89.

Schatzki 1996: T. Schatzki, Social practices. A wittgensteinian approach to Human activity and the social (New York 1996).

Schier 2010: W. Schier, Soziale und politische Strukturen der Hallstattzeit. Ein Diskussionsbeitrag. In: D. Krausse (ed.), „Fürstensitze" und Zentralorte der frühen Kelten. Abschlusskolloquium des DFG-Schwerpunktprogramms 1171 in Stuttgart, 12.-15. Oktober 2009. Forschungen und Berichte zur Vor- und Frühgeschichte in Baden-Württemberg 120 (Stuttgart 2010) 375-405.

Schumann 2015: R. Schumann, Status und Prestige in der Hallstattkultur. Aspekte sozialer Distinktion in ältereisenzeitlichen Regionalgruppen zwischen Altmühl und Save. Münchner Archäologische Forschungen 3 (Rahden/Westf. 2015).

Schußmann 2012: M. Schußmann, Siedlungshierarchien und Zentralisierungsprozesse in der Südlichen Frankenalb zwischen dem 9. und 4. Jh. v. Chr. Berliner archäologische Forschungen 11 (Rahden/Westf. 2012).

Steger 2003: M. Steger, Globalization. A very short introduction (Oxford 2003).

Teržan 2008: B. Teržan, Stična – Skizzen. In: St. Gabrovec/B. Teržan, Stična II/2. Gomile starejše železne dobe. Razprave. Grabhügel aus der älteren Eisenzeit. Studien. Katalogi in Monografije 38 (Ljubljana 2008 [2010]) 189-326.

Thomas 1991: N. Thomas, Entangled objects. Exchange, material culture, and colonialism in the Pacific (Cambridge, London 1991).

Torbrügge 1965: W. Torbrügge, Die Hallstattzeit in der Oberpfalz II. Die Funde und Fundplätze in der Gemeinde Beilngries. Materialhefte zur bayerischen Vorgeschichte 20 (Kallmünz/Opf. 1965).

Trachsel 2004: M. Trachsel, Studien zur relativen und absoluten Chronologie der Hallstattzeit. Universitätsforschungen zur prähistorischen Archäologie 104 (Bonn 2004).

Trachsel 2005: M. Trachsel, Kriegergräber? Schwertbeigabe und Praktiken ritueller Bannung in Gräbern der frühen Eisenzeit. In: R. Karl/J. Leskovar (eds.), Interpretierte Eisenzeiten. Fallstudien, Methoden, Theorie. Tagungsbericht der 1. Linzer Gespräche zur interpretativen Eisenzeitarchäologie. Studien zur Kulturgeschichte von Oberösterreich 18 (Linz 2005) 53-82.

Van der Vaart-Verschoof forthcoming: S. van der Vaart-Verschoof, Fragmenting the chieftain. A practice-based study of Early Iron Age Hallstatt C elite burials of the Low Countries and their relation to the Hallstatt Culture of Central Europe (forthcoming).

Willms 2002: Ch. Willms, Der Keltenfürst aus Frankfurt. Macht und Totenkult um 700 v. Chr. Archäologische Reihe 19 (Frankfurt am Main 2002).

Authors

Sasja van der Vaart-Verschoof
Faculty of Archaeology
Leiden University
Postbus 9515
2300 Leiden
The Netherlands
s.a.van.der.vaart@arch.leidenuniv.nl

Robert Schumann
University of Hamburg
Institute for Pre- and Protohistoric
Archaeology
Edmund-Siemers-Allee 1, West
20146 Hamburg
Germany
robert.schumann@uni-hamburg.de

Moravia – a connecting Line between North, West and South

To the supra-regional connections and formation of elites in the early Hallstatt period

Erika Makarová

Abstract

In the Early Iron Age the area of Moravia was divided into two parts, each of which was related to a different cultural sphere. The central and northern part were inhabited by members of the Platěnice culture related to the Lusatian culture complex, while the southern part was settled by the Horákov culture belonging to the eastern Hallstatt culture.

At the beginning of the Early Iron Age, southern Moravia was influenced by the first Hallstatt centres in the west. Soon after, the Horákov culture was influenced also by other regions, mainly from the south, and became an intermediator of these Hallstatt influences to its northern neighbour, the Platěnice culture. Prestige goods as well as new technologies and ideas were spreading through Moravia even more to the north, to Lower Silesia in Poland.

The impact of the Hallstatt environment can be seen mainly in changes of burial practices, including the grave construction and the composition of grave inventories in which increasing social differentiation and formation of local elites is reflected. Grave goods occurring mainly in the extraordinary chamber graves considered 'elite burials' or even 'princely graves', but also in the graves of 'higher middle class' point to the supra-regional connections of the Moravia region with distant areas in the north, west and south.

Zusammenfassung

In der älteren Eisenzeit war das Gebiet Mährens in zwei Bereiche untergliedert, die jeweils einer unterschiedlichen kulturellen Sphäre zugerechnet werden. Der zentrale und nördliche Teil war von der Platěnice Kultur besiedelt, die mit dem Lausitzer Kulturkomplex verwandt ist, wohingegen der südliche Part der Horákov Kultur zuzuweisen ist, die einen Teil der östlichen Hallstattgruppen darstellt.

Zu Beginn der älteren Eisenzeit stand das südliche Mähren unter Einfluss der ersten Hallstattzentren im Westen. Die Horákov Kultur sollte aber bald auch Einflüsse aus anderen Regionen, vor allem dem Süden, aufnehmen und wurde zu einem Vermittler dieser Hallstatteinflüsse in die nördlich angrenzende Region, die zum Siedlungsbereich der Platěnice Kultur zu zählen ist. Prestigegüter, ebenso wie neue Technologien und Innovationen wurden über Mähren bis ins südliche Schlesien in Polen vermittelt.

Die Auswirkung dieser hallstättischen Elemente sind vorrangig in Veränderungen in den Bestattungspraktiken, so der Konstruktion der Gräber und der Komposition der Grabbeigaben, zu sehen, in denen sich eine zunehmende soziale Differenzierung und eine Formierung lokaler Eliten widerspiegelt. Gerade in den Grabbeigaben aus den sogenannten Elite- oder Fürstengräbern, die vorrangig in herausragenden Kammergräbern bestattet wurden, ebenso wie in weiteren gehobenen aber weniger hervorstechenden Bestattungen, zeigen sich die überregionalen, nach Norden, Westen und Süden reichenden Kontakte des heutigen Mährens in der älteren Eisenzeit.

Introduction

The Moravian region, due to its advantageous geographical location between the Danubian and the Oder region, became a crossroad in different periods, including the Early Iron Age. A trade route led through the Brno basin as well as along the Moravia river through the Moravian gate up to the Oder and more to the north. The location of Moravia therefore had a significant impact on its development. While the southern part was tending to the Danubian region, central and northern Moravia was connected more with the Oder region. This trend could be traced from the beginning of the Urnfield period and remained even during the Hallstatt period when the division of the territory into two cultural areas continued. The central and northern part of Moravia was inhabited by the Platěnice culture that was related to the Lusatian culture complex. The southern part was settled by the Horákov culture and it was also inhabited by the Kalenderberg group in the very southern part of Moravia (Břeclav area), both belonged to the East Hallstatt culture (Fig. 1).

Since the beginning of the Early Iron Age the influence of the Hallstatt culture and the supra-regional contacts of both cultural areas were considerable, although not equally intense. The best evidence for that are cemeteries. Change of burial practices and a greater variability of burial customs including the construction of graves and the composition of grave inventories reflect a gradually increasing social differentiation. Building large-dimensional chamber graves equipped with luxury items imported from distant regions points to the rise of local elites. And the Amber road leading through the area of both cultures undoubtedly played an important role in it.

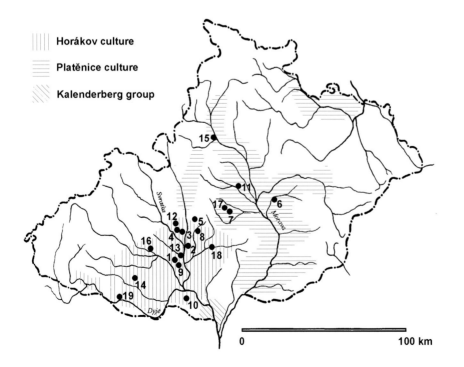

Fig. 1. Map of Moravia in Hallstatt C – D1 showing sites mentioned in the text.
1: Bratčice. – 2: Brno-Holásky. – 3: Brno-Obřany. – 4: Brno-Řečkovice. – 5: Býčí skála. – 6: Dobrčice. – 7: Drysice. – 8: Horákov-Hlásnica. – 9: Hrušovany u Brna. – 10: Klentnice. – 11: Kralice na Hané. – 12: Kuřim. – 13: Modřice. – 14: Morašice. – 15: Moravičany. – 16: Oslavany. – 17: Podivice. – 18: Slavkov u Brna. – 19: Znojmo.

Bronze Age/Iron Age transition

Lusatian culture

The Lusatian culture in Moravia developed smoothly and without any interruptions throughout the whole Urnfield period and the Bronze Age – Early Iron Age transition. At that time, the Silesian phase of the Lusatian culture was transformed into the Platěnice phase/culture under the influence of the Hallstatt culture. Burying continued until the end of the Late Hallstatt period in several burial grounds that had been founded in the Urnfield period, though the graves of the Platěnice culture were usually grouped slightly aside (Nekvasil 1964, 240).

Urnfield traditions persisted and were visible on the pottery and in the burial rite. These were influenced by the Hallstatt culture but certain patterns of the Lusatian Urnfield culture were maintained. The exclusive practice of cremation continued throughout the entire Hallstatt period. But, the 'hallstattization' of the Lusatian culture was manifested by the change of grave construction and composition of grave equipment. Besides the classical urn grave, a grave with an amphora-shaped storage jar as a dominant vessel started to appear from the earliest Iron Age, as grave 31 in Moravičany with a bronze vase-headed pin confirms (Nekvasil 1982, 23-24 pl. 10,6; Stegmann-Rajtár 1993, 455). So-called amphora graves were typical of the Hallstatt period and were created throughout the entire period of the Platěnice culture. The number of grave goods in them gradually increased and their richness culminated around Ha C2 – Ha D1. At that time, chamber tombs also started to appear (Baarová/Mikulková 2004, 305; Nekvasil 1983, 76; 1987, 115-118).

Horákov culture

The situation in the southern part of Moravia is a little bit more complicated; the Bronze Age/Iron Age transition and the creation of the Horákov culture is not fully clear there.

The most important grave of that period is grave 169 from Brno-Obřany. The cemetery is located in the northern part of the Brno basin, which is an area where the Podolí and Lusatian cultures overlapped (Stegmann-Rajtár 1994, 324). While the pottery was typical for the Urnfield culture (Podolí and Lusatian culture), metal finds, i.e. an iron flange-hilted sword and a bronze chape from a sword scabbard, point to southeastern Europe and the northern Black Sea region (Pare 1998, 388; Podborský 1970, 169; 177 pl. 59; Stegmann-Rajtár 1992b, 40-42 pl. 1-2; 1994, 324). Chronology and cultural affiliation of the grave has been the subject of several discussions (e.g. Golec 2005a, 40-42). Most researchers assign it to the end of the Podolí culture or to the transition of the southern Moravian Urnfield period to the Hallstatt period, i.e. to the 9th, at the latest to the beginning of the 8th century BC (e.g. Pare 1998, 388; Podborský 1970, 177; Stegmann-Rajtár 1986; 1992b, 40-42; 1993, 445; 1994, 324). On the contrary, M. Golec (2005a, 42) holds the view that the grave belongs to the early Hallstatt phase and together with grave 140 in this cemetery and graves 78 and 114 in the cemetery in Klentnice can be considered early Hallstatt 'princely' graves.

The latter two graves from the cemetery of Klentnice (Břeclav district) are believed to be the early Hallstatt graves in general (Pare 1998, 388-398; Podborský 1974; Říhovský 1970; Stegmann-Rajtár 1992b, 150; 1993, 447; 2009, 232-243).

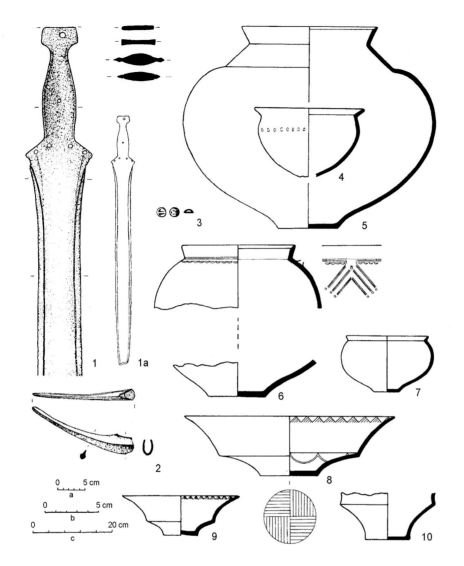

Fig. 2. Klentnice, Břeclav district, grave 78. 1-3: bronze; 4-10: pottery. Scale a: 4-10; scale b: 1-3; scale c: 1a (after Stegmann-Rajtár 1992a, pl. 67,5-6; pl. 68-69).

However, divergence of views in the interpretation of the grave goods led to the different points of view on the formation of the Horákov culture. A concept of an autochthonous development of the Horákov culture, smoothly developing from the previous Podolí culture, has prevailed among Moravian scholars. The Thrako-Cimmerian intervention into the Podolí culture at the end of the Bronze Age is considered to be one of the key impulses leading to the establishment of the Early Iron Age (e.g. Golec 2005a, 61; Nekvasil 1987, 115-116; Podborský 1970, 173-186; 1980a, 95; 1980b).

By contrast, continuous transition from the Urnfield period to the Hallstatt period in the southern Moravian region has been disputed by S. Stegmann-Rajtár (1992b, 166-167; 1993, 447; 1994, 327-330; 2009, 231-243). According to her, there is no evidence of domestic Urnfield tradition in the material of the southern Moravian settlements and cemeteries. Grave 78 of Klentnice (Fig. 2), containing a cremation provided with atypical grave goods for Podolí culture, is a pertinent example. There were carinated bowls (Fig. 2,8-9), parallels of which have been found in the cemetery of Kelheim, as well as a bronze Gündlingen sword (Fig. 2,1) and Prüllsbirkig chape (Fig. 2,2), also culturally connected to the territory of southern Germany. Moreover, she considers the grave a burial of a high-status man – an armed equestrian, who together with his companions left their homeland in southern Bavaria (Stegmann-Rajtár 2009, 240-241). Therefore, significant West Hallstatt elements are seen as evidence of the (invasive) western origin of the southern Moravian Hallstatt period. The conception of the beginning of the Horákov culture and periodisation of the Early Iron Age in the southern Moravian region presented by S. Stegmann-Rajtár has been criticised and denied (e.g. Golec 2003; Podborský 2002) but excavations of the last two decades have shed new light on this issue. Grave H895 in Modřice, corresponding with the early Hallstatt graves in Klentnice, consisted of pottery that indicates contacts with the eastern as well as western Hallstatt zone (Kos 2014). Close relations between southern Moravia and the upper Danubian region were confirmed mainly by ceramics, particularly bowls with cogwheel decoration found at cemeteries in Modřice (Kos 2009a, 119-120 fig. 4,17; 121 fig. 5,25; Kos/Přichystal 2013, 84-85), Znojmo or Hrušovany u Brna (Kos/Přichystal 2013, 87-91).

Wagon graves

Wagon burials were a typical sign of the western Hallstatt elites; the greatest concentration in the Ha C period was in Bohemia (Bylany and Hallstatt Tumulus culture) and southern Germany (Pare 1987, 190 fig. 1; 1991, fig. 4; 1992, 162 fig. 108). Despite the prevailing opinion on the absence of wagon graves in Moravia (e.g. Golec 2004, 553; Kolář 2007, 309; Podborský 1980a, 107; 2002, 168-170; Šolle 1955, 114), except for a few late Hallstatt wagons, or more likely just their parts, from the Býčí skála Cave (Barth 1995), there are some references to wagon burials in literature dealing with the issue of the Early Iron Age in southern Moravia.

The presence of a wagon in a grave was conceded by S. Stegmann-Rajtár (1992b, 134-135). She noted that wagon components were probably in Brno-Holásky, tumulus 2, but she did not assign a tumulus of Horákov-Hlásnica to the wagon graves for lack of evidence. In contrast, G. Kossack (1970, 126 fig. 13; 171) added both burial mounds to the list of the Early Iron Age wagon graves, while Ch. Pare (1987; 1991; 1992) did not mention any wagon graves from the Moravian region in his works concerning wagons and wagon graves, except for the find from the Býčí skála Cave.

The presence of wagon graves was not presupposed perhaps because it is generally accepted that the Horákov culture belongs to the northeastern Hallstatt culture and thus the finds, which might have been parts of a wagon from the tumulus in Horákov-Hlásnica (Skutil 1937; Stegmann-Rajtár 1992a, 16-17) or Brno-Holásky (Stegmann-Rajtár 1992a, 9-10) were overlooked.

Wagon graves sporadically occurred in the north-east of the Alps, as exemplified by tumulus 1 in Somlóvásárhely. The grave inventory consisted of finds suggesting connections with the western Hallstatt culture as well as the Illyrian and Greek area (Egg 1996b). Whether a wagon, real or symbolic, was present in the above-mentioned Moravian burial mounds, remains unknown due to the insufficient documentation. However, recent excavations in Brno and Znojmo districts showed that the custom of wagon burials had its place also in the environment of the Horákov culture (Fig. 3) in its early phase.

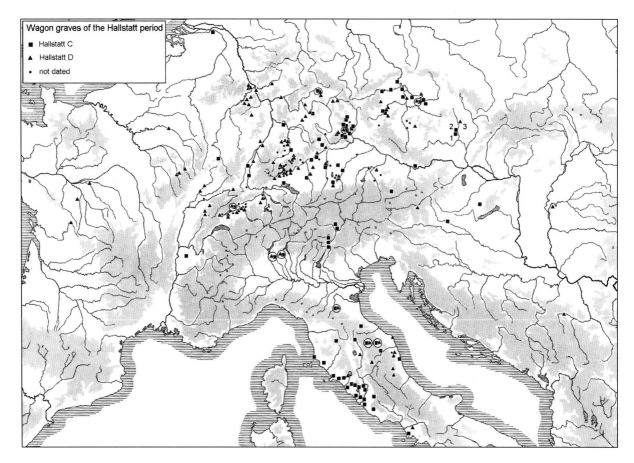

Remnants of a richly decorated yoke were found in biritual chamber grave H 1800 in Modřice. Small bronze studs with hemispherical heads arranged in a zig-zag ornament decorated a wooden yoke (Kos 2004a; 2009a, 129-130 fig. 3; Přichystal/Kos 2006, 53). The decorated yoke and a fragment of iron linchpin can be regarded as pars pro toto grave goods of a wagon. Richly decorated yokes and complete horse-gear were common parts of wagon graves of the Bylany culture (Dvořák 1938; Koutecký 1968).

Richly decorated yoke together with horse-gear appeared in another grave in Modřice, namely in grave H3815 (Kos 2009b, 310), and in the grave H1 in Hrušovany u Brna (Fig. 5) (Geisler 2009, 309; Kos 2011, 173-176; Kos/Přichystal 2013, 85-89). While small studs from Hrušovany were made of bronze, the ones from Modřice were made of iron. Two elongated hollows in the floor of a wooden chamber suggest that a real wagon may have been embedded in both graves. As there were no metal wagon components, an all-wooden wagon may have been placed in the grave. Another possibility is that the wagon was later taken out of the grave or that they were indeed only symbolic wagon graves. In both cases, they were large chamber graves of 6 x 4 m. Actually, they are some of the biggest and richest graves in the southern Moravian region. In grave H1 in Hrušovany u Brna, the yoke was located near the southern wall of the burial chamber and the wagon in the northern part of the grave (Fig. 4), exactly as it was common for wagon graves of the Bylany culture (Koutecký 1968, 464; Pare 1987, 208).

Four bronze Tutuli with small rings along the rim (Fig. 5,16) were part of the horse-gear found in the grave of Hrušovany u Brna. Another four Tutuli of this

Fig. 3. Distribution of wagon graves in the Hallstatt period. 1: Hrušovany u Brna. – 2: Modřice. – 3: Býčí skála Cave (after Pare 1987, 190 fig. 1, with additions).

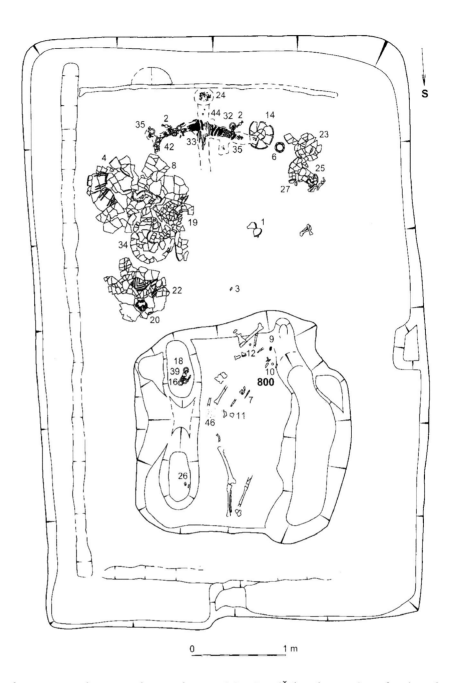

Fig. 4. Hrušovany u Brna, Brno-Country district, grave H 1 (after Kos 2011, 174 fig. 1).

0 _____ 1 m

form appeared in princely tumulus 1 in Morašice (Říhovský 1956, 17 fig. 4,2 a-b; Stegmann-Rajtár 1992a, 53 pl. 106,12). The centre of their concentration was the western Hallstatt zone – in Bohemia and southern Germany – where they were associated with graves of the Ha C containing a wagon and sword (Egg 1996b, 346 fig. 15; Kossack 1954, 121 fig. 2; 125 map 3) but they sporadically occurred in the eastern Alpine region as well (Somlóvásárhely tumulus 1: Egg 1996b, 346 fig. 4,4-7; Preloge grave IV/43: Tecco Hvala 2012, 160 fig. 61,6).

The grave in Hrušovany u Brna (Fig. 5) as well as the one in Modřice can be equated with Ha C1b (Kos 2009b, 310; 2011, 177; Kos/Přichystal 2013, 87). These graves, fitting into the period between the early Hallstatt graves of Klentnice and Podolí and the 'princely' graves of the middle Hallstatt period (Ha C2), play a

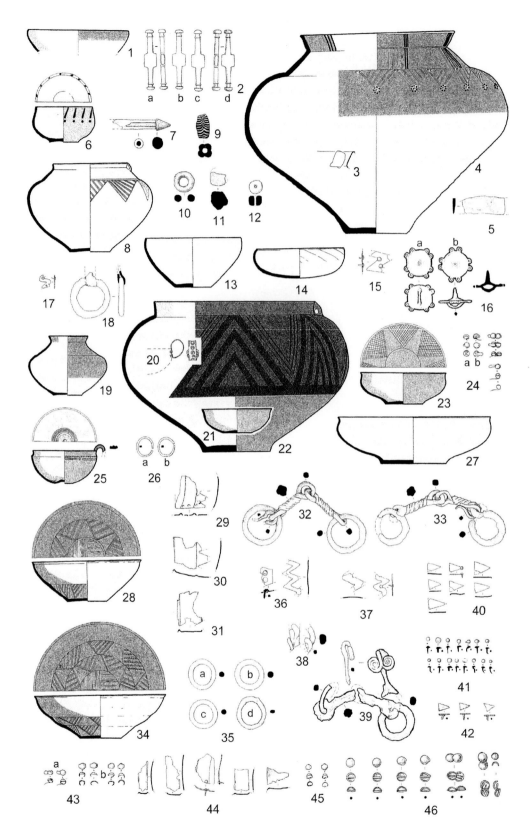

Fig. 5. Finds from grave H 1 in Hrušovany u Brna, Brno-Country district. 12: amber; 9: glass; 5, 11, 18, 32-33, 39: iron; 7 iron and wood; 10 lignite; 1, 3-4, 6, 8, 13-14, 19, 21-23, 25, 27-28, 34 pottery; otherwise bronze. Not to scale (after Kos 2011, 178 fig. 3).

key role in observing the development of the Horákov culture, as there was a lack of representative graves with metal finds from that period (Golec 2005b, 422).

The wagon as a symbol of exceptionality occurred even in the environment of the Platěnice culture, although somewhat later – in Ha D – as a depiction. A four-wheeled wagon drawn by a pair of yoked horses had been engraved on a drinking horn made of bone found in a grave in Dobrčice. The grave also contained an iron lance, bit and belt hook, two bronze bracelets and some pottery (Červinka 1938, 78-80 fig. 1). This grave, which represents one of the exceptional graves of the Platěnice culture, can be regarded as a burial of a man with high social status (Makarová 2013, 102-103).

Grave goods of 'princely' graves

The richest graves of the Horákov culture, that are considered princely graves (Podborský 1980a, 107-111) are the already mentioned tumulus in Horákov-Hlásnica (Fig. 6C), tumulus 1 (Fig. 6A) and 2 in Brno-Holásky (Fig. 6B) and tumulus 1 in Morašice. A grave from Bratčice (Fig. 7) also belongs to this group, although it is a little younger (Golec 2003, 512). These large chamber tombs covered by a barrow stood out due to the quantity and quality of grave goods. Apart from a large amount of pottery, they contained warrior equipment – weaponry (swords or lances), possibly protective armor ("remnants of an armour or a coat with fixed bronze knobs on" were allegedly found in the tumulus Horákov-Hlásnica; Skutil 1937, 3) and a horse harness as well as jewelry and clothes fittings. However, the most luxurious items of these graves were bronze vessels and iron spits that point to contacts with the southeast Alpine region and northern Italy (Golec 2003, 512).

Likewise, sheet-bronze vessels were the most splendid components of grave goods in the richest princely graves such as those in Pommer- and Kröllkogel near Kleinklein or in Strettweg (Egg 2006, 52), although they appeared in greater amounts in comparison with the Moravian graves.

There were broad-rimmed bowls decorated with birds and suns among the bronze vessels (Fig. 6,16, C11-12). The bowls were named by J. Nekvasil (1991, 15-16 pl. 5,30; pl. 6,31) as the Horákov type, named after the eponymous site, where two of them come from. Another bowl was found in one of the burial mounds in Brno-Holásky (Nekvasil 1991, 16 pl. 7,32). Distribution of these bowls is linked solely to the second half of the 7th century BC; they do not occur in Moravia in later periods (Golec 2003, 506). Fragments of broad-rimmed bowls without decoration were discovered in tumulus 1 in Morašice (Nekvasil 1991, 16-17 pl. 7,34) and a complete one was found in Bratčice (Fig. 7,5) (Čižmář *et al.* 2000, 131 fig. 104,1; Golec 2005a, 107-110 pl. 54; Kos 1995/1996, 337). The broad-rimmed bowls were spread in the western as well as the eastern Hallstatt culture, while the highest number of them were situated in the center of their distribution, namely at the cemetery of Hallstatt (Egg 1996a, 124-125 fig. 73). Despite their absence in the territory of the Platěnice culture in Moravia, they sporadically appeared more in the north, in the Lusatian culture in Polish Silesia (Józefowska/Łaciak 2012, 472).

The greatest number of sheet-bronze vessels was found in Bratčice. There was a situla, a cup and a ladle along with the above-mentioned undecorated broad-rimmed bowl. The situla (Fig. 7,7) had two ribs on the shoulders and a movable

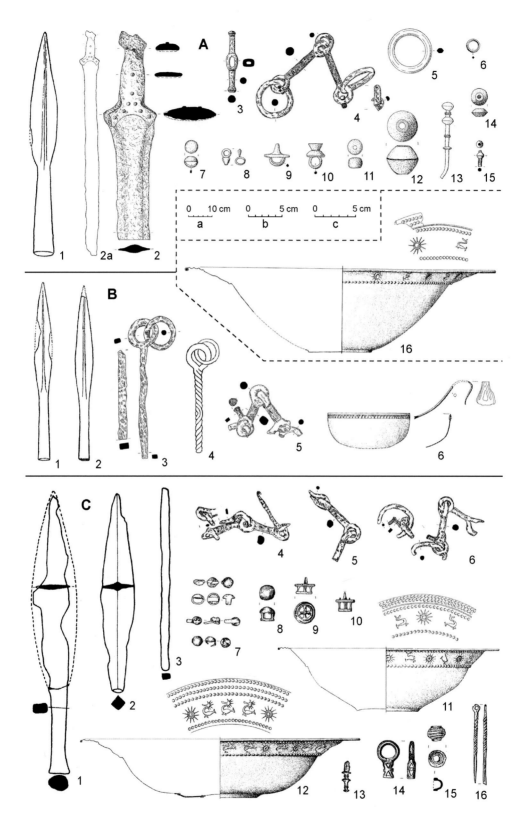

Fig. 6. Selection of finds from 'princely' graves. A Brno-Holásky, tumulus 1. – B: Brno-Holásky, tumulus 2. – C: Horákov-Hlásnica. A1-4, B1-5, C1-6: iron; A14-15: amber and bronze; otherwise bronze. Scale a – 2a; scale c – A5-15, C7-10; otherwise scale b (A1, B1-2 after Červinka 1948, 15 fig. 8,2; 18 fig. 10,1-2; 16, B6, C11-12 after Nekvasil 1991, pl. 5,30-7,32; pl. 8,35; otherwise after Stegmann-Rajtár 1992a, pl. 1; pl. 2,1-9; pl. 4,2-3; pl. 5,9; pl. 18,4-6; pl. 19,1-9; pl. 20,1-2; pl. 20,6).

handle. The closest parallels can be found in the Býčí skála Cave (Nekvasil 1991, 22 pl. 11,44; Parzinger 1995, 75 pl. 38,346) and Strettweg (Egg 1996a, 96 fig. 54,1), and its distribution is limited to the territory east of the Alps (Parzinger 1995, 75). The next two bronze vessels from Bratčice, a cup with engraved decoration and a strap handle rising above the rim (Fig. 7,8) and a ladle with a lever handle (Fig. 7,6), can be associated with this area as well. Another ladle with a lever handle was found in tumulus 2 in Brno-Holásky (Fig. 6,B6; Nekvasil 1991, 18 pl. 8,35).

Spits are considered indicators of high social status in male graves. They are also suggestive of cultural contacts with the Mediterranean region where the habit of their deposition into graves comes from (Egg 1996a, 139; Tomedi 2002, 134-136). Moreover, according to B. Teržan (2004), spits were not only ritual or status symbols but they may also have represented a sort of pre-monetary means of payment. Iron spits occurred in three graves of the Horákov culture, namely in Brno-Holásky tumulus 2 (Fig. 6,B3-4), Hlásnica near Horákov (Fig. 6,C3) and Bratčice (Fig. 7,4). In all these cases, these spits had a round ending, on which a ring was sometimes strung and they mostly had an alternately twisted upper part. Such spits occurred only in the eastern Alpine region and the ones from Moravia are the northern-most finds of these specimens (Egg 1996a, 143 fig. 83; Golec 2003-2004, 104 fig. 1). M. Egg (1996a, 145) pointed out the multiple occurrence of iron spits together with broad-rimmed bowls that probably were used for serving cooked or roasted meat. This occurred in Bratčice and tumulus 2 in Brno-Holásky.

Neither bronze vessels nor spits have been found in any graves of the Platěnice culture so far. Although such supra-regional contacts cannot be seen in the burial rite of the Platěnice culture, there is no doubt of their existence. Iron finds confirming contacts between the Platěnice culture and the southeastern Hallstatt culture area already in the Ha C1a phase were found at the hillfort in Podivice (Fojtík/Golec 2007). Moreover, there are hoards from the Ha D period, mostly found at settlements, suggesting the contacts with distant regions in the south as well as the north. A hoard unearthed at the settlement in Kralice na Hané (Prostějov district) consisting of several pieces of iron spits and eight bronze vessels is a great example of the contacts (three ladles with lever handle and five cups and bowls) (Přichystal/Kos 2006, 50, 209; Šmíd 2004, 170 fig. 3). The interesting thing is that in the area of the Lusatian culture in Poland, significant amounts of imports got there from the south through Moravia and the Moravian Gate (Bukowski 1992, 41-50; 1999, 151) during Ha C (Gedl 1991; Gerdsen 1986, 32; Józefowska/Łaciak 2012).

As multi-headed pins show, foreign fashionable elements became a part of the costume of the local nobility. These pins were typical components of a male costume in the eastern Alpine region and Po Valley in the period from the end of 8th to the beginning of the 6th century BC (Nebelsick 1996, 350; 1997, 95-97 fig. 40). In the area of the Horákov culture, they were present only in rich graves – in grave 1 in Oslavany (Říhovský 1979, pl. 68,1890; Stegmann-Rajtár 1992a, 24-25 pl. 45,10) and grave 2 in Hrušovany u Brna (Kos 2011, 177 fig. 4,12) and princely graves – in Brno-Holásky (probably tumulus 1; Fig. 6,A13) (Golec 2003, 504; Říhovský 1979, pl. 67,1866), and as a pin catch (Fig. 6,C13) indicates, in Horákov-Hlásnica too (Skutil 1937, 4 pl. 1,12; Stegmann-Rajtár 1992a, 17 pl. 19,7). An iron multi-headed pin was also found in grave 1099 at the cemetery of the Platěnice culture in Moravičany (Nekvasil 1982, pl. 298,17). Even though

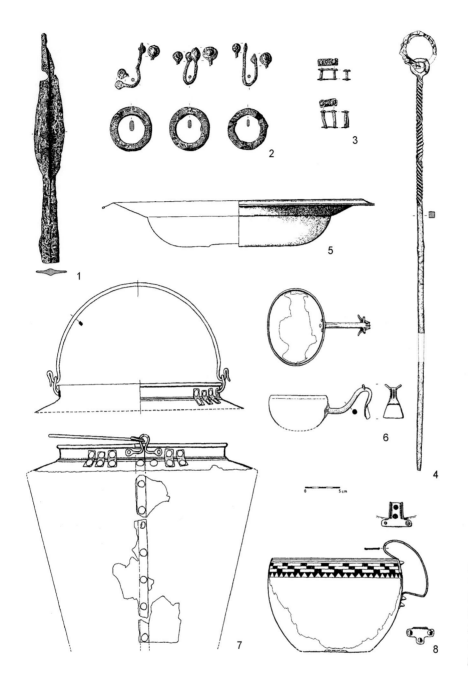

Fig. 7. Selection of finds from 'princely' grave in Bratčice, Brno-Country district. 1-4: iron; 5-8: bronze (after Golec 2005a, 110 pl. 54; 113 pl. 56; 124 pl. 65; 130 pl. 68,25-27, pl. 68,33).

the remnants of a wooden chamber were not recognised there, it bears a striking resemblance to grave 1100 identfied by J. Nekvasil (1982, 319) as a chamber grave. According to the pottery, both graves can be dated to Ha C2 so they represent the oldest chamber graves at the cemetery. The other chamber graves date to Ha D and are larger and richer.

Another significant component of a man's costume was a belt consisting of ring hangers, on which for example a whetstone or a knife might be suspended. They are known from the princely grave in Bratčice (Fig. 7,2) (Golec 2003, 507), Slavkov u Brna, grave 2 (Dobisíková *et al.* 2010, 71; 89 fig. 18,16; 27), Modřice, graves 3846 and 3815 (Kos/Přichystal 2013, 85) and Hrušovany, grave H 2 (Kos 2011, 176-180 fig. 4,23). Parallels can be found at the cemetery of Hallstatt (Kromer

1959, pl. 25,10; pl. 62,7; pl. 63,2; pl. 83,6; pl. 156,6; pl. 195,6) or cemeteries in Transdanubia (Golec 2003, 507-508), which belong to Ha C2 and Ha D1.

A belt, not just as a functional or decorative component of clothes but also as a status symbol, started to be used in a woman's costume as well. The belt, which was composed of a large number of small bronze rings, sometimes also coupled with ring pendants, was a typical item of female graves of Ha C2 – D1 belonging to high-ranking elites (Kos 2004b; Podborský 2002, 169-170; Přichystal/Kos 2006, 52; Štrof 2000, 43-44 fig. 41; fig. 42).

Foreign funerary architecture

Contacts between Moravia and the eastern Alpine region are not only manifested by grave goods but sporadically also by grave construction. The best example of foreign construction technique in the area of the Horákov culture is a timber-and-stone chamber grave in Morašice (Fig. 8) (Říhovský 1956). A parallel can be drawn between this and the territory of the Pannonian, Sulmtal and Dolenj groups (Dobiat 1985, 34-39 fig. 1-2; Egg 1996b; 2006, 47). There was a large grave pit 6.5 x 6.2 m in size under a barrow. Inside the grave pit there was a square shaped log-cabin burial chamber (4.4 x 4.4 m), which was enclosed by a 1 m wide stone wall (Říhovský 1956, 14-16). Revision of the archaeological context by M. Golec (2004) revealed that the wooden burial chamber had two stages and an entrance corridor – dromos – that led slightly diagonally from the southeastern corner of the upper part (about 1 m above the chamber floor) to the top. C. Dobiat (1985, 39) assumes that this kind of monumental funerary architecture, mostly the dromos, has its origin in the Etruscan funerary architecture. The Mediterranean area, especially Etruscan middle Italy, undoubtedly played an important role in forming the Central European elites in the Early Iron Age (Bouzek 2007, 260; Egg 2006, 47) and the Horákov culture in Moravia was also affected.

The construction technique was spread even more to the north, to the area of the Platěnice culture. In Drysice, a chamber tomb similar in construction, though smaller (4.6 m²) and without a dromos, was unearthed (Nekvasil 1962, 154-155). The grave is exceptional for its timber-and-stone burial chamber but as to the dimensions of the grave pit, the quantity and quality of grave goods, it can be ranked among average chamber tombs (Makarová 2013, 102).

Amber

Contacts with the north are mainly suggested by finds of amber. In comparison with, for example, the cemetery of Hallstatt, amber beads occur in much smaller amounts at the cemeteries of the Horákov and Platěnice cultures, though one must be mindful of the fact that most of the rich graves were robbed; it is quite possible that the amount of amber in graves had been much higher.

An amber bead or several amber beads were part of a necklace, which was usually also composed of glass and/or bronze beads, or as part of a pin. A bronze pin with an amber head was found in tumulus 1 in Morašice (Stegmann-Rajtár 1992, 53 pl. 106,16) and a pin with multiple amber heads in a grave in Modřice (Kos/Přichystal 2013, 86-87) and probably in tumulus 1 in Brno-Holásky, too (Fig. 6,A14-15). As many as 179 amber beads come from three chamber graves of the Platěnice culture in Pustiměř, which have been assigned to Ha C2 – D1 (Baarová 2007, 15-20

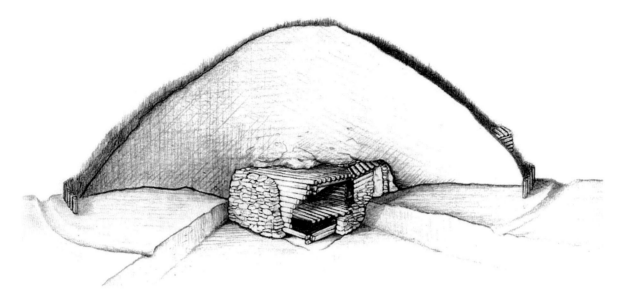

fig. 14). Exceptional are the more than 1800 beads from the Býčí skála Cave dating to the Late Hallstatt period (Parzinger 1995, 56, pl. 79-80).

The Moravia-Oder route was the main road by which most of the amber was transported until the early 6th century (Bouzek 1993, 143). In the late Hallstatt period, even the route along the Vistula regained its importance, which is related to the increase in the amount of amber and to the richer furnished graves in the late Lusatian cemeteries in Poland (Dąbrowski 1993, 112). The Moravian region, however, was not just a transitional area, through which the amber trade was most likely organised in stages (Bouzek 2007, 260-264), but it seems that raw amber was processed here as well. Amber processing was documented at the settlements of the classic stage of the Horákov culture (Ha C2 – D1) in Brno-Řečkovice (Tichý 1969) and Kuřim (Čižmář 1997). They are located in the Brno basin, where the highest concentration of rich graves, including princely ones is located. Many small fragments of amber come from a feature at the settlement in Polešovice, that has been preliminary dated to the Hallstatt – La Tène period (Snášil 1971, 36). Two amber workshops were also unearthed at the settlement of the Platěnice culture in Kralice na Hané. They contained a considerable amount of amber in all stages of processing – from raw material through half-finished goods to finished beads (Přichystal 2007, 212-222). Amber beads were even found in the Ha D hoards from settlements in Šarovy (Dohnal 1977, 163) and Prostějov-Čechůvky (Přichystal/Kos 2006, 50; Šmíd 2005, 264).

Fig. 8. Reconstruction drawing of tumulus 1 in Morašice, Znojmo district, showing a timber-and-stone chamber tomb with a dromos (after Golec 2004, 551 fig. 11).

Conclusion

The revision of old finds and new excavations has revealed that the location of the Horákov culture on the interface between the western and eastern Hallstatt zones had an essential impact on the formation of local elites, who took over traditions from both cultural zones. The amber route connecting the north to the south, leading through the Moravian region, also played an important role.

Connections with the western Hallstatt zone were significant at the beginning of the Early Iron Age. The graves of higher-status individuals of the Horákov culture contained western Hallstatt pottery as well as a wagon (or at least parts of it). The influence of the south started to dominate from the Ha C2 period. The impact of the southeastern Alpine region and northern Italy was manifested not only by grave inventories consisting of luxurious items such as sheet-bronze vessels or iron spits but also by the appearance of new funeral architecture (timber-and-stone chamber grave with dromos).

In the area of the Platěnice culture, objects reflecting the supra-regional contacts occur rather sporadically, even though it is fairly likely that they travelled to Silesia through Moravia. This may be explained, to some extent by the conservatism of the Platěnice culture, which is also manifested by their using cremation during the entire Hallstatt period. Change takes place at the turn of Ha C and Ha D, when richly furnished chamber graves started to occur. Apparently in this period, the Platěnice culture became involved in the amber route, as the workshops in the settlement of Kralice na Hané and some hoards of the late Hallstatt period indicate.

Bibliography

Baarová 2007: Z. Baarová, Platěnické pohřebiště s komorovými hroby v Pustiměři. In: M. Salaš/K. Šabatová (eds.), Doba popelnicových polí a doba halštatská. Příspěvky z IX. konference, Bučovice 3.-6. 10. 2006 (Brno 2007) 13-33.

Baarová/Mikulková 2004: Z. Baarová/B. Mikulková, Halštatské žárové pohřebiště v Drnovicích (okr. Vyškov). Pravěk Nová řada 14, 2004, 287-331.

Barth 1995: F. Barth, Die Wagenreste. In: H. Parzinger/J. Nekvasil/F. Barth, Die Býčí skála-Höhle. Ein hallstattzeitlicher Höhlenopferplatz in Mähren. Römisch-Germanische Forschungen 54 (Mainz 1995) 97-115.

Bouzek 1993: J. Bouzek, The shifts of the amber route. In: C. W. Beck/J. Bouzek (eds.), Amber in archaeology. Proceedings of the Second International Conference on Amber in Archaeology, Liblice 1990 (Praha 1993) 141-146.

Bouzek 2007: J. Bouzek, Von Bronzezeit zur Eisenzeit: Veränderungen in der prähistorischen Gesellschaft in Mitteleuropa unter den Einflüssen aus Süd, Ost und Nord. In: E. Kazdová/V. Podborský (eds.), Studium sociálních a duchovních struktur pravěku (Brno 2007) 257-268.

Bukowski 1992: Z. Bukowski, Tzw. szlak bursztynowy z wczesnej epoki żelaza na obrzarach na południe od Sudetów i Karpat w świetle importów pochodzenia południowego. In: S. Czopek (ed.), Ziemie polskie we wczesnej epoce żelaza i ich powiązania z innymi terenami. Materiały z konferencji – Rzeszów, 17-20. 09.1991 (Rzeszów 1992) 39-54.

Bukowski 1999: Z. Bukowski, Late Bronze Age and Early Iron Age amber finds from the catchment areas of the rivers Oder and Vistula. In: B. Kosmowska-Ceranowicz/H. Paner (eds.), Investigations into amber. Proceedings of the International Interdisciplinary Symposium: Baltic Amber and Other Fossil Resins, 2-6 September 1997, Gdańsk (Gdańsk 1999) 151-156.

Červinka 1938: I. Červinka, Nálezy z Přerovska. Ročenka Městského musea v Přerově 2, 1938, 78-86.

Červinka 1948: I. Červinka, Holásky (okr. Brno). Časopis Vlasteneckého spolku musejního v Olomouci 57, 1948, 5-19.

Čižmář 1997: Z. Čižmář, Bernstein auf der hallstattzeitlichen Ansiedlung in Kuřim. Ein Beitrag zur Frage der Bernsteinbearbeitung im Brünner Becken und dessen Umgebung. In: J. Čižmářová/Z. Měchurová (eds.), Peregrinatio Gothica. Supplementum ad Acta Musei Moraviae, Scientiae sociales 82 (Brno 1997) 17-34.

Čižmář et al. 2000: M. Čižmář/K. Geislerová/J. Unger (eds.), Výzkumy – Ausgrabungen 1993-1998 (Brno 2000).

Dąbrowski 1993: J. Dąbrowski, Amber trade in the Lusatian culture. In: C. W. Beck/J. Bouzek (eds.), Amber in archaeology. Proceedings of the Second International Conference on Amber in Archaeology, Liblice 1990 (Praha 1993) 110-116.

Dobiat 1985: C. Dobiat, Der Kröll-Schmiedkogel und seine Stellung innerhalb der ostalpinen Hallstattkultur. In: A. Reichenberger/C. Dobiat, Kröll-Schmiedkogel. Beiträge zu einem "Fürstengrab" der östlichen Hallstattkultur in Kleinklein (Steiermark). Kleine Schriften aus dem Vorgeschichtlichen Seminar der Philipps-Universität Marburg 18 (Marburg 1985) 29-61.

Dobisíková et al. 2010: M. Dobisíková/M. Geisler/J. Kala/P. Kos/B. Mikulková/D. Parma/A. Přichystal, Halštatské pohřebiště ze Slavkova u Brna (okr. Vyškov). In: V. Furmánek/E. Miroššayová (eds.), Popolnicové polia a doba halštatská. Zborník referátov z X. medzinárodnej konferencie "Popolnicové polia a doba halštatská", Košice, 16.-19. september 2008. Archaeologica Slovaca Monographiae XI (Nitra 2010) 57-99.

Dohnal 1977: V. Dohnal, Kultura lužických popelnicových polí na východní Moravě. Fontes Archaeologiae Moravicae 10 (Brno 1977).

Dvořák 1938: F. Dvořák, Knížecí pohřby na vozech ze starší doby železné. Praehistorica 1 (Praha 1938).

Egg 1996a: M. Egg, Das hallstattzeitliche Fürstengrab von Strettweg bei Judenburg in der Obersteiermark (Mainz 1996).

Egg 1996b: M. Egg, Einige Bemerkungen zum hallstattzeitlichen Wagengrab von Somlóvásárhely, Kom. Veszprém in Westungarn. Jahrbuch des Römisch-Germanischen Zentralmuseums Mainz 43, 1996, 327-353.

Egg 2006: M. Egg, Anmerkungen zu den Fürstengräbern im Osthallstattkreis. In: C. von Carnap-Bornheim/D. Krausse/A. Wesse (eds.), Herrschaft – Tod – Bestattung. Zu den vor- und frühgeschichtlichen Prunkgräbern als archäologisch-historische Quelle. Internationale Fachkonferenz, Kiel, 16.-19. Oktober 2003. Universitätsforschungen zur prähistorischen Archäologie 139 (Bonn 2006) 41-60.

Fojtík/Golec 2007: P. Fojtík/M. Golec, Časně halštatské hradisko na „Na valech" u Podivic, okr. Vyškov a jeho přínos k poznání stupně H C1 na Moravě. Pravěk Nová řada 16, 2007, 37-75.

Gedl 1991: M. Gedl, Die Hallstatteinflüsse auf den polnischen Gebieten in der Früheisenzeit. Zeszyty Naukowe Uniwersytetu Jagiellońskiego CMLXIX, Prace archeologiczne 48 (Warszawa, Kraków 1991).

Geisler 2009: M. Geisler, Hrušovany u Brna (okr. Brno-venkov). Přehled výzkumů 50, 2009, 309.

Gerdsen 1986: H. Gerdsen, Studien zu den Schwertgräbern der älteren Hallstattzeit (Mainz am Rhein 1986).

Golec 2003: M. Golec, Hlásnica u Horákova: kam s ní? Archeologické rozhledy 55, 2003, 500-516.

Golec 2003/2004: M. Golec, Rožně, řecko-etruské vlivy ve střední Evropě. Sborník prací Filozofické fakulty brněnské univerzity M 8-9, 2003/2004 (2004) 101-110.

Golec 2004: M. Golec, Ein Dromos in Mähren. Archeologické rozhledy 56, 2004, 532-560.

Golec 2005a: M. Golec, Horákovská kultura. Unpublished doctoral thesis (Brno 2005).

Golec 2005b: M. Golec, Chronologie horákovské kultury aneb stupně v pohybu. Pravěk Nová řada 15, 2005, 419-446.

Józefowska/Łaciak 2012: A. Józefowska/D. Łaciak, Cmentarzysko ludności kultury łużyckiej z wczesnej epoki żelaza na stanowisku Domasław 10-12, gm. Kobierzyce. In: S. Kadrow (ed.), Raport 2007-2008,1 (Warszawa 2012) 463-482.

Kolář 2007: F. Kolář, Životní styl halštatské a časně laténské aristokracie – možnosti interpretace. In: E. Kazdová/V. Podborský (eds.), Studium sociálních a duchovních struktur pravěku (Brno 2007) 285-329.

Kos 1995/1996: P. Kos, Bratčice (okr. Brno-venkov). Přehled výzkumů 39, 1995/1996 (1996) 337-338.

Kos 2004a: Kos, Modřice (okr. Brno-venkov). Přehled výzkumů 45, 2004, 173-176.

Kos 2004b: P. Kos, Pohřby žen z doby halštatské v Modřicích u Brna. In: Popelnicová pole a doba halštatská. Příspěvky z VIII. konference, České Budějovice 22.-24. 9. 2004. Archeologické výzkumy v jižních Čechách, Supplementum 1 (České Budějovice 2004) 271-292.

Kos 2009a: P. Kos, Hrob H 1800 z Modřic – doklad interakcí mezi oblastmi Moravy, Bavorska a JV Přialpím v době halštatské. Pravěk Nová řada 19, 2009, 113-159.

Kos 2009b: P. Kos, Modřice (okr. Brno-venkov). Přehled výzkumů 50, 2009, 310-311.

Kos 2011: P. Kos, Halštatské hroby z Hrušovan u Brna. In: R. Korený (ed.), Doba popelnicových polí a doba halštatská. Příspěvky z XI. konference, Příbram, 7.-10. 9. 2010. Podbrdsko – Miscelanea 2 (Příbram 2011) 173-184.

Kos 2014: P. Kos, K upřesnění datace hrobu H 895 z Modřic (Příspěvek k počátkům vývoje horákovské kultury na Brněnsku). Zborník Slovenského národného múzea 58 – Archeológia 24, 2014, 37-58.

Kos/Přichystal 2013: P. Kos/M. Přichystal, Doba halštatská. In: K. Geislerová/D. Parma (eds.), Výzkumy – Ausgrabungen 2005-2010 (Brno 2013) 74-94.

Kossack 1954: G. Kossack, Pferdegeschirr aus Gräbern der älteren Hallstattzeit Bayerns. Jahrbuch des Römisch-Germanischen Zentralmuseums 1, 1954, 111-178.

Kossack 1970: G. Kossack, Gräberfelder der Hallstattzeit an Main und fränkischer Saale. Materialhefte zur Bayerischen Vorgeschichte 24 (Kallmünz/Opf. 1970).

Koutecký 1968: D. Koutecký, Velké hroby, jejich konstrukce, pohřební ritus a sociální struktura obyvatelstva bylanské kultury. Památky archeologické 59, 1968, 400-487.

Kromer 1959: K. Kromer, Das Gräberfeld von Hallstatt (Firenze 1959).

Makarová 2013: E. Makarová, Chamber tombs of the Platěnice culture – elite burials? In: R. Karl/J. Leskovar (eds.), Interpretierte Eisenzeiten. Fallstudien, Methoden, Theorie. Tagungsbeiträge der 5. Linzer Gespräche zur interpretativen Eisenzeitarchäologie. Studien zur Kulturgeschichte von Oberösterreich 37 (Linz 2013) 95-105.

Nebelsick 1996: L. Nebelsick, Herd im Grab? Zur Deutung der kalenderberg-verzierten Ware am Nordostalpenrand. In: E. Jerem/A. Lippert (eds.), Die Osthallstatkultur. Akten des Internationalen Symposiums, Sopron, 10.-14. Mai 1994. Archaeolingua 7 (Budapest 1996) 327-364.

Nebelsick 1997: L. Nebelsick, Die Kalenderberggruppe der Hallstattzeit am Nordostalpenrand. In: L. Nebelsick/A. Eibner/E. Lauermann/J.-W. Neugebauer, Hallstattkultur im Osten Österreich (St. Pölten 1997) 9-128.

Nekvasil 1962: J. Nekvasil, Pronikání horákovské kultury do oblasti lužických popelnicových polí. Sborník Československé společnosti archeologické 2, 1962, 141-165.

Nekvasil 1964: J. Nekvasil, K otázce lužické kultury na severní Moravě. Archeologické rozhledy 16, 1964, 225-264.

Nekvasil 1982: J. Nekvasil, Pohřebiště lužické kultury v Moravičanech. Katalog nálezů. Fontes Archaelogiae Moravicae 14,1-2 (Brno 1982).

Nekvasil 1983: J. Nekvasil, Początki halsztatyzacji morawskiej grupy kultury łużyckiej. Silesia Antiqua 25, 1983, 61-83.

Nekvasil 1987: J. Nekvasil, Mähren in der Hallstattzeit. Mitteilungen der österreichischen Arbeitsgemeinschaft für Ur- und Frühgeschichte 37, 1987, 115-120.

Nekvasil 1991: J. Nekvasil, Hallstattzeitliche Bronzegefäße in Mähren. In: J. Nekvasil/V. Podborský, Die Bronzegefäße in Mähren. Prähistorische Bronzefunde 2,13 (Stuttgart 1991) 15-43.

Pare 1987: C. Pare, Der Zeremonialwagen der Hallstattzeit: Untersuchungen zu Konstruktion, Typologie und Kulturbeziehungen. In: F. E. Barth (ed.), Vierrädrige Wagen der Hallstattzeit – Untersuchungen zu Geschichte und Technik. Monographien Römisch-Germanisches Zentralmuseum 12 (Mainz 1987) 189-248.

Pare 1991: C. Pare, Swords, wagon-graves and the beginning of the Early Iron Age in Central Europe. Kleine Schriften aus dem Vorgeschichtlichen Seminar der Philipps-Universität Marburg 37 (Marburg 1991).

Pare 1992: C. Pare, Wagons and Wagon-Graves of the Early Iron Age in Central Europe. Oxford University Committee for Archaeology, Monographs 35 (Oxford 1992).

Pare 1998: C. Pare, Beiträge zum Übergang von der Bronze- und Eisenzeit in Mitteleuropa. Teil I: Grundzüge der Chronologie im östlichen Mitteleuropa (11.-8. Jahrhundert v. Chr.). Jahrbuch des Römisch-Germanischen Zentralmuseums 45, 1998, 293-433.

Parzinger 1995: H. Parzinger, Die Funde. In: H. Parzinger/J. Nekvasil/F. E. Barth, Die Býčí skála-Höhle. Ein hallstattzeitlicher Höhlenopferplatz in Mähren. Römisch-Germanische Forschungen 54 (Mainz am Rhein 1995) 16-92.

Podborský 1970: V. Podborský, Mähren in der Spätbronzezeit und an der Schwelle der Eisenzeit (Brno 1970).

Podborský 1974: V. Podborský, Die Stellung der südmährischen Horákov-Kultur im Rahmen des danubischen Hallstatt. In: B. Chropovský (ed.), Symposium zu Problemen der jüngeren Hallstattzeit in Mitteleuropa (Bratislava 1974) 371-426.

Podborský 1980a: V. Podborský, Dvě nová halštatská pohřebiště na jižní Moravě (Několik poznámek ke studiu společnosti lidu horákovské kultury). Sborník prací Filozofické fakulty brněnské univerzity E 25, 1980, 75-124.

Podborský 1980b: V. Podborský, Kulturní a sociální proměny jižní Moravy v době halštatské. In: B. Gediga/L. Leciejewicz/W. Wojciechowski (eds.), Rola oddziaływań kręgu halsztackiego w rozwoju społeczeństw epoki żelaza w Polsce Zachodniej na tle środkowoeuropejskim: materiały konferencyjne (Wrocław 1980) 47-57.

Podborský 2002: V. Podborský, Výpověď bohatých hrobů horákovské kultury. In: P. Čech/Z. Smrž (eds.), Sborník Drahomíru Kouteckému. Příspěvky k pravěku a rané době dějinné severozápadních Čech 9 (Most 2002) 167-176.

Přichystal 2007: M. Přichystal, Zpracování jantaru na sídlišti z halštatského období kultury lužických popelnicových polí v Kralicích na Hané (okr. Prostějov). In: M. Salaš/K. Šabatová (eds.), Doba popelnicových polí a doba halštatská. Příspěvky z IX. konference, Bučovice 3.-6. 10. 2006 (Brno 2007) 209-231.

Přichystal/Kos 2006: M. Přichystal/P. Kos, Doba halštatská. In: M. Čižmář/K. Geislerová (eds.), Výzkumy – Ausgrabungen 1999-2004 (Brno 2006) 49-54.

Říhovský 1956: J. Říhovský, Mohyla horákovské kultury v Morašicích na Moravě. Archeologické rozhledy 8, 1956, 13-18.

Říhovský 1970: J. Říhovský, Halštatské hroby na pohřebišti v Klentnici. In: B. Klíma (ed.), Sborník Josefu Paulíkovi k šedesátinám (Brno 1970) 43-54.

Říhovský 1979: J. Říhovský, Die Nadeln in Mähren und im Ostalpengebiet (von der mittleren Bronzezeit bis zur älteren Eisenzeit). Prähistorische Bronzefunde 13,5 (München 1979).

Skutil 1937: J. Skutil, Halštatské nálezy horákovské "Hlásnice". Šlapanský zpravodaj 4,3, 1937, 3-6.

Snášil 1971: R. Snášil, Další nálezy z halštatskolaténského sídliště u Polešovic (okr. Uherské Hradiště). Přehled výzkumů 1970, 1971, 36-37.

Stegmann-Rajtár 1986: S. Stegmann-Rajtár, Neuerkenntnisse zum Grab 169 von Brno-Obřany. In: Hallstatt Kolloquium Veszprém 1984. Mitteilungen des Archäologischen Instituts der Ungarischen Akademie der Wissenschaften 3 (Budapest 1986) 211-219.

Stegmann-Rajtár 1992a: S. Stegmann-Rajtár, Grabfunde der älteren Hallstattzeit aus Südmähren (Košice 1992).

Stegmann-Rajtár 1992b: S. Stegmann-Rajtár, Spätbronze- und früheisenzeitliche Fundgruppen des mittleren Donaugebietes. Bericht der Römisch-Germanischen Kommission 73, 1992, 29-179.

Stegmann-Rajtár 1993: S. Stegmann-Rajtár, Mitteldonauländische Hallstattkultur und Lausitzer Kulturkreis – Einige Bemerkungen zur Entwicklung gegenseitiger Beziehungen in Mähren. Bericht der Römisch-Germanischen Kommission 74, 1993, 444-459.

Stegmann-Rajtár 1994: S. Stegmann-Rajtár, Vývoj stredodunajských popolnicových polí v neskorej dobe bronzovej (HaB) a vznik halštatskej kultúry. Slovenská archeológia 42,2, 1994, 319-331.

Stegmann-Rajtár 2009: S. Stegmann-Rajtár, Von Bayern bis nach Südmähren: Zur Verbreitung weslicher Gefäßformen in Gräbern der südmährischen Hallstattkultur. In: L. Husty/M. M. Rind/K. Schmotz (eds.), Zwischen Münchshöfen und Windberg. Gedenkschrift für Karl Böhm. Internationale Archäologie, Studia honoraria 29 (Rahden/Westf. 2009) 227-246.

Šmíd 2004: M. Šmíd, Kralice na Hané (okr. Prostějov). Přehled výzkumů 45, 2004, 169-170.

Šmíd 2005: M. Šmíd, Prostějov (k. ú. Čechůvky, okr. Prostějov). Přehled výzkumů 46, 2005, 264.

Šolle 1955: M. Šolle, Jižní Morava v době halštatské. Památky archeologické 46, 1955, 101-133.

Štrof 2000: A. Štrof, Mladší doba bronzová a doba halštatská. In: M. Čižmář/K. Geislerová/J. Unger (eds.), Výzkumy – Ausgrabungen 1993-1998 (Brno 2000) 37-44.

Tecco Hvala 2012: S. Tecco Hvala, Magdalenska gora. Družbena struktura in grobni rituali železnodobne skupnosti. Magdalenska gora. Social structure and biritual rites of the Iron Age community. Opera Instituti Archaeologici Sloveniae 26 (Ljubljana 2012).

Teržan 2004: B. Teržan, Obolos – mediterrane Vorbilder einer prämonetären „Währung" der Hallstattzeit? In: B. Hänsel (ed.), Parerga Praehistorica: Jubiläumsschrift zur Prähistorischen Archäologie; 15 Jahre UPA. Universitätsforschungen zur prähistorischen Archäologie 100 (Bonn 2004) 161-202.

Tichý 1969: R. Tichý, Horákovské sídliště v Brně-Řečkovicích. Archeologické rozhledy 21, 1969, 168-177, 279-280.

Tomedi 2002: G. Tomedi, Das hallstattzeitliche Gräberfeld von Frög. Die Altgrabungen von 1883 bis 1892. Archaeolingua 14 (Budapest 2002).

Author

Erika Makarová
Department of Archaeology and Museology
Masaryk University
Arne Nováka 1
602 00 Brno, Czech Republic
erika.makarova@gmail.com

The Iron Age cremation cemetery of Wörgl in Tyrol and the early Hallstatt Mindelheim horizon

Markus Egg

Abstract

This paper considers large-scale interactions of elites during the early Hallstatt period based on Grave 5 of the Wörgl cemetery in Tyrol. This cemetery is located in the valley of the river Inn in the northeastern Alps. It is part of the inner Alpine Hallstatt groups, which are distinguished from the Hallstatt groups north of the Alps by differences in their burial rituals. For example, they lack the monumental burial mounds that are part of Hallstatt burials, while extensive pars pro toto depositions are characteristic. Even though Grave 5 of Wörgl is the result of a burial ritual characteristic of the inner Alpine Hallstatt groups, it yielded a huge amount of metal grave goods that allow an analysis on a European scale. In addition to the urn and another pottery vessel, a fragment of a sword, horse-gear, parts of a wagon, an iron pin and fragments of a situla were found in this grave. This combination of metal grave goods is typical of elite graves throughout Europe and therefor indicates large-scale interactions on a massive scale, from the Netherlands to Tyrol. An intensive evaluation of the distribution of these finds supports this.

Zusammenfassung

Dieser Beitrag beschäftigt sich mit großräumigen Kontakten älterhallstattzeitlicher Eliten ausgehend von Grab 5 des Gräberfeldes von Wörgl im Nordtiroler Inntal. Die Nekropole von Wörgl liegt im Nordtiroler Inntal und ist Teil der inneralpinen Hallstattgruppen. Diese grenzen sich von den nördlich der Alpen liegenden Hallstattgruppen unter anderem durch ein abweichendes Bestattungsritual ab. So werden in diesen Gruppen beispielsweise keine monumentalen Grabhügel errichtet. Zudem charakterisieren häufig pars pro toto beigegebene Funde diese Bestattungsplätze. In Grab 5 von Wörgl, dass eben diese inneralpinen Charakteristika des Bestattungsrituals aufweist, wurde eine große Anzahl an metallenen Grabbeigaben niedergelegt, die sich für eine großräumige Auswertung im ältereisenzeitlichen Europa eignet. Neben der Urne und einem weiteren Keramikgefäß fanden sich hier ein Fragment eines Schwertes, Pferdegeschirr, Teile eines Wagens, eine eiserne Nadel, ein eisernes Messer und Fragmente einer Situla. Diese Kombination an Beigaben ist typisch für Elitegräber dieser Zeit in weiten Teilen Europas und deutet großräumige Interaktionen dieser Eliten von den Beneluxländern bis in den circumalpinen Bereich an, was anhand der Verbreitung der entsprechenden Funde herausgearbeitet wird.

The cemetery of Wörgl

The Iron Age urnfield cemetery of Wörgl 'Egerndorfer Field' is situated a few kilometers to the east of Kufstein in the valley of the river Inn (Fig. 1). It was discovered as early as 1838 during stone quarry works (see Franz 1951, 5-11; Kneußl 1969, 147-148; Mérey-Kádár 1958, 450-451; Von Wieser 1911, 4-9 on the history of the discovery). The first excavations to recover a respectable amount

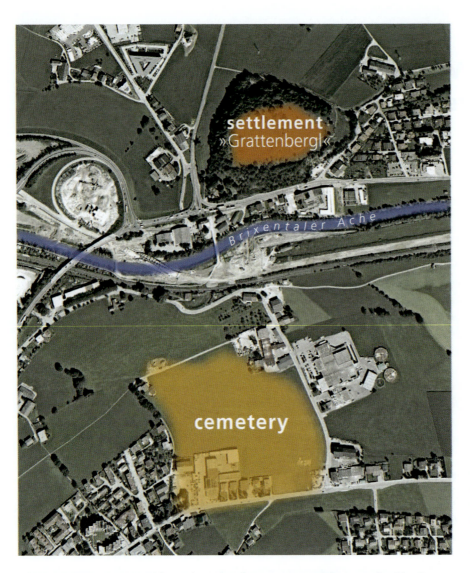

Fig. 1. The necropolis Egerndorfer Feld, district Wörgl and the Grattenbergl, district Kirchbichl (graphics M. Ober, RGZM based on a map of Google Earth).

of urn graves were carried out by a local Antiquities club in 1842-44. G. von Merhart, professor for Prehistory at the University of Marburg, led excavations between 1934 and 1937 (Von Merhart 1935-38a, 48-49; Von Merhart 1935-38b, 104; Lucke 1938, 150-157). A. Lang in Munich is currently preparing the ca. 90 cremation burials that were uncovered during Von Merhart's campaigns for publication.

Von Merhart realized the significance of this cemetery for Tyrol and southern Bavaria for it bridges the gap between the Urnfield period and the La Tène period. Furthermore the huge amount of metal grave goods interred in those burials reveals contact with Southern Germany, Upper Italy and the southeastern Alpine region.

Due to threatening and actual building activities in the area of the cemetery further excavations were carried out by L. Zemmer-Plank and W. Sölder (Tyrolean Landes Museum Ferdinandeum Innsbruck) between 1982 and 2004 in twelve campaigns that revealed some further 600 cremation burials[1]. After the field work

---

1   See the annual reports published in Veröffentlichungen des Tiroler Landesmuseums Ferdinandeum 61, 1981; 62, 1982; 63, 1983; 65, 1985; 66, 1986; 68, 1988; 71, 1991; 72, 1992; 72, 1993; 82, 2002; 83, 2004; 84, 2004.

the restoration of the huge amount of find materials turned out to be a challenge. Almost two-thirds of the burials of the modern excavations were restored in the laboratories of the Tyrolean Landes Museum Ferdinandeum. Subsequently a joint project between the museum in Innsbruck and the Römisch-Germanisches Zentralmuseum in Mainz (RGZM) was started. This project in Mainz was devoted to the restoration, documentation and scientific analysis of the remaining burials, most of which were recovered *en bloque*. This work is still in progress and the cemetery of Wörgl may still provide some surprises. The current state of research indicates that the cemetery was founded at the very beginning of the Early Iron Age (Ha C1a) and was used until the Early La Tène period (Lt A). Younger graves have not yet been discovered.

The associated settlement has been located. It was situated on the other side of the Brixentaler Ache, a small river, on a hilltop (Grattenbergl, municipality Kirchbichl) rising up in the middle of the valley of the river Inn (Fig. 1; Appler 2010, 76-81; Franz 1951, 20-21; Kneußl 1968, 149-150; Tomedi 1998, 49 fig. 9). The contemporaneousness of the burial site and the settlement was established by a noteworthy amount of stray finds and through two excavations on the Grattenbergl that were carried out by the Tyrolean State Museum in the 1970s[2]. In terms of the spatial distribution of sites of the Hallstatt and Early La Tène period around Wörgl it can be pointed out that the burial site on the Egerndorfer Feld was erected on the first natural terrace above the Brixentaler Ache. The distance between the burial site and the settlement is roughly 600 m and they show a good visibility to each other. The Brixentaler Ache divides the burial site from the settlement and needs to be crossed on the way from the settlement to the burial site. This striking separation of the world of the living and the dead by a flowing body of water may be linked to a perception of the division of the underworld from the living by a river, as testified in ancient Greek mythology. According to which one could reach the realm of the dead by crossing the river Acheron (also called Styx or Lethe). Similar perceptions may have led to the foundation of the burial site at its exact location.

Geographical background

The broad valley of the lower river Inn in northern Tyrol runs from southwest to northeast through the northeastern Alps. The terraces at the northern and southern fringes of the valley borders were settled in prehistoric times. Near Wörgl the Brixentaler Ache river flows into the Inn. Wörgl is therefore situated in an important location regarding transport geography (Fig. 2). The valley of the river Inn forms an east-west axis reaching from the Bavarian upland to the Maloja pass in Grisons (Switzerland). One can easily reach Italy by following the valley of Eisack and Etsch after passing the main chains of the Alps at the Brenner and Reschen pass. From the valley of the Eisack river one can reach the valley of the Drava river which runs to the southeastern Alpine region through the valley of the Puster river. The Brixentaler Ache as well as the Große Ache lead to the upper Salzach via the Grießen pass. From there one can easily get to Bischofshofen and the salt mining complex of Hallstatt via Bischofshofen and the valley of the river Enns.

---

2   See the annual reports published in Veröffentlichungen des Tiroler Landesmuseum Ferdinandeum 56, 1976, 343 and 59, 1979, 165 on those excavations.

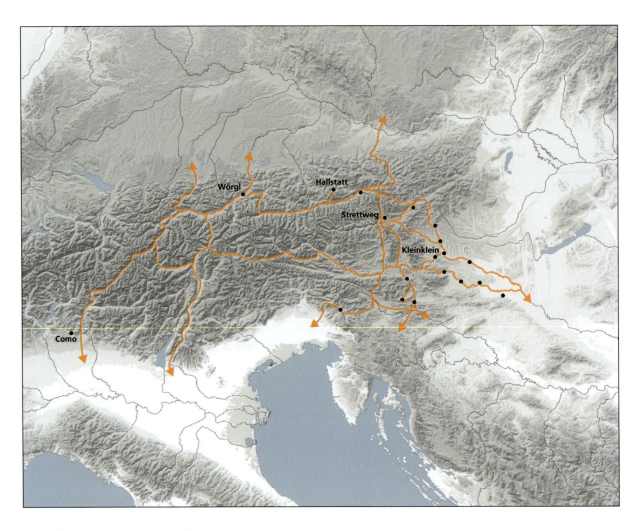

The inner Alpine Hallstatt groups

The cemetery of Wörgl is part of the inner Alpine Hallstatt groups (Fig. 3A; Moosleitner 1980, 205-226). One of the main characteristics of these groups is their continued use of the cremation and urnfield traditions of the Late Bronze Age (Fig. 4). This adherence distinguishes the inner Alpine Hallstatt groups from those north of the Alps. Thereby the inner Alpine region is not a single uniform culture but can rather be divided into several groups (Fig. 3A)[3]. The burial sites of Bischofshofen and Uttendorf form the Salzach group in Salzburg (see Lippert/Stadler 2009; Moosleitner 1982/83) and they are characterized by a strong influence from north of the Alps in their pottery and southeastern Alpine influences in their costumes. The sites in the valley of the river Inn show a strong Bavarian influence in the early Hallstatt period (Ha C) but lack the southeastern Alpine imprint concerning the costumes (Lang 1998, 216-224). In southern Tyrol and the Trentino located south of the main Alpine crest the Melaun group is situated, that is distinguished by their Laugen influences in the pottery (Von

Fig. 2. The transalpine route network in the eastern Alps (graphics M. Ober, RGZM).

Fig. 3 (opposite page). A: The inner Alpine Hallstatt culture groups and their neighbors in the Early Iron Age. – B: Cultural contacts in the necropolis of Wörgl (graphics M. Ober, RGZM).

3   According to the latest research conducted by G. Tiefengraber (Tiefengraber/Tiefengraber 1980, 206) the inner Alpine group in the valley of the upper Mur in Styria (Moosleitner 1980, 206) is not a part of the inner Alpine Hallstatt groups because it is dominated by the Sulmtal group, those centre is situated south of the alps.

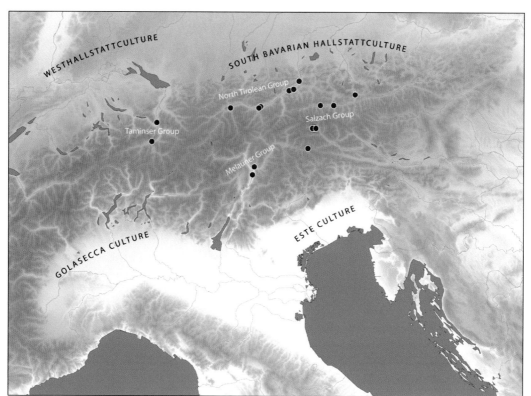

Merhart 1927, 67-79; Lunz 1974, 52-70; Gleirscher 1992, 117-134). The Tamins group is located in the Alpine Rhine Valley in Switzerland (see Rageth 1992, 176-184; Schmid-Sikimić 2002, 239-293), the pottery of which is influenced by the western Hallstatt culture as well as the Melaun group. Their costumes were heavily influenced by the Golasecca culture in Lombardia.

Wörgl is one of the northernmost necropoles of the inner Alpine Hallstatt groups and is located only a few kilometers to the south of the western Hallstatt culture in Bavaria, the tumulus groups of which are distributed to the north of Lake Chiem (Fig. 3A); *cf.* Kossack 1959, 7-11 fig. 1 pl. 149). In the preceding Urnfield culture southern Bavaria and northern Tyrol formed a cultural entity (Sperber 1992a, 55-56; 1992b, 37), especially with regard to the burial rituals which show strong similarities. With the beginning of the Hallstatt culture around 800 BC this entity slowly dissolved through the dissociation of northern Tyrol from southern Bavaria. While in Bavaria as well as north of the Alps in general, the burials of elites are monumentalized through the erection of tumuli, this innovation is not adopted by the societies of the inner Alpine Hallstatt groups. This lack of monumental burials might be part of a resistance against the Hallstatt elites, who are typical for the regions north of the Alps. Furthermore in northern Tyrol the number of vessels does not increase in the course of the burial ritual. While in Bavaria 30 or more vessels can be deposited in burials (Kossack 1970, 130-138; Krausse 1996, 322-330; Lüscher 1993, 127-139 fig. 62-66), most graves in Wörgl and Kundl yield only the urn and one further vessel.

The burial rites in Wörgl

The burial site of Wörgl is characterized by strongly uniform burial rituals. Every deceased was burned and interred in a pottery urn. These urns were deposited in round burial pits. In several cases stones were used to shore up the burial pits or were arranged in a circular pattern. In some cases larger stones were used to mark a burial above ground. The used stones were never worked. Large burial monuments comparable to the tumuli of the Hallstatt culture north of the Alps are not known from Wörgl, where the burials are too close together to allow larger monuments.

As mentioned above, many burials contained a single pottery vessel, a small bowl, in addition to the urn (Fig. 4). In only a few cases were one or two further vessels discovered, some of which survive only as fragments in the urn. This pattern of grave goods was strictly adhered to from the early Hallstatt period to the La Tène period.

A special feature of the necropolis on the Egerndorfer Feld is the vast amount of rich metal grave goods compared to general Alpine burial rituals. Prestigious finds such as rich costumes, weapons, parts of horse-gear and bronze vessels are found in the burials. In Wörgl it is only the metal finds that demonstrate social inequalities within the burial ritual. Large burial mounds or huge sets of vessels are not used for social distinction. The metals also testify large-scale culture contacts and interdependencies (Fig. 3B). From all cardinal directions material culture found its way to Wörgl: a special form of ankle rings (*Schaukelringe*) points to nearby Bavaria; forms of arm rings derive from southwestern Germany like the so called *Tonnenarmbänder*. Arm rings with circular extensions hint to the middle Rhine region. The fibula costumes from Wörgl consist of large

5 cm

5 cm

Fig. 4. Wörgl, Egerndorfer Feld, grave 224. 1: in situ block recovery. – 2: Pottery urn with accompanying bowl (photo R. Müller, RGZM).

amounts of spectacle shaped fibulae (*Brillenfibeln*) and half-moon shaped fibula (*Halbmondfibeln*) that testify an orientation on the eponymous site of Hallstatt in Upper Austria. In contrast, the female belt costumes with oval belt plates follow Italic notions. Some neck rings (Ösenhalsringe) and fibulae testify connections to Slovenia and the Carpathian basin. All these large-scale interdependencies indicated by the finds lead to the question to what extend the inhabitants of the Grattenbergl were involved in the lucrative exchange of goods in Early Iron Age

Europe. The exceptional position of Wörgl in these networks becomes even more evident when the grave goods are compared to other burial sites of the region, like the necropolis of Kundl located some ten kilometers to the west (see Lang 1998). Here only very few metal grave goods were found in the Early Iron Age burials.

Before one grave of Wörgl is presented in the context of connected elites, one specialty in the burial rituals of the necropolis needs to be emphasized: all the dead were burned on the pyre. Afterwards the cremated bones were collected, but only up to one or two handfuls were deposited in the urns. While for an adult one would roughly estimate around 1.5-2 kg of cremated bones, in Wörgl only up to 0.3 kg were deposited. In Kundl similar small amounts of cremation were interred in the graves (see Lang 1998, 48). The treatment of the remainder remains unknown.

In many cases, metal grave goods were bent or broken before they were placed in the urns (Fig. 5; 7). A good example for this practice is the iron knives. In some cases, they were only bent to up to 90° while in other cases, they were folded several times. This folding seems impossible without the use of tools. Other iron objects were also heavily bent, like La Tène swords or horse-bits. Bronze grave goods were treated in a similar way. Fibulae or rings were equally bent or broken prior to deposition. A very special treatment was reserved for arm and ankle rings that were interred in pairs: one was broken while the other one was left intact (Fig. 5).

Regularly, a *pars pro toto* was deposited in the grave, rather than the whole object. This rite is clearly illustrated by the fragment of a sword in Grave 5 (Fig. 7,8). The remainder was not interred in the urn. This custom is strikingly illustrated by Grave 58. In the urn two small fragments of tires with associated nails and felloe clamps were discovered. Such finds are parts of an early Hallstatt four-wheeled wagons and clearly illustrate the *pars pro toto*. Interestingly only one horse-bit was detected in this grave, even though a yoke and a harnessed team of two horses is needed for the use of the wagon. The *pars pro toto* custom was used far more intensively when compared to the Hallstatt culture north of the Alps (see Pare 1992, 198-200). It seems to be a characteristic of the inner Alpine Hallstatt groups, as described by A. Lang based on the cemetery of Kundl (Lang 1998, 50-51).

It needs to be discussed what happened to the parts of the grave goods that were not interred in the urns: did they remain on the pyre and in the case of the bronze objects were burned down to amorphous drops of bronze? A definite evaluation is hard to give as the pyres have not been located. It remains possible that those other parts of the objects were deposited at hitherto unknown places.

Fig. 5. Wörgl, grave 338. 1: complete bronze arm ring. – 2: intentionally broken bronze arm ring (drawings M. Weber, RGZM).

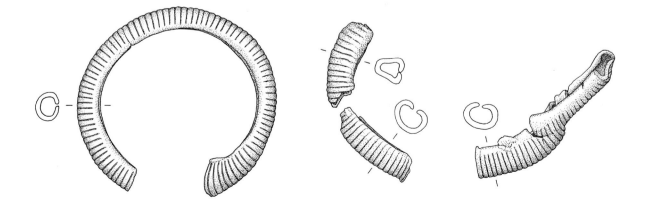

Another possibility is that they were kept by the mourners as a memento on the dead, but they could also have been remelted and reused later on.

Wörgl, Grave 5 and large-scale interdependencies in the early Hallstatt period

Although the funerary community of Wörgl did not employ the new burial customs that dispersed north of the Alps, there were close connections with southern Germany in the early Hallstatt period (Ha C). This becomes exceedingly evident in Grave 5, which will be presented in the following to illustrate the large-scale interdependencies of the cemetery of Wörgl.

As is common for the burial site of Wörgl, Grave 5 is a typical urn burial (Fig. 6). The urn was interred in a circular pit and encircled by some stones. All grave goods were found in the urn.

The Bavarian influence is already clearly depicted on the urn, which is only fragmentarily preserved. It shows a cone shaped neck and an ornament made of cherry red slip and graphite painting in a zigzag pattern (Fig. 7,10). Such vessels are type finds for the Hallstatt culture in southern Bavaria and the area around Inn and Salzach (Kossack 1959, 34-37; Stöllner 2002, 162-165) and are often testified in Wörgl as well. Inside the urn some cremated bones were discovered underneath a small pottery bowl (Fig. 7,11). As noted above, this combination of vessels is typical for the cemetery of Wörgl.

Fig. 6. Wörgl, Grave 5: plan of the grave (Tyrolean State Museum Ferdinandeum Innsbruck).

This grave also yielded a fragment of a bronze sword blade that was damaged by fire (Fig. 7,8). Although the grip is missing, which is usually important for a typological analysis, the width of the blade and its ribs hint towards a Mindelheim sword (Cowen 1967, 384-391; Schauer 1971, 194-195). The central rib fits best with the variant Wels-Pernau, as defined by P. Schauer (1971, 194-195 pl. 95).

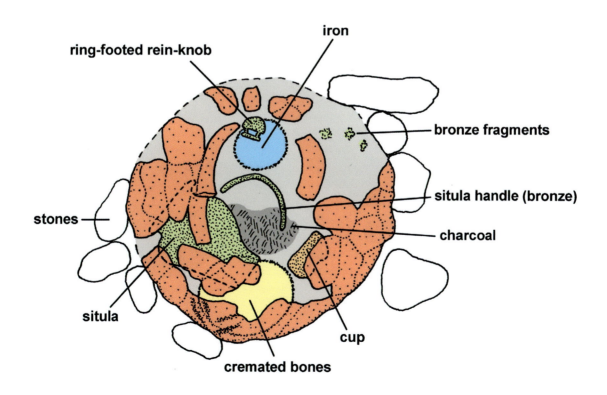

Fig. 7. Wörgl, grave 5, the grave goods. 1-2: iron horse-bits. – 3-6: bronze ring-footed rein-knobs 7: iron pin with multiple heads. – 8: fragments of a bronze sword blade. – 9: fragments of a bronze situla. – 10: fragments of the urn. – 11: accompanying pottery bowl (photo M. Egg, RGZM).

Due to the fragmentary state of preservation the schemes as proposed by P.-Y. Milcent and M. Trachsel cannot be applied (Milcent 2004, 87-95; Trachsel 2004, 124-132 fig. 65-67).

Mindelheim swords are generally made of iron, and the bronze versions are seen as the older variant of this weapon type. The bronze swords are much rarer than the iron examples. J.D. Cowen compiled them in 1967 (Fig. 8; Cowen 1967, 424-427 map A). Bronze Mindelheim swords are mostly found north of the Alps between Baden-Württemberg and Bohemia. Core areas can be found in Northern Bavaria and Upper Austria. The absence of such swords in the west seems noteworthy as they already do not appear in the Upper Rhine valley. The spread of swords found from Bohemia to southern Scandinavia is striking and can probably be seen in relation with the trade of amber. The sword of Wörgl is one of the southernmost swords of this type.

Mindelheim swords are a type find of Ha C1b – C2 (Hodson, 1990, 54-65 fig. 13; fig. 17; Kossack 1959, 17-22). The bronze swords date to the beginning of this period as clearly shown by R. Hodson in the cemetery of Hallstatt (Hodson 1990, 58 fig. 17). The presence of such a sword in Grave 5 dates this burial to an early stage of Ha C1b around 700 BC. Two iron horse bits with curved cheek-pieces tetragonal holes were also found (Fig. 7,1-2), which belong to G. Kossack classic type Ib[4]. Wörgl is the only site of the inner Alpine Hallstatt groups where cheek-pieces are testified in eight graves. In Grave 5 the cheek-pieces were found in a pair but as typical for Wörgl, in an incomplete state. These finds identify the deceased as a driver of a wagon.

Cheek-pieces of the type Ib are typical for Ha C1b in southern Germany as already noted by G. Kossack in 1954. The more recent studies of C. Metzner-Nebelsick (2002, 114) confirm this classification. The distribution map of these finds testifies their broad distribution from the Netherlands to Serbia with a clear concentration in southern Germany and Bohemia. The finds from Wörgl link up to this core area (Pare 1992, 142 fig. 101a).

Grave 5 also yielded four ring-footed rein-knobs without flanges (Fig. 7,3-6; Kossack 1954, 117 map 3; Pare 1992, 139-146 fig. 101b). C. Metzner-Nebelsick terms these as type AVa (Metzner-Nebelsick 2002, 311-318 fig. 139A, Va.). G. Kossack stressed that these ring-footed rein-knobs need to be counted to the group of burials with richly decorated horse-gear of the early Hallstatt period (Ha C) and are mostly associated with horse-bits of the types Ib or Ic (Fig. 9; Kossack 1954, 118-124), which is also the case in Grave 5 of Wörgl. Graves with such horse-gear are typical for Ha C1.

The simple ring-footed rein-knobs of the Hallstatt period are mostly found in southern Germany and Bohemia (Fig. 10; Pare 1992, 143 fig. 101b) and the finds from Wörgl form a southern periphery of this core area. Still, some such finds are scattered from the Netherlands to the Carpathian basin.

In terms of costume Grave 5 yielded a badly preserved iron pin with multiple heads separated from the shaft by a stop (*Faltenwehr*). The final head is lenticular in shape and is accompanied by two further heads (Fig. 7,7). At first glance, the use of iron seems unusual for such pins were usually cast in bronze, as for example in

---

4   Kossack 1954, 119-120 map 2; Pare 1992, 140-146 fig. 101a. – Two further cheek pieces of this type from Salzburg-Maxglan, grave 400 (Moosleitner 1996, 324 fig. 10,1-2) need to be added as well as two pieces tumulus 3 and 139 of Budinjak in Croatia (Škoberne 1999, pl. 8,3. – I would like to thank the excavator Ž. Škoberne (Zagreb) for the hint on the unpublished piece of Tumulus 3).

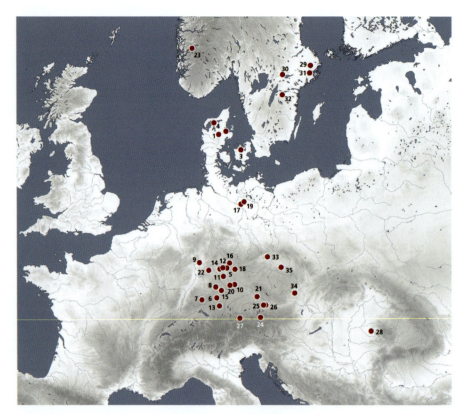

Fig. 8. Distribution of bronze Mindelheim Sword (mapped after Cowen 1967 with complements). 1: Bjerringbro. – 2: Fœllenslev. – 3: Holbaek-Slots. – 4: Limfjord. – 5: Bamberg. – 6: Bubesheim. – 7: Burladingen-Ringingen. – 8: Ellwangen-Röhlingen. – 9: Frankfurt-Oberrad. – 10: Ittelhofen-Freihausen. – 11: Kappel-Kemmathen. – 12: Knetzgau-Wertheim. – 13: Mindelheim. – 14: Mistelgau. – 15: Möttingen. – 16: Neuensee. – 17: Schönfeld. – 18: Schreez-Gosen. – 19: Steffenshagen. – 20: Thalmässing. – 21: Vilshofen. – 22: Wertheim. – 23: Lekve. – 24: Hallstatt. – 25: Wels-Pernau. – 26: Wels-Wimpassing. – 27: Wörgl. – 28: Batăr-Arpăşel. – 29: Ånsta. – 30: Hassle. – 31: Råsunda. – 32: Sjögestad. – 33: Bohušovice. – 34: Jarošavice. – 35: Kolin (graphics M. Ober, RGZM).

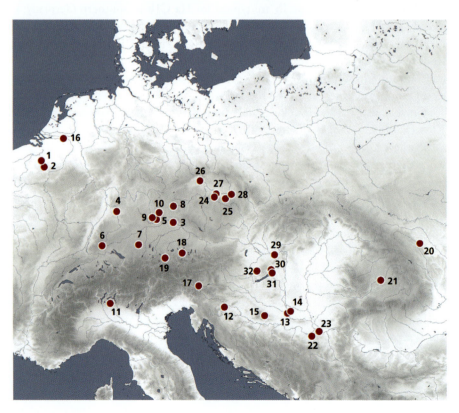

Fig. 9. Distribution of type Ib horse bits (mapped after Pare 1992 with complements). 1: Limal-Morimoine. – 2: Court-St.-Etienne. – 3: Aholfing. – 4: Bad Rappenau. – 5: Beilngries. – 6: Bittelbrunn. – 7: Mindelheim. – 8: Neukirchen-Gaisheim. – 9: Thalmässing. – 10: Unterwiesenacker. – 11: Como-Ca'Morta. – 12: Budinjak. – 13: Dalj. – 14: Erdut Veliki Varad. – 15: Kaptol. – 16: Oss. – 17: Rosegg-Frög. – 18: Salzburg-Maxglan. – 19: Wörgl. – 20: Cristeşti. – 21: Cipău. – 22: Boranja. – 23: Ritopek. – 24: Hradenín. – 25: Lhotka. – 26: Lovosice. – 27: Plaňany. – 28: Platěnice. – 29: Nagysomló-Dobai Ungarn. – 30: Sédvíz. – 31: Somlyóhegy. – 32: Somlyóvásárhely (graphics M. Ober, RGZM).

Fig. 10. Distribution of simple ring-footed rein-knobs (mapped after Pare 1992 with complements). 1: Albstadt-Ebingen. – 2: Albstadt-Tailfingen. – 3: Bittelbrunn. – 4: Breisach-Gündlingen. – 5: Dietfurt a. d. Altmühl. – 6: Eigeltingen-Honstetten. – 7: Emmerting-Bruck. – 8: Engstingen-Großengstingen. – 9: Estorf-Leeseringen. – 10: Forst Merzelbach. – 11: Gauting. – 12: Großeibstadt. – 13: Köngen. – 14: Lager Lechfeld. – 15: Leipheim. – 16: Maisach-Gernlinden. – 17: Mindelheim. – 18: Moritzbrunn. – 19: Neukirchen-Gaisheim. – 20: Neustetten-Wolfenhausen. – 21: Oberfahlheim. – 22: Reichenau. – 23: Riedenburg-Haidhof. – 23: Rorgenwies. – 24: Scheuring-Haltenberg. – 25: Sigmaringen-Laiz. – 26: Tannheim.- 27: Thann-Neuhaus. – 28: Unterwiesenacker. – 29: Vöhringen. – 30: Wehringen. – 31: Mailhac. – 32: Wijchen. – 33: Gilgenberg. – 34: Hallstatt. – 35: Wörgl. – 36: Stična. – 37: Vitina (Herzegowina). – 38: Dýšina. – 39: Horákov. – 40: Lhotka. – 41: Lovosice. – 42: Plaňany. -43: Straškov-Račiněves. – 44: Nagyberki-Szalacska. – 45: Százhalombatta (graphics M. Ober, RGZM).

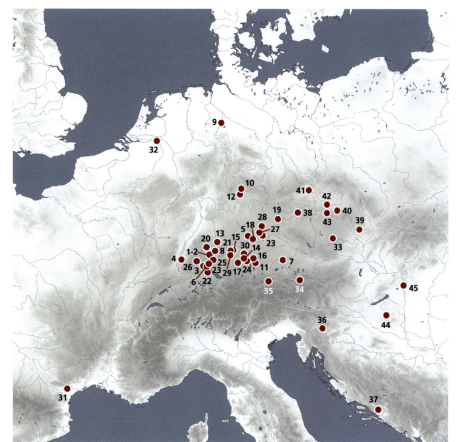

Hallstatt, Veneto or in Slovenia. In Wörgl pins with multiple heads were primarily made of iron, which conforms with other cemeteries of the inner Alpine Hallstatt groups, like Bischofshofen[5] or Uttendorf in the Pinzgau (Moosleitner 1982/83, 30 fig. 26,3.7) situated in federal state Salzburg or in Pfatten/Vadena in southern Tyrol (Marzatico 1997, 531-534 fig. 231-235 pl. 115,1284-1293). Those sites yielded several iron pins of that type, which indicates that this is typical for the inner Alpine Hallstatt groups. The choice of this material cannot be ascribed to a lack of copper in this region but can rather be seen as a conscious choice in appreciation of iron in the manufacture of costume.

The distribution map recently provided by Ž. Škoberne (2004, 213-218 fig. 4)[6] indicates that these pins are concentrated around the Caput Adriae, the southeastern Alpine region, the eastern Alps with the center of Hallstatt and along the valleys of Etsch and Inn. In smaller numbers they also appear in southern Bavaria and the area around Inn and Salzach north of the Alps.

Furthermore, fragments of a bronze situla with a short cylindrical neck were found in Grave 5 (Fig. 7,9). As with all situlae in Wörgl, it was fragmented and only a part of it was interred in the grave. The clearly pronounced shoulder was ornamented with a circular rib. The bottom of the situla was formed like a riveted bowl, which indicates an early dating of this situla, as these were replaced by

5　As much as six iron pins with multiple heads were discovered here. See Lippert/Stadler 2009, pl. 25,3.8; pl. 32,6; pl. 74,9; pl. 132,4; pl. 169,27.

6　In northern Tyrol one further piece of Langenkampfen-Marienkapelle needs to be added (Appler 2010, 80 fig. 39,8).

Fig. 11. Distribution of the discussed type of situlae (Situlen mit Steilhals, einnietiger Bandattasche und angenieteter Bodenschale). 1: Albate. – 2: Como-Ca'Morta. – 3: Ede. – 4: Hallstatt. – 5: Wörgl. – 6: Rvenice. – 7: Vaskeresztes (graphics M. Ober, RGZM).

situlae with grooved bottoms in the course of Ha D. The handle attachments of the situla feature one rivet and held a bow shaped handle ending in bird shapes

As the distribution map indicates (Fig. 11), there are only a few parallels for the situla of Grave 5 of Wörgl, among them the situla of Ede-Bennekom in the Netherlands (Kimmig 1962/63, 67 fig. 12). Such a connection, from Wörgl in northern Tyrol to the Netherlands, is quite striking as it connects the most distant parts of early Hallstatt elites with each other. The distribution of those situlae covers a broad area from upper Italy to the Netherlands and from Hungary to the western Alps. What stands out is that most of these situlae show two or three ribs on the shoulder. The only exceptions are Wörgl Grave 5, Grave 555 of Hallstatt (Prüssing 1991, pl. 35,162) and tumulus 1 from Vaskersztes in Hungary (Fekete 1985, 73 fig. 5,4), which feature a single rib. As already pointed out, these situlae chronologically derive from the early Hallstatt period (Ha C), (see Hodson 1990, 59 fig. 17 and Sievers 1982, 18 pl. 1,1 on the piece of Hallstatt as well as Fekete 1985, 74-75 and Patay 1990, 74 pl. 48 on the find from Vaskersztes). Those with multiple ribs seem to emerge in the Later Hallstatt period (Ha D). The example from Wörgl is a little older than its parallels and dates to an early section of Ha C1b, around 700 BC, due to the association with the horse-gear and the bronze Mindelheim sword blade.

Conclusion

Although interred in an urn in a flat grave, the metal grave goods of Wörgl Grave 5 – consisting of a sword, horse-gear, a wagon and even a bronze vessel – form an exclusive grave furnishing. This set of grave goods represents the classic endowment of the early Hallstatt Mindelheim horizon. This pattern of exclusive grave goods can be found in quite diverse cultural groups between Tyrol and the Netherlands. The elites of these cultures of different origin all used this set to show high prestige in burial rituals. These burials therefor clearly indicate large-scale interaction between elites in the early Hallstatt period on a European scale in this large area between Tyrol and the Netherlands. These elites were communicating and interacting with each other across Europe.

Bibliography

Appler 2010: H. Appler, Schatzfunde, Opferplätze und Siedlungen. Neue archäologische Forschungen zur Vorgeschichte und Römerzeit in Nordtirol 1 (Wattens/Wien 2010).

Cowen 1967: J. Cowen, The Hallstatt sword of Bronze: on the continent and in Britain. Proceedings of the Prehistoric Society 33, 1967, 377-454.

Fekete 1985: M. Fekete, Rettungsgrabung früheisenzeitlicher Hügelgräber in Vaskeresztes. Acta Archaeologica Hungarica 37, 1985, 33-77.

Gleirscher 1992: P. Gleirscher, Die Laugen-Melaun-Gruppe. In: P. Metzger/P. Gleirscher (eds.), Die Räter – I Reti (Bozen 1992) 117-125.

Franz 1951: L. Franz, Aus Wörgls vor- und frühgeschichtlicher Zeit. In: H. Federer (ed.), Wörgler Heimatschriftchen II. Von der Besiedlung (Wörgl 1951) 5-22.

Hodson 1990: R. Hodson, Hallstatt. The Ramsauer Graves – Quantification and Analysis. Monographien des Römisch-Germanischen Zentralmuseums 16 (Mainz 1990).

Kimmig 1962/63: W. Kimmig, Bronzesitulen aus dem Rheinischen Gebirge, Hunsrück-Eifel-Westerwald. Bericht der Römisch-Germanischen Kommission 43/44, 1962/63, 31-106.

Kneußl 1969: R. Kneußl, Studien an hallstättischer Keramik der Gräberfelder Egerndorfer Wald (Wörgl) und Haiming. In: O. Menghin (ed.), Beiträge zur Urgeschichte Tirols. Innsbrucker Beiträge zur Kulturwissenschaft, Sonderheft 29 (Innsbruck 1969) 145-235.

Kossack 1954: G. Kossack, Pferdegeschirr aus Gräbern der älteren Hallstattzeit Bayerns. Jahrbuch des Römisch-Germanischen Zentralmuseums 1, 1954, 111-178.

Kossack 1959: G. Kossack, Südbayern während der Hallstattzeit. Römisch-Germanische Forschungen 24 (Berlin 1959).

Kossack 1970: G. Kossack, Gräberfelder der Hallstattzeit an Main und Fränkischer Saale. Materialhefte zur bayerischen Vorgeschichte 24 (Kallmünz 1970).

Krausse 1996: D. Krausse; Hochdorf III. Das Trink- und Speiseservice aus dem späthallstattzeitlichen Fürstengrab von Eberdingen-Hochdorf (Kr. Ludwigsburg). Forschungen und Berichte zur Vor- und Frühgeschichte in Baden-Württemberg 64 (Stuttgart 1996).

Lang 1998: A. Lang, Das Gräberfeld von Kundl im Tiroler Inntal. – Studien zur vorrömischen Eisenzeit in den zentralen Alpen. Frühgeschichtliche und provinzialrömische Archäologie 2 (Rahden/Westf. 1998).

Lippert/Stadler 2009: A. Lippert/P. Stadler, Das spätbronze- und früheisenzeitliche Gräberfeld von Bischofshofen-Pestfriedhof. Universitätsforschungen zur prähistorischen Archäologie 168 (Bonn 2009).

Lucke 1938: W. Lucke, Zu einem Bronzefund mit Situla in Wörgl, Tirol. Germania 22, 1938, 150-157.

Lüscher 1993: G. Lüscher, Unterlunkhofen und die hallstattzeitliche Grabkeramik in der Schweiz. Antiqua 24 (Basel 1993).

Lunz 1974: R. Lunz, Studien zur End-Bronzezeit und älteren Eisenzeit im Südalpenraum (Florenz 1974).

Marzatico 1992: F. Marzatico, Il gruppo Fritzens-Sanzeno. In: Metzger / Gleirscher 1992, 213-233.

Marzatico 1997: F. Marzatico, I materiali preromani della valle dell'Adige nel Castello del Buonconsiglio. Patrimonio Storico e Artistico del Trentino 21 (Trento 1997).

Mérey-Kádár 1958: E. Mérey-Kádár, Funde aus dem Gräberfeld „Egerndorfer Wald" bei Wörgl im Tiroler Landesmuseum Ferdinandeum. Der Schlern 32, 1958, 450-452.

Metzger/Gleirscher 1992: P. Metzger/P. Gleirscher (eds.), Die Räter – I Reti (Bozen 1992).

Metzner-Nebelsick 2002: C. Metzner-Nebelsick, Der „thrako-kimmerische" Formenkreis aus der Sicht der Urnenfelder- und Hallstattzeit im südöstlichen Pannonien. Vorgeschichtliche Forschungen 23 (Rahden/Westf. 2002).

Milcent 2004: P.-Y. Milcent, Le premier âge du Fer en France Centrale. Mémoires de la Société Préhistorique Française 34 (Paris 2004).

Moosleitner 1980: F. Moosleitner, Der inner Alpine Raum in der Hallstattzeit. In: Die Hallstattkultur Symposium Steyr (Linz 1980) 205-226.

Moosleitner 1982/83: F. Moosleitner, Das hallstattzeitliche Gräberfeld von Uttendorf im Pinzgau. Ausstellungskat. Zell a. See u. Salzburg (1982 u. 1983).

Moosleitner 1996: F. Moosleitner, Zum Übergang von der Urnenfelderzeit zur Hallstattperiode im Salzburger Becken. In: E. Jerem/A. Lippert (eds.), Die Osthallstattkultur. Akten des internationalen Symposiums Sopron 1994. Archaeolingua (Budapest 1996) 315-325.

Pare 1992: C. Pare, Wagons and wagon-graves of the early iron age in Central Europe. Oxford Univ. Committee for Archaeology Monographs 35 (Oxford 1992).

Patay 1990: P. Patay, Die Bronzegefäße in Ungarn. Prähistorische Bronzefunde 2,10 (München 1990).

Prüssing 1991: G. Prüssing, Die Bronzegefäße in Österreich. Prähistorische Bronzefunde 2,5 (Stuttgart 1991).

Rageth 1992: J. Rageth, Zur Eisenzeit im Alpenrheintal. In: In: P. Metzger/P. Gleirscher (eds.), Die Räter – I Reti (Bozen 1992) 175-201.

Schauer 1971: P. Schauer, Die Schwerter in Süddeutschland, Österreich und der Schweiz I (Griffplatten-, Griffangel- und Griffzungenschwerter). Prähistorische Bronzefunde 4,2 (München 1971).

Schmid-Sikimić 2002: B. Schmid-Sikimić, Mesocco Coop (GR) Eisenzeitlicher Bestattungsplatz im Brennpunkt zwischen Süd und Nord. Universitätsforschungen zur prähistorischen Archäologie 88 (Bonn 2002).

Sievers 1982: S. Sievers, Die mitteleuropäischen Hallstattdolche. Prähistorische Bronzefunde 6,6 (München 1982).

Škoberne 1999: Ž. Škoberne, Budinjak kneževski tumul (Zagreb 1999).

Škoberne 2004: Ž. Škoberne, The find of an unusual multi-headed pin from the cemetery at Budinjak. Archäologisches Korrespondenzblatt 34, 2004, 211-227.

Sperber 1992a: L. Sperber, Zur Spätbronzezeit im Alpinen Inn- und Rheintal. In: P. Metzger/P. Gleirscher (eds.), Die Räter – I Reti (Bozen 1992) 53-74.

Sperber 1992b: L. Sperber, Zur Demographie des spätbronzezeitlichen Gräberfeldes von Volders in Nordtirol. Veröffentlichungen des Tiroler Landesmuseums Ferdinandeum 72, 1992, 37-74.

Stöllner 2002: T. Stöllner, Die Hallstattzeit und der Beginn der Latènezeit im Inn-Salzach-Raum. Archäologie in Salzburg 3,1 (Salzburg 2002).

Tiefengraber/Tiefengraber 2105: G. Tiefengraber/S. Tiefengraber, Zum Stand der Erforschung hallstattzeitlicher „Zentralsiedlungen" in der Obersteiermark. In. C. Gutjahr/G. Tiefengraber (eds.), Beiträge zur Hallstattzeit am Rande der Südostalpen. Akten 2. Int. Symposion Wildon 2010. Internationale Archäologie, Kongress 19 = Hengist-Studien 3 (Rahden/Westf. 2015) 217-275.

Tomedi 1998: G. Tomedi, Eine vorgeschichtliche Wanderung im Raum Wörgl. In: J. Zangerl (ed.), Wörgl ein Heimatbuch. (Wörgl 1998) 39-52.

Trachsel 2004: M. Trachsel, Untersuchungen zur relativen und absoluten Chronologie der Hallstattzeit. Universitätsforschungen zur prähistorischen Archäologie 104 (Bonn 2004).

von Merhart 1927: G. von Merhart, Archäologisches zur Frage der Illyrer in Tirol. Wiener prähistorische Zeitschrift 14, 1927, 65-118.

von Merhart 1935-38a: G. von Merhart, Wörgl, GB. u. VB Kufstein. Fundberichte aus Österreich 2, 1935-1938, 48-49.

von Merhart 1935-38b: G. von Merhart, Wörgl, GB. u. VB Kufstein. Fundberichte aus Österreich 2, 1935-1938, 104.

von Wieser 1911: F. von Wieser, Prähistorische und römische Funde bei Wörgl. In: Festschrift zur Feier der Markterhebungsfeier von Wörgl am 13. August 1911 (Innsbruck 1911) 3-9.

Author

Markus Egg
Römisch-Germanisches Zentralmuseum
Leibniz-Forschungsinstitut für Archäologie
Ernst-Ludwig-Platz 2
D – 55116 Mainz
Germany
egg@rgzm.de

Animals to honour the ancestors

On animal depositions in barrows of the northeast Alpine Hallstatt region

Petra Kmeťová

Abstract

This paper considers the character and role of animal depositions in graves of social elites in the northeast Alpine Hallstatt region. Only a small number of graves are included in the analysis due to the rather poor state of research. Collections of finds, however, differ in several aspects, such as animal species present and the amount and form of deposited remains. Animal depositions in graves of social elites are investigated from the point of horizontal social status of the deceased. They are also compared to animal remains in graves of individuals of assumed lower social rank. Finally, their role in burial rites of members of the social elites is discussed.

Zusammenfassung

Dieser Beitrag ist dem Charakter und der Rolle von Tierdeponierungen in Gräbern der sozialen Eliten in den nordostalpinen Hallstattgruppen gewidmet. Aufgrund des eher schlechten Forschungsstandes können dabei nur wenige Bestattungen analysiert werden. Nichtsdestotrotz lassen sich Unterschiede herausarbeiten, so in der Auswahl der Tierarten, der Menge und der Selektion der niedergelegten Teile. Die entsprechenden Befunde werden in diesem Beitrag auch in Hinblick auf den horizontalen Status der in den Bestattungen niedergelegten Individuen untersucht. Zudem werden die Tierdeponierungen der Elitegräber mit Bestattungen von sozial niedriger zu verordnenden Gruppen verglichen, bevor schlussendlich die Rolle von Tierdeponierungen in den Bestattungsriten der sozialen Eliten diskutiert wird.

Introduction

High social status and prestige of some individuals buried at cemeteries of the Hallstatt culture was indicated by monumental grave construction, variety of artefacts with additional symbolic meaning and also by complex burial rites. This paper examines whether animal depositions were another means of underlining the high status of deceased, or more precisely, what their function in graves of social elites was. It focuses on barrows of social elites in the northeast Alpine Hallstatt region (present-day Lower Austria and Burgenland, southern Moravia, south-western Slovakia, and northern and central Transdanubia, Hungary). Dominant barrows in this region date to period of Ha C – D1 after which they ceased to be built.

Animals were an irreplaceable part of life of Early Iron Age communities. They were not only a source of food (meat, fat, milk, etc.), but also a source of organic materials (wool, leather, fur, bone, horn, antler, perhaps even manure), domesticated ones were also working animals (draft power, means of transport, watching the property, herding, assistance in hunting, etc.), and some were even close human companions. The significance of some animals was reflected in art and the religious sphere. Research on the use of animals in early phases of the Hallstatt period based on skeletal remains is still rather sporadic or focuses on selected species. A similar situation exists in western Central Europe, with more sites researched, where majority of sites with analysed osteological material comes from Ha D (e.g. Müller-Scheeßel/Trebsche 2007, 63-65 tab. 1). The issue of animal remains in barrows of social elites in northeastern Alpine Hallstatt region has not yet been evaluated in its complexity. In this area few archaeozoologically researched grave finds are available; nevertheless, there are some find contexts that warrant attention. Despite certain limitations of the research (animal depositions without bones are undetectable by traditional methods), it can show certain tendencies in treating animal bodies for funeral purposes to honour the members of social elites.

Materials and state of research

This contribution is based on available information on archaeozoological investigation, closely linked to state of archaeological research. It focuses primarily on osteological finds that are well recorded, evaluated and published (including detailed archaeozoological determination, evaluation and interpretation; cf. e.g. Ambros 1975, 217; Stadler 2010, 26-33). Although, at present time it is a standard procedure, in the studied area only a small number of graves are evaluated in such detail (cf. Nebelsick 1997a, 50-58), namely barrows in Dunajská Lužná-Nové Košariská, south-western Slovakia (Pichlerová 1969; Ambros 1975), barrows 109 and 114 in Százhalombatta, western Hungary (Holport 1993; Vörös 1993), barrow 3 in Langenlebarn, Lower Austria (Preinfalk 2003; Pucher 2003), and barrow 1 in Zagersdorf, Burgenland (Rebay 2002).

In case of other barrows excavated in the 2nd half of the 20th century, archaeozoological analyses were published only briefly or were not realized/ published at all. Among them of special importance is a barrow in west Hungary, Süttő-Sáncföldek, excavated in 1978-82. Beside information on uncremated remains, also results of analyses of cremated animal remains were published (Vadász 1983; 1986). Publication of such analyses is rare until now in the area of the northeast Hallstatt region. Unpublished partial results (horse remains) of such analysis in barrows 1 and 3-6 in west Hungarian Fehérvárcsurgó-Eresztvény were provided by I. Vörös (pers. comm. 2008; cf. Jungbert 1993). Only some information from archaeozoological analysis was included in evaluation of a rich grave (barrow?) from south-Moravian Bratčice (Golec 2005, 93-140 esp. 99). In case of some other barrows only complete animal skeletal remains or their larger parts were specified (Gemeinlebarn, barrow 1, Vaszar-Pörösrét, barrows 4, 5 and 7, Modřice, female grave; Mithay 1980, 57-58; 64; 77; Offenberger 1980, 438; Kos/Přichystal 2013, 80-82).

The majority of dominant barrows in the region were unearthed in the 19th or first half of the 20th century when evidence, excavation and storage of animal remains were not in the focus of most researchers. If animal bones were mentioned, it is unclear whether they were determined by a specialist on zoological material and thus whether the information is accurate. These finds were therefore not included

cemetery	grave	cattle	sheep	sheep/goat, goat?	domestic pig	horse, equid	dog	red deer	wild boar	European hare	fox	domestic hen	greylag goose, goose	wild duck	bird egg	beaver	fish	indet.	references
Bad Fischau-Feichtenboden	barrow 10	X	X	X	X	1?		1						X					Klemm 1992, 372-393
Bad Fischau	barrow Hochholz	X	X																Klemm 1992, 443-464
Bratčice	grave	1?		1?		1													Golec 2005, 99-100
Dunajská Lužná-Nové Košariská	barrow 1	1	1																Ambros 1975
Dunajská Lužná-Nové Košariská	barrow 3	X	≥ 1	≥ 2	≥ 2		1			1?		1	2?	1	X		1?	X	Ambros 1975
Dunajská Lužná-Nové Košariská	barrow 4	≥ 1	≥ 1	≥ 1						1				X	1	1-2			Ambros 1975
Dunajská Lužná-Nové Košariská	barrow 6	≥ 1			≥ 3					1?			2-3						Ambros 1975
Gemeinlebarn	barrow 1				1													?	Offenberger 1980
Fehérvárcsurgó	barrow 1				X	1												?	Vörös 2008, pers. comm.
Fehérvárcsurgó	barrow 3					1												?	Vörös 2008, pers. comm.
Fehérvárcsurgó	barrow 4				X													?	Vörös 2008, pers. comm.
Fehérvárcsurgó	barrow 5				X													?	Vörös 2008, pers. comm.
Fehérvárcsurgó	barrow 6				X													?	Vörös 2008, pers. comm.
Langenlebarn	barrow 3	X	≥ 2	1?	X	1?								X			X		Pucher 2003
Modřice									X									?	Kos/Přichystal 2013, 80-82
Süttő-Sáncföldek	barrow	X	X		X	X	X												V. Vadász 1983; 1986
Százhalombatta	barrow 109	1	≥ 7	1?	1	1	1	X		1	1								Vörös 1993
Százhalombatta	barrow 114		1		2					X	2								Vörös 1993
Vaszar-Pörösrét	barrow 4				X													?	Mithay 1980
Vaszar-Pörösrét	barrow 5				2					X								?	Mithay 1980; Horváth 1969
Vaszar-Pörösrét	barrow 7				2												X		Mithay 1980
Zagersdorf	barrow 1	X		X	1?														Rebay 2002, 98

Table 1. Occurrence of animal species in barrows of elites in northeast Alpine Hallstatt region. Numbers state the number of detected individuals.

in this study, except barrows in Bad Fischau-Feichtenboden. Not only are the animal remains recorded rather precisely, but determinations from J. Szombathy's article (1924) practically correspond with results of archaeozoological analysis from the late 20th century (Klemm 1992). In the following analysis two large Bad Fischau barrows with outstanding grave goods are used, namely no. 10, and Hochholz excavated in the mid-20th century (Klemm 1992, 372-393; 443-467; Szombathy 1924, 186-187).

Animal species in barrows

Several animal species were present in all barrows excavated in the second half of the 20th century where palaeozoological material was analysed (Table 1). There were at least two, but mostly three and more species. The highest number (nine species) was detected in barrow 3 in Dunajská Lužná-Nové Košariská, following eight species in barrow 109 in Százhalombatta. Among these species, domestic animals and also game were included, namely mammals, birds and fish.

Three species occurred most frequently: cattle (*Bos taurus*), ovicaprid (sheep, *Ovis aries*, or goat, *Capra aegagrus hircus*, since their bones can be distinguished only sometimes), and domestic pig (*Sus scrofa domesticus*). In every grave with known and verified composition of animal remains at least two, but mostly all 'three' of these species were present. According to settlement and grave finds in wider Central Europe, they were essential to human meaty diet in the Early Iron Age (Benecke 1994, 131-133; Müller-Scheeßel/Trebsche 2007, 62-72; 75-83). In presented barrows, cattle were the most frequent found animal.

Regarding small ruminants, their remains were either undistinguishable, or, in several cases, were specified as remains of sheep (Table 1). Presence of goat bones is not confirmed in any of the presented barrows, only assumed in one grave (Bad

Fischau, barrow 10). The dominance of sheep in grave contexts compared to goat corresponds with its dominance in settlements and graves in most regions in wider Central Europe (Benecke 1994, 358 tab. 32; Müller-Scheeßel/Trebsche 2007, 66; Stadler 2010, 53).

The third most often occurring animal was domestic pig, which is also similar to the situation in breeding livestock in eastern Central Europe (Benecke 1994, 131; Müller-Scheeßel/Trebsche 2007). Its frequent occurrence in settlements of central character with developed crafts and exchange is associated with the ability to produce meat for a large number of people (Müller-Scheeßel/Trebsche 2007, 71-72).

Remains of 'best friends of humans', *ergo* horses and dogs, occurred less frequently. Horse remains (*Equus caballus*) are a rather frequent find in barrow graves; they come from nine or ten graves. Their higher proportion, however, might be only a reflection of uncomplete data (Fehérvárcsurgó, only information on horses available). Remains of dog (*Canis lupus familiaris*) were found only in three barrows.

Remains of wild animals were also less numerous. The most frequent was European brown hare (*Lepus europaeus*). Its bones were recorded in five barrows. Hare remains were also the most numerous game remains in Hallstatt and early La Tène settlements in Lower Austria and South Moravia, i.e. in the environment of wide open landscape, and frequent also at other sites (Trebsche 2013, 217; 225 fig. 10). Other wild mammals (red deer – *Cervus elaphus*, wild boar – *Sus scrofa*, and red fox – *Vulpes vulpes*) occur only sporadically. Artefacts made of red deer antler were found in two graves. Canine teeth of wild boar, used also as parts of artefacts, were detected in three graves. Fox bones were recognized in only one barrow. All of these animals were relatively frequent among game recorded in Hallstatt and early La Tène settlements (Trebsche 2013).

In barrows of northeast Alpine elites, remains of several birds (wild as well as domestic) were present. They were detected only in precisely excavated find contexts and in some of them several bird species were identified. The only certainly domestic species was hen (*Gallus gallus* f. *domestica*). A single wing bone comes from barrow 3 in Dunajská Lužná-Nové Košariská. In early Ha C2 (for dating see Parzinger/ Stegmann-Rajtár 1988, 168-169) hen was rather rare in this region. The earliest evidence of this domestic fowl in eastern Central Europe is currently dated to the final phase of the Bronze Age (Ha B3). In the Early Iron Age their breeding was more widespread, although still low-numbered (Kyselý 2010; Schmitzberger 2006, 346). The archaeozoologists have assumed that hens were bred mainly for their meat or other specific use, such as cock-fighting, since eggs were then produced only seasonally (Benecke 1994, 134; Kyselý 2010, 11; 20-21).

Goose remains were found in three barrows. It is discussed whether remains of geese in Early Iron Age contexts were of wild (*Anser anser*) or domesticated species (*Anser anser domesticus*; Ambros 1975; Benecke 1994, 116-119; Pucher 2003). In these cases both possibilities must be taken into account, since the first occurrence of domestic goose in Central Europe is dated to the turn of the Bronze and Early Iron Ages, similar to hen (Benecke 1994, 117). Goose was present in barrows by larger amount of skeletal remains than hen. The third bird in the barrows was wild duck (*Anas platyrhynchos*), detected in two graves. Waterfowl was also found in settlements from this era; however, in dependence on excavation methods (*cf.* Trebsche 2013, 222).

site	grave	find-group	cattle	sheep/goat	swine	horse	dog	European hare	domestic hen	goose	wild duck	bird egg	beaver	fish	indet.
Bratčice		SE part of grave	X (1?) f	X (1?) f											
		S corner				X (1) f									
Dunajská Lužná	barrow 1	1	X (1) f	X (1) f											
	barrow 3	A			X (1) n					X (1) f					X f
		B	X f	X (1) n f	X (2) n f					X (1) n				X (1) n?	X f
		C		X (1) n	X n		X (1) f	X f		X (1) f					X
		D	X? f											X (1) n?	
		E	X? f												
		F			X (1) n				X (1) f	X (1) f	X (1) f				
		G		X (1) f	X (2) n f										
		H (human remains)											X		
Dunajská Lužná	barrow 4	A	X (1) f												
		B											X (1) n	X (1)	
		C						X (1) n f				X			
		D	X f	X (2) n											
		E		X (1) n											
		F	X (1) f	X (2) n											X (1)
Dunajská Lužná	barrow 6	A	X (1) f		X (≥3) n f										
		B	X f												
		C	X f		X f				X n f	X (≥2) f					
		D	X f		X n?					X n f					
Langenlebarn	barrow 3	2	X f												
		9													X f
		11		X (1) n											
		13		X (1) n											
		21		X (2?) n											
		cleaning of grave	X f n		X n f	X? (1)				X					

Table 2. Character of animal remains in selected barrows according to their find context. Legend: X – presence of species; (1) – assumed number of individuals; f – fragmented remains (small pieces); n – not fragmented remains (whole bones, large fragments); n f – majority of remains not fragmented, some fragmented.

Careful excavations of Dunajská Lužná-Nové Košariská barrows yielded several finds of fish remains. These bones are known from two barrows (Table 1), both with the largest amount of animal species in the cemetery. In barrow 3 these remains were of pike (*Esox lucius L.*), while bones from barrow 4 could be determined only generally as infraclass *Teleostei*. In general, fishing must have been more frequent in the Early Iron Age Central Europe as identified fish remains suggest, especially when animal bones were obtained by hand collecting, not by floatation (Trebsche 2013, 223). In latter barrow beaver bones (*Castor fiber*) were also found. In the past, beaver was hunted for its meat, fur and glands. Its bones were frequently found in prehistoric settlements situated near rivers (Ambros 1959, 53; Trebsche 2013, 218).

In some graves a few indeterminable animal bones were also present; the occurrence of more animal species therefore cannot be excluded.

Form of animal remains and their role in grave

In the studied barrows of the northeast Alpine Hallstatt region, animal remains were present in a variety of forms. Smaller groups of bones and parts of animal bodies such as legs are most frequent. Bones are either whole or cut. Single bones or teeth and artefacts made of them or antler occurred less frequently. Intact skeletons and remains of whole bodies cut in portions were rather sporadic.

Intact bodies of animals were placed in presented barrows rather rarely. In barrow 1 at Gemeinlebarn a skeleton of a horse was found, lying in the corridor entering the burial chamber. Horses were also burned on funeral pyres as suggested by finds from two sites (Süttő and Fehérvárcsurgó). In the former, "high proportion of horse remains" in 17 kg of cremated osteological material was observed. A large amount of cremated horse remains, however, does not have to mean cremation of whole horses, as was proved by new detailed analyses of cremation remains from southeast Alpine Kleinklein-Kröllkogel in Styria. Specifically, horse cremation remains – with one exception – come exclusively from autopodia of one or several individuals (Grill/Wiltschke-Schrotta 2013, 44-52). From Süttő barrow, no detailed archaeozoological analyses were published so far. Nevertheless, in Fehérvárcsurgó barrows 1 and 3, cremated remains of a whole horse were recognized. On the contrary, only part of horse's body was cremated in barrow 5 and a few bones in barrows 4 and 6. Even when horsemeat was sporadically still consumed (Benecke 1994, 133), it seems less likely that horse remains in graves were offerings of meat. Horses were primarily used as a means of transport and was also perceived as an emblem of groups and individuals of high social rank (Kmeťová 2013; Metzner-Nebelsick/Nebelsick 1999). In funeral symbolism, these two functions have merged. Horse represented or underlined elevated rank of the deceased and served as the companion on his last journey (*psychopompos*), in order to transport him safely to the Otherworld (Kmeťová 2013; Milićević Bradać 2003).

In northeastern Alpine barrows with known animal remains there are only a few questionable finds of other animals deposited possibly in form of whole bodies (scattered remains in disturbed barrows, absence of published detailed osteological analyses). Therefore the practice of depositing intact animal bodies (pig in Vaszar, barrow 7, cattle in Százhalombatta, barrow 109, and pig, dog, and burned dog/s in Süttő) is, except of the horse, uncertain. However, a dog (with mutilated legs?) buried along with a child on the roof of burial chamber in Süttő seems to reflect its significance as *psychopompos*, an emblem of rebirth and also messenger of gods (Cooper 1986, 83). The same might apply to cremated dog(s), though in this case the aspect of companionship must be also taken into consideration.

Some animal remains are connected with food. Parts of animals rich in flesh (*cf.* Stadler 2010, 32 fig. 10), such as upper leg, rump, upper arm, shoulder, and parts of trunk were clearly grave offerings of meat. Remains of swine occur in this form most frequently. Pork was often placed in graves in large portions, in some graves entire or almost entire bodies were cut and split (Süttő, Vaszar barrow 5; similarly in south German sites: Stadler 2010, 57). Preference of pork in several graves was emphasized by deposition of body parts or entire bodies of at least two individuals (Table 1). Its function as meat grave offering is underlined by the age of pigs deposited in this manner: in most cases they were determined to be young, non-adult, or very young, only once as adult. Even the majority of ovicaprids' remains were of similar character. The most common are parts of front and hind legs rich in quality meat, or almost whole legs; back parts were less frequent. Also sheep or goats were slaughtered for the burial purposes preferably in young or sub-adult age which is ideal for getting tasty meat. In some graves at least two individuals were placed as well. Additionally, depositions of some other animals were also rich in meat. For example, waterfowl (goose, duck) were placed in graves mainly as intact larger part of the body, cut body or chopped meaty parts, such as legs or wings. Moreover, meaty parts of legs, chest and back of hare, whole bodies or large parts of fish and also upper front leg of a beaver suggest their function as a food.

Cattle were deposited in various forms. Parts of skeleton rich in meat were rather sporadic. Much more frequent were bones with less meat (ribs, vertebrae) or without meat (chopped joints). These bones and also some parts rich in meat were chopped in small pieces and some of them were even split (Dunajská Lužná-Nové Košariská barrows, Bad Fischau, Hochholz, Bratčice, Langenlebarn; Table 2). In Dunajská Lužná-Nové Košariská, these chopped cattle bones were sometimes placed together with similarly prepared bones of other animals. Osteological determinations usually do not state whether bones were raw or cooked. It cannot be excluded that remains of animals found in the same place and prepared in the same way were remains of a specific dish (*cf.* Lauwerier 1983; Schmitzberger 2006, 347). It can be speculated that in some cases, if they were originally placed in a wooden vessel (cattle remains were only rarely placed in ceramic vessels), it was a meal resembling stew. Such interpretation might be supported by finds of bowls near some of these piles (Pichlerová 1969, 24; 69-70; 96; 100). Furthermore, beef ribs, even with less meat on, are considered to be a delicacy. Finally, lack of bones rich in meat can be hypothetically explained by nature of beef portions which are frequently unboned. Hence, the presence of quality beef in graves cannot be excluded.

The difference between character of remains of pig and sheep/goat placed in graves (esp. meaty parts, frequently in larger portions) and those of cattle (esp. chopped in small pieces) is striking (Table 2). If character of cattle remains was not just associated with preparation of a specific meal, it could have had symbolic meaning. Dismemberment of something symbolically represented death and rebirth, in the sense of disintegration and reintegration, and was frequently associated with sacrifice to deities (Cirlot 1984, 83-84; Cooper 1986, 230). Moreover, cattle symbolism, especially of bulls, was a frequent part of northeast Alpine luxurious funeral pottery (bull protomes) and became one of the defining elements of the whole east Alpine region (Preinfalk 2003, 74-79; Siegfried-Weiss 1979). Interconnection of both aspects therefore cannot be excluded.

Bones poor in meat (*cf.* Stadler 2010, 32 fig. 10) are sometimes interpreted as a symbolic meal offering in the sense of *pars pro toto*. Burial rites of the Hallstatt culture were very complex and rich in symbolic grave goods. Hence, the parts poor in meat could have been of symbolic character, as a symbolic meal or animal offering. It is well-known that in the antiquity, along with sacrifice of animals to deities it was common that participants consumed the meaty parts. Offered remains were not regarded to have inferior value in the context of (also funeral) sacrifice. For example, animal bones and hide were a regular offering to deities (Węgrzynowicz 1982, 126-128; Stadler 2010, 78-79). Based on this assumption, such explanation would apply also to single bones, such as tarsal bones, vertebrae, fragments of bones, teeth etc. Deposition of a bone or body part could have replaced the deposition of a whole animal.

Such meaning must be also taken into consideration for a deposition of animal heads/skulls. In various cults the head represented vitality and the greatest symbolic value of living creature; hence it symbolized the whole being. Skull in general was also used as apotropaic object (Cooper 1986, 94-95; Węgrzynowicz 1982, 126; 133; 206). In presented barrows, several animal skulls were found of which some are questionable (also other bones of the animal present and the original contexts disturbed: two cattle skulls on the roof of burial chamber in Süttő and sheep skull in Százhalombatta, barrow 109). Three finds are more certain: a skull of a calf with the horns cut off placed in between two piles of human cremated remains on a clay bank within the burial chamber in Süttő, a swine (boar) skull in barrow 109, and skull of a young ram in barrow 114 in Százhalombatta. Only a few fragments of horse skull were originally placed in a grave chamber in Bratčice.

Similarly, teeth and jaw were parts of a skull but also had specific symbolic meaning as parts of a set of teeth. Animal teeth and jaws were frequently used as amulets or talismans in the past (Hansmann/Kriss-Rettenbeck 1966, 102). It is supposed that animal teeth given to deceased were there to help them reach the

Otherworld more easily. A few teeth and phalanx of equid(s?; probably horse) were deposited in barrow 10 in Bad Fischau. A fragment of lower jaw of a puppy comes from Dunajská Lužná-Nové Košariská, barrow 3.

Eggs of unidentified birds of which tiny shell fragments were collected in Dunajská Lužná-Nové Košariská barrows could have held several functions. First of all, egg was a nourishing food produced only seasonally (even domestic hens laid eggs only in the springtime; Kyselý 2010, 20-21). Nevertheless, bird eggs were also important symbols of creation, fertility, rebirth, renewal of life, and protection. In some cultures, such as Etruscan or Greek, eggs were frequently associated with the world of the dead and were a grave offering (e.g. Carpino 1996, 69-71; Omran 2015; Simoons 1994, 146; 156-159; Stadler 2010, 106). Considering the complexity of Hallstatt burial rites and position of shell fragments in both barrows (near human cremated remains – barrow 3; near hare bones among ceramic vessels – barrow 4; Pichlerová 1969, 51; 69) none of these functions can be excluded.

Some finds were represented only by remains of animal autopodia. In disturbed barrow 109 in Százhalombatta there were some bones of lower parts of legs of hare and a dog. Bones of animal autopodia are sometimes explained as remains of hide or fur, since they usually remain attached after the skinning (e.g. Stadler 2010, 35; Vörös 1993, 38). Hare is a typical fur-bearing animal and its hunting was not only done for meat but also for fur, which is also very likely for the Early Iron Age (Scheibner 2013, 26; Trebsche 2013, 217; 222). Use of dog's fur was even described by some classical writers (Scheibner 2013, 26). In the Százhalombatta barrow there were also leg remains of a fox but of more 'meaty' parts (humerus and ulna fragments). Though, I. Vörös (1993, 38) considers them to be remains of fur deposition. In general, it cannot be excluded that even remains of other animal species such as autopodia and skull or its fragments were remnants of fur or hides.

Some animal remains were deposited in graves as artefacts. The most numerous are astragali (talus bones). In northeastern Alpine barrows of elites there were only astragali of sheep and sporadically of sheep/goat. They were found in two dominant barrows in larger amount (Süttő, 39 specimens; Százhalombatta, barrow 109, 13 specimens; six left and seven right). All were perforated except one with traces of bronze. They were probably remnants of necklaces or other objects, forming personal possessions of a deceased (found in the remains of the funeral pyre). Astragali have been used as children's toys and components of a game, and also for magic (fortune-telling, amulet; Węgrzynowicz 1982, 129; Wiesner 2013, 99-103). For astragali from graves of the Urnfield culture it is, however, assumed that were rather *pars pro toto* representation of animals (Wiesner 2013, 103-106), to which also composition of left and right specimens from Százhalombatta refers. Tusks of wild boar were also used as artefacts. Large lower canines of wild boar from barrow 114 in Százhalombatta were transformed into horse bridles (Holport 1993, 25 fig. 1), similarly as most likely those from barrow 5 in Vaszar-Pörösrét (Horváth 1969, 125 fig. 24,1-2). On the other hand, a set of boar tusks found around skull of an inhumed female in grave in Modřice could have served as a headgear decoration or remnant of a ritual mask (Kos/Přichystal 2013, 81-82). Wild boar hunting was particularly dangerous and killing a wild boar was therefore appreciated and closely associated with heroism and kingship. Artefacts from its tusks (trophies?) were considered to bear the strength of the animal and were most likely connected to individuals/groups of elevated social rank (Eibner

2001). Red deer antler fragments most likely from horse harness were discovered in Százhalombatta's barrow 109 as well as fragments of some other antler artefacts. Artefacts made of red deer antlers come also from Bad Fischau, barrow 10.

Finally, it must be taken into consideration that in depositions of an animal body or its parts a symbolic meaning of the animal could have been present. A whole animal, not edible parts of the animal, or other forms of depositions (single bones or even artefacts) could have included also symbolic meanings of individual animals in the religious sphere. Animal species from presented barrows frequently occur in various religious systems with various symbolic meanings. They have been associated especially with deities and principles of heaven and sun (male principle) and/or earth, Underworld and moon (female principle). Some of them have rather been associated with male/heavenly/solar principle (bull, ram, horse, red deer, goose, rooster), other with female/earthly/lunar principle (hare, cow, fish, dog), but frequently these principles have merged (e.g. cow, bull, ram, swine, horse, rooster). It is remarkable that all of these animals share the association with fertility, life and/or rebirth (overcoming death in the Afterlife). Some animals had also apotropaic significance. Horse and dog were also human's life companions and were perceived as *psychopompoi*. Waterfowl as birds able to swim, sink under the water, fly, and their wild forms also seasonally migrating to the south and back were associated with heaven and also the Underworld, and therefore as connecting both of these worlds as well (Andrałojć 1993, 30-34; Carpino 1996, 71; Cooper 1986; Milićević Bradač 2003; Scheibner 2013, 62-64; Stadler 2010, 116-126). It seems that at least some animal depositions in graves symbolized a safe journey to the Otherworld, renewal and rebirth in eternal life. Some animal depositions, such as horses or artefacts from boar tusks, were also to enhance high social rank of the deceased or its reflection.

Furthermore, particular symbolic meaning could have been expressed also by a combination of various animal species. Except their significance in fertility and rebirth cults, individual species were also associated with various principles and aspects of life, and their sacrifice/offering could have had different (additional?) meaning. In many Indo-European cultures sacrifices of several appointed species were practised. For example, a wide-spread sacrifice of swine, sheep and cattle was in ancient Rome known as *suovetaurilia* and connected to an agrarian cult (Cato the Elder, CXLI,1-4; Stadler 2010, 116). Therefore, it cannot be excluded that every animal species and deposition form in a grave had a specific function.

Animal depositions in grave and their connection to the social rank of the deceased

Comparison of the deposition of animals in different types of graves most likely reflects different social groups (vertical social structure?) and can indicate whether and how their presence in a grave could have been related to the social rank of the deceased.

Animal depositions in barrows of northeast Alpine social elites cannot be associated with people of one or another gender exclusively. Such graves in this region contained mostly cremation burials of several individuals (*cf. e.g.* Klemm 1992, 170-175) and anthropological analyses are able to state sex of the deceased rather sporadically. It is also difficult to attribute the grave goods to individual piles of human remains (individual deceased?). Nevertheless, the available anthropological analyses and/or grave goods indicate that animals were part of funerary assemblages of men, women and children. A single burial of a male is evidenced by a single anthropological determination (Százhalombatta barrow 114; Holport 1993, 25). Male burials are also indicated by grave goods in a small number of graves (Dunajská Lužná-Nové Košariská, barrows 3 and 4, Gemeinlebarn barrow 1, Langenlebarn barrow 3; Kromer 1958; Pichlerová 1969, pl. 12-24; Preinfalk 2003, 47-95). Only two graves seem to be laid primarily for females and/or juveniles and children (Zagersdorf and Dunajská Lužná-Nové Košariská, barrow 6 where, however, no human remains were found in the primary burial, only a child/children in the secondary shaft; Pichlerová 1969, 95 fig. 56; 58-59; Rebay 2002, 93-97; Studeníková 2008, 91-92; 110-111). No patterns in animal depositions can be observed in any of these groups and therefore this situation is different to that in the western Hallstatt area where sheep predominated in graves of females, while male graves contained mostly pigs (Stadler 2010, 64-67; 70-72; cf. Table 1). Furthermore, in Süttő, several types of animal depositions were clearly related to the burial of a child of about eight years old on the chamber roof.

Remaining barrows contained remains of several human individuals, both of males and females. Although in some of them the burial of an adult male appears to be of principal position, while remains of other people seem to be accompanying burials/sacrifices, it cannot be excluded that at least some of them were buried subsequently. In conclusion, no specific animal species, or specific type of animal depositions can be connected to particular age or gender of the deceased, with one exception. Inhumation of a whole horse seems to be typical for males (Kmeťová 2014, 262).

All presented barrows belong to the largest and richest barrows in the region. They were of considerable size (diameter up to 50-60 m; Offenberger 1980, 383; Pichlerová 1969, 79), with elaborate construction of a burial chamber, built either solely of wood or using stone and wooden structures. Their outer grandeur corresponded with quantity and exceptionality of grave goods. They were especially rich in pottery vessels of various forms. The deceased were buried with elements of clothing and jewellery. Deposition of other metal artefacts depended on local burial practices: in some regions also horse harness and wagon components were placed in graves, in others, weapons were sporadic. Some artefacts were luxurious imports from other regions or were influenced by such artefacts. Furthermore, these barrows also frequently contained artefacts which had particular ritual significance (e.g. anthropomorphic and zoomorphic figurines and vessels, so-called Kalenderberg trias in female graves, wagon models, etc.). People buried in these graves are therefore considered to be representatives of the most elevated social group, individuals with supreme powers in the society, possessing also some significant roles in cult (Egg 1996; Studeníková 2008; Teržan 1986).

Animal depositions and vertical social structure

The animal depositions in graves of members of elevated social group have been analysed in detail, except for the frequency of their occurrence. Because of the state of research this aspect can be studied in a limited number of barrow cemeteries/ groups with a high proportion of excavated graves and recorded animal remains. In Dunajská Lužná-Nové Košariská animal remains were found in four out of five barrows. In Százhalombatta, they were in every barrow excavated in the late 1970s and 1980s (7 barrows; Holport 1993, 28; 33). In Fehérvárcsurgó, horse remains were found in five out of nine excavated barrows; presence of other animals is still unpublished. Accordingly, the occurrence of animal depositions in barrows of social elites was notably frequent. Moreover, the absence of osteological animal remains in some barrows cannot exclude the original presence of unboned animal depositions, for example unboned meat, since it can be evidenced only by methods of archaeological chemistry.

This situation will be compared with that in other types of cemeteries/graves in the region, in order to recognize the association of animal depositions with graves of social elites within wider vertical social structure.

Considering "flat" cemeteries (*cf.* Rebay 2006, 43-44) which are regarded as burial places for common population, only a few of them (those that were archaeozoologicaly analysed) are of any use for this study. Animal remains in these cemeteries were detected in a rather small number of graves. For example, in the large Statzendorf cemetery in Lower Austria they were recognized in 57 graves out of about 375, in relatively close Grafenwörth cemetery in four graves out of 21, in western Slovak Vrádište cemetery in 14 out of 28 graves, in Transdanubian Halimba-Cseres in four out of 24 graves and in Nagydém-Középrépáspuszta in twelve out of 23 graves (Ambros 1960; Lochner 1988; Nagy 1939; Pichlerová 1960; Rebay 2006; Schmitzberger 2006). No clear correlation between amount of grave goods and presence of animal remains are observed, since animal remains were found in 'rich' as well as 'poor' graves. The number of animal species in individual graves was also considerably lower than that in presented barrows. Remains of one species were the most frequent, while two were much more sporadic and three species in a grave were very rare. Regarding the variability of species, it seems that various species were placed in these graves, similarly to barrows. Namely, along with the three (or four) most frequent species, remains of horse, red deer, beaver or hen were also occasionally detected. Considering the forms of animal depositions, there were also various forms present (meat depositions, *pars pro toto* (?), astragali, single bones or teeth etc.), but mostly only one per grave. The amount of animal remains from individual species in a grave was also considerably lower than in barrows: usually there was a single bone or a couple of adjacent bones forming a portion of meat. Sporadically other parts of animal bodies occur. It must be pointed out that in none of these graves entire mammals were found and moreover, large parts were present extremely rarely. It is also of notice that remains of particular species were treated very similarly as in presented barrows (e.g. pork cuts, larger parts of sheep, even whole extremities, sheep astragali, chopped cattle remains). Finally, it seems that the main differences between the animal depositions in barrows of top social elites and deceased from 'flat' cemeteries were multiplicity and variability.

Similar tendencies can be observed in the south Moravian cemetery in Vojkovice, even though archaeozoological analyses were not carried out/published (Golec 2005, 141-267). It is a flat cemetery with a high proportion of chamber graves (19) compared to simple urn graves (2). Chamber graves are interpreted as of 'higher middle class', but also a rich female grave socially comparable to those from barrows was among them. Animal remains were recorded in twelve chamber graves, all with more grave goods than in remaining ones. Usually there was only a small amount of bones, only in graves with large number of grave goods or luxurious artefacts were there more animal remains or animal body parts, sporadically located even in a couple of places. In the rich female grave a piglet skeleton was found.

From barrows of smaller dimensions and smaller amount and variability of grave goods than in dominant barrows, those in Bad Fischau (Klemm 1992, 311-464; Szombathy 1924) are suitable for comparison as well as a single grave from Donnerskirchen (grave 1; Rebay 2005). In Bad Fischau animal remains were found/mentioned in eleven out of 16 barrows, two of them (no. 10, Hochholz) are considered above as dominant barrows. The number of animal species in a barrow was one or two. Remains of cattle, sheep and swine were the most frequent, while other species occurred rather rarely (ovicaprid, equid). The character of these remains resembles those in dominant barrows. They were present in graves of males as well as females.

In conclusion, it seems that the number of animal species, amount of their remains and the variability of forms of their depositions in a grave generally increase with higher social importance of buried person (if burial rites/grave type really reflected vertical social structure). It applies to animal remains interpreted as food, but also to other forms of animal depositions. However, accurate definition of situation in these 'less prestigious' types of graves requires further detailed and complex research.

Chronology of animal depositions

Diverse collections of animal depositions in individual barrows of social elites could have depended also on chronology. Their complex chronological evaluation is, however, problematic. The only usable site for the study of development of this practice is Dunajská Lužná-Nové Košariská cemetery with all barrows excavated and with well researched find contexts (on chronology see Parzinger/Stegmann-Rajtár 1988, 168-169). In the earliest barrow 2 no animal remains were detected. The following three barrows from Ha C2, no. 3, 4 and 6, respectively, contained a large amount of animal remains. Moreover, the first two contained a considerable number of species placed in several spots (5-8) within the burial chamber. In the latest barrow 1, dated to Ha D1, animals were deposited only in one place and comprised of two species. The multiplicity and variability of animal depositions in Ha C2 barrows correspond with situation in Transdanubian barrows Süttő and Százhalombatta 109. However, observed situation cannot be applied to all barrows of this type. For example, graves from Ha D1 (Langenlebarn 3, Bratčice) still contained several animal species (≥5, 3), although the amount of their remains appears to be smaller.

The determination of development of animal depositions in barrows of northeast Alpine social elites requires further research, including their forerunners in previous periods.

Conclusion

Although only a limited number of barrows of northeast Alpine Hallstatt elites were investigated due to limited information on animal remains, some tendencies relating to the manifestation of social importance of deceased from the barrows have clearly showed up.

It is evident that animal depositions were typical for this type of grave, despite the sporadic absence of animal remains in some of them. Further research is required to state whether this absence was caused by chronological development of this practice, insufficient state of research, or by other factors (e.g. unboned meat). Regarding the practice of animal deposition, the main difference between outstanding graves (the ones primarily analysed in this paper) and other ones was the multiplicity and variability of detected animal remains. Accordingly, barrows of social elites in this region generally contained higher number and variability of both the animal species and forms of their depositions. Usually several species were present in a grave, most frequently two or three main food-producing domestic animals (cattle, sheep or less likely goat, and swine), and several other domestic animals and/or game. Even though the presence of several species and several forms of animal depositions in a grave was not restricted to barrows of social elites, it was standard for them. Furthermore, presence of individual species was not exclusive for these barrows, except some deposition forms of particular animals (e.g. entire horse, wild boar tusks as parts of horse-bits).

Various forms of animal depositions are apparently related to their various functions in graves. First, some of them represented offerings of meat/meal, especially portions of pork, lamb (even whole legs), as well as parts of hare, waterfowl and fish. Moreover, animal furs or hides could have represented luxurious furnishing of the mortuary bed in the burial chamber or on the funeral pyre, or equipment of the deceased. This applies to the artefacts made of tusks or antlers as well. Numerous and various depositions of meat along with these artefacts were apparently associated with manifestation of opulence and hence of social significance of these people and/or their families (*cf.* Hayden 2009). The large amount of meat in these graves was similar to situations in central graves in southern Germany where it seems to refer to a certain status of the deceased (Schumann 2015, 103-104; Stadler 2010, 70-72; 74-76).

Some other animal depositions most likely reflected diverse symbolic aspects. Cattle body parts rich in flesh were detected only sometimes, while bones poor in meat or without meat, chopped in small pieces, clearly predominated. It has been speculated that these remains could have been either of a specific dish (stew?), similarly as some remains of other animals, or were offerings in the sense of *pars pro toto*, and/or reflected a specific practice associated with a cult (dismemberment). Animal heads/skulls placed in a grave could have also borne a specific symbolic meaning, similarly as single bones poor in meat, astragali(?) or teeth. They could have even stood for a particular animal. In connection with the burial rites, symbolic perception of these animals as emblems of safe passage to the Otherworld, rebirth and life stands out. For some species and deposition forms, it seems that several meanings have merged, such as horse as an emblem of privileged transport to the Otherworld and at the same time a reference to high social rank of the deceased. Eggs were also important symbols of life and rebirth as well as food.

Multiplicity and variability of animal depositions were similar to multiplicity and variability of some other grave goods in barrows of elites, especially ceramic vessel sets (*cf.* Nebelsick 1997a, 37-48). Grave goods from rich barrows in this region and rich sets of ceramic vessels in particular (as "drinking sets"; *e.g.* Preinfalk 2003, 66-68; on different function of vessels see Müller 2012, 357-359) could be linked to rites resembling the cult of Dionysus in the north

Mediterranean which was connected to a belief in resurrection (Nebelsick 1997b, esp. 384-387). Also some animal depositions (symbolizing life, death and rebirth) seem to reflect similar religious conception. For example, the bull, a significant emblem of northeast Alpine Hallstatt region, was also a part of Dionysian cult as was dismemberment of something (see dismembered cattle remains in barrows; *cf.* Cooper 1986, 230; Nebelsick 1997b, 386; these remains placed near vessel with bull-protomes: Pichlerová 1969, 25 fig. 12; pl. 6,2; Preinfalk 2003, 100; pl. 1-7). It seems that the issue of rebirth and resurrection was very important in the burial rites of deceased members of the social elites and was associated with their heroization. Accordingly, grave goods of ritual-symbolic meaning along with those indicating high social status or prestige (*cf.* Schumann 2015), as well as monumental grave construction and complex burial rite were supposed to helped them to complete the metamorphosis from the deceased members of social elites to powerful "ancestors" (Müller 2012, 359-361; Nebelsick 1997b, 384-386; Williams 2005, 37-38). Animal depositions were part of this cult, serving the deceased as food and objects of a personal nature during their life in the Otherworld, or rather in a period of "living dead" between their death and entrance to the Otherworld, and possibly also to funeral attendants during the funeral feast (Stadler 2012, 162-170; 174). They could also help them to get there safely. Some animal depositions were also necessary to ensure them new life as heroized ancestors with appropriate social identity.

Bibliography

Ambros 1959: C. Ambros, Zvieracie zvyšky z doby bronzovej z Gánoviec, okr. Poprad. Slovenská archeológia 7, 1959, 47-70.

Ambros 1960: C. Ambros, Zvieraci inventár halštatských hrobov vo Vrádišti. In: M. Pichlerová, Mladohalštatské popolnicové pohrebisko vo Vrádišti. Slovenská archeológia 8, 1960, 173-175.

Ambros 1975: C. Ambros, Tierreste aus den früheisenzeitlichen Hügelgräbern in Nové Košariská. Slovenská archeológia 23, 1975, 217-226.

Andrałojć 1993: M. Andrałojć, The phenomenon of dog burials in the prehistoric times on the area of Middle Europe. Ollodagos 1 (Bruxelles 1993).

Benecke 1994: N. Benecke, Archäozoologische Studien zur Entwicklung der Haustierhaltung in Mitteleuropa und Südskandinavien von den Anfängen bis zum ausgehenden Mittelalter. Schriften zur Ur- und Frühgeschichte 46 (Berlin 1994).

Carpino 1996: A. Carpino, Greek mythology in Etruria: An iconographical analysis of three Etruscan relief mirrors. In: J. F. Hall (ed.), Etruscan Italy: Etruscan influences on the civilizations of Italy from antiquity to the modern era (Provo, Utah 1996) 65-92.

Cato the Elder: Cato the Elder, De Agricultura. Translated by W. D. Hooper/H. B. Ash (Loeb Classical Library 1934).

Cirlot 1984: J. Cirlot, A dictionary of symbols (London/Henley 1984).

Cooper 1986: J. Cooper, Lexikon alter Symbole (Leipzig 1986).

Egg 1996: M. Egg, Zu den Fürstengräbern im Osthallstattkreis. In: E. Jerem/A. Lippert (eds.), Die Osthallstattkultur. Akten des Internationalen Symposiums, Sopron, 10.-14. Mai 1994. Archaeolingua 7 (Budapest 1996) 53-86.

Eibner 2001: A. Eibner, Die Eberjagd als Ausdruck eines Heroentums? Zum Wandel des Bildinhalts in der Situlenkunst am Beginn der Latènezeit. In: B. Gediga/A. Mierzwiński/W. Piotrowski (eds.), Sztuka epoki brązu i wczesnej epoki żelaza w Europie środkowej (Wrocław/Biskupin 2001) 231-279.

Golec 2005: M. Golec, Horákovská kultura. Unpublished dissertation (Brno 2005).

Grill/Wiltschke-Schrotta 2013: Ch. Grill/K. Wiltschke-Schrotta, Anthropologische und archäozoologische Untersuchungsergebnisse des Leichenbrandes. In: M. Egg/D. Kramer (eds.), Die hallstattzeitlichen Fürstengräber von Kleinklein in der Steiermark: der Kröllkogel. Monographien des Römisch-Germanischen Zentralmuseums 110 (Mainz 2013) 33-59.

Hansmann/Kriss-Rettenbeck 1966: L. Hansmann/L. Kriss-Rettenbeck, Amulett und Talisman. Erscheinungsform und Geschichte (München 1966).

Hayden 2009: B. Hayden, Funerals as feasts: Why are they so important? Cambridge Archaeological Journal 19,1, 2009, 29-52.

Holport 1993: Á. Holport, Kora vaskori halomsíros temető Érd-Százhalombatta határában. In: I. Poroszlai (ed.), 4000 év a 100 halom városában. Fejezetek Százhalombatta történetéből (Százhalombatta 1993) 23-34.

Horváth 1969: A. Horváth, A Vaszari és Somlóvásárhelyi Hallstatt-kori halomsírok. A Veszprém megyei múzeumok közleményei 8, 1969, 109-134.

Jungbert 1993: B. Jungbert, Early Iron Age (HC2) settlement centre at Fehérvárcsurgó. In: J. Pavúk (ed.), Actes du XIIe Congrès International des Sciences Préhistoriques et Protohistoriques, Bratislava, 1-7 septembre 1991 (Bratislava 1993) 191-197.

Klemm 1992: S. Klemm, Die Malleiten bei Bad Fischau in Niederösterreich. Monographie zu den Grab- und Siedlungsfunden der urgeschichtlichen Höhensiedlung. Ein Beitrag zur Kenntnis der Keramik der Urnenfelder- und der Hallstattzeit im Ostalpenraum. Unpublished dissertation (Wien 1992).

Kmeťová 2013: P. Kmeťová, The spectacle of the horse. On Early Iron Age burial customs in the eastern-alpine Hallstatt region. Archaeological Review from Cambridge 28, 2, 2013, 67-81.

Kmeťová 2014: P. Kmeťová, Deponovanie koní na pohrebiskách z doby halštatskej v priestore Panónskej panvy. Dissertationes Archaeologicae Bratislavenses 2 (Bratislava 2014).

Kos/Přichystal 2013: P. Kos/M. Přichystal, Doba halštatská/Hallstattzeit. In: K. Geislerová/D. Parma (eds.), Výzkumy/Ausgrabungen 2005-2010 (Brno 2013) 74-94.

Kromer 1958: K. Kromer, Gemeinlebarn, Hügel 1. Inventaria Archaeologica. Corpus des Ensembles Archeologiques, Österreich, 2 A 11 (Bonn 1958).

Kyselý 2010: R. Kyselý, Review of the oldest evidence of domestic fowl *Gallus gallus* f. *domestica* from the Czech Republic in its European context. Acta zoologica cracoviensia 53A,1-2, 2010, 9-34.

Lauwerier 1983: R. Lauwerier, A meal for the dead. Animal bone finds in Roman graves. Palaeohistoria 25, 1983, 183-193.

Lochner 1988: M. Lochner, Ein Flachgräberfeld der Hallstattkultur in Grafenwörth, pol. Bez. Tulln, Niederösterreich. Archaeologia Austriaca 72, 1988, 91-142.

Metzner-Nebelsick/Nebelsick 1999: C. Metzner-Nebelsick/L. Nebelsick, Frau und Pferd – ein Topos am Übergang von der Bronze- zur Eisenzeit Europas. Mitteilungen der Anthropologischen Gesellschaft in Wien 129, 1999, 69-106.

Milićević Bradać 2003: M. Milićević Bradać, Greek Mythological Horses and the World's Boundary. Opuscula Archaeologica, Zagreb 27, 2003, 379-391.

Mithay 1980: S. Mithay, A vaszari koravaskori temető és telephely. Archeológiai Értesitő 107, 1980, 53-78.

Müller 2012: S. Müller, Monumente der Ahnenverehrung? Zur Deutung der hallstattzeitlichen Grabhügel von Nové Košariská. Slovenská archeológia 60, 2012, 343-364.

Müller-Scheeßel/Trebsche 2007: N. Müller-Scheeßel/P. Trebsche, Das Schwein und andere Haustiere in Siedlungen und Gräbern der Hallstattzeit Mitteleuropas. Germania 85, 2007, 61-94.

Nagy 1939: L. Nagy, A középprépáspusztai (Veszprém megye) kora-vaskori temető. Folia Archaeologica 1-2, 1939, 39-57.

Nebelsick 1997a: L. Nebelsick, Die Kalenderberggruppe der Hallstattzeit am Nordostalpenrand. In: L. Nebelsick/A. Eibner/E. Lauermann/J.-W. Neugebauer, Hallstattkultur im Osten Österreichs (St. Pölten 1997) 9-128.

Nebelsick 1997b: L. Nebelsick, Trunk und Transzendenz. Trinkgeschirr im Grab zwischen der frühen Urnenfelder- und späten Hallstattzeit im Karpatenbecken. In: C. Becker/M. L. Dunkelmann/C. Metzner-Nebelsick/H. Peter-Röcher/M. Roeder/B. Teržan (eds.), Chronos. Beiträge zur prähistorischen Archäologie zwischen Nord- und Südosteuropa. Festschrift für Bernhard Hänsel. Internationale Archäologie, Studia honoraria 1 (Espelkamp 1997) 373-387.

Offenberger 1980: J. Offenberger, Gemeinlebarn. Fundberichte aus Österreich 19, 1980, 438-440.

Omran 2015: W. Omran, The egg and its symbolism in the Graeco-Roman period. Journal of Faculty of Tourism and Hotels, Fayoum University 9,1, 2015, 173-185.

Parzinger/Stegmann-Rajtár 1988: H. Parzinger/S. Stegmann-Rajtár, Smolenice-Molpír und der Beginn skythischer Sachkultur in der Südwestslowakei. Prähistorische Zeitschrift 63, 1988, 162-178.

Pichlerová 1960: M. Pichlerová, Mladohalštatské popolnicové pohrebisko vo Vrádišti. Slovenská archeológia 8, 1960, 125-182.

Pichlerová 1969: M. Pichlerová, Nové Košariská. Kniežacie mohyly zo staršej doby železnej (Bratislava 1969).

Preinfalk 2003: F. Preinfalk, Die hallstattzeitlichen Hügelgräber von Langenlebarn, Niederösterreich. Fundberichte aus Österreich, Materialheft A 12 (Wien 2003).

Pucher 2003: E. Pucher, Die Tierknochen. In: F. Preinfalk, Die hallstattzeitlichen Hügelgräber von Langenlebarn, Niederösterreich. Fundberichte aus Österreich, Materialheft A 12 (Wien 2003) 95.

Rebay 2002: K. Rebay, Die hallstattzeitliche Grabhügelgruppe von Zagersdorf im Burgenland. Wissenschaftliche Arbeiten aus dem Burgenland 107 (Eisenstadt 2002).

Rebay 2005: K. Rebay, Hallstattzeitliche Grabfunde aus Donnerskirchen. Burgenländische Heimatblätter 67,4, 2005, 165-210.

Rebay 2006: K. Rebay, Das hallstattzeitliche Gräberfeld von Statzendorf in Niederösterreich. Möglichkeiten und Grenzen der Interpretation von Sozialindexberechnungen. Universitätsforschungen zur Prähistorischen Archäologie 135 (Bonn 2006).

Scheibner 2013: A. Scheibner, Der Hund in der mitteleuropäischen Eisenzeit. Wirtschaftliche, rituelle und soziale Aspekte. Berliner Archäologische Forschungen 12 (Rahden/Westf. 2013).

Schmitzberger 2006: M. Schmitzberger, Tierknochen aus dem hallstattzeitlichen Gräberfeld von Statzendorf, NÖ. In K. C. Rebay, Das hallstattzeitliche Gräberfeld von Statzendorf in Niederösterreich. Möglichkeiten und Grenzen der Interpretation von Sozialindexberechnungen. Universitätsforschungen zur Prähistorischen Archäologie 135 (Bonn 2006) 342-355.

Schumann 2015: R. Schumann, Status und Prestige in der Hallstattkultur. Aspekte sozialer Distinktion in ältereisenzeitlichen Regionalgruppen zwischen Altmühl und Save. Münchner Archäologische Forschungen 3 (Rahden/Westf. 2015).

Siegfried-Weiss 1979: A. Siegfried-Weiss, Der Ostalpenraum in der Hallstattzeit und seine Beziehungen zum Mittelmeergebiet. Hamburger Beiträge zur Archäologie 6, 1979.

Simoons 1994: F. Simoons, Eat not this flesh: Food avoidances from prehistory to the Present. (Madison/Wisconsin/London 1994).

Stadler 2010: J. Stadler, Nahrung für die Toten? Speisebeigaben in hallstattzeitlichen Gräbern und ihre kulturhistorische Deutung. Universitätsforschungen zur prähistorischen Archäologie 186 (Bonn 2010).

Studeníková 2008: E. Studeníková, Výpoveď kalenderberských mohýl na Slovensku o vzťahu pohlaví. Acta archaeologica Opaviensia 3, 2008, 85-111.

Szombathy 1924: J. Szombathy, Die Tumuli im Feichtenboden bei Fischau am Steinfeld. Mitteilungen der Anthropologischen Gesellschaft in Wien 54, 1924, 163-197.

Teržan 1986: B. Teržan, Zur Gesellschaftsstruktur während der älteren Hallstattzeit im ostalpen-westpannonischen Gebiet. In: L. Török (ed.), Hallstatt Kolloquium Veszprém 1984. Antaeus 3 (Budapest 1986) 227-243.

Trebsche 2013: P. Trebsche, Hunting in the Hallstatt and early La Tène cultures: The economic and social importance. In: O. Grimm/U. Schmölcke (eds.), Hunting in northern Europe until 1500 AD. Old traditions and regional developments, Continental sources and continental influences. Papers presented at a workshop organized by the Centre for Baltic and Scandinavian Archaeology (ZBSA), Schleswig, June 16th and 17th, 2011. Schriften der Archäologischen Landesmuseums, Ergänzungsreihe 7 (Neumünster 2013) 215-238.

Vadász 1983: É. Vadász, Előzetes jelentés egy koravaskori halomsír feltárásáról Süttőn (Vorbericht über die Erschliessung eines früheisenzeitlichen Hügels in Süttő. Auszug). Communicationes Archaeologicae Hungariae 1983, 19-54.

Vadász 1986: É. Vadász, Das früheisenzeitliche Gräberfeld von Süttő. In: L. Török (ed.), Hallstatt Kolloquium Veszprém 1984. Antaeus 3 (Budapest 1986) 251-257.

Vörös 1993: I. Vörös, Temetési étel- és állatáldozat Százhalombatta 109. sz. halomsírjában. In: I. Poroszlai (ed.), 4000 év a 100 halom városában. Fejezetek Százhalombatta történetéből (Százhalombatta 1993) 35-40.

Węgrzynowicz 1982: T. Węgrzynowicz, Szczątki zwierzęce jako wyraz wierzeń w czasach ciałopalenia zwłok (Warszawa 1982).

Wiesner 2013: N. Wiesner, Astragali in Gräbern der mitteleuropäischen Urnenfelderkultur. Germania 91, 2013, 89-113.

Williams 2005: H. Williams, Animals, Ashes & Ancestors. In: A. Pluskowski (ed.), Just skin and bones? New perspectives on human-animal relations in the historical past. British Archaeological Reports, International Series 1410 (Oxford 2005) 19-40.

Author

Petra Kmeťová
Independent Researcher
kmetova.p@gmail.com

Hallstatt C sword graves in Continental Gaul

Rise of an elite or new system of representation of self in a context of crisis?

Pierre-Yves Milcent

*"Howbeit no huge barrow do I bid you rear with toil for him,
but such a one only as beseemeth"*
Homer, *Iliad*, XXIII, 245-246

Abstract

355 Hallstatt C swords are recorded in Gaul. With the exception of about 41 specimens found in rivers, these swords, for which the context of discovery is known, come from graves in barrows. These sword graves fall into two main geographically distinct groups of unequal size. The smallest group corresponds to about 34 cremation burials found in the northeast of Gaul, possibly extending towards the northwest. It spreads from Champagne in France to south Gelderland in the Netherlands and was called the Mosan group by E. Warmenbol. This group presents cultural characteristics of Atlantic and Nordic affinities. The second group, numerically larger, corresponds to 170 inhumation burials distributed from the Upper Rhine to the southwest of the Massif Central. It is this group, belonging to Hallstatt cultures, that we will primarily address.

In each of these two groups of sword graves, the deposited and preserved artifacts are sparse. In the inhumation burials the sword is placed with a scabbard or a textile cover next to the deceased, often on the right side of the body, alone or accompanied by one to three vessels. A razor and bracelet regularly are associated with the body. Other categories of objects are rare. The deceased and the accompanying artifacts are arranged under a barrow, whose architecture varies by region, but whose size remains modest. The layouts associated with the barrow, including enclosures, are simple.

In the past, archaeologists connected these sword graves with an emerging elite, of either foreign (before the 1980s, the dominant theory being invasions by eastern horsemen) or local origin. Some even considered that they were the beginning of an ongoing and increasingly complex socioeconomic process that would culminate with the princely wagon burials at the end of the first Iron Age.

The perspective, given by taking into account more global data not only from the beginning of the first Iron Age but also the end of the Late Bronze Age, today suggests a very different interpretation of this phenomenon. Aside from five graves generally attributable to the late Ha C (Chavéria, Magny-Lambert, Marainville-sur-Madon, Ohnenheim, Poiseul-la-Ville), the Ha C sword inhumations finally appear rather poor; and, register in a context of profound break with the Late Bronze Age, apparently even inside a context of a crisis with multiple causes (the crisis of the 8th century BC). These sword tombs therefore do not demonstrate the development of a more powerful elite than in preceding period; quite the contrary, but, a new self-representation system through the adoption of a renewed material culture and the recomposition of funeral practices with standardized rules.

Résumé

Sur l'ancien territoire de la Gaule, 355 épées du Hallstatt C sont répertoriées. A l'exception de 41 exemplaires trouvés dans des cours d'eau ou des milieux humides, les épées dont le contexte de découverte est connu proviennent de tombes sous tumulus. Ces tombes à épée se répartissent principalement en deux groupes géographiquement bien distincts et de taille inégale. Le groupe le plus petit correspond à une quarantaine de sépultures à crémation que l'on trouve dans le nord-est de la Gaule, avec une possible extension en direction du nord-ouest. Il s'étend de la Champagne, en France, au sud du Guelderland dans les Pays-Bas et a été qualifié de groupe Mosan par E. Warmenbol car il couvre surtout le bassin de la Meuse. Ce groupe mosan présente principalement des caractéristiques culturelles d'affinités atlantiques et nordiques. Le second groupe, plus important numériquement, correspond à 170 sépultures à inhumation distribuées du Rhin supérieur au sud-ouest du Massif central. C'est de ce groupe, appartenant aux cultures hallstattiennes, que nous parlerons. Dans chacun de ces deux groupes de tombes à épée, le mobilier déposé et conservé est peu abondant. Dans les tombes à inhumation, l'épée est placée auprès du défunt, généralement dans un fourreau et au côté droit, seule ou plus souvent accompagnée de vases (entre un et trois vases). Un rasoir et un bracelet sont régulièrement associés. Les autres catégories d'objets sont rarement déposées. Le défunt et le mobilier de ces sépultures sont disposés sous un tumulus, dont l'architecture varie selon les régions, mais dont la taille reste modeste. Les aménagements associés au tumulus, enclos notamment, sont simples. Par le passé, les archéologues ont souvent mis ces sépultures à épée en relation avec l'émergence d'une élite, qu'elle soit supposée d'origine étrangère (théorie dominante des invasions de peuples cavaliers orientaux avant les années 1980), ou locale. Certains ont même considéré qu'elles marquaient le début d'un processus continu de complexification socio-économique qui culminerait avec les tombes à char princières de la fin du premier âge du Fer.

Le recul donné par une prise en compte plus globale des données pour le début de l'âge du Fer, mais aussi la fin de l'âge du Bronze final, permettent aujourd'hui de proposer une interprétation très différente du phénomène. A part cinq sépultures dont quatre attribuables à l'extrême fin de la période (Chavéria, Magny-Lambert, Marainville-sur-Madon, Ohnenheim, Poiseul-la-Ville), les tombes à épée du Ha C apparaissent finalement assez pauvres et s'inscrivent dans un contexte de profonde rupture avec l'âge du Bronze final, apparemment même dans un contexte de crise aux causes multiples, la crise du VIIIe s. av. J.-C. Elles ne manifestent donc pas le développement d'une élite plus puissante qu'aux époques précédentes, bien au contraire, mais un nouveau système de représentation de soi, à travers l'adoption d'une culture matérielle renouvelée et la recomposition des pratiques funéraires selon des normes strictes et interrégionales.

Introduction

This paper summarizes the context and interpretation of Ha C sword deposits in Gaul[1]. I focus on the contexts of Hallstattian graves, that is to say the inhumations from the south and east of Gaul. In the past, archaeologists connected these sword graves with the emergence of elites of either foreign (before the 1980s, the dominant theory being invasions by eastern horsemen) or local origin. Some even considered them as the beginning of an ongoing and increasingly complex socioeconomic process culminating in the princely wagon burials at the end of the first Iron Age. By taking into account global data not only from the beginning of the first Iron Age but also the end of the Late Bronze Age, a very different interpretation is suggested.

---

1   Gaul is considered here in a pure geographic sense according to the definition given by Julius Cesar in the opening of the *Bellum Gallicum*. Therefore it is the geographic area between Pyrenees, Alps and Rhine. This area shows no cultural or ethnic homogeneity at the beginning of the Iron Age.

History, contexts, and geography of discoveries

The first exploitable discoveries of Ha C swords in Gaul date back to the early 19th century, but most were made in the last third of the 19th century and in the 1960-90s. Funeral documentation was collected by H. Gerdsen during the 1980s (Gerdsen 1986). Recent work has improved and enriched this body of work (Beylier 2012; Cicolani *et al.* 2015; Dhennequin 2005; Milcent 2004).

The swords of the Ha C are distributed mostly in eastern Gaul, are rare in western Gaul and unknown in the southwest of France (355 Ha C swords are known, found in France (288), Belgium (24), Netherlands (24), western Germany (12), western Switzerland (6) and 1 in the Italian Alps near the French border; Fig. 1). In northwest Gaul, the near-absence of archaeologically identifiable burials explains this contrast, rather than a lack of research. In these western regions funerary practices were different during the first Iron Age and generally informal and archaeologically invisible. The elites of these Western regions are nevertheless identifiable archaeologically, but in different forms from those known elsewhere. Large enclosed residences often with palisades, similar to the *Herrenhöfe* of Bavaria, are found in much of the Atlantic Gaul during the first Iron Age (as early as the 8th century BC). These elite residences remain almost without equal in Hallstattian Gaul (Milcent forthcoming 1). Two metal hoards in Pfalz yielded a few swords (5?). Elsewhere in Gaul, no hoard contains a piece of a Ha C sword, as demonstrated by J. Gomez de Soto (2014).

But we now know that there are very few metal hoards from the Ha C in Gaul (in France for example, most of the Armorican axe hoards and the Launacian hoards date Ha D1-2: Milcent forthcoming 2). 41 swords (11.5% of the total) come from rivers or wetlands without any significant concentration, excepting perhaps northern Gaul, and were found especially in areas where there has been a lot of dredging and archaeological surveys. Today, we mainly interpret these water finds as the result of involuntary losses during Ha C, unlike during Late Bronze Age (Cicolani *et al.* 2015).

The other swords (276: 77.7% of the total) come from 272 (probable) burials where the context of discovery is known. These swords come mainly from southern and eastern Gaul, and we only know the burial custom for 213 graves. These graves belong to two main groups of unequal size.

The first consists of 34 cremation burials in the northeast, usually buried in a medium-sized barrow. Swords are often broken or bent and cremated bones are deposited in urns. These homogeneous burials are spread in and around the Mosan basin and referred to as the Mosan group by E. Warmenbol (1993). The grave goods show many affinities with the Atlantic cultures, especially during the first part of Ha C, but the funeral practices are more or less similar to those from northwest Germany. With few exceptions at the very end of Ha C, the links with the *stricto sensu* Hallstattian groups appear superficial.

The other 170 graves are inhumations buried in barrows or pits probably covered by a barrow, in central, eastern and southern Gaul. These burials are characteristic of cultural Hallstattian groups from Gaul. These are the ones that I will study.

The Hallstattian sword graves of Gaul are clearly differentiated from those found in the *Osthallstattkreis*. To a lesser extent, they are also distinct from the sword tombs of the upper basin of the Danube. This is why the traditional

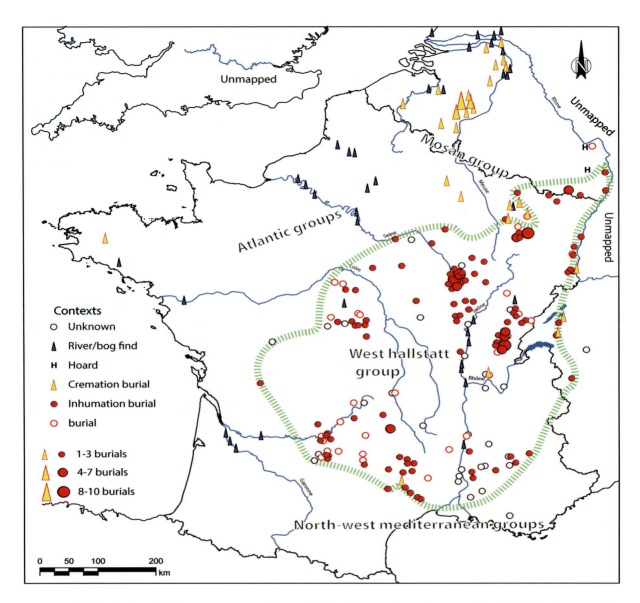

Fig. 1. Distribution map of the Ha C swords in Gaul.

Contexts

- ○ Unknown
- ▲ River/bog find
- H Hoard
- ▲ Cremation burial
- ● Inhumation burial
- ○ burial

▲ ● 1-3 burials
▲ ● 4-7 burials
▲ ● 8-10 burials

concept of *Westhallstattkreis* presents a problem of definition and no longer seems relevant. This concept actually gives an impression of continuity and even cultural homogeneity, that would run from the centre of France to Bavaria. As demonstrated by W. Reinhard (1993; 2003), this continuity does not exist; from one side to the other of the upper Rhine Valley, the differences in rituals and burial furnishings among sword tombs are marked (see Reinhard 2003, 43 fig. 24). To take another criteria, the forms and patterns of the fine ceramics of the Ha C show that products discovered in the Hallstattian areas west of the Rhine have simple decoration (Fig. 2,2), and have little in common with those from Central Europe that are richly engraved and painted (Fig. 2,4). The case of sword graves of Gaul will reinforce this point of view and will show that it is probably necessary to distinguish not two, but three large Hallstattian areas: Eastern (middle basin of the Danube), Central (upper basin of the Danube) and Western (regions from the upper Rhine to the southern Massif central).

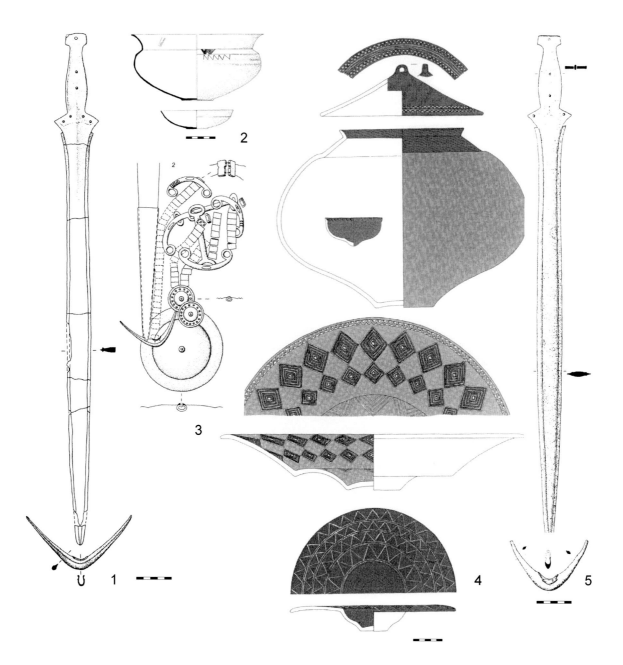

Fig. 2. Examples of decorated fine ceramics deposited in Early Ha C sword burials from eastern Gaul (1-3: Chavéria T.16, Jura) and south Germany (4-5: Wehringen barrow 8, Bavaria). 1-2: after Vuaillat 1977; 3-4: after Hennig 1995).

First, however, the chronology and the production groups of these swords need to be reviewed.

Chronology and evolution of swords of the Gündlingen family

Almost all Ha C swords in Gaul belong to the family of swords with leaf-shaped blade and flat tanged grip, called Gündlingen (from my point of view, the Gündlingen swords do not indicate a type, but a family of weapons characteristic of Ha C in temperate Europe and encompass all models of swords from Ha C, including the Mindelheim type).

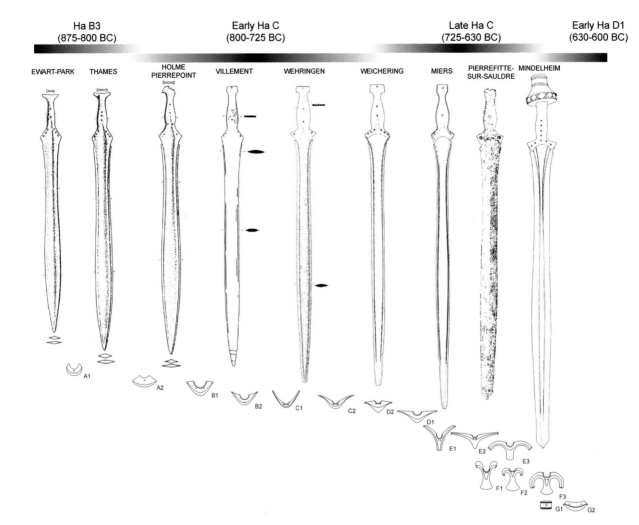

Ha B3 (875-800 BC)		Early Ha C (800-725 BC)			Late Ha C (725-630 BC)			Early Ha D1 (630-600 BC)
EWART-PARK	THAMES	HOLME PIERREPOINT	VILLEMENT	WEHRINGEN	WEICHERING	MIERS	PIERREFITTE-SUR-SAULDRE	MINDELHEIM

Fig. 3. Chronological evolution of the Gündlingen sword family during Ha C, with their Atlantic Late Bronze Age prototypes and their chapes.

Their relative chronology today is accurate, at least for the bronze ones which are much better preserved than iron specimens (Milcent 2004, 95-107). The general shape of the swords and chapes are the best indicators of chronology: the associations of different types of swords and chapes enable us to identify two major stages: the Early Ha C and the Late Ha C, with a short transitional horizon between the two (Fig. 3).

The Early Ha C (equivalent to Ch. Pare's (1999) Ha C0) is represented by the successive sword types Holme Pierrepoint, Villement and Wehringen, and their iron equivalents, as well as by bag and V-shaped chapes from the 8th century BC. The Weichering type, associated with open V-shaped chape, is at the transition between Early and Late Ha C. This Early Ha C stage is not well documented, except in the northwestern regions of Europe. Therefore, it is rarely understood and taken into consideration in summary works which prefer to focus either on the end of the Late Bronze Age or the Late Ha C. Today it is clear that the swords of the Gündlingen family are essentially part of a weaponry tradition of the Atlantic Late Bronze Age, developed first in the British Isles and northern Gaul. The geographic distribution of the oldest Gündlingen swords and their chapes (Fig. 4), their affinities with earlier Atlantic models of the Ewart Park type from the Atlantic Late Bronze Age clearly exhibit this North Occidental origin.

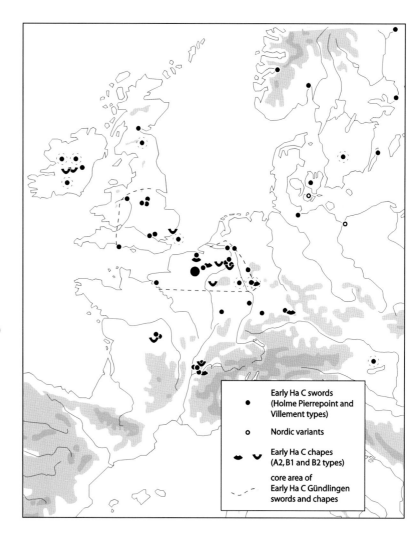

Fig. 4. Distribution map in Europe of the earliest Gündlingen family swords and their chapes at the beginning of Early Ha C (800-750 BC). After Milcent 2004, 109-110, fig. 57-58, with additions: Belgium: Aalst (East Flanders) „Hofstade" (Holme Pierrepoint sword and A2 chape); Germany: Stolzenau (Niedersachsen) (Holme Pierrepoint sword); Great Britain: Jackfield (Shropshire) River Severn (Villement sword); Weymouth (Dorset) 'Backwater' (Villement sword); Ireland: Edenderry (Villement sword), Holme Pierrepoint sword and Villement with no precise location; Netherlands: Maastricht-Vroendal (Limburg) (Villement sword and B2 chape).

This is not an isolated case: many other Hallstattian objects have prototypes in the Atlantic Late Bronze Age (Milcent 2009a, 246 fig. 14). Therefore, the adjective „Hallstattian" generally used to describe these Ha C swords is problematic and purely conventional. These facts therefore contradict the traditional hypotheses that these weapons were brought by invasions of horsemen from Eastern Europe. Swords of the Gündlingen family, moreover, are never associated with harnesses of ridden horses, but only with parts of horse tack related to a four-wheeled wagon. To the east of the Rhine, on the other hand, swords of family Gündlingen of Early Ha C are rare (the tomb of Wehringen barrow 8 is the best-known; Friedrich/ Hennig 1996; Fig. 2,4-5) and correspond to imports or to Atlantic imitations. Save for these exceptions, the contemporary swords of the Early Ha C in Central Europe carry on the Continental tradition of swords with a massive bronze grip from the end of the Bronze age (for example types Mörigen, Weltenburg, Tachlovice; Milcent 2009a, fig.7,1-9).

The Late Ha C (equivalent to Ha C1-2) is represented by sword types Miers and Pierrefitte-sur-Sauldre, often made of iron (Fig. 3). Their chapes have more or less curved wings or, for the latest, a sub-rectangular shape. These date from the end of the 8th century or the first two thirds of the 7th century BC. East of the Rhine the beginning of the Late Ha C corresponds to the generalization of these swords of Atlantic tradition and the abandonment of styles inherited from the tradition of the Central European Late Bronze Age (we only know a few exceptions like the burial of München-Trudering „Am Mitterfeld" in Bavaria, where an evolved Weltenburg sword is still associated with a Late Ha C chape of F1 type).

At the end of Late Ha C, very long swords in bronze or iron appear: the Mindelheim type. These swords are late models imported from Central Europe and exhibit oriental technical characteristics. The latest swords of Ha C are also the longest. They are sometimes even accompanied by artifacts characteristic, in principal, of the beginning of the Ha D1: snake shaped fibula at Viala-du-Pas-de-Jaux (Aveyron), first antennae daggers at Nuits-Saint-Georges (Côte-d'Or) „Concoeur et Corboin", crescent razors with high extremities like at Magny-Lambert (Côte-d'Or) „Montceau Laurent". Therefore this Mindelheim horizon belongs to the transition from Late Ha C to Early Ha D1. I emphasize the importance of this late dating of the longer swords, since, as in the past, the Mindelheim horizon had been mistakenly attributed to an older stage. The Mindelheim horizon is not only well documented in Central Europe, but also in the East and northeast of Gaul because it sees the development of rich graves, with wagon and bronze dishes. Similarly, it is marked out in Northern Europe by exceptional non-funerary metal deposits (hoard of Hassle in Sweden with an Etruscan cauldron and cordoned situlae from the second half of the 7th century BC especially). In the western regions, on the other hand, it is documented only by relatively poor sets of artifacts. In all, this chronological evolution shows the early appearance of iron swords and a late continuation of bronze swords: there is no succession, but rather a coexistence of two very different technical traditions (Atlantic and Continental) over almost two centuries, the Atlantic one gradually taking the ascendancy over the other with mixing on the Continent. During Ha C, swords become longer. One may even wonder whether the longest swords at the end of the period, were still functional for combat (in the Gomadingen burial found in 1885 (Baden-Württemberg), an unusable repaired Mindelheim sword was deposited for example). In Gaul, their study does not allow one to establish a clear relationship with either usage on horseback or from a wagon, as one might have thought in the 20th century. The geographic distribution of the Early Ha C bronze swords in a burial context shows no true concentration in Gaul. We cannot identify a clear diffusion direction. This configuration without polarity is characteristic of a network development. On the other hand, this deduction cannot yet be made for iron swords whose detailed history is much more difficult to reconstruct due to their degradation by oxidation.

Dominant characteristics of the inhumation burials with swords in Hallstattian Gaul

Let us now look at the principal characteristics of inhumation burials with Ha C sword. Regarding the dead, we have very little information due to the ancientness of most of the excavations. The dead are buried on their back in a stretched out position, and half the time with the head pointing north or south; west orientations are avoided with exceptions (Fig. 2,5). The sword is always parallel to the body, very often on the right side of the body (43/60 known cases), often with the tip pointing toward the feet (25/40 known cases) (Fig. 5,2). One good example

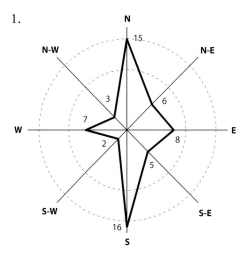

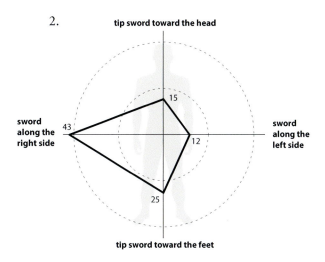

Fig. 5. 1: Graphic of the orientation frequency (according to the cardinal points) of the head of the deceased buried with a sword during the Ha C in Gaul. – 2: Graphic of the position frequency of the sword in the inhumation burials during the Ha C in Gaul. – 3: A tomb under barrow representative of the most common funerary practices in Hallstattian Gaul: Jaulnes (Seine-et-Marne) "Le Bas des Hauts Champs"; burial of an elderly man, with his head toward the North, an iron sword on the right side with the tip toward the feet and a bracelet on the left wrist; the tomb is located on a more ancient barrow. (Photography N. Ameye, Inrap).

comes from a recent excavation at Jaulnes in Seine-et-Marne (Fig. 5,3). However, it should not be assumed that the sword was in a functional position: indeed, there was no trace of suspension elements (in contrast for example to the sword tombs of the Late Bronze Age from Saint-Romain-de-Jalionas and Chavéria) and the substantial length of many swords is not in agreement with the hypothesis of a normal arrangement along the leg and hip. Numerous cases of swords found with the point near the head or the grip at head height of the deceased also show that these were not deposited in a functional manner. On a daily basis, one could imagine that these swords would be worn instead at either an angle or horizontally on the chest or back, or even on the shoulder, as was the case in some Mediterranean cultures.

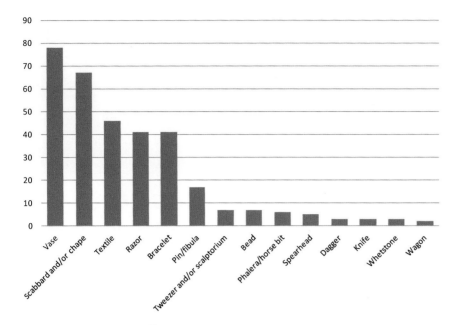

Fig. 6. Histogram of the frequency of the types of objects deposited in Ha C sword burials in Gaul.

Biological age and sex are very rarely determined with confidence. All 21 decedents for which the age is known were adults. There were six adults with no precise determination and only three young adults. In contrast, twelve dead were 30 years old or more (three of them were probably 50 years old or more). Among these cases, we know that ten dead were males (no females are determined). In other burials, the lack of typically feminine objects and the frequency of razors, objects certainly masculine and for adults, lends support to these general rules. Swords and objects from burial tombs under tumuli are deposited according to rather homogeneous and widely spread geographically funeral codes. Swords are deposited intact, with six exceptions corresponding to burials located along the margins of Hallstattian Gaul (Haroué in Lorraine, Cazevieille and Chabestan in Mediterranean France). The presence of a scabbard is regularly attested by imprints on the blade or the association with a chape (67 cases; Fig. 6). Textiles are often observed (46 cases) on the blade and sometimes the grip of the sword, especially on iron specimens because organic matter is preserved more easily by mineralization when in contact with iron oxidation. Among well-studied cases, six show the association of two different fabrics. The identified fabrics are woven in flax, hemp, nettle, or wool, without identifying a genuine preference for one of these fibers. These textiles might well have been part of the scabbard or part of a wrapping: the distinction between the two cases is rarely possible without a very precise study.

In burials the swords are regularly accompanied by other objects, but in limited number (two on average[2]). In descending order of frequency, we first find drinking vessels (three per tomb at a maximum in 78 cases except in the Rhine Valley and the surrounding area where the number of vessels can be higher as it is common for more easterly regions[3]). W. Reinhard has already pointed out, in fact, that the upper Valley of the Rhine constitutes a limit for Hallstattian sword tombs notably from the point of view of deposits of vessels (Reinhard 2003, 41 fig. 24). West

---

2   I do not take into account the many rings known in the sword tombs because they could have had very different purposes and are often directly related to the hanging of other objects, razors in particular.

3   Exceptions: Wörth in the Pfalz, Obenheim and Ohnenheim in Alsace, Matran in the Fribourg's canton.

of the Rhine, these deposits are scaled down and correspond to an individual drinking service, while to the east, the vessels are more numerous and form rather a drinking and dining service for few people. This distinction in funeral rituals also explains the general absence of remnants of deposits of solid foods, for example in the form of connecting animal bones or a meat knife, in Hallstattian tombs from Gaul unlike the Central and eastern provinces of the Hallstattian world. The vessels of these tombs are often represented by a pot for liquids, more or less globular, and a drinking cup. Their decoration, if it exists, is limited to a few grooves, incisions and sometimes graphite painting. Most are in ceramic; but 14 tombs yielded at least one bronze vessel of local or imported origin.

Grooming utensils are the next best represented objects with 40 tombs with razors in bronze or iron, six tombs with other grooming utensils (*scalptorium* or tweezers) and one tomb with a razor and grooming utensils combined. We generally find these utensils near the head or pelvis. If the razor tombs are dispersed evenly geographically, we observe that the tombs with *scalptorium* and/or tweezers are rather concentrated in southern Gaul. Once more, it had already been noted that the deposit of the razor was rather a funeral practice specifically widespread in regions of Hallstattian Gaul (Olivier/Reinhard 1993, 108 fig.3; Reinhard 2003, 41 fig. 19; 60 fig. 37). The deposits of bracelets, observed in 41 sword tombs, is almost as common as that of a grooming instrument. With exceptions, the armring, which could be made of iron or bronze, was worn by itself, on the left wrist (16 cases) rather than on the right wrist (five cases) of the deceased. Staying on the topic of clothing and jewelry, the presence of a pin or a fibula is distinctly less common with 17 cases. These recurrent associations give a simple uniformity to the burials from Gaul in comparison with sword graves in Central and Eastern Europe which have more grave goods (especially with drinking and eating ceramics), and diverse and less standardized artifacts. Indeed other objects appear in sword inhumations from Gaul, but in a more or less anecdotal fashion:

- beads (one or two in each burial, made from ceramic, amber, glass or gold) for seven cases,
- *phalerae* and/or pairs of horse-bits for six cases and two in association with a four wheeled wagon,
- spearheads for four or five cases;
- knives for three or four cases,
- daggers for three cases,
- whetstones for three cases,
- fingerring for two or three cases,
- axe for one possible case.

The scarcity of pins, metallic items for sword suspension and other weapons also shows that these items were selected according to fairly strict interregional customs and were not a full deposit of personal equipment. I also stress the absence of objects for eating meat or solid food. The deceased is not presented in the tomb as a real warrior with all his functional equipment, nor as an important person who could host ceremonial meals, but rather as a person whose status is evoked by a conventional selection of few grave goods. This evocation seems metonymic or very connotative, which poses, of course, interpretation problems. Here we have a very different funeral ideology from those that were at work at the same time in Central Europe for some very rich burials.

The sword tomb in its burial context

I am now going to expand the research focus to the barrows and necropolises that sheltered these sword tombs. Once again, accurate information is often lacking. However, we know that the documented inhumations were always sheltered by a barrow. This tumulus never appears isolated because it belongs to a necropolis.

Inside the mound, the tomb can occupy three types of positions:

- central and founding location, in a pit dug in the ground: this is rare;
- central and founding location, but on older ground: this is the most frequent case;
- adventitious location to an older barrow, usually dated from the Chalcolithic. This is common in the south of France where Chalcolithic and Early Bronze Age burial mounds are very numerous.

The last two cases pose a well-understood conservation problem: if the mound is eroded, the sword tomb disappears as well. Barrow architecture is poorly documented. The variability seems high and depends a lot on the natural environment, notably geology. Earth, clumps of turf and wood are used where stone is rare, and vice and versa. The founding burial tombs with sword, and with no other burials in quite small barrows: around 8 to 15 m in diameter and 50 cm to 2 m high (between three and 85 m³; Fig. 7). This is true as well of the rich sword tombs, as for example at Poiseul-la-Ville (Chaume/Feugère 1990). Larger mounds exist, but they are not so widely represented. These bigger barrows always show traces of successive expansion: some older barrows are enlarged to accommodate the sword burial, or Ha C barrows are enlarged later to deposit more recent tombs, notably at the Ha D. The latter case is known at Marainville-sur-Madon in Lorraine where two tumuli with central sword tombs had been significantly expanded in order to install female tombs with wagon (Olivier 2002). As for the reused mounds of the Chalcolithic period or from the beginning of the Bronze Age in the South of the Massif Central, one could see the desire to associate themselves with a place of memory and in this way obtain additional prestige for the deceased in the Ha C. More prosaically, it is noted that many other tombs from the early Iron Age reuse the oldest mounds in this area and that they are not distinguished by artifacts or funerary practices in particular. The reoccupation of the oldest mounds for sword burials does not appear as a limited privilege. It seems rather dictated by expediency of not having to build a new monument at the time of burial. In summary, the little data available shows a rather limited investment in materials and working time, even if the barrows containing the sword tombs are not the smaller ones from Ha C. The great princely mounds in Gaul, which required a lot of investment arose before or after Ha C: they date from the Early Bronze Age (like the Plouvorn „Kernonen" or Lannion „La Motta" barrows), Late Bronze Age (like the Saint-Romain-de-Jalionas, Chavéria T.3 and T.9, or Sublaines barrows) or from the end of the first Iron Age and the beginning of the La Tène period (barrows from Apremont, Vix, Bourges, Lavau for example).

In extensively excavated necropolis, the sword mounds do not appear segregated or in any particular position. The same necropolis, whether large or small, often yields several sword tombs. This is the case at Chavéria and Doucier (Jura), Poiseul-la-Ville (Côte-d'Or) and Rubenheim (Saar) with four tombs, at Saint-Georges (Cantal) with five tombs, Diarville (Meurthe-et-Moselle) with six tombs, Clayeures (Meurthe-et-Moselle) with seven tombs, at Magny-Lambert

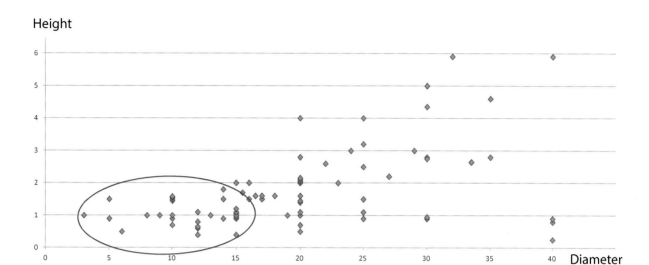

Height

Diameter

Fig. 7. Graphic of the size of the tumulus of inhumation sword tombs whose diameter and height are known in Gaul. The ellipse corresponds to the barrows which we think were set up for Ha C sword tombs and have not been reused or expanded for future burials.

(Côte-d'Or) with ten tombs. One could think that we are dealing in several of these cases with necropolises used by several family clans.

But what one should take away is that sword tombs relate to necropolises which, for the most part, seem created during the Ha C or even reactivated through the construction of tumuli. Rare indeed are the examples of strict continuity with the Late Bronze age. Indeed, during the Late Bronze Age, burials rarely formed a grouped necropolis that was used over a long period. On the other hand, recurring discoveries of tombs from Ha D and Lt A1 in necropolises with Ha C sword graves demonstrate that the use of these sites extended beyond Ha C and that these necropolises were probably designed to last. Therefore, many of the deceased buried with a sword in Ha C might have been considered founding ancestors. Since the works of A. Saxe and L. Goldstein (Morris 1991), the idea that the creation (or reactivation) of a necropolis is a way for a community to affirm ancestral rights over a territory and its resources in a context of competition has been emphasized. The transition from rather scattered graves or loose necropolises, during the Late Bronze Age, to rather concentrated graves in dense necropolis (re)starting from the Ha C, certainly signaled a profound change in value related to the territory. This relationship to the territory where the dead play an important role was interpreted, by Saxe and Goldstein, in terms of accentuated pressure on land resources and even development of land ownership by groups rather patrilineal and patrilocal (Morris 1991). What we know of the identity of the deceased accompanied with a sword would agree with this interpretation.

Synthesis: wealth and status of the deceased

By way of summary, I now examine the wealth of artifacts and funerary investment in order to try to identify the status of the deceased accompanied by a sword. The objective criteria to try to clarify this status are the abundance, quality and origin of the artifacts, and their degree of rarity. It is also the size of the grave and the barrow that covers it. Other criteria should be taken into account, but the gaps from the old documentation frequently do not allow this. One can think, for example, of the techniques in making the artifacts, especially swords, or the quality of the funerary architecture. Similarly, it should be possible to work out the relationship of the sword tombs to the settlements, landscape, territory or other tombs.

Overall, most sword inhumation tombs in Gaul represent a medium or a low investment: the construction of the tomb and mound required little work and very few items. These funerary objects are rather simple and mundane like ceramics and small metal objects. Gold, for example, the metal representing power and wealth par excellence, is represented in only one burial in the form of a small bead (Diarville T.3 S.1). In this case, would the sword be the exception and the only prestige good in the tomb? Probably not, in fact: swords, with some exceptions, most likely have a regional origin, as shown by small local typological variations. These swords show no particular enrichment, neither in the material used, nor the decoration, which would show them to be anything other than a weapon for warfare, except perhaps for the latest and longest (Mindelheim swords for

Fig. 8. Distribution map of the rich Ha C sword inhumations in Hallstattian Gaul. In addition: rich burials of Ha C, more or less destroyed before or during their discovery (with Ha C sword at the origin?).

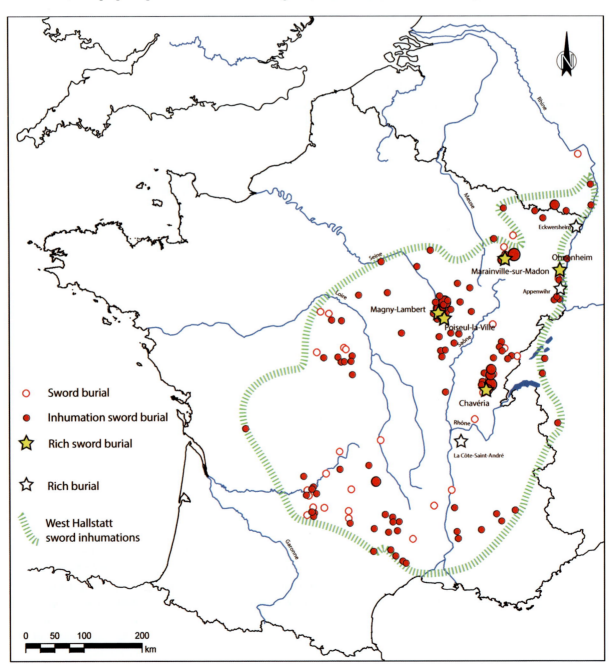

Sword burial

Inhumation sword burial

Rich sword burial

Rich burial

West Hallstatt sword inhumations

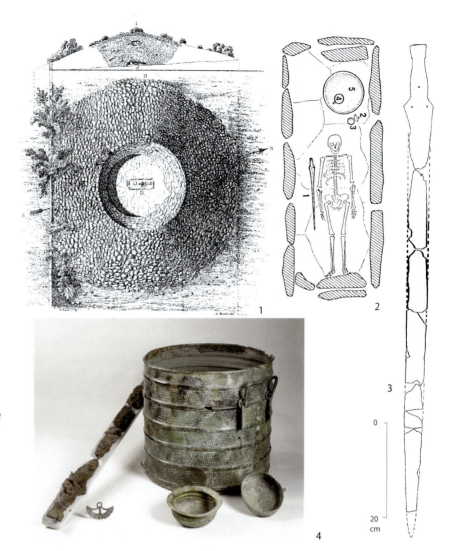

Fig. 9. Barrow, burial and grave goods of a Late Ha C – beginning Ha D1 rich sword inhumation: Magny-Lambert (Côte-d'Or) 'Montceau Laurent' (barrow 4 on the necropolis plan). Notice that the barrow shows a complex stratigraphy, reoccupation and clear evidence for a successive expansion. (Plan of the barrow and the burial by A. Maître, sword drawing after Nicolardot 1987 63 fig.68, photography of the Grave goods by H. Lewandowski (RMN)).

example). This is not a real surprise because swords usually do not belong to the category of rare and precious objects since the Late Bronze Age in Gaul. These are relatively common items, especially if we compare them to the truly exceptional objects and prestige goods of Late Bronze Age, which are, for example, bronze helmets and cuirasses, gold jewels, bronze flesh hooks and rotary spits, or large bronze buckets and cauldrons. The end of the Bronze Age in Gaul shows that communities already had a fairly large stock of metal and were able to produce large quantities of swords: a few thousand are indexed and these constitute a very small part of what existed. It is likely that tens of thousands of swords were produced at this time. During Ha C the development of iron metallurgy made this production easier. It thus becomes impossible to seriously argue the idea that these Ha C swords would be rare to the point of representing prestige goods. However, these Ha C swords were certainly not available to everyone and would remain costly items. But it is necessary not to simplify this picture. Indeed, there exists a small group of burials in Hallstattian Gaul that differ from all others by a rich funeral deposit (Fig. 8):

- at Chavéria (Jura), barrow 16 contained an Early Ha C burial with a bronze Wehringen sword and a harness for a two horse team (Vuaillat 1977; Fig. 2,1-3);

- at Magny-Lambert (Côte-d'Or), the Montceau Laurent inhumation with a very long iron sword and a crescent bronze razor had a drinking service in bronze (Nicolardot 1987; Fig. 9). One beaker is in a local form. Two other bronze vessels were imported from the north of Italy, perhaps from the region around Bologna, where we find comparable vessels: one is a large ribbed situla with fixed grips and the second is a ladle. The wide situla is well-dated by its zoomorphic pendants of the Bisenzio type from the late 8th to the beginning of the 7th century BC (Chaume 2004). The same can be said of the ladle. Wear and tear of the imported vessels, especially the ladle which shows traces of cracks and repairs, implies that these luxury items had been used for a long time before becoming part of the funeral deposit. The highly developed form of the sword and the razor[4] reinforces the idea that the Montceau Laurent tomb belongs to the very end of the Late Ha C;

- at Poiseul-la-Ville (Côte-d'Or), the burial of barrow 3 has given a very long iron sword, a bronze armring, two iron razors, and a set of bronze Etruscan vessels: a Kurd type bucket and a Colmar type phiale, dated in Italy from the end of the 8th to the first quarter of the 7th century BC (Chaume/Feugère 1990). Like the Montceau Laurent burial, this inhumation is dated by the sword around the end of Late Ha C and it shows a long use of the vessels before the deposit;

- at Ohnenheim in Alsace, an adventice tomb with a Mindelheim sword with an ivory pommel from the very end of Late Ha C was linked with a four-wheeled wagon. The wagon of Ch. Pare type 4 is richly decorated with bronze appliqués and perhaps imported from southern Germany (Pare 1992). It is probable that the inventory of the tomb is incomplete due to the mediocre conditions of the excavations;

- at Marainville-sur-Madon in Lorraine, we are dealing with the richest tomb from Hallstattian Gaul (Olivier 2002). It contained a long iron sword of the Mindelheim type imported from Central Europe at the end of Late Ha C (Fig.10,2). The ivory pommel had amber incrustations. A large bronze cauldron and a carinated bronze cup were both imported from central Italy (Fig. 10,3-4). A harness (Fig. 10,5-6) and a four-wheeled wagon of Ch. Pare type 5A, with Austrian style decorations and imported from Central Europe, completed the funerary artifacts (Fig. 10,7-8).

---

4   The same type of razor is indeed associated with an antennae dagger from the beginning of the Ha D1, in the tomb of Saint-Hélier in Côte-d'Or.

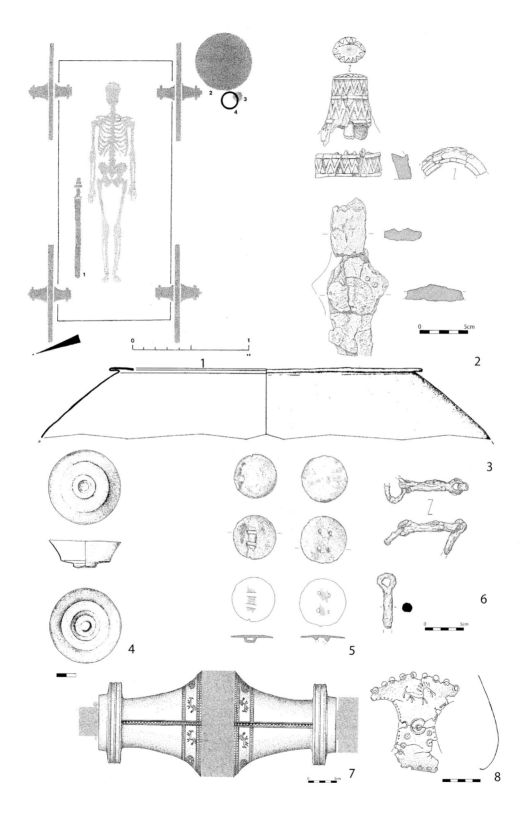

Fig. 10. Plan and grave goods of a Late Ha C/beginning Ha D1 rich sword inhumation: Marainville-sur-Madon (Vosges) „Sous le Chemin de Naviot" (after Olivier 1988, 276 fig. 2; 2002, 67 fig 15).

To sum up, there are only 5 sword inhumations[5] out of 170 that stand out. Except for Chavéria T.16, these richest burials date from the end of the Late Ha C or even from the early Ha D1. They are scattered in the eastern regions of Gaul, that is to say, in contact with the central Hallstattian domain, like for Marainville-sur-Madon. For Ohnenheim, very close to the river Rhine, the burial could in fact belong to the central Hallstattian domain because the limit with the west Hallstattian domain was not precisely on the Rhine in Alsace, but probably on the Vosges. This very small group of rich burials in Gaul thus appears even more marginal.

Discussion

To sum up, sword inhumations under tumuli from Ha C in Hallstattian Gaul show a great homogeneity over a very large area (600 km from the Vosges to the Charente, 700 km from the Saar to the south Massif central). The codification of the funerary practices appears standardized and strict, favoring limited artifact deposition in both variety and number of objects. The burials that deviate from the norm, that is to say, the richest, are rare (~3%), arising late in the Ha C and geographically limited. One could wonder what such a homogeneity of funerary practices represents: is it the manifestation of a social reality (existence of an elite claiming a social class identity?), or a cultural reality, even ethnic? Aside from the sword deposits, these burials hardly stand out. One notes that, indeed, other burials from Hallstattian Gaul present fairly homogeneous features: the majority are inhumations under tumulus with modest funerary deposits. This uniformity and this soberness of funerary practices could thus derive primarily from a cultural characteristic. This is why it would be tempting to correlate this vast funerary province from Hallstattian Gaul (Fig. 8) to what we know of the geography of the Celtic people of Gaul and their neighbors just as ancient writers (Strabo and Julius Caesar mainly) drew it for the end of the Iron Age. More or less, the area encompassing sword inhumations under barrow overlaps indeed with Celtic Gaul, while the regions where they are absent correspond to those that have been attributed to the Belgians, Armoricans, Aquitanians and Ligurians. We can also ask ourselves more precisely about the place occupied in the societies of Hallstattian Gaul, of those buried with a sword while they were still alive. The first point to emphasize is that the Ha C sword burials belong to a mundane or common phenomenon. They are possibly as numerous as La Tènian sword tombs in Gaul during the Middle La Tène period. Except for some very specific and rare cases, they do not demonstrate an exceptional investment in grave goods or construction

---

5   It is possible that there are a few others. In Alaise „Combe Beron" in the Doubs, we point to the discovery of a bronze (lost) bucket with an antennae sword from the transition of the Late Ha C/ Ha D1. In Alsace, the Kastenwald burial at Appenwihr with an etruscan pyxis, a Colmar type phiale and a footed bronze cup (Jehl/Bonnet 1966), as well as the tomb in Eckwersheim „Burgweg Rechts", with a Kurd type bucket and a hemispherical cup, delivers italic luxury dishes that remind one of deposits known in the rich sword tombs of the Late Ha C (Poiseul-la-Ville and Frankfurt Stadtwald especially). No swords were reported in these Alsatian tombs, but that could be a problem of differential preservation (the tomb of Eckwersheim was partially destroyed). The same problem is raised with the tomb with the 4 bronze casted wheeled wagon and Etruscan bronze dishes (a Kurd type bucket and a basin) from La Côte-Saint-André (Isère): indeed, only a portion of these artifacts are known (Chapotat 1962). On the other hand, among the rich sword tombs, we do not set aside those which were accompanied by a simple goblet or a locally made bronze cup, notably the group from the South of the Massif Central (Milcent/Delrieu 2007). The tomb of Chaffois (Jura) is also set aside because it is probably a female inhumation from the Ha D1 in which a piece of a sword pommel of the Mindelheim type figured as an amulet (Milcent 2013b).

of the barrow. One can imagine that each masculine head of a family or clan could be buried with a sword. This sword, which was a weapon, could also become a marker of a dominant social status, even if, with some exceptions, this is absolutely not a luxury good in a strict sense. It is also a deposit which demonstrates the elites' enhanced values, through funerary practices, of a warrior like, heroic and patriarchal ideology. Moreover, some additional values are affirmed: the deposit of drinking vessels in small number expresses the valorization of commensality practices of drinking together, but in small groups, and not those of the banquet as in Central Europe. The presence of toiletries (razor, tweezers,…) with hanging systems show that they could be carried and exhibited daily showing a certain idea of body care.

However, I admit we should remain cautious regarding the extent of these interpretations: funerary practices also form a message to the community, and above all, the graves teach us what societies were willing to disclose of themselves through choices motivated by diverse reasons: practical, individual, socio-economical, political and cultural. What I mean to say is that the marked difference in wealth that appears between the sword tombs of Hallstattian Gaul and those known in Central Europe does not necessarily signify a very differentiated socio-economic reality. It would be naive to interpret this difference in burial deposits as indicating that the societies west of the Rhine were poorer and less hierarchical than those to the East. One could envisage for example that the Hallstattian elites in Gaul had made the choice (or had been forced) to drastically limit the importance of funerary deposits and the investment in the development of the tomb. Even if it is in a very different socio-political context, one will recall that sumptuary laws existed in Greece and Rome, in slightly later periods, which restricted the exhibition of wealth and splendor for funerals. To reiterate a distinction made by A. Testart (2001), the tombs of Hallstattian Gaul could also indicate the choice by the elites of a funeral policy of redistribution during the funeral while the elites of Central Europe, not necessarily richer or more powerful, clearly made the choice of a funerary policy of deposits, with sumptuous burials. The relative modesty of the sword tombs in Hallstattian Gaul should be interpreted first as a choice, taking into account fairly strict rules governing the selection of funerary deposits, rather than as a reflection of a possible poverty, even if, objectively, contemporary settlements[6] do not allow, for the moment, to consider the existence of very rich or powerful elites.

Now the relative modesty of the vast majority of elite tombs from Ha C must be placed in its historical context. During Early Ha C, in the first two thirds of the 8th century BC, a climatic, socio-economic, and cultural value crisis actually impacts Hallstattian societies in Gaul. This crisis marks the break between the Bronze and Iron Ages. It corresponds to deep changes: abandonment of settlements on high positions and fortified sites, scattering of settlements, disappearance of metallic hoards on land, scarcity of metallic objects immersions in rivers, dislocation of

---

6   Only one significant Ha C elite residence is identified today in Hallstattian Gaul, while, to this day, many domestic dwellings have been excavated in the centre and east of France. The elite residence mentioned above is a small, fortified site with large buildings from Early Ha C located in Villiers-sur-Seine (Seine-et-Marne) and of which the foundation dates back to the end of the Bronze Age (Peake *et al.* 2009). We do not yet know which of the two phases of occupancy (Ha B3 and the Early Ha C) is the richest. Some other sites fairly nearby and contemporary, for example at Préfontaines in Loiret (Milcent 2009b, 472 fig. 21,2), are perhaps also of high status judging by their protection by means of a palisade.

long distance networks from the Late Bronze Age, moving from cremation without tumulus to inhumations under mounds, real development of iron metallurgy, disappearance of „pictogram" style decoration on fine potteries and abandonment of the Late Bronze Age Continental elite set, etc. (Cicolani *et al.* 2015; Milcent 2004; 2009b). At this time, only the network connecting eastern and southern Gaul to the medio- and north-Atlantic cultures seems to have been maintained. This is visible with the strong Atlantic influences on elite equipment (swords, razors, horse harness and wagons, feasting items, etc.). This network has a very large scope since the elite metallic productions of medio- and North Atlantic style find their way everywhere from the British Isles to Austria and from Scandinavia to the South of France (Milcent 2009a). With the end of 8th and especially with the 7th century BC, the Late Ha C marks a slow recovery, as evidenced by the very rare sword tombs which are richer than the others. The exotic objects discovered in these rich tombs show that the network of connections were reoriented and that relationships are now preferentially oriented toward the middle basin of the Danube on one hand and toward northern and central Italy on the other hand (Milcent 2004, 113-115).

Conclusion

The Ha C sword graves in Hallstattian Gaul do not correspond to the emergence of an elite, as these elites already existed in the Late Bronze Age. They also do not correspond to their development, quite the contrary. These burials mark a way to represent a dominant social status with different methods than those in effect during the Late Bronze Age. This is first a change of funerary ideology that suddenly makes a social group visible in the eyes of archaeologists. These funerary representation elements are not really new. They are rooted, in fact, in an earlier tradition anterior to the Late Bronze Age which dates back to the Middle or Early Bronze Age. These periods are also known for male inhumations under a barrow and accompanied by a rapier or dagger. So this is a reactivation of a past funerary ideology, perhaps following a period of crisis that required a reshaping and new legitimization of the elites. However, it is likely that the sword tombs, as a likely vector of the (re)creation of necropolises with barrows, correspond to a structuring mutation of the elites. We note, in particular, the hypothesis of Saxe/Goldstein in considering that they could indicate new economic forms of differentiation and control, changing through land appropriation or claim for the benefit of certain elite families. In a certain fashion, the sword tombs from Hallstattian Gaul would be the symmetric counterpart to the rise of a phenomenon which we observe at the same time in Atlantic Gaul, namely the emergence of large real estates identified by important enclosed settlements, often with palisades, associated with large storage capacity (storage pits and especially raised granaries) and set up for managing and pasturing cattle (Milcent forthcoming 1). This emergence or development of large land ownership probably, constituted for the elites, a new way to solve the problems caused by the crisis of the 8th century BC.

Finally, there is a remarkable fact. The sword graves of Ha C do not really carry forward into the next period. In Ha D, the weapon graves effectively almost disappear in Hallstattian Gaul. Going forward, it is essentially the women who bring rich artifacts into their graves, notably metallic. These female burials seem neither less numerous nor wealthier than those before. But unlike previous male graves, these are used even more often as founding tombs for barrows which are enlarged to become family burial necropolis (Milcent 2003; 2013). In the same way, we do not perceive any strong link between the sword tombs of Ha C and the development, clearly much later, of true princely tombs. The sword tombs of Ha C are therefore a fairly original phenomenon in Gaul, which has no real immediate past and no immediate posterity.

Acknowledgments

My thanks to Harry and Marie Pugh for the translation of this article.

Bibliography

Beylier 2012: A. Beylier, L'armement et le guerrier en Méditerranée nord-occidentale au premier âge du Fer. Monographies d'Archéologie Méditerranéenne 31 (Lattes 2012).

Chapotat 1962: G. Chapotat, Le char processionnel de la Côte-Saint-André (Isère). Gallia XX, 1962, 33-78.

Chaume 1993: B. Chaume, La nécropole de Magny-Lambert (Côte-d'Or). Historique des fouilles et étude topographique. Revue Archéologique de l'Est 44, 1993, 181-189.

Chaume 2001: B. Chaume, Vix et son territoire à l'Age du Fer. Fouilles du mont Lassois et environnement du site princier. Protohistoire européenne 6 (Montagnac 2001).

Chaume 2004: B. Chaume, La place de la France orientale dans le réseau des échanges à longues distances du Bronze final au Hallstatt final. In: M. Guggisberg (ed.), Die Hydria von Grächwil. Zur Funktion und Rezeption mediterraner Importe in Mitteleuropa im 6. und 5. Jahrhundert v. Chr. Schriften des Bernischen Historischen Museums (Bern 2004) 79-106.

Chaume/Feugère 1990: B. Chaume/M. Feugère, Les sépultures tumulaires aristocratiques du Hallstatt ancien de Poiseul-la-Ville (Côte-d'Or). Revue Archéologique de l'Est, supplement 10 (Dijon 1990).

Cicolani et al. 2015: V. Cicolani/E. Dubreucq/M. Melin/P.-Y. Milcent, Aux sources de la Douix : objets et dépôts métalliques en milieu aquatique au Premier âge du Fer en France à partir de l'exemple d'un site remarquable. In: F. Olmer/R. Roure (eds.), Les Gaulois au fil de l'eau. Actes du 37e colloque international de l'AFEAF (Montpellier, 8-11 mai 2013), volume 1. Communications (Bordeaux 2015) 719-756.

Dhennequin 2005: L. Dhennequin, L'armement au premier âge du Fer en Europe tempérée. Unpublished doctoral thesis (Paris 2005).

Friedrich/Hennig 1996: M. Friedrich/H. Hennig, A dendrodate for the Wehringen Iron Age wagon grave (778±5 BC) in relation to other recently obtained absolute dates for the Hallstatt period in southern Germany. Journal of European Archaeology 4, 1996, 281-303.

Gerdsen 1986: H. Gerdsen, Studien zu den Schwertgräbern der älteren Hallstattzeit (Mainz am Rhein 1986).

Gomez de Soto 2014: J. Gomez de Soto, Des éléments du Hallstatt C dans les derniers dépôts français de l'horizon métalique de l'épée en langue de carpe? Un examen critique. Bulletin de la Société Préhistorique Française 111,4, 2014, 727-738.

Gruat 1994: P. Gruat, Les épées protohistoriques découvertes dans le département de l'Aveyron. Vivre en Rouergue 8, 1994, 123-135.

Hennig 1995: H. Hennig, Zur Frage der Datierung des Grabhügels 8 „Hexenbergle" von Wehringen, Lkr. Augsburg, Bayerische-Schwaben. In: B. Schmid-Sikimic/Ph. Della Casa (eds.), Trans Europam, Beiträge zur Bronze- und Eisenzeit zwischen Atlantik und Altaï. Festschrift für Margarita Primas. Antiquitas 3,34 (Bonn 1995) 129-145.

Jehl/Bonnet 1966: M. Jehl/C. Bonnet, Le tumulus de Wolfgantzen, forêt de Kastenwald. Cahiers Alsaciens d'Archéologie, Art et Histoire X, 1966, 43-46.

Milcent 2003: P.-Y. Milcent, Le contexte historique. In: C. Rolley (dir.), La tombe princière de Vix (Paris 2003), 327-366.

Milcent 2004: P.-Y. Milcent, Le premier âge du Fer en France centrale. Société Préhistorique Française, mémoire XXXIV (Paris 2004).

Milcent 2009a: P.-Y. Milcent, A l'Est rien de nouveau. Chronologie des armes de poing du premier âge du Fer médio-atlantique et genèse des standards matériels élitaires hallstattiens et laténiens. In: A. Lehoërff (ed.), Construire le temps. Histoire et méthodes des chronologies et calendriers des derniers millénaires avant notre ère en Europe occidentale. Actes du XXXe colloque international HALMA-IPEL, Lille 7-9 décembre 2006. Bibracte 16 (Glux-en-Glenne 2009) 231-250.

Milcent 2009b: P.-Y. Milcent, Le passage de l'âge du Bronze à l'âge du Fer en Gaule au miroir des élites sociales : une crise au VIIIe siècle av. J.-C.? In: A. Daubigney/ P.-Y. Milcent/ M. Talon/ J. Vital (eds.), De l'âge du Bronze à l'âge du Fer en France et en Europe occidentale (Xe-VIIe s. av. J.-C.). La moyenne vallée du Rhône aux âges du Fer. Actes du XXXᵉ colloque international de l'AFEAF, co-organisé avec l'APRAB (Saint-Romain-en-Gal, 26-28 mai 2006). Revue Archéologique de l'Est, supplément 27 (Dijon 2009) 453-476.

Milcent 2013a: P.-Y. Milcent, La nouvelle place des femmes dans l'espace funéraire en Gaule : des tombes à épée hallstattienne aux tombes à riche parure féminine. In: St. Verger/ L. Pernet (eds.) Une Odyssée gauloise. Parures de femmes à l'origine des premiers échanges entre la Grèce et la Gaule. Errance (Paris 2013) 136-141.

Milcent 2013b: P.-Y. Milcent, Le pommeau d'épée en ivoire et ambre de Chaffois (Doubs). In In: St. Verger/ L. Pernet (eds.) Une Odyssée gauloise. Parures de femmes à l'origine des premiers échanges entre la Grèce et la Gaule. Errance (Paris 2013) 188-189.

Milcent forthcoming 1: P.-Y. Milcent, The atlantic Early Iron Age in Gaul. In: A. Lehoërff (ed.), Au-delà des frontières. Voyager, échanger, communiquer. Actes du colloque de Boulogne-sur-Mer 2013 (forthcoming).

Milcent forthcoming 2: P.-Y. Milcent, Echanges prémonétaires et immobilisation fluctuante de richesses métalliques en Gaule atlantique (XIIIe-Ve s. av. J.-C.). Dynamiques et décryptage des pratiques de dépôts métalliques non funéraires. In: B. Toune/ E. Warmenbol (eds.), Choice pieces. The destruction and manipulation of goods in the Later Bronze Age: from reuse to sacrifice. Actes du colloque de Rome 2012. Academia Belgica (forthcoming).

Milcent/Delrieu 2007: P.-Y. Milcent/F. Delrieu, Tertres et archéologie funéraire en Haute Auvergne dans le contexte du premier âge du Fer en Gaule méridionale (VIIIe-Ve s. av. J.-C.). In: Chr. Mennessier-Jouannet/Y. Deberge (eds.), L'archéologie de l'âge du Fer en Auvergne. Actes du XXVIIᵉ colloque international de l'AFEAF, Clermont-Ferrand, 29 mai-1ᵉʳ juin 2003, Monographies d'Archéologie Méditerranéenne (Lattes 2007) 43-70.

Morris 1991: I. Morris, The archaeology of ancestors: The Saxe/Goldstein hypothesis revisited. Cambridge Archaeological Journal 1,2, 1991, 147-169.

Nicolardot 1987: J.-P. Nicolardot, Le tumulus du Montceau-Laurent à Magny-Lambert. Trésors des princes Celtes. In: Catalogue de l'exposition des Galeries nationales du Grand Palais (Paris 1987) 62-66.

Olivier 1988: L. Olivier, Le tumulus à tombe à char de Marainville-sur-Madon (Vosges). Premiers résultats. In: Les princes celtes et la Méditerranée. Rencontres de l'Ecole du Louvre, La Documentation Française (Paris 1988) 271-301.

Olivier 2002: L. Olivier (dir.), Princesses celtes en Lorraine. Sion, trois millénaires d'archéologie d'un territoire (Nancy 2002).

Olivier/Reinhard 1993: L. Olivier/W. Reinhard, Les structures socio-économiques du premier Age du Fer dans le groupe Sarre-Lorraine : quelques perspectives. In: A. Daubigney (ed.), Fonctionnement social de l'Age du Fer. Opérateurs & hypothèses pour la France. Table ronde internationale de Lons-le-Saunier 1990 (Besançon 1993) 105-130.

Pare 1992: C. Pare, Wagons and wagons-graves of the Early Iron Age in Central Europe. Oxford University for Archaeology Monographs 35 (Oxford 1992).

Pare 1999: C. Pare, Beiträge zum Übergang von der Bronze zur Eisenzeit in Mitteleuropa. Teil II : Grundzüge der Chronologie im westlichen Mitteleuropa (11.-8. Jahrhundert v. Chr.). Jahrbuch des Römisch-Germanischen Zentralmuseums 46, 1999, 175-315.

Peake *et al.* 2009: R. Peake/G. Allenet/G. Auxiette/F. Boisseau/Chr. Chausse/S. Coubray/C. Leroyer/C. Pautret-Homerville/J. Perrière/F. Toulemonde, Villiers-sur-Seine, Le Gros Buisson : un habitat aristocratique de la fin de l'âge du Bronze et du début du premier âge du Fer. In: A. Daubigney/P.-Y. Milcent/M. Talon/J. Vital (eds.), De l'âge du Bronze à l'âge du Fer en France et en Europe occidentale (Xe-VIIe s. av. J.-C.). La moyenne vallée du Rhône aux âges du Fer. Actes du XXXe colloque international de l'AFEAF, co-organisé avec l'APRAB (Saint-Romain-en-Gal, 26-28 mai 2006). Revue Archéologique de l'Est, supplément 27 (Dijon 2009) 559-564.

Reinhard 1993: W. Reinhard, Gedanken zum Westhallstattkreis am Beispiel der Ha C-zeitlichen Schwertgräber. Blesa 1, 1993, 359-387.

Reinhard 2003: W. Reinhard, Studien zur Hallstatt- und Frühlatènezeit im südöstlichen Saarland. Blesa 4 (Bliesbrück-Reinheim 2003).

Testart 2001: A. Testart, Deux politiques funéraires. Trabalhos de Antropologia e Etnologia 41,3-4, 45-66.

Vuaillat 1977: D. Vuaillat, La nécropole tumulaire de Chavéria (Jura). Annales Littéraires de l'Université de Besançon 139 (Besançon 1977).

Warmenbol 1993: E. Warmenbol, Les nécropoles à tombelles de Gedinne et Louette-Saint-Pierre (Namur) et le groupe „mosan" des nécropoles à épées hallstattiennes. In: F. Boura/J. Metzler/A. Miron (eds.), Interactions culturelles et économiques aux Ages du Fer en Lorraine, Sarre et Luxembourg. Actes du XIe colloque de l'A.F.E.A.F., Sarreguemines 1987. Archaeologia Mosellana 2 (Metz 1993) 83-114.

Author

Pierre-Yves Milcent
University of Toulouse Jean Jaurès
UMR 5608-TRACES
5 allées Antonio Machado
31058 Toulouse cedex 9
France
milcent@univ-tlse2.fr

Hallstatt elite burials in Bohemia from the perspective of interregional contacts

Martin Trefný

Abstract

In large parts of Bohemia during the early Hallstatt period (Ha C – D1) elites are represented in tumuli burials. The individuals buried in these chamber graves frequently are equipped with wagons or parts of thereof and other valuable and prestigious items. Most of these are imports from other regions of the Hallstatt culture or even from the Mediterranean world. Thus, these burials show interregional contacts between early Hallstatt Bohemia and other regions.

Dealing with the origin of such imports, it appears, that individual Bohemian regions show evolutionary affinity especially to the geographically adjacent areas. Namely there is a clear relation between central and northwestern Bohemia with its population of Bylany culture, south and western Bohemia with its Hallstatt tumulus culture and the Hallstatt civilization of southwestern Germany. On the other hand the east Bohemian Silesia-Platěnice culture evinces significant tendency to the cultures of the East Hallstatt area.

It may be argued that some imports represent the products of more distant areas, for example from the Etruscan or southeast Alpine regions. But also in these cases it is highly probable, that these items reached their final destination coming through the above mentioned adjacent areas, where they are also well represented. Such situation thus reflects again the significance of the proximity of these important evolutional centres, such as southwest Germany or the east Alpine area.

Regarding the character of proper contacts, we are today already far away from the idea of the interpretation of various importations in the terms of direct encounter of the various ethnicities, although in some cases it cannot be completely excluded. More probably the existence of the luxurious imported goods in the Bohemian elite graves features an adoption of a certain behavioral pattern in the environs of the Central European early Hallstatt social elite, which reflects an economical potential as well as political power.

Zusammenfassung

Soziale Eliten der älteren Hallstattzeit (Ha C – D1) manifestieren sich in weiten Teilen Böhmens in reichen Kammergräbern unter Grabhügeln und durch Grabausstattungen mit Wagen oder Teilen von Wägen. Die Inventare dieser Gräber bestehen zumeist aus wertvollen und prestigeträchtigen Objekten, die als typisch für die Mitglieder der herrschenden sozialen Klassen gelten können. Die Mehrheit dieser Prestigegüter stammt aus benachbarten Regionen der Hallstattkultur oder aus dem mediterranen Raum. Damit zeigen sich in diesen Gräbern großräumige Kontakte im ältereisenzeitlichen Böhmen.

Betrachtet man die unterschiedlichen großräumigen Beziehungen, so zeigt sich, dass einzelne Regionen in Böhmen Affinitäten zu unterschiedlichen geographisch angrenzenden Regionen aufweisen. So gibt es deutliche Beziehungen mit Südwestdeutschland in Zentral- und Nordwestböhmen mit der Bylany-Kultur und Süd- und Westböhmen mit der hallstättischen Grabhügelkultur. Auf der anderen Seite zeigt der ostböhmische Raum mit der schlesischen Platěnice-Kultur signifikante Affinitäten zum osthallstättischen Bereich.

Eine Objekte mögen aus deutlich entfernteren Reginoen stammen, so beispielsweise aus Etrurien oder dem Südostalpenraum. Es ist aber wahrscheinlich, dass diese eher über die benachbarten Gebiete, in denen derartige Funde regelhaft auftreten, in den böhmischen Raum gelangten, worin sich die Bedeutung der Nachbarschaft zu diesen wichtigen Zentren in der älteren Eisenzeit zeigt.

Im Hinblick auf den Charakter dieser Kontakte ist die Forschung mittlerweile weit über die Idee der direkten Verknüpfung mit ethnischen Identitäten hinweg, auch wenn diese in einigen Fällen nicht komplett ausgeschlossen werden kann. Wahrscheinlicher erscheint, dass das Auftreten der luxuriösen Importgüter in den Elitegräbern in Böhmen eine Übernahme eines gewissen Verhaltensmuster der zentraleuropäischen Elite der Hallstattkultur darstellt, in dem sich ökonomische Potenzial und politische Macht widerspiegeln.

Introduction

Social elites of the early Hallstatt period (Ha C – D1) are represented in most of contemporary Bohemia by the rich chamber graves, frequently equipped with wagons or part thereof and marked by tumuli. Grave inventories in most cases consist of valuable and prestigious items, typical for the members of the leading social class. The majority of these prestigious finds is represented by the imports from other areas of the contemporary Hallstatt or Mediterranean world. The inventories of such graves thus represent distinctive indications of the interregional contacts of early Hallstatt Bohemia with other regions, realized by using the network of long distance routes.

Between various groups of material culture of possible exogenous provenance occuring in the Bohemian Hallstatt elite graves may be listed for example parts of wagons, parts of horse harness, jewelery, pins, toiletries, pincushions, weapons, amber or glass. Of course this contribution cannot comprehend all of these classes in detail. For this reason it focusses on the categories with special significance or brand new finds, enriching our present state of knowledge in the appropriate field. These categories include firstly bronze vessels. Although the Etruscan or Picene bronze bowls with pearl studded rims of the Hohmichele type from the graves in Hradenín or Slatina have already been examined many times (Dvořák 1936, 67-74, 130; 1938, 33-39; Koutecký 2003, pl. 2,17; Siegfried-Weiss 1991, 112-113; Trefný *et al.* 2012), this contribution focuses in this category (bronze vessels) on new finds or earlier finds still unpublished. This paper also presents initial information on the finds of iron grates, first of a kind in the Bohemian territory. This contribution also generally aims to discuss several finds from the rich graves of Ha C – D1 such as trunnion axes, some kinds of pendants or fibulae, also documenting the important relations to the various adjacent areas (*cf.* Fig. 1).

Bronze vessels

Bucket from Prague-Letňany

The specialists of the Archaeological Institute of the Czech academy of Sciences in Prague uncovered two rich chamber graves of the Bylany culture during the november and december 2014 in the territory of the municipal quarter Letňany (Frolíková 2015)[1]. One of them (Fig. 2,1) included the remains of a four wheeled funeral wagon, horse harness, armring, 21 ceramic vessels, two iron grates, remains

---

1   Both graves are presently being studied and the majority of the finds still have not been fully conserved. However this fact should not influence in any way the chronological and typological classification of the bucket as well as grates (see below), which also were part of the grave inventory. I am very obliged to Mrs. Frolíková – excavator of the graves – for the possibility to study these graves already in this 'early' phase.

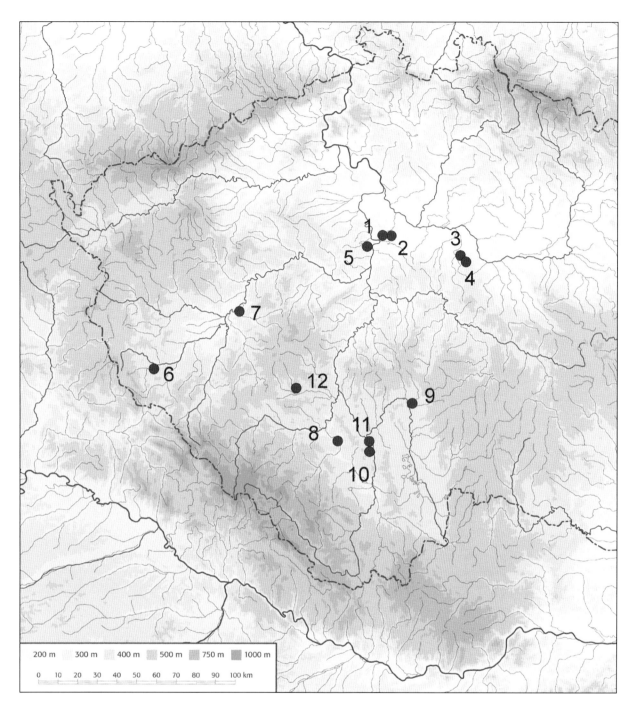

Fig. 1. Sites mentioned in text.
1: Prague-Letňany. –
2: Prague-Vinoř. – 3: Plaňany.
– 4: Hradenín. – 5: Prague-
Střešovice. – 6: Mašovice-
Meclov. – 7: Dýšina. –
8: Protivín. – 9: Dobronice. –
10: Litoradice. – 11: Týn nad
Vltavou. – 12: Bezdědovice.

of animals serving as a food for the deceased, parts probably from the sword, including the imprints of textile, visible in the superficial corrosion product and numerous remains of a bronze bucket without handles (*henkelloser Eimer*).

The bucket (Fig. 3,1) has a conical shape, with a sharply offset horizontally ribbed shoulder and perpendicular low neck. Characteristic high bottom, the lower third of vessel attached to the body with rivets, as well as specific profilation of the neck indicates certain affinity with types occuring frequently in the Hallstatt necropolis. Fine examples of such elements may be represented for example by the buckets from the graves no. 495, 827 or 458 (Prüssing 1991, pl 50,183; pl.

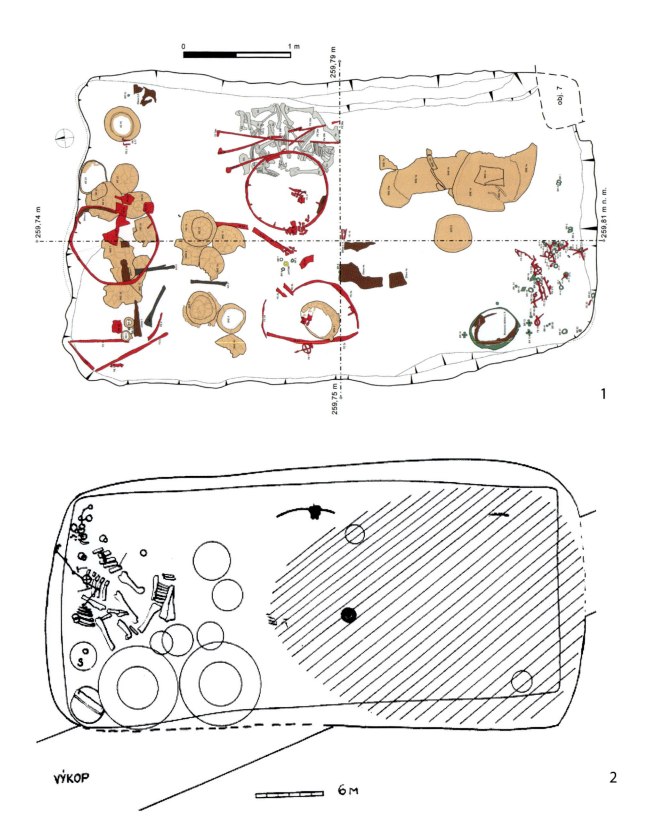

Fig. 2. Above (1): Prague-Letňany-Bylany culture grave with remnants of four wheeled wagon and bronze bucket (after Frolíková 2015, 18). – Below (2): Prague-Vinoř-Bylany culture grave with remnants of four wheeled wagon and bronze situla (after Fridrichová 1988).

52,185; pl. 57,190). Based on this preliminary classification, the Prague Letňany bucket may be considered a product of the Hallstatt area. With regard to the chronology of the bucket, the example from the grave No. 458 in Hallstatt is dated to phase Ha D (Prüssing 1991, 70; Sievers 1982, 44). Various characteristics of the inventory of the Prague-Letňany grave and the number of clay vessels indicate that this grave falls in the transition of Ha C/D or in the phase Ha D1.

The bronze bucket from Prague-Letňany is unique in one feature. The major part of its surface is covered by a black substance, reminiscent of paint. However use of a black paint on the surface of the metal vessels during the Hallstatt period is not common, but rather rare. It is known from a rich tumulus grave in Klein-Klein-Pomerkogel in southeastern Austria, a newly excavated tumulus in Rovná in southern Bohemia (Chytráček *et al.* 2015, 82 fig. 12; 84 fig. 14,1), Erkbolzheim in Elsace and Hallstatt[2]. The Prague-Letňany bucket is only the second case in this territory. A sample of this paint has been analysed in the laboratories of the Czech technical university and based on its composition it is possible to conclude that it contains aliphatic esters (waxes), occuring in natural bonding agents[3]. Regarding the chemical analyses of other paints, also the composition of the sample from Klein-Klein was studied. According to M. Egg (pers. comm.), the composition is equal or similar to betulin. This extract from the bark of birch or birch sap occurs in birch pitch, which has been used due to its effect as a glue or adhesive. This is also for example the case of fabulous find of the Iceman Ötzi in the Ötztaler Alps, where this substance was used to fix some parts of weapons (Sauter *et al.* 2000). Also the black paint of the ribbed cist from Rovná has been studied, but the results have been not yet published. In this respect it is neccessary to point out that the quality of the Rovná paint substantially differs from the paint of the Prague-Letňany bucket. The former is more coloid, while the later one is coarser. This distinction may indicate different chemical composition of the paints.

Since, the research on the black paint on several Hallstatt metallic vessels is in its initial phase, the interpretation of it is highly speculative. While in the case of Rovná or Klein-Klein the function of decoration may be considered, the purpose of paint on the Prague-Letňany bucket remains unknown and will be a matter of future studies (c.f. Kozáková et al. forthcoming).

Situla from Prague-Vinoř

The bronze situla (*Steilhalssitula*) was part of the inventory of the rich Bylany culture princely grave of Prague-Vinoř (Fridrichová 1988; Trefný 2012, fig. 1) (Fig. 4,1; 2,2). These situlae have hitherto been known only from Dobřany in western Bohemia or Rvenice in northwestern Bohemia (Siegfried-Weiss 1991, 115-117). Except for these, the remains of the bucket with sickle shaped handles, imported from Picenum, have been found in Břasy (Siegfried-Weiss 1991, 116). A few years ago a rich tumulus of the west Bohemian Hallstatt tumulus culture was excavated in Rovná, near Strakonice in southern Bohemia. In addition to other kinds of bronze vessels, the inventory included also one Tessin type situla (Chytráček *et al.* 2015, 83 fig. 13).

Although the Prague-Vinoř situla was found in 1988, it was kept a long time in the National museum of Prague because of restoration works. This is why it was

---

2   Author is obliged for oral information to M. Egg.
3   Autor is obliged for the analysis and interpretation to K. Drábková.

Fig. 3. 1 Prague-Letňany-bronze bucket from one of the graves; 2 iron grates from the same grave.

not included in the compendium by A. Siegfried-Weiss, dedicated to the Hallstatt bronze vessels in Bohemia (1991), and why it practically vanished from the sight of professional archaeologists, unless being typologically and chronologically classified.

The vessel was found not intact but as a cluster of distorted metal sheets. During the restoration individual parts were set on a core formed by metal net. Unfortunately during the restoration the superficial corrosion layer had been removed, unless being properly examined because of eventual imprints of the textile, as was for example the case of Rvenice situla (Siegfried-Weiss 1991, 116). Today only very little parts of original surface may be examined in this sense.

The situla was made of bronze metal sheet with thickness of ca. 0.3 mm. It was assembled from five parts (Fig. 4,2-3), with the body consisting of two segments, each riveted from two parts. The bottom, produced from one piece of metal, is attached to the lower part with rivets. The rim of the situla is curved outwards, with the core wire preserved in major parts of the rim. The remains of the handles, formed by the bent wire, are visible below the rim in two places. During the reconstruction of the vessel, a small puzzle occured, because one handle is made of iron, and is so described also in the unpublished excavation report from M. Fridrichová (1988), held in the Prague Municipal Museum. One handle made of bronze and the second one from iron would represent a certain problem. But finally this puzzle was solved with a contribution of the museum's archaeologist M. Kostka, who informed me that the iron attache has been erroneously added to the group of finds from Prague-Vinoř, whereas it comes from totally different Medieval site.

Typologically and technologically the Prague-Vinoř situla differs from the known Bohemian examples. The Dobřany situla (Kimmig 1962, 84; Pleinerová 1973, 291 fig. 15; Siegfried-Weiss 1991, 116; von Merhart 1952, Taf. 22,1) is assembled from only of two halves, joined by eleven rivets. The bottom (*Falzboden*) is attached to the body. The situla is different even by the decoration of the neck, because this one, contrary to the Prague-Vinoř situla neck, is decorated by horizontal ribs. The situla from Rvenice (Pleinerová 1973, 280 fig. 4,11.6-8) is also made of two halves, with bottom made of one piece and attached to the lower part of the body with rivets. The diameter of the omphalos on the Rvenice situla is similar to the Prague-Vinoř situla, though they differ in that the situla Rvenice situla has horizontal ribs on the neck.

The bucket with sickle shaped handle-attachments (Píč 1900, pl. 29,1; Šaldová 1968, 367; Siegfried-Weiss 1991, 116) is very fragmented, moreover only the upper part is preserved. Thus the detailed comparison of individual parts is not possible. Finally, the newly discovered situla from the tumulus grave from Rovná, dated Ha D3 (Chytráček et. al. 2015, 83 fig. 13) has also a so-called *Falzboden*, where the bottom is not made of one piece with part of the body, but separately and is attached to the walls of vessel not by rivets but by bending of walls around the bottom[4]. The body of this situla is formed by two halves. Also the overall shape of the situla is little different from the Prague-Vinoř one.

Regarding the occurence of technologically fitting analogies outside of the Bohemian area, it is possible to exclude from this comparison so-called Tessin situlae, produced in the area of the Golasecca culture (*cf.* Kimmig 1962). Similar form comes from grave no. 759 in the necropolis of San Vitale in Bologna (Pincelli/Morigi Govi 1975). This situla is also assembled from five parts (two parts each made of two halves plus bottom) and also the bottom is made of one piece. However, the most numerous parallels may be found in the Hallstatt necropolis. It may also be emphasised, that here we generally find a high number of vessels with bottom with omphalos, which is riveted to the lower part of the body, as is the case of Prague-Vinoř situla (Prüssing 1991, pl. 24-35; pl. 38-63). Moreover, *Falzboden* is here an exogenous element, occuring alternatively in the later period (Kimmig 1962, 85). Probably the closest example is the situla from grave no. 12 (Prüssing 1991, pl. 55,188). Although this situla has no handles and is also a little bit bigger (48 cm), its manner of construction as well as the number of parts are the same. It also has an outcurved rim and also corresponds in the overall shape.

Presented comparisons indicate the origin of the Prague-Vinoř situla may be sought directly in Hallstatt or its surroundings. So this situla is the second piece of this provenance (after the Rvenice situla; Pleinerová 1973, 294), occuring in Bohemian territory. The Dobřany situla shows certain affinities with situlae of southeast Alpine provenance (Kimmig 1962, 85) and the bucket from Břasy is most likely the product of the Picenum workshops in central Adriatic Italy.

Chronology of the Prague-Vinoř situla may be derived from comparison with the example from grave no. 12 in Hallstatt. This situla was found together with a cauldron, classified as 'type Hallstatt' (*Kessel der Form Hallstatt*). The cauldron of this type is represented in Austria by only one other piece found in Dürrnberg. Chronologically the Hallstatt piece should be earlier than that one from Dürrnberg, which was found together with fibulae with decorated foot (*Fusszierfibel*) and a tambourine fibulae (*Paukenfibel*) and dated to Ha D3 (Prüssing 1991, 76). Regarding the chronological possition of the Prague-Vinoř situla, it is worth of noting that the number of the vessels in the Prague-Vinoř grave as well as its

---

4   In 2016 the lastest find of a Bohemian situla was published (John 2016). The find of a Tessin situla from Vlkov in south Bohemia represents the same type as the situla from Rovná.

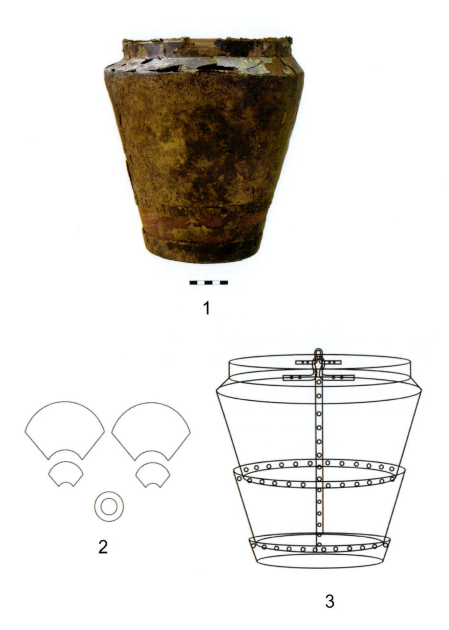

1

2

3

Fig. 4. Prague-Vinoř. 1: bronze situla after restoration (after Trefný 2012). – 2-3: scheme of the design of the situla.

overall nature was characteristic for Ha D1. This is not in contradiction with the mentioned date of its Hallstatt counterpart.

Iron spits from Prague-Letňany

The rich Bylany culture grave from Prague-Letňany included also two iron spits (Fig. 3,2), which represent the first find of this kind in the Bohemian territory. This is not a case in Moravia, where some finds of spits occured in the milieu of Horákov culture, where they are known from rich graves of Bratčice, Brno-Holásky 2 and Hlásnica u Horákova (Golec 2003/04, 101 fig. 1; 106 fig. 2,1-4) (Fig. 5,1-2). The spits are significantly concentrated in the east Hallstatt region (Fig. 5,1), where they occur as an Italic or Etruscan influence, since here they are known already in the end of the 8th century BC in warrior graves (Stary 1979, 40). From central Italy they spread to the north with a concentration in the Este area and then to Slovenia and the eastern Alps. Some of the spits were exported from northern Italy also to southwestern Germany (Egg 1996, 143-144; Frey 1980, 98).

Iron spits with the terminal eylet are a specific type known only in the East Hallstatt zone, and unknown in the West Hallstatt zone. Their production centres are sought in the region of Caput Adriae in Slovenia or in northern Italy (Golec 2003/04, 105). Such spits may thus be interpreted as inspirations made under ideological influence of Italic forms, rather than directly Etruscan or generally Italic imports.

The spits from the Prague-Letňany grave have a distorted upper part, while the rest of the shaft is plain and rectangular in cross-section. From the point of view of their construction they are comparable with pieces from Strettweg, Bratčice or Hallstatt grave 12/1889 (Egg 1996, 139-151; Golec 2003/04, 106 fig. 2,1.5.9; Kromer 1959, pl. 206). The Moravian finds may be also helpful with chronology of the Prague-Letňany finds. They all fall into the second half of the 7th century BC – Ha C2 – in the case of Bratčice even later-beginning of Ha D (Kos 1999). The supposed date of the Prague-Letňany exemples, second half of the 7th -beginning of the 6th century BC is also in compliance with other indices in this grave, as for example the date of the bronze bucket or the number of clay vessels, characteristic for this period.

Of course, the Prague-Letňany iron spits represent important evidence of the interregional contacts of the central Bohemian area with the region of their origin. If their southeast alpine origin is accepted, then they could be interpreted as a significant demonstration of the long distance connection to that area. In this way such transfer recalls other similar reminiscences as for example trunnion axes, coming to the Bohemian basin from the east or important example of the semi crested fibula of southeast Alpine origin from Předměřice in eastern Bohemia (see below). However, the character of this connection or contact may be more likely interpreted as non-direct, respectively transfer in more phases over more significant centres. Finally it could be interpreted rather as a direct contact of the Bohemian basin with the south Moravian region, considering that this is the nearest area with the representation of similar spits. Anyhow, the occurence of the Prague-Letňany grates in the Bylany culture area is also of a special significance for the West Hallstatt zone. According to the contemporary state of knowledge, it seems that they represent the first finds of this type in this area.

The Prague-Letňany spits also have great importance for the questions of the contemporary social hierarchy. The find contexts with spits from Italy, Slovenia, east Alpine region and finally from Moravia, where three mentioned sites belong to the richest tombs of the Horákov culture, clearly demonstrate their connection with the contemporary elite. Such connections and their use in the milieu of the court symposia or ceremonies could be indicated in the iconography, such as on the fabulous situla from Certosa (Golec 2003/04, 108; Kastelic 1964, fig. 17). It cannot be excluded that items worn by one man in the second register, laid on his shoulder, represented spits.

Other types of finds

The trunion axes represent important material evidence for the contacts of the Bohemian basin with the east or southeast (Trefný forthcoming). They have been in use for a long time. The bronze examples belong to the 2nd millenium BC, the

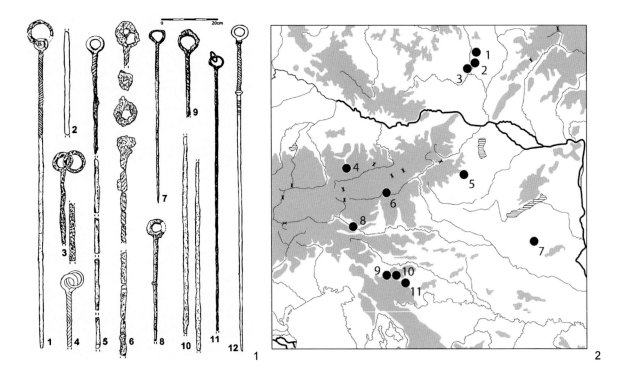

Fig. 5. Left (1): Spits of the east Alpine region. 1: Hlásnica u Horákova. – 2: Bmo-Holásky. – 3: Bratčice. – 4: Hallstatt. – 5: Schandorf. – 6: Strettweg. – 7: Nagyberki-Szálacka. – 8: Rosseg-Frög. – 9: Magdalenska gora. – 10: Stična. – 11: Dolenjske Toplice. Right (2): Finds of the grates with an eyelet in the east Alpine region. 1: Bratčice. – 2: Hlásnica u Horákova. – 3-4: Bmo-Holásky. – 5: Strettweg. – 6: Nagyberki-Szálacka. – 7, 9: Hallstatt, grave 12/1889.- 8: Schandorf. – 10: Dolenjske Toplice. – 11: Stična, tumulus 6, grave 18. – 12: Magdalenska gora, tumulus 1, grave 38. Right (2): Distribution of the grates with an eyelet in the east Alpine region. (after Golec 2003/04, 106 fig. 2).

iron ones are later. Their origin is sought in the Carpathian basin and Greece. Later they occur in the east Hallstatt zone and in Silesia (Filip 1936/37, 98, 126; Foltiny 1961; Hoernes 1917; Horedt 1964; Hošek *et al.* 2007, 336; Kromer 1959; Mayer 1977; Parzinger *et al.* 1995, 66, 267, Abb. 23:1; Rieth 1942, 18-20; Wesse 1990, map 1). Generally, the later iron examples are known in Moravia, Silesia, central Poland, the Carpathian basin, the Balkan penisula, Ukraine, the Upper Danube area, northern Italy or Slovenia (*cf.* Wesse 1990, map 15) (Fig. 6,1).

The Bohemian finds of iron axes (13 pieces) are mostly represented by isolated finds or finds derived from metal detector seekers (Michálek *et al.* 2015, 125-127 fig. 10). The only piece (Fig. 6,2) from a chronologically fixed context, which is the grave of the Bylany culture in Plaňany in central Bohemia, is dated to Ha C2 (Dvořák 1933, 36 tab. III,26; Filip 1936/37, 126 fig. 76; Hošek *et al.* 2007, 336; Pleiner/Rybová 1978, 475 fig. 143,22). This date correpsonds with the typological classification of A. Wesse, according to which it should be close to the subgroup III3C1, dated to Ha C2 – D2. The occurence of this axe in a site near to the borderline between central and eastern Bohemia need not be accidental. Although the Plaňany region still belongs to the Bylany culture area strongly affiliated with the Hallstatt culture in southwest Germany, it is located already very close to the territory of the east Bohemian Silesia Platěnice culture-part of the East Hallstatt zone. Here we register one notable artefact of southeast provenance – a semilunar fibula from grave no. 34 in Předměřice, which may be dated to

Ha C2 (Filip 1936/37, 126 fig. 74; Vokolek 1999, 16; 119 pl. 94,9; Venclová *et al.* 2008, 91 fig. 50,21). Such fibulae are very significantly concentrated in the southeast Alpine region (De Marinis/Guštin 1975, 245 fig. 8). They occur there already since the period of Santa Lucia Ia (Ha B3) and then spread to Italy and other regions (Trefný forthcoming). The axe from the Plaňany grave as well as the fibula from Předměřice indicate that, although significant eastern influence in the Bohemian territoitory is typical for Ha D, the beginnings of eastern or southeastern contact may be sought already in beginnings of the Early Iron Age.

Two important finds, absolutely unique in the Bohemian territory, have been a part of the inventory of one of the graves in Hradenín, east Bohemia (Fig. 6,3-4). These bronze pendants are very similar in form to an extensive category of bronze pendants, known as Graeco-Macedonian bronzes or bird cage bronzes (*cf.* Bouzek 1971; 1974), named according to their shape, where substantial part is characteristic as a globular or conical openwork, complemented by other elements. The nearest site with similar finds is the famous Býčí skála cave in southern Moravia. However local finds may be compared with Hradenín ones only very formally (Parzinger *et al.* 1995, pl. 20; Trefný 2002, 371 fig. 10,12). This type is found in Switzerland, France and Italy. A suitable analogy may be represented by one piece from Bex in Switzerland (Bouzek 1997, fig. 235,17). But it must be stressed that the rectangular eyelet of the Hradenín examples still differs from the oval eyelet of the mentioned piece from Bex. Regardless of their origin in the Alpine region or in the Balkans, both pendants represent important and unique evidence for transfer of material culture between the Bohemian basin and mentioned areas.

Significant evidence for the interregional contacts in the Bohemian elite graves of Ha C – D1 can be witnessed also in some types of fibulae. Early Iron Age spectacle fibulae of a distinct form (*Doppelbrillenfibeln mit Achterschleife*) are represented in the Bohemian area by three pieces dated to Ha C – D1 (Fig. 6,5-7). One comes from a Bylany culture grave in the necropolis of Prague-Střešovice (Fridrichová *et al.* 1999, 333 fig. 4,9), a second one from the upland settlement of Meclov-Mašovice in western Bohemia (Chytráček/Metlička 2004, 192, fig. 65,1; Venclová *et al.* 2008, 75 fig. 36,3) and the third one from the rich grave of the west Bohemian tumulus culture from Dýšina (Šaldová 1974, 459 fig. 5,9). All three pieces may be classified as exemples of Schrotzenhofen type. Although the origin of the spectacle fibulae may be generally seen in the Carpathian basin (*cf.* for example Sundwall 1943; Alexander 1965; Betzler 1974; Bader 1983; Pabst 2012; Romano/Trefný 2015), it need not be so in case of individual variants. Such assumptions may also be applied to the Schrotzenhofen type fibulae, which are concentrated especially in southwestern Germany and Bohemia. Thus their occurence in the Bohemian basin indicates rather an evidence of the contacts to the southwestern Germany, which corresponds with the evolutionary affinities of most of the Bohemian territory during the Hallstatt period.

The five four-spiral fibulae (*Vierpassfibeln*) are in Bohemia represented by finds from Protivín, Dobronice, Litoradice, Týn and Vltavou and Bezdědovice in south Bohemia (Michálek 1981, 150 fig. 1; 152 fig. 2)[5]. All these finds (Fig. 7,1-6)

5 According to the oral information of J. Michálek, new pieces of four spiral fibulae, still unpublished, have been discovered within some last decades. These unknown finds will be included in a complex compendium of southern Bohemian Early Iron Age prepared by him. I am very obliged to J. Michálek for this information.

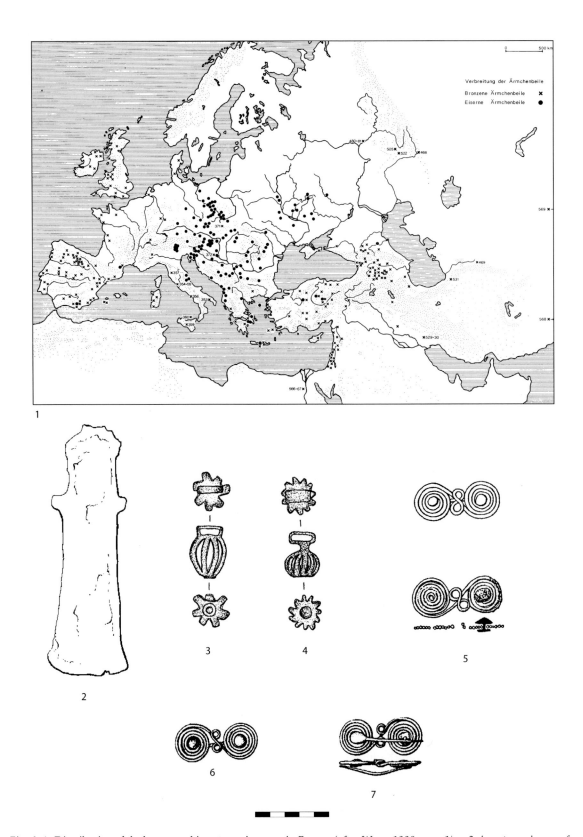

Fig. 6. 1: Distribution of the bronze and iron trunnion axes in Europe (after Wesse 1990, map 1). – 2: iron trunnion axe from the grave of the Bylany culture in Plaňany (after Pleiner/Rybová 1978, 475 fig. 143,22). – 3-4: 'bird cage' bronze pendants from Hradenín (after Venclová et al. 2008, 57 fig. 20,29-30). – 5: spectacle fibula from Mašovice-Meclov. – 6: spectacle fibula from Dýšina. – 7: spectacle fibula from Prague-Střešovice (after Venclová et al. 2008, 58 fig. 21,17).

belong to two variants and were originally parts of inventory of rich tumuli graves, dated to Ha D1 (Michálek 1981, 151). But some exemplars may be slightly later (*cf.* Říhovský 1993, 74). Three of them, pieces from Protivín, Dobronice and Litoradice, represent intact exemples. The Protivín fibula was first classified as a Maiersch type (Venclová *et al.* 2008, 74), then re-classified as a type very close to the find from the grave no. 74 in Hallstatt (Trefný 2016, 143-145), which is a little different from the pieces of Maiersch type (*cf.* Berg 1962; Michálek 1981, 153 fig. 3,4; Betzler 1974, pl. 66,972; Kromer 1959; Michálek 1981, 153 fig. 3,5; Betzler 1974, pl. 66,973). The fibula from Dobronice has a very suitable counterpiece in the example found in fabulous Moravian Bull´s rock cave (Říhovský 1993, pl. 13,117). But it seems that except for the Moravian example, this fibula has no precise analogy. In this respect one fibula from Longane in Sicilia may be mentioned (Lo Schiavo 2010, 858 pl. 654,7854B). It has a characteristic rhomboid plate in its middle, but is constructed in a different way than the fibulae from Dobronice and Bull´s rock cave. The fibula from Litoradice is a one-piece fibula made in metal sheet. The analogies to that piece occur more frequently in Moravia, for example in Budkovice (Ondráček 1971, 17; Říhovský 1993, pl. 13,119). Similar fibulae have been found also in grave no. 1001 in Hallstatt (Betzler 1974, pl. 72,993-994). These fibulae are classified as Oberkrumbach type, which is close to the finds from the Upper Palatinate or Slovenia (Betzler 1974, 147).

The typology of the Bohemian four-spiral fibulae clearly indicates the relationships with the area of Moravia, Upper Austria or alternatively with southwestern Germany. Also the fibulae thus represent an important indicator of mutual relationships of the Bohemian area, represented by the contemporary social elite burried in rich graves, to the mentioned regions.

Conclusion

Regarding the origin of various sorts of mentioned imports, it appears that individual Bohemian regions show evolutionary affinity especially to the geographically adjacent areas. Firstly, there is a clear relation between central and northwestern Bohemia with its population of Bylany culture, south and western Bohemia with its Hallstatt tumulus culture and the Hallstatt civilization of southwestern Germany. On the other hand the East Bohemian Silesia-Platěnice culture evinces notable affinity with the cultures of the East Hallstatt area.

It may be argued that some imports represent the products of more distant areas, for example from the Etruscan or southeast Alpine regions. But also in these cases it is highly probable, that these items reached their final destination through the above mentioned adjacent areas, where they are also well represented. This situation thus reflects again the significance of the proximity of these important evolutionary centres, such as southwest Germany or the east Alpine area.

Regarding the character of proper contacts, we are today already far away from the idea of the interpretation of individual importations in the terms of direct encounter of the various individuals, although it cannot be in some cases completely excluded. From this point of view it would be perhaps more suitable to talk about the diffusion of exogenous material culture, than about 'interregional contacts' which evokes rather the encounter of different ethnicities. More likely the existence of the luxurious imported goods in the Bohemian elite graves features an adoption of a certain behavioral pattern in the environs of the Central

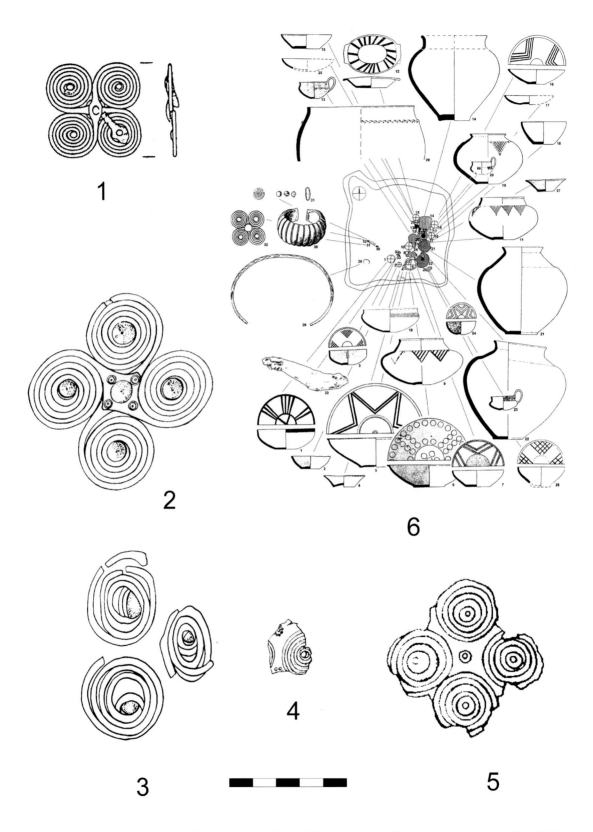

Fig. 7. Four-spiral fibula. 1: Protivín. – 2: Dobronice. – 3: Týn nad Vltavou. – 4: Bezdědovice. – 5: Litoradice (after Michálek 1981, 152 fig. 2). – 6: scheme of the grave from Protivín with one four spiral fibula (after Venclová et al. 2008, 81 fig. 42).

European early Hallstatt social elite, which reflects an economical potential as well as political power.

Bibliography

Alexander 1965: J. Alexander, The spectacle fibulae of Southern Europe. American Journal of Archaeology 69,1, 1965, 7-23.

Bader 1983: T. Bader, Die Fibeln in Rumänien. Prähistorische Bronzefunde XIV,6 (München 1983).

Berg 1962: F. Berg, Das Flachgräberfeld der Hallstattkultur von Maiersch, Mitteilungen der österreichischen Arbeitsgemeinschaft für Ur- und Frühgeschichte 4 (Wien 1962).

Betzler 1974: P. Betzler, Die Fibeln in Süddeutschland, Österreich und der Schweiz I (Urnenfelderzeitliche Typen). Prähistorische Bronzefunde XIV,3 (München 1974).

Bouzek 1971: J. Bouzek, Openwork „bird-cage" bronzes. In: J. Boardman/M. A. Brown/T. G. E. Powell (eds.), The European community in later prehistory. Studies in honour of C.F.C. Hawkes (London 1971) 77-104.

Bouzek 1974: J: Bouzek, Graeco-Macedonian bronzes (Prague 1974).

Bouzek 1997: J. Bouzek, Greece, Anatolia and Europe: Cultural interrelations during the Early Iron Age (Jonsered 1997).

Chytráček/Metlička 2004: M. Chytráček/M. Metlička, Die Höhensiedlungen der Hallstatt- und Latenezeit in Westböhmen. Památky Archeologické, Supplementum 16 (Praha 2004).

Chytráček et al. 2015: M. Chytráček/O. Chvojka/M. Egg/J. John/R.Kyselý/J. Michálek, S. Ritter/P. Stránská, Zu einem Fürstengrab aus der Späthallstattzeit mit zweirädrigem Wagen und Bronzegefäßen bei Rovná in Südböhmen – ein Vorbericht. Archäologisches Korrespondenzblatt 45, 2015, 71-89.

De Marinis/Guštin 1975: R. de Marinis/M. Guštin, Qualche considerazione sulla cronologia e diffusione delle fibule semilunate. Preistoria Alpina 11, 1975, 237-253.

Dvořák 1933: F: Dvořák, Kostrový hrob bylanského typu z Plaňan. Památky Archeologické 39, 1933, 35-38.

Dvořák 1936: F Dvořák, Pravěk Kolínska a Kouřimska (Kolín 1936).

Dvořák 1938: F: Dvořák, Knížecí pohřby na vozech ze starší doby železné. Praehistorica I (Praha 1938).

Egg 1996: M. Egg, Das hallstattzeitliche Fürstengrab von Strettweg bei Judenburg in der Obersteiermark. Monographien des Römisch-Germanischen Zentralmuseums 37 (Mainz 1996).

Foltiny 1961: S. Foltiny, Athens and the East Hallstatt Region: Cultural Interrelations at the Dawn of the Iron Age. American Journal of Archaeology 65, 1961, 283-297.

Filip 1936/37: J. Filip, J. Popelnicová pole a počátky železné doby v Čechách (Praha 1936/37).

Frey 1980: O. Frey, Der Westhallstattkreis im 6. Jahrhundert v. Chr. In: Die Hallstattkultur, Frühform europaischer Einheit (Linz 1980) 80-116.

Fridrichová 1988: M. Fridrichová, Praha 9 Vinoř-Bohdanečská. Nálezová zpráva. Muzeum Hlavního Města Prahy (Praha 1998).

Friedrichová *et al.* 1999: M. Fridrichová/D. Koutecký/M. Slabina, Die Gräberfeld der Bylaner Kultur in Praha – III. Teil. Památky Archeologické 90, 1999, 319-397.

Frolíková 2015: D. Frolíková, Dva hroby „knížat" z doby halštatské v Praze-Letňanech. Akademický Bulletin AV ČR 6, 2015, 18-20.

Golec 2003/04: M. Golec, Rožně, řecko-etruské vlivy ve střední Evropě. Sborník Prací Filosofické Fakulty Brněnské Univerzity 8/9, 2003/04, 101-110.

Hoernes 1917: M. Hoernes, Eine höchst seltene Form von Bronzebeilen. Wiener Prähistorische Zeitschrift 4, 38-44.

Horedt 1964: K. Horedt, Die Verwendung des Eisens in Rumänien bis in das 6. Jahrhundert v. Chr.. Dacia 8, 1964, 119-139.

Hošek *et al.* 2007: J- Hošek/Z. Smrž/A. Šilhová, Sekera s raménky z vrchu Ostrý (k. ú. Března, okr. Litoměřice) v Českém středohoří, Alena. Archeologické Rozhledy 59, 2007, 336-352.

John 2016: J. John, Analýza prvkového složení halštatské situly z veselí nad lužnicí. Archeologické výzkumy v jižních Čechách 29, 2016, 29-32.

Kastelic 1964: J. Kastelic, Situlenkunst (Wien, München 1964).

Kos 1999: P. Kos, Bratčice (Bmo-venkov), Přehled Výzkumů 39, 1995/1996 (1999) 337-338.

Kimmig 1962: Kimmig, Bronzesitulen aus dem Rheinischen Gebirge, Hunsrück-Eifel-Westerwald. Bericht der Römisch Germanischen Komission 43/44, 1962, 31-106.

Koutecký 2003: D. Koutecký, Příspěvky k době halštatské v severozápadních Čechách. Příspěvky k Pravěku a Rané Době Dějinné Severozápadních Čech 13 (Most 2003).

Kromer 1959: K. Kromer, Das Gräberfeld von Hallstatt (Firenze 1959).

Kozáková et al. forthcoming: R. Kozáková/R. Kyselý/M. Trefný/K. Drábková/P. Kočár/D. Frolíková/R. Kočárova/R. Moravcová, Food offerings, flowers, a bronze bucket and a wagon: A multidisciplinary approach of the Hallstatt princely grave from Prague-Letnany, Czech Rep. (forthcoming).

Lo Schiavo 2010: F. Lo Schiavo, Le fibule dell'Italia meridionale e della Sicilia: dall'eta del bronzo recente al VI secolo a. C. Prähistorische Bronzefunde XIV,14 (Stuttgart 2010).

Mayer 1977: E. Mayer, Die Äxte und Beile in Österreich. Prähistorische Bronzefunde IX/9 (München 1977).

Von Merhart 1952: G. von Merhart, Studien über einige Gattungen von Bronzegefässen. In: Festschrift des Römisch-Germanischen Zentralmuseum in Mainz (Mainz 1952) 1-71.

Michálek 1981: J. Michálek, Čtyřspirálové spony halštatské mohylové kultury v jižních Čechách. Praehistorica 2, 149-155.

Michálek *et al.* 2015: J. Michálek/J. Fröhlich/O. Chvojka, Halštatský depot z Třebanic u Netolic (okr. Prachatice). Archeologické výzkumy v jižních Čechách 28, 119-138.

Ondráček 1971: J. Ondráček, Horákovský hrob z Budkovic (okr. Brno-venkov). Přehled Výzkumů 1969 (1971) 17.

Pabst 2012: S. Pabst, Die Brillenfibeln. Untersuchungen zu spätbronze- und ältereisenzeitlichen Frauentrachten zwischen Ostsee und Mittelmeer. Marburger Studien zur Vor- und Frühgeschichte 25 (Rahden/Westf. 2012).

Parzinger *et al.* 1995: H. Parzinger/J. Nekvasil/F. Barth, Die Býčí skála-Höhle. Römisch-Germanische Forschungen 54 (Mainz 1995).

Píč 1900: J. Píč, Starožitnosti země České I,2 (Praha 1900).

Pincelli/Morigi Govi 1975: R. Pincelli/Morigi Govi, La necropoli villanoviana di San Vitale (Bologna 1975).

Pleiner/Rybová 1978: R. Pleiner/A. Rybová (eds.), Pravěké dějiny Čech (Praha 1978).

Pleinerová 1973: I. Pleinerová, Bronzové nádoby v bylanské kultuře. Památky Archeologické 64, 1973, 272-300.

Prüssing 1991: G. Prüssing, Bronzegefässe in Österreich. Prähistorische Bronzefunde 2,5 (Stuttgart 1991).

Říhovský 1993: J. Říhovský, Die Fibeln in Mähren. Prähistorische Bronzefunde XIV,9 (München 1993).

Rieth 1942: A. Rieth, Die Eisentechnik der Hallstattzeit. Mannus Bibliothek 70 (Leipzig 1942).

Romano/Trefný 2015: S. Romano/M. Trefný, Notes upon the distribution of spectacle fibula between Central Europe and Balkan Peninsula in the Late Bronze and beginnings of the Early Iron Age. Aristonothos 9, 2015, 197-225.

Šaldová 1968: V. Šaldová, Halštatská mohylová kultura v západních Čechách – Pohřebiště Nynice. Památky Archeologické 59, 1968, 297-399.

Šaldová 1974: V. Šaldová, Östliche Elemente in der westböhmischen hallstattzeitlichen Hügelgräberkultur. In: Symposium zu Problemen der jüngeren Hallstattzeit in Mitteleuropa (Bratislava 1974) 447-468.

Sauter *et al.* 2000: F. Sauter/U. Jordis/A. Graf/W. Werther/K. Varmuza, Studies in Organic Archaeometry I. Identification of the Glue Used by the "Tyrolean Iceman" to Fix his Weapons. Archive for Organic Chemistry 1,5, 2000, 735-747.

Siegfried-Weiss 1991: A. Siegfried-Weiss, Bronzegefässe in Böhmen. In: O. Kytlicová, Die Bronzegefäßein Böhmen. Prähistorische Bronzefunde II,12 (Stuttgart 1991) 106-118.

Sievers 1982: S. Sievers, Die mitteleuropäischen Hallstattdolche, Prähistorische Bronzefunde VI,6 (München 1982).

Stary 1979: P. Stary, Feuerböcke und Bratspiesse aus eisenzeitlichen Grabem der Apennin – Halbinsel. Kleine Schriften aus dem Vorgeschichtlicher Seminar Marburg 5 (Marburg 1979) 40-61.

Sundwall 1943: J. Sundwall, Die älteren italienischen Fibeln (Berlin 1943).

Trefný 2002: M.Trefný, Bronzefunde aus der Býčí skála-Höhle und ihre Beziehungen zum Südostalpenraum und Italien. In: A. Lang/V. Salač (eds.), Fernkontakte in der Eisenzeit (Liblice 2002) 360-378.

Trefný 2012: M. Trefný, Čechy a střední Evropa v pozdní době halštatské až časné době laténské a jejich vztah k oblasti antického Středomoří. In: J. Valentová/M. Tisucká/P. Belaňová (eds.), Ve stínu Olympu (Praha 2012) 21-43.

Trefný *et al.* 2012: M. Trefný/R. Korený/J. Frána, K problematice halštatských mís s perlovitě vybíjeným okrajem v Čechách. Archeologické Rozhledy 64, 2012, 320-332.

Trefný forthcoming: M. Trefný, Notes on eastern elements of the Hallstatt culture at Bohemia. In: Das nördliche Karpatenbecken in der Hallstattzeit (forthcoming).

Trefný 2016: M. Trefný, Notes on some Hallstatt fibulae finds in Bohemia. In: J. Juchelka (ed.), Doba popelnicových polí a doba halštatská ve střední Evropě II (Opava-Brno 2016) 143-158.

Venclová *et al.* 2008: N. Venclová/P. Drda/M. Chytráček/D. Koutecký/J. Michálek/V. Vokolek/P. Sankot, Doba halštatská. Archeologie pravěkých Čech 6 (Praha 2008).

Vokolek 1999: V. Vokolek, Východočeská halštatská pohřebiště (Pardubice 1999).

Wesse 1990: A. Wesse, Die Ärmchenbeile der Alten Welt: ein Beitrag zum Beginn der Eisenzeit im östlichen Mitteleuropa. Universitätsforschungen zur prähistorischen Archäologie 3 (Bonn 1990).

Author

Martin Trefný
Charles University Prague
Thákurova 3
166 00 Prague 6
Czech Republic
trefnymartin@seznam.cz

A cluster of chieftains' graves in the Netherlands?

Cremating and inhumating elites during Ha C on the Maashorst, NL

Richard Jansen and Sasja van der Vaart-Verschoof

Abstract

An iconic find from Dutch late Prehistory is the famous Chieftain's burial of Oss with its exceptional Mindelheim sword with gold-inlayed hilt. This burial, however, does not lie in isolation. It is but one of several exceptional elite burials found on the Maashorst, a high-lying plateau in the eastern part of the southern Netherlands which has a long history of use for burials, including Ha C elite graves. In this paper four exceptional Early Iron Age elite burials and the cemeteries in which they were created are discussed and brought together. Each grave is unique, but created through burial rituals with many similarities.

Zusammenfassung

Einer der ikonischen Funde der späteren Vorgeschichte in den Neiderlanden ist das berühmte Fürstengrab von Oss mit seinem herausragenden Mindelheim-Schwert mit goldenen Einlagen auf dem Griff. Dieses Grab ist aber kein isolierter Fund, es ist vielmehr eines von mehreren außergewöhnlichen Elitebestattungen auf dem Maashorst. Dieses hochgelegene Plateau im östlichen Teil der südlichen Niederlande hat eine lange Geschichte als Bestattungsplatz, auch für elitäre Bestattungen der älteren Hallstattzeit (Ha C). In diesem Beitrag werden vier ältereisenzeitliche Elitebestattungen und die Bestattungsplätze, in denen diese niedergelegt wurden, vorgestellt und diskutiert. Jedes Grab ist einzigartig, aber die Begräbnisrituale zeigen deutliche Gemeinsamkeiten.

The Maashorst

The Maashorst-area forms the northern zone of the geological formation known as the Peel Blok, a high lying plateau in the eastern part of the southern Netherlands (Fig. 1). Due to tectonic processes this plateau rises several millimeters each year. In the last Ice Age, melt water ran off the flanks, creating large and shallow valleys (Jansen/Van der Linde 2013). Furthermore the area is characterized by fault lines and wet areas where groundwater seeps to the surface (*kwelwater* in Dutch). In general the subsoil on the Maashorst consists of fluviatile gravel and coarse sand depositions, locally covered by a thin layer of wind-blown cover sand. The gravel and coarse sand are older Rhine and Meuse deposits which are situated at the surface due to tectonic movement.

Large mounds and (contemporary) cemeteries, dating from the Late Neolithic onwards are situated within this prominent landscape. Several barrow groups

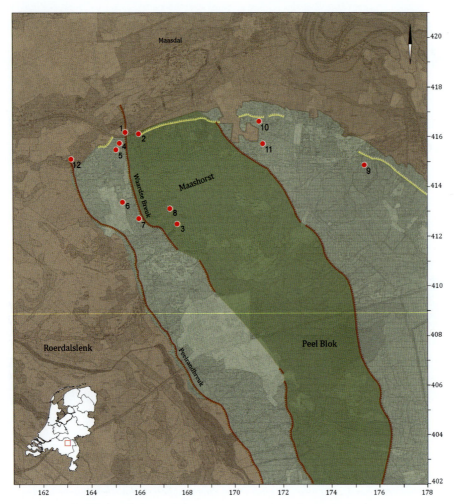

Fig. 1. The geomorphological characteristics of the Maashorst showing the high-lying plateau (green). The fault lines are indicated in brown, the terrace sides in yellow. 1 Oss-Vorstengraf; 2 Oss-Zevenbergen; 3 Uden-Slabroekse Heide; 5-12 other barrow groups/urnfields (after Jansen/Van der Linde 2013, 36 fig. 2.2).

and small urnfields are known on the flanks of the ridges in the northwestern corner of the Maashorst, including the Chieftain's grave of Oss-Vorstengraf and two monumental mounds of Oss-Zevenbergen (Fokkens *et al.* 2009; Fokkens/ Jansen 2004; Fontijn *et al.* 2013c; Jansen/Fokkens 2007; Van der Vaart-Verschoof forthcoming). The Early Iron Age urnfield of Slabroekse Heide is located at the center of a ridge in the heart of the Maashorst, approximately 4 km south of Vorstengraf and Zevenbergen (Jansen forthcoming).

The Chieftain's burial of Oss

Probably the most iconic find from Dutch Prehistory – as well as the Netherlands' original claim to Hallstatt fame – is the Chieftain's grave of Oss. Besides a Mindelheim sword with gold inlayed handle, this burial also contains bronze and iron components of two decorated bridles and a yoke, as well as an iron knife and socketed axe, and some kind of stone tool. Two iron razors, three dress pins and a fair amount of high quality textile (see also Grömer this volume) also survived. A number of carved wooden fragments are probably the remains of a ribbed drinking bowl. All this was brought together in the bronze situla that was used as urn.

The Chieftain's burial was discovered in 1933 when two local men encountered a bronze bucket during leveling works at the extensive heaths south of Oss. The

Grave	Date(s)	Human remains	Objects	Mound	Context
Chieftain's grave Oss	Ha C1-2	Cremation (almost complete)	Bronze bucket, iron mindelheim sword with gold-inlayed handle, iron horse-bit (2x), bronze hemispherical sheet-knobs (>12x), bronze tubular cross-shaped object, bronze *Tutulus*, bronze harness decoration (?), bronze rings (3x), iron ring (fragments; > 12x), bronze yoke rosettes (2x), iron toggle (2x), iron knife with leather and textile remains adhered, iron socketed axe, (whet)stone (?), iron razor (2x), bronze & iron bombenkopf pin (3x), wood, leather, bone, antler and textile fragments	53 m; built with plaggen sods; urn in burial pit	MBA barrows; small EIA urnfield
Oss-Zevenbergen Mound 3	Ha C2 – LTA	One fragment of cremated bone	Bronze sword fragment with plastic decoration, iron pin fragment, iron pin-like object, bronze fragment	30 m; built with plaggen sods; burned planks in center	MBA/LBA barrows; small EIA urnfield
Oss-Zevenbergen Mound 7	Ha C1-2	Cremation (partial deposition)	Schräghals-urn, bronze studs (>1000x), bronze ring (fragments; 4x), decorated bone fragment, iron fragment	36 m; built with plaggen sods; urn sited next to pyre remains	
Uden-Slabroekse Heide	Ha C1-2	Inhumation	Bronze anklet (2x), bronze bracelet (3x), hair rings, bronze tweezers, iron nail-cutter, iron ring, bronze pin, iron pin, amber bead, textile	No mound; inhumation in large and deep 'burial chamber' constructed with charred wood	MBA barrows; large EIA urnfield; Roman Period graves

Table 1. The main characteristics of the four exceptional EIA burials of the Maashorst.

archaeologists J.H. Holwerda and F.C. Bursch from the National Museum of Antiquities were called to Oss, encased the bucket in plaster, lifted it as a block and brought it to the Museum in Leiden. When the objects from the Chieftain's burial were removed from their bronze urn in the Museum in 1933 they were in very poor condition and at that time many were still unrecognizable. Later in the 1960s and 1990s new restorations were undertaken, and each one revealed new objects (Modderman 1964). Recent consideration of a number of fragments that had never been published uncovered a few new items as well. By combining the museum's documentation of this burial through the 80 years that it has been in their collection with detailed study of the objects, restoration notes and X-rays, it was possible to reconstruct (to some extent) the manner in which the objects ended up in the bronze bucket (Van der Vaart 2011). The whole showed that this was a deliberate burial ritual in which the cinerary urn was created in a structured manner and, as such, in a way transformed into a small burial chamber (described below).

A year after the bronze urn was lifted, the Museum returned to Oss to (partly) excavate the remains of the mound. The excavation proved that the Chieftain's burial was covered with an extremely large mound surrounded by a ditch 53 m in diameter (Holwerda 1934). Photographs show that the mound was built of sods placed in a very structured manner. Interesting is a second ditch (diameter 16 m) surrounding the burial and the a-central position of the burial pit (see below). The following year two other Bronze Age mounds were excavated in the direct vicinity, illustrating that the Chieftain's burial of Oss was not a solitary mound (Bursch 1937). The latter was confirmed by later researches in 1972 and 1998 whereby several (contemporary) burials were uncovered (Jaarverslag Heemkundekring Maasland 1975, 23-24; Jansen/Fokkens 2007, 46-54). Also some (Early Iron Age) urns found at this location before the unearthing of the Vorstengraf possibly derive from the larger cemetery (Fokkens/Jansen 2004, 33-35).

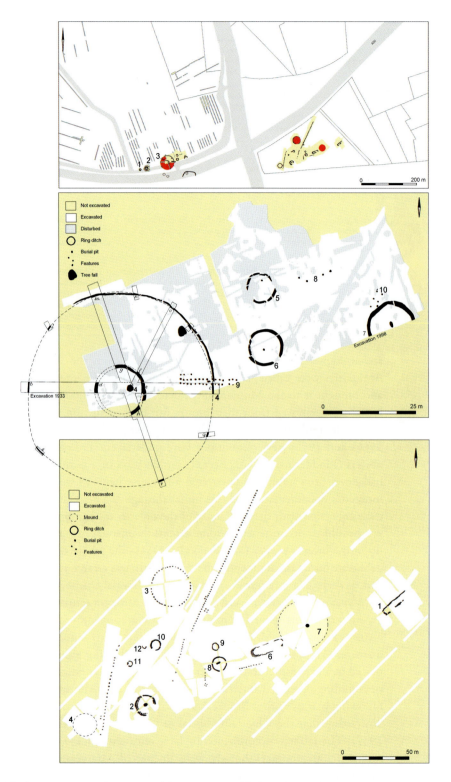

Fig. 2. Top: The barrow group and cemetery of Oss-Vorstengraf (left) and Zevenbergen (right). 2 and 3: Middle Bronze Age
burial mounds; – Middle: The excavation plans of the Chieftain's burial of Oss from 1933 and 1997/98 combined. 4: Early Iron
Age Ha C Chieftain's mound; 5-7: Early Iron Age graves; 8: Early Iron Age flat graves; 9: post alignment; 10: post structure.
For the grave goods see figure 3 in Van der Vaart-Verschoof/Schumann this volume. -Bottom: The barrow group and cemetery
of Oss-Zevenbergen. 2, 4 and 8: Middle Bronze Age mounds; 1 and 6: Late Bronze Age-Early Iron Age mounds; 9-12 and
internments in 2 and 8: Early Iron Age graves; 3 and 7: Early Iron Age Ha C mounds.

A larger cemetery

The earliest known burial monument at the site is a Middle Bronze Age A barrow that covered an urn placed within a ring ditch (Fokkens *et al.* 2012, 191-192; Jansen/Fokkens 2007, 84). Some 50 m to the west two more barrows (Mounds 8 and 9) were erected and marked by multiple post circles during the Middle Bronze Age B (Bursch 1937) (Fig. 2: Mounds 2 and 3). One of these barrows was re-used already in the Middle Bronze Age for a secondary burial (Jansen/Fokkens 2007, 84). A Bronze Age double and partly triple post alignment some 15 m long (with about one m between the rows) lay oriented more or less east-west on the Middle Bronze Age A barrow, and has been interpreted as a relic of ancestral rituals that may relate to funerary ritual (Fokkens *et al.* 2012, 197). There was also a six-post structure that is interpreted as some kind of funerary structure (*dodenhuisje* in Dutch) but it is unclear how this dates (Jansen/Fokkens 2007, 86-87).

Later, likely during the Early Iron Age, a small urnfield was created to the southeast of the Middle Bronze Age barrows. Six circular ditches and four urns without a structure were found but the extent of the urnfield could not be established. It was noted that it was rather small with an 'open' character, which may be a regional variant. Apparently it had been used selectively over a long period, contrasting with the general layout of contemporaneous urnfields that are continuously used by a local community (Fokkens *et al.* 2012, 197).

The most easterly Middle Bronze Age barrow was selected during the Early Iron Age to bury the Chieftain[1] in – a mound already a thousand years old at the time. They purposefully dug the Chieftain's burial pit off-center – avoiding and respecting the ancient central burial. The Early Iron Age mourners were aware that they were burying the Chieftain in a funerary monument and it appears that this was a deliberate act intended to link the new burial with the ancestral one (Jansen/Fokkens 2007, 86). The Bronze Age barrow was then covered with the largest barrow known in the Low Countries.

Burying the Chieftain of Oss

The Chieftain of Oss was cremated, but it appears that his grave goods did not accompany him on the pyre. His cremated remains were collected from the pyre and eventually placed in the bronze urn. The mourners were extremely thorough in their collecting – not only is there a lot of cremated bone in this burial, just about all skeletal elements are represented (except for his teeth; Lemmers *et al.* 2012; *pers. comm.*). It is one of the most 'complete' prehistoric cremations ever found in the Low Countries.

Iron rings were removed from a wagon or yoke and wrapped up tightly in textile, and the package thus created was placed on the bottom of the bronze urn. Next to it a bridle, incorporating an iron horse-bit and bronze trappings was placed. On top of this an iron knife, probably wrapped in another piece of textile, was placed together with an iron socketed axe. Next to this the second bridle, also with an iron horse-bit and bronze trappings, was placed. The bronze yoke rosettes and iron toggles were removed from the yoke and placed in the bucket at well. Two iron razors were then placed on top of the yoke components.

---

1   This is a historically evolved name to refer to the individuals buried in these graves and the term is used as such in this paper.

The magnificent iron sword with gold-inlayed handle was bent round, wrapped in yet another piece of cloth, was placed in the bucket, hilt down. Against the wrapped sword lay a packet of extremely high quality imported cloth, a precious and prestigious grave good in its own right (see also Grömer this volume; Grömer in Van der Vaart-Verschoof forthcoming). Lastly, the cremated remains of the Chieftain were placed in the urn, perhaps also wrapped in textile.

The situla-urn thus created was dug into a Bronze Age barrow, and covered with the largest barrow known in the Low Countries, 53 m in diameter. *This is significant* – this barrow is so massive that the mourners could have chosen to bury a complete wagon and yoke or place the sword alongside the bucket in its original straight form. Yet they chose to expend time and effort in getting everything relevant, or at least components of those relevant objects, to fit into this bucket.

Two neighboring monumental mounds: Oss-Zevenbergen

The Chieftain's burial is not the only monumental burial mound at Oss. There are two more Early Iron Age barrows with extraordinary contents some 450 m to the east at Oss-Zevenbergen, known as Mound 3 and Mound 7. This site was also excavated in multiple campaigns (in 1964/65, 2004 and 2007), with the result being that the two Ha C barrows, as well as a number of other mounds *and* the areas in between them were excavated according to modern standards, in total ca. 2 ha (Fokkens *et al.* 2009; Fontijn *et al.* 2013a; 2013c; Verwers 1966). This makes it one of the few Ha C elite burial sites with excellent context information.

Mounds 3 and 7 lay in a structured, ritual landscape with several post-alignments and a long use-history, very similar to Oss-Vorstengraf. The earliest funerary monuments are three Middle Bronze Age A round barrows erected in a row on a sandy ridge. All three were reused for secondary burials, and heightened as well (Fontijn *et al.* 2013b, 286). Two long barrows (Mounds 1 and 6) were erected during the Late Bronze Age or Early Iron Age at the northern end of the barrow row, with the latter having two use-phases in which a post circle and ditch were added (Valentijn 2013; Van Wijk *et al.* 2009, 72-74; 115-119; Verwers 1966). Prior to the creation of these long barrows it had likely been quite some time since monuments had been erected at this location (Fontijn *et al.* 2013b, 287). These long mounds flank a natural elevation that would later be incorporated into Mound 7 (see below). By building monuments on either side of this elevation it appears that the Late Bronze Age/Early Iron Age mourners were respecting and lengthening the barrow row. As has been argued previously (Fontijn *et al.* 2013b, 293), the mourners may have perceived the roundish natural elevation as one of the burial mounds of this already ancient barrow row. At some time prior to the erection of Mound 7, an unusual nine-post structure (two parallel rows of four posts each with a 'blocking' post at one end) was created on the west flank of the natural elevation (Fontijn *et al.* 2013b, 292). This post-structure is strikingly similar in design to the one at Oss-Vorstengraf (Fokkens 2013, 142-145; Fig. 2). A small urnfield was also created at this site, likely during the Early Iron Age. To the north of the barrow row lay four ring ditches ('Mounds' 9-12), of which two yielded Early Iron Age urns. Internments were found in the Bronze Age Mounds 2 and 8. In Mound 8 a circular ditch at the base of the barrow accompanied the interment. In Mound 2 only an urn with cremation remains with a set of grave goods was found: two fragments of a whetstone, three fragments of bone objects (jewelry) and a piece of siltstone with traces of ochre (Van Wijk *et al.* 2009, 84-86). It is unclear whether these EIA graves were created before or after the exceptional Ha C mounds.

In addition to the graves there are five singular alignments of widely spaced post rows that vary in orientation and in size from eight to 116 m long and are sometimes flanked by small four-post constructions (Fokkens 2013; Fokkens *et al.* 2007, 131-139; Van Wijk *et al.* 2007). The rows are dated to the Early Iron Age phase and based on their spatial orientation they seem to divide the cemetery in compartments (Fokkens 2013, 146-148; Fontijn *et al.* 2013c).

The natural elevation was eventually selected for the cremation and burial of a man during the Early Iron Age. As already noted, it is highly plausible that the Early Iron Age people took this roundish elevation positioned in a barrow row to be an ancient burial mound, and that their intention was to bury the man of Mound 7 in an ancestral mound, similarl to what was done with the Chieftain of Oss so close by. Following the cremation ritual, which is described below, a large barrow was erected which incorporated the natural elevation (Fontijn *et al.* 2013c).

Mound 3 was likely built after mound 7 and was erected on a flat spot at the northern edge of the high lying area. It was the only barrow not created on the barrow row, and appears to have been separated from the other barrows by the post rows. It was also marked with a post-circle, which is rather rare for Early Iron Age barrows (Fontijn *et al.* 2013b, 304). This barrow also covered an unusual deposit.

Mound 7 – burying a second Chieftain?

Mound 7 was 36 m in diameter and was erected on top of an existing natural dune. This dune was roundish in appearance and located in a barrow row (Fig. 3). Two opposing quadrants of the mound were excavated, including the central burial. Rather than a straightforward central grave, this barrow covered a massive spread of charcoal, and a complex assemblage of bronzes and other material.

This central find assemblage was so complex and the material so delicate, that the entire assemblage was lifted professionally in blocks and excavated in a lab by restorers (Kempkens 2013). The main component of this assemblage turned out to consist mostly of tiny bronze studs (Fig. 3). Several bronze rings and ring fragments were also found, as well as decorated bone fragments.

Analysis of the blockliftings, the excavation and restorations records (including X-rays of the blocks) revealed a unique burial event whereby a young man was cremated here, on top of a dune in a barrow row, which may have been interpreted as a barrow itself, with a dismantled yoke, decorated with over a thousand tiny bronze studs, located alongside the pyre (Fontijn *et al.* 2013). After cremation the pyre was searched through, with charcoal beams being placed to one side and the stud-decorated yoke components being shoved to the other side. Most of the cremated remains were collected and placed in an urn, and buried by the pyre remains. However, several cremation remains were also deliberately left behind amongst the pyre remain. The same was done with the objects. A bronze ring was broken, and only part was deliberately left behind. The whole complex of charcoal and bronze including the urn with cremation remains was then carefully covered with sods and the mound erected (Fontijn/Van der Vaart 2013).

Fig. 3. Mound 7 in excavation (top) and some of the finds found here (bottom; urn 1:7, others 1:1). The X-ray (middle) shows the block-lifted concentration of studs (X-ray and photographs finds by Restauratieatelier Restaura, Haelen).

We emphasize that by excavating by hand and blocklifting the central complex we can be sure that nothing preserved was missed. The manner of excavation here means that an absence of evidence *is* evidence of absence. So once again we have a burial ritual that involved intentional dismantling, manipulation and very clearly fragmentation and *pars pro toto* deposition of both grave goods and the deceased. An even more extreme example of this practice was found at nearby Mound 3.

Mound 3 – extreme pars pro toto monument

This large barrow was also built from sods and appears to date slightly later than Mound 7, which itself seems to either be contemporaneous or slightly later than the Chieftain's burial (Van Wijk *et al.* 2009; Van der Vaart-Verschoof forthcoming, Ch. 3). The sod-built barrow Mound 3 was encircled with a post circle, which is uncommon for the Early Iron Age. The singular circle consists of 48 posts with seven double posts encircling a 30 m wide mound carefully constructed with *plaggen* sods (De Leeuwe 2007, 207-208). The mound is built 'within' the post circle. The center had not been disturbed and was completely excavated, together with the mound itself. In the center lay a charred plank, cut from a very old and substantial tree that originally would have had a diameter of at least 2 m (Van Wijk *et al.* 2009, 92-98). Around this plank lay four fragments of metal objects and a single piece of cremated human bone. The objects include two unrecognizable fragments, an iron pin and a deliberately broken fragment of a bronze sword of unknown type. The only conclusion can be that the objects were intentionally deposited in a fragmented state (Fokkens *et al.* 2012, 192).

As with Mound 7, in this case the complete excavation means that absence of evidence *is* evidence of absence. This burnt plank, these four object fragments and the single piece of human cremation is all that was deposited. It would seem that here we are dealing with an extreme *pars pro toto* deposition, probably an extreme *pars pro toto* grave.

A barrow landscape

Some 800 m to the south of Oss-Vorstengraf and -Zevenbergen two other barrow groups are known. Of each group one mound has been excavated, dating to the Late Neolithic and Middle Bronze Age B respectively (Bursch 1937; Van Wijk/ Jansen forthcoming). Both clusters, however, contain more mounds wherein the possible presence of another Chieftain's grave cannot be excluded beforehand. This extensive barrow landscape, situated at a very prominent and visible location, has been used for burials for many generations. Research in the larger area, especially to the north shows no sign of habitation. To the south the nearest probable Iron Age settlements are located at a distance of app. 800-1000 m (Jansen/Van der Linde 2013). Even further south more cemeteries are known. One of them, the Slabroekse Heide site, contains our fourth Ha C elite burial.

An elite inhumation grave at Slabroekse Heide

The urnfield of Slabroekse Heide, located in the heart of the Maashorst, was discovered and partly excavated in 1923. At that time the mounds were still visible in the extensive early 20th century heath landscape. Archaeologist A.E. Remouchamps of the National Museum of Antiquities (partly) excavated 38 barrows, discovering ca. 22 urns, occasionally with some 'modest' grave goods like small pots (Remouchamps 1924). Photos of the excavation show the excellent preservation of the mounds and features (Fig. 5). The ditches surrounding the mounds are clearly visible in the sandy soil. The profile of one of the mounds

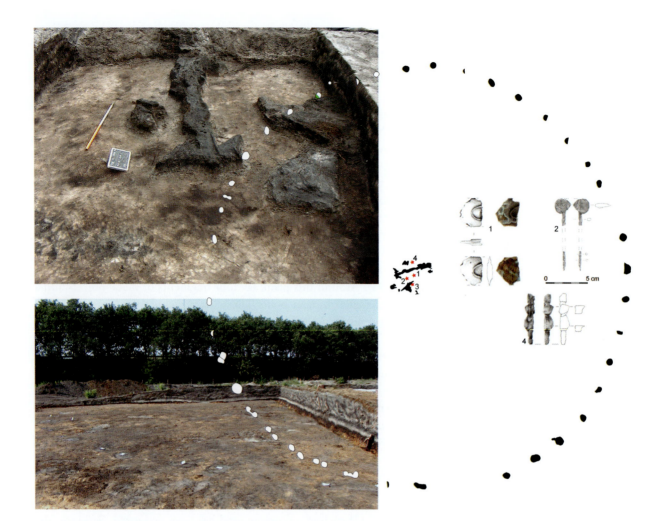

Fig. 4. Mound 3 in excavation with the plank and the object fragments found around it.

undoubtedly displays the carefully placed sods with which the mounds were constructed (the common practice in this area).

The overall drawing of the urnfield illustrates the specific excavation method. In general small trenches were dug out by hand, which in most cases run through the centers of the mounds (Remouchamps 1924). After the excavation in 1923 the mounds were erased from the landscape as the area was transformed into an agricultural field.

The area was eventually researched again, in 2005 and 2010, as the Dutch Forest State Service was transforming the Maashorst-area (back) into a forest and heath landscape. An important conclusion of the trial trench campaign in 2005 was that the conservation of the features had decreased dramatically (Van Wijk/Jansen 2010). The features were hardly visible anymore. Only the soil activity (*bodemwerking* in Dutch) underneath the features was observable and it looked like the ploughing activities had thoroughly erased the soil archive. Burials were not found.

It was apparent that the remaining features would soon disappear forever, so the decision was made to excavate the last remnants of the urnfield Slabroekse Heide. During the 2 ha excavation in 2010 it soon became clear that Remouchamps in fact did not excavate the whole cemetery. Eight 'new' (cremation) burials were unearthed (Jansen *et al.* 2011; Jansen/Louwen forthcoming). In general the Early Iron Age graves were buried in urns or cloths. One grave yielded a large amount

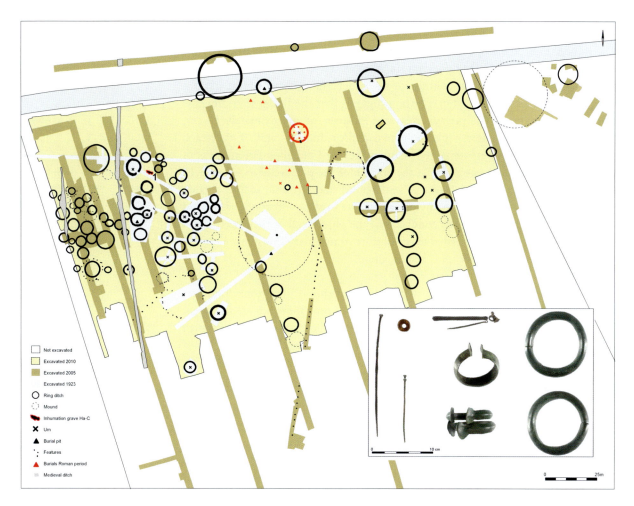

Fig. 5. The barrow group
and cemetery of Uden-
Slabroekse Heide with
inset of the finds from the
inhumation burial (nr. 1)
(excavation plan by Archol
BV and find photographs by
Restauratieatelier Restaura,
Haelen).

of cremation remains which had probably been placed in a cloth, and a thin iron bracelet. The undecorated jewelry was carefully placed among the cremation remains. Lastly a single line of at least 32 posts was found comparable to those at Oss-Zevenbergen. The post row at Slabroekse Heide runs to one of the larger mounds in the center of the cemetery and (also) seems to divide the cemetery into two compartments, like at Zevenbergen (Jansen/Louwen forthcoming).

It is clear that the cemetery of Uden-Slabroekse Heide was much larger than previously thought with at least 110 known graves (Fig. 5). The cemetery continues to the west (and possibly other directions), though a recent trial trench campaign indicates that the cemetery ends here within a 100 m (Van Wijk/ Jansen forthcoming). Comparable to the cemeteries of Oss-Vorstengraf and -Zevenbergen, the Slabroekse Heide urnfield also has a long history of use, with at least one or two Bronze Age barrows as its earliest phase. One of these mounds is still visible and has partly been excavated in 2005. The central grave was not found but pollen analysis and OSL-dating suggests a (Middle) Bronze Age date (De Kort/Van Mourik 2005; Van Wijk/Jansen 2010, 45-50).

Different is the fact that the Early Iron Age urnfield of Slabroekse Heide is significantly larger than the relatively small ones of Oss-Vorstengraf and -Zevenbergen. The latter seem to be used extensively, in contrast to the intensively used urnfield of Slabroekse Heide. Lastly one elite grave contemporaneous with Oss-Vorstengraf and -Zevenbergen diverges from the 'norm' of cremating the dead.

The Ha C inhumation burial of Slabroekse Heide

The inhumation burial of Slabroekse Heide was discovered in a small open area within the urnfield, bordered by several ring ditches. Here we found a rectangular pit with charcoal (Fig. 5). In contrast to the other graves, it was most likely a flat grave, although the lack of overcutting suggests that the burial was somehow marked above ground. The pit was excavated in layers of approximately 10 cm. Each layer was documented – photographed and/or drawn – and, if necessary, sampled. Twelve layers were excavated before we reached the inhumation burial of which only the outline was visible. At the bottom of the pit several metal objects, already indicated by a metal detector, were found. Comparable to the organic remains the metal objects were badly preserved due to the context of coarse sand and gravel. Considering the poor condition of the objects, all of them were lifted in small blocks. X-rays were needed to reveal the extraordinary finds: bracelets and anklets, hair rings, a toilet set, pins and an amber bead.

A unique find was the presence of several fragments of textile. Cloth was preserved around and in some cases within the corrosion of the bronze bracelets and anklets, and underneath a fragment of the bronze pin. Some fragments appear to be part of the deceased's clothes, with a second textile that was probably used to cover the deceased (see also Grömer this volume; Grömer in Van der Vaart-Verschoof forthcoming).

Based on the thorough *top-down* excavation and descriptions we are able to reconstruct a unique burial event from 2700 years ago in detail.

A burial event: a bottom-up reconstruction

As with the burials described above, the elite burial event at Slabroekse Heide can be divided in several 'actions'. After the burial location was selected, a large rectangular pit was dug. This must have taken considerable effort considering the soil conditions and the depth of the pit. Then a small rectangular burial chamber (approximately 3 x 1 m) was created with oaken blocks at each end and planks. All wood had been charred in a controlled manner prior to use (the unburnt parts of the wood had rotted away, only the charcoal lines were visible) (Van Hees forthcoming). In a settlement context wood is charred to make it more sustainable, and this may have been the intention here as well. In any case, the charring of the wood was a deliberate act that required building a fire, probably somewhere in the surroundings.

The deceased was placed between thick oaken blocks at both ends of the burial pit. Unfortunately the sex could not be determined as only a corpse shadow remained in the soil. Human bone fragments were found only within the bronze bracelets and anklets, but these were too fragmented for any analysis (Lemmers forthcoming). It was only possible to measure the length of the deceased in the field. He or she was relatively short, around 1.60 m.

The deceased was buried wearing an extraordinary set of ornaments, representing a specific kind of personal appearance, as well a number of toiletry items. His or her arms were adorned with bronze bracelets with one on the right wrist and two on the left wrist. The bracelets at the left wrist had been worn together so long that they displayed heavy use-wear where they touched. The legs were adorned with bronze anklets.

By the right arm lay an iron pin with a twisted decoration and a small bronze ring. A toilet set was found at the left shoulder. It consisted of an iron nail cutter and tweezers that likely dangled from an iron ring. Close by the set lay an amber bead. The use-wear traces on the bead are consistent with use as a closing for some kind of pouch. Underneath this set a fragmented bronze pin was found. The distribution of these fragments indicates that the pin was broken deliberately prior its placement in the grave. Finally, metal-spiraled rings were found near the head (see also Bourgeois/Van der Vaart-Verschoof this volume).

A very special feature of the burial is the preservation of textile. Fragments of woolen cloth survived in the bronze corrosion around the anklets and bracelets, and also inside the bracelets. The textile fragments indicate that the deceased was buried wearing a garment with long sleeves, and that a shroud was placed on top of the body (see also Grömer this volume; Grömer in Van der Vaart-Verschoof forthcoming).

Eventually the entire burial chamber was sealed off with charred planks covering the body. Ultimately the pit from at least 1.5 till 2 m deep was back-filled with soil and more charred oaken branches. Whether the burial was marked above ground is unknown. It can only be said that it was never overbuilt by other grave monuments and/or opened again, until its excavation in 2010.

Inhumation – beyond the norm?

While it can be debated whether the Slabroek elite burial can be referred to as a 'Chieftain's burial' (Jansen 2011 vs. Roymans 2011), an archaeological type of grave generally characterized by the presence of bronze vessels, weaponry, horse-gear and/or wagon components among the grave goods, the perceived 'difference' of the Slabroek grave can also not be dismissed by labeling the deceased an import-bride (as done for example by Roymans 2011). When this grave is considered from a more practice-based, rather than only a object-based, approach it conforms in many ways to the Early Iron Age elite burials and customs of the southern Netherlands (see Bourgeois/Van der Vaart-Verschoof this volume). Also the context conforms to the other Maashorst elite graves making the Slabroekse Heide inhumation grave definitely a Ha C elite grave, as suggested before (Jansen 2011; Jansen forthcoming).

Inhumation burials in general are a recently revealed element of Dutch Iron Age burial ritual. Until 20 years ago archaeologists thought the Iron Age urnfields and cemeteries were exclusively the domain of cremation burials. Cremation was the standard ritual for disposal or discarding of the body after death (Hessing/Kooi 2005; Gerritsen 2003, 118-150). Nowadays we know of at least 48 inhumation burials, most of them in the Dutch Central River Area (Jansen forthcoming; Van den Broeke 2008, 166 table 6). Six Early Iron Age cemeteries with cremation burials and inhumations lie around the city of Nijmegen, another cluster more to the west. South of the rivers Rhine and Meuse, on the sand soils, five inhumation burials from the Early Iron Age are known, in all cases one inhumation per urnfield (Fig. 6). The inhumations explicitly date to the Early Iron Age and first part of the Middle Iron Age, more specifically from approximately 700 till 375 BC (Van den Broeke 2008, 172-174). No inhumations are known from Late Bronze Age urnfields. Also after this period inhumation burials are not known until the later Roman Period.

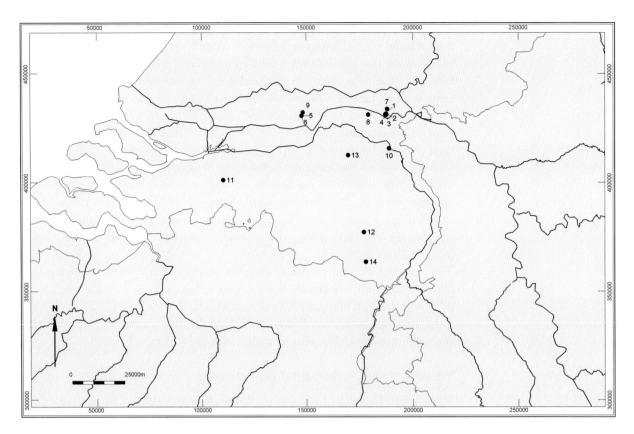

At first sight, considering the known tens of thousands of Early Iron Age urnfield graves in the southern Netherlands, the small number of inhumation graves seems insignificant. However these are meaningful exceptions. In general the inhumation burials show the same variation as contemporaneous cremation burials; they are never more elaborate, in most cases just simple flat graves, some of them contain no grave goods, others do like for example ornaments. It is striking that the ornaments in inhumation graves tend to be rather fragile. It is thinkable that in the case of a cremation where these objects were burned mourners may have overlooked them, or even the excavators may have overlooked them.

A preliminary research of isotopes of inhumations from Nijmegen gives reason to believe that *some* of the deceased that are buried as inhumations are non-local. Perhaps they were buried according the funeral customs of their homeland (Van den Broeke 2008, 176-178). But not every inhumation proved to be non-local. The same is true for cremation burials; we cannot prove that every cremation is local. Therefore we want to state that, until future research proves the opposite, inhumations are *not* by definition immigrants and/or import-brides. We argue that the same is true for the only inhumation Ha C elite grave in the Netherlands known so far (Jansen 2011; Roymans 2011). The inhumation graves are part of Early Iron Age burial ritual norm, and the Slabroekse Heide elite grave inhumation fits within this norm. Perhaps immigrants were integrated in society in such a way that they were buried conform local traditions.

Fig. 6. Distribution of Early and Middle Iron Age inhumation graves in the southern Netherlands. 1: Lent – Lauwerikstraat; 2: Lent – Steltsestraat; 3: Lent – Lentseveld; 4: Oosterhout – De Eeuwige Lente; 5: Meteren – Plantage; 6: Meteren – De Bogen; 7: Ewijk – Keizershoeve (Beuningen); 8: Ressen – Zuiderveld; 9: Geldermalsen – Middengebied; 10: Cuijk – Nutricia (Grotestraat); 11: Breda – Steenakker; 12: Someren – Waterdael; Uden – Slabroekse Heide; Weert – Raak (figure by Archol BV).

A cluster of chieftain's graves at the Maashorst

In conclusion, it is apparent from the above that the Maashorst region was repeatedly selected as a final resting place during later Prehistory for exceptional individuals who warranted being interred through elaborate burial rituals. There are three monumental Early Iron Age barrows at the northern edge of the Maashorst plateau, each extraordinary and unusual in their own way. All built in an existing barrow landscape with a long history, located no more than a couple hundred meters from each other. All three created through burial rituals that involved fire, dismantling, bending and breaking of objects and/or *pars pro toto* depositions. While we cannot with certainty determine which burial was created first, when the second and third were constructed, people would still have known what happened at the previous ones.

At the same time, someone special was also buried in an exceptional manner some 4 km to the south, further into the heartland of the Maashorst. At first glimpse the Slabroekse Heide inhumation burial appears to deviate from the norm. (S)he has been seen as an example of an immigrant, or even an import-bride, originating from a region where inhumation was a customary funerary practice (Roymans 2011). When considered in more detail, especially the burial practice, it conforms in many ways to the known Early Iron Age burials of the southern Netherlands (see also Bourgeois/Van der Vaart-Verschoof this volume; Jansen forthcoming). In this case not within the inconspicuous majority of urnfield graves, but within the exceptional elite burials – with the Slabroekse Heide as the first example of an elite *inhumation* grave.

Together with the Chieftain's grave of Oss-Vorstengraf and the monumental Oss-Zevenbergen mounds, the Slabroekse Heide inhumation is part of an extraordinary cluster of Hallstatt C elite graves in the Maashorst-region in the Low Countries. These, in turn fit into a larger pattern of elite burials where fire, manipulation and fragmentation were key (see also Bourgeois/Van der Vaart-Verschoof this volume; Van der Vaart-Verschoof forthcoming). Within the dominant burial practice, each burial has its unique, perhaps almost personal character.

Bibliography

Bursch 1937: F. Bursch, Grafheuvels te Oss. Oudheidkundige Mededelingen uit het Rijksmuseum van Oudheden te Leiden 18, 1937, 1-3.

De Kort/van Mourik 2005: J.-W. de Kort/J. van Mourik, Palynologisch onderzoek Slabroekse Heide. In: I. M. van Wijk/R. Jansen (eds.), Het urnenveld Slabroekse Heide op de Maashorst. Een verkennend en waarderend archeologisch proefsleuvenonderzoek. Archol rapport 72 (Leiden 2005) 57-66.

De Leeuwe 2007: R. de Leeuwe, Twee grafheuvels in het prehistorische dodenlandschap van Oss-Zevenbergen, circa 1800-500 v. Chr. In: R. Jansen/L. Louwe Kooijmans (red.), 10 jaar Archol. Van contract tot wetenschap (Leiden 2007) 205-220.

Fokkens 2013: H. Fokkens, Post alignments in the barrow cemeteries of Oss-Vorstengraf and Oss-Zevenbergen. In: D. R. Fontijn/A. Louwen/S. van der Vaart/K. Wentink (eds.), Beyond barrows. Current research on the structuration and perception of the prehistoric landscape through monuments (Leiden 2013) 141-154.

Fokkens/Jansen 2004: H. Fokkens/R. Jansen, Het vorstengraf van Oss: een archeologische speurtocht naar een prehistorisch grafveld (Utrecht 2004).

Fokkens *et al.* 2009: H. Fokkens/I. van Wijk/R. Jansen (eds.), Het grafveld Oss-Zevenbergen. Een prehistorisch grafveld ontleed. Archol rapport 50 (Leiden 2009).

Fokkens *et al.* 2012: H. Fokkens/S. van der Vaart/D. Fontijn/S. Lemmers/R. Jansen/I. van Wijk/P. Valentijn, Hallstatt burials of Oss in context. In: C. Bakels/H. Kamermans (eds.), The end of our fifth decade. Analecta Praehistorica Leidensia 43/44, 2012, 183-204.

Fontijn/van der Vaart 2013: D. R. Fontijn/S. A. van der Vaart 2013, Dismantled, transformed and deposited – prehistoric bronze from the centre of mound 7, In: D. Fontijn/S. A. van der Vaart/R. Jansen (eds), Transformation through Destruction. A monumental and extraordinary Early Iron Age Hallstatt C barrow from the ritual landscape of Oss-Zevenbergen (Leiden 2013) 151-194.

Fontijn *et al.* 2013a: D. Fontijn/R. Jansen/Q. Bourgeois/C. van der Linde, Excavating the seventh mound. In: D. Fontijn/S. van der Vaart/R. Jansen (eds), Transformation through Destruction. A monumental and extraordinary Early Iron Age Hallstatt C barrow from the ritual landscape of Oss-Zevenbergen (Leiden 2013) 69-118.

Fontijn *et al.* 2013b: D. Fontijn/R. Jansen/S.van der Vaart/H. Fokkens/I. van Wijk, Conclusion: the seventh mound of seven mounds – long-term history of the Zevenbergen barrow landscape. In: D. Fontijn/S. van der Vaart/R. Jansen (eds), Transformation through Destruction. A monumental and extraordinary Early Iron Age Hallstatt C barrow from the ritual landscape of Oss-Zevenbergen (Leiden 2013) 281-316.

Fontijn *et al.* 2013c: D. Fontijn/S. van der Vaart/R. Jansen (eds.), Transformation through Destruction. A monumental and extraordinary Early Iron Age Hallstatt C barrow from the ritual landscape of Oss-Zevenbergen (Leiden 2013).

Gerritsen 2003: F. Gerritsen, Local Identities. Landscape and community in the late prehistoric Meuse-Demer-Scheldt region. Amsterdam Archaeological Studies 9 (Amsterdam 2003).

Grömer in Van der Vaart-Verschoof forthcoming: K. Grömer, Hallstatt period Textile Finds from the Netherlands. In: S. van der Vaart-Verschoof, Fragmenting the Chieftain. A practice-based study of Early Iron Age Hallstatt C elite burials of the Low Countries and their relation to the Hallstatt Culture of Central Europe (forthcoming).

Hessing/Kooi 2005: W. Hessing/P. Kooi, Urnfields and cinerary barrows. Funerary and burial ritual in the Late Bronze and Iron Ages. In: L. Louwe Kooijmans/P. van den Broeke/H. Fokkens/A. van Gijn (eds.), The Prehistory of the Netherlands (Amsterdam 2005) 631-654.

Holwerda 1934: J. H. Holwerda, Een vroeg Gallisch vorstengraf bij Oss (N.B.). Oudheidkundige Mededelingen uit het Rijksmuseum van Oudheden te Leiden 15, 1934, 39-53.

Jaarverslag Heemkundekring Maasland 1975 (1976) 23-24.

Jansen 2011: R. Jansen, Vorstengraf of graf van een lokale leider? What's in a name. Archeobrief 15, 2011, 37-38.

Jansen/Fokkens 2007: R. Jansen/H. Fokkens, Het Vorstengraf van Oss re-considered. Archeologisch onderzoek Oss-Vorstengrafdonk 1997-2005. Archol rapport 49 (Leiden 2007).

Jansen/Louwen forthcoming: R. Jansen/A. Louwen, Het prehistorisch grafveld Slabroekse Heide – de resultaten van de opgraving in 2010. In: R. Jansen (ed.), Heuvels op de Heide. Een urnenveld met inhumatiegraf uit de vroege ijzertijd en grafveld uit de Romeinse tijd op de Maashorst (forthcoming).

Jansen/van der Linde 2013: R. Jansen/C. van der Linde, The physical and archaeological landscape of the Oss-Zevenbergen barrow group. In: D. Fontijn/S. van der Vaart/R. Jansen (eds.), Transformation through Destruction. A monumental and extraordinary Early Iron Age Hallstatt C barrow from the ritual landscape of Oss-Zevenbergen (Leiden 2013) 35-46.

Jansen et al. 2011: R. Jansen/Q. Bourgeois/A. Louwen/C. van der Linde/I. van Wijk, Opgraving van het grafveld Slabroekse Heide. In: R. Jansen/K. van der Laan (eds.), Verleden van een bewogen landschap – Landschaps en bewoningsgeschiedenis van de Maashorst (Utrecht 2011).

Jansen forthcoming: R. Jansen, Heuvels op de Heide. Een urnenveld met inhumatiegraf uit de vroege ijzertijd en grafveld uit de Romeinse tijd op de Maashorst (forthcoming).

Lemmers et al. 2012: S. Lemmers/M. Janssen/A. Waters-Rist/B. Grosskopf/M. Hoogland/L. Amkreutz, The Chieftain of Oss: new perspectives on an Iron Age individual with DISH. Poster presentation (Lille 2012).

Lemmers forthcoming: S. Lemmers, Osteologisch onderzoek naar het botmateriaal van een Vroege IJzertijd inhumatie uit het grafveld Slabroekse Heide. In: R. Jansen (ed.), Heuvels op de Heide. Een urnenveld met inhumatiegraf uit de vroege ijzertijd en grafveld uit de Romeinse tijd op de Maashorst (forthcoming).

Modderman 1964: P. Modderman, The chieftain's grave of Oss reconsidered. Bulletin van de Vereeniging tot Bevordering der Kennis van de Antieke Beschaving 39, 1964, 57-62.

Remouchamps 1924: A. Remouchamps, Opgravingen van een urnenveld te Uden. Oudheidkundige Mededelingen uit het Rijksmuseum van Oudheden te Leiden 5, 1924, 69-76.

Roymans 2011: N. Roymans, Een nieuw graf van een ijzertijdvorst of – vorstin in Zuid Nederland? Over ethische grenzen in de publieksvoorlichting. Archeobrief 15, 2011, 36-37.

Valentijn 2013: P. Valentijn, 'Mound' 6: a post and ditch aligned long barrow. In: D. Fontijn/S. van der Vaart/R. Jansen (eds.), Transformation through Destruction. A monumental and extraordinary Early Iron Age Hallstatt C barrow from the ritual landscape of Oss-Zevenbergen (Leiden 2013) 47-68.

Van den Broeke 2008: P. van den Broeke, Inhumation burials: new elements in Iron Age funerary ritual in the southern Netherlands. In: A. Cahen-Delhaye/G. de Mulder (eds.), Des Espaces aux Esprits. L'organisation de la mort aux ages des Métaux dans le nord-ouest de l'Europe. Etudes et Documents Archéologie 32, 2008, 161-184.

Van der Vaart 2011: S. van der Vaart, Hail to the Chieftain. A detailed examination of grave goods from Dutch chiefly burials and their role in funerary rituals during the Hallstatt period. Unpublished Master Thesis (Leiden 2011).

Van der Vaart-Verschoof forthcoming: S. van der Vaart-Verschoof, Fragmenting the chieftain. A practice-based study of Early Iron Age Hallstatt C elite burials of the Low Countries and their relation to the Hallstatt Culture of Central Europe (forthcoming).

Van Hees forthcoming: E. van Hees, Brandstof voor levenden en doden – houtskoolresten uit kuilen uit het mesolithicum en een grafveld uit de ijzer- en Romeinse tijd op de Slabroekse Heide (Noord-Brabant). In: R. Jansen (ed.), Heuvels op de Heide. Een urnenveld met inhumatiegraf uit de vroege ijzertijd en grafveld uit de Romeinse tijd op de Maashorst (forthcoming).

Van Wijk/Jansen 2010: I. Van Wijk/R. Jansen, Het urnenveld Slabroekse Heide op de Maashorst. Een verkennend en waarderend archeologisch proefsleuvenonderzoek. Archol rapport 72 (Leiden 2010).

Van Wijk/Jansen forthcoming: I. van Wijk/R. Jansen, Op zoek naar de grenzen van het urnenveld van Slabroekse Heide. Inventariserend Proefsleuvenonderzoek te Uden-Slabroekse Heide. Archol rapport (forthcoming).

Van Wijk et al. 2009: I. van Wijk/H. van Wijk/H. Fokkens/D. Fontijn/R. de Leeuwe/L. Meurkens/A. van Hilst/C. Vermeeren, Resultaten van de definitieve onderzoek. In: H. Fokkens/I. van Wijk/R. Jansen (eds.), Het grafveld Oss-Zevenbergen. Een prehistorisch grafveld ontleed. Archol rapport 50 (Leiden 2009) 36-140.

Verwers 1966: G. Verwers, Tumuli at the Zevenbergen near Oss, gemeente Berghem, province of North Brabant. Analecta Praehistorica Leidensia 2, 1966, 27-32.

Authors

Richard Jansen
Faculty of Archaeology
Leiden University
Einsteinweg 2
P.O. Box 9515
2300 RA Leiden
The Netherlands
r.jansen@arch.leidenuniv.nl

Sasja van der Vaart-Verschoof
Faculty of Archaeology
Leiden University
Einsteinweg 2
P.O. Box 9515
2300 RA Leiden
The Netherlands
s.a.van.der.vaart@arch.leidenuniv.nl

Textile symbolism in Early Iron Age burials

Christoph Huth and Monika Kondziella

Abstract

Textile symbolism is a central element in Early Iron Age burials of the Hallstatt and Villanova groups. Textiles and their imagery can be found in almost all well-equipped graves, even in the Low Countries. Most princely burials contain precious textiles that were used to enshroud the grave goods. In addition, weaving and other forms of manufacturing are a common motif in pictorial representations from Italy to the south-east Hallstatt groups. Weaving equipment like distaffs, spindle whorls, bobbins and the like is a standard feature of Villanovan and Hallstatt graves. In south-west Central Europe bronze belts clearly imitate textile patterns. This is also the case with the richly decorated pots of the so-called Alb-Hegau style, while further to the east ceramic pots display stylized forms of weaving looms. The Alb-Hegau decoration possibly mimics real textiles which were used to wrap grave-goods in rich burials. It is suggested that textile elements in burials refer to the high standing of women in Early Iron Age society. A case is made that burials are staged like a marriage, with drinking and textiles as core symbols. The rich burials of the Low Countries fit perfectly well into this Early Iron Age ideology. Insofar that they are by no means a peripheral phenomenon.

Zusammenfassung

Textile Symbolik ist ein elementarer Bestandteil der früheisenzeitlichen Kulturen im Hallstatt- und Villanovabereich. Textilien, Geräte zu ihrer Herstellung und einschlägige Bilddarstellungen finden sich in praktisch allen gut ausgestatteten Gräbern, nicht zuletzt auch in den Niederlanden. In den Prunkgräbern verhüllte man die Beigaben mit kostbaren Tüchern. Darüber hinaus sind das Weben und andere Schritte der Textilherstellung ein geläufiges Motiv unter den Bilddarstellungen in Italien und in der Osthallstattkultur. Geräte wie Rocken, Spindeln, Spulen und anderes mehr gehören zu den Standardbeigaben in Villanova- und vielen Hallstattgräbern. In der westlichen Hallstattkultur findet man in den Gräbern Bronzeblechgürtel, die offensichtlich textile Muster nachahmen. Auch die reich verzierte Alb-Hegau-Keramik imitiert textilen Dekor, während man in Nordbayern stilisierte Webstühle auf der Grabkeramik abbildete. Vielleicht sollten die Alb-Hegau-Bemalungen Tücher abbilden, wie man sie in den Prunkgräbern zum Verhüllen der Beigaben verwendete. Vermutlich repräsentierten die textilen Symbole den hohen Status der Frauen in der frühen Eisenzeit. Gräber waren wohl wie Hochzeiten inszeniert, mit Trinkservicen und Textilien als zentralen Symbolen. Die reichen Gräber der Niederlande fügen sich in diese Vorstellungswelt der frühen Eisenzeit nahtlos ein. Insofern handelt es sich bei ihnen keineswegs um eine Randerscheinung der Hallstattkultur.

The emergence of lavish burials in the Early Iron Age has attracted much attention among researchers. Actually the focus on burials mounds and rich grave goods has been so strong that simple flat graves in between the burial mounds have been overlooked for a very long time. Only recently has systematic research of Hallstatt burial grounds started bringing simple flat graves to light, primarily cremation graves with few to no grave goods. Meanwhile more than 500 of the simple cremation burials are known in southern Germany (Müller-Scheeßel 2013, 123-125), and one starts to wonder whether the mounds with rich grave goods really are the standard burial type of the time. As a matter of fact the simple graves are the traditional form of burial of the preceding urnfield period. Seen from this angle the Iron Age burial grounds are nothing else than traditional urnfields with burial mounds spotted amidst the simple graves. It is perhaps no coincidence to find a very similar situation in the Low Countries, where in the Early Iron Age lavish burials covered by mounds appear among the simple cremation graves of Bronze Age tradition. Admittedly, the contrast is much starker in the Low Countries counting both types of burial by numbers, yet from a structural point of view it is by no means different.

As in southern central Europe the conspicuous burial monuments of the Low Countries were seemingly of greater interest to researchers than the simple graves. However, due to their comparatively small number they were regarded as exotic, not to say as intrusive in an otherwise unchanged landscape of Bronze Age tradition. For a long time these burials seemed to be the leftovers of Hallstatt invaders or at least immigrants. Only with time the perception changed and the burial goods were taken as imports by a native population. Nevertheless, they were still seen as peripheral with regard to the Hallstatt core area (for changing perspectives on this matter cf. Fontijn/Fokkens 2007; Mariën 1952, 275-304; Roymans 1991).

In the following it will be suggested that this may not be true, taking up a thread laid out by Sasja van der Vaart in her intriguing study on the elite burials of the Early Iron Age in the Low Countries (Van der Vaart 2011). However, attention will be drawn away from the standard elite elements of these graves, i.e. drinking equipment, weapons and wagons plus horse-gear, in other words away from all those supposedly male paraphernalia of an Early Iron Age aristocracy. Instead the focus will be laid on allegedly female grave goods, i.e. textiles, including manufacturing equipment and pictorial representations of cloths and cloth production. These elements, which are easily overlooked for obvious reasons, seem to be ubiquitous in burials of the Iron Age communities of Central Europe, Italy and beyond. As a matter of fact, they were present in the Dutch elite burials of Oss, Rhenen and Wijchen (Van der Vaart 2011, 97-98; 109; 134-135).

Textiles, tools and images in burials and beyond

The perishable physical characteristics of textiles do not mean that cloth was of lesser importance with regard to the remaining grave goods. There can be little doubt that precious textiles were an easily recognizable sign of material wealth. Presumably some textiles also demonstrated prestigious contacts to the outside world. In general, textiles may be seen as an emblem of high standing, particularly for women. Over and above these material qualities textiles had a strong symbolic meaning in Iron Age burials, very much like the drinking equipment, the wagon and all the other prestige goods.

Only recently have textiles received the attention they deserve (e.g. Gleba 2008; Gleba 2011; Gleba/Pásztókai-Szeöke 2013; Grömer 2010; Grömer et al. 2013). The most famous example for the presence of textiles in burials are the wrapped grave goods of Hochdorf (Banck-Burgess 1999). To this may be added

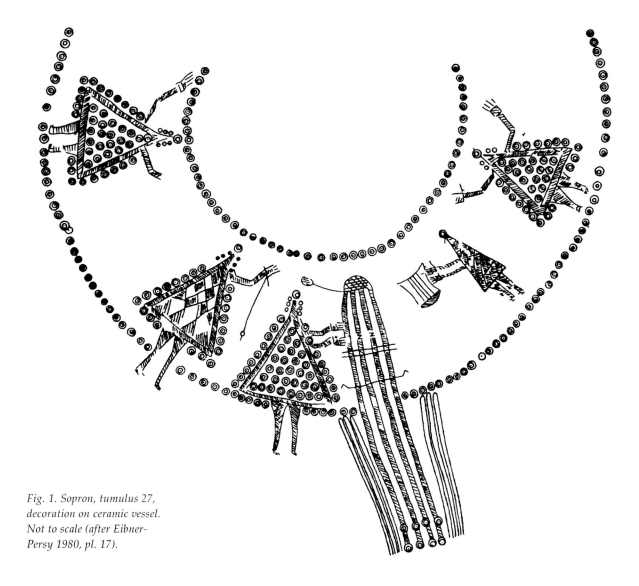

Fig. 1. Sopron, tumulus 27, decoration on ceramic vessel. Not to scale (after Eibner-Persy 1980, pl. 17).

the main burial of the Glauberg (Baitinger/Pinsker 2002). Both burials are recent excavations and therefore perfectly documented. Taking a closer look at the older discoveries however, it turns out that most of the elite burials of the Hallstatt and early La Tène period contained textiles indeed (Banck-Burgess 1999, 34-51 for further examples; for the princely tomb of Vix see Moulhérat 2003). In addition to textiles, manufacturing tools like spindles and whorls occur in graves. In some regions, like northern Italy they are a standard element in Villanova burials (Bartoloni 1989). Additionally there is a whole range of images, either showing textile manufacture itself or its equipment, and sometimes figural objects like fibulae or pendants in the shape of weaving looms (Fath/Glunz-Hüsken 2011).

Not surprisingly the archaeological evidence is turning richer and more complex the further south one gets. Villanovan Italy stands out among the communities of Early Iron Age Europe while it is part of a *koinè* of groups using a surprisingly uniform symbolic language and imagery. Therefore, a short overview of images and artefacts has to start in Italy. A well-known example of textile symbolism in a burial is the *tintinnabulum* of the Tomba degli ori in Bologna, showing richly dressed women weaving and spinning and related activities (Morigi Govi 1971). No less impressive is the throne in Grave 89 in Verucchio, with various scenes of textile production, including weaving women sitting on thrones with footstools (von Eles 2002). Mario Torelli compared the central scene in the lower register with Etruscan *cippi* from Chiusi. These *cippi* depict women exchanging precious textiles as part of a wedding arrangement (Torelli 1997, 70 fig. 56).

Famous representations of textile manufacturing come from Sopron in west Hungary, with a vessel in tumulus 27 showing a spinning woman and another one standing at the weaving loom (Eibner-Persy 1980, pl. 16,2; pl. 17). The weaving beam has the shape of a bird-boat, very much like in Verucchio (Fig. 1). The central picture on a vessel from nearby Várishegy compares best to the Bologna *tintinnabulum* (Dobiat 1982, 295 fig. 12). The pattern and the borders of the women's clothes are carefully depicted. This is remarkable, because the pictures are otherwise rather sketchy and resemble stick figures. People on these vessels seem to wear sumptuous clothes in general, sometimes lavishly embellished. Some are adorned with large earrings. Either a checkered piece of cloth or a different kind of weaving loom can be seen in Rabensburg in Lower Austria (Dobiat 1982, 86 fig. 4,1; 312; 314; Grömer 2010, 140-142). An entire weaving loom together with spindle whorls and spindles has been discovered in Frög in Carinthia, actually a double burial of a man and a woman (Gleirscher 2009).

While entire weaving looms seem to be the exception, pictorial representations of looms are quite common (Bergonzi 2007). Again most of them are found in Italy. In grave 149 in Este Casa di Ricovero pendants hanging from a brooch indisputably resemble a weaving loom (Ruta Serafini 2004, 279 fig. 3). The warp threads are made of glass beads, the trapezoidal loom weights are made of sheet bronze. The beams are once again shaped like bird-boats, lending a religious connotation to the whole arrangement. Brooches of this type have been reported from Sirolo near Ancona and other places (Nava/Salerno 2007, 175 fig. III,124). In Frög rectangular bronze sheets with a plaid pattern may stand for the piece of cloth already woven, with the warp threads and the weights hanging below. A similar pattern can be observed on a couple of brooches from Hallstatt, again with chains and trapezoidal pendants (Fath/Glunz-Hüsken 2011).

Real weaving equipment is found in many graves (Gleba 2011; Gambacurta/ Ruta Serafini 2007). Some distaffs are clearly lavish objects like the bronze and bone distaffs in Este Casa di Ricovero grave 149 and Villa Benvenuti graves 78 and 89 (Ruta Serafini 2004, 279 fig. 4). In Frög, grave 186 colored glass beads were used (Gleirscher 2011, 73 fig. 2), the distaff from Dürrnberg near Hallein has wrongly been taken as a scepter (Moscati 1991, 168). At any rate they appear to be precious objects that were highly esteemed. Spindle whorls and bobbins on the other hand are almost ubiquitous (Bartoloni 1989). They seem to be so trivial that they hardly ever attract attention. Some burials contain equipment for tablet weaving.

To conclude this *tour d'horizon* through the Early Iron Age communities of Central Europe and especially of Italy mention must be made of objects revealing a close connection between textiles and the religious sphere. Textiles, or rather images of textiles, are also known as votive objects from the sanctuary in Este-Caldevigo (Pascucci 1990, 227 fig. 80). The bronze sheets wear plaids like real textiles, and some of the sheets were folded together like real cloth. The Reitia sanctuary nearby yielded loom weights, spindle whorls and bobbins. A religious context furthermore may be assumed for the countless pictures of weaving looms

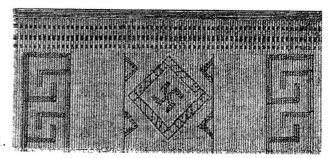

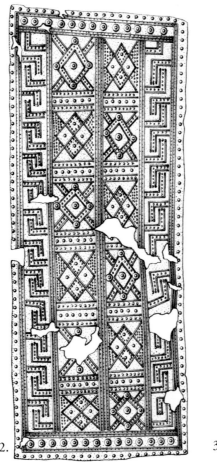

Fig. 2. 1: Hohmichele, grave 6, cloth. Not to scale. – 2: Hettingen, bronze belt plate. Not to scale. – 3: Mörsingen, tumulus 4, grave 3, bronze belt plate. L = 25.6 cm (after Banck-Burgess 1999,62 fig. 33; Kilian-Dirlmeier 1972, pl. 44,416, pl. 28,333).

1.

2.

3.

in the Valcamonica (Anati 1994). And last but not least one must not forget the Daunian *stelae*, which are the best and most impressive example of textile lavishness, with brooches imitating weaving looms and pictures of women sitting at weaving looms (Norman 2011). To sum up, there are manifold allusions to the manufacture of textiles in burials of the Early Iron Age, and there are many hints to a religious context of spinning and weaving.

Textile symbolism on bronze belts

A more subtle connection between textile symbolism and burial rites can be observed in the western Hallstatt province. Lavishly decorated bronze belts are a common grave good of the Early Iron Age in south-western Germany, eastern

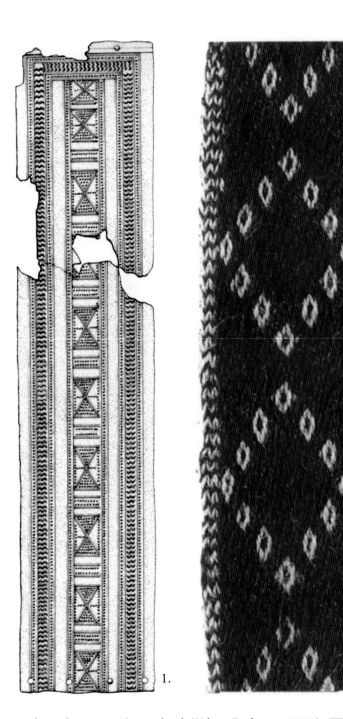

Fig. 3. 1: Büsingen, Tiefental tum. 10, bronze belt plate. L. = 35,5 cm. – 2: Hochdorf, cloth. Not to scale. (after Kilian-Dirlmeier 1972, pl. 27,322; Banck-Burgess 1999, 78 fig. 47).

France and north-western Switzerland (Kilian-Dirlmeier 1972). While some of them display figural pictures like horses, deer or men, most of them are all over covered with geometric motifs. The eye-catching density of the decoration may result from a certain *horror vacui*, yet it seems much more probable that these belts are meant to resemble textiles.

Comparing a piece of cloth from the Hohmichele princely burial close to the Heuneburg with a bronze belt plate from Mörsingen, which is just 17 km away, striking similarities in both patterns and their arrangement are immediately evident (Fig. 2). Both display lozenges (or rather diamonds) framed by little triangles. The lozenges on the belt plate are separated by ladder-like ornaments

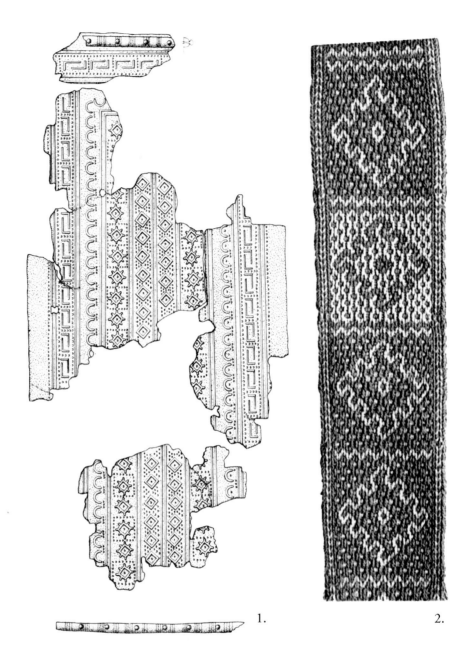

1. 2.

which resemble the selvedge of the Hohmichele cloth (Banck-Burgess 1999, 62
fig. 33; Kilian-Dirlmeier 1972, pl. 28,333). On the belt plate from Hettingen
(Kr. Sigmaringen) we find the same border ornaments of meanders and in the
center again diamonds separated by vertical stripes (Kilian-Dirlmeier 1972, pl.
44,416). Border ornaments with counter-pieces among textiles are vertical rows
of M-shaped motifs like on the belt plate from Büsingen (Kr. Konstanz) (Kilian-
Dirlmeier 1972, pl. 27,322) and the cloth from the wagon in Hochdorf (Banck-
Burgess 1999, 78 fig. 47) (Fig. 3).

Sometimes it is not only the motifs and their combination that seem to be
borrowed from textiles. It may also be the weaving technique itself that has been
translated into an image covering a bronze sheet. A bi-colored piece of cloth made
by tablet weaving from Hochdorf shows the typical dotted surface which recurs in

the very same manner on a belt plate from Mölsheim near Worms (Banck-Burgess 1999, 78 fig. 45; Kilian-Dirlmeier 1972, pl. 47,441) (Fig. 4).

The ornaments found on bronze belts in any case resemble real textiles, as do their combination, arrangement and density and texture, to put it that way. However there remains the question why belt plates should be imitating textiles, all the more as they are worn on top of cloth.

Textile symbolism on pottery

Apart from belt plates textile ornaments can be found on ceramic vessels of the so-called Alb-Hegau type, a ceramic style widely found in south-west Germany and surrounding areas (Zürn 1987; Brosseder 2004, 159-216). Alb-Hegau pottery is ubiquitous in burials of the early and middle Hallstatt period. The resemblance of the geometric pottery decoration and textile ornaments has been acknowledged for a long time. As a matter of fact, many ceramic vessels share the same ornaments as textiles, including their composition and combination and their serial arrangement, i.e. repeating the same motif all over or rather all around the vessel. Basically all burials of the south-western Hallstatt province have a whole set of richly decorated pots, among them large containers for drinks and small cups for drinking. In general the ceramic sets are doubled, i.e. all important vessels occur twice. On the richly decorated pots we find diamonds, vertical strips, horizontal borders and so on, everything very much like on the textiles and the bronze belts for that matter (Fig. 5). Sometimes, like on a bowl from Steinkirchen (Kr. Deggendorf), the ornament resembles the texture of cloth like twill, which in this particular case seems to be framed by a border with a zig-zag pattern on the rim of the bowl (Brosseder 2004, 165 fig. 111). A similar ornament consisting of alternating triangles combined with the well-known rows of diamonds can be found on a pot from Zainingen. A further ornament consists of parallel zig-zag lines with left-open diamonds like in Kirchensittenbach (Brosseder 2004, 201 fig. 132; 233 fig. 154).

Not all of the motifs known from textiles in south-west Germany occur on pottery. For example there is no counterpart for the tablet-woven cloth from the cauldron in Hochdorf. However, the hook-like motive on the cloth is matched by painted ceramic vessels of the east Hallstatt province (Fig. 6). In general, textile decoration is not as easy to spot on east Hallstatt pottery. Nevertheless reticulate ornaments like on pots from Nové Kosariská do resemble textiles (Pichlerová 1969). Very often the main decoration of the pot is framed by a border-like ornament on the neck. In most cases, however, it is the manufacture of textiles itself that is shown on pottery in the east Hallstatt province, like in Sopron (see above).

A peculiar situation prevails in northern Bavaria. Again textile decorations are not as easily recognizable as among the Alb-Hegau pottery of the south-west, although there can be no doubt that many motifs found on ceramic vessels are derived from textiles. Instead the weaving equipment is depicted on the vessels, very much like in the Kalenderberg province. A shared feature of both groups is the depiction of the activities that seem to go along with it, like lyre players or people raising their arms in some kind of adoration gesture. Several large pots show weaving looms on their shoulder (Stroh 1979, pl. 60,4; pl. 130,8; pl. 131,12; Stroh 1988, pl. 78,2; pl. 94,2; Stroh 2000a, pl. 8,4-5; Stroh 2000b, pl. 26,8; Torbrügge 1979, pl. 26,5; pl. 107,5; pl. 166,10). Sometimes they

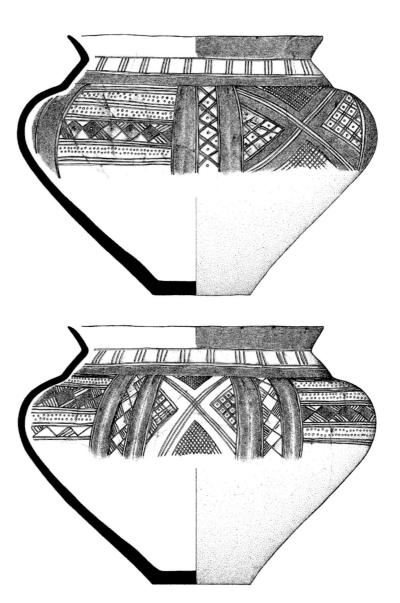

Fig. 5. Mehrstetten, Flur Fleckenhau, richly decorated ceramic of Alb-Hegau type. H = 26.5 cm (after Zürn 1987, pl. 247,1a – b).

are found as decoration on the inside of bowls. Admittedly the depictions are rather stylized, but it is certainly not mere coincidence to find them exactly in those places where the human representations are situated as well (Fig. 7). On top of that, the patterns match the patterns found on cloth, like zig-zag textures or reticular patterns. Garland patterns hanging from the shoulder of some pots strongly resemble textiles as well.

Wrapping pots with textiles is a common practice in the Early Iron Age. Hochdorf and Glauberg are just the most spectacular examples (Banck-Burgess 1999; Baitinger/Pinsker 2002). Dressing pots is also widely known from Italy (Gleba 2008, 87-88; Putz 2007, 86-87; von Eles 2006), and north of the Alps particularly from eastern communities like the Billendorf group (Nebelsick/ Coblenz 1997, 19-20). There all that is left is a dress pin lying next to the urn. This is where it dropped down after the cloth wrapped around the urn had decayed. Earlier examples can be found among the cremations in southern German urnfields of the Late Bronze Age (Wirth 1998, 27; 32).

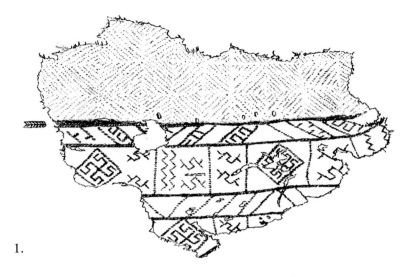

1.

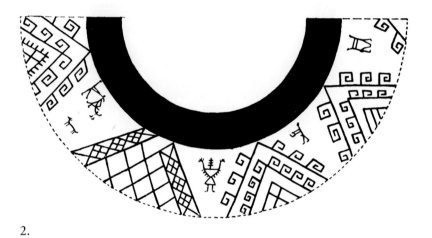

2.

Fig. 6. 1: Hochdorf, cloth. Not to scale. – 2: Nové Košariská, tum 1, decoration on ceramic vessel. Not to scale (after Banck-Burgess 1999, pl. 27,2; Pichlerová 1969, pl. 3,b).

The elite burials of the Netherlands and Belgium are no exception. There textiles were used for wrapping the grave goods, like the items placed in the bucket in Oss (Van der Vaart 2011, 100-105). In this respect, the rich Hallstatt burials of the Lower Rhine area seem to follow rules that were valid over large parts of Early Iron Age Europe, particularly so among the Hallstatt communities and in Italy, but equally in the Billendorf communities of eastern Germany and Poland.

There has been a lot of speculation as to the reasons of wrapping grave-goods in textiles, reaching from a generous display of wealth by showing off lavish textiles to the other extreme, i.e. by hiding away the precious grave-goods from the eyes of the mourners (Banck-Burgess 1999, 28-32). Some prefer more profane reasons like protecting the grave goods from possible damage on the journey to the Otherworld. Quite obviously, there is some sort of perplexity with regard to the matter.

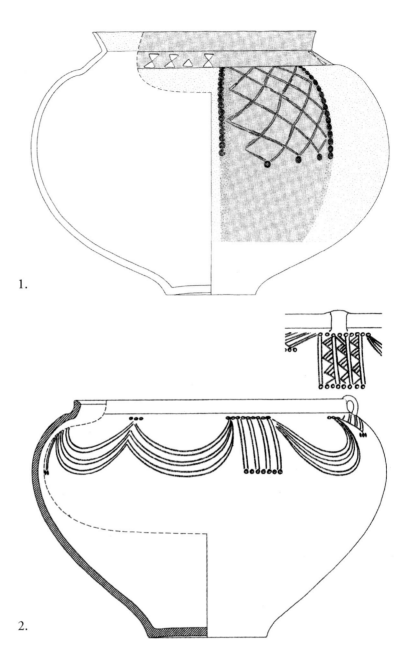

Fig. 7. 1: Schirndorf, tum. 200. H. = 30 cm. – 2: Schirndorf, tum. 59. H = 23.2 cm. Decoration on ceramic vessels (after Stroh 2000b, pl. 26,8; Stroh 1988, pl. 78).

1.

2.

Weaving, wedding and access to power

Mention must be made of the manifold symbolic meanings of textiles and their manufacture in antiquity (Wagner-Hasel 2000). Artemis and Athene carried golden spindles and supposedly passed their knowledge of textile manufacture to young women. Spinning and weaving were regarded as sacred activities. They both formed an integral part of the high standing of aristocratic women. Precious clothes played a central role as dowry, and certainly had a strong erotic connotation, for example as wedding coats. And of course the fates and their thread must not be forgotten. On a more profane level textiles may stand for material wealth, for prestigious contacts with other groups, particularly those in the Mediterranean world as the swastika ornaments of the Hochdorf textiles seem to demonstrate.

It seems as if the pottery of the east Hallstatt province may give some clues to the possible meaning of the textiles in Early Iron Age burials. Some of the ceramic vessels with human representations show a couple holding their hands. The couple can be found in the grave with the weaving loom in Frög (Gleirscher 2009, 205-206 fig. 2-3) as well as in Nové Kosariská, tumulus 1 and 4 (Pichlerová 1969, pl. 3; pl. 5; pl. 20,4), or in tumulus 28 in Sopron (Eibner-Persy 1980, pl. 28-29). Most researchers take these couples either as men involved in some ritual fight or as dancers or mourners (Gleirscher 2009). Once again a look to the south reveals a further possibility. In grave B/1971 of the Lippi necropolis in Verucchio a carved piece of wood shows an upright standing couple making love (von Eles 2007, 152 fig. 4). Evidently the couple is meant to symbolize a wedding, more conceivably a *hieros gamos*. Depictions of weddings are indeed quite common in the Mediterranean and beyond. Typically one figure touches the chin of the other or the breasts or right away the genitals (Säflund 1993, 37-46). Weddings are a central motif in situla art (Huth 2003, 160-220) as well as on the throne of grave 89 in Verucchio (von Eles 2002) or on the cart incense burner from Bisenzio Olmo Bello (Woytowitsch 1978, pl. 24).

A recently discovered situla from Pieve d'Alpago near Belluno underlines the close relationship between wedding, weaving and, for that matter, access to power (Gangemi *et al.* 2016). Several depictions of sexual encounters are followed by a woman giving birth to a child (Fig. 8). The scenery is enriched by a variety of symbols and paraphernalia of high status like the richly ornamented dress of the women, large earrings, belts, scepters and last but not least weaving equipment like a loom. A couple of footstools underneath the lovers' bed reminds the beholder that all this wedding business is about access to power. While on the *oinochoe* from Tragliatella a pair of thrones awaits the lovers (Torelli 1997, 29 fig. 15), in situla art footstools seem to be a common shorthand code for sitting on a throne. Pairs of footstools can be found on several *situlae* (always placed below the lovers' bed), like on a newly discovered cist from Montebelluna. Here two spinning women stand right next to the couple making love (Bianchin-Citton 2014). Other vessels in situla art show a man or a woman serving a drink to the couple on the bed. In addition footstools are accessories of weaving women sitting on a throne, like on the throne from Verucchio or the *tintinnabulum* of the tomba degli ori in Bologna (von Eles 2002; Morigi Govi 1971). Sometimes, however, the *hieros gamos* itself takes place on a throne, as is the case on the belt plate from Brezje (Barth 1999).

In Italian research it is generally accepted by now that the events depicted in situla art are meant to legitimize power (Sassatelli 2013). There is a clear link between drinking and marriage in situla art, and there is an equally clear link between textiles and marriage in situla art. It seems that textiles played a crucial role in weddings, showing that a woman was prepared to marry and demonstrating her high social standing.

Burials of the Early Iron Age, especially so rich burials, seem to be staged like a marriage, with the grave goods telling a story very similar to the events depicted in situla art (Huth 2003; 2015). One element is never missing in burials of the Early Iron Age, and this is drinking. Other elements like weapons or a wagon may be present, but they do not have to be. In situla art the drink served by a woman with precious clothes to a man sitting on a throne (or lying in a bed, after all) is one of the central events. The other one is the sexual intercourse with this woman.

The second element that may not be missing, at least in all burials that are carefully excavated, is precious cloth, sometimes used for enshrouding the grave

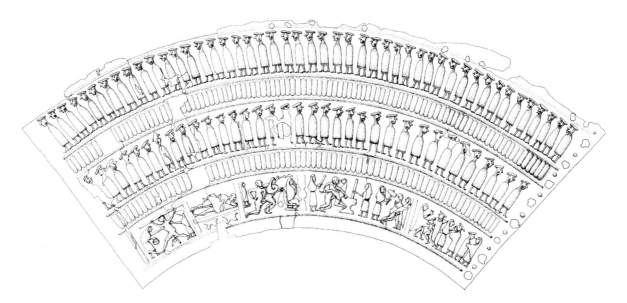

Fig. 8. Pieve d'Alpago near Belluno, decoration on bronze situla. Not to scale (after Gangemi et al. 2016, pl. 1).

goods. Sometimes the act of weaving is shown by pictorial representations like in the Kalenderberg group or in northern Bavaria. One may therefore wonder if the rich decoration on pots like in south-western Germany is not meant to represent textiles wrapped around the drinking vessels, or urns for that matter.

Drinking and making textiles are integral and indispensable elements of the marriage symbolism of Early Iron Age burials. The close relationship between drinking and making textiles can be seen on the pendant of the large drinking horn in Hochdorf, which has the shape of a weaving loom (Fath/Glunz-Hüsken 2011, 263 fig. 9,1).

The rich burials in the Low Countries fit perfectly well into the ideological realm of the Early Iron Age communities further to the south and east. They tell exactly the same story about divine descent as the supposedly princely graves and many of the better equipped Hallstatt and Villanova burials do (Huth 2015). Hence the grave-goods are by no means exotic. They may be unusual with regard to the simple burials, but this is very much the same case with the rich burials and the long neglected simple burials of the Hallstatt core area.

Bibliography

Anati 1994: E. Anati, Valcamonica. Una storia per l'Europa. Il linguaggio delle pietre (Capo di Ponte 1994).

Baitinger/Pinsker 2002: H. Baitinger/B. Pinsker (eds.), Das Rätsel der Kelten vom Glauberg (Stuttgart 2002).

Banck-Burgess 1999: J. Banck-Burgess, Hochdorf IV. Die Textilfunde aus dem späthallstattzeitlichen Fürstengrab von Eberdingen-Hochdorf (Kreis Ludwigsburg) und weitere Grabtextilien aus hallstatt- und latènezeitlichen Kulturgruppen. Forschungen und Berichte zur Vor- und Frühgeschichte in Baden-Württemberg 70 (Stuttgart 1999).

Barth 1999: F. Barth, Zu den im Situlenstil verzierten Gürtelblechen aus Brezje. Archäologisches Korrespondenzblatt 29, 1999, 57-59.

Bartoloni 1989: G. Bartoloni, Marriage, Sale and Gift. A proposito di alcuni corredi femminili dalle necropoli populoniesi della Prima Età del Ferro. In: A. Rallo (ed.), Le donne in Etruria (Roma 1989) 35-54.

Bergonzi 2007: G. Bergonzi, Donne del Piceno dall'età del Ferro all'orientalizzante. In: P. von Eles (ed.), Le ore e i giorni delle donne. Dalla quotidianità alla sacralità tra VIII e VII secolo a.C. (Verucchio 2007) 87-95.

Bianchin-Citton 2014: E. Binachin-Citton, Topografia e sviluppo di un centro preromano della fascia pedemontana veneta. Il caso di Montebelluna. In: G. Baldelli/F. Lo Schiavo, F. (eds.), Amore per l'Antico. Dal Tirreno all'Adriatico, della Preistoria al Medioevo e oltre (Roma 2014) 999-1006.

Brosseder 2004: U. Brosseder, Studien zur Ornamentik hallstattzeitlicher Keramik zwischen Rhônetal und Karpatenbecken. Universitätsforschungen zur prähistorischen Archäologie 106 (Bonn 2004).

Dobiat 1982: K. Dobiat, Menschendarstellungen auf ostalpiner Hallstattkeramik. Eine Bestandsaufnahme. Acta Archaeologica Academiae Scientiarum Hungaricae 34, 1982, 279-322.

Eibner-Persy 1980: A. Eibner-Persy, Hallstattzeitliche Grabhügel von Sopron (Ödenburg). Wissenschaftliche Arbeiten aus dem Burgenland 62 (Eisenstadt 1980).

Fath/Glunz-Hüsken 2011: B. Fath/B. Glunz-Hüsken, Textilien und Symbole für ihre Herstellung in eisenzeitlichen Gräbern Mitteleuropas. Griechenland – Este – Frög – Sopron. Prähistorische Zeitschrift 86,2, 2011, 254-271.

Fontijn/Fokkens 2007: D. Fontijn/H. Fokkens, The emergence of Early Iron Age 'chieftain's graves' in the southern Netherlands: reconsidering transformations in burial and depositional practices. In: C. Haselgrove/R. Pope (eds.), The earlier Iron Age in Britain and the near Continent (Oxford 2007) 354-373.

Gambacurta/Ruta Serafini 2007: G. Gambacurta/A. Ruta Serafini, Dal fuso al telaio. Profili di donne nella società di Este nell'età del Ferro. In: P. von Eles (ed.), Le ore e i giorni delle donne. Dalla quotidianità alla sacralità tra VIII e VII secolo a.C. (Verucchio 2007) 45-53.

Gangemi et al. 2016:G. Gangemi/M. Bassetti/D. Voltolini (eds.), Le signore dell'Alpago. La necropoli preromana di "Pian de la Gnela" Pieve d'Alpago (Belluno) (Treviso 2016).

Gleba 2008: M. Gleba, Textile Production in Pre-Roman Italy (Oxford 2008).

Gleba 2011: M. Gleba, The 'Distaff-Side' of Early Iron Age Aristocratic Identity in Italy. In: M. Gleba/H.W. Horsnæs (eds.), Communicating Identity in Italic Iron Age Communities (Oxford 2011) 26-32.

Gleba/Pásztókai-Szeöke 2013: M. Gleba/J. Pásztókai-Szeöke (eds.), Making textiles in pre-Roman and Roman times. People, places, identities (Oxford 2013).

Gleirscher 2009: P. Gleirscher, Sopron – Nové Košariská – Frög. Zu den Bildgeschichten der Kalenderberg-Kultur. Prähistorische Zeitschrift 84, 2009, 202-223.

Gleirscher 2011: P. Gleirscher, Die Hügelgräber von Frög. Ein eisenzeitliches Herrschaftszentrum in Rosegg (Klagenfurt 2011)

Grömer 2010: K. Grömer, Prähistorische Textilkunst in Europa. Geschichte des Handwerks und Kleidung vor den Römern. Veröffentlichungen der prähistorischen Abteilung 3 (Wien 2010).

Grömer et al. 2013: K. Grömer/A. Kern/H. Reschreiter/H. Rösel-Mautendorfer, Textilien aus Hallstatt. Gewebte Kultur aus dem bronze- und eisenzeitlichen Salzbergwerk. Archaeolingua 29 (Budapest 2013).

Huth 2003: Ch. Huth, Menschenbilder und Menschenbild. Anthropomorphe Bildwerke der frühen Eisenzeit (Berlin 2003).

Huth 2015: Ch. Huth, Deux mariages et un enterrement. Réflexions sur la signification du mobilier des tombes aristocratiques du début de l'âge du Fer. In: A. Esposito (ed.), Autour du "banquet". Modèles de consommation et usages sociaux (Dijon 2015) 203-218.

Kilian-Dirlmeier 1972: I. Kilian-Dirlmeier, Die hallstattzeitlichen Gürtelbleche und Blechgürtel Mitteleuropas. Prähistorische Bronzefunde XII,1 (Munich 1972).

Mariën 1952: M.-E. Mariën, Oud-België. Van de eerste landbouwers tot de komst van Caesar (Antwerpen 1952).

Morigi Govi 1971: C. Morigi Govi, Il tintinnabulo della tomba degli ori dell'Arsenale Militare di Bologna. Archaeologia Classica 23, 1971, 211-235.

Moscati 1991: S. Moscati (ed.), The Celts (Milano 2003).

Moulhérat 2003: C. Moulhérat, Les vestiges textiles. In: C. Rolley (ed.), La tombe princière de Vix (Paris 2003) 286-295.

Müller-Scheeßel 2013: N. Müller-Scheeßel, Untersuchungen zum Wandel hallstattzeitlicher Bestattungssitten in Süd- und Südwestdeutschland. Universitätsforschungen zur prähistorischen Archäologie 245 (Bonn 2013).

Nava/Salerno 2007: M. Nava/A. Salerno (eds.), Ambre. Trasparenze dall'antico (Milano 2007).

Nebelsick/Coblenz 1997: L. Nebelsick/W. Coblenz, Das prähistorische Gräberfeld von Niederkaina bei Bautzen 1 (Stuttgart 1997)

Norman 2011: C. Norman, Weaving, Gift and Wedding. A Local Identity for the Daunian Stelae. In: M. Gleba/H.W. Horsnæs (eds.), Communicating Identity in Italic Iron Age Communities (Oxford 2011) 34-49.

Pascucci 1990: P. Pascucci, I depositi votivi Paleoveneti. Per un'archeologia del culto. Archaeologia Veneta 13 (Padua 1990).

Pichlerová 1969: M. Pichlerová, Nové Košariská. Kniežacie mohyly zo staršej doby železnej (Bratislava 1969).

Putz 2007: U. Putz, Früheisenzeitliche Prunkgräber in Ober- und Mittelitalien. Archäologische Forschungen zur Entstehung temporärer Eliten. Regensburger Beiträge zur prähistorischen Archäologie 15 (Regensburg 2007).

Roymans 1991: N. Roymans, Late Urnfield Societies in the Northwest European Plain and the expanding networks of Central European Hallstatt Groups. In: N. Roymans/F. Theuws (eds.), Images of the past. Studies on ancient societies in nortwestern Europe (Amsterdam 1991) 9-89.

Ruta Serafini 2004: A. Ruta Serafini, Il mondo Veneto nell'età del Ferro. In: F. Marzatico/P. Gleirscher (eds.), Guerrieri, Principi ed Eroi fra il Danubio ed il Pò dalla Preistoria all'Alto Medioevo (Trento 2004) 276-283.

Säflund 1993: G. Säflund, Etruscan imagery. Symbol and meaning (Jonsered 1993).

Sassatelli 2013: G. Sassatelli, L'arte delle situle. In: M. Gamba/G. Gambacurta/A. Ruta Serafini/V. Tiné/F. Veronese (eds.), Venetkens. Viaggio nella terra dei Veneti antichi (Venezia 2013) 98-105.

Stroh 1979: A. Stroh, Das hallstattzeitliche Gräberfeld von Schirndorf, Ldkr. Regensburg III. Materialhefte zur bayerischen Archäologie 35 (Kallmünz/Opf. 1979).

Stroh 1988: A. Stroh, Das hallstattzeitliche Gräberfeld von Schirndorf, Ldkr. Regensburg III. Materialhefte zur bayerischen Archäologie 36 (Kallmünz/Opf. 1988).

Stroh 2000a: A. Stroh, Das hallstattzeitliche Gräberfeld von Schirndorf, Ldkr. Regensburg III. Materialhefte zur bayerischen Archäologie 37 (Kallmünz/Opf. 2000).

Stroh 2000b: A. Stroh, Das hallstattzeitliche Gräberfeld von Schirndorf, Ldkr. Regensburg IV. Materialhefte zur bayerischen Archäologie 38 (Kallmünz/Opf. 2000).

Torbrügge 1979: W. Torbrügge, Die Hallstattzeit in der Oberpfalz. Materialhefte zur bayerischen Vor- und Frühgeschichte 39 (Kallmünz/Opf. 1979).

Torelli 1997 : M. Torelli, Il rango, il mito e l'immagine. Alle origine della rappresentazione storica romana (Milano 1997).

Van der Vaart 2011: S. van der Vaart, Hail to the Chieftain. A detailed examination of grave goods from Dutch chiefly burials and their role in funerary rituals during the Hallstatt period. Unpublished Research Master thesis (Leiden 2011).

Von Eles 2002: P. von Eles (ed.), Guerriero e sacerdote. Autorità e comunità nell'età del ferro a Verucchio. La tomba del trono (Firenze 2002).

Von Eles 2006: P. von Eles, Il rituale funerario nel Villanoviano dell'Emilia Romagna: considerazioni alle luce di nuovi scavi e nuovi studi. In: P. von Eles (ed.), La ritualità funeraria tra età del Ferro e Orientalizzante in Italia (Pisa 2006) 67-78.

Von Eles 2007: P. von Eles, Le ore del sacro. Il femminile e le donne, soggetto e interpreti del divino? In: P. von Eles (ed.), Le ore e i giorni delle donne. Dalla quotidianità alla sacralità tra VIII e VII secolo a.C. (Verucchio 2007) 149-156.

Wagner-Hasel 2000: B. Wagner-Hasel, Der Stoff der Gaben. Kultur und Politik des Schenkens und Tauschens im archaischen Griechenland (Frankfurt 2000).

Wirth 1998: S. Wirth, Grabfunde der späten Bronzezeit und der Urnenfelderzeit von Augsburg-Haunstetten und Friedberg in Bayern. Ein Beitrag zur vorgeschichtlichen Besiedlung des Unteren Lechtals. Augsburger Beiträge zur Archäologie 1 (Augsburg 1998).

Woytowitsch 1978: E. Woytowitsch, Die Wagen der Bronze- und frühen Eisenzeit in Italien. Prähistorische Bronzefunde XVII,1 (Munich 1978).

Zürn 1987: H. Zürn, Hallstattzeitliche Grabfunde in Württemberg und Hohenzollern. Forschungen und Berichte zur Vor- und Frühgeschichte 25 (Stuttgart 1987).

Author

Christoph Huth
Institut für Archäologische
Wissenschaften
Abteilung Urgeschichtliche
Archäologie
Universität Freiburg
79085 Freiburg im Breisgau
christoph.huth@archaeologie.uni-
freiburg.de

Monika Kondziella
Institut für Archäologische
Wissenschaften
Abteilung Urgeschichtliche Archäologie
Universität Freiburg
79085 Freiburg im Breisgau
kondziella.monika@gmail.com

Identification and chronological aspects of western influence in northeast Alpine region of Hallstatt culture

Ladislav Chmelo

Abstract

The borders of Lower Austria, Burgenland, southern Moravia, southwestern Slovakia and Hungarian Transdanubia geographically determine the northeast alpine region of Hallstatt culture, territories of the Kalenderberg and Horákov cultures (ca. 800-400 BC). The Danube was intensively used for communication, and numerous interactions with the west-Hallstatt environment can be observed from the beginning of the Hallstatt period in this region. This contribution identifies objects and elements, which could be assessed as influences from the western Hallstatt culture into the northeastern Alpine region. It discusses the rate of acceptance and integration of western components into the development and representation of the Hallstatt culture. It analyses chronological and chorological aspects of these relations, which are projected on distribution maps. The most important communication route mediating those impulses was the Danube communication, which was intensively used during the Early Iron Age.

Zusammenfassung

Die nordostalpinen Hallstattgruppen (Kalenderberg- und Horákovkultur) finden sich geographisch im heutigen Niederösterreich, dem Burgenland, Südmähren, der südwestlichen Slowakei und dem ungarischen Transdanubien. Seit dem Beginn der Hallstattzeit lassen sich in der Region zahlreiche Interaktionen mit dem westlichen Hallstattkreis aufzeigen. Der Fokus dieses Beitrags liegt in der Identifizierung von Objekten und Merkmalen, die als westliche Einflüsse auf die nordostalpine Region angesehen werden können. Diskutiert werden zudem die Art und Intensität der Akzeptanz und Integration westlicher Komponenten in diese Gruppen. Anhand von Verbreitungskarten wird die choro- und chronologische Dynamik dieser Einflüsse herausgestellt. Hierbei zeigt sich klar die Bedeutung der Donau als Kommunikationsweg in der älteren Eisenzeit.

Introduction

The Early Iron Age is a dynamic period full of social and economic changes after almost a millennium of Urnfield culture developments. One of the dominant cultures from this period is the Hallstatt culture, spanning from Champagne and Ardennes to southwest Slovakia, during the 8th – 5th centuries BC. However, it was not a unified entity, but rather a conglomerate of multiple regionally limited cultural groups sharing basic similarities (Weiss 1999, 10-11). Cultural groups from this period are characterized by openness to cultural impulses in the material and ideological sphere. Numerous interactions of increasing intensity occurred in Europe, which could influence the environment or groups. Contacts with the Ancient World, which are more characteristic for its western *facies*, increased too.

On a theoretical level, I follow E. Studeníková's (1987) determination of the northern Alpine region of the Hallstatt culture, geographically covering Lower Austria, Burgenland, Transdanubia, southwestern Slovakia and southern Moravia. On the northern boundary, it encounters the Lusatian culture, the western boundary is formed by the river Enns and Bohemian-Moravian Highlands, and on the south it stretches towards the Styria and Balaton. The eastern boundary is the faintest and is determined by the expansion of so-called "Hallstatt culture of the central and northeastern Transdanubia" (Stegmann-Rajtár 2009, 57-116). From the cultural aspect, this region is represented by the expansion of Kalenderberg culture and Horákov culture and part of the Central and northeastern Transdanubian culture. Furthermore, from the terminological level of the text I could not avoid frequent use of the term 'western influence'. It refers to an object or phenomenon, which is within the observed time and space a foreign element and it comes directly or indirectly from the western Hallstatt environment. It can be adopted and utilized by the native population, but its origin is the western Hallstatt territory. This term is accepted in the archaeological literature (for example "westlicher Einfluss" in Rebay 2005). I realize its shortcomings (mainly in the meaning of the word influence) and treat it only as an auxiliary term.

This paper aims to identify objects and elements that could be influences from the western Hallstatt region, i.e. foreign non-domestic elements, penetrating into the studied area through cultural impulses as a material or ideological import from the western facies of the Hallstatt culture. These artifacts are valuable only within their basic typological categories. I am not dealing with the more detailed typology, definition of types and their variants, since it is irrelevant within the context of my paper. The ornamentation motifs are evaluated along with the pottery. In most cases I concentrate on closed archaeological contexts, which have greater information value and therefore can be anchored (although sometimes only in general terms) in a chronological development. For the integrity of complex archaeological discoveries and the sought objective to create a thorough database for these kinds of items it is secondarily supplemented also with the rescue excavations and the settlement material. Finds and find contexts are briefly described as deeper description would go beyond the extent of an article. In addition, as items of the western influence I consider also the profiled amber pearls, lignite bracelets, some specific parts of horse harness with analogies in the western Hallstatt territory, four-rosette fibulae and toiletries. The expansion and origins of these artifacts in their original environment, besides in the western Hallstatt territory and the argumentation of reasons why they should be identified as the western influence was already addressed by several authors (e.g. Kossack 1959; Stegmann-Rajtár 1992b; Studeníková 1987). Therefore, I do not individually describe their genesis, especially considering the limited extent of this contribution. I also will not discuss the appearance of the inhumation burial rite, which is very complex and complicated problematics of interactions between western and eastern regions of Hallstatt culture and its periphery. This contribution is first of a series of articles concerning western influence in northeastern Alpine region of Hallstatt culture and it is focused only on identification and chronological aspects of those relations. It also touches on the variable nature, cause and interpretation of western influence.

Swords

The northeastern Alpine territory of the Hallstatt culture represents the eastern peripheral zone of expansion of the bronze and iron Hallstatt swords (Studeníková 1987, 13). They are very rare and very few come from closed archaeological contexts. Moreover, many were found long ago, even without any archaeological context, or represent isolated finds. Despite this they are, thanks to their overall occurrence and being well-processed, a great dating resource.

Perhaps the best preserved bronze specimen is an isolated find from Trakovice (Paulík 1962, 119-122 fig. 1). It is a variant Muschenheim (Schauer 1971, 207), with a parallel in the bronze Gündlingen type sword from the flat cremation grave no. 78 in Moravian Klentnice dated to Ha C1a (Říhovský 1970, 43-54). The trinity of almost completely preserved bronze swords in the northeastern Hallstatt territory is concluded with an isolated find of a bronze sword from Dorog in Komárom-Esztergom county (Patek 1993, 93 fig. 73,12). I do not include the bronze sword from Čičovo (Barta/Willvonseder 1934, 4 fig. 1,1), because it resembles Bronze Age swords and may not date to the Hallstatt period. In addition, two fragments from the cremation double-grave with a stone cladding (tumulus X) from Bad Fischau can be determined as bronze swords (Szombathy 1924, pl. X,887), as can perhaps a triangular fragment of a blade point from tumulus VI in Nové Košariská, which were originally interpreted (Pichlerová 1969, 119; 180 pl. XLIII,1) as fragments of a dagger with an antenna-shaped pommel. However, Studeníková (1987, 14) refuted this interpretation. The original artifact cannot be reevaluated, but from the publication its interpretation as a sword is questionable. She also claims that the group of lightweight bronze Hallstatt swords developed in the more western parts of Central Europe. Their overall development scheme was elaborated by P. Schauer (1972, 261-270).

One of the most significant iron finds comes from Gemeinlebarn, tumulus 1. This burial mound excels within the given area nearly with all its characteristics. Its inventory has clear parallels in the western Hallstatt environment. It is an iron Mindelheim type sword with a wider tongue-shaped hilt and a long tang for securing a button (Kromer 1958, I a – b). The grave is thus dated to the Ha C1b – 2 (Tomba Database). Another sword from Somlóvásárhelyi tumulus 1, however, is lost (Egg 1996b, 330 fig. 3,1; Horváth 1969, 114 fig. 9). Similarly, this burial mound with a stone chamber and an entrance in the form of 'dromos' has one of the wealthiest inventories in this area, and can be related to barrows in southern Germany. An iron sword from Brno-Holásky tumulus 1 can also be assigned to the Mindelheim type (Červinka 1948, 13-19 fig. 7). Again, it was a skeletal grave under a mound with a wooden chamber in the environment of Horákov culture. From the cadastral area of Somlószőlős, location Séd, on the slope of the hill Somlóhegy (tumulus Doba I) and the cadastral area of village Doba (tumulus Doba II) originate two iron swords from disturbed burial mounds (Darnay *et al.* 1895, 317-324). The tumulus I, dated Ha C1b (Trachsel 2004, 421; Tomba Database) is stated to be in an inhumation grave, although many authors question this, arguing that this burial rite is absent Transdanubia (see the Tomba Database). The grave chamber of tumulus II had a rectangular, stone cladding. At first it was dated Ha C1 (Trachsel 2004, 421), but is currently dated Ha C2 (Tomba Database).

Further, the iron swords could include a badly preserved specimen from grave C from the flat burying ground in Maiersch (Berg 1962, pl. 311) with a

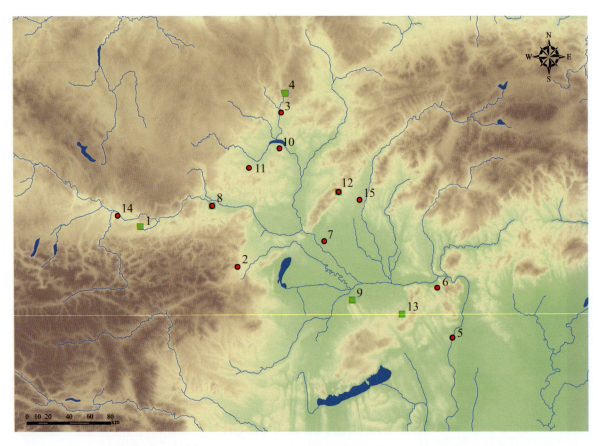

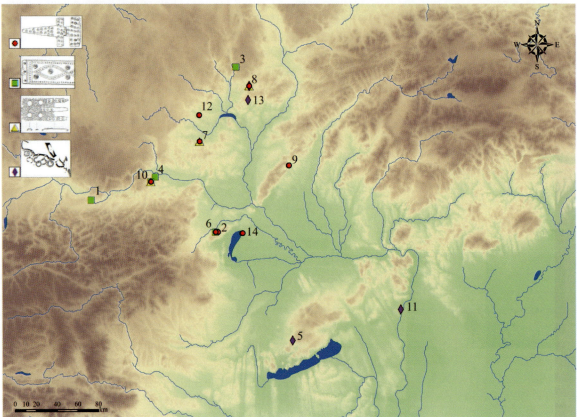

mushroom-shaped pommel on the hilt and an isolated find from St. Pantaleon in Lower Austria, where remains of organic material attached with two rivets have been preserved on the tang (Harreither/Kremslehner 1990, 208). From Slovakia an iron sword fragment is know from house no. 24 in the hill-fort Smolenice-Molpír (Dušek/Dušek 1984, pl. 181,17), which could be dated to the start of the 6th Century BC according to the accompanying material.

Discoveries of Hallstatt swords in the territory of the northeastern Hallstatt culture (Fig. 1) are western elements in the material culture in this area. The western nature of these artifacts is noticeable, for example, in the case of a specimen from grave 78 in Klentnice, where the entire accompanying inventory has parallels in the western Hallstatt territory. G. Kossack (1959, 23-24) writes, that they are a typical representative of the stage Ha C with the peak concentration in its first half. However, in the northeastern Hallstatt territory they can be observed during the entire Ha C phase. Furthermore, numerous swords can be observed in the Horákov culture, where they can be understood as a result of the influence from more western parts of Central Europe (Studeníková 1987, 15).

The occurrence of swords both in Germany and at the burial grounds in Hallstatt concentrates mainly in the wealthiest warrior graves (Kossack 1959; Kromer 1959). The situation in the Bylany culture is similar (Koutecký 1968, 400-401) and also in the northeastern Alpine territory (apart from isolated finds). Generally, they are accompanied by other weapons (spear, axe). Their representation on the flat burial grounds suggests a social stratification even within this type of burials (Romsauer 1976, 167).

Wagons and wagon parts

This kind of discovery are among the rarest within the northeastern Alpine territory (Fig. 1), but can be confirmed in only a few cases. However, the tradition of depositing wagons in graves is very typical throughout the entire western Hallstatt area.

The first known discovery is from Amstetten (Kromer 1960, 105-108), where poorly preserved 2.4 cm wide fragments of forged wheel parts were found. What is significant is the geographic localization of Amstetten on the fringe of the Lower Austria. The character of the burial and its inventory indicate stronger ties with southern Germany than with the northeastern Hallstatt territory.

Perhaps the best preserved is the wheel ironwork from the four-wheeled wagon from Somlóvásárhely, tumulus I. P. Romsauer analyzed this tumulus' inventory and compared it with the inventory of barrows from southern Germany. The newest dating of Somlóvásárhely tumulus I are Ha C1b (Tomba Database) or Ha C1 according to M. Trachsel (2004, 423). However, the excavation, as in the case of a specimen from Amstetten, was carried out at the beginning of the 20th century and its documentation is highly unclear. The capacity and quality of information about these burials make it impossible to analyses the grave plan or general archaeological context.

Two pieces of an axle-cap were discovered in Gemeinlebarn, tumulus 1 during a revision excavation, as well as a horse skeleton, two wheel hubs, scorched bronze fragments and a fire pit (Neugebauer 1997, 195-198).

Furthermore, also the flat bronze or iron rings, found in several archaeological contexts in the northeastern Hallstatt territory, are often considered wagon

Fig. 1 (previous page). Swords (circle), wagons and wagon parts (square):
1: Amstetten. – 2: Bad Fischau. – 3: Brno-Holásky. – 4: Býčí skála. – 5: Doba. – 6: Dorog. – 7: Dunajská Lužná-Nové Košariská. – 8: Gemeinlebarn. – 9: Györujbarát-Nagybarát. – 10: Klentnice. – 11: Maiersch. – 12: Smolenice-Molpír. – 13: Somlóvásárhely. – 14: St. Pantaleon. – 15: Trakovice.

Fig. 2 (previous page). Belts and belt parts. Bronze plate belts (square), belts with plate caps (triangle), belts consisting of rings (diamond) and organic belts with metal belt buckle (circle, i.e. double-crossed – 2, 6, 8, 10; wired – 10; "T"-shaped – 10, 12; rhombic – 7, 9). 1: Amstetten. – 2: Au am Leithagebirge. – 3: Býčí skála. – 4: Franzhausen. – 5: Halimba. – 6: Loretto. – 7: Maiersch. – 8: Slavkov u Brna. – 9:- Smolenice-Molpír. – 10: Statzendorf. – 11: Százhalombatta. – 12: Těšetice. – 13: Velké Hostěrádky. – 14: Weiden am See.

components. One of the discoveries, which presumably belongs to components of a wagon, is a set of these rings from Györujbarát-Nagybarát (Börzsönyi 1909, 245-253). E. Studeníková (1994, 25-47; Dušek/Dušek 1984, pl. 192,21) considers a bronze ring with triangular pendants from the hill-fort in Smolenice-Molpír as part of a linchpin, although, this interpretation is questionable. Other finds of these rings worth mentioning come from Vaszar (Horváth 1969, 125 fig. 25,1-3), Szalacska (Kemenzei 1974, 9 fig. 6,10), Csönge (Lazár 1955, pl. XXXII,14.16), including their southern parallel as well (Novo Mesto; Gabrovec 1968, 182). Their usage is so diverse, that unless they are accompanied by a linchpin, they cannot be included in this group with a certainty (Studeníková 1987, 54). Within the context of these finds, P. Romsauer speculates about the existence of a specific kind of a wagon, with different construction than the south German or Bylany specimens, which would be typical for the middle Danube basin (Romsauer 1976, 177). However, no more convincing evidence has been found, and neither the excavation documentation nor the artifacts are sufficient to assess whether we can speak of two or four-wheel wagons. The latter mentioned type is documented in the area of the Bylany culture and in southern Germany, where the character of finds from Somlovásárhely I and Amstetten incline to.

From the very end of the Hallstatt period, from the environments of Horákov culture, originates the reconstructed four-wheel wagon from the Býčí skála (Parzinger *et al.* 1995, pl. 103,1; pl. 112), which was analysed in detail and reconstructed by F.E. Barth (Parzinger *et al.* 1995, 97-115). It was discovered in a unique archaeological context with varying interpretations. It was reconstructed based on the remains of a wheel and ironwork from its body. However, it is presumed, that they represented parts from several incomplete wagons (different types of the wheel forgings). This wagon is dated to the stages Ha D2-3. It belongs to Pare's (1992, 159; 175-176) type 7 and is associated with the Late Hallstatt development. F.E. Barth (Parzinger *et al.* 1995, 182) further provides information on the austere remains of another wagon, type 3 according to Pare (1992, 152; 175-176), which is older and is represented exclusively in Ha C.

Moreover, we have other sources about wagons from the northern Hallstatt territory. Illustrations of the four-wheel wagons appear already on the ritual pottery from the older Hallstatt phase. On the neck of an amphora vessel from Sopron tumulus 80 (Gallus 1934, pl. II,5) is a wagon, on which stands a particular kind of a pyramid. The wagon from this illustration is part of an *ekphora*. An engraved scene on the neck of a vessel from tumulus 28 from the same site is similar (Eibner-Persy 1980, pl. 27-28). The surface of the wagon of this vessel is covered with a simplified checkerboard pattern, which according to E. Studeníková (1987, 56) can be considered a funeral cover by its context. Therefore, she assumes, that the use of wagons at least by the highest levels of society, and not only for funeral purposes, should be foreseen during the Hallstatt period. Furthermore, she contemplates that for the needs of a funeral ceremony (or placing to the burial chamber), symbolic whole-wooden wagons were made. Eventually, wagons were represented only by their individual components. In this context, rather interesting is the discovery of a cult wagon from a burial mound at Fertöendréd (Gomori 2010, 61-73) in Burgenland, several kilometres southeast of lake Neusiedl and only 22 km east of the Sopron barrow. This wagon is presented as a classic Kalenderberg pot-like vessel with a sculptural decoration on four wheels. The tumulus contained a cremation grave in a wooden chamber. Unfortunately, it was disturbed and it was impossible to observe the exact localization of the wagon. A highly similar vessel is known from Kánya (Csalog 1943, 41-49). This site is located to the south of Balaton and is generally dated to the Hallstatt period. The burial from Kánya exhibits similar inventory as previous cases, although it includes a larger number of vessels. The vessel has similar artworks already in previous period. Csalog (1943, 49) speaks of the continual surviving tradition of the cult of the dead in terms of the placement of wagon models into a grave. The context of the contempory bronze wagons from Strettweg (Egg 1996a), Frög (Egg 1987, 181-187), south Styrian Radkersburg (Egg 1986, 211 fig. 9) and already mentioned Kánya, can form a kind of parallel with the tradition of burials with wagons in the southern periphery of the northern Alpine up to the north of the southern Alpine territory. Yet, this tradition excludes a find interpreted as a wheel of such a wagon from Nová Dedinka (Studeníková 1994, 25-47 fig. 12,8-11). Its classification as a cult wagon is questionable. Another fragment of a wheel hub from a bronze wagon model comes from the hill-fort Smolenice-Molpír (Studeníková 1994, 25-47 fig. 12,2). E. Studeníková also addresses the wheel motif and associates it with the moon-shaped idols of the Kalenderberg culture. She mentions specimens from Chorvátsky Grob, where the wheels had multiple spikes and pronounced wheel hubs, which fully correspond with wheels from Hallstatt wagon (Studeníková 1987, 55-56).

E. Studeníková (1987, 55) further states that burials with wagons and its components occur on a vast territory from the Caucasus to the Iberian peninsula and also by the Mediterranean groups. Nonetheless, in the Hallstatt culture, they are typical for the territory of the southern Germany and Bylany culture (Koutecký 1968, 442; Pare 1992), G. Kossack (1970, 125; 129) presumes an easterly origin based on wagon construction details. Wagon wheels are in his opinion similar to Assyrian-Elamite wheels. Nevertheless, certain specimen from the northern Hallstatt environments are most likely related to their western parallels.

Belts and belt parts

In the inventory of the graves, these kinds of items also appear, of which several types can be determined as forms of the western influence. The most distinctive and simultaneously most sporadic are bronze plate belts (Fig. 2), often with rich decoration. Currently known specimens concentrate in Lower Austria with a unique exception in the Burgenland. They are completely absent in the central part of the northeastern Hallstatt territory. According to E. Studeníková (1987, 59), this phenomenon is associated with the use of a different type of garment and its components in the entire territory in general.

A bronze plate belt decorated with a point-pearl pattern was discovered in the already mentioned grave in Amstetten (Kromer 1960, pl. II,1a – b). The distribution map of the bronze plate belts (Kilian-Dirlmeier 1972, pl. 82) displays the concentration of this type of belts in the western Hallstatt territory, from where they spread northward to Thuringia and Saxony and eastward along the Danube (in this context, perhaps, Amstetten) and to Hallstatt itself. G. Kossack (1959, 71) correlates this with the main trade routes for salt or graphite, leading through Bavaria.

This claim has a broader application. It is not limited to belts and can be considered as one of the means of the distribution of Bavarian elements, or elements of southern German character to the northeastern Hallstatt territory. At this point it should therefore be noted that it is impossible to assess whether they represent the distribution of the elements directly from the southern Bavarian region or intermediated by the communities living in the area of the Salzkammergut in Austria. This relation can be observed while closely inspecting the belt from Amstetten. Although this group of artefacts indicates relationships with southern Germany, the decorative motifs on the belt have their parallels exclusively in the belts from the Hallstatt necropolis (Kromer 1959, pl. 226,1; pl. 230,15).

Another bronze plate belt comes from the wealthy grave A14 on the necropolis in Statzendorf, which was dated Ha D1 in older works according to the accompanying inventory to the stage (Dungel 1908, 13 fig. 46-53). After revision it is dated to phase 3-4 of Statzendorf, which represents Ha C1 – C2 (Rebay 2005, 290). It features a T-shaped plate buckle, with parallels in the Hallstatt necropolis (Romsauer 1976, 179). I. Killian-Dirlmeier (1972, 91-92) named it type Statzendorf and she also provides three specimens from the Hallstatt necropolis – grave 9, 367 and an unknown grave and one from Traubing – tumulus 11. The whole group is dated Ha D1. However, the belt was not discovered in its functional position, but near the deceased's feet (Rebay 2005, 171). A probable parallel with similar decoration is a severely damaged, burned plate belt from the Loretto cemetery which extends the distribution of these belts to the Burgenland area (Rebay 2005, 71).

Part of a Hallstatt period flat burial ground was discovered during highway construction in Traisental on the site Franzhousen. Only a brief report from this excavation was submitted, which states that a bronze plate belt decorated with a stud-shaped motif was found in the inhumation grave Verf. 524 (Neugebauer/ Gattringer 1988, 68 fig. 18,3-4). Only a photographic documentation of the grave is provided in the report, where the belt is visible only in rough outlines. J. W. Neugebauer (1993, fig. 31,2) mentions another dislocated belt from this site (by means of the contemporary "plundering"), discovered in pieces in archaeological contexts 747, 768 and 847, which was decorated with hallmarks. It most likely came from a cremation grave. Franzhausen is only 7 km from Statzendorf towards the Danube to the NE, from which it is only 3.5 km (even closer than Amstetten). It could represent yet another example of the distribution of these belts by means of the established trade routes. All of these belts, including their parallels, are primarily Ha D. T. Stöllner (2002, 94) sees their predecessors in the belts with a tongue-shaped buckle from this area.

Contrasting with the fully bronze specimens, are the belts from organic material with a plate belt buckle, decorated with bronze studs of various diameters arranged in patterns (Fig. 2). The most common is a domestic pattern in the form of a sun. It is most abundant in the territory of Lower Austria and is more widespread than the fully bronze belts (Studeníková 1987, 62). Their concentration in the Lower Austria is again explained by the close vicinity to the western Hallstatt territory, which assumes the appropriate conditions for the adaptation of the cultural elements streaming from the west. Romsauer (1976, 180) already created an inventory. They occur in tumulus I and II in Gemeinlebarn (Dungel/Szombathy 1890, 54), on the flat burial ground in Maiersch in grave 24 and 37 (Berg 1962, pl. 4,3; pl. 13,3-5) and in Statzendorf (Dungel 1908, 30 fig. 143; fig. 145-147). Studs from Statzendorf were discovered in the grave C001, which K. Rebay (2005, 290) dates to phase 3-4 of the necropolis, which corresponds with Ha C.

In the context of the elements of the western character found in the inventory of this grave, it is necessary to mention several ceramic shapes, for instance the ridged bowl, which had origins in the southern Bavaria and in Swiss environment (Kossack 1959, pl. 15; Stegmann-Rajtár 1992b, 67 fig. 18). The inventory of Gemeinlebarn tumulus I is dated Ha C2 (Stegmann-Rajtár 1992b, 85-86). It is therefore possible to accept the opinion of P. Romsauer (1976, 180), who claims that the absence of the rhomboid belt buckles indicates that they presumably are not younger than Ha D1.

This type of the belt fitting was identified also in Moravia in the environment of the Horákov culture. On the necropolis Slavkov u Brna, a wide and originally leather belt with applied studs and studs forming a geometric pattern was documented in grave 1. It featured a massive rectangular iron plate buckle (Dobisíková et al. 2010, 63 fig. 13,1-4). Although it has a different buckle and pattern, it consists of the same components as the belt from Maiersch grave 24. It was found in an inhumation grave, which was anthropologically assessed as presumably female. Due to this analysis and a pair of harp-shaped fibulae this belt is classified as part of the female garb (Dobisíková et al. 2010, 88). An analogical specimen preserved like this has not yet been discovered in Moravia. However, based on the specimen from grave 1 in Slavkov u Brna, authors interpret grave 6 from the same site in a similar manner (Dobisíková et al. 2010, 78 fig. 24,20). Their dating corresponds with other discoveries of this type of the belt fitting, namely Ha C2 in the case of grave 1 and generally Ha C in the case of grave 6 (Dobisíková et al. 2010, 93).

It is interesting, that Trachsel (2004, 440) classified completely analogical garnitures among the components of the horse trappings and wagons in the category "Besatz 01b Typ Thalmässing", principally as the applications of this element on the leather parts of horse trappings and yokes and they are also dated Ha C. Comparable function of the application of this element is on one analogy in the environment of the Bylany culture on the site Hradenín in grave 24 (Dvořák 1938, 46).

Another group, which occurs simultaneously with the previous one (e.g. mentioned Statzendorf C001), or without the decorative studs, are the organic belts with a metal belt buckle (Fig. 2), made either from plate or wire. These belts are geographically relatively widely distributed, although, they are most abundantly represented in the burial grounds of southern Germany (Kossack 1959, pl. 90,7; Torbrügge 1979, pl. 44,14; pl. 65,1).

The wirework specimens, consisting of fine wire, generally have T-shaped ends. A plainer specimen comes from grave A013 on the necropolis in Statzendorf (Rebay 2005, pl. 13), dated by the accompanying pottery to the turn of Ha C1/Ha C2 (Rebay 2005, 290). An almost identical belt buckle was found in grave A104 (Rebay 2005, pl. 78). Unfortunately, only a negligible and fire-damaged fragment was preserved. P. Romsauer (1976, 182) looks for parallels for the specimen from Statzendorf grave A013 in northern Italy, Este, Bologna-Savenna and Bologna-San Vitale. One of the most evolved shapes of this type of buckle was found in the tumulus in Nagybarát (Börzsönyi 1909, 250 fig. 3).

Belts with bronze or iron plate buckles come in various shapes. Rhombic shapes, shapes in the form of the letter "T", rectangular and doubled cross plates are all documented.

Very distinctive are the doubled cross plates. One bronze specimen decorated with concentric rings was discovered in the already mentioned Statzendorf grave C001 (Dungel 1908, 30 fig. 143; Rebay 2005, pl. 149), accompanied by studs of the previous group. It was repaired in the past – there are two broken parts visible, reconnected with a bronze rivet. A parallel was found in grave 120 on necropolis in Loretto, Burgenland, (Rebay 2005, 172) and in Au am Leithagebirge, only 2 km from Loretto (Seracsin 1929, 229-237 fig. 6,6). P. Romsauer (1976, 182) states that these buckles appear in Slovenia already during the Urnfield culture, where they are reflected in the variant Slepšek and with the onset of the Hallstatt period they appear in Austria, with the highest concentration in Hallstatt. In my opinion, these belt buckles could have spread into the northeastern Alpine territory through the Hallstatt necropolis, where they are relatively numerous (e.g. Kromer 1959, pl. 3,31; pl. 17,1; pl. 32,8; among others). A cross-shaped iron plate buckle from grave C003 can be considered a simpler variant of this type (Dungel 1908, 33 fig. 155; Rebay 2005, pl. 152). Rebay assigned this type to the plates with T-shaped buckles. This variant is represented in the Horákov culture in Těšetice grave 5 (Podborský 1960, 643-650) and was documented at Slavkov u Brna in the cremation grave of an adult dated to the Ha C phase and was accompanied by pottery of western character, influenced by the Bylany culture and southern Bavaria (Dobisíkova et al. 2010, 72 fig. 21,14; 78 fig. 24,11-12.16).

Younger are rhombic shaped variants. Two specimens were found in a grave at Maiersch (Berg 1962, pl. 18,5.7). Both had their ends bent to outwards, forming the T-shape. One rhombic-shaped buckle comes from the Smolenice-Molpír hill-fort (Dušek/Dušek 1995, pl. 25,11). According to Kossack (1959, 32 pl. 154C) they are typical in southern Bavaria during Ha D, where they also reach the highest concentration.

The last variant of the belt buckles with a rectangular metal plate. They are again represented in the Maiersch necropolis (Berg 1962, pl. 13,1-2.6). They extend the variety of the belt on this necropolis, where this type of artefact is considerably abundant. Another, significantly corroded specimen was found at Weiden am See in Burgenland (Pescheck 1943, 152 pl. 6,9). They represent one of the simplest shapes and cannot be exactly narrowly dated (Romsauer 1976, 183).

Entirely different type of the belt garniture consists of rings (mainly iron), which usually have eyelets pinned with tiny rivets and are fashioned at the ends (Fig. 2). They are probably all that survived of belts made from organic material – presumably leather. For instance, a visible textile imprint was preserved in the corrosion of the specimen from Slavkov u Brna grave 2 (Dobisíkova at. al. 2010, 68 fig. 18,16). It was documented *in situ* in its functional position. This grave also yielded two heavily corroded spears and an iron bit, i.e. the typical male inventory. This is supported also by the anthropological designation of "probably male" (Dobisíkova *et al.* 2010, 89). A similar case from the Horákov culture can be observed in the wealthy grave in Bratčice, where this belt garniture appears in connection with a warrior's equipment (Kos 1999, 337-338). Fragmentary parts of these belts were also found in Transdanubia. Eyelets with rivets on rings, combined with pendants in the shape of a bird head were found in Györujbarát-Nagybarát, tumulus I (Patek 1993, 112 fig. 91,10.12-13,15-18). It should be noted, that yet again, components of the horse trappings, two axes and as stated above, questionably interpreted parts of a wagon were discovered here too. In addition, possible components of this type of belt were found in Százhalombatta in barrow 118 (Patek 1993, 137 fig. 110,19) and in Halimba-Cseres, graves 1 and 14 (Patek 1993, 88 fig. 68,22-25; 90 fig. 70,1-5.8). Both graves are dated Ha C2 (Patek 1993, 49 fig. 34). Identical dating for Halimba, in general, is also given by Stegmann-Rajtár, who also dates the site Györujbárt-Nagybarát to the same period (1992b, 100; 106). Furthermore, components of these belts are represented at the Hallstatt necropolis in graves 192, 388 and 469 (Kromer 1959, pl. 8,16; pl. 25,10; p. 62,5-11; pl. 83,5-6) and also in the environment of the Bylany culture at Rvenice (Koutecký 2003, pl. 11,3-4; pl. 14B). This type of belt is, however, insufficiently processed and it is necessary to review all the older discoveries with the aim to identify the components of this type of belt in other grave contexts, because, as it is clear from the situation sketched by Dobisíkova *et al.* (2010, 88-89), they can be expected in this territory.

The belt garnitures mentioned above, are geographically concentrated in Lower Austria, although it seems that it will be possible to observe them in several regional areas. A certain overlap from Lower Austria is appearing on its boundary with Burgenland and another concentration is also in Moravia in the environment of the Horákov culture. It can be assumed, that the garb from Lower Austria in certain aspects closely approached the garb of the western Hallstatt cultural territory. This statement can be partially applied to the area of southern Moravia, which along these lines exhibits numerous relations with the Lower Austrian area, though with their own regional traditions.

Pins

The vast majority of garment pin types originate from domestic contexts, already present in the Late Urnfield culture and continuously existing during the Hallstatt period (e.g. pins with a double-conical head, with a small rounded head). Some types come from the templates in the Adriatic and southeastern Alpine territory (pin with a multiple head and conical clasp). Apart from those groups, garment pins of the western provenance also appear.

The younger pins with bowl-shaped heads (Fig. 3) and straight bodies are based on those with bowl-shaped heads and ribbed bodies from Ha B1-3. Their development is evidenced in Beckerloch, tumulus 10 in Bavaria through a transitory form with a hemispherical head and a small rib under the neck. In the northeastern Alpine territory it is represented by two examples at the Statzendorf necropolis. One specimen is from cremation grave A023 and dated to Ha C (Rebay 2005, 27 pl. 21). In the second case, J. Říhovský (1979, 216 pl. 65,1792) only states that it was found in a flat burial ground. Its archaeological context is, therefore, unknown. A fragment of an analogous pin was found as a solitary discovery in the territory of the Horákov culture at Sobůlky (*Říhovský 1979, 216 pl. 65,1790*). Their distribution was processed by K. Tackenberg (1934, 188-189 map 40). The largest concentration can be observed in the area to the north and east of the town Harz in central Germany, between the rivers Ems and Hase and in northern Germany around Lüneburg. From here, they were further distributed to the north of Holstein, Denmark and southern Scandinavia and, being isolated, even to eastern Germany. A smaller number of pins of this type is represented in the Czech Republic and to the north of the Krušné Hory (Říhovský 1979, 217). In Upper Austria they were found in the cemetery of Linz-St. Peter (Adler 1965, 170-171 fig. 3).

Pins with a swan-shaped neck (which can have various tips; Fig. 3) are primarily found in the western Hallstatt territory. Two distinctive concentrations appear in the Horákov cultural environment and in Lower Austria. Within settlement contexts, these pins are documented at Brno-Obřany, where it was found in feature 4 along with five spindle whorls, on the site Troubsko and on the elevated settlement in Křenovice, dating to the younger Hallstatt period (Říhovský 1979, 224-225 pl. 67,1852-1853.1863). One specimen is known from the Horákov culture cremation grave in Určice and Dolnoplazy. Two specimens come from the wealthy inhumation grave 2 in Vedrovice (Stegmann-Rajtár 1992a, pl. 137,6-7) and in Dobšice, where it was accompanied by a pin with a double-spiral head and bracelet with spiral-ends (Říhovský 1979, pl. 67,1861). They were also represented in in graves 22 (2 pieces) and 25 (1 piece) at Vojkovice (Golec 2005, 166). In Lower Austria, two specimens from the flat burial ground in St. Andrä are known. One comes from grave 2, the other from grave 6 and they are both dated to Ha C (Krenn 1935, 76 fig. 10,18). In grave A024 of Statzendorf a variant with a spherical head was found (Rebay 2005, 284 pl. 22). In addition, they are represented in eastern Austria by one specimen from the site Waidendorf, which lies by the river Moravia (Hahnel 1985/86, 253 fig. 322). Garment pins with a swan-shaped neck occur in several variants, primarily dating Ha C, with a continuation to the end of the Hallstatt period. They are widespread across Central Europe and in southern Sweden. However, their main area of expansion is central and northern Germany, Pfalz and Bavaria (Říhovský 1979, 227).

Although, the issue is the provenance of the pins with a double-spiral head. Kossack (1959, pl. 153B) states that they are of western origin. J. Říhovský associates them with Greater Poland, as demonstrated by the fact, that within Slovak contexts, with the exclusion of Šarovce, they can be evidenced only in the Lusatian culture (Novotná 1980, 162-164) and that they correlate with the older period. M. Novotná seeks their origins in Eastern Europe. The pins with a large double-spiral head form a closely related group, which has its center undoubtedly in the western territory (southern Bavaria, Salzburg). In the northeastern Hallstatt territory, in addition to the already mentioned artefacts, is represented another pin in Dobšice and in Statzendorf grave A023. Taking a closer look at the accompanying inventory brings out an interesting fact. In both graves artefacts of western character were among the accompanying inventory. In the case of Dobšice it is the already mentioned pin with a swan-shaped neck and in Statzendorf the pin with a bowl-shaped head and straight body and also the pottery of western provenance.

The last type of garment pin which indicates relations with the western environments is a pin with a rosette head (Fig. 3). Its occurrence within the northeastern Hallstatt territory is rather sporadic and contextual information only fragmentary. Two specimens were documented. One is the solitary discovery from Bad Deutsch-Altenburg (Adler 1987, 220 fig. 308). The second comes from the Gemer region from the year 1882, presumably from a deposit (Novotná 1980, 156 pl. 44,1040). These finds correspond with artefacts from the areas of Upper Palatinate in sites Oberwiesenacker and Beratzhausen and with the solitary discovery from Starý Kolín in the Czech Republic (Novotná 1980, 157).

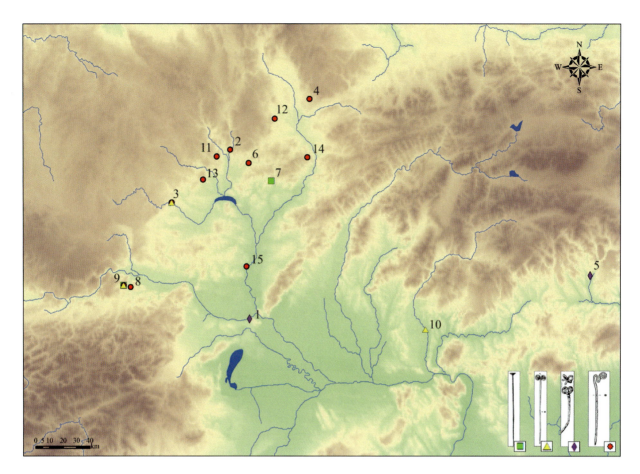

Pottery

The foreign elements appear even in this type of artefacts of material culture in the northeastern Alpine territory. A part of them is of western provenance. They can be divided into two groups. The first consists of ceramic shapes of a non-domestic origin, which include ridged bowls, so called *Knickwandschalen*, plate-like bowls, bowls with a funnel-shaped mouth, larger bulbous shapes with a collar-shaped mouth, bowls with ridged bottom, amphora-like vessels with shortened conical neck and funnel-shaped mouth and archaic vessels with funnel-shaped mouth set on a bulbous body (Fig. 4). The second group is represented by the decorative motifs, which are applied not only on the foreign shapes and forms, but also on the classic vessels of the Kalenderberg culture. These are motifs created by a decorating wheel tool, stamped motifs, garland motifs, grid, rhombus and also black and red paint. The issue of imported or domestic production of these articles is complex, nevertheless, some domestic shapes with the application of western elements assist in its resolution. The general transport of pottery in such abundance, as can be observed in the northeastern Hallstatt territory, is improbable at greater distances due to the fragile nature of the material. Deeper analyses of pottery will be focus of further articles.

Discussion

Diffusion of foreign elements from the western cultural environment can be observed in the northeast Alpine region from the beginning of the Early Iron Age. Process of appearance and acceptance of those impulses did not occur simultaneously in the whole area. Most significantly in terms of acceptance of elements are Lower Austria concentrating in the Traisen river valley and the territory of Horákov culture of southern Moravia. The process of hallstattization occurred similarly in both areas. This is certainly connected with their geographic position on the borders of western Hallstatt culture area. After evaluation of those processes and their projection to culture it needs to be concluded that elements of western influence appear in the northeast Alpine region in multiple levels with whole different character.

Early in the Hallstatt period in this region there must have been individuals or small groups coming down the Danube river stream to area of Lower Austria and south Moravia. They are manifested by burials with specific inventories, which fully consist of artefacts of western influence both in pottery and garniture. Inhumation burial rite is not required (for example graves Statzendorf A035 and A062; Rebay 2005, 37; 57; Klentnice 78 and 114; Říhovský 1970, 43-54). Those individuals are bearers of cultural impulses previously unknown in the area. Question of cause and purpose of their presence cannot be answered yet. The largest part of cultural exchange and penetration of cultural impulses in this direction took the Danube Road. They could have been merchants or craftsmen in motion within newly formed conditions of Hallstatt period or prospecting activity in order to find new resources. The Traisen river valley stands out in this context. It benefits on the one hand from its geographical position, on the other hand can be considered important due to its wealth of mineral resources. The Traisen river valley forms the eastern border of Dunkelsteinwald, which is a natural source of graphite. On the western edge of the valley, on the Danube terrace is situated Melk with imports from western Hallstatt culture, even though there are no modern excavations because of recent infrastructure. Although evidence of prehistoric mining from around Dunkelsteinwald is not proven yet, in my opinion this cannot be excluded. The Traisen river valley could in some sense also fulfil a trade-exchange-manufacturing

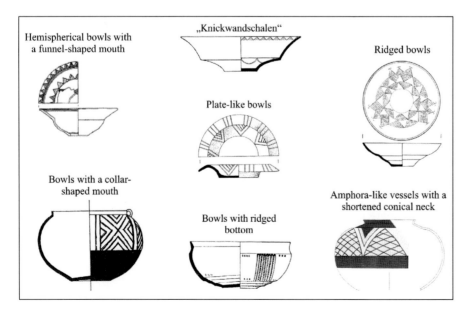

Fig. 4. Western types of pottery in northeast Alpine region. Hemispherical bowls with a funnel-shaped mouth (after Hellerschmidt/Penz 2004, 183 Abb. 5,7); "Knickwandschalen" (after Stegmann-Rajtár 1992a, pl. 68,1); Ridged bowls (after Stegmann-Rajtár 1992a, pl. 27,2); Plate-like bowls (after Stegmann-Rajtár 1992a, pl. 4,8); Bowls with a collar-shaped mouth (after Berg 1962, pl. 17,2); Bowls with ridged bottom (after Stegmann-Rajtár 1992a, pl 45,3); Amphora-like vessels with a shortened conical neck (after Lochner 1988, 124 Taf. 7,1).

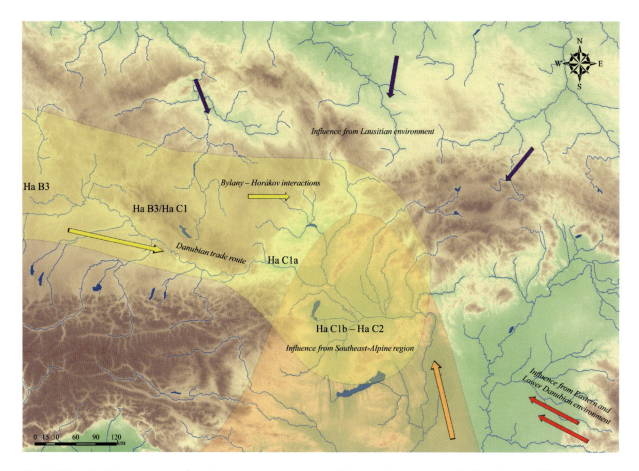

Fig. 5. Chronological aspect of western influence in Northeast-Alpine region.

function. In concentration of sites in lower parts of valley, there is Wagram an der Traisen with more than 12,000 objects, inhabited since the Late Urnfield period until Early La Tène, with plentiful evidence of manufacturing (Neugebauer 1997, 185-186). However this settlement was not fully excavated. A similar situation can be observed in the Smolenice-Molpír hillfort.

A second level of interpretation is connected with the rate of acceptance of those cultural impulses by indigenous populations. It needs to be stressed that acceptance of such elements is possible only by a population with a stabilized and consolidated environment. I suppose that their acceptance was a part in the process of consolidation of relations in the beginning of the Hallstatt age. This statement is primarily valid for the most western part of northeast Alpine region. Cultural processes there are part of the transformation of Late Bronze Age society to its Hallstatt form. A class of people, who are able to accept those impulses is separated from the rest of society during Ha C. As this process disrupted long and strict traditions in burial rites, it had to represent in-depth transformation. This change largely chronologically and chorologically corresponds with the emergence of artefacts with western influence. Based on the finds from Lower Austria and southern Moravia I assume that in the case of indigenous population this can be perceived as 'change from above', even though these processes can be observed already at the beginning of formation of so-called 'elites'. This group of people or social *strata* reshapes and transforms their thinking, beliefs, traditions and way of life under foreign models. It is reflected in archaeological sources in adopting and inclusion of specific parts of garniture. Populations adapt to the newly formed

Hallstatt era and accept ideological and cultural impulses flowing to this area from the centers of the Hallstatt culture. Remote contacts are supported by large-scale social interactions. That is why values and ideological ideas also are shared to a limited extent. The find contexts do not only indicate that the western environment in northeast Alpine region is reflected in imports and acceptance of several types of pottery and garniture, but it definitively influenced thinking and habits of forming eastern Hallstatt culture, which is displayed also in the metaphysical sphere and art. Together with strong urnfield 'base' and tradition they are main components of genesis and shape of Hallstatt culture in western parts of the northeast Alpine region.

Social differentiation intensifies later on with the appearance of rich tumuli of the elite in the second half of Ha C1 and Ha C2. Those tumuli already combine influences from different regions. In the eastern part of the region the Urnfield culture tradition survived slightly longer. Development is disrupted by intervention of a nomadic component coming from the east during the Bronze – Iron Age transition. Consolidation of relations is established in younger stages of Hallstatt culture. However those are dominated by influence from south and southeastern centers, which behaves similarly as western influence in western part of northeast Alpine region in Ha C1. The Lower Danube river stream region also played a significant role in the development of this eastern part.

Conclusion

Within the space of the northeastern Alpine territory, foreign elements and cultural impulses appear at the beginning of the Hallstatt period. The paramount communication, mediating these impulses, was the Danube Road, which was intensively used during this period. It is possible to observe a clear route of the spread of the western elements, which originates mainly in Bavaria, Pfalz and northeastern Switzerland. These elements are gradually distributed along the flows of the Danube to Upper Austria with a significant concentration around Linz (Fig. 5). As indicated, the archaeological contexts from Lower Austria and southern Moravia exhibit strong relations to this territory, what is a logical consequence of their neighbouring geographical localization. Through the Danube Road, these elements were distributed to Lower Austria, with the highest concentration in the valley of the lower flow of the river Traisen. This region presumably benefited from its advantageous geographical localization on the Danube. I stress that the results could be biased by intensive research activities during the construction of the highway which leads right through this valley, and it is possible that the solitary finds on the Austrian river bank of the Moravia may reflect only the state of research and not reality. However, it seems, that the majority of the western elements can be traced in the area of distribution of the 'Statzendorf-Gemeinlebarn' type and to the south and east the intensity of these relations decreases. This influence spreads into the territory of the Horákov culture through the digressions of the Danube Road as well as by numerous interactions with the Bylany culture, as can be observed in the grave inventories of the Horákov culture. Furthermore, it is possible to trace the chronological aspect of these relationships. Many of the elements described are already represented in southern Bavarian during the Urnfield culture in Ha B3. In Upper Austria around Linz, they can be observed in the earliest graves from the Hallstatt period in Ha B3 – C1. They expand to the western parts of the northeastern Alpine territory in Ha C1a. Nevertheless, the development of the eastern part of the northeastern Alpine territory is slightly different. The traditions from the Late Urnfield culture survive here, even during the older Hallstatt period. In the stage Ha C1b, but mainly in Ha C2, it is possible to trace the western influence even in Transdanubia, regarding the wealthiest warrior barrows, in which it represents the imported luxurious and status-related items. The inventory of these graves, however, consists of various components. A strong component which manifests not only in the material culture, but in the construction of the burial chambers from the quarried stone with a dromos, can be credited to the influence from the southern Alpine territory. The consolidation of relationships occurs mainly during the Late Hallstatt period. In connection with the development of the production forces along with the culmination of the social differentiation, new hill-forts are built, which probably acted as the centres of power. Their strong social and economic status is evidenced by the high concentration of the luxurious items, which are uncommon in this territory (Smolenice-Molpír, Velem). This territory exhibits signs of strong relations with the southern Alpine territory, although, the western influence spreads even to the wider Bratislava region and to the hill-fort Smolenice-Molpír. The cultural impulses of southeastern character become dominant during the later Hallstatt period. They also reach Lower Austria and are reflected in the material culture (e.g. bow-shaped fibulae, boat-shaped fibulae).

Acknowledgments

This publication is a part of the author's master thesis, which was led by prof. P. Romsauer, CSc. at the Department of archaeology, Constantine the Philosopher University, Nitra and is the result of the implementation of the project VEGA MŠ SR Reg. No. 1/0208/15: "Man and mountains over time – from prehistoric hill-forts to medieval castles" and the project UGA I-15-203-02 "Vývoj spoločnosti a kultúrne kontakty v mladšom praveku na území stredného Podunajska".

Bibliography

Adler 1965: H. Adler, Das Urgeschichtliche Gräberfeld Linz-St. Peter 1. Linzer Archäologische Forschungen 2 (Linz 1965).

Adler 1987: H. Adler, Bad Deutsch Altenburg. Grafenwörth. Fundberichte aus Österreich, 1987, 26, 219.

Barta/Willvonseder 1934: H. Barta/K. Willvonseder, Zur ur- und frühgeschichtlichen Besiedlung der Grossen Schütt. Sudeta 19, 1934, 1-22.

Berg 1962: F. Berg, Das Flachgräberfeld der Hallstattkultur von Maiersch. Mittielungen der Österreichischen Arbeitsgemeinschaft für Ur- und Frühgeschichte 4 (Wien 1962).

Börzsönyi 1909: A. Börzsönyi, Györmegyei emlékek a hallstatti korszakból. Archaeologiai Értesítő 29, 1909, 245-253.

Csalog 1943: Z. Csalog, Hallstattzeitliche Wagenurne aus Kánya. Komitat Tolna, Ungarn. Archaeologiai Értesítő, 1943, 41-49.

Červinka 1948: I. Červinka, Holásky (okr. Brno). Mohyly s halštatskými hroby na "Čtvrtích od Tuřan". Časopis Vlastenekého spolku musejního v Olomouci, 57, 1948, 13-19.

Darnay et al. 1895: K. Darnay/K. Kleiszl/A. Száraz, Két Nagy-Somló-Melléki lelet a Hallstatt Korból. Archaeologiai Értesítő, 15, 1895, 317-324.

Dobisíková *et al.* 2010: M. Dobisíková/M. Geisler/J. Kala/P. Kos/Z. Mikulková/D. Parma, Halštatské pohřebiště ze Slavkova u Brna (okr. Vyškov). In: Popolnicové polia a doba halštatská. Zborník referátov z X. medzinárodnej konferencie "Popolnicové polia a doba halštatská". Košice, 16.-19. September 2008 (Nitra 2010) 57-97.

Dungel 1908: A. Dungel, Die Flachgräber der Hallstattzeit bei Statzendorf in Niederösterreich. Mitteilungen der Prähistorischen Kommission 2,1, 1908, 1-39.

Dungel/Szombathy 1890: A. Dungel/J. Szombathy, Die Tumuli von Gemeinlebarn. Mitteilungen der Prähistorischen Kommission 1, 1890, 49-79.

Dušek/Dušek 1984: M. Dušek/S. Dušek, Smolenice-Molpír. Befestigter Fürstensitz der Hallstattzeit I (Nitra 1984).

Dušek/Dušek 1995: M. Dušek/S. Dušek, Smolenice-Molpír. Befestigter Fürstensitz der Hallstattzeit II (Nitra 1991).

Dvořák 1938: F. Dvořák, Knížecí pohřby na vozech ze starší doby železné (Praha 1938).

Egg 1986: M. Egg, Zum "Fürstengrab" von Radkersburg (Südsteiermark). Jahrbuch des Römisch-Germanischen Zentralmuseums 33, 1986, 199-214.

Egg 1987: M. Egg, Zum Bleiwagen von Frög in Kärnten. In: Vierrädige Wagen der Hallstattzeit Monographien des Römisch-Germanischen Zentralmuseums 12 (Mainz 1987) 181-187.

Egg 1996a: M. Egg, Das Hallstattzeitliche Fürstengrab von Strettweg bei Judenburg in der Obersteiermark. Monographien des Römisch-Germanischen Zentralmuseums 37 (Mainz 1996).

Egg 1996b: M. Egg, Einige Bemerkungen zum hallstattzeitlichen Wagengrab von Somlóvásárhely, Kom. Veszprém in Westungarn. Jahrbuch des Römisch-Germanischen Zentralmuseums 43, 1996 (1998) 327-353.

Eibner-Persy 1980: A. Eibner-Persy, Hallstattzeitliche Grabhügel von Sopron (Ödenburg). Wissenschaftliche Arbeiten aus dem Burgenland 62 (Eisenstadt 1980).

Gabrovec 1968: S. Gabrovec, Grob s trinožnikom z Novego mesta. Archeološki vestnik 19, 1968, 157-188.

Gallus 1934: S. Gallus, A soproni Burgstall alakos urnái. Archaeologia Hungarica 13, 1934, 53-54.

Golec 2005: M. Golec, Horákovská kultura. Unpublished doctoral dissertation (Brno 2005).

Gomori 2010: J. Gomori, Ein Grab der Osthallstattkultur mit Kultwagen aus Fertoendréd (Kom. Sopron, Ungarn). In: E. Jerem/M. Schönfelder/G. Wieland: Nord-Süd, Ost-West. Kontakte während der Eisenzeit in Europa. Akten der Internationalen Tagungen der AG Eisenzeit in Hamburg und Sopron 2002. Archaeolingua 17 (Budapest 2010) 61-73.

Hahnel 1985/86: B. Hahnel, Waidendorf. Fundberichte aus Österreich 24/25, 1985/86, 250.

Harreither/Kremslehner 1990: R. Harreither/K. Kremslehner, St. Pantaleon. Fundberichte aus Österreich 29, 1990, 208.

Hellerschmidt/Penz 2004: I. Hellerschmidt/M. Penz, Die Befestigte Siedlung Stillfried a. d. March am Übergang von der Bronze- zur Eisenzeit. In: Popelnicová pole a doba halštatská. Příspěvky z VIII. konference, České Budějovice 22. 24. 9. 2004. Archeologické výzkumy v jižních Čechách Supplementum 1. Jihočeské muzeum (České Budějovice 2004) 167-192.

Horváth 1969: A. Horváth, A vaszari és somlóvásárhely Hallstattkori halomsírok. A Veszprém megyei muzeumok kozleményei 8, 1969, 109-134.

Kemenzei 1974: T. Kemenzei, Ujabb leletek a nagyberki-szalacskai koravaskori halomsírokból. Archaeologiai Értesítő 101, 1974, 3-14.

Killian-Dirlmeier 1972: I. Killian-Dirlmeier, Die hallstattzeitlichen Gürtelbleche und Blechgürtel Mitteleuropa. Prähistorische Bronzefunde XII,1 (München 1972).

Kos 1999: P. Kos, Bratřice (okr. Brno). Přehled Výskumů 39, 1999, 337-338.

Kossack 1959: G. Kossack, Südbayern während der Hallstattzeit. Römisch-Germanische Forschungen 24 (Berlin 1959).

Kossack 1970: G. Kossack, Gräberfelder der Hallstattzeit an Main und Fränkischer Saale. Materialhefte zur bayerischen Vorgeschichte 24 (Kallmünz/Opf 1970).

Koutecký 1968: D. Koutecký, Velké hroby, jejich konstrukce, pohřební ritus a sociální struktura obyvatelstva bylanské kultury. Památky archeologické 69, 1968, 400-484.

Koutecký 2003: D. Koutecký, Příspěvky k době halštatské v severozápadních Čechách (Most 2003).

Krenn 1935: K. Krenn, Hallstattzeitliche Flachgräber von St. Andrä, N. Ö. Wiener prähistorische Zeitschrift 21, 1935, 63-73.

Kromer 1958: K. Kromer, Gemeinlebarn Hügel l. Inventaria Archaeologica, Österreich 2A,11 (Bonn 1958).

Kromer 1959: K. Kromer, Das Gräberfeld von Hallstatt (Firenze 1959).

Kromer 1960: K. Kromer, Ein hallstattzeitliches Wagengrab aus Amstetten, NÖ. Mitteilungen der Anthropologischen Gesellschaft Wien, 1960, 90, 105-108.

Lazár 1955: J. Lazár, Hallstattkori tumulusok a Sághegy távolabbi környékéröl. Archaeologiai Értesítő 82, 1955, 202-211.

Lochner 1988: M. Lochner, Ein Flachgräberfeld der Hallstattkultur in Grafenwörth, pol. Bez. Tulln, Niederösterreich. Archaeologia Austriaca 72, 1988, 91-142.

Neugebauer 1993: J. W. Neugebauer, Rettungsgrabungen im Unteren Traisental in den Jahren 1992 und 1993. Fundberichte aus Österreich 32, 1993, 443-460.

Neugebauer 1997: J. W. Neugebauer, Beiträge zur Erschliessung der Hallstattkultur im Zentralraum Niederösterreichs. In Nebelsick/Eibner/Lauermann/Neugebauer (eds.): Hallstattkultur im Osten Österreichs (St. Pölten-Wien 1997) 165-190.

Neugebauer/Gattringer 1988: J. W. Neugebauer/A. Gattringer, Rettungsgrabungen im Unteren Traisental im Jahre 1988. Fundberichte aus Österreich 27, 1988, 65-98.

Novotná 1980: M. Novotná, Die Nadeln in der Slowakei. Prähistorische Bronzefunde XIII,6 (München 1980).

Paulík 1962: J. Paulík, Bronzový halštatský meč z Trakovíc. Študijdné Zvesti AÚ SAV 9, 1962, 119-122.

Pare 1992: C. Pare, Wagons and wagon-graves of the Early Iron Age in Central Europe. Oxford University Commitee for Archaeology Monographs 35 (Oxford 1992).

Parzinger *et al.*1995: H. Parzinger/J. Nekvasil/F. Barth, Die Býčí Skála-Höhle. Ein hallstattzeitlicher Höhlenopferplatz in Mähren. Römisch-Germanische Forschungen 54 (Mainz am Rhein 1995).

Patek 1993: E. Patek, Westungarn in der Hallstatzeit. Acta humaniora, Quellen und Forschungen zur prähistorischen und provinzialrömischen Archäologie 7 (Weinheim 1993).

Pescheck 1943: C. Pescheck, Die junghallstättischen Grabhügelfunde von Krensdorf, Marz und Weiden am See, Mitteilungen der Prähistorischen Kommission 4/6, 1943, 152-186.

Pichlerová 1969: M. Pichlerová, Nové Košariská. Kniežacie mohyly zo staršej doby železnej (Bratislava 1969).

Podborský 1960: V. Podborský, Halštatské pořebiště v Těšeticích na Moravě. Archeologické rozhledy 12, 1960, 643-650.

Rebay 2005: K. Rebay, Das hallstattzeitliche Graberfeld von Statzendorf, Niederosterreich. Universitätsforschungen zur Prähistorischen Archäologie 135 (Bonn 2005).

Romsauer 1976: P. Romsauer 1976, Počiatky a vývoj doby halštatskej v strednom Podunajsku, kandidátska práca (Bratislava 1976).

Říhovský 1970: J. Říhovský, Halštatské hroby na pohřebišti v Klentnici. In: Sborník Josefu Poulíkovi k šedesátinám (Brno 1970) 43-54.

Říhovský 1979: J. Říhovský, Die Nadeln in Mähren und im Ostalpengebiet. Prähistorische Bronzefunde XIII,5 (München 1979).

Seracsin 1929: A. Seracsin, Das Hallstattgräberfeld von Au am Leithagebirge. Wiener prähistorische Zeitschrift 20, 1929, 229-237.

Schauer 1971: P. Schauer, Die Schwerter in Süddeutschland, Österreich und der Schweiz. Prähistorische Bronzefunde IV,2 (München 1971).

Schauer 1972: P. Schauer, Zur Herkunft der bronzenen Hallstatt-Schwerter. Archäologisches Korrespondenzblatt 2, 1972, 261-170.

Stegmann-Rajtár 1992a: S. Stegmann-Rajtár, Grabfunde der älteren Hallstattzeit aus Südmähren (Košice 1992).

Stegmann-Rajtár 1992b: S. Stegmann-Rajtár, Spätbronze- und früheisenzeitliche Fundgruppen des mittleren Donaugebietes. Bericht der Römisch-Germanischen Kommission 73, 1992, 29-179.

Stegmann-Rajtár 2009: S. Stegmann-Rajtár, Žiarové pohrebisko východohalštatskej a vekerzugskej kultúry v Nových Zámkoch. Slovenská archeológia.57, 1 2009, 57-116.

Studeníková 1987: E. Studeníková, Kultúrne kontakty juhozápadného Slovenska v dobe halštatskej, kandidátska práca (Bratislava-Nitra 1987).

Studeníková 1994: E. Studeníková, Záchranný výskum halštatskej mohyly v Novej Dedinke. Zborník Slovenského Národného Múzea – Archeológia 4, 1994, 25-47.

Stöllner 2002: T. Stöllner, Der prähistorische Salzbergbau am Dürrnberg bei Hallein II : Die Funde und Befunde der Bergwerksausgrabungen zwischen 1990 und 2000. Dürnberg Forschungen 3 (Rahden/Westf. 2002).

Szombathy 1924: J. Szombathy, Die Tumuli in Feichtenboden bei Fischau am Steinfeld. Mitteilungen der Anthropologischen Gesellschaft Wien 54, 1924, 163-197.

Tomba Database: Tomba Database (http://www3.rgzm.de/tomba/; 20.04.2016).

Torbrügge 1979: W. Torbrügge, Die Hallstattzeit in der Oberpfalz I. Materialhefte zur bayerischen Vorgeschichte 39 (Kallmünz/Opf 1979).

Trachsel 2004: M. Trachsel, Untersuchungen zur relativen und absoluten Chronologie der Hallstattzeit. Universitätsforschungen zur prähistorischen Archäologie 104 (Bonn 2004).

Trackenberg 1934: K. Trackenberg, Die Kultur der frühen Eisenzeit in Mittel- und Westhannover. Die Urnenfriedhöfe in Niedersachsen 1 (Leipzig 1934).

Weiss 1999: R. M. Weiss, Die Hallstattzeit in Europa. Die Altertümer im Museum Für Vor- und Frühgeschichte Berlin 2 (Mainz 1999).

Author

Ladislav Chmelo
Department of Archaeology
Constantine the Philosopher University
Hodžova 1
SK-949 74 Nitra
lchmelo@gmail.com

Elites before the *Fürstensitze*

Hallstatt C sumptuous graves between Main and Danube

Manuel Fernández-Götz and Bettina Arnold

Abstract

The appearance of large fortified Early Iron Age centers, traditionally known as Fürstensitze, represents one of the main developments of the first millennium BC north of the Alps. For a long time, their emergence was seen mainly as a result of increasing contacts with the Mediterranean world and in particular as a reaction to the foundation of the Greek colony of Massalia around 600 BC. However, rich burial evidence from the 8th and 7th centuries BC demonstrates that the increase in social hierarchisation and the development of powerful local elites predated by more than a century the arrival of the Greek colonists in southern France, implying that the social processes concerned were primarily of an indigenous nature. This paper will consider the evidence for Hallstatt C elite burials between Main and Danube, including outstanding examples such as the Gomadingen grave on the Swabian Alb and the sumptuous burial from Frankfurt-Stadtwald. The main conclusion is that we need to move away from Mediterraneo-centric perspectives and simplistic applications of core-periphery models, by acknowledging the importance of endogenous factors and the complexity of Early Iron Age networks.

Zusammenfassung

Das Aufkommen von großen befestigten Zentren der frühen Eisenzeit, den sogenannten „Fürstensitzen", stellt eine der wichtigsten Entwicklungen des 1. Jahrtausends v. Chr. nördlich der Alpen dar. Lange Zeit wurde ihre Entstehung vornehmlich als das Ergebnis von zunehmenden Kontakten mit der mediterranen Welt und insbesondere als eine Reaktion auf die Gründung der griechischen Kolonie von Massalia um ca. 600 v. Chr. interpretiert. Reiche Gräber aus dem 8. und 7. Jahrhundert v. Chr. bezeugen aber, dass der Anstieg der sozialen Hierarchisierung und die Herausbildung von mächtigen lokalen Eliten der Ankunft der griechischen Kolonisten in Südfrankreich um mehr als ein Jahrhundert vorausgingen, so dass die damit verbundenen sozialen Prozesse von primär endogener Natur waren. Im Rahmen des vorliegenden Aufsatzes werden reiche Hallstatt C Elitebestattungen zwischen Main und Donau vorgestellt, darunter herausragende Beispiele wie das Grab von Gomadingen auf der Schwäbischen Alb und das Prunkgrab von Frankfurt-Stadtwald. Die wichtigste Schlussfolgerung ist, dass wir uns von mittelmeerzentrischen Sichtweisen und vereinfachten Anwendungen von Zentrum-Peripherie-Modellen distanzieren müssen, um die Wichtigkeit von endogenen Faktoren und die Komplexität der früheisenzeitlichen Netzwerke anzuerkennen.

Fingerprinting the Origins of the *Fürstensitze*: Looking Back to See Ahead

In previous studies of the Early Iron Age, most of the attention has traditionally concentrated on Hallstatt D, a period characterized by the development of large *Fürstensitze* and famous sumptuous graves such as Hochdorf or Vix. However, in order to be able to understand the roots of these processes we must examine the previous stage, Hallstatt C, which has received much less attention despite the existence of early sumptuous graves such as Oss in the Low Countries (Fontijn/ Fokkens 2007; see contributions in this volume) or Frankfurt-Stadtwald in the Main region (Willms 2002; see below).

The emergence of large fortified Hallstatt centers, the so-called *Fürstensitze* ('princely seats' in English, '*résidences princières*' in French), represents one of the main developments in the history of Iron Age Central Europe (Fernández-Götz *et al.* 2014; Fernández-Götz/Krausse 2016). The last two decades have witnessed a spectacular increase in research on these centers, including the large-scale project of the German Research Foundation *Frühe Zentralisierungs- und Urbanisierungsprozesse – Zur Genese und Entwicklung frühkeltischer Fürstensitze und ihres territorialen Umlandes* (*cf.* Krausse 2008; 2010). Thanks to the new data, it can be stated that the first urban and proto-urban centers north of the Alps were not the Late La Tène *oppida*, but in fact already the Early Iron Age central places that developed between the end of the 7th and the 5th centuries BC in an area stretching from Bohemia to Central France (Brun/Chaume 2013; Fernández-Götz/Ralston forthcoming; Fig. 1).

The spectacular research results indicate that the political and demographic dimensions of these societies were much larger than traditionally thought (Fernández-Götz/Krausse 2013; Ralston 2010; Verger 2015). This is particularly

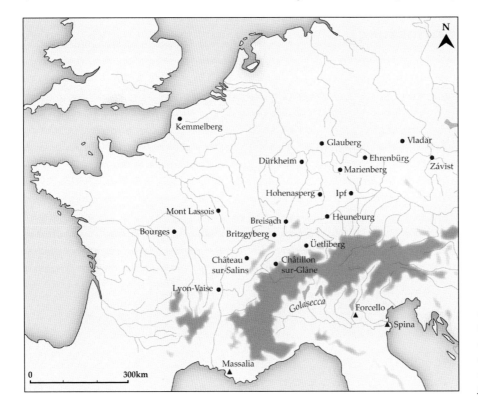

Fig. 1. Distribution map of the Fürstensitze north of the Alps and selected sites in Mediterranean Europe (after Fernández-Götz/Ralston forthcoming).

exemplified by the cases of the Heuneburg in southwest Germany and Bourges in the Berry region of Central France. Extensive survey projects and excavations have attested that the agglomeration of the Heuneburg (citadel, lower town and outer settlement) had an area of ca. 100 hectares during the mudbrick wall phase, with an estimated population of around 5,000 inhabitants (Krausse *et al.* 2015). In the case of Bourges, the whole settlement complex covered several hundred hectares in the 5th century BC, during which time it probably acted as a large tribal capital (Milcent 2007; Ralston 2010).

The association between the main Hallstatt D and La Tène A centers and cemeteries with elite burials (e.g. Gießübel-Talhau, Grafenbühl, Hochdorf, Kleinaspergle, Sainte-Colombe or Vix) suggests that the *Fürstensitze* served political and administrative functions. These were hierarchically organized societies, structured around central places – mostly fortified settlements – which were in turn surrounded by groups of tumuli containing the burials of elite members and their retinues (Arnold 2010a; Fernández-Götz/Ralston forthcoming). The rich burials of some children, for example as found in the Bettelbühl necropolis at the Heuneburg or at Bourges, indicate the establishment of hereditary principles based on social rank and status at this time (Krausse 2006; Kurz/Wahl 2005; Fig. 2). Furthermore, the composition and quality of the burial inventories of at least the richest Late Hallstatt and Early La Tène graves allows them to be interpreted as the burials of kings or high-ranking aristocrats (Verger 2015). In some cases, for example at Hochdorf or the Glauberg, we can even propose the presence of a type of sacred kingship since the deceased are outfitted according not only to the execution of their political functions, but also as holders of religious office (Fernández-Götz/Krausse forthcoming).

As stated above, during the last two decades our understanding of the *Fürstensitze* has evolved enormously. However, the processes that led to the genesis of these Hallstatt D centers remain poorly understood. This is at least partly linked to a more general methodological problem in the interpretation of the

Fig. 2. Gold items from the rich child burial from the Bettelbühl necropolis near the Heuneburg (after Kurz/Wahl 2005, 82 fig. 66).

archaeological record. As K. Kristiansen has rightly stated: "Social and cultural changes cannot be fully observed until they have actually taken place and have materialized. Their genesis in a preceding period is, however, difficult to observe" (Kristiansen 1998, 26). In fact, it is likely that such shifts in power structures must be masked initially in order to be possible at all, especially in societies that retain a tribal and kin-based structure while reaching population sizes that are commensurate with those of states (Arnold 2011).

For a long time, the processes of centralization and hierarchisation materialized in the *Fürstensitze* and the rich elite burials of the Late Hallstatt period were interpreted mainly as a result of increasing contacts with the Mediterranean world and in particular as a reaction to (or even result of) the foundation of the Greek colony of *Massalia* around 600 BC (see *e.g.* Kimmig 1983a). However, burial evidence from the 8th and 7th centuries BC clearly shows that the increase in social inequalities and the development of powerful local elites had begun much earlier than the arrival of the Greek colonists in southern France; moreover, there is considerable continuity between Hallstatt C and Hallstatt D status markers (Schumann 2015). Therefore, these processes of increased social complexity and stratification should be considered primarily of an indigenous nature. In what follows we will present the evidence for some of the most important Hallstatt C elite burials between Main and Danube, including outstanding examples such as the sumptuous burial from Frankfurt-Stadtwald, the Gomadingen grave on the Swabian Alb, and the early elite burials in the vicinity of the Heuneburg.

Early status markers: Wagons and swords

Broadly speaking, a key common element linking Hallstatt C (mainly cremation) and Hallstatt D (mainly inhumation) elite central burials is one primary object category, the four-wheeled wagon (Pare 1991; 1992). Already during the Urnfield period wagon-related finds are known from a large number of localities in West-Central Europe, in particular the Hart-an-der-Alz group of burials (Pare 1987, 33-34). There are 30 assemblages from 23 different localities in this group based on the most recent update by C. Pankau (2013), ranging from Lake Geneva to the Chiemgau (Fig. 3), but as usual the degree of preservation and accuracy of recording leaves much to be desired. Nineteen of these wagon complexes are burials or burial-like depositions (Pankau 2013, 115).

Hart an der Alz itself, the type site for this group, and a burial in Mengen excavated in 1955, are the two best-preserved and were probably both wooden chamber burials. The remains of cremated bone, ash and charcoal as well as burned pottery and bronze were found in concentrated piles suggesting the presence of an organic container (Pare 1987, 39). Unfortunately the fragments of wagon fittings, in many cases damaged by fire or removed from the wagon before the cremation, are rarely in their original positions, so drawing conclusions about wagon size, style or quality is challenging if not impossible (Pankau 2013, 115). The earliest examples, dated to Bronze D on the basis of distinctive grave goods in the form of weapons and pins, are Essenbach, Königsbronn, Mengen, Oberottmarshausen, Poing und Publy, but the majority can be dated to Hallstatt A1-2, representing a 200 year period during which this type of burial was practiced in this region. Unfortunately the burning of many of the objects in these graves with the body

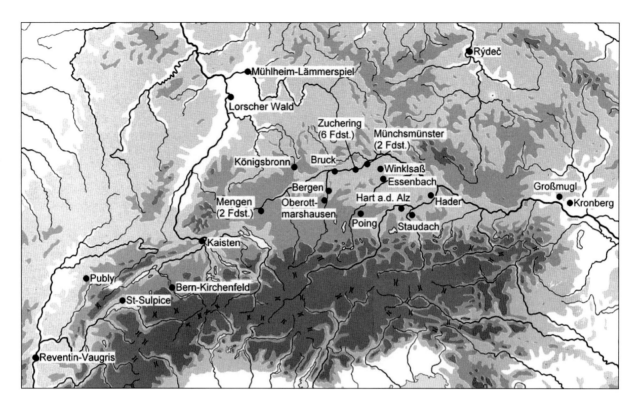

Fig. 3. Distribution map of Bronze D – Hallstatt A wagon graves (after Pankau 2013, 117 fig. 1).

means that our knowledge of the presence of potential imports is quite limited (Pare 1987, 40).

Swords seem to have been a particularly important rank symbol in Hallstatt C burials throughout the region between the Rhine and the Danube, with especially impressive bronze or iron examples recovered from elite graves at Rottenburg-Baisingen and Sternberg-Gomadingen; the sword in the latter was 108 cm long with a gold-plated handle (Stadelmann 1983, 68-69). Evidence for contacts well outside the region are found in the form of inlays of ivory, amber and gold that characterize the handles of a select few of these swords, especially those of Mindelheim type (Pare 2004, 540-542). The burial mounds near the Rhine appear to have been strategically located near natural fords, evidence of territorial marking on the part of local elites (Plouin 1996, 21). Just over 300 bronze swords are known from this region and an even larger number of iron swords also dated to Hallstatt C have been recorded but are less often published or studied due to their poor preservation.

The top of the top: From Frankfurt to Gomadingen

Among the best examples of a rich Hallstatt C burial in Central Europe is the elite grave of Frankfurt-Stadtwald in the Main region. It was discovered in 1966-67 and contained the remains of a 50± year old man who was buried around 700 BC (Fischer 1979; Hofmann 2010; Willms 2002). This spectacular grave is more than 150 years older than Hochdorf and more than 250 years older than the Glauberg *Fürst*. The burial chamber was covered by a monumental tumulus of about 36 m in diameter which was about 3.5 m high. The deceased was buried with a selection of rich grave goods which mark his prominent social position at the pinnacle of his community. The objects recovered included some bronze pins and rings, two

*Fig. 4. Drinking service
from the sumptuous grave of
Frankfurt-Stadtwald (after
Willms 2002, 52).*

iron knives, a large bronze sword, the remains of horse-gear and a yoke which
point towards the existence of a wagon, and finally different elements of feasting
and drinking equipment consisting of ceramic and bronze bowls and a bronze
situla with a capacity of 20 liters (Fig. 4).

Wagons, weapons and luxury vessels associated with drinking are characteristic
attributes of elite burials in many societies and reflect the widespread importance
of war, feasting and hospitality in the aristocratic ideology of Iron Age Europe
(Arnold 1999; Diepeveen-Jansen 2001; Fernández-Götz 2014a, 85-89; 184-
185). This leads us to a further consideration, namely that the traditions seen
in the rich Hallstatt D elite graves have clear roots in the previous Hallstatt C
period; the shape of items may change but the ideology behind them shows many
clear continuities between both periods (Schumann 2015, 256-273). Moreover,
the fact that the early Hallstatt sumptuous grave from Frankfurt-Stadtwald was
constructed at the same location as previous burials from the Middle and the Late
Bronze Age (Fischer 1979; Hofmann 2010, 68) suggests an attempt to establish

Fig. 5. Geometric designs on a ceramic plate from Gomadingen (after Hoppe/ Schorer 2012, 209 fig. 264).

links with ancestral memories and resembles the situation found at other sites such as Oss in the Netherlands (Fontijn *et al.* 2013; Fokkens *et al.* 2012).

Equally outstanding in terms of grave goods is the elite burial of Gomadingen in the Swabian Alb. This cremation grave of a male individual was discovered under a tumulus near the present day village of Gomadingen (Zürn 1987, 125). It dates to around 700-650 BC and is therefore roughly contemporaneous with Frankfurt-Stadtwald. The most famous item from the Gomadingen burial is without a doubt the 108 cm long sword of Mindelheim type with a gold-plated handle. However, the grave also contained several ceramic vessels, including two particularly richly decorated pots with geometric designs which were probably manufactured specifically as showpieces for burial. An oblique viewpoint illustrates the complex stepped shape and decorations particularly well (Fig. 5).

Elites before the *Fürstensitze*: The case of the Heuneburg region

In keeping with the area of the Swabian Alb, another revealing example of early Hallstatt elites comes from the Heuneburg and its environs. Until recently evidence for Hallstatt C interactions in the Heuneburg region was relatively poorly documented. The general consensus at the moment is that between the 12th and the late 7th centuries BC the hillfort at least appears to have been largely abandoned (Fernández-Götz 2014b, 26-27; Krausse *et al.* 2015, 44-51), making it unlikely that extra-regional Hallstatt C contacts were a major factor in the transition to the Early Iron Age in this area. Even during the Hallstatt D phase of occupation the evidence for imported ceramics is concentrated in the period after the destruction of the mud-brick wall, that is, post-540 BC (Arnold 2010b; Shefton 2000).

The excavations directed between 1999 and 2002 as part of the 'Landscape of Ancestors' project in two mounds of the Hohmichele 'Speckhau' group have provided some important new evidence on Hallstatt C elite burials in the area of the Heuneburg (Arnold 2002; Arnold 2012; Arnold/Murray 2015; Arnold *et al.* forthcoming). The *in situ* cremation in the center of Tumulus 18 is attested by the ditches that supported the lowest level of the pyre platform and are clearly visible in spite of extensive damage by looters who redeposited more than 12 ceramic vessels in their excavation trenches, including several large and elaborately decorated *Kegelhalsgefäße*. Two of these vessels are distinctively Hallstatt C in date and one is unusual in both its size and its decoration, consisting of a matte gray slip with graphite inclusions and linear incised as well as rolled-wheel impressions. The use of the rolled-wheel, which produces regularly spaced rectangular punctuated decorations that were probably originally filled with white paste, is more typical of northeastern Bavaria and the Upper Palatinate but the decorative fields and their composition is not distinctive enough to definitively state that this piece was an import. On the other hand, the extremely rich ceramic assemblage from the central cremation in this mound, which contained at least one and possibly two adults, indicates that status differentiation in this period was already clearly marked.

The same is true of the central cremation in Tumulus 17. Like Tumulus 18 this mound had a diameter of about 20 m and an original height of around 3 m, roughly a quarter the size of the nearby Hohmichele tumulus. The remains of the central cremation were deposited in an extremely large chamber or enclosure of 5 x 5 m and included fragments of iron as well as extensive organic material (Fig. 6). The shaft and blade fragments of two spears as well as an iron spear shoe were recovered, as were fragments of a long iron knife. Large fragments of iron, probably the remains of a four-wheeled wagon, indicate that this was the burial of a high-status individual; embedded within one of these corroded clumps were large black animal hairs that could be identified as the remains of a bear skin (Rast-Eicher in Banck-Burgess forthcoming), which was presumably lying on the floor of the chamber under the wagon when the looters broke in. This is the first physical evidence of the use of body parts from this animal species as a status marker in an Iron Age West-Central European burial context and indicates that the cremated individual, probably male, was of some importance.

In summary, the central graves from Tumuli 17 and 18 of the Hohmichele 'Speckhau' group testify to the existence of elites in the environs of the Heuneburg in Hallstatt C, thus predating the foundation of the *Fürstensitz* agglomeration around 630 BC. This also means that the Hohmichele, while much larger and in close proximity, was founded later than the two smaller mounds, raising interesting questions about how the central interments in these tumuli were related to one another and to the founding of the Iron Age Heuneburg itself. It was presumably the circle of the most important families and settlement groups who were responsible for initiating the construction of the Heuneburg in the course of the

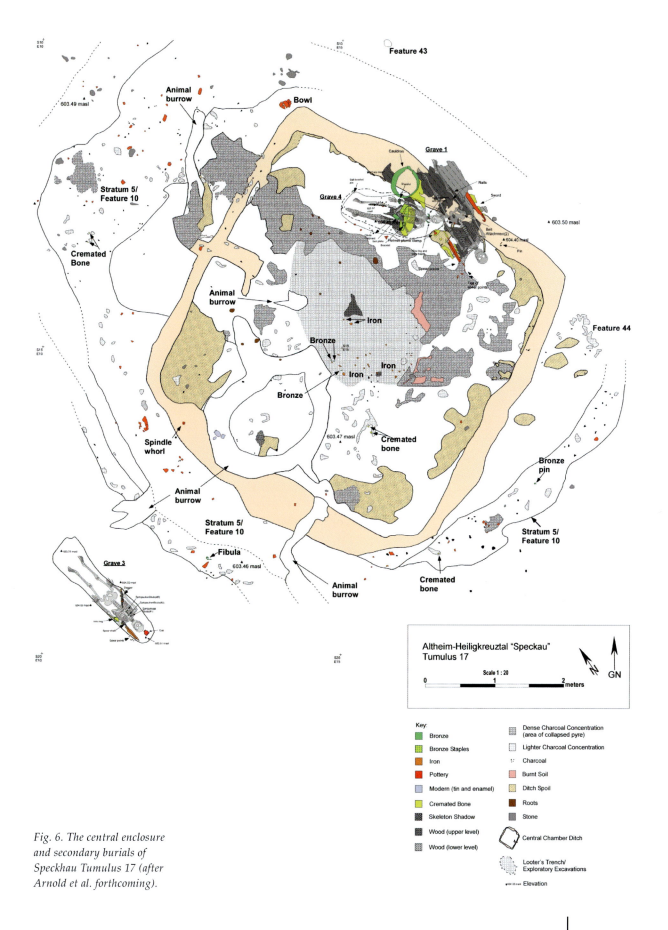

Fig. 6. The central enclosure and secondary burials of Speckhau Tumulus 17 (after Arnold et al. forthcoming).

Inside the figure:

S10 E10
S10 E15
Feature 43
603.49 masl
Animal burrow
Bowl
Grave 1
Cauldron
Stratum 5/ Feature 10
Grave 4
Nails
Sword
Cremated Bone
603.50 masl
Belt Attachment(2)
604.40 masl
Pin
Animal burrow
Iron
Feature 44
Bronze
Iron
Iron
Bronze
Cremated bone
603.47 masl
Spindle whorl
Bronze pin
Animal burrow
Stratum 5/ Feature 10
Stratum 5/ Feature 10
S15 E10
Fibula
603.46 masl
Grave 3
Cremated bone
Dagger
Animal burrow
Spear shaft
Spear points
Cup
S20 E10
S20 E15

Altheim-Heiligkreuztal "Speckau"
Tumulus 17
Scale 1 : 20
0   1   2 meters
N
GN

Key:
Bronze
Bronze Staples
Iron
Pottery
Modern (tin and enamel)
Cremated Bone
Skeleton Shadow
Wood (upper level)
Wood (lower level)
Dense Charcoal Concentration (area of collapsed pyre)
Lighter Charcoal Concentration
Charcoal
Burnt Soil
Ditch Spoil
Roots
Stone
Central Chamber Ditch
Looter's Trench/ Exploratory Excavations
Elevation

second half of the 7th century BC. The heads of different households and lineage groups must have joined together in a process that led to the construction of the hillfort and the outer settlement (Fernández-Götz 2014b; Krause *et al.* 2015).

Sword and wagon burials in the Rhine region

Moving on to the West, the Rhine river appears to have acted as a cultural boundary during the Hallstatt C period based on ceramic assemblages as well as funerary ritual, which seems to have involved much more extensive feasting equipment than burials east of the river. This may provide a clue as to the regionally distinct role played by elite commensality in this early period of consolidation of socio-political power (Lüscher 1996, 18). Initially sword graves are found in tumuli of modest size that were frequently erected in earlier periods, again showing an attempt to establish links with the past. It is not until the end of Hallstatt C/early Hallstatt D that we see a new phase of status marking emerge in the form of mega-mounds erected to accommodate elite central burials that also include wagons and horse trappings.

Six wagon burials dating to the Hallstatt period are known east of the Rhine in Baden, part of a wider phenomenon of about 250 Early Iron Age wagon burials found across France, the Netherlands, Switzerland, southern Germany, Bohemia, Austria and Hungary (Pare 1992, 1996, 31). The ornamental metal attachments on the Hallstatt C2 Ohnenheim wagon (Alsace) have been linked to stylistically similar examples from wagons found in Wijchen, Ins and Birmentorf, for example, while ivory inlay was found in the remains of the sword pommel from the Ohnenheim wagon grave (Egg 1987; Pare 1996, 33). The three ivory lathe-turned tube ornaments found in the March-Buchheim Bürgle tumulus also have been interpreted as imports not only on the basis of the material of which they are made but also their style (Pare 1996, 38).

Clearly these burials were part of a gradual process of elite power consolidation that begins in the late Urnfield period with wealthy sword burials in tumuli clustered in precisely the same region in which the *Fürstengräber* eventually appear; the trend is toward amplification as well as innovation within the elite burial panoply, from swords to swords and wagons to daggers, wagons, gold and Mediterranean imports, with the sword/dagger and wagon combination as the main common denominator (Pare 1996, 43).

Social complexity in Early Iron Age Europe: Mediterranean influence or indigenous?

In conclusion, we would like to provide some brief remarks on the processes of social differentiation and centralization that took place during the course of the Hallstatt period. First of all, trade with the Mediterranean does not seem to have been the prime mover of cultural change during the Early Iron Age, but rather a consequence of demographic growth and increasing internal inequalities which had their roots in Hallstatt C. The appearance of Mediterranean imports in graves and settlements can be regarded as an effect rather than a cause of endogenous processes that were already in progress well before the founding of Greek colonies in southern France. The role of demographic increase in the development of more centralized forms of power has been stressed since the influential work of R. Carneiro on early state formation (Carneiro 1967; 1970). Population numbers in relation to carrying capacities are important, but the key aspect is the associated increase in 'social density', that is, the frequency of communication and interaction occurring between individuals and groups through their social, political and economic networks (*cf.* Ortman *et al.* 2014; see also Brun 1995, 122-123).

In his critique of S. Frankenstein and M. Rowlands' (1978) prestige goods model, C. Gosden showed that in predominantly agrarian societies such as those of the Hallstatt period in West-Central Europe, power and status would have depended mainly on land and animal ownership and the control of local production (Gosden 1985), a conclusion that is underpinned by more recent

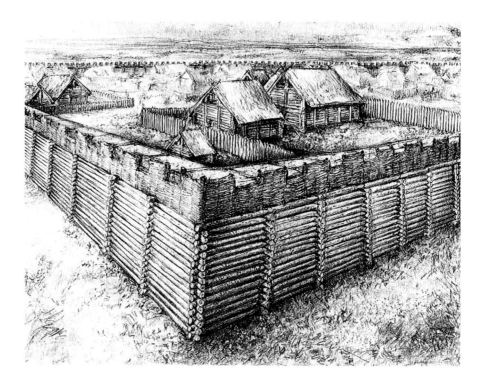

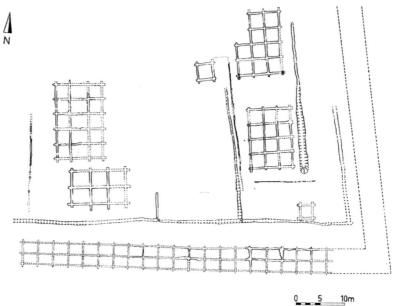

Fig. 7. Reconstruction and plan of the southeast corner of the Heuneburg plateau during period IVc, predating the construction of the mudbrick wall (after Kimmig 1983b, 69 fig. 33).

work (*cf.* Karl 2015). B. Arnold (2010a) has suggested that the organization of the mortuary landscape, where mounds are clustered and burials within and between mounds distributed in structured ways, indicates a social system based on kinship ties, while ceramic analyses indicate that these complex intra- and inter-regional groupings emerge as early as Ha C (Brosseder 2004). Moreover, by over-emphasizing contacts with the Mediterranean traditional interpretations have underestimated the importance of East-West and North-South interactions between the communities of Central and Northern Europe.

Analysis of the vegetational history indicates that in the 6th century BC for the first time there was dense settlement in several highland regions north of the Alps, areas with relatively poor climatic and agricultural conditions. This settling of new land must have been immediately preceded by a period of population increase, a process that is well-documented in the pollen diagrams of the Hunsrück-Eifel region (Fernández-Götz 2014a, 105-107; Krausse/Nakoinz 2000). We can assume that apart from technical innovations such as iron production and politico-organizational improvements, a period of climatically favorable conditions in the 7th and 6th centuries BC also led to a growth in population and the settlement of new areas. These factors – population increase and the opening up of new areas to agriculture and other economic resources – formed the real basis of the wealth of the social elite that is so impressively visible to us in the form of sumptuous graves (Krausse 2006).

In the case of the Heuneburg, the first settlement phase, Period IVc in the stratigraphic sequence of the site (Fig. 7), started around 630 BC, at the very beginning of Hallstatt D1 (Arnold 2010b; Fernández-Götz 2014b, 26-27; Gersbach 1995, 4-9; 98-108). This early settlement predates the mudbrick wall which was probably constructed about 600 BC; it is very likely that the enormous outer settlement also begins in this earliest phase. Therefore, the process of synoikismos that led to the development of the Heuneburg clearly predates by at least one generation the foundation of *Massalia*. Moreover, in the case of the Heuneburg, and leaving aside the mudbrick wall, evidence for Mediterranean contact and influence is minimal until the restructuring that took place after the major destruction event by fire around 540 BC (Arnold 2010b). B. Shefton dates the earliest ceramic imports at the site to 550 or 570 BC but describes this interaction as an episodic and non-Attic luxury import trickle (Shefton 2000, 34).

The above reflections are not to deny the existence and influence of contacts with the Mediterranean world: the regions north and south of the Alps were never isolated from each other, and one of the challenges for the future is precisely to overcome the artificial academic division between Classical and Late Prehistoric archaeology. But at the same time we need to move away from Mediterraneo-centric perspectives and simplistic applications of core-periphery models (Dietler 2010). For this task, one of the main challenges is to pay greater attention to the developments that took place in the Hallstatt C period. Although there is still a long way to go, the present volume represents an important step in the right direction.

Addendum

The recent discovery in 2016 of a rich Hallstatt C grave under tumulus at Unlingen, about 11 km from the Heuneburg, provides further archaeological proof for the presence of elites in the region preceding the foundation of the agglomeration. The burial was part of a larger necropolis that remained in use until Hallstatt D3 (Meyer/König 2016).

Bibliography

Arnold 1999: B. Arnold, 'Drinking the feast': Alcohol and the legitimation of power in Celtic Europe. Cambridge Archaeological Journal 9, 1999, 71-93.

Arnold 2002: B. Arnold, A landscape of ancestors: the space and place of death in Iron Age West-Central Europe. In: H. Silverman/D. Small (eds.), The space and place of death. Archaeological Papers of the American Anthropological Association 11 (Arlington 2002) 129-144.

Arnold 2010a: B. Arnold, Memory maps: The mnemonics of central European Iron Age burial mounds. In K. T. Lillios/V. Tsamis (eds.), Material mnemonics: Everyday memory in prehistoric Europe (Oxford 2010) 147-173.

Arnold 2010b: B. Arnold, Eventful archaeology, the Heuneburg mud-brick wall and the Early Iron Age of southwest Germany. In D. Bolender (ed.), Eventful archaeologies: New approaches to social transformation in the archaeological record (Albany 2010) 100-114.

Arnold 2011: B. Arnold, The illusion of power, the power of illusion: Ideology and the concretization of social difference in Early Iron Age Europe. In: R. Bernbeck/R. McGuire (eds.), Ideologies in archaeology (Albuquerque 2011) 151-174.

Arnold 2012: B. Arnold, Gürtelfrauen und Dolchmänner: Zwei Hügel der Speckhau-Hohmichele-Gruppe. In: Die Welt der Kelten. Zentren der Macht – Kostbarkeiten der Kunst (Ostfildern 2012) 127-129.

Arnold/Murray 2015: B. Arnold/M. Murray, Zwei hallstattzeitliche Grabhügel der Hohmichele-Gruppe im „Speckhau". In D. Krausse/I. Kretschmer/L. Hansen/M. Fernández-Götz, Die Heuneburg. Keltischer Fürstensitz an der oberen Donau. Führer zu archäologischen Denkmälern in Baden-Württemberg 28 (Darmstadt 2015) 114-117.

Arnold et al. forthcoming: B. Arnold/M. Murray/T. Kreß, A landscape of ancestors: Archaeological investigations of two Iron Age burial mounds in the Hohmichele Group, Baden-Württemberg. Forschungen und Berichte zur Vor- und Frühgeschichte in Baden-Württemberg (Stuttgart, forthcoming).

Brosseder 2004: U. Brosseder, Studien zur Ornamentik hallstattzeitlicher Keramik zwischen Rhônetal und Karpatenbecken. Universitätsforschungen zur Prähistorischen Archäologie 106 (Bonn 2004).

Brun 1995: P. Brun, Oppida and social «complexification» in France. In J. D. Hill/C. G. Cumberpatch (eds.), Different Iron Ages. Studies on the Iron Age in temperate Europe. British Archaeological Reports, International Series 602 (Oxford 1995) 121-128.

Brun/Chaume 2013: P. Brun/B. Chaume, Une éphémère tentative d'urbanisation en Europe centre-occidentale durant les VIe et Ve siècles av. J.C.? Bulletin de la Société Préhistorique Française 110,2, 2013, 319-349.

Carneiro 1967: R. Carneiro, On the relationship between size of population and complexity of social organization. Southwestern Journal of Anthropology 23, 1967, 234-243.

Carneiro 1970: R. Carneiro, A theory of the origin of the state. Science 169, 1970, 733-738.

Dietler 2010: M. Dietler, Archaeologies of colonialism: Consumption, entanglement and violence in ancient Mediterranean France (Oakland, CA 2010).

Diepeveen-Jansen 2001: M. Diepeveen-Jansen, People, ideas and goods. New perspectives on 'Celtic Barbarians' in Western and Central Europe. Amsterdam Archaeological Studies 7 (Amsterdam 2001).

Egg 1987: M. Egg, Das Wagengrab von Ohnenheim im Elsass. In: Vierrädrige Wagen der Hallstattzeit. Untersuchungen zu Geschichte und Technik. Monographien des Römisch-Germanischen Zentralmuseums 12 (Mainz 1987) 77-102.

Fernández-Götz 2014a: M. Fernández-Götz, Identity and power: The transformation of Iron Age societies in northeast Gaul. Amsterdam Archaeological Studies 21 (Amsterdam 2014).

Fernández-Götz 2014b: M. Fernández-Götz, Understanding the Heuneburg: A biographical approach. In M. Fernández-Götz/H. Wendling/K. Winger (eds.), Paths to complexity: Centralisation and urbanisation in Iron Age Europe (Oxford 2014) 24-34.

Fernández-Götz/Krausse 2013: M. Fernández-Götz/D. Krausse, Rethinking Early Iron Age urbanisation in Central Europe: The Heuneburg site and its archaeological environment. Antiquity 87,336, 2013, 473-487.

Fernández-Götz/Krausse 2016: M. Fernández-Götz/D. Krausse (eds.), Eurasia at the dawn of history: Urbanization and social change (Cambridge 2016).

Fernández-Götz/Krausse forthcoming: M. Fernández-Götz/D. Krausse, Sacred kingship and ancestor worship: A re-evaluation of religious and political leadership in the Late Hallstatt and Early La Tène periods. In B. Arnold (ed.), The Oxford handbook of the archaeology of the continental Celts (Oxford, forthcoming).

Fernández-Götz/Ralston forthcoming: M. Fernández-Götz/I. Ralston, Complexity and fragility of Early Iron Age urbanism in temperate Europe. Journal of World Prehistory (forthcoming).

Fernández-Götz et al. 2014: M. Fernández-Götz/H. Wendling/K. Winger (eds), Paths to complexity: Centralisation and urbanisation in Iron Age Europe (Oxford 2014).

Fischer 1979: U. Fischer, Ein Grabhügel der Bronze- und Eisenzeit im Frankfurter Stadtwald. Schriften des Frankfurter Museums für Vor- und Frühgeschichte 4 (Frankfurt 1979).

Fontijn/Fokkens 2007: D. Fontijn/H. Fokkens, The emergence of Early Iron Age 'chieftains'graves' in the southern Netherlands: Reconsidering transformations in burial and depositional practices. In: C. Haselgrove/R. Pope (eds.), The earlier Iron Age in Britain and the near continent (Oxford 2007) 354-373.

Fontijn et al. 2013: D. Fontijn/S. van der Vaart/R. Jansen (eds.), Transformation through destruction. A monumental and extraordinary Early Iron Age Hallstatt C barrow from the ritual landscape of Oss/Zevenbergen (Leiden 2013).

Fokkens 2012: H. Fokkens, Access to origins: On the meaning of continuity and discontinuity in the use of barrow 'cemeteries'. In: D. Bérenger/J. Bourgeois/M. Talon/S. Wirth (eds.), Gräberlandschaften der Bronzezeit. Paysages funéraires de l'âge du Bronze (Darmstadt 2012) 553-572.

Frankenstein/Rowlands 1978: S. Frankenstein/M. J. Rowlands, The internal structure and regional context of Early Iron Age society in South-Western Germany. Bulletin of the Institute of Archaeology 15, 1978, 73-112.

Gersbach 1995: E. Gersbach, Baubefunde der Perioden IVc-IVa der Heuneburg. Heuneburgstudien IX = Römisch-Germanische Forschungen 53 (Mainz 1995).

Gosden 1985: C. Gosden, Gifts and kin in Early Iron Age Europe. Man 20, 1985, 475-493.

Hofmann 2010: K. Hofmann, Das hallstattzeitliche Fürstengrab vom Frankfurter Stadtwald. In: E. Wamers (ed.), Fürsten, Feste, Rituale. Bilderwelten zwischen Kelten und Etruskern (Frankfurt 2010) 67-74.

Hoppe/Schorer 2012: T. Hoppe/B. Schorer, Geometrisches Ornament. Die Kunst der Hallstattzeit. In: Die Welt der Kelten. Zentren der Macht – Kostbarkeiten der Kunst (Ostfildern 2012) 209-225.

Karl 2015: R. Karl, Labour procurement in pre-monetary Europe. In: B. Danielisova/M. Fernández-Götz (eds.), Persistent economic ways of living. Production, distribution, and consumption in late prehistory and early history. Archaeolingua 35 (Budapest 2015) 21-36.

Kimmig 1983a: W. Kimmig, Die griechische Kolonisation im westlichen Mittelmeergebiet und ihre Wirkung auf die Landschaften des westlichen Mitteleuropa. Jahrbuch des Römisch-Germanischen Zentralmuseums 30, 1983, 5-78.

Kimmig 1983b: W. Kimmig, Die Heuneburg an der oberen Donau. Führer zu archäologischen Denkmälern in Baden-Württemberg 1 (Stuttgart² 1983).

Krausse 2006: D. Krausse, Prunkgräber der nordwestalpinen Späthallstattkultur. Neue Fragestellungen und Untersuchungen zu ihrer sozialhistorischen Deutung. In C. von Carnap-Bornheim/D. Krausse/A. Wesse (eds), Herrschaft – Tod – Bestattung. Zu den vor- und frühgeschichtlichen Prunkgräbern als archäologisch-historische Quelle. Universitätsforschungen zur prähistorischen Archäologie 139 (Bonn 2006) 61-80.

Krausse 2008: D. Krausse, (ed.), Frühe Zentralisierungs- und Urbanisierungsprozesse. Zur Genese und Entwicklung frühkeltischer Fürstensitze und ihres territorialen Umlandes. Forschungen und Berichte zur Vor- und Frühgeschichte in Baden-Württemberg 101 (Stuttgart 2008).

Krausse 2010: D. Krausse (ed.), „Fürstensitze" und Zentralorte der frühen Kelten. Forschungen und Berichte zur Vor- und Frühgeschichte in Baden-Württemberg 120 (Stuttgart 2010).

Krausse et al. 2015: D. Krausse/I. Kretschmer/L. Hansen/M. Fernández-Götz, Die Heuneburg. Keltischer Fürstensitz an der oberen Donau. Führer zu archäologischen Denkmälern in Baden-Württemberg 28 (Darmstadt 2015).

Krausse/Nakoinz 2000: D. Krausse/O. Nakoinz, Binnenkolonisation und Zentralisation. Überlegungen zur latènezeitlichen Besiedlungs- und Bevölkerungsentwicklung im Mittelgebirgsraum nordwestlich der Mosel. In: V. Guichard/S. Sievers/O. H. Urban (eds.), Les processus d'urbanisation à l'âge du Fer. Eisenzeitliche Urbanisationsprozesse. Collection Bibracte 4 (Glux-en-Glenne 2000) 127-140.

Kristiansen 1998: K. Kristiansen, Europe before history (Cambridge 1998).

Kurz/Wahl 2005: S. Kurz/J. Wahl, Zur Fortsetzung der Grabungen in der Heuneburg-Außensiedlung auf Markung Ertingen-Binzwangen, Kreis Biberach. Archäologische Ausgrabungen in Baden-Württemberg 2005, 78-82.

Lüscher 1996: G. Lüscher, Die frühe Hallstattzeit (Ha C) am Oberrhein/Le Hallstatt ancient (Ha C) dans le fossé rhénan supérieur. In S. Plouin (ed.), Trésors Celtes et Gaulois. Le Rhin supérieur entre 800 et 50 avant J.-C. Exposition présentée au musée d'Unterlinden du 16 mars au 2 juin 1996 (Colmar 1996) 17-20.

Meyer/König 2016: M. Meyer/J. König, Mit Reiter und Wagen ins Jenseits – außergewöhnliche Grabfunde aus keltischen Grabhügeln bei Unlingen. Archäologische Ausgrabungen in Baden-Württemberg 2016, 120-123.

Milcent 2007: P.-Y. Milcent (ed.), Bourges-Avaricum: Un centre proto-urbain celtique du Ve s. av. J.-C. (Bourges 2007).

Ortman et al. 2014: S. Ortman/ A. Cabaniss/J. Sturm/L. Bettencourt, The pre-history of urban scaling. PLoS ONE 9, 2014, 1-10.

Pankau 2013: C. Pankau, Neue Forschungen zu den Wagengräbern der Hart an der Alz-Gruppe. In: L. Husty/K. Schmotz (eds.), Vorträge des 31. Niederbayerischen Archäologentages (Rahden/Westf. 2013) 113-147.

Pare 1987: C. Pare, Der Zeremonialwagen der Bronze- und Urnenfelderzeit. Seine Entstehung, Form und Verbreitung. In: Vierrädrige Wagen der Hallstattzeit. Untersuchungen zu Geschichte und Technik. Monographien des Römisch-Germanischen Zentralmuseums 12 (Mainz 1987) 25-67.

Pare 1991: C. Pare, Swords, wagon-graves and the beginning of the Early Iron Age in Central Europe. Kleine Schriften aus dem Vorgeschichtlichen Seminar Marburg 37 (Marburg 1991).

Pare 1992: C. Pare, Wagons and wagon-graves of the Early Iron Age in Central Europe. Oxford University Committee for Archaeology 35 (Oxford 1992).

Pare 1996: C. Pare, Fünf hallstattzeitliche Wagengräber am südlichen Oberrheingraben/ Cinq tombes à char halltattiennes du Rhin supérieur. In: S. Plouin (ed.), Trésors Celtes et Gaulois. Le Rhin supérieur entre 800 et 50 avant J.-C. Exposition présentée au musée d'Unterlinden du 16 mars au 2 juin 1996 (Colmar 1996) 31-43.

Pare 2004: C. Pare, Schwert – Hallstattzeit. Reallexikon der Germanischen Altertumskunde 27, 2004, 537-545.

Poulin 1996: S. Plouin, Les tombes à épées/Die Schwertgräber. In: S. Plouin (ed.), Trésors Celtes et Gaulois. Le Rhin supérieur entre 800 et 50 avant J.-C. Exposition présentée au musée d'Unterlinden du 16 mars au 2 juin 1996 (Colmar 1996) 21-26.

Ralston 2010: I. Ralston, Fragile states in mid-first millennium B.C. temperate Western Europe? The view from Bourges. Social Evolution & History 9,2, 2010, 135-159.

Rast-Eicher forthcoming: A. Rast-Eicher, Fasern aus Altheim. In: J. Banck-Burgess, Textilien und andere organische Reste aus Hügel 17 und 18 der Grabhügelgruppe Altheim-Heiligkreuztal „Speckhau". In: B. Arnold/M. L. Murray, A landscape of ancestors: Archaeological investigations of two Iron Age burial mounds in the Hohmichele Group, Baden-Württemberg. Forschungen und Berichte zur Vor- und Frühgeschichte in Baden-Württemberg (Stuttgart, forthcoming).

Schumann 2015: R. Schumann, Status und Prestige in der Hallstattkultur. Aspekte sozialer Distinktion in ältereisenzeitlichen Regionalgruppen zwischen Altmühl und Save. Münchner archäologische Forschungen 3 (Rahden/Westf. 2015).

Shefton 2000: B. Shefton, On the material in its northern setting. In: W. Kimmig (ed.), Importe und mediterrane Einflüsse auf der Heuneburg. Heuneburgstudien XI = Römisch-Germanische Forschungen 59 (Mainz 2000) 27-41.

Stadelmann 1983: J. Stadelmann, Die Metallzeiten: Bronze- und Eisenzeit. In: S. Albert (ed.), Tübingen und das Obere Gau. Führer zu archäologischen Denkmälern in Deutschland 3 (Stuttgart 1983) 56-74.

Verger 2015: S. Verger, L'Âge du Fer ancien: l'Europe moyenne avant les Celtes historiques (800-400). In: O. Buchsenschutz (ed.), L'Europe celtique à l'âge du Fer (VIIIe-Ier siècle) (Paris 2015) 75-176.

Willms 2002: C. Willms, Der Keltenfürst aus Frankfurt. Macht und Totenkult um 700 v. Chr. Archäologische Reihe 19 (Frankfurt 2002).

Zürn 1987: H. Zürn, Hallstattzeitliche Grabfunde in Württemberg und Hohenzollern. Forschungen und Berichte zur Vor- und Frühgeschichte in Baden-Württemberg 25 (Stuttgart 1987).

Authors

Manuel Fernández-Götz
School of History, Classics and Archaeology
University of Edinburgh
William Robertson Wing
Old Medical School, Teviot Place
Edinburgh EH8 9AG
United Kingdom
M.Fernandez-Gotz@ed.ac.uk

Bettina Arnold
Department of Anthropology
University of Wisconsin-Milwaukee
Sabin Hall 229
3413 N. Downer Ave
Milwaukee, WI 53201
USA
barnold@uwm.edu

The Early Iron Age in Belgium

Earth and fire, and also water

Eugène Warmenbol

Abstract

The Belgian sword burials of Court-Saint-Etienne and neighboring villages, Gedinne and Harchies, to which one might add the more recent discoveries of Aalst-Hofstade and Neerharen-Rekem, are recognized as a very important group of elite burials of the Early Iron Age in Northwest Europe. The burials of the Court-Saint-Etienne area also produced many horse trappings, but it appears that they are a relatively late feature here as elsewhere, with, to us, the 'Chieftain's grave' in Oss in the southern Netherlands as a classic example. The present paper proposes to contextualize these burials, often used to show the 'contrast' between the Late Bronze Age and the Early Iron Age, while there is no question that change came quite gradually. There are very clear indications, for instance, that hoarding and wet depositions are, in the southern Netherlands and Belgium, very much a feature of the Late Bronze Age and of the Early Iron Age as well, but it is also true that they get less and less conspicuous as time goes on. Many urnfields in use at the end of the Bronze Age continue for a few generations into the Early Iron Age, showing that the 'advent' of the social and economic order of the Iron Age is very much an endogenous, 'Atlantic' phenomenon, with some confirmation through traditional typo-chronology. An (new) opening towards southern Germany and eastern France and, beyond, the Mediterranean, seems to occur during the 6th century BC, with the Kemmelberg as a possible Fürstensitz, probably thriving on the North Sea salt trade.

Résumé

Les tombes à épées de Court-Saint-Etienne et de certaines communes proches, de Gedinne et Harchies, auxquelles ont ajoutera les découvertes plus récentes de Aalst-Hofstade et Neerharen-Rekem, constituent un ensemble important de tombes "des élites" du Premier âge du Fer à l'échelle de l'Europe nord-occidentale. Les sépultures de la région de Court-Saint-Etienne ont aussi produit un certain nombre de pièces de harnachement, mais celles-ci semblent relativement tardives, avec la tombe "du chef" de Oss dans le Sud des Pays-Bas comme exemple classique. L'article que voici propose de contextualiser ces sépultures, souvent utilisées pour souligner les "contrastes" entre l'âge du Bronze final et le Premier âge du Fer, alors que les choses changent fort graduellement. Ainsi, contrairement aux clichés en la matière, les dépôts en pleine terre, comme les dépôts dans les rivières, sont troujours pratiqués au Premier âge du Fer, tout en devenant, apparemment, progressivement plus rares. Beaucoup de nécropoles en utilisation à la fin de l'âge du Bronze, le sont encore pour quelques générations appartenant au Premier âge du Fer, ce qui signifie sans doute que les phénomènes sociaux-économiques qui caractérisent ce dernier sont endogènes, "atlantiques", ce que la traditionnelle typo-chronologie vient d'ailleurs confirmer. Une nouvelle ouverture vers le Sud de l'Allemagne et l'Est de la France et, au-delà, vers la Méditerranée, semble se produire dans le courant du VIème siècle avant notre ère, avec le site du Mont Kemmel comme exemple vraisemblable de Fürstensitz, florissant grâce au commerce du sel de Mer du Nord.

Introduction

We presented a *status quaestionis* about the 'transition' from the Bronze to the Iron Age some ten years ago (Warmenbol/Leclercq 2009); but both Bronze Age and Iron Age studies in Belgium have made major strides forwards since (Guillaume 2013; Warmenbol 2015). Though a lot of the new or rediscovered material is unpublished yet, a new *status quaestionis* seems fully justified, the more so because most of the new material does *not* come from burial sites and thus finally allows for some contextualization of these, putting them into a (cultural) landscape. We will focus in this paper on old and new finds with absolute dates, which will enable us to better understand the large-scale interactions that seem to be so typical of this period.

Burials

Radiocarbon dating has been possible on burned bones for more than ten years now (De Mulder *et al.* 2007), and we thus have now a number of dated burials, exclusively cremations, from this period. Those that concern us, of course, mostly fall in the infamous 'Hallstatt-plateau'. We gladly refer to the contribution by Guy De Mulder (this volume) regarding these matters.

The most interesting date, no doubt, remains the one for *Graf* 72 in Neerharen-Rekem (Limburg) (Van Impe 1980), an urnfield in use at the end of the Bronze Age and the beginning of the Iron Age, which was the subject of a doctoral thesis some years ago (Temmerman 2007). This grave produced the remains of three individuals, allegedly two young men and a young woman, accompanied by three broken and burned swords of Gündlingen/Villement type, three broken (?) and burned spearheads and two chapes, one of the Coplow Farm type, the other of the Sion Reach type (Warmenbol 1988, 248-250) (Fig. 1). There are two dates, in fact, the medium value of which is 2675 ± 40 BP (GrA-17787/19062) (Lanting/Van der Plicht 2002, 225), i.e. something like 840-795 cal BC (at 95.4 % probability), which is, of course, surprisingly early.

On the contrary, the dates for the tombs in Wijshagen (Limburg) are definitely late. A first set of dates was obtained through the Groningen laboratory, a second set, quite recently, through the Brussels laboratory. Two tumuli with situlae (C and E), dated 2420 ± 30 BP (GrA-14279) or 2496 ± 45 BP (RICH-20578), and 2440 ± 40 BP (GrA-14281) or 2371 ± 32 BP (RICH-20577) tend to put both incineration tombs not in the Hallstatt but in the La Tène period. The same is true of tumulus H, with its *cista a cordoni* and horse trappings, dated 2430 ± 30 BP (GrA-14284) or 2275 ± 32 BP (RICH-20589), which, of course, is not unexpected (De Mulder *et al.* 2016, with bibliography).

Another interesting new find, as far as burial places go, though it did not produce any elite material – no material at all, in fact – is the giant circular ditch in Edegem 'Buizegem' (Antwerpen), about 53 to 54 m in diameter, 1.10 to 2.60 m wide and 1.10 to 1.70 m deep, probably surrounding a massive tumulus (Fig. 2). It was immediately compared to the one surrounding the *Fürstengrab* in Oss (Noord-Brabant), and just as here, there is a centrally placed, smaller circular ditch underneath, which in both cases delimited another, older tumulus, the one in Edegem associated with a single Beaker fragment (Vandevelde *et al.* 2007, 13-24). No ¹⁴C-dates were produced.

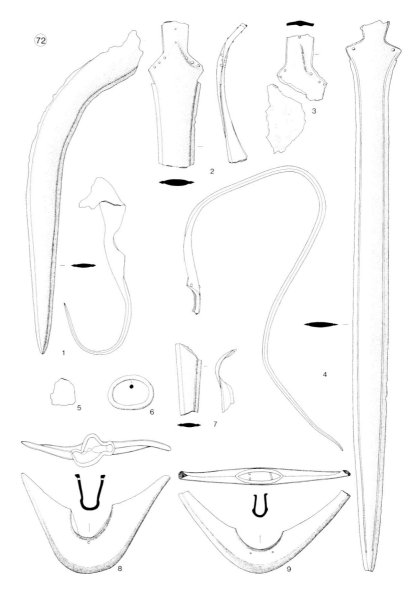

Fig. 1. The bronze swords
and chapes from tomb 72 in
Neerharen-Rekem (Limburg)
(after Van Impe 1980, pl. XII).

Burial goods

Bronze swords and their chapes are, of course, one of the most characteristic grave
goods of the Early Iron Age in Belgium and the southern Netherlands. It has
now been generally accepted that these bronze swords and chapes are the direct
descendants of the Late Bronze Age ones (Milcent 2004, 108-113; Warmenbol
1988), and recent discoveries even show some overlap in the deposition of 'Late
Bronze Age' and 'Early Iron Age' types in urnfields that quite often stay in use at
least during the 8th century BC.

At least two of the swords of Harchies (Hainaut), if not all of them, could
definitely be considered to be Ewart Park, or Holme Pierpoint rather than
Gündlingen swords, or, at least, are 'proto-Hallstatt' rather than 'Hallstatt'-swords
(Leblois 2010; Mariën 1999).

A recent find from Marche-en-Famenne 'La Campagnette' (Namur) (Lecarme/
Warmenbol 2015), belonging to an urnfield that remains to be excavated, deserves

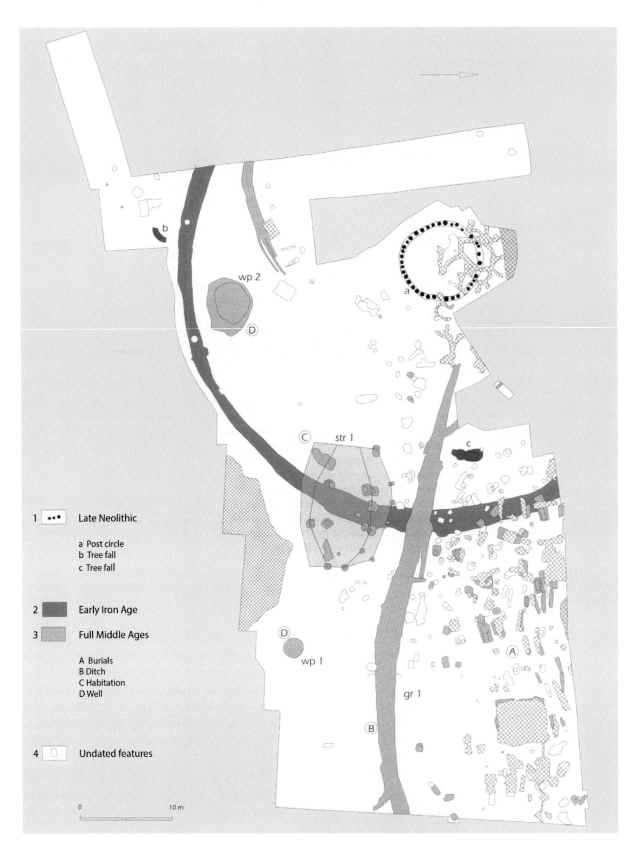

Fig. 2. The Fürstengrab from Edegem 'Buizegem' (Antwerpen), built over a Beaker barrow (after Vandevelde et al. 2007, fig. 44, legend translated by the author).

1 ●●● Late Neolithic

    a Post circle
    b Tree fall
    c Tree fall

2   Early Iron Age

3   Full Middle Ages

    A Burials
    B Ditch
    C Habitation
    D Well

4   Undated features

0   10 m

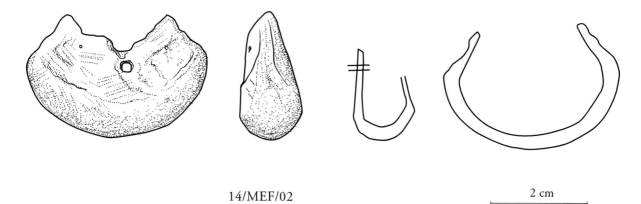

14/MEF/02

2 cm

to be mentioned here too. This is a bag-shaped chape of 'Han-sur-Lesse' type (Milcent 2012, plate 9,18; plate 63,17), so called because four of them have been found at the bottom of the river Lesse in the cave there, 'accompanying' three swords of Ewart Park or Thames type (Mariën 1975, 14-18) (Fig. 3).

We know of only one other from an urnfield, the chape excavated in Weert 'Boshoverheide' (Limburg), where three Gündlingen swords (allegedly) were also found, though not with the chape (Gerdsen 1986, 168 plate 33).

The most interesting new find, is the fragmented sword with its chape in Hofstade 'Kasteelstraat' (Aalst, Oost-Vlaanderen), deposited with a cremation within an urnfield currently being excavated by Ghent Archaeological Team bvba. The sword (Laloo et al. 2014, 26 fig. 20; 28 fig. 24) is a Gündlingen type (Villement or Wehringen, more exactly), the chape (Laloo et al. 2014, 27 fig. 23) is a rare example of a 'naviform' (type A 2), for which we know only one parallel, namely in Court-Saint-Etienne 'La Quenique' (Brabant wallon) (Mariën 1958, 73 fig. 10,109).

Settlements

Twenty years ago, it would have been difficult to 'fill in' a chapter about Early Iron Age settlements in Belgium, then undated, or undiscovered. A few ^{14}C-dates will help us, as traditional typochronology applied to ceramics has somewhat been discredited, not always with good reasons (there certainly is hope: see, for instance Bardel et al. 2013).

A most interesting recent excavation was that of Hermalle-sous-Huy 'Campagne de la Gérée' (Liège), where two buildings, of apparently Early Iron Age date, were discovered, one of which (B.14) was ^{14}C-dated (charcoal from one of its posts: 2600 ± 60 BP (Beta-206972) (Frébutte et al. 2007). It has three naves, is 21.60 m long and 6.40 to 6.80 m wide. The second building was probably similar, but is not so well preserved (Fig. 4). Several pits with what appears to be Early Iron Age pottery were excavated aux abords et au sein (around and within) the two buildings. There is nothing 'aristocratic' about them.

Slightly older dates, rather Late Bronze Age, were obtained for two wells with a woven wooden casing discovered in Sint-Gillis-Waas (Oost-Vlaanderen) (Hoorne 2004, with bibliography), one (n° 282) ^{14}C-dated to 2690 ± 30 BP (IRPA-1244), the other one (no n°) to 2660 ± 40 BP (KIA-10549) (Warmenbol/Leclercq 2009, 379). The other structures on the site, houses and granaries, though, are not necessarily strictly contemporary (Bourgeois 2003), and could/should in fact be

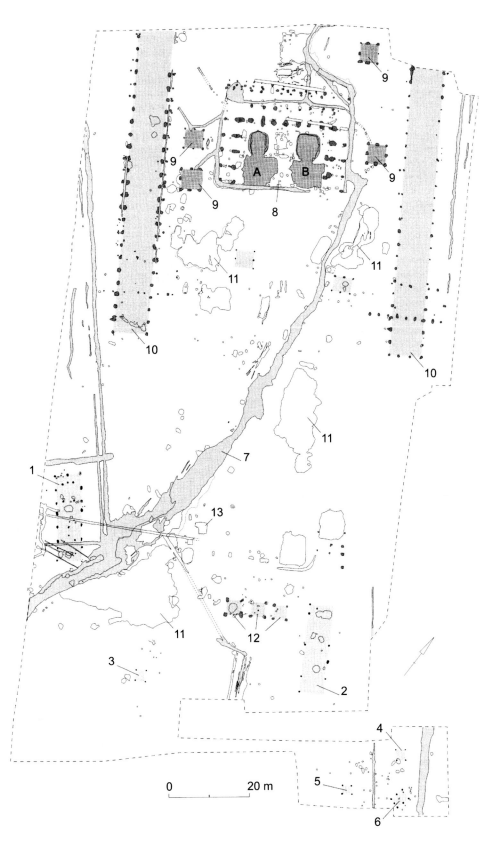

Fig. 4. The Early Iron Age houses (1,2) and granaries (3-6) in Hermalle-sous-Huy 'Campagne de la Gérée'(Engis, Liège), 7 is a natural gully and 8-13 make up a gallo-roman tile-factory (after Frébutte/Gustin 2007, 130).

somewhat younger. These Early Iron Age houses again have three naves, but seem to be shorter than Late Bronze Age examples, which can be read as 'change' but we should avoid generalizations (Bourgeois/Cherreté 2005, 62-65). Again, there is nothing aristocratic about this hamlet…

Slightly older dates than the ones from Hermalle-sous-Huy, suggest the settlement at Ekeren 'Schriek' (Antwerpen), might again be Late Bronze Age rather than Early Iron Age. The three-naved house was only partially excavated, was much eroded, and was dated through charcoal from of a centrally (?) placed pit 2690 ± 25 BP (KIA-20896). An associated (?) granary (B), was dated 2565 ± 25 BP (KIA-20897), another one (D), 2880 ± 30 BP (KIA-20895), which shows matters are not simple (Minsaer 2003; 2004).

Mostly, the archaeological structures are much eroded, and every so often disturbed by later occupations, as is the case in Orp-Jauche 'Le Tierceau' (Brabant wallon), where we have Late Bronze Age material, but also Early Iron Age material (Ha C2, most probably), in distinct excavated structures from silo to waste-pit (Hanut/Goffioul 2015, 107 fig. 2; 108 fig. 3). A comparable site is 'Ghislenghien IV' in Ath/Ghislenghien (Hainaut), where Early Iron Age material was found (Ha C2 and Ha D), and Middle Iron Age material (La Tène A2 and B1), but in loose association with the pits and posts excavated here (Danèse *et al.* 2015)

Elite settlements?

A few fortified sites in Southern Belgium also produced dates somewhere at the end of the Bronze Age or in the beginning of the Early Iron Age, while most of these sites are attributed to the end of the Late Iron Age, not always with much pertinence.

The Cheslé of Bérismenil (Samrée, Luxembourg), which encloses 13 ha within a meander of the river Ourthe, thus produced a series of interesting radiocarbon dates, related to the actual wall, at different points of its line, such as 2650 ± 40 BP (IRPA-1002), 2640 ± 50 BP (KIK-1172/Utc-9271), 2610 ± 40 BP (IRPA-1208) and 2600 ± 60 BP (KIK-44/Utc-1349) (Warmenbol/Leclercq 2009, 379, with bibliography).

The Cheslé de Bérismenil is to be found in the near vicinity of the gold-panning sites along the Amblève and the Salm, with traces of gold washing going back to the (Early?) Iron Age (recently: Detaille/Van Eerdenburg 2014).

This is certainly the place to mention the Kemmelberg (West-Vlaanderen), which can be found on most distribution maps as the most north-westerly *Fürstensitz* (see now Bourgeois *et al.* 2006), but it is actually quite difficult to assess its true importance, due to massive destruction of the archaeological site during the First World War. Most of what is known from the site is dated in the very early 5th century BC, including the only fragment of Attic pottery ever found in Belgium (Van Doorselaer *et al.* 1987, pl. II,1). The Kemmelberg also produced its own high quality red painted pottery, also found on a few other sites, sometimes more than 100 km away (Dimitrakopoulou *et al.* 2014).

A gilded bronze bead, slightly biconical in shape (L : 2.1 cm) and one small piece of gold foil with (possibly) a palmette-like decoration in repoussé (1.6 x 1.4 cm) are part of the discoveries made here, and they are the only gold finds made on a fortified site of Iron Age date in Belgium (Van Doorselaer *et al.* 1987, plate II, 4.6).

We do not know an exact parallel of the Kemmelberg bead, but it does remind us of the massive, cylindrical beads from the 'Bettelbühl' near the Heuneburg (district Sigmaringen), which were deposited something like a century earlier than the Kemmelberg bead (Krausse/Ebinger-Rist 2012, 124 fig. 134).

River finds

The occurrence of bronze swords of the Early Iron Age in rivers (the Meuse, in particular) is a well-known phenomenon in the southern Netherlands (Fontijn 2003, 171-173), and quite an exceptional one in Belgium, as here they are classically grave goods, with no known bronze example in a wet context (in the Scheldt).

Two iron swords, though, have been dredged from the Dyle in Battel, near Mechelen (Antwerpen) (Warmenbol/Leclercq 2009, 381 fig. 6). One has to remember here that the tumuli from Court-Saint-Etienne (Brabant wallon) are also along the Dyle (Mariën 1958).

One of them has a bronze hilt and an iron blade. The best parallel we found for this curious piece is the sword from Port-Sainte-Foy 'Gué de Chantier' in Périgord, dredged from the Dordogne river. These are swords with the hilt cast and modeled over the tang ending the iron blade, just like the one from tumulus III in Chavéria (Jura) or the one from tumulus I in Vescles (Jura), also part of this small group of 'transitional' weapons (Warmenbol/Leclercq 2009, 382).

The other sword probably had a hilt in perishable material and its iron is in a quite exceptional state of preservation. It confirms the importance of the finds made in the years 1930-1932 at the confluence of the Dyle and the Vrouwenvliet, which did not get any attention yet, though these finds are still available (Georges Hasse archives, Museum Vleeshuis, Antwerpen).

The chape of type Beratzhausen allegedly dredged from the Scheldt near Schoonaarde (Oost-Vlaanderen) (Warmenbol 2000, 106 fig. 4), is problematical, considering it does not have a 'typical' river patina. The same site did produce a razor of type Feldkirch/Bernissart (Warmenbol 1992, 98 note 84), also known from Early Iron Age tombs in Belgium (Jockenhövel 1980, 174).

Objects associated with bronze or iron swords in Early Iron Age graves are rarely found elsewhere, that is true, but this might give us a distorted view of what still went into rivers or hoards in the Early Iron Age, and this applies in particular to tools and ornaments. Linear-faceted axes like the one in tomb 3 from Court-Saint-Etienne 'Champ de la Ferme Rouge' (Brabant wallon) are known from the Scheldt near Wichelen (Oost-Vl) Another one was dredged in the Aisne near Rethel (Ardennes françaises), a second one in the Oise, near Compiègne, and a third one in the Seine near Villeneuve-Saint-Georges (Warmenbol 1992, 80, note 58, with bibliography). The new hoard from Beerse 'Beekakkers' (Antwerpen) had one (see further on), as did the one from Wattenheim (Kr. Bad Dürkheim) (Kibbert 1984, 156-158 plate 56,734; 98C – 99). So we know, as they occur together in Beerse, they were contemporary with Sompting axes, which again appear in rivers as well as in hoards. Several were dredged in the Scheldt near Wichelen (Oost-Vlaanderen) (Desittere 1976, 87 fig. 6,5-6), one of which was dated 2465 ± 35 BP (Utc-3917) (Warmenbol 1992, 80 note 59; Verlaeckt 1996, 66). They are known from hoards to be dated obviously in the Early Iron Age such as the one from Llyn Fawr (Glamorgan) (O'Connor 1980, 420-421) and the type

Wesseling one from Bingen (Kr. Mainz), with two type Gündlingen swords, as cast (Kibbert 1984,130 plate 47, 616; 100A).

Caves and elite deposits?

The well-known cave of Han-sur-Lesse (Namur) produced three fragments of at least two (judging by the colour) golden hollow beads or pinheads, made up of two hemispherical elements, approximately 1.5 cm in diameter and 0.5 cm in height. One of the elements slid into the other one, the join being masked by a flat twisted wire, upon which rest small triangular grapes of granulation. At one end of what we believe to be pinheads, rather than anything else, a rosace was made of two concentric round wires, the outer one doubled on the inside and (?) the outside by granulation, the inner one completely filled up with granulation. The source of inspiration for these jewels is definitely Mediterranean, but their manufacture is possibly non-Mediterranean (Warmenbol 2004, with bibliography) (Fig. 5).

The closest parallels (materially and geographically) are the pendants from Anet (Ins) 'Grossholz' (Kt. Bern) and Jegenstorf 'Hurst' (Kt. Bern) (Furger/Müller 1991, 114; 117), both dated to the middle or third quarter of the 7th century BC. The hollow gold pinheads, without filigree and granulation though, from Urtenen 'Grauholz' (Kt. Bern) (Furger/Müller 1991, 116) could be mentioned here too, as should the gold beads, just with filigree, from the 'Bettelbühl' near the Heuneburg (Kr. Sigmarigen) (Krausse/Ebinger-Rist, 2012, 124 fig. 134; 125 fig 136), but all these are half a century younger, or more.

Curiously, if a date somewhere around 650-550 BC is correct for the fragments found at the Trou de Han in Han-sur-Lesse, this would mean that they stand almost alone for the period, at least they alone have been identified as Early Iron Age material from here, but one could take a lead from here. At the entrance of the tourist circuit through the cave, the 'Caveau' did yield one bi-perforated lug-handle typical of the late 7th or 6th century (or Ha D1) (Zeebroek/Warmenbol 2016). A human skull found isolated in this same part of the cave could be contemporary, though its radiocarbon date is a good example of what the 'Hallstatt-plateau' means: 2515 ± 30 BP (KIA-23755), i.e. 800 cal BC to 520 cal BC (Warmenbol 2007, 541). Another human skull (terebrated!), from the nearby 'Tienne des Maulins' in Eprave (Namur), could be of the same period (Groenen 2006, 14 fig. 2), with a radiocarbon date of 2430 ± 30 BP (KIA-25233), though the sample could be contaminated. The skull was indeed found with the remains of at least sixteen other individuals, which produced dates in the Late Neolithic (Toussaint *et al.* 2014).

And the bi-perforated lug-handle from Han-sur-Lesse is certainly not the only pot sherd from the Early Iron Age to be found in a cave in Southern Belgium. A new study of the pottery from Cave n° 1 from Les Avins (Clavier, Liège) shows a considerable part of it can be dated in the Early Iron Age (Fig. 6), but it is not yet clear if the human remains apparently stratigraphically associated, are indeed of the same date (Hubert/Jadot 1986; see also Cauwe 2004, table 1).

Back to burials

The bi-perforated lug handles such as the one from Han-sur-Lesse occur quite often in Saint-Vincent 'Grand-Bois' (Luxembourg) (Mariën 1964, 43 fig. 22; 59 fig. 37; 67 fig. 46; 87 fig. 65; 113 fig. 88; 115 fig. 90; 119 fig. 92), where

Fig. 5. One of the granulated and filigreed gold jewels from Han-sur-lesse (Rochefort, Namur) (photo G. Focant).

tomb 61 yielded a hollow-headed pin, up to a point comparable to the golden ones mentioned previously, except this one is in iron (Mariën 1964, 96 fig. 73; see also Mariën 1964, 128 fig. 99 for a second one, without context). Three very similar pins were discovered in the well-known 'Chieftain's grave' of Oss (Noord-Brabant), which also yielded a Mindelheim type sword with its hilt and pommel decorated with gold strips, drawing geometrical motifs (Fokkens/Jansen 2004, 65). We are aware of the fact the 'Chieftain's grave' recently produced two radiocarbon dates, one on wood, one on cremated bone (dates communicated by Sasja van der Vaart-Verschoof, and many thanks for that!). We feel the one on wood is tricky to use, as it could not be identified as being from an object, and so does not *necessarily* belongs to the grave, is just possibly alder, and is by all means too old, with a date of 2785 ± 30 BP (GrA-55555), calibrating to 1007-854 cal BC, definitely a Late Bronze Age date. Only the bone sample seems, to us, to relate to the grave, and it obviously does, as it pertains to the human remains, with a date of 2500 ± 30 BP (GrA-55551), calibrating to 788-537 cal BC which could suit the high date favored by Sasja van der Vaart-Verschoof, but also the low date we favor (Warmenbol 1993, 104 proposes a date between 600 to 550; Fokkens/Jansen 2004, 68 suggest one between 625 and 575 BC). To us, it seems obvious the 'Chieftain's grave' of Oss cannot be much older or much younger than tomb 3 of Court-Saint-Etienne 'La Ferme Rouge' (Brabant wallon) (Mariën 1958, 109-111 fig. 17-19, several elements of its assemblage (including an antenna-sword) pointing to a date not earlier than the 7th century (Sievers 1982, 10 strangely makes of the sword an exception to the rule) (Fig. 7). Whatever date one prefers, they all seem to imply that the 'Chieftain's' sword was a heirloom, which should not come as a great surprise, and some of the material in Court-Saint-Etienne 'La Ferme Rouge' could fit the same description. The use of gold on the handle and/ or pommel of swords like the one found in Oss is quite exceptional, but occurs in Hallstatt itself, as in grave G 299 or tomb G 573 (see elsewhere in this volume).

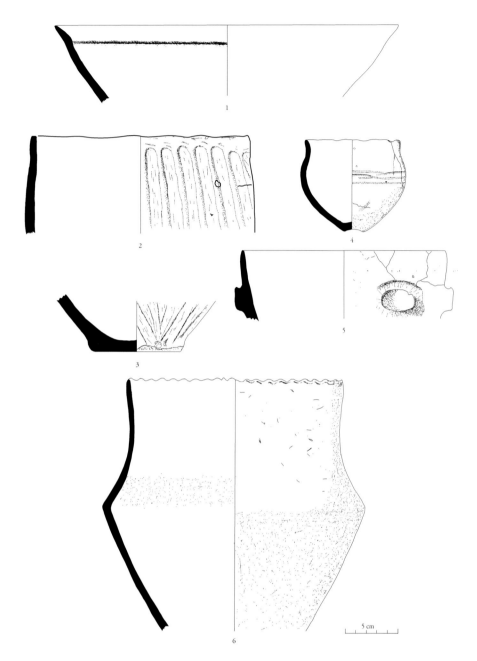

Fig. 6. Iron Age ceramics from Cave n° 1 in Les Avins (Clavier, Liège) (drawing and DAO W. Leclercq, Université libre de Bruxelles).

A very interesting cemetery, which awaits full publication, is the one from Kaulille 'Dorperheide' (Limburg), excavated in 1983-1984, and attributed, through typo-chronology to the 'transition' of Ha C to Ha D. As so often seems the case, there seem to be more metal objects here, than what one might expect in a Bronze Age cemetery. Most of them are bronze jewelry, but here is also a *Schwanenhalsnadel* in iron (Vanbutsele/Van Impe 2007). This iron pin from tomb 34, with a hollow head, is, up to a point, comparable with the above-mentioned pins from Oss and Saint-Vincent.

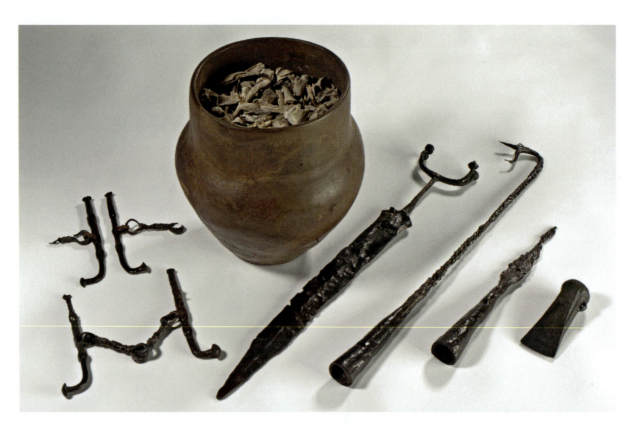

Fig. 7. *Part of the material from tomb 3 in Court-Saint-Etienne 'La Ferme Rouge' (Brabant wallon), including the linear-faceted axe (right) (photo Musées royaux d'Art et d'Histoire, Bruxelles).*

Fig. 8. *The hoard found in Beerse 'Beekakkers', with two bronze-sheet hollow rings and two axes (a Sompting-type, and a linear-faceted one) (photo S. Dewickere).*

Hoards

A very important, though small hoard was discovered recently in Beerse 'Beekakkers' (Antwerpen), in one of the post-holes of a small building that was part of an Early Iron Age farmstead. Four bronze objects were buried there: two socketed axes and two fragmentary hollow rings (about 155 mm in diameter) (Van Impe *et al.* 2011; Delaruelle *et al.* 2013, 122-125; Warmenbol 2015, 72 fig. 4,27) (Fig. 8). The rings have been compared to the Scandinavian and north German *Hohlwulstringe* (Schacht 1982), but could as well be compared to south German *Holstwulstringe* (Nagler-Zanier 2005, 154-158). The first axe is obviously a linear-faceted axe, the second one an axe of Sompting type (the published drawing is poor). This is a rather strange, or at least exceptional, combination. A *terminus post quem* (ca. 800 BC) is available for the deposition: charcoal left by the post was dated to 897-802 cal BC (KIA-43333: 2680 ± 30 BP). As we have seen, these axes also occur as river finds, and one was found in Court-Saint-Etienne 'Ferme Rouge' tomb 3.

Another grave find is to be mentioned here, the one from Rhenen 'Koerheuvel' (Utrecht), where a 'princely' grave to be dated in (the second half?) of the 7th century, produced a bronze situla, bronze and iron horse-gear, and half of a (recently broken) bronze axe of type Wesseling, the 'German' equivalent to the 'British' Sompting type, often with the same rib and pellet decoration (Van Heeringen 1999; see also, more generally, Verger 1997).

One of these is to be found in the already mentioned Bingen (district Mainz-Bingen, Rhineland-Palatinate) hoard (?), associated, among other things, with two *Rohgüsse* of bronze tanged swords, assuredly close to the Gündlingen/Villement type(s) (Kibbert 1984, 129-130 no 616 plate 100A).

Another German hoard (but again with a '?'), the one from Wattenheim (district Bad Dürkheim, Rhineland-Palatinate) is to be referenced here, this one with an axe close to the 'linear-faceted' ones mentioned before. All were found during works for the *Reichsautobahn*, in 1937, and one cannot but regret there was no follow-up. There is bronze, there is iron, much has been deliberately broken, and/or has been touched by fire. One of the most remarkable finds here, certainly in our perspective, is the iron flesh-hook, very close to the one from Court-Saint-Etienne 'Ferme Rouge' tomb 3, which, as we have seen, also has a linear-faceted axe (Kibbert 1984, 154-155 no 734 plate 99).

Beerse 'Beekakkers' is not the only Belgian hoard datable to the Early Iron Age. We have little doubt that the socketed axes of Geistingen type are to be dated in the Early Iron Age (though this cannot yet be 'proven', for lack of associations (Butler/Steegstra 2003, 303-309). A new study of some of these thin-walled axes from the eponymous hoard (Kinrooi, Limburg) confirmed that they are made of a non-functional copper alloy (Nienhuis *et al.* 2013). This reminds us, as far as the founder's intention goes, of the (quite different) non-functional alloys of the better-known axes of so-called Armorican types (recently: Rivallain 2012, 130-140; Rivallain 2013). We have no doubt at all about their Iron Age date (late Ha C or rather Ha D) (Gomez de Soto 2015), but many doubts about the authenticity of the finds with a Belgian or Dutch provenance, especially the so-called 'hoards' from Hoogstraten and Turnhout (Antwerpen) (Butler/Steegstra 2003, 309-316; Warmenbol 2013; forthcoming).

Conclusion

This is a work in progress, and it would be risky to present 'conclusions', as yet. It seems pretty obvious to us that the passage from the Late Bronze Age to the Early Iron Age is a very progressive one. The sword burials give an impression of abrupt change, but this is assuredly a false impression. Some material has been misdated, which partially explains why so many authors created a kind of divide between the Bronze and, at least, the beginning of the Iron Age. A clear indication of continuity is that many urnfields remain in use at least for a few generations, all the finds showing an endogenous evolution, and strong 'Atlantic' affinities. Horse-gear is indeed the herald of actual change, something that happens not in the beginning or the middle of the 8th century BC, but rather at the end of the 8th century BC, or during the 7th century BC (Milcent 2004, but see also Trachsel 2004). Scholars are dealing with a lot of old finds in Belgium, which means that the importance of a new excavation of an important urnfield, such as the one at Hofstade 'Kasteelstraat', cannot be overestimated.

Acknowledgments

We would like to thank the many colleagues who helped us with the collection of the materials presented here, especially Guy De Mulder (Universiteit Gent), Alain Guillaume (Service Public Wallon), Walter Leclercq (Université libre de Bruxelles), Stephan Delaruelle (Erfgoed Noorderkempen), and Georges Michel (Commission Wallonne d'Etude et Protection des Sites Souterrains).

A special mention goes to Mathieu Boudin and Mark Van Strydonck (Institut Royal du Patrimoine Artistique), who provided us and others with many precious ^{14}C-dates.

Bibliography

Bardel *et al.* 2013: D. Bardel/N. Buchez/A. Henton/E. Leroy-Langelin/A. Sergent/C. Gutierrez/L. Géant, Du répertoire hallstattien au répertoire laténien dans le Nord de la France. Première analyse typologique, chronologique et culturelle des corpus céramiques du Hallstatt D à La Tène A1 (VIIe-Ve s. av. J.-C.). Revue du Nord, 95, 2013, 143-192.

Bourgeois/Cherreté 2005: J. Bourgeois/B. Cherretté. L'âge du Bronze et le Premier âge du Fer dans les Flandres occidentale et orientale (Belgique): Un état de la question. In: J. Bourgeois/M. Talon (eds.), L'âge du Bronze du Nord de la France dans son contexte européen. Actes des congrès nationaux des sociétés historiques et scientifiques, 125e, Lille, 2000 (Paris 2005) 43-81.

Bourgeois *et al.* 2006: J.Bourgeois/G. De Mulder/J.-L. Putman, De Kemmelberg en verwante elitesites in Centraal- en Westeuropa (6de-5de eeuw): Perspectieven voor toekomstig onderzoek / The Kemmelberg and related elite sites in Central and Western Europe (6th-5th century) : Perspectives for future research (Ieper-Kemmel 2006).

Butler/Steegstra 2003: J. Butler/H. Steegstra, Bronze Age metal and amber in the Netherlands (III :II) : Catalogue of the socketed axes. Part A. Palaeohistoria 43/44, 2003, 263-319.

Cauwe 2004: N. Cauwe, Les sépultures collectives néolithiques en grotte du Bassin mosan. Bilan documentaire, Anthropologica et Praehistorica 115, 2004, 217-224.

Danèse *et al.* 2015: V. Danèse/F. Hanut/M. Van Assche, Vestiges d'occupation du premier et du second âge du Fer dans la zone d'activité économique d'Ath/Ghislenghien (Ghislenghien IV) (prov. de Hainaut, Belgique). Lunula, Archaeologia protohistorica XXIII, 2015, 153-161.

Delaruelle *et al.* 2013: S. Delaruelle/R. Annaert/M. Van Gils/L. Van Impe/J. Van Doninck (eds), Vondsten vertellen. Archeologische parels uit de Antwerpse Kempen (Turnhout 2013).

De Mulder *et al.* 2007: G. De Mulder/M. van Strydonck/M. Boudin/W. Leclercq/N. Paridaens/E. Warmenbol, Re-evaluation of the Late Bronze Age and Early Iron Age Chronology of the Western Belgian Urnfields based on C14 dating of cremated Bones. Radiocarbon 49,2, 2007, 499-514.

De Mulder *et al.* 2016: G. De Mulder/M. Van Strydonck/M. Boudin/L. Van Impe/G. Creemers, De ^{14}C-dateringen van het grafveld van Wijshagen (gem. Meeuwen-Gruitrode, prov. Limburg, België). Lunula, Archaeologica protohistorica XXIV, 2016, 173-177.

Detaille/Van Eerdenbrugh 2014: J. Detaille/B. Van Eerdenbrugh, Chercheurs d'or en Belgique. Les miettes des miettes (Liège 2014).

Dimitrakopoulou *et al.* 2014: A. Dimitrakopoulou/K. Delanghe/J. Bourgeois/P. Vandenabeele/G. De Mulder, Red painted pottery from the Kemmelberg (prov. West-Flanders, Belgium. Lunula, Archaeologia protohistorica XXII, 2014, 123-132.

Fokkens/Jansen 2004: H. Fokkens/R. Jansen, Het vorstengraf van Oss. Een archeologische speurtocht naar een prehistorisch grafveld (Utrecht 2004).

Fontijn 2003: D. Fontijn, Sacrificial Landscapes. Cultural biographies of persons, objects and 'natural' places in the Bronze Age of the southern Netherlands, c. 2300-600 BC. Analecta Praehistorica Leidensia 33/34 (Leiden 2003).

Frébutte *et al.* 2007: Chr. Frébutte/M. Gustin/J.-P. Marchal/O. Collette/A. Defgnée/C. Laurent, Occupation du Hallstatt C à la « Campagne de la Gérée », à Hermalle-sous-Huy, Engis (province de Liège). Lunula, Archaeologia protohistorica XV, 2007, 97-105.

Furger/Müller 1991: A. Furger/F. Müller, L'or des Helvètes. Trésors celtiques en Suisse (Zurich 1991).

Frébutte/Gustin 2007: C. Frébutte/M. Gustin, Engis/Hermalle-sous-Huy: fouille d'une installation protohistorique et d'une tuilerie gallo-romaine à la "Campagne de la Gérée". Chronique de l'Archéologie wallonne 14, 2007, 129-131.

Gerdsen 1986: H. Gerdsen, Studien zu den Schwertgräberen der älteren Hallstattzeit (Mainz 1986).

Gomez de Soto 2015: J. Gomez de Soto, Les haches à douilles de type armoricain: Une production strictement de l'âge du Fer. Critique des sources documentaires afférant à leur chronologie. Bulletin de la Société préhistorique Française 112, 2015, 117-136.

Groenen 2006: M. Groenen, La grotte-abri du Tiène des Maulins. In: L'archéologie à l'Université Libre de Bruxelles (2001-2005). Matériaux pour une histoire des milieux et des pratiques humaines, Bruxelles. Etudes d'Archéologie 1 (Bruxelles 2006) 13-20.

Guillaume 2003: A. Guillaume, 150 années de recherches hallstattiennes en Wallonie. Les rites funéraires. Bulletin du Cercle archéologique Hesbaye-Condroz XXVII, 2003, 3-184.

Guillaume 2013: A. Guillaume, Le Premier âge du Fer. In A. Guillaume (ed.), L'archéologie en Wallonie. Les âges des Métaux. Carnets du Patrimoine 111 (Namur 2013) 27-42.

Hanut/Goffioul 2015: F. Hanut/C. Goffioul, Périodisation du mobilier céramique issu des fouilles TGV dans le village protohistorique du « Tierceau » (Orp-Jauche : prov. du Brabant wallon, Belgique). Lunula, Archaeologica protohistorica XXIII, 2015, 105-114.

Hoorne 2004: J. Hoorne, Brons- en IJzertijdwaterputten in België. Lunula, Archaeologia protohistorica XII, 2004, 21-28.

Hubert/Jadot 1986: F. Hubert/M. Jadot, Une grotte-ossuaire « Champs d'Urnes » à Clavier. Archaeologia Belgica II, 1986, 19-21.

Jockenhövel 1980: A. Jockenhövel, Die Rasiermesser in Westeuropa. Prähistorische Bronzefunde VIII,3 (München 1980).

Kibbert 1984: K. Kibbert, Die Äxte und Beile im mittleren Westdeutschland II. Prähistorische Bronzefunde IX,13 (Müchen 1984).

Krausse/Ebinger-Rist 2012: D. Krausse/N. Ebinger-Rist, Jenseits der Donau – Das neue « Fürstinnengrab » von der Heuneburg. In : Die Welt der Kelten. Zentren der Macht – Kostbarkeiten der Kunst (Ostfildern 2012) 124-126.

Laloo et al. 2014: P. Laloo/J. Sergeant/J. Cryns/J. De Reu/L. Allemeersch/G. De Mulder, Hofstade – Kasteelstraat. Rapportage van het archeologisch proefsleuvenonderzoek. Gate-rapport 72 (Evergem 2014).

Lanting/van der Plicht 2002: J. Lanting/J. van der Plicht, De ^{14}C-chronologie van de Nederlandse pre-en protohistorie, IV : Bronstijd en Vroege Ijzertijd. Palaeohistoria 43-44, 2002, 117-262.

Leblois 2010: E. Leblois, La nécropole hallstattienne d'Harchies « Maison Cauchies » : un bilan et des perspectives (province de Hainaut, Belgique). Lunula, Archaeologia protohistorica 18, 2010, 107-111.

Lecarme/Warmenbol 2015: M. Lecarme/E. Warmenbol, Nouveaux objets métalliques de l'âge du Bronze final en provenance de Marche-en-Famenne 'La Campagnette' (prov. de Luxembourg, Belgique), Lunula. Archaeologia protohistorica XXIII, 2015, 75-79.

Mariën 1958: M.-E. Mariën, Trouvailles du Champ d'Urnes et des Tombelles hallstattiennes de Court-Saint-Etienne. Monographies d'Archéologie Nationale 1 (Bruxelles 1958).

Mariën 1964: M.-E. Mariën, La nécropole à tombelles de Saint-Vincent. Monographies d'Archéologie Nationale 3 (Bruxelles 1964).

Mariën 1975: M.-E. Mariën, Epées de bronze proto-hallstattiennes et hallstattiennes découvertes en Belgique. Helinium XV, 1975, 14-37.

Mariën 1999: M.-E. Mariën, Nécropole hallstattienne à tombelles dans le « Bois de la Taille des Vignes » à Havré (Hainaut, Belgique). In: B. Chaume/J.-P. Mohen/P. Perin (eds.) Archéologie des Celtes. Mélanges à la mémoire de René Joffroy (Montagnac 1999) 227-242.

Milcent 2004: P.-Y. Milcent, Le premier âge du Fer en France centrale. Mémoires de la Société Préhistorique Française 34 (Paris 2004).

Milcent 2012: P.-Y. Milcent, Le temps des élites en Gaule atlantique. Chronologie des mobiliers et rythmes de constitution des dépôts métalliques dans le contexte européen (XIIIe – VIIe s. av. J.-C.) (Rennes 2012).

Minsaer 2003: K. Minsaer, Van de Leugenberg tot het Laar. Bewoningssporen uit de late bronstijd, de ijzertijd en de Gallo-Romeinse periode aan de goederenspoorlijn te Ekeren. Interimverslag. In: G. Cuyt/K. Sas (eds.), Vlekken in het zand. Archeologie in en rond Antwerpen (Antwerpen 2003) 115-123.

Minsaer 2004: K. Minsaer, Bewoningssporen uit de late Bronstijd en de IJzertijd te Ekeren. Voorlopige resultaten van het archeologisch onderzoek in 2002 naar aanleiding van de uitbreiding van goederenspoor 27A. Lunula, Archaeologia protohistorica XII, 2004, 109-115.

Nagler-Zanier 2005: C. Nagler-Zanier, Ringschmuck der Hallstattzeit aus Bayern. Prähistorische Bronzefunde X,7 (München 2005).

Nienhuis et al. 2013: J. Nienhuis/H. Postma/G. Creemers, Four remarkable socketed axes from the Geistingen hoard. In: G. Creemers (ed.), Archaeological Contributions to Materials and Immateriality. Atuatuca 4 (Tongeren 2013) 8-21.

O'Connor 1980: B. O'Connor, Cross-Channel Relations in the Later Bronze Age. Relations between Britain, North-Eastern France and the Low Countries during the Later Bronze Age and the Early Iron Age. British Archaeological Reports, International Series 91 (Oxford 1980).

Rivallain 2012: J. Rivallain, Les haches à douille revisitées. Apports des travaux et des études de la deuxième moitié du XXe siècle en Bretagne. Les Dossiers du Centre Régional d'Archéologie d'Alet AI (Rennes 2012).

Rivallain 2013: J. Rivallain, Le plomb et les haches à douille armoricaines en Bretagne. Antiquités Nationales 44, 2013, 65-76.

Schacht 1982: S. Schacht, Die Nordischen Hohlwulste der frühen Eisenzeit (Halle 1982).

Sievers 1982: S. Sievers, Die mitteleuropäischen Hallstattdolche. Prähistorische Bronzefunde VI,6 (München 1982).

Temmerman 2007: B. Temmerman, Het urnenveld van Neerharen-Rekem: Onderzoek naar de ethnografie, sociaal-economische verhoudingen en ideologie van een prehistorische gemeenschap tijdens de Late Bronstijd/Vroege Ijzertijd in Westeuropa. Unpublished doctoral thesis (Brussel 2007).

Toussaint et al. 2014: M. Toussaint/I. Jadin/S. Pirson, Aperçu de la préhistoire de Rochefort. In: C. Frébutte (ed.), Coup d'œil sur 25 ans de recherches archéologiques à Rochefort, de 1989 à 2014. Namur 2014, 32-47.

Trachsel 2004: M. Trachsel, Untersuchungen zur relativen und absoluten Chronologie der Hallstattzeit. Universitätsforschungen zur prähistorischen Archäologie 104 (Bonn 2004).

Vanbutsele/Van Impe 2007: N. Vanbutsele/L. Van Impe, Het urnenveld uit de vroege ijzertijd op de 'Dorperheide' te Kaulille (Gemeente Bocholt, provincie Limburg). Lunula, Archaeologia protohistorica XV, 2007, 113-119.

Vandevelde et al. 2007: J. Vandevelde/R. Annaert/A. Lentacker/A. Ervynck/M. Vandenbruaene, Vierduizend jaar bewoning en begraving in Edegem-*Buizegem* (prov. Antwerpen). Relicta 3, 2007, 9-67.

Van Doorselaer et al. 1987: A. Van Doorselaer/J.-L. Putman/ K. Van der Gucht/F. Janssens, De Kemmelberg, een Keltische bergvesting. Westvlaamse Archaeologica, Monografieën III (Kortrijk 1987).

Van Heeringen 1999: R. M. Van Heeringen, Burial with Rhine view: The Hallstatt situla grave on the Koerheuvel at Rhenen. Berichten van de Rijksdienst voor het Oudheidkundig Bodemonderzoek 43, 1999, 69-97.

Van Impe et al. 2011: L. Van Impe/S. Delaruelle/S. Hertoghs/S. Scheltjens/ G. Bervoets, Een bronsdepot uit de vroege ijzertijd aan de Beekakkers in Beerse (prov. Antwerpen, België). Lunula, Archaeologica protohistorica XIX, 2011, 3-10.

Van Impe 1980: L. Van Impe, Graven uit de Urnenveldenperiode op het Hangveld te Rekem. I: Inventaris. Archaeologia Belgica 227 (Brussel 1980).

Verger 1997: S. Verger, L'incinération en urne métallique : un indicateur des contacts aristocratiques transalpins. In: P. Brun/B.Chaume (eds.), Vix et les éphémères principautés celtiques. Les VIe et Ve siècle avant J.-C. en Europe centre-occidentale. Actes du Colloque de Châtillon-sur-Seine (27-29 octobre 1993) (Paris 1997) 223-238.

Verlaeckt 1996: K. Verlaeckt, Between River and Barrow. A reappraisal of Bronze Age metalwork found in the province of East-Flanders (Belgium). British Archaeological Reports, International Series 632 (Oxford 1996).

Warmenbol 1988: E. Warmenbol, Broken bronzes and burned bones. The transition from Bronze to Iron Age in the Low Countries. Helinium XXVIII, 1988, 244-270.

Warmenbol 1989: E. Warmenbol, De l'âge du Bronze à l'âge du Fer en Belgique et dans le Sud des Pays-Bas. In: La civilisation de Hallstatt, bilan d'une rencontre, Liège 1987. Etudes et Recherches de l'Université de Liège 36 (Liège 1989) 133-140.

Warmenbol 1992: E. Warmenbol, Le matériel de l'âge du Bronze : le seau de la drague et le casque du héros. In: E. Warmenbol/Y. Cabuy/V. Hurt/N. Cauwe, La collection Edouard Bernays. Néolithique et âge du Bronze, époques gallo-romaine et médiévale. Monographie d'Archéologie Nationale 6 (Bruxelles 1992) 66-122.

Warmenbol 2000: E. Warmenbol, Passes d'armes. Les objets de l'âge du Bronze dragués dans l'Escaut. In: L. Bonnamour (ed.), Archéologie des fleuves et des rivières (Paris 2000) 103-106.

Warmenbol 2004: E. Warmenbol, Gold pickings and PIXE analysis. More about the Bronze Age gold found in the cave of Han-sur-Lesse (Namur, Belgium). Nuclear Instruments and Methods in Physics Research, Section B,226, 2004, 208-221.

Warmenbol 2007: E. Warmenbol, Le dépôt d'ossements humains en grotte aux âges des Métaux en Belgique. Nouvelles questions. In: Ph. Barral/A. Daubigney/C. Dunning/G. Kaenel/ M.-J. Roulière-Lambert (eds.), L'âge du Fer dans l'arc jurassien et ses marges. Dépôts, lieux sacrés et territorialité à l'âge du Fer. Actes du XXIXe colloque international de l'AFEAF, Bienne, 5-8 mai 2005. Annales Littéraires de l'Université de Franche-Comté 826 (Besançon 2007) 537-548.

Warmenbol 2013: E. Warmenbol, La hache à douille « de Nismes » (Viroinval, province de Namur, Belgique). Quelques réflexions autour des haches armoricaines avec une provenance belge. Archéo-Situla 32-33, 2013, 3-8.

Warmenbol 2015: E. Warmenbol, The Later Bronze Age and Early Iron Age in the southern Low Countries: Where east meets west. In F. Hunter/I. Ralston (eds.), Scotland in Later Prehistoric Europe (Edinburgh 2015) 47-83.

Warmenbol forthcoming: E. Warmenbol, Les haches à douille des types Couville et Maure, d'Arlon à Wetteren, et pourquoi pas Zelzate. Nouvelles réflexions autour des haches armoricaines avec une provenance belge. Mélanges Marc Bar (Bruxelles forthcoming).

Warmenbol/Leclercq 2009: E. Warmenbol/W. Leclercq, Les débuts de l'âge du Fer en Belgique. Chronologie relative, chronologie absolue. In: M.-J. Lambert-Roulière/A. Daubigney/P.-Y. Milcent/M. Talon/J. Vital (eds.), De l'âge du Bronze à l'âge du Fer en France et en Europe occidentale (Xe-VIIe siècle av. J.-C.). La moyenne vallée du Rhône aux âges du Fer, actualité de la recherche. Actes du XXXe Colloque International de l'Association Française pour l'Etude de l'Âge du Fer, Saint-Romain-en-Gal/Vienne (Rhône), 25-28 mai. Revue archéologique de l'Est, supplément 27 (Dijon 2009) 373-384.

Zeebroeck/Warmenbol 2016: M. Zeebroeck/E. Warmenbol Une occupation fin VIe/début Ve siècle av. n. ère à Heinsch « La Pierre Celtique » (Arlon, prov. de Luxembourg, Belgique). Lunula, Archaeologia protohistorica XXIV, 2016, 149-152.

Author

Eugène Warmenbol
Centre de Recherches en Archéologie et Patrimoine
Université libre de Bruxelles
Avenue F.D. Roosevelt, 50 – CP 133/01
1050 Bruxelles
Belgium
ewarmenb@ulb.ac.be

Textiles as Early Iron Age prestige goods – a discussion of visual qualities

Karina Grömer

Abstract

In archaeological research, the topic 'prestige and representation' usually is discussed by means of bronze objects in graves, but textiles also fit in this topic. Similar to the famous textiles from the princely burial of Hochdorf, recently analyzed textile finds from the graves from Oss-Vorstengraf and Uden-Slabroek in the Netherlands demonstrate that textiles themselves can serve as prestige grave goods. In this paper some theories about visual qualities with regard to textile finds are also discussed. It is asked whether we can identify a visual code for representative expression of elite identities via textiles. The Hallstatt period fabrics are of high quality, and very decoratively designed with weave structures, colors, patterns and elaborately made borders. Within the Early Iron Age, the interplay between textiles and metal objects displayed on them reached a very high standard – expressing wealth and beauty. The visual complexity of textile objects, with their bright colors and interesting patterns, can be demonstrated, at least by original textile finds from the salt mine of Hallstatt. This development was perhaps fostered by the emergence of differentiated social structures at the beginning of the Iron Age.

Zusammenfassung

In der archäologischen Forschung werden Themen wie Prestige und Repräsentation meist anhand von Bronzeobjekten in Gräbern diskutiert – hier soll gezeigt werden, dass ebenso Textilfunde dazu herangezogen werden können. Ähnlich wie beim berühmte Fürstengrab von Hochdorf zeigen auch die erst kürzlich untersuchten Textilreste von den Gräbern Oss-Vorstengraf und Uden-Slabroek in den Niederlanden, dass Gewebe durchaus als repräsentative Grabbeigaben dienen konnten. Im folgenden Beitrag werden nun einige Theorien bezüglich der visuellen Erscheinungsbilder und Qualitäten von Textilien diskutiert, vor allem, ob eventuell bestimmte visuelle Codes zur Repräsentation von Eliten durch Textilien festgemacht werden können. Hallstattzeitliche Gewebe haben eine hohe Qualität, sie zeigen komplexe Muster mit Webstrukturen, Färbungen und kunstvoll gefertigten Webkanten. Vor allem das Zusammenspiel zwischen Textilien und damit verwendeten Metallobjekten (vor allem Schmuck, Trachtbestandteile) wurde in der Älteren Eisenzeit gezielt eingesetzt, um Reichtum und Schönheit zu zeigen. Die visuelle Komplexität der Textilien mit ihren intensiven Farben und Mustern kann hierbei am besten durch die Funde aus dem Salzbergwerk Hallstatt aufgezeigt werden, da die Gewebe dort noch organisch erhalten sind. Generell kann diese Entwicklung zu sehr prachtvollen Textilien auch im Rahmen der sozialen Struktur in der Eisenzeit gesehen werden, die offenbar eine derartige Repräsentationskultur begünstigte bzw. erforderte.

Introduction: textiles and contexts in the first half of the 1st millennium BC

Textiles survived under and are present in various conditions in the archaeological record of the first half of the 1st millennium BC in temperate Europe. They are found attached to metal grave goods in both cremation and inhumation burials. Similar to graves, the metal items in hoards can provide hints for textiles. It is together with those metal objects that organic finds can survive. Textiles themselves are rarely preserved in settlements, but sometimes imprints of fabrics on potsherds survive. Nevertheless, the tools found in settlements give a good chance to study the production of woven fabrics. For Central Europe, salt mines are also of importance for the study of textiles and other organic finds.

Grave finds

Intensive research of the last decades demonstrated that textiles are relatively common finds in Early Iron Age graves in Central Europe (Banck-Burgess 1999, 196-223; Belanová-Štolcová 2012; Gleba 2008, 45-63; Grömer 2014, 45-46; 192-206; Rast-Eicher 2008), depending of the abundance of metal elements in them. Textiles were used to wrap grave goods, as shrouds, and even as decoration of the grave chamber during burial rites (Gleba 2014). The latter has been impressively demonstrated by J. Banck-Burgess (2012, 44-45) with the analysis of the elite burial from Eberdingen-Hochdorf. A high quality diamond twill textile, folded several times and placed together with other grave gifts in a situla is known from Oss (Bender Jørgensen 1992, 218; also see the unpublished report: Grömer/van der Vaart-Verschoof 2015; Grömer in Van der Vaart-Verschoof forthcoming). The wrapping of objects seems to be an integral part of burial rites in the Early Iron Age (Gleba 2014). As can be seen for example in the cemetery of Uttendorf im Pinzgau, where knives and other grave goods were found wrapped in woven bands (Grömer 2014, 44 fig. 24).

Fig. 1. Textile and clothing related objects, Iron Age: jewelry and textile tools (spindle whorl and spools) from Bad Fischau, shoe-fibula from Leopoldau, textiles from Hallstatt, figurine with short tunic from Idria pri Bači (photo A. Schumacher, © NHM Vienna).

Inhumation graves, which become common from Ha C and Ha D onwards, provide even more information: if fibulae or metal belts are placed correctly on the body and textiles are attached on them – they might be the remains of the garment worn by the deceased (see Grömer 2016, 324-329). A patterned twill textile, for example, was found on the inner side of the bracelets on both arms of the burial of Slabroek in the Netherlands. The patterned textiles were probably part of a long-sleeved garment and the bracelets were worn over it (Grömer in Van der Vaart-Verschoof forthcoming).

Textiles usually survive in graves due to mineralization processes, attached on metal items (see Chen *et al.* 1998). We can clearly see a difference between rich burials and poorer graves, because in 'poor' graves with few or no metal in it, textiles hardly survive. We are therefore better informed about textiles of rich burials.

Settlements

Direct records of woven fabrics are scarce from Iron Age settlements. The organic textiles that were in use within the settlement usually do not survive, but sometimes we find imprints of textiles on clay objects (e.g. Grömer 2014, 46; 193). The latter finds can tell something about the production process of the clay objects. There are, however, indirect hints for textiles that might have been used in settlements as well. Some wall hangings, floor coverings, pillows and mattresses from the princely burial Hochdorf, (Banck-Burgess 2012, 44-45), for example may also have been used by the living persons to make their houses more comfortable. These kinds of soft furnishing are also depicted on works of situla art, which was a way of self-representation by wealthy strata of society in the southern and eastern Alpine region between the 6th and 4th century BC, *e.g.* on the mirror of Modena-Castelvetro (Lucke/Frey 1962, pl. 21).

Early Iron Age settlements are multifaceted – we know of large hilltop settlements, sometimes fortified, which served as central places for the elites (e.g. Heuneburg: Fernández-Götz 2015). There are also smaller lowland villages and single farmsteads. With regard to the topic of 'prestige goods' it would be very interesting to compare the kinds of textiles used in fortified hillforts and smaller villages. This could only be done through textiles found in burials associated with the specific settlement types. It is hoped that such extensive studies will be possible in future.

There have been some efforts to understand what kinds of textiles were produced within the different types of settlements. Textile tools from hilltop settlements, especially in situ finds of loom weights, have been studied in comparison with lowland settlements. As we know now *e.g.* for the eastern Hallstatt area, spindle whorls of different shapes and sizes occur in all types of settlements.

Different sizes of looms were in use in the Early Iron Age (Belanová-Štolcová/ Grömer 2010, 17), and one could think that the use of extra-wide looms (3-4 m wide fabrics have been made on one loom) exceeds domestic requirements and hint towards specialized, representative or even ritually motivated production. The first example of such a very wide loom was found on the fortified hilltop settlement Kleinklein in Austria (Dobiat 1990), which is the central place for the Sulmtal necropolis. This evidence seemed to prove the exclusive and representative use of big looms in an elite context. Within the last decades, however, more finds of such big looms occurred, but also in lowland settlements such as Freundorf and Hafnerbach in Austria (Belanová-Štolcová/Grömer 2010, 17). So, the art of representative weaving of large size cloth is not restricted to hilltop settlements. Nevertheless, there must have been some production centers where high quality textiles were made, such as Smolenice-Molpír or Nové Košariská in modern Slovakia (Belanová-Štolcová 2012, 312-314).

Salt mines

For material culture studies of textiles, one at first glance unusual find context has to be considered: salt mines. The salty environment combined with constant climate and humidity prevents the decay of organic materials. As a result countless wooden artifacts are known from the salt mines Hallstatt (Kern *et al.* 2009) and Dürrnberg in the Austrian Alps (Stöllner 2005), as well as leather items, fur and textiles. Both salt mines were economic centers and the local inhabitants who lived and worked there (and left the textiles back in the mine) were among the wealthy communities of their time. This can be proved by studying the grave goods as well.

The Early Iron Age mining at Hallstatt dates between the 9th and 4th century BC, the salt mining activities at Dürrnberg begin in the 6th century, but mainly can be dated in the Late Iron Age.

Both sites together have more than a thousand textiles which are still colorful and offer a good overview of the textile techniques in use, but also of colors, dyes and patterns (e.g. Grömer *et al.* 2013; Stöllner 2005). The textiles were used in the salt mines as working material, maybe miners' clothing and carrying bags. But there are also textiles that were not directly made to be used for salt mining, also rags were brought into the mine to serve different purposes such as makeshift binding material. Amongst the salt mine finds there are also high quality products with complicated patterns. They might have been representative textiles in their primary use, but they ended up in the salt mine after wear and tear and recycling. Both at Hallstatt and Dürrnberg we are not restricted to organic textile finds from the salt mines, there are also some textiles in the graves. So we are able to compare the 'textile culture' used by the living with those used for burial rites. As far as we know now, they are similar in weave-type and quality (seen in thread count and yarn diameter), although the textiles in the graves do not offer colour information.

Visual qualities of objects – Theoretical background

To understand the visual qualities of objects, firstly we to have mention the recent studies by P. Wells (2008; 2012). He tries to understand the visual basis of communication in the Iron Age with the help of recent research in cognitive neuroscience and cognitive psychology. His main approach is that people in prehistoric Europe did see, experience and perceive things in a different way than we do today. With this, he responds to the concepts of the "cognitive map" and the "visual world" after J. Gibson (1950; see also Wells 2008, 32). The cognitive map is the essential model of the world that we have in our brains and to which we compare everything we see. In seeing things, interpreting what we see, and responding to our interpretations, our expectations play a vital role. The visual system and the cognitive map depend to a great extent on the early childhood experiences with vision and touch. Every individual´s cognitive map is unique, but the more similar the environments in which a group of individuals are raised, the more similar their cognitive maps and their visual experience will be. That means that for a person living in the 8th century BC the visual experience of a person located in Central Europe will differ completely from, for example, someone in contemporary Egypt, where monumental stone buildings and temples covered with hieroglyphs and other very complex visual impressions. In both contexts the person has to 'learn' what to see and how to interpret the incoming information – what the visual codes are for a high ranked person, for a person with a specific function within society (e.g. an Egyptian priest). This means that the cognitive map prehistoric people had and their former visual experience were vital to identifying representative goods. To take it boldly: you have to know how a kermes dyed textile looks like and that kermes is a precious dyestuff coming from far away – only with that information you are able to identify a person wearing a kermes-red gown as high-ranked. The cognitive map is key for sorting out visual codes.

Visual codes (see Chandler 2002) are a subcategory of nonverbal communication. Primarily, a code is a visual, audio or technical element that an audience has learnt implies meaning. The process of encoding converts information from a source into symbols for communication or storage. Decoding is the reverse process, converting code symbols back into a form that the recipient understands. All codes have a denotation and a connotation. The denotation is the literal meaning of a code, the connotation is a symbolic meaning of a code. Visual codes like colors, physical appearance and clothing, but also body language are unconsciously read by audiences who then understand them and sort information out about what they see. There are also specialized connotational and ideological codes to reflect particular social, political, moral, and aesthetic values.

Visual qualities of textiles

What kinds of visual qualities were created in textile art in the first half of the 1st millennium BC? There are different kinds of structure, texture, borders and weave types (see *e.g.* Grömer 2016, 121 fig. 67; 128 fig. 72; 135 fig. 76; 177 fig. 99). Here we concentrate on the most important of them for our specific topic about prestige goods: colour, patterns and the use of gold and metal together with textiles.

We often tend to think of prehistoric times as drab, but there is accumulating evidence that Iron Age peoples used many bright colors, at least for elite members of societies. For the Early Iron Age in Central Europe, the textiles from the Hallstatt salt mines are the prime source of information about colour and dyes (see Hofmann-de Keijzer 2016). Due to the mineralization-process it is not easy to detect dyestuffs in textiles that survived in graves, but some recent attempts from Hochdorf are promising (see Walton Rogers 1999) or Verucchio (Stauffer 2002, 216-219). Interestingly, primarily blue and red colors could be analyzed from grave-contexts (Hofmann-de Keijzer 2016, 149 fig. 84), deriving from plant dyes like woad or madder. For precious red colour insect dyestuffs were also used such as Kermes or the Polish cochineal. This could be proven from textiles found in princely burials like Hochdorf, Hohmichele (Walton Rogers 1999, 244) and Glauberg (Balzer *et al.* 2014, 2-8).

Fig. 2. Blue dyed textile from the salt mine Hallstatt, with polychrome repp ribbon (HallTex 100). Detail of blue dyed fibers (photos A. Rausch and R. Hofmann-de Keijzer, © NHM Vienna).

Fig. 3. Situla from Kuffarn and chequered textiles from the salt mine Hallstatt (HallTex 74, 91, 181, 203) (photos A. Schumacher and A. Rausch, © NHM Vienna).

Dye analyses on textiles from Hallstatt (Fig. 2) as well as dyeing experiments have demonstrated that the entire colour palette from yellow, orange and red shades to green, blue and black was available to Early Iron Age people and revealed how they could have achieved them (Hofmann-de Keijzer 2016). Blue was dyed with woad by vat dyeing. Yellow dyes were obtained by a dye-bath from various plants like weld, saw-wort or scentless chamomile, and red dyes derived from madder or bedstraw. Mordants may have been used to fix the dyes. Also tannins in combination with iron were used to obtain black colors. Different dyeing techniques were applied to a single textile to obtain specific shades, *e.g.* dyeing first yellow and the over-dye with blue in vat-dyeing to get a green colour. In Early Iron Age, patterns and even the use of gold also played an important role. This is discussed in the following paragraph.

Visual codes in textiles

Without written sources it is difficult to decode how Iron Age people perceived their surroundings. For sure, colour, patterns and decorations are important carrier of visual codes. In pre-industrial societies, where things were made by hand, all decoration was chosen consciously. Decoration is intended to draw and hold the attention of our brain. It helps us to see and recognize familiar motifs and therefore "situates us in social space" (Brett 2005, 62). Decoration is part of what D. Brett calls "visual ideology", it provides a link between the producers and the technology of an object as well as the observers and the material world in which they live, move and interact. Decoration thus serves as a communication medium, and in the context of prehistoric art it also serves as communication medium about elites. Decorated textiles of high quality may be a medium to express social status.

What kinds of textile decoration are common in the first half of the 1st millennium BC? We know of specific design principles: on the one hand spin patterning (use of groups of s- and z-twisted yarn to create a tone-on-tone pattern) is very common, but also dyeing textiles and colour patterns. The latter are of interest here. Early Iron Age textiles tend to be decorated during the weaving process (Banck-Burgess 1999), *e.g.* in tablet weaving or by using groups of different twisted or coloured threads in warp and/or weft to create checks or stripes (see *e.g.* Hallstatt salt mine Grömer 2016, 177 fig. 99; Grömer *et al.* 2013). There are a few examples of colour patterns from graves between the 8th and 6th century BC, like Verucchio in Italy (Stauffer 2002; 2012) or Uden-Slabroek in the Netherlands (unpublished report Grömer/Van der Vaart-Verschoof 2015; Grömer in Van der Vaart-Verschoof forthcoming), where alternating small groups of red (?) and blue threads in both thread systems form a houndstooth pattern. Checkered cloth is also depicted on contemporary high-status bronze objects such as situlae (e.g. Kuffarn, Fig. 3; Lucke/Frey 1962).

Late Hallstatt period elite burials provide us with further kinds of visually striking patterns: floating threads applied during weaving in weft-wrap (soumak) techniques or embroidered after weaving offer the chance for a free design-process and therefore patterns. A recent find from Glauberg tumulus 1, grave 1 allowed the identification of an embroidered pattern with a plait-like structure (Balzer *et al.* 2014, 5 fig. 6). The Hohmichele textile (Fig. 4) from grave VI is a well-known example for the weft-wraps (Hundt 1962, Taf. 36-39). It shows on a repp ground weave doubled square with swastika motive, accompanied by triangles. All of that repeated to form a band of a pattern. Weft wrap technique was also employed for some textiles from Hochdorf (Banck-Burgess 2012, 35; 55; 57) to create diamonds with swastikas or an element in the form of the letter Z. The base weave for these textiles were twill and tablet weaving.

Fig. 4. Textile pattern from Hohmichele on a reconstruction of the chariot from Býčí skála cave, kept at the NHM Vienna (photo K. Grömer, © NHM Vienna).

Tablet weaving also was applied in the Hallstatt period to create amazing polychrome decorations. From the salt mine Hallstatt we know of bands decorated with meanders, filled lozenges and triangles (Grömer 2016, 181-184 fig. 102-104). Even tablet woven items from graves, rust-brown due to their mineralized state, demonstrate through their structure, that they formerly have been wonderful colour patterns (e.g. Apremont in France: Banck-Burgess 1999, 69 fig. 40-41). Even more complex are the tablet woven items from Hochdorf (Banck-Burgess 2012, 34-35; 52-53) with meander or checkerboard patterns with tiny lozenges, again swastikas form the main motif at Hochdorf.

A specific part of the visual code is the use of metal together with textiles. For Early Iron Age the most common case is that for example fibulae or metal belt elements were attached to garments made of woven cloth. Thus, the soft textile often formed a background, contrast and ideal surface for shiny metal objects (Gibson 1980, xii-xiii; Wells 2008, 68; 78). In the Iron Age, bright dyed colors like blue, yellow, bluish-black and red underline that concept.

The interplay between textiles and metal can also be gold threads woven in or buttons sewn on – forming very precious and high status textiles. Impressive examples of this were found in elite burials such as Hohmichele or Grafenbühel in Germany (Banck-Burgess 1999, 39 fig. 10). The Grafenbühel find consists of very fine gold strips only 0.2-0.3 mm wide. The sharp folds that can be seen on the strips indicate that they belonged to a tabby fabric where they were woven in. There are some bends which suggest that they were used to create a brocaded pattern where the strips float over several (2-4) warp threads to form a sophisticated pattern. An 11.5 cm wide sash with gold stripes woven in is mentioned in the early excavation reports of Hohmichele, grave 1 (Hundt 1962, 211 Taf. 1,4).

Textiles were also decorated with metal applications, a custom that we often find for the wealthy strata of societies in Early Iron Age. Famous examples come from Hallstatt, Stična and Mitterkirchen, all Ha C. In grave 360 from Hallstatt (Grömer 2016, 199 fig. 116) 3,000 small bronze buttons found on the upper body region

Fig. 5. Mitterkirchen grave X, burial chamber 2, woman with bronze buttons, archaeological evidence and replica (© Oberösterreichisches Landesmuseum).

Fig. 6. Spin patterned textile from the salt mine Hallstatt (HallTex 31). Visibility of a spin pattern according to vantage point and light angle (photos A. Rausch, © NHM Vienna).

of a woman may have belonged to a precious upper garment. At Mitterkirchen in grave X/2 (Pertlwieser 1987, 55-70) a woman was buried and thousands of bronze knobs were found on the upper body and leg region, additionally between the knees and toes they were lined with a double zigzag row of tiny bronze elements. Traces of leather and animal fibers suggest that the buttons were attached to a splendid leather/fur cloak (Fig. 5). At the burials in Stična however it was possible to identify patterns made with the bronze buttons, such as triangles, lozenges or flower-like arrangements (Hellmuth 2010, 63-68 fig. 2-5).

Visibility from different vantage points

What happens at different vantage points (Wells 2008, 60; 67) – if you look at a costume or a textile from far or near?

Interestingly, texture can look very different depending on the vantage point, as noted by P. Wells (2008, 44). For textiles this means that most of the textures like zigzag or diamond twill or repp done as monochrome cloth would look like a simple, plain surface from far away, while from close by the lines of the twill or the ribbed structure of the repp can be seen. The same holds true for textiles with spin-patterns and other subtle tonal patterns. Thus, the elements requiring the most skill can only be appreciated in close proximity to the object. The creative expertise of the maker is demonstrated at the intimate personal level, not at a distance.

Colour and patterns, as described before, can be seen clearly from a distance, but there are other techniques of patterning like spin pattern, which are only visible from nearby. A lot of thought and design work was spent on them, but the patterns are almost invisible. For a spin pattern (Fig. 6), the difference of spinning direction was exploited to provide decoration, for otherwise identical S- and Z-spun threads laid side by side will catch the light differently and give a subtle tonal pattern. This created a special visual effect: stripes or bands created by alternating groups of S- and Z-spun threads.

One of the earliest such pieces comes from the copper mine Mitterberg in Austria (transition Early/Middle Bronze Age, 1600 BC) (Grömer 2012, 31 fig. 1,2) and is a finely made woolen repp-band (warp-faced) made with plied yarn. The special effect of the band is caused by the irregular change of groups of S- and Z-twisted plied yarns for the warp. So this is a first hint of spin-patterning from 1600 BC. Spin pattern especially is a very common pattern type in Central European Hallstatt culture (Banck-Burgess 1999; Bender Jørgensen 2005), a hint to creative choices of pattern effects in Central European Region, but also in Iron Age Italy, as we know *e.g.* from the finds of Verucchio (Stauffer 2002; 2012).

So we have to think about who was allowed to come near enough to see complex twill types or spin patterns? The same also applies to other delicately worked objects such as fibulae. They can have surfaces textured by incised lines that are so fine that the unaided human eye can barely make them out. Are those again visual codes for 'insiders'? You have to know high quality items and be near to see them. P. Wells (2008, 60) calls that a 'visual privilege', whereby some members of the community were permitted to see something from a distance, whilst others were allowed to view objects up close to examine details.

Light

Light also plays a very important role in visual appearance and the perception (Wells 2012, 48-51), especially in the perception of prestige goods. Light changes affect how objects appear. This can be demonstrated very easily with for example the representative costume of an elite member (Fig. 7). A typical Early Iron Age high status woman's ensemble are two fibulae worn on the shoulders and a belt (see also Grömer 2016, 390-394), in the most luxurious case one of bronze sheet. A dress worn together with it might be for example blue, which is a perfect background for the shiny golden bronze dress attire. Also – as we know from the situla art, some colorful patterned ribbons might be attached on the neckline, the sleeves and the lower hem (e.g. situla from Vače: Lucke/Frey 1962, table. 7).

During daylight, more so in direct sunlight, the viewer's attention recognizes the shiny metal objects, but also the blue colour and the patterned braid. This view changes completely in a dark environment that is only lit by fire. That means again that the perception of textiles, their colour and especially their pattern is not the same under different lightning conditions. This also applies to the textiles with woven-in gold threads or sewn-on metal buttons. If for example gold was worked into a bright blue dyed textile, under moderate lightning conditions both colors could be recognized. In direct sunlight the gold elements start to glitter on their nicely visible blue background, while in a dark surrounding only a fire, taper or torch light the metal objects while the textile remains a dark and dull mass.

So – when and where were what kinds of luxurious textiles and garments chosen for representation? This also refers to the light conditions that were presence in the residences of the elites.

Textiles – visual expression of elites

Conventional studies on prestige goods usually focus on metal objects. This is the same with the recent work by R. Schumann (2015, 23-24), who also discussed the definitions of status and prestige. Related to prestige goods is the question: what are elites? It is accepted that Iron Age society was hierarchical (Fernández-Götz 2015, 75-76). When P. Wells wrote his 2008 book "Image and Response in Early Europe", he focused on metal objects and mainly on elite contexts. By 'elites' he (Wells 2008, 11) refers to individuals and groups of people with greater authority, power and wealth than the majority of people, but he also mentions that there might be specific kinds of social and political systems. M. Fernández-Götz (2015, 75) writes "population growth and an increase in available arable land and other economic resources formed the real basis of the wealth of the social elite that is so impressively visible to us in the form of the so-called "princely graves" (*Fürstengräber*)". These, the top strata of society, are accompanied by other wealthy groups. We are not sure whether 'princely elite', a concept mainly used for the western Hallstatt area, can also be applied to persons buried at the Hallstatt cemetery (Kern *et al.* 2009), but there a wealthy population can definitely be identified who expressed their status and prestige via precious vessels, jewelry and – of course textiles.

As we have seen, textiles – although rare finds in comparison with other object groups like pottery, jewelry or weapons – have the potential to add to our knowledge about prestige goods. We know that in contemporary Greece pieces of cloth and garments formed an essential part of the dowry, served as representative goods for gift-exchange between elites and were high-ranked offerings to the gods (Wagner-Hasel 2000, 152-163; 2006, 257-269). Moreover, in Greek contexts status definition and the visualization of social status was achieved through textiles and clothing. The Greek epics attest that the visual potency of a person *"charis"* was also tied to their clothing.

For the Central European textile material which was presented here, we have to discuss: what are elite and luxurious items (see also Schumann 2015, 36-39 about the problems in identifying status and prestige objects)? For the present discussion, textiles with metal sewn-on or gold strips woven-in are seen as

Fig. 7. Reconstruction of dress accessories from the cemetery Hallstatt, grave 551, blue textile and patterned braid after finds from the salt mine Hallstatt. Model: Gloria Lekaj (photo A. Schumacher, © NHM Vienna).

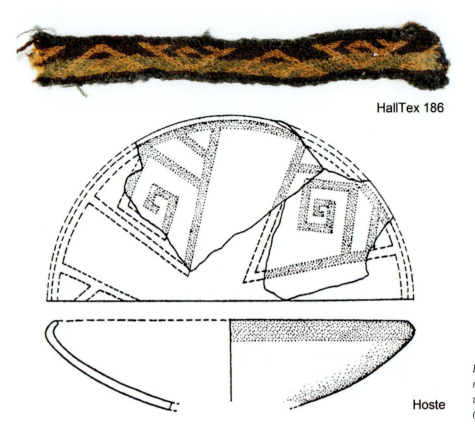

HallTex 186

Hoste

Fig. 8. Textile from the salt mine Hallstatt in comparison with a vessel from Hoste (© NHM Vienna).

luxurious objects. Insect dyes, which have to be imported from the south or east, are also precious. The exclusive materials in combination with craft skills indicate so in these cases. Are we also allowed to see luxurious goods – prestige goods – in objects with complex visuality, such as tablet woven bands or the textiles patterned with soumak techniques or embroidery? Such items have similar visual codes like high ranked pottery that can be found in graves as well and amongst hillfort settlements. The meander-motif, filled lozenges and triangles of the patterned tablet woven bands from Hallstatt are also known from Hallstatt period pottery *e.g.* from Hoste (Fig. 8) or Leobendorf (Griebl 1997, 96 fig. 33; Schappelwein 1999, 110; 214). This means that this kind of decoration was positioned in the cognitive map of the time and the specific meanings and even value was clearly understood. In the case of textiles it is a fact that highly complex items require specific skills, know-how and their production is usually time-consuming (see Grömer 2016, 184-185). For textile patterns we cannot know, which connotation (symbolic meaning of the visual code; Chandler 2002) was attached to specific kinds of colors or patterns. Which one was a 'sign' of a specific rank within the hierarchy? For the Roman period we know, for example, that the colour purple had a specific connotation, it functioned as visual code for the rank of a senator and later for the emperor.

Conclusion

Textiles can be found in various contexts in the European Early Iron Age, the most striking and numerous finds are known from the salt mine Hallstatt. But textiles also survive in graves, especially those with metal items – the most famous among these is the evidence from the princely grave of Hochdorf. Sophisticated excavation and analytical techniques employed during the last centuries allow us to gather more and more data. The material presented indicates that textiles and clothing played an important role in the Early Iron Age in temperate Europe for the expression of wealth, and as status symbols and prestige goods for the elites. The Hallstatt period textile culture is characterized by a lot of variations in weave types, patterns and textile qualities. Also, the textile patterns fit in the 'visual world' they belong to – carrying codes and information which should also be understood.

Handcraft skills in combination with precious raw materials create a powerful visual code that was worn on the body and thus carried around. Furthermore, textiles with colors, patterns and applied decoration represent the idea of creative work with textile material, according to the knowledge, the skill and rules of the society.

Specific colors and/or patterns were perhaps understood in the Iron Age as visual codes, to express the 'social space', group relationships – hierarchical, regional, or supra-regional. It is striking, that for the most complicated pattern techniques like soumak or tablet weaving in some cases specific patterns appear. For the elite burials related to the Heuneburg, *e.g.* Hohmichele and Hochdorf, it is the Swastika-motif. Maybe with this we can detect the visual code of the elite in the modern Baden-Württemberg area. In contrast – for the Eastern Hallstatt area (and 'border' line between East and West: Hallstatt and Mitterkirchen) we can see the use of applications to embellish textile surfaces, famous examples are the cloak with buttons from Mitterkirchen and the marvelous decorated garment from Stična. Especially the glittering bronze and sometime gold objects attached to (eventually dyed in bright, contrasting colors like deep red or blue) textiles allow a distinct visual appearance – even from far away. That visual code highlights rich women in that area.

For the visual appearance of textiles two further interesting matters are the vantage point and the light conditions. Did elites use special colors and/or colour patterns to mark their status and prestige to the masses of people looking at them from farer away? Who then was allowed to come near enough to see sophisticated details such as the spin patterns discussed?

Bibliography

Balzer *et al.* 2014: I. Balzer/C. Peek/I. Vanden Berghe, Neue Untersuchungen an den eisenzeitlichen Textilfunden der "Fürstengräber" vom Glauberg. Denkmalpflege und Kulturgeschichte 3, 2014, 2-10.

Banck-Burgess 1999: J. Banck-Burgess, Hochdorf IV. Die Textilfunde aus dem späthallstattzeitlichen Fürstengrab von Eberdingen-Hochdorf (Kreis Ludwigburg) und weitere Grabtextilien aus hallstatt- und latènezeitlichen Kulturgruppen. Forschungen und Berichte zur Vor- und Frühgeschichte in Baden-Württemberg 70 (Stuttgart 1999).

Banck-Burgess 2012: J. Banck-Burgess, Instruments of power. Celtic textiles – Mittel der Macht. Textilien bei den Kelten (Stuttgart 2012).

Belanová-Štolcová 2012: T. Belanová-Štolcová, Slovak and Czech Republic. In: M. Gleba/U. Mannering (eds.), Textiles and textile production in Europe from Prehistory to AD 400. Ancient Textiles Series 11 (Oxford 2012) 306-333.

Belanová-Štolcová/Grömer 2010: T. Belanová-Štolcová/K. Grömer, Weights, spindles and textiles – Textile production in Central Europe from Bronze Age to Iron Age. In: E. Andersson Strand/M. Gleba/U. Mannering/C. Munkholt/M. Ringgaard (eds.), North European symposium for archaeological textiles X (Oxford 2010) 9-20.

Bender Jørgensen 1992: L. Bender Jørgensen, North European textiles until AD 1000 (Aarhus 1992).

Bender Jørgensen 2005: L. Bender Jørgensen, Hallstatt and La Tène textiles from the archives of Central Europe. In: P. Bichler/K. Grömer/R. Hofmann-de Keijzer/A. Kern/H. Reschreiter (eds.), Hallstatt textiles. Technical analysis, scientific investigation and experiment on Iron Age textiles. British Archaeological Reports Int. Series 1351 (Oxford 2005) 133-150.

Brett 2005: D. Brett, Rethinking decoration: Pleasure and ideology in the visual arts (Cambridge 2005).

Chandler 2002: D. Chandler, Semiotics: The basics (London 2002).

Chen et al. 1998: H. Chen/K. Jakes/D. Foreman, Preservation of archaeological textiles through fibre mineralization. Journal of Archaeological Science 25, 1998, 1015-1021.

Dobiat 1990: C. Dobiat, Der Burgstallkogel bei Kleinklein I. Die Ausgrabungen der Jahre 1982-1984. Marburger Studien zur Vor- und Frühgeschichte 13 (Marburg 1990).

Fernández-Götz 2015: M. Fernández-Götz, The rise of urbanism in early Europe: A dialogue. Kleos. Amsterdam Bulletin of Ancient Studies and Archaeology 1, 2015, 73-81.

Gibson 1950: J. Gibson, The perception of the visual world (Boston 1950).

Gibson 1980: J. Gibson, A prefatory essay on the perception of surfaces versus the perception of markings on a surface. In: M.Hagen (ed.): The perception of pictures 1 (New York 1980) XI – XVII.

Gleba 2008: M. Gleba, Textile production in pre-roman Italy. Ancient Textiles Series 4 (Oxford 2008).

Gleba 2014: M. Gleba, Wrapped up for safe keeping: "Wrapping" customs in Early Iron Age Europe. In: S. Harris/L. Douny (eds.), Wrapping and unwrapping material culture. University College London, Institute of Archaeology Publications 64 (Walnut Creek 2014) 135-146.

Griebl 1997: M. Griebl, Siedlungsobjekte der Hallstattkultur aus Horn (Niederösterreich). Mitteilungen der Prähistorischen Kommission 31 (Wien 1997).

Grömer 2012: K. Grömer, Austria: Bronze and Iron Ages. In: M. Gleba/U. Mannering (eds.), Textiles and textile production in Europe from prehistory to AD 400. Ancient Textiles Series 11 (Oxford 2012) 27-64.

Grömer 2014: K. Grömer, Römische Textilien in Noricum und Westpannonien – im Kontext der archäologischen Gewebefunde 2000 v. Chr. – 500 n. Chr. in Österreich. Austria Antiqua 5 (Graz 2014).

Grömer 2016: K. Grömer, The art of prehistoric textile making – The development of craft traditions and clothing in Central Europe. Veröffentlichungen der Prähistorischen Abteilung 5 (Vienna 2016).

Grömer *et al.* 2013: K. Grömer/A. Kern/H. Reschreiter/H. Rösel-Mautendorfer (eds.), Textiles from Hallstatt. Weaving culture in bronze and Iron Age salt mines. Archaeolingua 29 (Budapest 2013).

Grömer/van der Vaart-Verschoof 2015: K. Grömer/S. van der Vaart-Verschoof, Hallstatt period textile finds from the Netherlands. Natural History Museum, Unpublished Report Textile Archaeology 2015/7 (Vienna 2015).

Grömer in Van der Vaart-Verschoof forthcoming: K. Grömer, forthcoming, Hallstatt Period Textile Finds from the Netherlands. In: S. van der Vaart-Verschoof, Fragmenting the Chieftain. A practice-based study of Early Iron Age Hallstatt C elite burials of the Low Countries and their relation to the Hallstatt Culture of Central Europe.

Hellmuth 2010: A. Hellmuth, Zur Rekonstruktion des Prunkgewandes aus Stična Grab 27, Hügel 48. In: S. Gabrovec/B. Teržan (eds.), Stična II/2. Grabhügel aus der Älteren Eisenzeit. Studien. Catalogi et Monographiae 38 (Ljubljana 2010) 61-68.

Hofmann-de Keijzer 2016: R. Hofmann-de Keijzer, Dyeing. In: K. Grömer, The art of prehistoric textile making – The development of craft traditions and clothing in Central Europe. Veröffentlichungen der Prähistorischen Abteilung 5 (Vienna 2016) 140-169.

Hundt 1962: H.-J. Hundt, Die Textilreste aus dem Hohmichele. In: G. Riek, Der Hohmichele. Ein Fürstengrabhügel der späten Hallstattzeit bei der Heuneburg. Römisch-Germanische Forschungen 25 (Mainz 1962) 199-214.

Kern *et al.* 2009: A. Kern/K. Kowarik/A. Rausch/H. Reschreiter, Kingdom of Salt. Veröffentlichungen der Prähistorischen Abteilung 3 (Wien 2009).

Lucke/Frey 1962: W. Lucke/O.-H. Frey, Die Situla in Providence. Römisch-Germanische Forschungen 26 (Berlin 1962).

Pertlwieser 1987: M. Pertlwieser, Frühhallstattzeitliche Wagenbestattungen in Mitterkirchen. In: Prunkwagen und Hügelgrab. Kataloge des Oberösterreichischen Landesmuseums N.F. 13 (Linz 1987) 55-70.

Rast-Eicher 2008: A. Rast-Eicher, Textilien, Wolle, Schafe der Eisenzeit in der Schweiz. Antiqua 44 (Basel 2008).

Schappelwein 1999: C. Schappelwein, Vom Dreieck zum Mäander. Untersuchungen zum Motivschatz der Kalenderbergkultur und angrenzenden Regionen. Universitätsforschungen zur Prähistorischen Archäologie 61 (Bonn 1999).

Schumann 2015: R. Schumann, Status und Prestige in der Hallstattkultur. Aspekte sozialer Distinktion in ältereisenzeitlichen Regionalgruppen zwischen Altmühl und Save. Münchner archäologische Forschungen 3 (Rahden/Westf. 2015).

Stauffer 2002: A. Stauffer, Tessuti. Abiti ceremoniali. Frammenti della cremazione. Catalogo. In: P. Von Eles (ed.), Guerriero e sacerdote. Autorità e nell`età der ferro a Verucchio. La tomba der Trono (Firenze 2002) 192-215.

Stauffer 2012: A. Stauffer, Case study: The textiles from Verucchio, Italy. In: M. Gleba/U. Mannering (eds.), Textiles and textile production in Europe from prehistory to AD 400. Ancient Textiles Series 11 (Oxford 2012) 242-253.

Stöllner 2005: T. Stöllner, More than old rags – Textiles from the Iron Age salt-mine at the Dürrnberg. In: P. Bichler/K. Grömer/R. Hogmann-de Keijzer/A. Kern/H. Reschreiter (eds.), Hallstatt textiles. Technical analysis, scientific investigation and experiment on Iron Age textiles. British Archaeological Reports Int. Series 1351 (Oxford 2005) 161-174.

Wagner-Hasel 2000: B. Wagner-Hasel, Der Stoff der Gaben. Kultur und Politik des Schenkens und Tauschens im archaischen Griechenland. Campus Historische Studien 28 (Frankfurt 2000).

Wagner-Hasel 2006: B. Wagner-Hasel, Gift exchange: Modern theories and ancient attitudes. In: S. Deger-Jalkotzy/I. S. Lemos (eds.), Ancient Greece: From the Mycenaean palaces to the age of Homer (Edinburgh 2006) 257-269.

Walton Rogers 1999: P. Walton Rogers, Dyes in the Hochdorf textiles and report on tests for dye in samples from the Iron-Age (Hallstatt) site at Hohmichele, Germany. In: J. Banck-Burgess, Hochdorf IV. Die Textilfunde aus dem späthallstattzeitlichen Fürstengrab von Eberdingen-Hochdorf (Kreis Ludwigburg) und weitere Grabtextilien aus hallstatt- und latènezeitlichen Kulturgruppen. Forschungen und Berichte zur Vor- und Frühgeschichte in Baden-Württemberg 70 (Stuttgart 1999) 240-246.

Van der Vaart-Verschoof forthcoming: S. van der Vaart-Verschoof, Fragmenting the Chieftain. A practice-based study of Early Iron Age Hallstatt C elite burials of the Low Countries and their relation to the Hallstatt Culture of Central Europe.

Wells 2008: P. Wells, Image and response in early Europe (London 2008).

Wells 2012: P. Wells, How ancient Europeans saw the world: Vision, patterns and the ahaping of the mind in prehistoric times (Princeton 2012).

Author

Karina Grömer
Natural History Museum Vienna
Prehistoric Department
Burgring 7
1010 Vienna
Austria
Karina.groemer@nhm-wien.ac.at

'Elite graves' in Bavaria

Considerations of practices, status and communication of early Hallstatt communities

Melanie Augstein

Abstract

In undisturbed 'rich' graves of the Early Iron Age in Bavaria, we regularly find wagons or parts of wagons, items of horse-gear, large sets of ceramic vessels and sometimes metal vessels. The connection between Late Bronze Age respectively the Urnfield period and early Hallstatt 'elite graves' is not only documented by such objects or a motif that is reminiscent of the so-called 'sun-bird-boat', but by practices as well. In an even distinct mode, in rich equipped Ha C graves there is regularly something missing, ensembles are not complete, there are only single objects representing the whole, items are non-functional or even destroyed. Against this background, research into Early Iron Age graves should not focus only on objects or object groups and their spread. The practices they are involved in – selection, pars pro toto, mechanical manipulation, fragmentation – are significant as well for an understanding of Ha C burial rites.

Résumé

Dans les tombes riches, non perturbées du Premier âge du Fer en Bavière se trouvent régulièrement des chars ou des pièces de chars, des éléments du harnais du cheval et des larges services en céramique et même en bronze. Le rapport entre le Bronze final, ou bien la Civilisation des champs d'urnes et les tombes 'élitaires' du Hallstattien ancien ne deviennent pas seulement apparentes dans ces objets ou un motif qui rapelle à la 'barque solaire aux oiseaux', mais également dans les pratiques. Les ensembles funéraires riches du Hallstattien ancien montrent encore d'une façon plus prononcés que quelques objets sont incomplets, inutilisables et même détruits. Dans ce contexte, il est proposé de ne pas regarder que les objets eux-mêmes et leur répartition. Les pratiques, dans lesquelles ils sont impliqués comme la sélection, le pars pro toto, la destruction mécanique et la fragmentation, ont la même importance pour la compréhension des rites funéraires hallstattiennes.

Hallstatt C research in Bavaria

Research concerning the early Hallstatt period respectively Ha C in Bavaria has not been a key topic for years now. The situation seems to change with, for example, recent finds like the rich grave of Otzing in Lower Bavaria (e.g. Claßen *et al.* 2013; Gebhard 2015; Gebhard *et al.* 2016). This publication also shows that Ha C is returning 'into the debate'[1].

---

1   Moreover, especially Late Bronze Age or Early Iron Age cemeteries like the urnfield from Cottbus (Gramsch 2010) or the complex structures in Oss in the Low Lands (e.g. Fokkens *et al.* 2012; Fontijn *et al.* 2013a) were the basis for an approach that brought topics like *rites de passage* or 'practice-orientation' into discussion.

Even if Bavaria is traditionally said to be part of the 'Westhallstattkreis' or at its margin, recent research sees the whole construction of 'West'- and 'Osthallstattkreis' more nuanced (e.g. Müller-Scheeßel 2000; Stöllner 1999). One should understand the Hallstatt culture not as a closed unit, but as a heterogeneous assembly of different regional phenomena, regional trends and characteristics. It should be seen more as a communication system with similar socio-economic basis, direct group relations and common cultural orientations (*cf.* Stöllner 1999, 446).

Especially German Hallstatt archaeology is focused on the so-called *Fürstenphänomen.* Therefore, the focus of research lies in a *temporal perspective* on the late Hallstatt period. Recent research projects are concerned with questions of centralization and urbanization and mainly interested in the political organization of the leading groups[2]. As Bavaria was outside the spread of 'princely seats' and 'princely graves' during that time and Mediterranean imports and objects from precious metal are generally absent, this area takes a marginal position in that discourse.

Bavaria plays, compared to southwest Germany, rather a subordinated role in recent research in a *spatial perspective* as well, even though there are quite a lot of graves from the early Hallstatt period. Some of them are from old excavations[3], and for those it is obviously hard to assess whether ensembles are complete, how the grave was constructed or how the graves fit in the general topography of the cemetery. And further, there is hardly any anthropological data that can help us to understand the role of age and gender for Early Iron Age burial practices.

At the same time, however, there is a range of burial sites extensively excavated according to modern standards (but sometimes not conclusively published yet), like Schirndorf (Hughes 1999; 2001; Stroh 1978; 1988; 2000a; 2000b), Untereggersberg (Nikulka 1998), Dietfurt (Augstein 2015; Röhrig 1994), Landersdorf (Hoppe 1987), Kinding (Meixner *et al.* 1995; Meixner *et al.* 1996; Schaich 2001), Großeibstadt I (Kossack 1970), Großeibstadt II (Schifferdecker/Wamser 1982; Wamser 1980; 1981), Bruckberg (Meixner 2004) or Niedererlbach (Koch 1992; 2001). Against this background it seems surprising that Bavaria hardly plays a role in the assessment of social structure and political organization of the Hallstatt period (Augstein 2015, 307; Schußmann 2008, 314; *cf.* Schier 2010).

Once, however, Bavaria played an important role in research – namely for the discussion of the 'character' of Ha C. Especially W. Torbrügge and G. Kossack are to be named here. G. Kossack's subdivision of the phase Ha C into Ha C1 and Ha C2 (Kossack 1957; 1959), mainly based on changes in ceramic form and decoration, was rejected firmly by W. Torbrügge (1979, 191-214; 1991). Today assessment of the chronological situation seems to depend on academic background of the researchers, but it can be noted that a division of Ha C into two or even three parts is widely accepted. But it was not only that discussion that is notable here. Especially W. Torbrügge was, abridged, concerned with whether Ha C is a chronological phenomenon or rather an 'equipment pattern'. He positioned Ha C *next to* instead of *between* Ha B and Ha D (Torbrügge 1979, 207; see also Torbrügge 1991).

---

2   For a concise overview of the controversial positions see Schier 2010, esp. 375-378.
3   *Cf.* the local workups for Upper Palatinate (Torbrügge 1965; 1979), Middle Franconia (Hoppe 1986) and Upper Franconia (Ettel 1996).

'Elite' graves?

Richly equipped Ha C graves generally are interpreted as 'elite graves', without, however, disclosing the mode of interpretation clearly. It has to be asked first, what constitutes an elite – 'religious' or 'knowledge' elites, for example, do not necessarily correspond to 'economic elites'. To what extent are the status of the buried – on the vertical as well as horizontal level – and the structure of society visible in the grave?

The identification of hierarchies and elites is a major aim of prehistoric archaeology[4]. Elites commonly are associated with increasing social complexity and social stratification, with establishing far-reaching networks, having differential access to power, wealth and knowledge and the organization and control of collective work (Kienlin 2012, 15-16; *cf.* Egg/Quast 2009). In the general mode of interpretation, rich graves of nearly any period are identified as the material reflections of elites (*cf.* Steuer 2006), and the differences in grave goods or the richness of the grave equipment are usually interpreted in terms of ranking or economic power (Hofmann 2013, 274; Veit 2013, 211; *cf.* Egg/Quast 2009).

Recently T. Kienlin (2012) pleaded for a perspective 'beyond elites'. His remarks are not to deny ranking throughout history, but to keep in mind a more diverse ancient reality (Kienlin 2012, 18). As emphasis is put on vertical political differentiation and hierarchical systems, other aspects stay unilluminated (*cf.* Kienlin/Zimmermann 2012). In many prehistoric societies, group authority especially referred to kinship. That does not mean that ancient societies were egalitarian – a lack of institutionalized ranking does not mean a group is not complex (Kienlin 2012, 19; Veit 2013, 210; *cf.* Schier 2010). There can be manifold identities, manifold ways people interact.

That means far-reaching networks are not necessarily established by elites; in kinship-based societies as well networks are tying individuals – on the basis of common descent, be it real or fictional – even across larger distances (Kienlin 2012, 23). The spread of objects shows that communication is proceeding and a sense of 'identity' is constituted – the 'mode' of communication and its 'agents', however, are in the first instance unknown. In the following remarks the term 'elite' is to be understood in this sense.

Ha C 'elite graves' – some examples

In the following, four examples will be introduced to give a general view on 'rich' graves of that period – that are said to be 'elite graves' – in the area of today's Bavaria. Focus is on the graveyard structure (as far as we know), on the objects and the practices they were involved in. I am very much aware of the little data applied, that there perhaps would have been other or even better examples, perhaps such that would challenge my theses. The examples chosen should still serve to bring some questions about the 'character' of these graves into the debate.

---

[4]   In the last years a perspective focusing 'the lower classes' can be recognized as well (Trebsche *et al.* 2007), but according to U. Veit (2013, 210) it is to be asked if this still upholds the concept of hierarchical structures and elites, only with other signs.

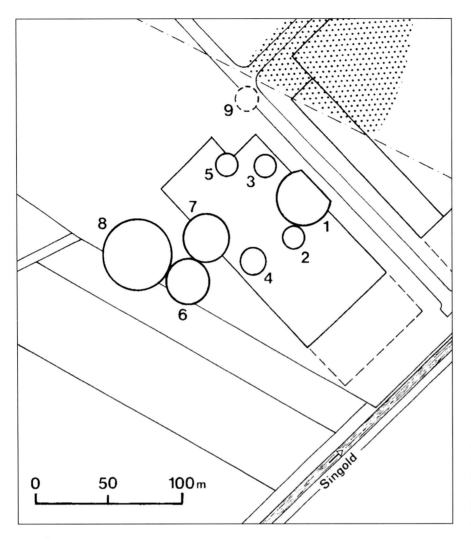

Fig. 1. Wehringen-Hexenbergle. Plan of the burial ground with the eight mounds still visible in the post-war period (after Hennig 2001, 254 fig. 130).

1: Wehringen-Hexenbergle

The first example is that of Wehringen-Hexenbergle mound 8, in Swabia. In this case, we have an idea about the general topography of the burial ground. It once consisted of at least 18 mounds (Hennig 2001, 254 with fig. 130). Eight of these mounds were still visible in the post-war period (Fig. 1), but only mound 8, the largest of them, was disturbed just on its surface. None of the mounds contained later burials. Mound 8 had a diameter of 46 m and a preserved height of 1.10 m. The chamber (Fig. 2) measured 5.20 by 4.50 m. It was built from oak planks on the surface, with a nearly centric support post (Hennig 2001, 259-268).

In the southwest corner a densely packed set of vessels was positioned, composed of several smaller or bigger bowls and four vessels with a cone-shaped neck and corresponding lids and scoops inside. Because of the sometimes oversized shape and the thin walls, the pottery is said to be non-functional (Hennig 2001, 102; 263). One of the vessels is extraordinary (Fig. 3), as this one is a small, thin-walled (0.02 mm wall thickness) gold bowl. In form and ornament it can be compared to the so-called 'Goldkegel' respectively 'Goldhüte' of the Late Bronze Age or Urnfield period (Hennig 2001, 88). Because of the only paper-thin walls, this bowl is also said to be non-functional. On the northwest chamber wall, three large plates and

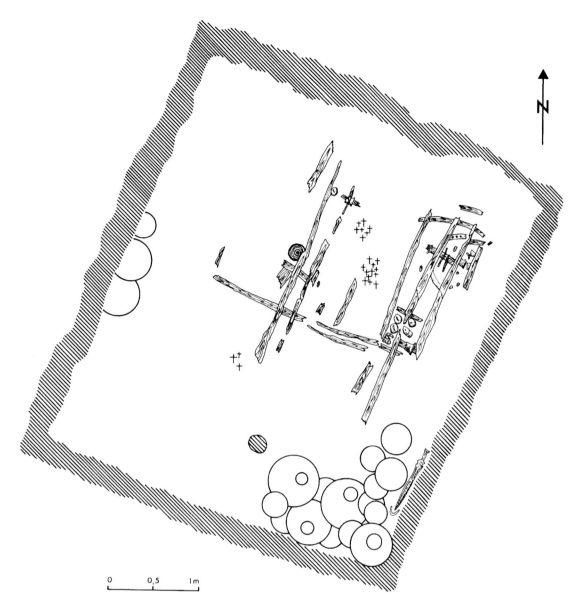

N

0   0,5   1 m

Fig. 2. Wehringen-
Hexenbergle, mound 8. Plan
of the chamber (after Hennig
2001, 260 fig. 134b).

one fragment of another were found. The ceramic vessels are very similar and seem to be intended as a set and made for the burial (Hennig 2001, 102; 263).

A four-wheeled wagon was arranged in the northeast corner. Several wooden and metal fragments from the wheels, fellows and naves as well as bronze fittings are recorded. The naves are associated with the Urnfield period dated Bad Homburg type (Hennig 2001, 88; see in detail Pare 1987). H. Hennig (2001, 102) describes this vehicle as non-functional, even as a 'fake' ("*Attrappe*").

Between the vessels in the southwest corner and the eastern chamber wall, a bronze sword from Gündlingen type (Fig. 4) was deposited. Gündlingen swords are to be set at the very beginning of the Iron Age (Pare 1987, 478; 1991; 2004a, 542), with close relations to late Urnfield types (Pare 1987, 478). Except for the wagon with 'Urnfield character', this sword marks the special chronological position of the Wehringen grave (Pare 1987, 477).

Fig. 3. Wehringen-Hexenbergle, mound 8. Gold bowl (© Archäologische Staatssammlung München. Fotograf: M. Eberlein; GD 2001-21).

The cremation remains were positioned in two separate small heaps between the wheels of the wagon and a third heap next to the right front wheel. They had a weight of only 443 gr, so this seems to be too little to represent the whole individual. The analysis of cremation remains by P. Schröter showed one individual, male, adult (Hennig 2001, 261)[5].

Concluding, we have an undisturbed grave that became the paragon for a Ha C sword and wagon grave and is a very important anchor for the absolute chronology of the Early Iron Age, as there is a dendro-date at 778 ± 5 BC (Hennig 2001, 263). And as there are objects in the grave that are formally associated with the Urnfield period as well as objects that are perceived to be already Early Iron Age (Hennig 2001, 86; 88; 263), this special equipment seems to mark the transition or continuity (Pare 1987, *e.g.* 475) from Urnfield period to the early Hallstatt period.

2: Unterwiesenacker

Unterwiesenacker mound 4, in Upper Palatinate, was found during excavations taking place at the beginning of the 20th century, and additionally, the objects from Unterwiesenacker may belong to the cemetery of Niederhofen (Torbrügge 1979; 271; 319-320). As the find contexts are very cloudy, it seems likely that the following ensemble is fragmentary. Nevertheless, this grave shows some more interesting details for understanding the 'character' of early Hallstatt graves.

The grave equipment contains parts of horse-gear as well as parts of the wagon fittings. Further, there are two bronze bowls, on the brim a sequence of birds and sun symbols that are to be seen in the tradition of the Urnfield symbolism of the 'sun-bird-boat' (Fig. 5), two bronze scoops with perhaps theriomorphic handle, one bronze bowl with omphalos bottom, four small bone disks with circle decoration, two needle bearings and parts of two toilet sets[6]. Then, there are more

---

5   There are two very different results from the analysis of the cremation remains. Departing from Schröters results, O. Röhrer-Ertl exposed even three deceased, one male/adult, one female/adult, and the third infans (Hennig 2001, 261). The latter results hardly play a role in Hallstatt research.

6   According to W. Torbrügge (1979, 191), needle bearings and toilet sets are often found as a dyad.

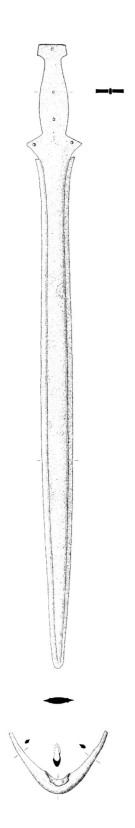

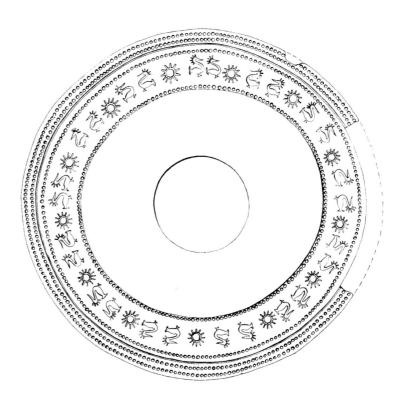

Fig. 5. Unterwiesenacker, mound 4. Bronze bowl with a sequence of birds and sun symbols (after Torbrügge 1979, pl. 90,1).

than 200 small bronze studs. The large number and their special appearance indicate that they may belong to the harness or to a yoke. Finally, apart from several ceramic vessels, the grave contained one iron sword.

3: Großeibstadt I

The Großeibstadt I graves in the Grabfeldgau in Lower Franconia were excavated in 1954. Six individuals[7], all men between 25 and 40 years old at the time of death (Kossack 1970, 155), were buried in a separate burial site that has become a paragon for 'elite graves' of the Early Iron Age apart from the 'princely graves' of the 'Westhallstattkreis' (*cf.* Metzner-Nebelsick 2009, 248).

Like Wehringen, we have a general idea about the topography of the graveyard (Fig. 6a), as it seems it was excavated completely (Kossack 1970, pl. 28,1)[8]. Principles of construction, like the massive stone packing, form and size of the burial chambers as well as selection and staging of grave goods show a pattern. For all men a two-horse four-wheeled wagon seems to have been arranged in the chamber – but remarkably, the wagons were represented by *pars pro toto* items in several cases.

The grave structure and goods from grave 1 (Fig. 7) are discussed as an example (Kossack 1970, 45-61; Pare 1992, 289-290). The chamber measured 5.80 by 2.80 m, the north part of the pit was found to be deeper. The burial was

Fig. 4. Wehringen-Hexenbergle, mound 8. Bronze Gündlingen sword (after Hennig 2001, pl. 113,24-25).

7   Seven 'grave-like structures' were found, but 'grave 6' seems to be a cenotaph (Kossack 1970, 92).
8   Kossack 1970, 45. – C. Pare (1992, 289) claims that the cemetery could have been larger, especially to the west of the excavated area.

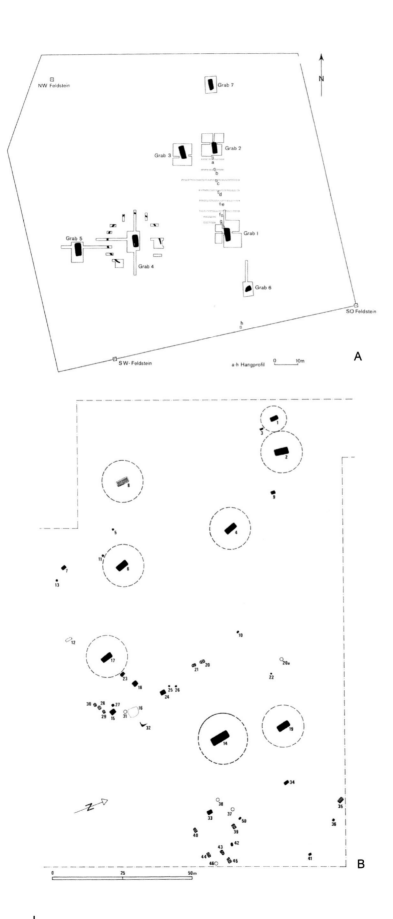

Fig. 6. A: Großeibstadt I. Plan of the burial ground with six graves (after Kossack 1970, pl. 28,1). – B: Großeibstadt II. Plan of the burial ground with 48 graves (after Wamser 1982, 41 fig. 34).

an inhumation, apparently a male of about 40 years old at the time of death. In addition to an iron sword, there were several fragments of iron tires and nave fittings. The grave was further equipped with three bronze vessels and 34 ceramic vessels. In the middle of the southern half lay a yoke covered with small bronze studs, and the horse harness, two bronze bits and several rings, knobs and fittings.

Interesting is the condition of the wagon[9]. It seems to be complete, although there are no metal fittings from the wagon box. The wheels seem to be mounted on their axles, but even the two intact wheels had too few clamps and the navestock-rings, axle-caps and linchpins are missing (Pare 1992, 289-290). G. Kossack (1970, 48-49) suggested that the wagon was deposited in a non-functional condition[10].

Except for grave 1 and grave 4, all other graves were equipped only with parts of the harness. G. Kossack noticed a remarkable detail in the equipment of grave 3 that should be mentioned in this context. In addition to a set of 19 ceramic vessels and an iron knife, there were several iron and bronze elements of a bridle. One of the two bits seems to have been broken into pieces, apparently at or even before the time of deposition. As both inner joints are nor destroyed nor connected, they must have been assembled from different sets (Kossack 1970, 71) – "…man hatte Nutzbares und Unbrauchbares zu seltsamen Geschirren zusammengeflickt, um es gleichsam als Atrappe [sic!] dem Toten mitzugeben" (Kossack 1970, 167). He interprets this in the same context of meaning as the phenomena in the other Großeibstadt I graves, where either crucial elements for functionality regularly are missing, or the wagon is represented only by *pars pro toto* items or references to the draft horses[11]. One can say, all ensembles are – in variations – incomplete.[12]

4: Großeibstadt II

All graves introduced thus far reflect male, often armed individuals – and that was said to be true for the phenomenon Ha C in general for a long time[13]. Recently, C. Metzner-Nebelsick brought together women's graves from the Early Iron Age with associated items of women's dress and bridle, including examples from Bavaria (Metzner-Nebelsick 2009).

An appropriate example could be Großeibstadt II[14] that was excavated by modern standards between 1980 and 1982, but never conclusively published (see the preliminary reports: Schifferdecker/Wamser 1982; Wamser 1980; 1981). All in all, there were about 50 graves (Fig. 6b). Besides a range of simpler cremation burials, eight of them were inhumation burials in large chamber graves (Schifferdecker/Wamser 1982, 59), very much like those of Großeibstadt I, 1.5 km

---

9   For the construction of the wagon see in detail Kossack 1970, 48-52; Uenze 1987; Pare 1992, 289-292.

10   H. P. Uenze (1987, 75) wants to put up for discussion if the missing elements could also be traced back to the long-time use of the vehicle.

11   The horses are never part of the grave goods – for Bavaria (and the 'Westhallstattkreis' in general) there are only two known exceptions from Swabia (Hennig 2001, 64-67).

12   G. Kossack (1970, 157) framed it like this: "*Vollständigkeit der Teile war offensichtlich bei keinem der Geräte beabsichtigt, vielleicht hat man sie sogar bewußt vermieden: außer den obligatorischen Trensen ist Unvollständigkeit der hervorstechendste Grundzug aller Inventare*". – H. Hennig (2001, 101-102) as well emphasises the distinguished practices visible in richly equipped Ha C graves.

13   That changed with, for example, grave X/1 from Mitterkirchen in Upper Austria (*cf.* Pertlwieser no year).

14   Bad Königshofen, Kirchenreinbach and Oberpfahlheim can be mentioned as well, but they are either from old excavations or find contexts are discussed controversially (Metzner-Nebelsick 2009, 238; 248; Torbrügge 1979, 124-140, esp. 139-140).

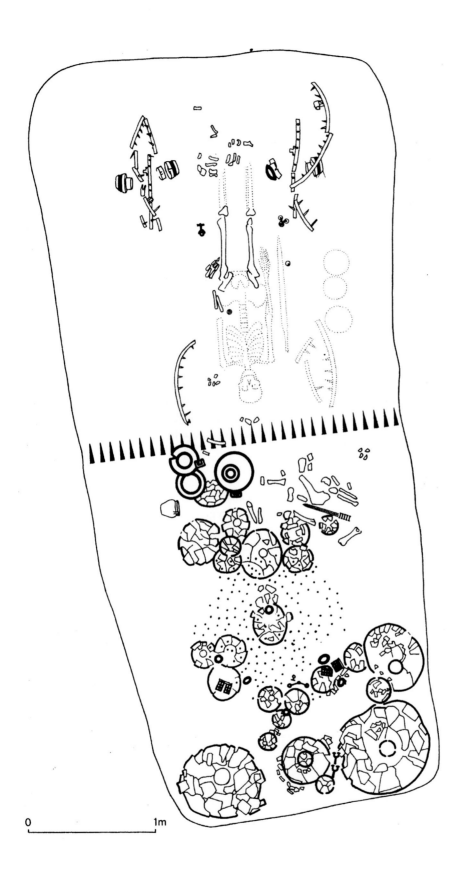

Fig. 7. Großeibstadt I, grave 1. Plan of the chamber (after Kossack 1970, pl. 30).

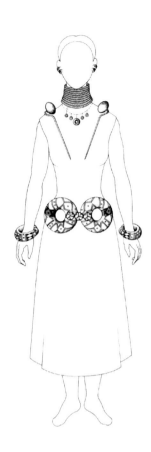

Fig. 8. Großeibstadt II, grave 19/1981. Reconstruction of the dress (after Wamser 1982, 40 fig. 33).

away. In one case, the deceased was buried with a wagon (Wamser 1981, 104 fig. 88). Generally, these graves were equipped with large sets of ceramic vessels, in some cases with metal bowls and elements of horse-gear. This means that they were arranged as wagon graves as well, and again we can recognize *pars pro toto* practices as often only the naves or the linchpins were interred (Schifferdecker/ Wamser 1982, 59).

What is different from Großeibstadt I is the fact that two of these chamber graves (17/1981 and 19/1981) contained paired horse-gear, as well as rich women's equipment (Wamser 1981, 104; Schifferdecker/Wamser 1982, 60). A reconstruction of the very rich dress of the woman from grave 19/1981 is the only one published (Fig. 8). She wore two iron swan's neck pins, four so-called "*Segelohrringe*", a set of ten neck rings with amber and jet beads, two lower arm-rings and two large so-called "*Hohlwulstringe*" (Wamser 1981, 40 fig. 33). Further, she was equipped with paired horse-gear as *pars pro toto* for the whole harness (Metzner-Nebelsick 2009, 248).

Objects and practices

The examples introduced above show that in undisturbed 'rich' graves of the Early Iron Age, we regularly find – in different compositions – wagons or parts of wagons, items of horse-gear, large sets of ceramic vessels, sometimes metal vessels[15]. Weapons, especially swords, are part of that equipment pattern, but they are limited to male graves.

Concluding, we should have a closer look at the material again. First, for an understanding of Ha C graves and communities, the Late Bronze Age or the Urnfield period have to be considered as well. On the one hand, there is a connection between Late Bronze Age/Urnfield period and early Hallstatt 'elite graves', documented by items like swords, horse-gear, wagons[16] or reminiscence of the so-called 'sun-bird-boat'.

But what is more, there is a connection in terms of *practices* as well. In every Late Bronze Age/Urnfield period grave, some of the grave goods are burnt – that means they were fragmented through fire. The burial of Eching near Munich showed, besides the cremation remains, a large ensemble of ceramic vessels. Most of them were complete, but some were evidently fragmented at the time of deposition in the grave. Furthermore, there are only a few bronze items, but one of them is a piece of the grip of a solid-hilted sword that is said to be a *pars pro toto* item (Winghart 1998, 358)[17]. Similar practices are observed in wagon graves like Poing (Bz D) or in Hart an der Alz (Ha A1)[18]. The wagon of the undisturbed and excavated by modern methods burial of Poing is represented by the burned

---

15 For the North Bavarian area, Walter Torbrügge (1987, 20) added figural representations; see also Winghart 1998, 370; Augstein forthcoming.

16 "Der damit [mit der Beigabe von reichen Geschirrsätzen aus Keramik bzw. bronzenen Gefäßen, Schwertern und/oder Trensen und einen vierrädrigen Wagen; comm. M. A.] symbolisch beanspruchte Status der Eliten des 13./12. Jahrhunderts und derjenigen des 8./7. Jahrhunderts ist dabei ein auffällig gleicher…" (Winghart 1998, 356).

17 This reminds of mound 3 at Oss-Zevenbergen that is interpreted as an extreme *pars pro toto* grave. Besides one single fragment of cremated bone, there were only four pieces of metal found. One of them has similarities to the hilt-blade transition of a bronze sword (Fontijn *et al.* 2013b, 303).

18 For chronology see Winghart 1999, 527.

bronze fitting. All items were out of their functional context, and smaller pieces were put in the hollows of bigger ones with great force (Winghart 1999, 517)[19].

Practices of selection are documented in Hart, where only three of the four axle-caps were found, and in Poing, where there are two different pairs of axle-caps (Pare 2004b, 360). Concerning the vessels, there seem to be sets as well, but in Poing, some of the vessels were destroyed intentionally and sometimes incomplete when they were used to cover the bronze items (Winghart 1998, 359-360; 1999, 526).

There is a hiatus – that is 'bridged' in a way by the 'sun-bird-boat' motif that has its focus in the middle and late Urnfield period in terms of Ha A2 – B1 (Pare 2004b, 363; 365) respectively its reminiscence – between Bz D/Ha A1 and Ha C in terms of changing equipment patterns regarding the occasional exclusion of status indicators (Winghart 1998, *e.g.* 356; 367; 371; Trachsel 2005, 63; 75), but the observation of practices in the latter period leads to one very important point concerning Ha C 'elite graves' in Bavaria. What is most striking here in an even more distinct mode is not the fact that we have similar equipment patterns in most of the graves, but the indication that there is regularly something missing, ensembles are not complete, there are only single objects representing the whole, items are non-functional.

M. Trachsel (2005, 68) pointed out that many of the Ha C swords – up to two-thirds – were broken intentionally[20]. And, as the cremation remains sometimes show, even here only a part of the whole is present. It is indeed fragmentation that seems to be the connecting element of all of these in detail different graves.

Generally, decedents who are buried in the described modes are said to be elites. First, one has to ask for the possibilities of reconstructing the status of persons, and further, if and how these elites are connected to each other. I want to agree with T. Kienlin (2012, 27) that "a framework has to be established that broadens our view for the wider range of organizational possibilities" that includes a perspective 'beyond elites', from the household level to kinship groups, without yet denying higher-order forms of power.

What is also important is the idea that questions concerning the 'degree' of connection and communication of early Hallstatt communities cannot focus only on objects or object groups and their spreading. Beside quality and quantity of the grave goods, 'context' plays an important role in interpretation. Graves can only be seen in their spatial order. This means that the topography of burial sites is very important. As a lot of the graves are from old excavations and there is no information regarding the structure of cemeteries, we therefore have to gain more information from modern excavated and documented sites.

But first and foremost: It has to be asked whether distribution of certain objects, but above all the ritual practices as well as certain staging patterns documented in rich Ha C graves can be seen as the same expression of complex transformation processes and whether they reflect far-reaching communication mechanisms, in spite of variety and regional differences. Objects do not have a single, fixed meaning. They rather undergo complex processes of decontextualizing and re-contextualizing. So the *practices* they are involved in – selection, *pars pro toto*,

---

19   See also the table with objects that were destroyed intendedly in the Late Bronze Age (Bz D) wagon burial of Königsbronn (Pankau 2013, 7 tab. 1).

20   His remarks refer to bronze swords, because it is hard to judge if iron swords are intentionally broken as well, because they have no metal core any more (Trachsel 2005, 67).

mechanical manipulation, fragmentation – are perhaps as much or even more meaningful than the objects themselves,[21] as stabilization and transformation of social order highly depend on performance and practices – that is true especially for funerary rituals.

Acknowledgements

First of all, I want to thank the organizers for giving me the opportunity to participate in the illuminating workshop and this publication. Further, I am indebted to Stefan Burmeister and Maria Kohle for helpful comments and Matthias Meinecke for translating the abstract into French.

Bibliography

Augstein 2015: M. Augstein, Das Gräberfeld der Hallstatt- und Frühlatènezeit von Dietfurt an der Altmühl ('Tankstelle'). Ein Beitrag zur Analyse einer Mikroregion. Universitätsforschungen zur Prähistorischen Archäologie 262 (Bonn 2015).

Augstein forthcoming: M. Augstein, Das Tier und sein Kontext. Tierdarstellungen und Tierfunde der Hallstattzeit Nordostbayerns. In: V. Brieske (ed.), Tiere und Tierdarstellungen. Kolloquium im Gedenken an Prof. Dr. Torsten Capelle. Veröffentlichungen der Altertumskommission für Westfalen (Münster, forthcoming).

Claßen et al. 2013: E. Claßen/S. Gussmann/G. von Looz, Regulär und doch außergewöhnlich – Eine hallstattzeitliche Bestattung mit Zuggeschirr von Otzing, Lkr. Deggendorf. In: L. Husty/K. Schmotz (eds.), Vorträge des 31. Niederbayerischen Archäologentages (Rahden/Westf. 2013) 191-214.

Egg/Quast 2009: M. Egg/D. Quast, Vorwort. In: M. Egg/D. Quast (ed.), Aufstieg und Untergang. Zwischenbilanz des Forschungsschwerpunktes "Studien zu Genese und Struktur von Eliten in vor- und frühgeschichtlichen Gesellschaften". Monographien des Römisch-Germanischen Zentralmuseums 82 (Mainz 2009) VII-IX.

Ettel 1996: P. Ettel, Gräberfelder der Hallstattzeit aus Oberfranken. Materialhefte zur Bayerischen Vorgeschichte A 72 (Kallmünz/Opf. 1996).

Fokkens et al. 2012: H. Fokkens/S. van der Vaart/D. Fontijn/S. Lemmers/R. Jansen/I. van Wijk/P. Valentijn, Hallstatt burials of Oss in context. Analecta Praehistorica Leidensia 43/44, 2012, 183-204.

Fontijn et al. 2013a: D. Fontijn/S. van der Vaart/R. Jansen, Transformation through destruction: A monumental and extraordinary Early Iron Age Hallstatt C barrow from the ritual landscape of Oss-Zevenbergen (Leiden 2013).

Fontijn et al. 2013b: D. Fontijn/R. Jansen/S. van der Vaart/H. Fokkens/I. van Wijk, Conclusion: the seventh mound of the seven mounds – Long-term history of the Zevenbergen barrow landscape. In: D. Fontijn/S. van der Vaart/R. Jansen, Transformation through destruction: A monumental and extraordinary Early Iron Age Hallstatt C barrow from the ritual landscape of Oss-Zevenbergen (Leiden 2013) 281-316.

---

21 G. Kossack (1970, 157) too referred to *practices* of the community, like the standardized construction of the graves, the selection in terms of age and gender of the deceased (adult men), burial rite (inhumation) and the standardized grave equipment with sets of vessels, but also with elements of horse-gear that symbolize horse and carriage.

Gebhard 2015: R. Gebhard, Otzing – Ein Grab voller Geheimnisse. In: L. Husty/K. Schmotz (eds.), Vorträge des 33. Niederbayerischen Archäologentages (Rahden/ Westf. 2015) 163-170.

Gebhard *et al.* 2016: R. Gebhard/C. Metzner-Nebelsick/R. Schumann, Excavating an extraordinary burial of the Early Hallstatt period from Otzing, Eastern Bavaria, in the museum laboratories. PAST – The Newsletter of the Prehistoric Society 82, 2016, 1-3.

Gramsch 2010: A. Gramsch, Ritual und Kommunikation. Altersklassen und Geschlechterdifferenz im spätbronze- und früheisenzeitlichen Gräberfeld Cottbus Alvensleben-Kaserne (Brandenburg). Universitätsforschungen zur Prähistorischen Archäologie 181 (Bonn 2010).

Hennig 2001: H. Hennig, Gräber der Hallstattzeit in Bayerisch Schwaben. Monographien der Prähistorischen Staatssammlung München 2 (Stuttgart 2001).

Hofmann 2013: K. Hofmann, Gräber und Totenrituale: Zu aktuellen Theorien und Forschungsansätzen. In: M. K. H. Eggert/U. Veit (eds.), Theorie in der Archäologie: Zur jüngeren Diskussion in Deutschland. Tübinger Archäologische Taschenbücher 10 (Münster 2013) 269-298.

Hoppe 1986: M. Hoppe, Die Grabfunde der Hallstattzeit in Mittelfranken. Materialhefte zur Bayerischen Vorgeschichte A 55 (Kallmünz/Opf. 1986).

Hoppe 1987: M. Hoppe, Das hallstatt- und frühlatènezeitliche Gräberfeld von Landersdorf, Gde. Thalmässing, Mittelfranken. Mitteilungen der Österreichischen Arbeitsgemeinschaft für Ur- und Frühgeschichte 37, 1987, 121-127.

Hughes 1999: R. Hughes, Das hallstattzeitliche Gräberfeld von Schirndorf, Lkr. Regensburg VI: Studien zu den Geschirrausstattungen. Materialhefte zur Bayerischen Vorgeschichte A 79 (Kallmünz/Opf. 1999).

Hughes 2001: R. Hughes, Das hallstattzeitliche Gräberfeld von Schirndorf, Lkr. Regensburg V. Materialhefte zur Bayerischen Vorgeschichte A 78 (Kallmünz/Opf. 2001).

Kienlin 2012: T. Kienlin, Beyond elites: An introduction. In: T. L. Kienlin/A. Zimmermann (eds.), Beyond elites. Alternatives to hierarchical systems in modelling social formations. Universitätsforschungen zur Prähistorischen Archäologie 215 (Bonn 2012) 15-32.

Kienlin/Zimmermann 2012: T. Kienlin/A. Zimmermann (eds.), Beyond elites. Alternatives to hierarchical systems in modelling social formations. Universitätsforschungen zur Prähistorischen Archäologie 215 (Bonn 2012).

Koch 1992: H. Koch, Grabfunde der Hallstattzeit aus dem Isartal bei Niedererlbach, Lkr. Landshut. Bayerische Vorgeschichtsblätter 57, 1992, 49-57.

Koch 2001: H. Koch, Niedererlbach, Gde. Buch a. Erlbach, LA (BY). In: S. Rieckhoff/J. Biel (eds.), Die Kelten in Deutschland (Stuttgart 2001) 432-434.

Kossack 1957: G. Kossack, Zur Chronologie der Älteren Hallstattzeit (Ha C) im bayerischen Alpenvorland. Germania 35, 1957, 207-223.

Kossack 1959: G. Kossack, Südbayern während der Hallstattzeit. Römisch-Germanische Forschungen 24 (Berlin 1959).

Kossack 1970: G. Kossack, Gräberfelder der Hallstattzeit an Main und Fränkischer Saale. Materialhefte zur Bayerischen Vorgeschichte 24 (Kallmünz/Opf. 1970).

Meixner 2004: G. Meixner, Die hallstattzeitliche Nekropole von Bruckberg, Lkr. Landshut. Beiträge zur Archäologie in Niederbayern 2, 2004, 125-281.

Meixner et al. 1995: G. Meixner/M. Schaich/S. Watzlawik, Ausgrabungen in einem hallstattzeitlichen Grabhügelfeld zwischen Kinding und Ilbling. Das Archäologische Jahr in Bayern 1995, 65-68.

Meixner et al. 1996: G. Meixner/K. Rieder/M. Schaich, Das hallstattzeitliche Grabhügelfeld von Kinding/Ilbling, Gemeinde Kinding, Landkreis Eichstätt, Oberbayern. Das Archäologische Jahr in Bayern 1996, 90-93.

Metzner-Nebelsick 2009: C. Metzner-Nebelsick, Wagen- und Prunkbestattungen von Frauen der Hallstatt- und frühen Latènezeit in Europa. Ein Beitrag zur Diskussion der sozialen Stellung der Frau in der älteren Eisenzeit. In: J. Bagley/C. Eggl /D. Neumann/M. Schefzik (eds.), Alpen, Kult und Eisenzeit. Festschrift für Amei Lang zum 65. Geburtstag. Internationale Archäologie, Studia honoraria 30 (Rahden/Westf. 2009) 237-270.

Müller-Scheeßel 2000: N. Müller-Scheeßel, Die Hallstattkultur und ihre räumliche Differenzierung: Der West- und Osthallstattkreis aus forschungsgeschichtlich-methodologischer Sicht. Tübinger Texte 3 (Rahden/Westf. 2000).

Nikulka 1998: F. Nikulka, Das hallstatt- und frühlatènezeitliche Gräberfeld von Riedenburg-Untereggersberg, Lkr. Kelheim, Niederbayern. Archäologie am Main-Donau-Kanal 13 (Rahden/Westf. 1998).

Pankau 2013: C. Pankau, Das spätbronzezeitliche Wagengrab von Königsbronn (Lkr. Heidenheim). Jahrbuch des Römisch-Germanischen Zentralmuseums 60, 2013, 1-103.

Pare 1987: C. Pare, Wagenbeschläge der Bad Homburg-Gruppe und die kulturgeschichtliche Stellung des hallstattzeitlichen Wagengrabes von Wehringen, Kreis Augsburg. Archäologisches Korrespondenzblatt 17, 1987, 467-482.

Pare 1991: C. Pare, Swords, Wagon-Burials and the Beginning of the Early Iron Age in Central Europe. Kleine Schriften aus dem Vorgeschichtlichen Seminar Marburg 37 (Marburg 1991).

Pare 1992: C. Pare, Wagons and Wagon-Graves of the Early Iron Age in Central Europe. Oxford University Committee for Archaeology, Monograph 35 (Oxford 1992).

Pare 2004a: RGA² XXVII 537-545 s. v. Schwert. §2 Hallstattzeit (C. Pare).

Pare 2004b: C. Pare, Die Wagen der Bronzezeit in Mitteleuropa. In: St. Burmeister/M. Fansa (conc.), Rad und Wagen. Der Ursprung einer Innovation. Wagen im Vorderen Orient und Europa. Wissenschaftliche Begleitschrift zur Sonderausstellung vom 28. März bis 11. Juli 2004 im Landesmuseum für Natur und Mensch Oldenburg (Oldenburg 2004) 355-372.

Pertlwieser no year: M. Pertlwieser, Frühhallstallstattzeitliche Wagenbestattungen in Mitterkirchen. In: M. Pertlwieser (ed.), Prunkwagen und Hügelgrab. Kultur der frühen Eisenzeit von Hallstatt bis Mitterkirchen. Kataloge des Oberösterreichischen Landesmuseums N. F. 13 (Linz no year) 55-70.

Röhrig 1994: K.-H. Röhrig, Das hallstattzeitliche Gräberfeld von Dietfurt a. d. Altmühl. Archäologie am Main-Donau-Kanal 1 (Buch am Erlbach 1994).

Schaich 2001: M. Schaich, Kinding, EI (BY). In: S. Rieckhoff/J. Biel (eds.), Die Kelten in Deutschland (Stuttgart 2001) 395-399.

Schier 2010: W. Schier, Soziale und politische Strukturen der Hallstattzeit. Ein Diskussionsbeitrag. In: D. Krausse (ed.), "Fürstensitze" und Zentralorte der frühen Kelten. Abschlusskolloquium des DFG-Schwerpunktprogramms 1171 in Stuttgart, 12.-15. Oktober 2009. Forschungen und Berichte zur Vor- und Frühgeschichte Baden-Württembergs 120 (Stuttgart 2010) 375-405.

Schifferdecker/Wamser 1982: M. Schifferdecker/L. Wamser, Die Ausgrabungen 1982 in der hallstattzeitlichen Nekropole II bei Großeibstadt, Landkreis Rhön-Grabfeld, Unterfranken. Das Archäologische Jahr in Bayern 1982, 59-61.

Schußmann 2008: M. Schußmann, Die östlichen Nachbarn der Hallstattfürsten – Siedlungshierarchien und Zentralisierungsprozesse in der Südlichen Frankenalb zwischen dem 9. und 4. Jh. v. Chr. In: D. Krausse (ed.), Frühe Zentralisierungs- und Urbanisierungsprozesse. Zur Genese und Entwicklung frühkeltischer Fürstensitze und ihres territorialen Umfelds. Forschungen und Berichte zur Vor- und Frühgeschichte Baden-Württembergs 101 (Stuttgart 2008) 299-318.

Steuer 2006: H. Steuer, Fürstengräber, Adelsgräber, Elitegräber: Methodisches zur Anthropologie der Prunkgräber. In: C. von Carnap-Bornheim/D. Krausse/A. Wesse (eds.), Herrschaft – Tod – Bestattung: Zu den vor- und frühgeschichtlichen Prunkgräbern als archäologisch-historische Quelle. Universitätsforschungen zur Prähistorischen Archäologie 139 (Bonn 2006) 11-25.

Stöllner 1999: RGA² XIII, 446-453 s. v. Hallstattkultur und Hallstattzeit (T. Stöllner).

Stroh 1979: A. Stroh, Das hallstattzeitliche Gräberfeld von Schirndorf, Lkr. Regensburg I. Materialhefte zur Bayerischen Vorgeschichte A 35 (Kallmünz/Opf. 1979).

Stroh 1988: A. Stroh, Das hallstattzeitliche Gräberfeld von Schirndorf, Lkr. Regensburg II. Materialhefte zur Bayerischen Vorgeschichte A 36 (Kallmünz/Opf. 1988).

Stroh 2000a: A. Stroh, Das hallstattzeitliche Gräberfeld von Schirndorf, Lkr. Regensburg III. Materialhefte zur Bayerischen Vorgeschichte A 37 (Kallmünz/Opf. 2000).

Stroh 2000b: A. Stroh, Das hallstattzeitliche Gräberfeld von Schirndorf, Lkr. Regensburg IV. Materialhefte zur Bayerischen Vorgeschichte A 38 (Kallmünz/Opf. 2000).

Torbrügge 1965: W. Torbrügge, Die Hallstattzeit in der Oberpfalz II: Die Funde und Fundplätze der Gemeinde Beilngries. Materialhefte zur Bayerischen Vorgeschichte A 20 (Kallmünz/Opf. 1965).

Torbrügge 1979: W. Torbrügge, Die Hallstattzeit in der Oberpfalz I: Auswertung und Gesamtkatalog. Materialhefte zur Bayerischen Vorgeschichte A 39 (Kallmünz/Opf. 1979).

Torbrügge 1987: W. Torbrügge, Kunst im Bild. Europäische Vorzeit (München 1987).

Torbrügge 1991: W. Torbrügge, Die frühe Hallstattzeit (Ha C) in chronologischen Ansichten und notwendige Randbemerkungen. Teil I: Bayern und der "Westliche Hallstattkreis". Jahrbuch des Römisch-Germanischen Zentralmuseums 38, 1991 (1995) 223-463.

Trachsel 2005: M. Trachsel, Kriegergräber? Schwertbeigabe und Praktiken ritueller Bannung in Gräbern der frühen Eisenzeit. In: R. Karl/J. Leskovar (eds.), Interpretierte Eisenzeiten. Fallstudien, Methoden, Theorie. Tagungsbeiträge der 1. Linzer Gespräche zur interpretativen Eisenzeitarchäologie. Studien zur Kulturgeschichte Oberösterreichs 18 (Linz 2005) 53-82.

Trebsche *et al.* 2007: P. Trebsche *et al.* (eds.), Die Unteren Zehntausend – Auf der Suche nach den Unterschichten der Eisenzeit. Beiträge zur Ur- und Frühgeschichte Mitteleuropas 47 (Langenweissbach 2007).

Uenze 1987: H. Uenze, Der Hallstattwagen von Großeibstadt. In: Vierrädrige Wagen der Hallstattzeit. Untersuchungen zu Geschichte und Technik. Monographien des Römisch-Germanischen Zentralmuseums 12 (Mainz 1987) 69-75.

Veit 2013: U. Veit, 'Gesellschaft' und 'Herrschaft': Gleichheit und Ungleichheit in frühen Gesellschaften. In: M. K. H. Eggert/U. Veit (eds.), Theorie in der Archäologie: Zur jüngeren Diskussion in Deutschland. Tübinger Archäologische Taschenbücher 10 (Münster 2013) 191-228.

Wamser 1980: L. Wamser, Neue Kammergräber der Hallstattzeit von Großeibstadt, Landkreis Rhön-Grabfeld, Unterfranken. Das Archäologische Jahr in Bayern 1980, 100-101.

Wamser 1981: L. Wamser, Die Ausgrabungen 1981 in hallstattzeitlichen Nekropolen bei Großeibstadt, Landkreis Rhön-Grabfeld, Unterfranken. Das Archäologische Jahr in Bayern 1981, 104-105.

Winghart 1998: S. Winghart, Zu spätbronzezeitlichen Traditionsmustern in Grabausstattungen der süddeutschen Hallstattzeit. In: H. Küster/A. Lang/P. Schauer (eds.), Archäologische Forschungen in urgeschichtlichen Siedlungslandschaften. Festschrift für Georg Kossack zum 75. Geburtstag. Regensburger Beiträge zur Prähistorischen Archäologie 5 (Regensburg 1998) 355-371.

Winghart 1999: S. Winghart, Die Wagengräber von Poing und Hart a. d. Alz. Evidenz und Ursachen spätbronzezeitlicher Elitenbildung in der Zone nordwärts der Alpen. In: Eliten in der Bronzezeit 2. Ergebnisse zweier Kolloquien in Mainz und Athen. Monographien des Römisch-Germanischen Zentralmuseums 43 (Mainz 1999) 515-532.

Author

Melanie Augstein
Professur für Ur- und Frühgeschichte am Historischen Seminar
Universität Leipzig
Ritterstraße 14
D-04109 Leipzig
Germany
melanie.augstein@uni-leipzig.de

New approaches to tracing (landscape) connections on the southeastern fringes of the Alps in the Early Iron Age

The state of (integrated) research in eastern Slovenia

Matija Črešnar

Abstract

This paper explores new approaches to tackling old questions about social and regional connections in the Early Iron Age. The case study area is eastern Slovenia, at a time when new technologies and methodologies became a vital part of archaeological studies. Consequently, are the old questions and approaches still suitable, or do we have to re-evaluate our viewpoints and possibly supplement them with new ones? This article explores some of the possible new datasets connected to Iron Age landscape on different scales, when sites are not only dots on maps, pathways are not only imaginary and individual structures can and have to be evaluated also in their relations with others. But, are we able to intertwine these new data and integrate them into our archaeological interpretations?

Zusammenfassung

In diesem Beitrag werden neue Ansätze zur Klärung alter Fragen bezüglich der sozialen und regionalen Beziehungen in der älteren Eisenzeit am Beispiel des östlichen Sloweniens vorgestellt. In einer Zeit, in der neue Technologien und methodologische Ansätze eine wichtige Rolle in der archäologischen Forschung spielen, muss hinterfragt werden, ob alte Fragestellungen und Ansätze noch zeitgemäß erscheinen, oder ob unsere Sichtweisen verändert oder zumindest durch neue ergänzt werden müssen. Diesbezüglich werden in diesem Beitrag neue Daten zu eisenzeitlichen Landschaften auf verschiedenen Ebenen untersucht, bei denen Fundstellen nicht nur als Punkte auf Verbreitungskarten erscheinen, Verbindungswege nicht nur imaginär sind und einzelne Strukturen im Zusammenhang mit anderen bewertet werden. Zu fragen bleibt, wie derartige Ansätzen in die bestehenden archäologischen Interpretationen nicht nur zur älteren Eisenzeit eingebunden werden können.

The research traditions we are building on

Already in the first half of the 19th century Early Iron Age sites in eastern Slovenia were the focus of various investigations. An important milestone emphasizing this evolution was the foundation of the Museum Joanneum in Graz in 1811. It was however followed by decades during which individual 'romantic' research activities prevailed. Various regions of Slovenia faced different fates. Nevertheless, the evolution of prehistoric archaeology as a research discipline is clearly linked to the developments that took place in Vienna. Mention has to be made of the foundation of the Vienna Anthropological Society (*Anthropologische Gesellschaft in Wien*) in 1870, with the research of barrows as one of its main tasks. This was followed by the establishment of the Prehistoric Commission (*Prähistorische Kommission*) at the Academy of Sciences, and the Anthropological-Prehistoric Collection (*Anthropologisch-prehistorische Sammlung*) of the Natural History Museum in Vienna shortly after (Dular 2003, 13-41; Mihelič *et al.* 2015; Teržan 1990b, 13-20).

By skipping all but the last few decades of research, we do not intend to diminish the work of our predecessors – it is however outside the scope of this paper to list all the giants on whose shoulders we stand. We shall, however, mention some of the most remarkable works of the last decades, which are fundamental to the next steps in our research.

A key figure was S. Gabrovec who, with his well-established international connections, not only brought the new approaches of the German 'von Merhart school' to Slovenia, but furthermore recognized the specifics of the area (Fig. 1), which is clearly seen in his research and published studies (e.g. Gabrovec 1964/65; 1966; 1974; 1987; 1994). He also introduced new excavation techniques, most clearly presented in international excavations at the Stična hillfort and the monumental barrow 48 just below it. They still stand out as one of the biggest projects in Slovenian Iron Age studies and were just recently integrally published (Gabrovec 1994; 2006; Gabrovec/Teržan 2010; Grahek 2016). His successors, namely B. Teržan and J. Dular, both successfully continued to deepen our knowledge of the Early Iron Age in the southeastern fringes of the Alps. B. Teržan published work on Early Iron Age Styria and its position between the Alps, the Panonnian plain and the Balkans (Teržan 1990b), as well as numerous works on chronology, social structure, social connections, burial rites etc. (e.g. Teržan 1976; 1978; 1980; 1985; 1987; 1990a; 1990b; 1994; 1995; 1997; 2001; 2010). J. Dular, on the other hand, until recently focused primarily on the Dolenjska region (southeastern Slovenia), where he invested long years of systematic (field) work on the holistic study of this region, with all its known Iron Age sites, and in particular, its hillforts and barrow cemeteries. Furthermore, he has intensively studied settlement patterns, and thereby introduced landscape studies into Early Iron Age research in Slovenia (e.g. Dular 1993; 2003; Dular/Tecco Hvala 2007 with references on all the previous publications). Their work clearly positioned the Early Iron Age of Slovenia as an important part of the mosaic of the Hallstatt period in southeastern Europe, and helped us to move forward in our understandings of technological, artistic, ideological, social, political, and other connections and changes that this period brought about.

Last, but not least are more recent excavations, preceding the building of Slovenian highways, leading to the investigation of over 150 previously mainly unknown archaeological sites, some of which date to the Early Iron Age. Though the number is not particularly large, these sites are important, as they opened 'a Pandora's box' of under-researched lowlands and integrated them into discussions of the Early Iron Age in this region (e.g. Gerbec 2014; Guštin/Tiefengraber 2001; Kerman 2014; Murgelj 2014; Šavel/Sankovič 2014).

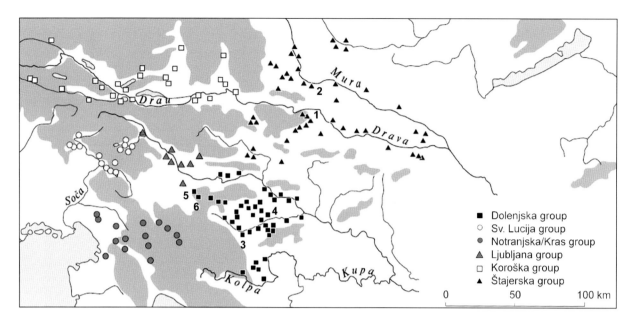

Fig. 1. Major Early Iron
Age regions and sites in
Slovenia, marked with those
sites addressed in the text. 1:
Poštela near Maribor. –
2: Novine above Šentilj. –
3: Cvinger near Dolenjske
Toplice. – 4: Veliki Vinji vrh.
– 5: Molnik. – 6: Magdalenska
gora (adapted from Gabrovec
1999, 150 fig. 1).

New methods and techniques we are using

Recent years have been marked by the growth and development of different
remote sensing and geophysical methods, and thus a widening of our associated
questions about the Early Iron Age in Slovenia. As such, whole landscapes have
become important objects of archaeological investigation; landscapes which were
previously only theoretically debated became tangible categories for study (e.g.
Črešnar et al. 2015; Doneus 2013, 241-335).

Airborne laser scanning (ALS) has proved one of the most successful tools
for landscape survey. It allows for the creation of precise 3D maps of the surface
of the Earth, even where it is covered by dense vegetation (e.g. Opitz 2013).
It is therefore very useful in the heavily forested landscapes of Slovenia, where
it has revolutionized archaeological prospection (e.g. Mlekuž 2013a; 2013b). It
was first applied as part of an Iron Age research project in Slovenia at Poštela,
near Maribor, in 2009, where it proved powerful in 'this landscape of hillforts
and barrows' (Fig. 2). Further analytical steps have helped us to differentiate
between natural phenomena and later human interventions and natural activities,
which have created the modern, multi-layered landscape around the hillfort. The
results were exceptional and the analysis has given us a new perspective of this
archaeological site complex. We had not previously observed an Early Iron Age
landscape in such an extent, including holloways leading up the hillfort ramparts,
passing barrow groups and the flat cremation cemetery and entering the settlement
via a previously unknown entrance corridor. The results of further analysis of
this data have influenced our work ever since, including geophysical prospection
and other elements of our integrated research strategy (Mušič et al. 2015b). It
also allowed us to better consider the wider hillfort landscape, and to disentangle
various elements, such as the different barrow groups, in order to gain a better
understanding of the logic behind the landscape organization patterns observed
(Mlekuž/Črešnar 2014).

One of the most important findings was, without doubt, the recognition of
ring-ditches around every barrow of the associated cemeteries. That was even more
surprising given the fact that the barrows, predominantly containing individual

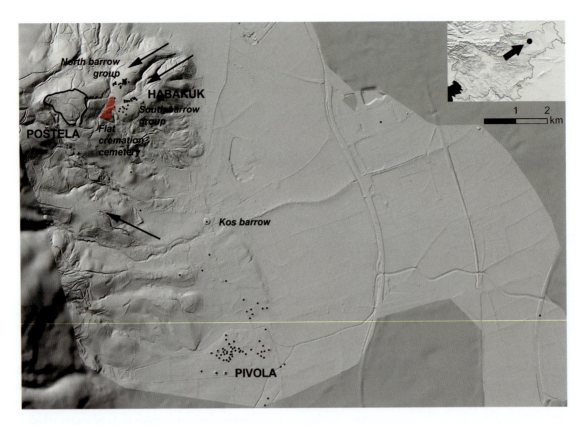

Fig. 2. The Poštela hillfort complex: hillfort with associated cemeteries on the Habakuk plateau, on the slopes towards the valley and in the valley itself, with the most prominent group at Pivola. Arrows indicate probable lines of approach to the hillfort settlement (ALS data manipulation: D. Melkuž).

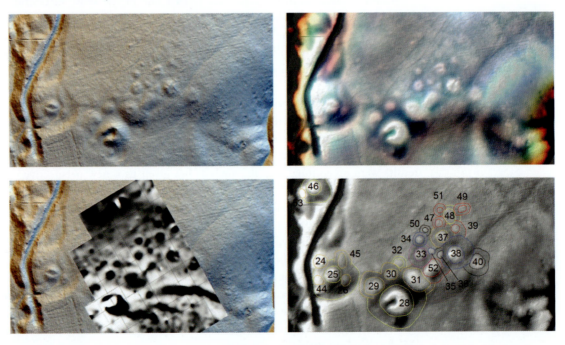

Fig. 3. Analysis of the northern barrow group on the Habakuk plateau below Poštela. A: Hill-shaded relief of the broader area with holloways on the ridges. – B: Analysis of local relief changes (by: D. Mlekuž). – C: Results of magnetic data analysis (by: B. Mušič). – D: 'Horizontal stratigraphy' of the barrow group with proposed relative chronological phases (from earliest to latest): yellow – orange – red – magenta – blue (barrows outlined with black lines do not yield enough information for their positioning).

burials in central chambers, have been known and researched for over a century, and their ditches never recognized (Črešnar/Mlekuž 2014, 27 fig. 4.5; Teržan 1990, 307-337). This recognition is, in the first instance, important for our understanding of the ways in which the barrows were erected, which, from this perspective, does not differ so fundamentally from the barrows recently discovered in the lowlands of eastern Slovenia and beyond, although central burial chambers of stone seem only to be a feature of the barrows associated with more prominent settlements (because the ring-ditches of the barrows often cut each other, or later barrows were erected on the edges and in ditches of earlier, often bigger, 'central' barrows, these relationships allow us to tease out previously invisible chronological information, also in the lowlands, *e.g.* at Rogoza, we have studied such examples e.g. Teržan *et al.* 2015).

As an example, we can take the northern barrow group on the Habakuk plateau below the Poštela hillfort (Fig. 3A). To interpret all the barrows, we have combined ALS and geophysical data (Fig. 3C), historical maps and field documentation. In addition, we applied various analytical procedures to the data, which made it possible to identify at least five stages of cemetery development (Fig. 3), although not all relations can be interpreted satisfactorily. In some aspects, the growth of the cemetery appears to have been linear, with the biggest barrows in the center of the clusters (e.g. nos. 25, 28) and the smaller ones surrounding them. However, barrow 38 follows a different logic, since it is one of the latest barrows, yet was placed in the middle of the group. Its creation damaged at least two earlier barrows (nos. 36, 40) and over-cut the ring-ditches of at least three more (nos. 37, 39 and 52). The female buried in barrow 38 was adorned with rich bronze attire and is therefore considered to be a high-status member of some of the last generations to be buried at this cemetery during Ha C – Ha D1 (Teržan 1990b, 66-70 tab. 61). The typology of the finds therefore supports the interpretation of the ALS data.

From a different perspective, the ring-ditches cutting each other most probably sketch out symbolic connections between buried individuals. As already stated, the individual barrows were mostly erected for single burials – thus, the grouping of barrows probably expressed affiliations between the individual in the central barrow and/or to a family/lineage/clan living in the hillfort and burying their deceased in these burial grounds.

An important part of our systematic research strategy was the geophysical investigation. The broad range of methods used (e.g. magnetic method, magnetic susceptibility, low-frequency electromagnetic method, ground penetrating radar (50-400 MHz antennas), electrical resistivity tomography) enabled us to adopt a strategy based on the local geology, and the type of expected archaeological structures etc. Listing of all results from the geophysical investigations is outside the scope of this paper (e.g. Medarić *et al.* 2016; Mušič *et al.* 2014; Mušič *et al.* 2015a; Teržan *et al.* 2015;), but results in particular shed additional light on the topic in hand.

As already shown (Fig. 3C), the analysis of the magnetic method measurements from the barrow cemeteries concords well with the picture presented by analysis of lidar data. It is clearly discernible that the barrows are encircled with distinctive ring-ditches. Furthermore, we can observe the form of central (stone) chamber constructions and other structures not visible in relief. The results of the magnetic method also support the study of lesser and denuded barrows, which are hardly noticeable in the field or in the ALS data (e.g. Fig. 3C-3D: barrows 48-49).

The interest in understanding different burial customs of the Poštela community has driven us further into detailed study of the flat cremation cemetery, which has been previously investigated in part (Pahič 1974; Teržan 1990b, 307-316). Our multi-method geophysical survey, combined with trial-trenching and innovative analysis of geophysical data, has brought us reliable new results (Fig. 4). After completing our analysis, we estimate that the cemetery contains at least 100 flat cremation graves (Medarić *et al.* 2016), which are, in form and equipment, closely related to the preceding Urnfield period graves of this region (e.g. Müller-Karpe 1959, 99-133; Pahič 1972; Teržan 1999). These results, to some degree, change our understanding of the foundation and the early phase of the hillfort, where the traditions of the Urnfield period must have played a much stronger role than previously thought. Although a close correlation in material culture and burial rite had previously been recognized, the ratio between the graves in the 'old' burial custom in the flat cemetery and the 'new' ones, with the erection of a barrow above them, now seems to have been far more complex (Medarić *et al.* 2016).

Although measurements of physical properties of the surface, combined with geophysics and targeted excavations often produce direct results, it is also the careful systematic GIS analysis that can deliver more 'than meets the eye'. In addition to geophysical surveys, we have used GIS analysis to understand the logics of erecting individual monuments in certain positions.

There was no doubt that the hillfort's location was dictated by its dominant position approximately 250 m above the plain. With such a position, it had good visual control over a large part of the Drava river plain, until the next important settlement at Ptuj to the southeast, and likewise had visual control and/or communication with areas all the way into the Mura valley on the Slovenian-Austrian border (e.g. Plački vrh/Platsch and Novine/Bubenberg). The logic behind the location of specific burial grounds below the hillfort was, however, far less clear.

After various GIS analyses we can conclude that the locations of these burial grounds were carefully selected. These monuments were purposefully positioned in specific parts of the landscape, to first and foremost afford views of the hillfort, but selectively also to other barrow groups. The spatial relations between barrow groups/barrows and hillfort suggest all sought to express their belonging to the Poštela community. The interrelations between the barrow groups suggest, however, a more nuanced story. The fact that the barrows were in use in the same

Fig. 4. Interpretation of the flat cremation cemetery, on the basis of the results of the magnetic measurements on the Habakuk plateau below Poštela hillfort (after Medarić et al. 2016, 85-86 fig. 14-15).

period, but have been positioned in various places with different visual envelopes, suggests that they were intended to convey different groups/populations/identities within the Poštela community. Consequently, we are experiencing various social groups populating the same hillfort, however, when meeting death, the deceased had to be buried on specific locations (Mlekuž/Črešnar 2014). Similar conclusions had been observed previously, from a different perspective, when B. Teržan recognized that the excavation reports of the southern barrow group on the Habakuk plateau always mentioned pieces of brown iron ore, often associated with stone tools and iron fragments, whereas only the latter are regularly present also in the northern group. It is however more abundant with artifacts associated with females, loom-weights, spindle-whorls, bracelets, whereas the presence of an axe and spears also represents the manly warrior note, which is also different to the southern craft-oriented finds with manly connotation. Furthermore, the flat cremation graves, which express a more traditional practice, also show at least two distinct groups. The eastern group seems to mainly include individuals buried in large urns, with all the grave goods gathered in the urn, whereas the others are mostly represented by smaller urns and other grave goods mostly in the grave around the urn (Teržan 1990b, 60-70; 308-316).

The holloways, recognized on the ridges ascending from the plain, lead us to the conclusion that the approach-routes to the hillfort also played a part in the division of space around Poštela. Following our study, we can discern at least three lines of approach or approach corridors (Fig. 2). The northern two can be associated with the two barrow groups on the Habakuk plateau, which have, through the study of grave goods and the GIS analysis, shown significant differences. An important marker in the landscape was also the monumental 'Kos barrow', located in the lowland, where southernmost line of the approach began to ascend to the hillfort's southern entrance (Fig. 2).

Complementary research approaches, integrated into one study, have encompassed a broad variety of data, which help to elucidate the different groups inhabiting the Poštela landscape, and who expressed their individuality in various ways. These differences might, in some aspects (e.g. burial rite), seem profound; yet, the deceased buried according to various different customs, were nevertheless buried almost side by side. And although the barrow groups were located some distance from one another, had different viewsheds, and were associated with different approach-paths, the interventions on the south edge of the Habakuk plateau made it possible that the most southern barrow on the plateau (Mlekuž/Črešnar 2014, 206 fig. 6) was visible on the horizon from the valley barrow group at Pivola. That is despite the differences a subtle, but clear statement that the sense of connectedness and belonging together was at least as strong as the differences which existed.

This is not an isolated example, and other Early Iron Age complexes in the Štajerska region, *e.g.* Novine near Šentilj (Vinazza *et al.* 2015, 167 fig. 1), or in the neighboring Dolenjska region, Veliki Vinji vrh (Mason/Mlekuž 2016) and Cvinger near Dolenjske Toplice (Fig. 5), reveal even more complex narratives.

At the Cvinger near Dolenjske Toplice complex, the holloways ascending the hill from the plain appear to unite at the barrow cemetery. Characteristic barrows in this group (Fig. 1: Dolenjska group) contain remains of inhumed individuals, who were buried in concentric circles around the center of the barrow. The center of the barrow can be empty or can contain the grave of a high-status individual (e.g. Teržan 2010, 191-232). The biggest barrows are often located outside of the

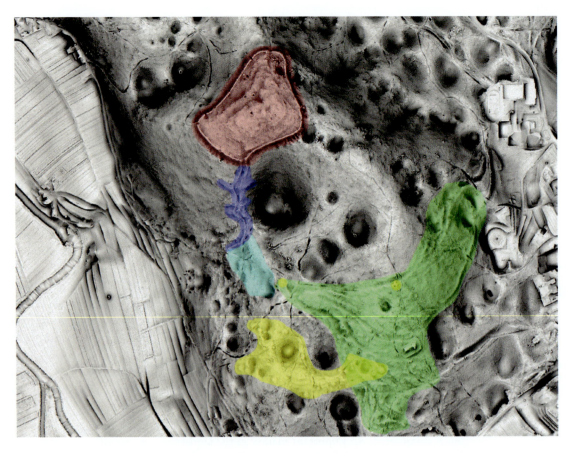

Fig. 5. Cvinger near Dolenjske Toplice (red – hillfort, blue – embanked entrance corridor, turquoise – metallurgical zone, yellow – barrows, green – holloways).

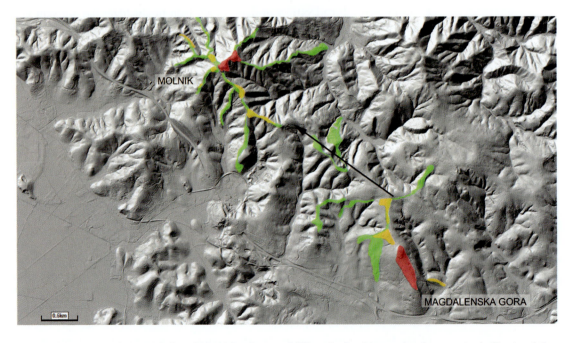

Fig. 6. Iron Age complexes Molnik and Magdalenska gora: hillforts (red) with associated cemeteries (yellow) and the better preserved holloways on the ridges (green). The arrow marks the main ridge connecting the two sites.

main groups, as is also the case at Cvinger. One of them, barrow V, contained, among 46 graves two of the most richly furnished warrior graves in the region (Teržan 1976, 393-413 pl. 24-26; pl. 29-31). The barrows seem to line the approach corridor, which runs westwards and then turns to the north. The various routes unite at the north-westernmost barrow, and follow the eastern edge of the metallurgical zone, with over 100 detected iron-smelting furnaces (Dular/Križ 2004; Mušič/Orengo 1998). The approach path continued through a complex embanked corridor with multiple transverse retaining walls leading towards the monumental entrance. The site is currently the subject of further research, but, as can be discerned from other examples, it seems to have been necessary to present visitors with an image of ancestral glory and thriving community.

We have focused primarily on holloways lying only a short distance outside the various Early Iron Age archaeological complexes. There are a number of reasons for this. Firstly, the environment radically changes upon reaching the fertile plains, where intensive agriculture has erased most traces completely. Secondly, the fact that they can be associated with daily activities in the inhabited landscapes which they ran through, and not only with wholesale movement from A to B (Mlekuž 2013b, 40-41), this presents some uncertainty as to their function and date. As such, these are multi-temporal, multi-causal features, which, even if once serving a particular function, have been transformed at a later date. These are just a few sources of uncertainty in their interpretation.

As ALS data is available for the entirety of Slovenia, we have attempted to 'connect the elites' using their roads. As modeled a decade ago, with the help of GIS analysis (e.g. Dular/Tecco Hvala 2007, 220-223), we naively expected that people were always acting similarly in the landscape. However, the studied examples, have taught us that the direction and course of routeways were not chosen only in light of geological factors or the most 'cost effective' routes. At sites like Vinkov vrh and Veliki Vinji vrh, both above the Krka valley, we encountered routeways mainly on ridges, whereas in previous studies, the valley was expected to have hosted the majority of travellers (Dular/Tecco Hvala 2007, 221 fig. 128).

One of the most informative examples can be observed just outside Ljubljana, on the ridges to the east of Ljubljansko barje (*Ljubljana marshes*) (Fig. 1). One of the hillforts of interest is Magdalenska gora, which dominated this northeastern part of the Dolenjska group. It is located on sloping terrain above the plain and is associated with three barrow cemeteries (Tecco Hvala 2012; Tecco Hvala *et al.* 2004). Its neighboring site was Molnik (Puš 1991), also one of the most prominent sites in the region (Dular/Tecco Hvala 2007, 155-195), which is significant in the fact that it is positioned in the border area between two 'cultural groups'. It is located in a more remote location, which would initially appear to lie away from the main routeways (on the plain). However, when studying the locations of barrow groups around the site, we can clearly see that the location of the ridges dictated their positioning. The same goes for the holloways, which all ran along the ridges, and although some descend onto the plains, it seems that most barrows and the most intensively used corridors of movement ran along the ridge connecting the two settlement complexes/sites (Fig. 6).

Although earlier studies are known (e.g. Doneus 2013, 318-335), this is the first example of the identification of a very probable physical connection between two Iron Age hillforts in Slovenia. It is both inspiring and challenging, that we lack a systematic strategy for approaching such topics and thus elucidating a more complete picture is still somewhat at arm's length.

Looking for connections... or should we start at a (new) beginning?

The various Slovenian landscapes which we have presented in our study have provided us with some answers, though they have rarely been the ones we expected, and when we apply our findings to new sites and new regions, different patterns emerge. We have developed a systematic approach which can be used in various landscapes (Mušič *et al.* 2015b), many of which have yet to be explored in detail.

If we want to be able to understand the connections between places on wider scale, and move beyond the current state of knowledge, we must first take one or two steps backwards. Do we even understand individual sites, their growth and evolution, the influences from abroad and the individual decisions which led to their existence as we see and evaluate them now? What about their surroundings? These were not static entities but evolving 'organisms', with their own biographies, which were founded, grew and/or shrank and were eventually abandoned. Their status within the region can be estimated by measuring their sizes, evaluating their positions, and/or assessing their relative material wealth (Dular/Tecco Hvala 2007, 155-195). It is the best we can do for now, but we are still only scratching the surface of this complex task.

For the purposes of this article, we omitted discussions of various other data-sets, gained by the use of the natural sciences. Through analyses of *e.g.* human remains, pottery and metal artifacts etc. (e.g. Žibrat Gašparič/Dolenec 2015; Nicholls/Buckberry 2016; Nicholls/Koon 2016; Teržan/Črešnar 2014; Büster *et al.* 2016), further layers of information will be integrated into this multi-disciplinary archaeological study.

We now have many tools by which to connect Iron Age people/populations/elites, the task now is to combine the right data with the right questions to push us further in our quest to understand the dynamics of Early Iron Age life in this region. Seemingly, it has never been easier. However... in fact it has never been so difficult...

Acknowledgements

The latest research at Poštela was initiated in 2011 within the framework of the *Continuity and Innovation in Prehistory – Case study between the Alps and the Pannonian Plain for the period 1300-600 BC* (N6-0004) project financed by the Slovenian Research Agency and led by Biba Teržan, whom we thank for the research opportunity we were given. The research was continued within the framework of the *Encounters and Transformations in Iron Age Europe (ENTRANS)* project, led by Ian Armit, with the Slovenian and Croatian principal investigators, Matija Črešnar and Hrvoje Potrebica. It was financially supported by the HERA Joint Research Programme (www.heranet.info) which is co-funded by AHRC, AKA, BMBF via PT-DLR, DASTI, ETAG, FCT, FNR, FNRS, FWF, FWO, HAZU, IRC, LMT, MHEST, NWO, NCN, RANNÍS, RCN, VR and The European Community FP7 2007-2013, under the Socio-economic Sciences and Humanities programme.

Bibliography

Armit et al. 2016: I. Armit/H. Potrebica/M. Črešnar/P. Mason/L. Büster (eds.), Cultural encounters in Iron Age Europe. Archaeolingua, Series Minor 38 (Budapest 2016).

Büster et al. 2016: L. Büster/I. Armit/A. Evans/R. Kershaw, Developing the 3D imaging of the Iron Age art in the ENTRANS Project. In: I. Armit/H. Potrebica/M. Črešnar/P. Mason/L. Büster (eds.), Cultural encounters in Iron Age Europe. Archaeolingua, Series Minor 38 (Budapest 2016) 23-38.

Črešnar/Mlekuž 2014: M. Črešnar/D. Mlekuž, Identities of the Early Iron Age in north eastern Slovenia. In: C. N. Popa/S. Stoddart (eds.), Fingerprinting the Iron Age: approaches to identity in the European Iron Age: Integrating South-Eastern Europe into the debate (Oxford 2014) 18-32.

Črešnar et al. 2015: M. Črešnar/M. Mele/K. Paitler/M. Vinazza (eds.), Archäologische Biographie einer Landschaft an der steirisch-slowenischen Grenze / Arheološka biografija krajine ob meji med avstrijsko Štajersko in Slovenijo. Schild von Steier, Beiheft 6 (Graz, Ljubljana 2015).

Doneus 2013: M. Doneus, Die hinterlassene Landschaft – Prospektion und Interpretation in der Landschaftsarchäologie. Mitteilungen der prähistorischen Kommission 78 (Wien 2013).

Dular 1993: J. Dular, Začetki železnodobne poselitve v osrednji Sloveniji. Arheološki vestnik 44, 1993, 101-112.

Dular 2003: J. Dular, Halštatske nekropole Dolenjske / Die hallstattzeitlichen Nekropolen in Dolenjsko. Opera Instituti Archaeologici Sloveniae 6 (Ljubljana 2003).

Dular 2013: J. Dular, Severovzhodna Slovenija v pozni bronasti dobi / Nordostslowenien in der späten Bronzezeit. Opera Instituti Archaeologici Sloveniae 27 (Ljubljana 2013).

Dular/Križ 2004: J. Dular/B. Križ, Železnodobno naselje na Cvingerju pri Dolenjskih Toplicah / Eisenzeitliche Siedlung auf dem Cvinger bei Dolenjske Toplice. Arheološki vestnik 55, 2004, 207-250.

Dular/Tecco Hvala 2007: J. Dular/S. Tecco Hvala, South-Eastern Slovenia in the Early Iron Age. Settlement, economy, society / Jugovzhodna Slovenija v starejši železni dobi. Poselitev, gospodarstvo, družba. Opera Instituti Archaeologici Sloveniae 12 (Ljubljana 2007).

Gabrovec 1964/65: S. Gabrovec, Halštatska kultura Slovenije / Die Hallstattkultur Sloweniens. Arheološki vestnik 15/16, 1964/65, 21-63.

Gabrovec 1966: S. Gabrovec, Zur Hallstattzeit in Slowenien. Germania 44, 1966, 1-48.

Gabrovec 1974: S. Gabrovec, Die Ausgrabungen in Stična und ihre Bedeutung für die Südostalpine Hallstattkultur. In: Symposium zu Problemen der jüngeren Hallstattzeit in Mitteleuropa (Bratislava 1974) 151-187.

Gabrovec 1987: S. Gabrovec, Jugoistočnoalpska regija sa zapadnom Panonijom. In: Praistorija jugoslavenskih zemalja 5. Željezno doba (Sarajevo 1987) 29-119.

Gabrovec 1994: S. Gabrovec (ed.), Stična 1. Naselbinska izkopavanja / Siedlungsausgrabungen. Katalogi in monografije 28 (Ljubljana 1994).

Gabrovec 1999: S. Gabrovec, 50 Jahre Archäologie der älteren Eisenzeit in Slowenien. Arheološki vestnik 50, 1999, 145-188.

Gabrovec 2006: S. Gabrovec (ed.), Stična 2/1. Gomile starejše železne dobe / Grabhügel der älteren Eisenzeit. Katalog. Katalogi in monografije 37 (Ljubljana 2006).

Gabrovec/Teržan 2010: S. Gabrovec/B. Teržan (eds.), Stična II/2, Gomile starejše železne dobe, Razprave / Grabhügel aus der älteren Eisenzeit, Studien. Katalogi in monografije 38 (Ljubljana 2010).

Gerbec 2014: T. Gerbec, Hotinja vas pri Mariboru. In: B. Teržan/M. Črešnar (eds.), Absolute dating of the Bronze and Iron Ages of Slovenia / Absolutno datiranje bronaste in železne dobe na Slovenskem. Katalogi in monografije 40 (Ljubljana 2014) 275-286.

Grahek 2016: L. Grahek, Stična. Železnodobna naselbinska keramika / Iron Age Settlement Pottery. Opera instituti archaeologici Sloveniae 32 (Ljubljana 2016).

Guštin/Tiefengraber 2001: M. Guštin/G. Tiefengraber, Prazgodovinske najdbe z avtocestnega odseka Murska Sobota – Nova tabla / Vorgeschichtliche Funde aus dem Autobahnabschnitt bei Murska Sobota – Nova tabla. Arheološki vestnik 52, 2001, 107-116.

Kerman 2014: B. Kerman, Kotare pri Murski Soboti. In: B. Teržan/M. Črešnar (eds.), Absolute dating of the Bronze and Iron Ages of Slovenia / Absolutno datiranje bronaste in železne dobe na Slovenskem. Katalogi in monografije 40 (Ljubljana 2014) 107-139.

Kiszter et al. 2015: S. Kiszter/D. Mlekuž/M. Mori, Rezultati raziskav z metodami daljinskega zaznavanja ob meji / Forschungsergebnisse der Fernerkundungsmethoden an der Grenze. In: M. Črešnar/M. Mele/K. Paitler/M. Vinazza (eds.), Archäologische Biographie einer Landschaft an der steirisch-slowenischen Grenze / Arheološka biografija krajine ob meji med avstrijsko Štajersko in Slovenijo. Schild von Steier, Beiheft 6 (Graz, Ljubljana 2015) 58-85.

Mason/Mlekuž 2016: P. Mason/D. Mlekuž, Negotiating space in the Early Iron Age landscape of south eastern Slovenia: The case of Veliki Vinji vrh. In: I. Armit/H. Potrebica/M. Črešnar/P. Mason/L. Büster (eds.), Cultural encounters in Iron Age Europe. Archaeolingua, Series Minor 38 (Budapest 2016) 95-120.

Medarić et al. 2016: I. Medarić/B. Mušič/M. Črešnar, Tracing flat cremation graves using integrated advanced processing of magnetometry data (case study of Poštela near Maribor, NE Slovenia) In: I. Armit/H. Potrebica/M. Črešnar/P. Mason/L. Büster (eds.), Cultural encounters in Iron Age Europe. Archaeolingua, Series Minor 38 (Budapest 2016) 67-94.

Mihelič et al. 2015: M. Mihelič/D. Modl/M. Vinazza, Forschungsgeschichte / Zgodovina raziskav. In: M. Črešnar/M. Mele/K. Paitler/M. Vinazza (eds.), Archäologische Biographie einer Landschaft an der steirisch-slowenischen Grenze / Arheološka biografija krajine ob meji med avstrijsko Štajersko in Slovenijo. Schild von Steier, Beiheft 6 (Graz, Ljubljana 2015) 28-56.

Mlekuž 2013a: D. Mlekuž, Messy lendscapes: lidar and the practices of landscaping. In: R. Opitz/D. Cowley (eds.), Interpreting Archaeological Topography: Airborne Laser Scanning, 3D Data and Ground Observation (Oxford 2013) 88-99.

Mlekuž 2013b: D. Mlekuž, Roads to nowhere? Disentangling meshworks of holloways. In: Z. Czajlik/A. Bödőcs (eds.), Aerial archaeology and remote sensing from the Baltic to the Adriatic. Selected papers of the Annual Conference of the Aerial Archaeology Research Group 13th-15th September 2010, Budapest, Hungary (Budapest 2013) 37-41.

Mlekuž/Črešnar 2014: D. Mlekuž/M. Črešnar, Landscape and Identity politics of the Poštela hillfort. In: S. Tecco Hvala (ed.), Studia Praehistorica in Honorem Janez Dular. Opera Instituti Archaeologici Sloveniae 30 (Ljubljana 2014) 197-211.

Müller-Karpe 1959: H. Müller-Karpe, Beiträge zur Chronologie der Urnenfelderzeit nördlich und südlich der Alpen. Römisch-Germanische Forschungen 22 (Berlin 1959).

Murgelj 2014: I. Murgelj, Podsmreka. In: B. Teržan/M. Črešnar (eds.), Absolute dating of the Bronze and Iron Ages of Slovenia / Absolutno datiranje bronaste in železne dobe na Slovenskem. Katalogi in monografije 40 (Ljubljana 2014) 437-450.

Mušič/Orengo 1998: B. Mušič/L. Orengo, Magnetometrične raziskave železnodobnega talilnega kompleksa na Cvingerju pri Meniški vasi. / Magnetic Investigation of the Iron Age Iron-Smelting Complex at Cvinger near Meniška vas. Arheološki vestnik 49, 1998, 157-186.

Mušič *et al.* 2014: B. Mušič/M. Črešnar/I. Medarić, Possibilities for geophysical research on sites dated to the Early Iron Age. Case study of Poštela near Maribor (Slovenia) / Možnosti geofizikalnih raziskav na najdiščih iz starejše železne dobe: primer Poštele pri Mariboru. Arheo 31, 2014, 19-47.

Mušič et al 2015a: B. Mušič/I. Medarić/M. Mori/E. Nass, Geofizikalne raziskave na Novinah in Plačkem vrhu / Geophysikalische Untersuchungen auf dem Bubenberg (Hoarachkogel) und dem Platsch. In: M. Črešnar/M. Mele/K. Paitler/M. Vinazza (eds.), Archäologische Biographie einer Landschaft an der steirisch-slowenischen Grenze / Arheološka biografija krajine ob meji med avstrijsko Štajersko in Slovenijo. Schild von Steier, Beiheft 6 (Graz, Ljubljana 2015) 86-119.

Mušič *et al.* 2015b: B. Mušič/M. Vinazza/M. Črešnar/I. Medarić, Integrated non-invasive research and ground trothing. Experiences from prehistoric sites in north-eastern Slovenia / Integrirane neinvazivne razsikave in terensko preverjenje. Izkušnje s prazgocovinskih najdišč severovzhodne Slovenije. Arheo 32, 2015, 37-64.

Nicholls/Buckberry 2016: R. Nicholls/J. Buckberry, Death and the body: Using oseological methods to investigate the later prehistoric funerary archaeology of Slovenia and Croatia. In: I. Armit/H. Potrebica/M. Črešnar/P. Mason/L. Büster (eds.), Cultural encounters in Iron Age Europe. Archaeolingua, Series Minor 38 (Budapest 2016) 121-143.

Nicholls/Koon 2016: R. Nicholls/H. Koon, The use of stable light isotopes as a method of exploring the homogeneity and heterogeneity of diet in Late Bronze Age and Early Iron Age Temperate Europe: a preliminary study. In: I. Armit/H. Potrebica/M. Črešnar/P. Mason/L. Büster (eds.), Cultural encounters in Iron Age Europe. Archaeolingua, Series Minor 38 (Budapest 2016) 145-164.

Opitz 2013: R. Opitz, An overview of airborne and terrestrial laser scanning in archaeology. In R. Opitz/D. Cowley (eds.), Interpreting Archaeological Topography: Airborne Laser Scanning, 3D Data and Ground Observation (Oxford 2013) 13-31.

Pahič 1972: S. Pahič, Pobrežje. Katalogi in monografije 6 (Ljubljana 1972).

Pahič 1974: S. Pahič, Poštelsko grobišče. *Časopis za zgodovino in narodopisje* 10, 1974, 4-72.

Puš 1991: I. Puš, Molnik. Sedež prazgodovinskih knezov (Ljubljana 1991).

Šavel/Sankovič 2014: I. Šavel/S. Sankovič, Trimlini pri Lendavi. In: B. Teržan/M. Črešnar (eds.), Absolute dating of the Bronze and Iron Ages of Slovenia / Absolutno datiranje bronaste in železne dobe na Slovenskem. Katalogi in monografije 40 (Ljubljana 2014) 65-77.

Tecco Hvala 2012: S. Tecco Hvala, Madalenska gora. Družbena struktura in grobni rituali železnodobne skupnosti / Social structure and burial rites of the Iron Age community. Opera instituti archaeologici Sloveniae 26 (Ljubljana 2012).

Tecco Hvala et al. 2004: S. Tecco Hvala/J. Dular/E. Kocuvan, *Železnodobne gomile na Magdalenski gori / Eisenzeitliche Grabhügel auf der Magdalenska gora*. Katalogi in monografije 36 (Ljubljana 2004).

Teržan 1976: B. Teržan, Certoška fibula / Die Certosafibel. Arheološki vestnik 27, 1977, 317-536.

Teržan 1978: B. Teržan, O halštatski noši na Križni gori / Über das Trachtzubehör auf Križna gora. Arheološki vestnik 29, 1978, 55-63.

Teržan 1980: B. Teržan, Posodje v grobovih halštatskih veljakov na Dolenjskem. In: Zbornik posvečen Stanetu Gabrovcu ob šestdesetletnici. Situla 20-21 (Ljubljana 1980) 343-352.

Teržan 1985: B. Teržan, Poskus rekonstrukcije halštatske družbene strukture v dolenjskem kulturnem krogu / Ein Rekonstruktionsversuch der Gesellschaftsstruktur im Dolenjsko-Kreis der Hallstattkultur. Arheološki vestnik 36, 1985, 77-105.

Teržan 1987: B. Teržan, The Early Iron Age chronology of the Central Balkans. Review from the viewpoint of the southeastern alpine Hallstatt. Archaeologia Iugoslavica 24, 1987, 7-27.

Teržan 1990a: B. Teržan, Polmesečaste fibule – o kulturnih povezavah med Egejo in Caput Adriae / Die Halbmondfibeln. Über die Kultureverbindungen zwischen der Ägäis und dem Caput Adriae. Arheološki vestnik 41, 1990, 49-88.

Teržan 1990b: B. Teržan, Starejša železna doba na Slovenskem Štajerskem / The Early Iron Age in Slovenian Styria. Katalogi in monografije 25 (Ljubljana 1990).

Teržan 1994: B. Teržan, Überlegungen zum sozialen Status des Handwerkers in der frühen Eisenzeit Südosteuropas. In: C. Dobiat (ed.), Festschrift für Otto-Herman Frey zum 65. Geburtstag. Marburger Studien zur Vor- und Frühgeschichte 16 (Marburg 1994) 659-669.

Teržan 1995: B. Teržan, Handel und sociale Oberschichten in früheisenzeitlichen Südosteuropa, In: B. Hänsel (ed.), Handel, Tausch und Verkehr im Bronze- und früheisenzeitlichen Südosteuropa. Prähistorische Archäologie in Südosteuropa 11 = Südosteuropa-Schriften 17 (Berlin, München 1995) 81–159.

Teržan 1997: B. Teržan, Heros der Hallstattzeit. Beobachtungen zum Status an Gräbern um das Caput Adriae. In: C. Becker/M. L. Dunkelmann/C. Metzner-Nebelsick/H. Peter-Röcher/M. Roeder/B. Teržan (eds.), Χρόνος: Beiträge zur prähistorischen Archäologie zwischen Nord- und Südosteuropa, Festschrift für Bernhard Hänsel. Internationale Archäologie, Studia honoraria 1 (Espelkamp 1997) 653–669.

Teržan 1999: B. Teržan, An Outline of Urnfield Culture Period in Slovenia / Oris obdobja kulture žarnih grobišč na Slovenskem. Arheološki vestnik 50, 1999, 97-143.

Teržan 2001: B. Teržan, Die spätbronze- und früheisenzeitliche Besiedlung im nordöstlichen Slowenien. Ein Überblick. In: A. Lippert (ed.), Die Drau-, Mur- und Raab-Region im 1. vorchristlichen Jahrtausend: Akten des internationalen und interdisziplinären Symposiums vom 26. bis 29. April 2000 in Bad Radkersburg. Universitätsforschungen zur Prähistorischen Archäologie 78 (Bonn 2001) 125-35.

Teržan 2010: B. Teržan, Stiške skice / Stična Skizzen. In: S. Gabrovec/B. Teržan (eds.), Stična II/2, Gomile starejše železne dobe, Razprave / Grabhügel aus der älteren Eisenzeit, Studien. Katalogi in monografije 38 (Ljubljana 2010) 189-325.

Teržan/Črešnar 2014: B. Teržan/M. Črešnar (eds.), Absolute dating of the Bronze and Iron Ages of Slovenia / Absolutno datiranje bronaste in železne dobe na Slovenskem. Katalogi in monografije 40 (Ljubljana 2014).

Teržan *et al.* 2015: B. Teržan/M. Črešnar/B. Mušič, Early Iron Age barrows in the eyes of complementary archaeological research. Case study of Poštela near Maribor (Podravje, Slovenia). In: Ch. Gutjahr/G. Tiefengraber (eds.), Beiträge zur Hallstattzeit am Rande der Südostalpen, Akten des 2. Wildoner Fachgespräches vom 10. bis 11. Juni 2010 in Wildon / Steiermark (Österreich). Internationale Archäologie. Arbeitsgemeinschaft, Symposium, Tagung, Kongress 19 = Hengist-Studien 3 (Rahden/Westf 2015) 61-82.

Vinazza *et al.* 2015: M. Vinazza/ T. Nanut/M. Mihelič/M. Črešnar, Arheološka izkopavanja na slovenski strani Novin pri Šentilju / Archäologische Grabungen auf der slowenischen Seite des Bubenbergs (Hoarachkogels) bei Spielfeld. In: M. Črešnar/M. Mele/K. Paitler/M. Vinazza (eds.), Archäologische Biographie einer Landschaft an der steirisch-slowenischen Grenze / Arheološka biografija krajine ob meji med avstrijsko Štajersko in Slovenijo. Schild von Steier, Beiheft 6 (Graz, Ljubljana 2015) 166-205.

Žibrat Gašparič/Dolenec 2015: A. Žibrat Gašparič/M. Dolenec, Ceramic petrography of pottery and clays from Novine (Hoarachkogel) and Plački vrh (Platsch). In: M. Črešnar/M. Mele/K. Paitler/M. Vinazza (eds.), Archäologische Biographie einer Landschaft an der steirisch-slowenischen Grenze/Arheološka biografija krajine ob meji med avstrijsko Štajersko in Slovenijo. Schild von Steier, Beiheft 6 (Graz, Ljubljana 2015) 246-262.

Author

Matija Črešnar
Department of Archaeology
Faculty of Art
University of Ljubljana
Aškerčeva 2, 1000 Ljubljana
Slovenia
Institute for the Protection of Cultural Heritage of Slovenia
Centre for Preventive Archaeology
Poljanska 40, 1000 Ljubljana
Slovenia
matija.cresnar@gmail.com

Elites in the cemetery at Hallstatt, Upper Austria

Bettina Glunz-Hüsken

Abstract

The necropolis of Hallstatt is of outstanding significance for the Early Iron Age and renowned for its large number of rich, seemingly pretentious graves connected – by most different items and sometimes also by their interpretation – to other rich graves of the circumalpine Iron Age. However, we are not only dealing with socially defining physical products, but also with religiously inspired grave goods in the shape of innovative ensembles or unique objects virtually anchoring the buried person in a mythical way and/or addressing her/him as ritually authorized.

Zusammenfassung

Die für die ältere Eisenzeit so bedeutende Nekropole von Hallstatt liefert bekanntermaßen eine ganze Reihe reicher, prunkhaft anmutender Bestattungen, die sich über verschiedenste Objekte, teils auch deren Deutung mit anderen reichen Gräbern der zirkumalpinen Eisenzeit verbinden lassen. Dabei handelt es sich jedoch nicht nur um sozial definierendes Sachgut, sondern auch um religiös motivierte Beigaben, innovative Gefüge und Solitäre, die die bestattete Person gewissermaßen mythisch verankern und/oder sie als kultisch befugt ansprechen lassen.

Introduction

The large eponymous necropolis in a geographically isolated high valley at Lake Hallstatt in the Salzkammergut region (some 1000 m above MSL of the Adriatic Sea) is well-known for its numerous opulently furnished Ha C and D graves. It was these that inspired, long ago, the naming of an entire epoch, the so-called Hallstatt period. The population buried there in the 7th and 6th centuries BC occupied as yet unknown settlement and owed their wealth to the mining of the salty rock formation outcropping from the local mountain, which was a much sought-after and vital commodity. Obviously this salt was traded over long distances as is attested *e.g.* by numerous brooches in the cemetery that must be considered "foreign" at their find spot (Glunz 1997). Some 1,000 inhumations and cremations (of a total of 5,000 to 6,000 according to recent estimates; Kern *et al.* 2008, 121) were excavated mainly in the 2nd half of the 19th century and did not survive completely due to the archiving methods at that time: bones from inhumations, cremated remains, and the pottery in particular were not kept and therefore are not available as source material. This fact in combination with the particular geological conditions of the Alps, the overlapping of graves, the possibly erroneous attributions of objects caused thereby, and the permutations (of a later date in museums) all restrict the scientific value, but only to a limited degree – except for the loss of the pottery (Glunz-Hüsken 2017; Hodson 1990) and bones.

The question how elites presented themselves at Hallstatt in particular, can hardly be answered in a satisfactory way if we restrict ourselves to social parameters as has often been the case in past archaeological studies. These usually focused on 'rich' graves from socially vertical or horizontal aspects, calculated their significance within the necropolis or – when possible – in comparison to matchable inventories abroad and labeled the result, recently in a differentiated way, with terms such as "status" or "prestige" (Burmeister 2003; Schumann 2015).

However, at Hallstatt such an exclusively social view seems to do only partial justice to the important constants of a mythical-religious nature in the representation of elites, such as *e.g.* the complexes of horse and wagon, banquet, weaponry, anthropomorphic images etc., because elites connected themselves through the ages with their ancestors and hereby ultimately implied their divine descent (e.g. Egg/Kramer 2013, 440). To be specific, quite a number of rich graves at Hallstatt are characterized by grave goods and/or signs demanding a dominantly religious interpretation, *e.g.* fibulae adorned with miniature vessels, daggers, belts and belt chains, anthropomorphic dagger hilts implying the pose of a *pothnia theron* (Glunz-Hüsken/Schebesch 2015), three-dimensional bull figurines partly with earrings or supposedly sacrificial axes which, at the same time, demonstrated the socially esteemed activities of horse riding and horse breeding. It is exactly such material goods that demonstrate the close interweaving of a social and religious-mythical or ritual element. Finally I arrive to cultural relationships in general and ritual objects in specific.

Social and religious elites

If we page through K. Kromer's relevant publication of 1959 (Kromer 1959) under the general aspect of "elite", the most striking observation is a number of inventories with bronze vessels, i.e. equipment for the symposium in the possession of women and men. What we might additionally enumerate as remarkable and certainly socially definitive, is the large number of sheet metal belts sometimes with attached chains and jingles, swords decorated with gold and amber, daggers with anthropomorphic hilts, various gold objects, so-called ring pendants or otherwise unique fibulae, *e.g.* with miniature vessels or figural sculpture. A recent revision has established a complex of some 100 graves with one to six bronze vessels, ca. 210 graves with very different belts, 28 sword and 55 dagger graves, as well as 38 inventories containing gold (Glunz-Hüsken 2017). These can be differentiated into objects usually counted amongst common grave goods of rich female and male burials (such as *e.g.* feasting vessels, weapons) on the one hand and rather rare objects on the other hand, such as *e.g.* lattice disc brooches or crescent fibulae with bird protomes elsewhere deposited in materially superior graves, according to local scale.

Additionally a distinction should be made between the large mass of probably local products (Ha C: swords, bronze vessels; Ha D: daggers, belts, fibulae) and some supposed imports. Generally the following items are believed to be of foreign origin: the golden plate fibula with a bone pad from grave 505 from Greece or *Magna Graecia* (Glunz 1994), the bowl with pictures of probably Phoenician origin (grave 682), the bronze lid (grave 697) and amphora stand (grave 507) possibly from northern Italian workshops, the golden earring from Etruria (grave 13/1889), the golden trefoils ornaments from Slovenia (grave 505), the glass cups from the eastern Alpine region (graves 502, 733), just to mention the archaeological highlights of the necropolis which, at the same time, illustrate the southern and southeastern contact zones since Ha C.

The import of textiles is thought possible, too, to be specific in the case of tablet woven braids perhaps brought from Italy. Not so obvious but rather more cryptic and yet of polysemous meaning are graves with – once probably very precious – textiles (or leather items) partly covered by bronze ornaments. However, they elude a classification as garments, grave covers or ritual wrapping of certain grave goods, not to mention a differentiation between local products and imported goods. As an example I quote grave 236 (Fig. 1) with two (rare) bronze plates placed on top of each other and obviously covered by a cloth (or leather cover) decorated with small metal knobs or grave 136 in which the skeleton featured perforated tiny limestone discs on the humerus which probably attesting a corresponding garment once decorated with them. Textiles symbolize interpersonal relationships and thus emotion, patterns and pictures woven into them warrant (probably not only in Greece) the handing down of norms and transport signs of communication. Textile production was costly in many respects (procurement, possible import of raw materials, and – if necessary – of dyes/*Kermes vermilio*), it required 'international' contacts in some cases, craftsmanship, time, and therefore expenses. Apart from their practical purpose, textiles represent a multifaceted symbolism and they are the subject of symbolic and religious behavior. Technical procedures of weaving were used by ancient writers as metaphors for political action (Wagner-Hasel 2000c, 322-325; 2000a; 2000b). Jewelry pendants from rich graves, usually of women, mainly from Italy but sometimes also deposited north of the Alps, can be interpreted as representations of cloths on the loom. However, they are sometimes found in male ensembles (Hochdorf), too, emphasizing the importance of weaving for both sexes (Fath/Glunz-Hüsken 2011). Crescent brooches with bird protomes can also be attributed to this group, a possibility making B. Teržan's hypothesis more precise that female individuals thus equipped held a hieratic office (Teržan 1990, 73; 88) (Fig. 2).

Meanwhile, natural scientific analyses of the Bronze Age and Iron Age textiles used in the high valley have revealed that some of them had been dyed with animal dye (natural carminic acid) which means that either the dye insects, the coloured yarn or the finished dyed cloths had actually been imported, because no suitable *coccoidea* are known from around Hallstatt (Hofmann-de Keijzer *et al.* 2013, 128). From this point of view, textiles in graves deserve at least as high an appreciation as bronze vessels, weapons or tools (see Grömer in this volume), a complex the discussion and significance of which were quite considerably fostered by the textile evidence from the grave at Hochdorf (Banck-Burgess 1999).

Additionally, the reduced representation of a two-axle wagon – the only one in the cemetery – by four locally made linchpins (grave 507) should be mentioned, as should the perhaps symbolic display of a woman using a wagon by means of a ring pendant with the very naturalistic image of a wheel hub (grave 121). A singular object including a possibly reused hub fitting came from the – according to archaeological classification – female Ha D1 grave 669. It symbolically combined the components of wagon, vessel, and twisted cross beam, features that have been used since time immemorial for the characterization of cauldron wagons and have been fused here into an innovative symbol (Glunz-Hüsken 2013).

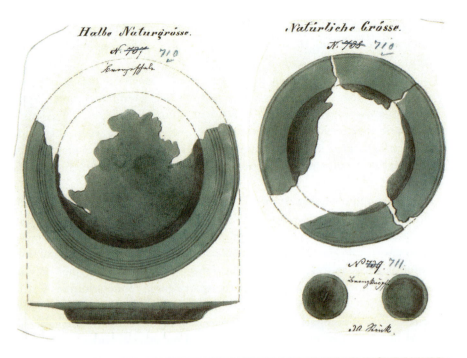

Fig. 1. Hallstatt grave 236, detail (after Mahr's register, © NHM-Wien).

We may also list burials with tools such as fishhooks or harpoons, rasps and chisels – elsewhere attested in both modest and very rich graves (Stöllner 2007) – and *e.g.* huntsmen's equipment with arrows (and perhaps mostly decayed quivers of organic materials): three such "huntsmen" were additionally distinguished by golden ring jewelry (graves 11/1889, 15/1938, 13/1939) but without any closer definition of this apparently 'mythical' elite, since golden rings – similar to tools – connect quite a number of rich graves at Hallstatt (and other sites as well) without comparable weapons.

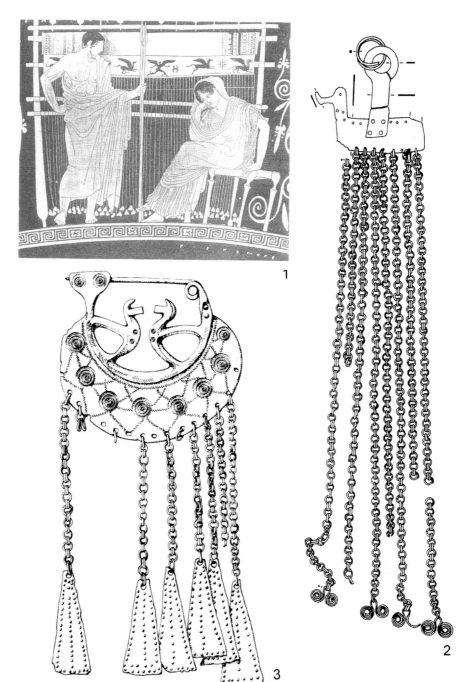

Fig. 2. 1: Loom scene on a red-figure skyphos by the Penelope Painter (after Wagner-Hasel 2000a, 332 Abb. Q 115). – 2: Pendant jewelry from Novilara/Servici 85 (after Beinhauer 1980, pl. 139). – 3: Crescent brooch from Hallstatt grave 606 (after Hodson 1990, pl. 47,1).

To sum up, we are dealing with provisions for the afterlife of a social upper class that had become rich by their command of a monopoly (salt) and entertained a local, probably mainly economic network, the original size and function of which can probably only be sketched rudimentarily yet by archaeological and natural scientific methods (e.g. Kern *et al.* 2008, 82-147).

Imports from afar enabled their few owners to demonstrate social status or prestige and to visualize and materialize their created network of contacts, presumably presented during obsequies in particularly. Apart from the aforementioned exotica, the rich grave inventories at Hallstatt do by all means fit in with the *habitus* of other graves with supra-local equipment and partly ostentatious character, as is illustrated *e.g.* by the topics of horse and wagon, banqueting, hunting and fishing, weaving and textiles. The 'destruction' of great wealth by deposition in graves ultimately underlines once more the social position of the person thus portrayed and his/her entire ancestral family circle (whether this be defined genetically or otherwise) which, of course, is also true for locally made products according to their equivalent hierarchy.

It is remarkable that rich graves can be found in the high valley side by side with more modest ones, i.e. that no spatial separation or concentration of either quality level can be observed. Whether this was only due to the shortage of space in the narrow valley or actually reflect the organization of the (supposedly montane) society in any way remains unsolved as does the question whether those buried with rich grave goods had worked in the salt mine themselves. With regard to this it is only the lack of source material, namely the lack of anthropological material from the early excavations that prevents the desired elucidation, because from the time of the main excavator, Johann Ramsauer, not a single bone survives (statistical analyses of groups without individual examination: Pany 2003). Moreover, many rich graves of Ramsauer's days were cremations which would not have formed a sufficient basis for individual analyses even if they had survived. The anthropological result of analyses of three 'richly' equipped children from graves 33/1997, 20/1938, and 8/1939 provided a first clue that even adolescents might have worked in the mine (Pany-Kucera *et al.* 2010). Even in these cases, it remains unknown, where the youths had obtained the observed wear marks on their bones, because we must also take into consideration the possibility of stays abroad – a field for future research. However, a sociological model argues against the hypothesis claiming that the formation of social elites always relies on the mobilization of other labor and not on personal effort (Veblen 1997), respectively that elites demonstratively consume (precious) goods not immediately derived from personal labor, which ultimately can be seen by prominently exclusive grave goods or rather precisely by their emphatic destruction. This still unsolved and thrilling complex of questions will only be solved by modern excavations of similarly equipped grave inventories.

Cultural relationships

If we now focus only on the regional bearing of some selected, generally elitist grave goods of presumably local production, we obtain a broad context, which at the same time, clarifies the origin of the postulated cultic elements. Let me first consider only the purely spatial perspective: both the gold-sheet applications and the amber inlays in bell-shaped hilts from Ha C graves at Hallstatt (graves 299 and 573) possess close parallels far away in swords from Gomadingen, distr. Reutlingen, and Oss, Northern Brabant, or in the wagon graves of Marainville-sur-Madon, dép. Vosges, Losheim, and Chaffois, dép. Doubs respectively (Gomadingen, Marainville-sur-Madon, Oss: Stöllner 2002, 268 note 686; Van der Vaart-Verschoof/Schumann this volume; Losheim: Haffner 1969. Chaffois, dép. Doubs: Hansen 2010, 246, no. 98). Therefore they are clearly identified as a means of demonstrating status, not prestige (after Schumann 2015). Ha D daggers with an anthropomorphic hilt in winner's posture (e.g. Hallstatt graves 203/204, 65/2002, 574, 559, 682, 836) are found in great number in southern

German graves such as Kappel, distr. Biberach, Gößweinstein-Morschreuth an der Pegnitz, distr. Forchheim, and Veringenstadt, distr. Sigmaringen, daggers implying the pose of *potnia theron* at the Dürrnberg Mountain, in southern Bavaria, and particularly in Baden-Württemberg (Glunz-Hüsken/Schebesch 2015). Large numbers of situlae with bent handle attachments (Hallstatt grave 697) are only known from central Italy and the southern fringe of the Alps (Dehn *et al.* 2005, 163). A cauldron with iron handle rings from grave 12/1889 belongs to the rare group with a folded rim also including objects from Uffing am Staffelsee, distr. Garmisch-Partenkirchen, and at Hallein-Dürrnberg, federal state of Salzburg. Consequently, the production area of the type has been assumed to be on the eastern edge of the Western Hallstatt Circle. The cauldron type with four variants itself is considered a type fossil of Ha D and occurs in renowned princely burials of southwest Germany together with wagons and golden torcs (Dehn *et al.* 2005, 140-141). The eleven Ha C-graves with bowl-shaped helmets (*Schüsselhelm*) from Hallstatt link the necropolis to the Slovenian region of Lower Carniola, Dolenjska, (Egg *et al.* 1998) although it is impossible to determine whether we are dealing with imports or local products after foreign models (Glunz-Hüsken 2013, 18-19). The same is true for the golden trefoils in the rich female grave 505 with multi-regional connections (Ha D1) parallels for which can be found in Slovenia (Libna, Podzemelj, Malence, Šmarjeta, and Črnomelj), Mezőcsát in Hungary, and in the northern Caucasus Mountains (Teržan/Hellmuth 2008, 177). As is generally known, grave 27 of tumulus 48 at Stična contained quite similar lamellae which formed part of a diadem or a multi-part headdress (Hellmuth 2008). In these cases they tangibly prove the continuity of southeastern contacts from Ha C until Ha D. So-called ring pendants with a handle are considered objects of a markedly 'magic' nature in female graves at Hallstatt (46, 393, 443, 495, 611, 672, 793, 890). Parallels to them are known at Mittelreinbach, Upper Palatinate, Heidenheim, Baden-Württemberg, Kronstorf-Thaling, Linz, and probably St. Panthaleon, Lower Austria (Egg 1988/89). According to their distribution and R. Schumann's (2015) classification, these ring pendants with a handle count, quite like bronze vessels, as the prestigious objects – if we were to judge them by a social measure – which, however, certainly does not do justice to them, at least not to the ring pendants, since they are highly symbolic objects. Last but not least one might hint at the unique quatrefoil fibula from grave 324 at Hallstatt and its counterpart in grave 57 at Riedenburg-Untereggersberg (Glunz 1997, 114-115; Hoppe 1991; Nikulka 1998, 277-279) (Fig. 3). The latter one was a definitely female ensemble according to anthropological analysis which was additionally striking for its prominent belt rare in the area and therefore possibly imported (type with "large closed zones" (*große geschlossene Felder*) after I. Kilian-Dirlmeier 1972). Golden jewelry in the shape of a coil made of sheet gold with longitudinal ribs (found at the neck) underlines the elitist character of this likewise female individual. The spirals riveted to the quatrefoil brooch from grave 324 at Hallstatt actually have no parallels yet, except in distant Campania where they form part of large disc fibulae with theriomorphic and anthropomorphic fittings (Lo Schiavo 2010, *e.g.* pl. 710-726).

Furthermore we may quote the pompous crescent fibula from grave 94/1873 at Hallstatt with good parallels at Wörgl and Stanz near Landeck, both Tyrol. Its convex disc pendants have close counterparts at Tarquinia, prov. Viterbo (Wörgl and Stanz: Zemmer-Planck 1990; Tarquinia: Iaia 1999, fig. 16,B8), and thus

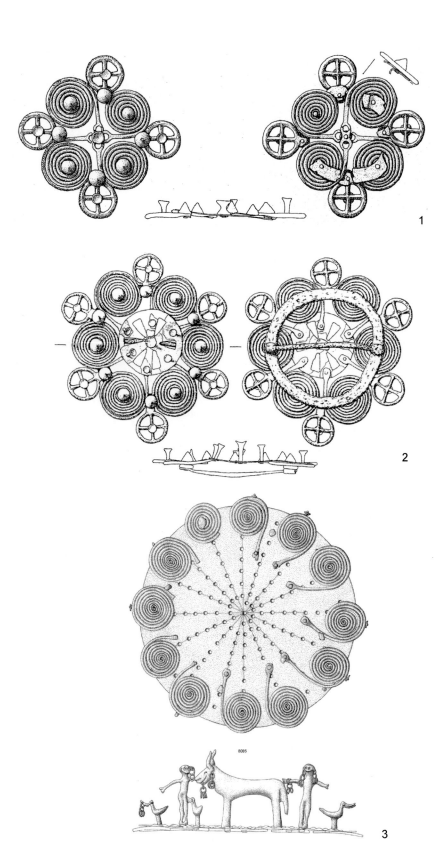

Fig. 3. 1: Suggested reconstruction of the brooch from grave 324 (after Hoppe 1991, 502 Abb. 1). – 2: Fibula from grave 57 at Riedenburg-Untereggersberg (after Nikulka 1998, pl. 86). – 3: Brooch from Cumae (after Lo Schiavo 2010, pl. 718 no. 8085).

indicate the southern origin of the idea behind the fibula which I have associated with the representation of a holy cloak elsewhere (Glunz-Hüsken 2017).

While these objects and groups of objects, only punctually chosen here, reflect generally known and well investigated cultural relationships, this is not the case with plain ring pendants with antithetic animal protomes (graves 46, 443, 495, 672, 793, 890). These obviously had their roots in Greece and possibly came northwards across the Balkans or over the Adriatic Sea (Glunz-Hüsken 2008, 54-55), because of their patchy distribution and perhaps also the regional difference in the state of research. At Hallstatt their isolated appearance with unmistakable formal dependence is surprising but their local production in the high valley (in Ha C) can hardly be doubted. What remains a matter of speculation, however, both in Greece and at the salt mountain, is the conceptual content of the symbolic pendants, demonstratively worn on the chest. Anyhow, the pendants were restricted to presumably female burials and combined with bronze vessels (graves 495, 890), textiles or belts with metal fittings (495, 672), amulets from horse-gear (672), and earrings (793) definitely reflecting their elitist character, too. Archaeologists willingly considered the rings a piece of evidence for the ritual competence of the deceased, a hypothesis not supported by any independent clue from the ensemble of grave goods apart from perhaps the pair of earrings in grave 793 (each consisting of three bronze rings hanging in each other). B. Teržan has collected quite a number of different examples (grave goods, sculpture) which *summa summarum* support the idea that pairs of earrings made of gold or bronze were sacred signs of a special dress characterizing women during the practice of cults (Teržan 2003). Grave 793 from Hallstatt might therefore casually be added to her well-chosen supporting documents, whereby we have reached the question of religious markers mentioned at the beginning, which I will discuss below once more by the example of two striking groups of objects.

Ritual objects

It is generally known that five three-dimensional bull figurines with strong horns have been found in four graves at Hallstatt (Barth 1973; Wells 1978). In grave 507 they had been deposited in two pottery bowls, probably wrapped in a cloth decorated with bronze beads in each case. Therefore it will hardly be doubted that we are dealing with the symbolic representation of sacrificial animals whose power the participants believed to incorporate by drinking. The alleged persons (female and male) buried in grave 507 are thus presented as owners of sacrificial animals. It remains disputed, however, whether the combined miniature axe with a theriomorphic sculpture was used as an 'appropriate' ritual tool for sacrifice which is perhaps implied, once more, by the small axe (of an identical type but with an individual imprint) from grave 641 that has been found in a – now lost – bronze bowl and has thus allowed a conclusion by analogy as to function for all the other miniature axes without a find context.

The missing animal figurine from the female Ha C grave 340 (containing two bronze vessels, two belts, spiraled gold wire etc.) provided another hint illuminating the genesis and meaning of these sculptures.

The animal wore an earring and can thus be connected to humans and animals with rings represented on scenically arranged Campanian brooches which are difficult to read but probably attest fertility rites (Fig. 3,3) – at least this is what

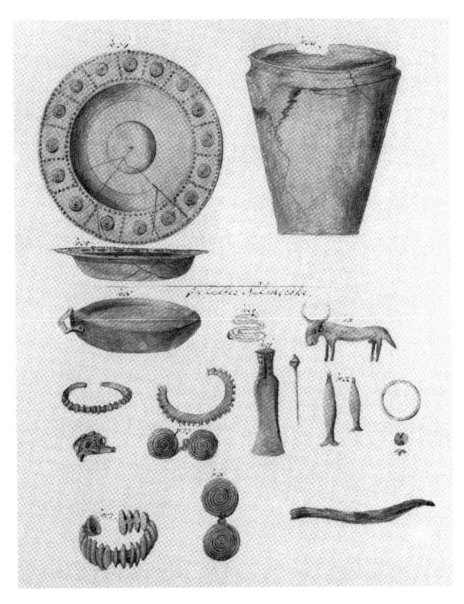

G. Kossack (1999, 23-24) believed at that time. Although no other narrative sceneries apart from the cult wagon from Strettweg, which significantly also features protagonists wearing earrings, have yet been found north of the Alps, the aforementioned bull figurine from grave 340 seems to indicate cultic procedures in a highlighted, reduced, and probably substitutional way. A lost flanged axe (probably of type Hallstatt) made of bronze and decorated with a ring-and-dot pattern from this female grave supports this interpretation insofar as both would make sense as an ensemble in a representation of a sacrifice (Fig. 4).

Additionally, there are quite a number of miniature vessels playing a meaningful role attached to fibulae, daggers (Glunz-Hüsken/Schebesch 2015, 302; 315), and belts. Although bronze or pottery vessels of reduced size can be found in the entire Hallstatt area, whether it be on local brooches (e.g. as a foot ornament, sometimes in scenic arrangement as in graves 574, 577 or 667 at Hallstatt), Italian bronze vessels or Eastern Alpine pottery, their accumulation on bronzes from Hallstatt remains unique indeed (Glunz-Hüsken 2017). As an example I concentrate on the

Fig. 5.: Belt chain and detail from grave 669 (photograph A. Schumacher, © NHM Vienna).

rich female Ha D1 grave 669 (belt type Schrotzhofen, gold and amber beads, wheel amulet, Italian Sanguisuga brooch) standing out because of its unique forged belt chain surviving in a heavily fragmented state (Fig. 5). It is characterized by two miniature trays each holding two equally small vessels (imitations of local high necked bowls); isolated vessels are attested, too. Whether these dishes recall the actual banquet and/or the sacrifice connected to it or whether the miniature vessels contained intoxicants remains uncertain. The usually female individuals with belt chains in northern Greece, the Balkans, and Italy are considered representatives of ritual acts in any case (Kilian-Dirlmeier 2012, 170-173).

Although it is futile to search for stylistically really comparable belt pendants in the closer and wider vicinity and in Italy, one ultimately comes across the probably slightly earlier female inhumation grave 15 from Marvinci-Lisičin Dol near Valandovo, Republic of Macedonia (Ha C). The woman buried with so-called Paeonian ritual bronzes was also wearing a long belt chain (Fig. 6), the miniature pyxis with bird protomes which is said to have contained raw opium (opium poppy) (Kilian-Dirlmeier 2012, 172; Mitrevski 1996/97, 106; Mitrevski 2007). The sickle handles from the belt chain might represent sacrificial instruments but also symbolic tools for harvesting, i.e. ultimately symbols of fertility. Both ladies, who certainly were neither relatives nor immediately connected to each other, thus flaunted liturgical equipment on their belts, respectively belt chains, and were probably protagonists in a ritually motivated performance the spiritual content of which eludes us both here and there.

These few examples do not only demonstrate regional connections between elite graves or individual grave goods at Hallstatt but also characterize certain individuals as obviously ritual office-holders, whether they recalled religious-ritual procedures or represented them (miniature vessels), whether certain persons had symbolic command of sacrificial animals and tools (no matter whether they only owned them or slaughtered them by themselves) or whether they were involved in supposed rites of fertility or sacrifice (individuals with earrings) in analogy to ringed creatures from Lower Italy, which cannot be described more precisely (Kossack 1998, 82; 1999, 23). What has been passed down to us is only certain scattered, but recurrent distinctive marks that might also signal the congruency of concepts behind them.

(*Translation: J. Fries-Knoblach, Dachau*)

Fig. 6: Marvinci Lisičin Dol, grave 15 (reconstruction after Kilian-Dirlmeier 2012, 173 Abb. 75).

Bibliography

Banck-Burgess 1999: J. Banck-Burgess, Die Textilfunde aus dem späthallstattzeitlichen Fürstengrab von Eberdingen-Hochdorf (Kr. Ludwigsburg) und weitere Grabtextilien aus hallstatt- und latènezeitlichen Kulturgruppen. Forschungen und Berichte zur Vor- und Frühgeschichte in Baden-Württemberg 70 (Stuttgart 1999).

Barth 1973: F. Barth, Zur Identifizierung einiger Gegenstände aus dem Gräberfeld von Hallstatt in der Sammlung Johann Georg Ramsauer. Mitteilungen der Anthropologischen Gesellschaft Wien 103, 1973, 48-54.

Beinhauer 1980: K. Beinhauer, Untersuchungen zu den eisenzeitlichen Bestattungsplätzen von Novilara, Provinz Pésaro und Urbino, Italien. Archäologie, Anthropologie, Demographie; Methoden und Modelle (Frankfurt 1980).

Burmeister 2003: S. Burmeister, Die Herren der Ringe: Annäherung an ein späthallstattzeitliches Statussymbol. In: U. Veit/T. Kienlin/C. Kümmel/S. Schmidt (eds.), Spuren und Botschaften: Interpretationen materieller Kultur. Tübinger archäologische Taschenbücher 4 (München 2003) 265-296.

Dehn *et al.* 2005: R. Dehn/M. Egg/R. Lehnert, Das hallstattzeitliche Fürstengrab im Hügel 3 von Kappel am Rhein. Monographien des Römisch-Germanischen Zentralmuseums 63 (Mainz 2005).

Egg 1988/89: M. Egg, Ein hallstattzeitliches Ringgehänge im Römisch-Germanischen Zentralmuseum. Mitteilungen der Anthropologischen Gesellschaft Wien 118/119, 1988/89, 259-285.

Egg et al.1998: M. Egg/U. Neuhäuser/Ž. Škoberne, Ein Grab mit Schüsselhelm aus Budinjak in Kroatien. Jahrbuch des Römisch-Germanischen Zentralmuseums 45, 1989, 435-472.

Egg/Kramer 2013: M. Egg/D. Kramer, Die hallstattzeitlichen Fürstengräber von Kleinklein in der Steiermark: Der Kröllkogel. Monographien des Römisch-Germanischen Zentralmuseums 110 (Mainz 2013).

Fath/Glunz-Hüsken 2011: B. Fath/B. Glunz-Hüsken, Textilien und Symbole für ihre Herstellung in eisenzeitlichen Gräbern Mitteleuropas. Griechenland – Este – Frög – Sopron. Prähistorische Zeitschrift 86, 2011, 254-271.

Glunz 1994: B. Glunz, Zu mitteleuropäischen Plattenfibeln unter spezieller Berücksichtigung der goldenen Fibel aus Hallstatt Grab 505. Archäologisches Korrespondenzblatt 24, 1994, 283-288.

Glunz 1997: B. Glunz, Studien zu den Fibeln aus dem Gräberfeld von Hallstatt. Linzer Archäologische Forschungen 25 (Linz 1997).

Glunz-Hüsken 2008: B. Glunz-Hüsken, Neue Fibeln aus der Nekropole von Hallstatt. Mit einem Nachtrag zur Fibelstudie von 1997, einem Exkurs zu Symbolen an hallstattzeitlichen Gewandverschlüssen und einem Vergleich der Friedhöfe Hallstatt – Bischofshofen. Archaeologia Austriaca 92, 2008, 35-71.

Glunz-Hüsken 2013: B. Glunz-Hüsken, Sparsam in der Grube! – Reich im Grab? Varianten und Aspekte sekundär verwendeter Beigaben aus dem Gräberfeld von Hallstatt, Oberösterreich. In: R. Karl/J. Leskovar (eds.), Interpretierte Eisenzeiten. Fallstudien, Methoden, Theorie. Tagungsbericht der 5. Linzer Gespräche zur interpretativen Eisenzeitarchäologie. Studien zur Kulturgeschichte von Oberösterreich 37 (Linz 2013) 9-25.

Glunz-Hüsken 2017: B. Glunz-Hüsken, Religiöse Symbolik in reichen Gräbern der Nekropole von Hallstatt, Oberösterreich. Freiburger Archäologische Studien 8 (Radhen/Westf. 2017).

Glunz-Hüsken/Schebesch 2015: B. Glunz-Hüsken/A. Schebesch, Körpersprachliche Signale hallstattzeitlicher, anthropomorph gestalteter Dolchgriffe. Prähistorische Zeitschrift 90, 2015, 301-317.

Haffner 1969: A. Haffner, Ein Gräberfeld der jüngeren Hunsrück-Eifel-Kultur von Losheim, Kr. Merzig-Wadern. Bericht der staatlichen Denkmalpflege im Saarland 16, 1969, 61-103.

Hansen 2010: L. Hansen, Hochdorf VIII. Die Goldfunde und Trachtbeigaben des späthallstattzeitlichen Fürstengrabes von Eberdingen-Hochdorf (Kr. Ludwigsburg). Forschungen und Berichte zur Vor- und Frühgeschichte in Baden-Württemberg 118 (Stuttgart 2010).

Hellmuth 2008: A. Hellmuth, Zur Rekonstruktion des Prunkgewandes aus Stična Grab 27, Hügel 48. In: St. Gabrovec/B. Teržan (eds.), Stična II. Gomile starejše železne dobe. 2: Razprave. Katalogi in Monografije 38 (Ljubljana 2008 [2010]) 61-68.

Hodson 1990: F. Hodson, Hallstatt – The Ramsauer graves. Quantification and Analysis. Monographien des Römisch-Germanischen Zentralmuseums 16 (Bonn 1990).

Hofmann de Keijzer *et al.* 2013: R. Hofmann-de Keijzer/M. van Bommel/A. Hartl/K. Grömer/H. Rösel-Mautendorfer/H. Reschreiter/K. Kania/I. Joosten/A. Gaibor/R. Erlach/E. Lachner/M. Wandl/M. de Keijzer, Coloured Hallstatt Textiles: 3500 Year-old Textile and Dyeing Techniques and their Contemporary Application. In: J. Banck-Burgess/C. Nübold (eds.), NESAT XI, The North European Symposium for Archaeological Textiles 1981-2011 (Rahden/Westf. 2013) 125-130.

Hoppe 1991: M. Hoppe, Ein singuläres Fibelpaar der Hallstattzeit aus Riedenburg-Untereggersberg. Mit einem Beitrag zu den Fibeln aus Hallstatt, Grab 324. Archäologisches Korrespondenzblatt 21, 1991, 501-505.

Iaia 1999: Ch. Iaia, Simbolismo funerario e ideologia alle origini di una civiltà urbana. In: F. Marzatico/P. Gleirscher (eds.), Guerrieri Principi ed Eroi fra il Danubio e il Po della Preistoria all`Alto Medioevo (Trento 2004).

Kern *et al.* 2008: A. Kern/K. Kowarik/A. Rausch/H. Reschreiter (eds.), Salz-Reich. 7000 Jahre Hallstatt. Veröffentlichungen der Prähistorischen Abteilung 2 (Wien 2008).

Kilian-Dirlmeier 1972: I. Kilian-Dirlmeier, Die hallstattzeitlichen Gürtelbleche und Blechgürtel Mitteleuropas. Prähistorische Bronzefunde XII,1 (München 1972).

Kilian-Dirlmeier 2012: I. Kilian-Dirlmeier, Körper- und Ringschmuck, Pektorale und Gürtel als Würdezeichen. In: H.-G. Buchholz (ed.), Erkennungs-, Rang- und Würdezeichen. Arch. Homerica. Die Denkmäler und das frühgriechische Epos (Göttingen 2012) 159-202.

Kossack 1998: G. Kossack, Von der verborgenen Lebenskraft der Dinge. Nordtiroler Gehängefibeln aus der frühen Eisenzeit als sakrale Zeichen. Veröffentlichungen des Tiroler Landesmuseums Ferdinandeum 78, 1998, 71-87.

Kossack 1999: G. Kossack, Religiöses Denken in dinglicher und bildlicher Überlieferung Alteuropas aus der Spätbronze- und frühen Eisenzeit (9.-6. Jh. v. Chr. Geb.). Bayerische Akademie der Wissenschaften, Philosophisch-Historische Klasse, Abhandlungen N. F. 116 (München 1999).

Kromer 1959: K. Kromer, Das Gräberfeld von Hallstatt (Firenze 1959).

Lo Schiavo 2010: F. Lo Schiavo, Le Fibule dell'Italia meridionale e della Sicilia dall'età del bronzo recente al VI secolo a. C. Prähistorische Bronzefunde XIV,3 (Stuttgart 2010).

Mitrevski 1996/97: D. Mitrevski, Fyrom, Lisičin Dol Grab 15. Macedoniae Acta Archaeologica 15, 1996/97, 69-79.

Mitrevski 2007: D. Mitrevski, Pogrebuvanja na svešteničkite vo železno vo Makedonija. In: M. Blečić/M. Črešnar/B. Hänsel/A. Hellmuth/E. Kaiser/C. Metzner-Nebelsick (eds.), Scripta praehistorica in honorem Biba Teržan. Situla 44 (Ljubljana 2007) 563-583.

Nikulka 1998: F. Nikulka, Das hallstatt- und frühlatènezeitliche Gräberfeld von Riedenburg-Untereggersberg, Lkr. Kelheim, Niederbayern. Archäologie am Main-Donau-Kanal 13 (Rahden/Westf. 1998).

Pany 2003: D. Pany, Mining for the miners? An analysis of occupationally-induced stress markers on the skeletal remains from the ancient Hallstatt cemetry. Unpubl. Diplomarbeit (Wien 2003).

Pany-Kucera *et al.* 2010: D. Pany-Kucera/H. Reschreiter/A. Kern, Auf den Kopf gestellt – Überlegungen zu Kinderarbeit und Transport im prähistorischen Salzbergwerk Hallstatt. Mitteilungen der Anthropologischen Gesellschaft Wien 140, 2010, 39-68.

Schumann 2015: R. Schumann, Status und Prestige in der Hallstattkultur. Aspekte sozialer Distinktion in ältereisenzeitlichen Regionalgruppen zwischen Altmühl und Save. Münchner archäologische Forschungen 3 (Rahden/Westf. 2015).

Stöllner 2002: T. Stöllner, Die Hallstattzeit und der Beginn der Latènezeit im Inn-Salzach-Raum. Auswertung. Archäologie in Salzburg 3,1 (Salzburg 2002).

Stöllner 2007: T. Stöllner, Handwerk im Grab – Handwerker? Überlegungen zur Aussagekraft der Gerätebeigabe in eisenzeitlichen Gräbern. In: R. Karl/J. Leskovar (eds.), Interpretierte Eisenzeiten. Fallstudien, Methoden, Theorie. Tagungsbericht der 2. Linzer Gespräche zur interpretativen Eisenzeitarchäologie. Studien zur Kulturgeschichte von Oberösterreich 19 (Linz 2007) 227-252.

Teržan 1990: B. Teržan, Die Halbmondfibeln. Über die Kulturverbindungen zwischen der Ägäis und dem Caput Adriae. Arheološki vestnik 41, 1990, 49-88.

Teržan 2003: B. Teržan, Goldene Ohrringe in der späten Bronze- und frühen Eisenzeit – Zeichen des Sakralen? Anzeiger des Germanischen Nationalmuseums Nürnberg 2003, 68-82.

Teržan/Hellmuth 2008: B. Teržan/A. Hellmuth, Noch einmal zum goldenen Diadem aus Stična. In: S. Gabrovec/ B. Teržan (eds.), Stična II. Gomile starejše železne dobe. 2: Razprave. Katalogi in Monografije 38 (Ljubljana 2008 [2010]) 173-189.

Veblen 1997: T. Veblen, Theorie der feinen Leute. Eine ökonomische Untersuchung der Institutionen [Original 1899: The Theory of the Leisure Class] (Köln 1997).

Wagner-Hasel 2000a: B. Wagner-Hasel, Der Stoff der Gaben. Kultur und Politik des Schenkens und Tauschens im archaischen Griechenland (Frankfurt, New-York 2000).

Wagner-Hasel 2000b: B. Wagner-Hasel, Die Reglementierung von Traueraufwand und die Tradierung des Nachruhms der Toten in Griechenland. In: T. Späth/B. Wagner-Hasel (eds.), Frauenwelten in der Antike. Geschlechterordnung und weibliche Lebenspraxis (Darmstadt 2000) 53-81.

Wagner-Hasel 2000c: B. Wagner-Hasel, Arbeit und Kommunikation. In: T. Späth/B. Wagner-Hasel (eds.), Frauenwelten in der Antike. Geschlechterordnung und weibliche Lebenspraxis (Darmstadt 2000) 311-335.

Wells 1978: P. Wells, Eine bronzene Rinderfigur aus Hallstatt. Archäologisches Korrespondenzblatt 8, 1978, 107-109.

Zemmer-Planck 1990: L. Zemmer-Planck, Zwei Neufunde aus Tirol. Veröffentlichungen des Tiroler Landesmuseums 70, 1990, 331-346.

Author

Bettina Glunz-Hüsken
Albert-Ludwigs-Universität Freiburg, Institut für Archäologische Wissenschaften/ Abt. Urgeschichtliche Archäologie
Belfortstraße 22
D-79085 Freiburg
Germany
bettina.glunz_huesken@t-online.de

French elite burials of the Early Iron Age

Laurie Tremblay Cormier

Abstract

This contribution aims at a general synthesis of elite graves of the Early Iron Age (Ha C/Ha ancien) within the borders of France. Based on a corpus of more than 200 graves, of which some are only partially known, the main characteristics of elite graves are proposed: preponderance of weapons (swords) and ad hoc presence of wagons, harness equipment and metallic vessels. The result is a great homogeneousness of the sets, however with a general differentiation of the oriental margin going from Alsace to the Jura, and of the extreme south-west (Languedoc). This homogeneousness can be refined through the integration of non-prestigious objects regularly found within these graves (arm rings, razors, pottery), although regional variations are still slight.

Thanks to the uniformity of the representation scheme, it is possible to define margins for the group of the central-eastern French elite graves. The practice of cremation and the handling of weapons in some Lorraine graves tends to relate this region – at least partially – to the Mosan group. Likewise, the Upper Rhine might also be linked to a group centered on southern Bavaria, where wagons and metallic vessels have a more important role in the funerary set. In the actual state of art, it is hard to estimate the southern border of the French group; but, regarding some of the finds, the Alps can be integrated into this pattern. The Languedoc, with its Iberic traditions, figures as the south-western margin, while the absence of graves in the Atlantic regions does not permit the identification of any elite funerary representation mode. The sharing of practices and ideas by individuals of the same social status, over such a wide geographical extent, leads to the identification of a strong interactions network between the elites and a sense of belonging to a privileged group going beyond the frontiers.

Résumé

Cet article fait une synthèse générale des tombes de l'élite du Ha C (Ha ancien) dans les limites administratives actuelles du territoire français. À partir d'un corpus de plus de 200 sépultures, dont certaines ne sont connues que partiellement, les traits généraux définissant les tombes de l'élite sont proposés : présence majoritaire de l'armement (épée), et ponctuelle du char, d'éléments de harnachement et de vaisselle métallique. Il en résulte une très grande homogénéité des ensembles, avec toutefois une différenciation générale de la bordure orientale allant de l'Alsace au Jura, et de l'extrême sud-ouest (Languedoc). Cette homogénéité peut être affinée par la prise en compte d'objets non-prestigieux régulièrement représentés dans ces tombes (bracelet, rasoir, céramique), bien que les variations régionales restent légères.

Grâce à l'uniformité de ce schéma de représentation, il est possible de définir des marges au groupe des tombes de l'élite de France centre-orientale. La pratique de la crémation et de la déformation de l'arme, dans certaines tombes lorraines, tend ainsi à rattacher cette région – au moins partiellement – au groupe mosan. De même, la question du rattachement du Rhin supérieur à un groupe centré sur le sud de la Bavière est ouverte, où les chars et récipients métalliques ont plus d'importance dans l'assemblage. Dans l'état actuel des connaissances, il est difficile d'estimer une limite méridionale; cependant, au vu de découvertes ponctuelles, on peut inclure le massif alpin au phénomène hallstattien. Le Languedoc aux traditions ibériques matérialise la frontière sud-ouest, tandis que l'absence de tombes dans les régions atlantiques ne permet pas d'identifier le mode de représentation funéraire des élites. Le partage de pratiques et d'idées par des individus de statut social équivalent, dans une aire géographique aussi vaste, conduit à l'identification d'un étroit réseau d'interactions entre les élites, et un sentiment d'appartenance à un groupe privilégié transcendant les frontières.

Introduction

Thanks to the search for the remains of the Gaul War in the 19th century sponsored by the emperor Napoleon III, hundreds of barrow cemeteries have been excavated in France. Even today, these finds form the main part of our knowledge of the Early Iron Age elite graves; this knowledge, unevenly distributed over half the country, is therefore of unequal accuracy and density.

However, the homogeneousness of the French elite graves is striking. Variations of personal goods, burial practices and offerings are so faint, that it can be hard to distinguish two remote graves on the sole evidence of their remains. This paper intends to sketch out common traits and regional differences, and the role of long-distance interactions in the construction of the elite funerary representation. The margins of the group are also discussed, being directly related to the recognition of this precise pattern of elite expression.

Criteria for the identification of elite graves

What gives a grave this special nature that differentiates it from the more common segment of the population as being an individual of a privileged top layer? Several elements can be put forward, although these are not always available in the archaeological record. At the outset, the size and the architecture of the barrow are two of them, as they indicate the expense of energy from the group and the desire to stage the grave within the landscape. Unfortunately, the size and structure of the barrows were seldom observed during ancient excavations; at best the building materials are – unevenly – described (sand, stone plates, rocks, earth, wood), and these usually vary according to the local geological resources and regional traditions.

The same can be said about the splendors of the funeral ceremony, which already leave little to no archaeological traces. The lack of observations, together with the practice of inhumation instead of cremation, makes it hard to identify a special treatment of the body and objects prior to their final deposition. Except for the wrapping traces found on a few objects that are, in France, mainly swords and wagon parts (Médard 2015, 87), no evidences of a particular handling of grave elements that could be used to define elite graves are known.

The remaining available criteria are thus based on the grave goods themselves. Their prestige can be related to one or more of the following: luxury materials like gold, ivory or amber; a distant origin, from a far-off region; high technical skills involved in their making leading to an uncommon quality; and a symbolic status associated with upper social classes, like weapons, wagons, harnesses and metallic vessels – even if the latter is more or less linked to our conception of what might have been restricted to the elites. On the contrary, some other object types found within these graves cannot be considered as identification criteria. Indeed, even if they are frequently associated with prestigious goods, razors, arm rings, knives and potteries are also found in more humble graves. It is likely that a detailed study of

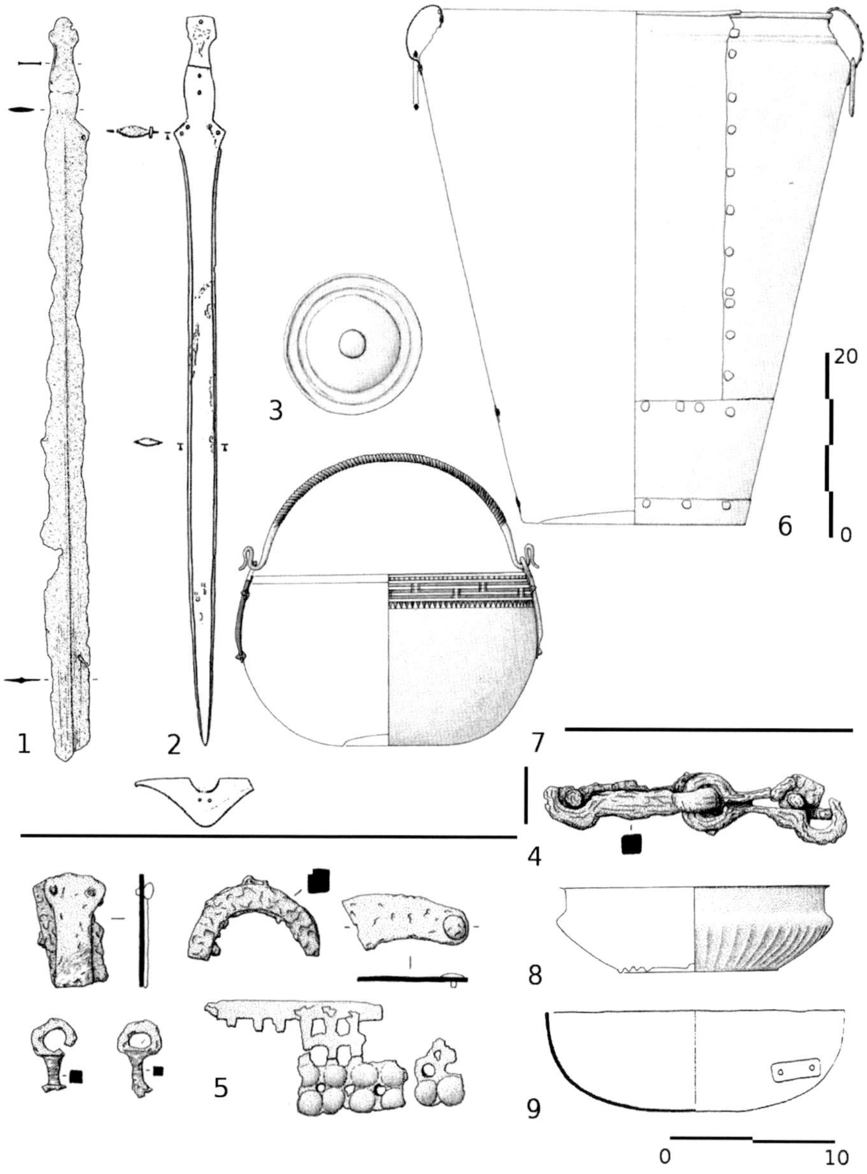

Fig. 1. Prestigious objects found in French elite graves. 1: Iron sword, Poiseul Barrow 3 (Chaume/Feugère 1990, 14 fig. 12,2). – 2: Bronze sword and chape, Dompierre, Barrow 4 (Bichet/Millotte 1992, 38 fig. 21). – 3: Phalera, Poiseul Barrow 2 (Chaume/Feugère 1990, 11 fig. 8,4). – 4: Horse bits, Saint-Louis (Pare 1992, pl. 8B12). – 5: Wagon (selection of pieces), Saint-Louis (Pare 1992, pl. 8B). – 6-9: Metallic vessels (selection); 6: Situla, Poiseul Barrow 3 (Chaume/Feugère 1990, 15 fig. 13,3). – 7: Cauldron, Poiseul Barrow 1 (Chaume/Feugère 1990, 8 fig. 5,5). – 8: Ribbed cup, Poiseul Barrow 3 (Chaume/Feugère 1990, 14 fig. 12,4). – 9: Cup, Sévérac-le-Château, Roumagnac (Gruat 1993, 211 fig. 12,2).

these objects would shed light on particular productions that were reserved to the elites; but, without such information, they should nowadays be set apart (Fig. 1).

Following these very restrictive criteria, 219 elite graves can be identified in France, mainly located in its large eastern half (Fig. 2, see the list below). Their composition is not always totally reliable, and the presumed existence of a grave is sometimes only based on the discovery of an object usually found in a funerary context. Nevertheless, they are largely sufficient to analyze the general representation pattern and its regional variations.

Bronze and iron swords

Swords are the main element defining French elite graves; in fact, they are found within more than 90% of the graves, being the most obvious criteria for their identification. Bronze and iron swords share a similar distribution, even though

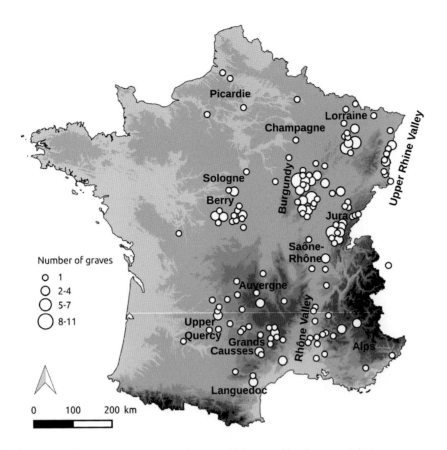

Number of graves
○ 1
○ 2-4
◯ 5-7
◯ 8-11

0   100   200 km

Fig. 2. Map of the Early Iron Age elite graves in France and natural regions mentioned in the text.

the latter are far more numerous; this parallel use of both materials is common to a wider area, going up to the Czech Republic. The Villement, Wehringen, Miers and Weichering types, first equated with the bronze Gündlingen form, can be considered as earlier than the Mindelheim type and the majority of iron swords (Milcent 2004, 99; Pare 1991, 4-6; 1996, 103). Oldest types are counted as Atlantic productions, originating from an area going from south-east England to the Seine River, and up to the Lower Rhine (Milcent 2009, 240). But a series of mutual technological transfers with Central Europe quickly lead to the making of Continental variants and types, which can be seen in morphological and technical details. In this perspective, Mindelheim swords are one of the representatives of these Continental productions, as well as probably most of the iron swords (Brun *et al.* 2009, 480). However, the lack of a typology of the latter, due to preservation problems, is a serious impediment to locating their region of origin; French iron swords might then be local, as well as imports.

On a smaller level, the distribution of bronze and iron swords varies. Only a few regions really share both materials: Jura, southern Burgundy and northern Berry; the others do not, and are defined by the presence of bronze or iron swords, which testifies local preferences (Milcent 2004, 101). As sword accessories, chapes are almost absent from southeastern France and the Rhone valley, and associated with iron swords only in the south-west, in Burgundy and Jura (Fig. 3).

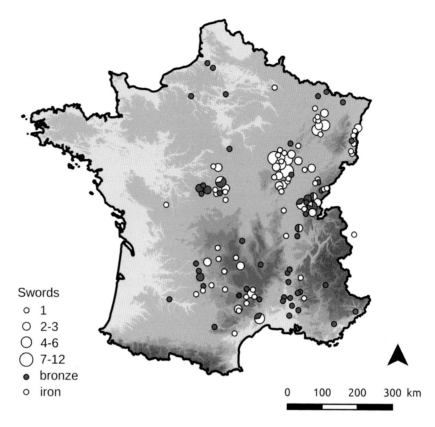

Fig. 3. Sword graves and swords with unknown context from the Early Iron Age (completed from Beylier 2012; Bichet/Millotte 1992, 97-98 fig. 73-74; Blanchet 1984; Milcent 2004; Mohen 1980).

Swords
- ○ 1
- ○ 2-3
- ○ 4-6
- ◖ 7-12
- ● bronze
- ○ iron

0   100   200   300 km

Wagons and harness equipment

Unlike in southern Germany, northern Austria and Czech Republic, French elite graves are not characterized by wagons, except for three burials. The grave from La Côte-Saint-André associates a Kurd situla with Late Bronze Age massive bronze wheels, which preserved wooden tires (obviously a late repair) date to 745-735 BC (^{14}C; Bocquet 1990, 36). The remaining two graves are clustered in the Upper Rhine valley: Ohnenheim, deposited with an iron sword, and the Lisbühl barrow in Saint-Louis. They fully take part in a more extended group of wagon-graves covering Central Europe (Pare 1992, 139), of which they are the western margin.

The Lisbühl barrow does not feature weapons, but did yield horse harness equipment. The distribution of horse-bits is somewhat similar to wagons and still limited to the eastern fringe of the country, with the two Alsatian wagon-graves and the Chavéria barrows IX and XVI. At the opposite end, a complete harness and bits are also known in the Mailhac cemetery (graves 68 and 99); but the characteristics of Languedocian graves (cremation, pottery and metal objects forms, grave goods associations) undoubtedly exclude them from the group described in this paper, relating them more to the Iberian regions than to Continental ones, as discussed later regarding geographical margins.

Phalerae have a wider, but not heavier distribution. The Chavéria XVI *phalerae* can be seen as the remains of Late Bronze Age productions (Pare 1991, 12), the only other burial with this equipment being the Poiseul barrow 2. The Saulce-Champenoises grave, more to the west in the Champagne region, completes the distribution together with the pieces of a yoke. The larger distribution of *phalerae* could be explained by the crossing, in France, of influences from Central Europe and the Atlantic: harnesses mainly come with wagons, through an eastern funerary representation pattern, and are thus limited to the oriental fringe; while *phalerae* are part of this scheme but also of the Atlantic elites' representation pattern, which enlarge their scope. This hypothesis is supported by the practice of cremation in the Saulce-Champenoises grave, and its cultural belonging to a northwestern area going up to Belgium and the Netherlands (Milcent 2015, 27; 35).

Metallic vessels

Metallic vessels are not evenly represented in French elite graves, but are once more clustered in the eastern half and in the extreme southwest. In regions where they are absent, they might have been replaced by ceramic counterparts; thus, a study on the production of prestigious potteries, designated for the elites, would be welcome to test this possibility.

At the moment, no case of use as a cinerary urn is known, which tends to point towards their use as consumption elements for liquid and/or solid food items. In eastern France, the main characteristic of these vessels is that they are imports; apart from their external provenance, they rarely share the same category or type. Regions of origin do differ, although they cannot always be precisely circumscribed; still some are better represented than others, showing privileged interactions with particular remote regions.

South of the Alps, Etruria is represented by two ribbed cups and mixed influences on the Appenwihr *pyxides*, and is probably the provenance region of Kurd *situlae*. Five basins with pellets-decorated rims, within which three in the Alps, can also be considered imitations of italic models, as well as imports. The north of the Adriatic completes the Mediterranean imports, with a comparison in Este for the small pointed sieve from Appenwihr and, very likely, the production of three cauldrons from northern Burgundy (Adam 1997; Chaume/Feugère 1990, 34-38). The other main provenance of metal vessels is the oriental Alps, where some forms are clustered: the cist from Magny-Lambert, the large-rim cup and spherical ladle from Appenwihr, and the jug from Avançon. The *pyxides* from Appenwihr also show strong influences of this area, both in technique and ornamentation.

In the Languedoc and Grand Causses region, the scheme is totally different: some elite graves do present metallic vessels, but of a local form – except for one basin with pellets-decorated rim in Mailhac – Grand Bassin, grave 14. Indeed, the *simpulum* of the graves 68 and 99 from the latter cemetery are characteristic elements of a very regional pattern of banquet items, and can be found in great numbers in cremation graves of the northeastern Iberian peninsula, in particular in weapon-graves (Graells i Fabregat 2009, 203-204). Same goes for the small, non-decorated bronze cups of the Grand Causses, the form of which is clearly inspired by local potteries and is limited to this region (Gruat 1993, 214-215).

Regional variations and margins

Therefore French elite graves follow quite a minimalistic trend: the core is composed of a barrow, the practice of inhumation, and a bronze or iron sword. Other criteria for the identification of elite graves are either rare and/or limited to the east of the country, as could be seen through the distribution of wagons, harnesses, *phalerae* and metallic vessels. The preference for bronze or iron swords is, at the moment, the only elite marker which shows regional differences; thus, the question of composition variations must be completed by the use of non-prestigious objects found within these graves.

On the other hand, thanks to this very same homogeneousness, the margins of this group can be quite easily discussed. But its geographical extension calls for caution, as some neighboring regions often considered as 'outside the area' might just rather be poorly documented.

Non-prestigious elements

The association of a razor and arm rings in sword graves is typical for an area centered on northern Burgundy, which reaches southern Lorraine, Berry and Jura. Types and materials of both objects do not seem to be quite related to geography. Razors and arm rings are only found in sword graves; they are indeed absent from graves with only metallic vessels, wagons or horse-gear, with the exception of Serres (barrow 1 grave 3) and the Viala-du-Pas-de-Jaux barrow, which tends to correlate them to the presence of a weapon. Taken alone, razors can be found in Alsace, southern Lorraine, Burgundy, eastern Berry and Languedoc. Arm rings share the same distribution, in addition to northern Lorraine, Jura and the whole Berry region. These elements allow for distinguishing regions which share the same pattern when only taking account of prestige objects, though the differences are still quite minor.

A great help in distinguishing regional variations in the graves could come from potteries, which are evenly distributed between the regions. Unfortunately, no large-scale study is available at the moment for comparing the ceramics deposited within elite graves. As previously observed, this could lead to the identification of productions restricted to the elite graves, increasing their visibility; but this could also help in understanding the funerary rites, through the characterization of the food and liquid offerings and, perhaps, the funerary banquet.

Boundaries of reality or limits of research?

On the behalf of some unusual graves, the northern half of Lorraine must be related to a distinct group better known in Belgium and in the Netherlands as the Mosan group, which also includes the Saulce-Champenoise cremation barrow (Warmenbol 1993). Indeed, the grave 1 from Moncel-sur-Seille associates the practices of cremation and the bending of an iron sword; the barrow VI from Pont-à-Mousson, built on a layer of ashes, also shows cremation and an iron sword, although it is not mentioned whether the latter was also cremated, broken or bent (Thévenin 1981). The barrow 20 from Haroué can be added to these Mosan graves, but with more caution: in the barrow, once more built on a layer of ashes (cremation?), an intentionally broken iron sword was found, but said to be placed on the legs of an individual, so the question of the main funerary practice remains (Millotte 1965, 84).

The Mosan group might have extended beyond Lorraine, mixing with the French graves, as is clearly the case in Apremont (Jura). During the excavation of the La Motte aux Fées barrow, what seems to be an earlier cremation was discovered under the wooden chamber of the Ha D wagon-grave; on a thin layer of ashes, cremated remains where gathered together with an iron sword, described as "coiled" ("*enroulée sur elle-même*"; Castan 1879, 382-383). Thus this set is quite different from the other graves in the vicinity, defined by the classical burial and unbroken sword. The doubts regarding it dating to the Late Iron Age (Warmenbol 1993, 92) can also be lifted, thanks to the stratigraphic observations, which allow its inclusion into the Mosan group.

To the east, the wagon-graves and harnesses of Ohnenheim and Saint-Louis play in favor of a rapprochement between Alsace and southern Germany. As previously said, these barrows are the western limit of a greatest group going up to the Czech Republic; the Appenwihr grave, with its oriental Alps influences, can be added to this neighboring pattern. However, it is unsure whether the La Côte-Saint-André wagon-grave and Chavéria barrows IX and XVI are also part of it, or are only a testimony of mixed influences in the Jura and the Rhône valley. A better knowledge of the graves between the Saône and Rhône rivers is needed to answer this question, although hardly reachable due to the ancient destruction of many barrows, in particular near the confluence.

This lack of information affects other regions such as the north of the Massif Central, the Morvan massif and the Alps. It is therefore difficult to trace the southern border of the French group; yet, the discovery of many swords in the Lower Rhône valley indicates that it might extend more to the south than previously thought, to maybe less than 50 km from the Mediterranean coast. The recent discovery of a sword burial barrow in Aosta, a few kilometers from the actual frontier (Regione Valle d'Aosta 2016) and the barrows cemetery of Avançon (Musée départemental de Gap 1991) strongly encourage, at the least, the integration of the Alps in the French group.

In the south-west, the Languedoc elite graves can be excluded, because of their affiliation to a cultural group spread on the northeastern coast of the Iberian Peninsula. Even if the Mailhac graves 68 and 99 also have metallic vessels and harnesses, the practice of cremation, the forms of metal objects and ceramics and the complexity of the vessels set – elements also observed in the other graves of the Languedoc region – clearly express their foreign origin (Janin *et al.* 2002). The southern limit can probably be assigned to the Grand Causses, on the limit of the Massif Central, a region where "hallstattian" influences are strong in the composition of the graves (Gruat 1993, 215).

The western limit can be set after the Haut Quercy and Berry groups, following the almost total disappearance of graves in the third-part of France, which is not due to a lack of research but is an archaeological reality. Even if elite markers such as weapons, feasting equipment and metallic vessels are known in this wide area, they do not come from funerary contexts (Milcent 2012; 2015) – except if one wants to consider the hoards and isolated objects as evidences of such practices. Nevertheless, the absence of body remains does not permit the inclusion of the western regions into the group studied here, as it is based upon the characterization of graves.

Construction through interactions

Inside the margins, the French elite graves display a deep homogeneousness in their particular refined, simple way. Regional variability sparsely affects the elite representation, but rather the local traditions to which the elite patterns adhere, and the more modest graves that surround them. Following this uniformity and its geographical consistency, this wide group can be considered as one: the 'central-eastern French group' (*groupe de France centre-orientale*). A deeper study of the non-prestigious finds, especially pottery, should permit the tracing of subgroups to a more regional scale (Fig. 4).

Thus, the sharing of the same representation pattern, or 'what must the grave of an elite look like', goes beyond regional cultural particularities and geographical distance. It is therefore the result of sustained relations between individuals, not following their physical proximity, but their social linkage. This implies a tight network between individuals of similar rank, through which ideas – and, indirectly, objects – circulated. This is one great example of the globalization that took place during the Early Iron Age in the elite sphere, where interactions led to the construction of similar ideology and practices (Fontijn/Van der Vaart-Verschoof 2016).

But what about the role of external influences? Are the imports just evidence of the exchange networks, or do they emphasize external inputs crucial to the elite representation pattern? Although it is hard to say who started first, the importance of swords in France during the Late Bronze Age supports the idea that, in the Early Iron Age, sword burial was not a foreign thing. The Late Bronze Age sword burial barrows in Burgundy, Jura and the Saône-Rhône confluence are certainly the core of this phenomenon, which later extends to more southern and western regions (Pare 2003), where swords were already present – but not yet associated with the practice. However, this local construction integrates exogenous productions. The various types and origins of swords, horse-gear and metallic vessels nevertheless indicate that most important is the presence of the object itself, more than its place of provenance. Moreover, a distant origin can be sufficient to make an object prestigious, as it becomes exotic and rare; its possession also shows that its owner

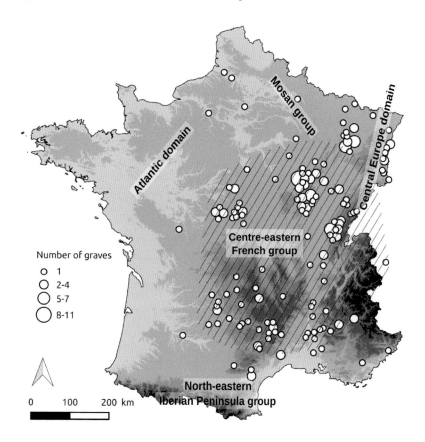

Fig. 4. Map of the extension of the central-eastern French group and neighboring groups.

has far-away relations, which is a good way to get above the more modest ones of the community.

So the provenance of imports rather indicates the great influences ensuing from exchange networks and their crossing in the central-eastern French group, than an external trigger for the construction of the elite representation pattern. Thus, the distribution of Atlantic types of swords and *phalerae* mainly concerns the center, up to Lorraine, while the oriental vessels, swords, wagons and harnesses are clustered in the east. The few Mediterranean objects are only found in regions where the interactions with Austria and Bavaria are strong, which adds to the idea that imports from Etruria or the Adriatic probably came to France not directly, but through intermediaries. Thus, a circulation through the Swiss and Austrian alpine passes, and then the Upper Danube, is much more likely than a premature use of the Rhône valley; unfortunately, the actual lack of information in the French Alps does not permit to assess the role of French-Italian alpine passes. This form of interaction networks has already been proposed as an explanation key for the composite set of the Appenwihr grave (Adam 1997, 12), and could be applicable to a wider extent.

Hence, the central-eastern French group finds its consistency through strong interactions between elites, around the diffusion of a representation pattern originating from traditions of the Late Bronze Age. Despite its local roots and homogeneity, this group is not withdrawn nor closed to external contacts, as testifies the importation of the major part of the prestige objects (swords, wagons, horse-gear, metallic vessels). However, the dynamics presented in this paper only concern a limited part of the population, which is also the most visible and, certainly, unrepresentative one. This calls for a study and comparison of the graves from the more common people, in order to replace the elites in their real social background, and to see how – and if – the globalization phenomenon affects whole communities.

Bibliography

Adam 1997: A.-M. Adam, Nouvelles observations sur le matériel d'importation du tumulus I d'Appenwihr (Haut-Rhin). Cahiers alsaciens d'archéologie, d'art et d'histoire XL, 1997, 5-15.

Beylier 2012: A. Beylier, L'armement et le guerrier en Méditerranée nord-occidentale au premier âge du Fer. Monographies d'archéologie méridionale 31 (Lattes 2012).

Bichet/Millotte 1992: P. Bichet/J.-P. Millotte, L'âge du fer dans le haut Jura: les tumulus de la région de Pontarlier, Doubs. Documents d'archéologie française 34 (Paris 1992).

Blanchet 1984: J.-C. Blanchet, Les premiers métallurgistes en Picardie et dans le nord de la France : Chalcolithique, âge du Bronze et début du premier âge du Fer. Mémoire de la Société Préhistorique Française XVII (Paris 1984).

Bocquet 1990: A. Bocquet, Le char de La Côte-Saint-André. In: Les premiers princes celtes, 2000 à 750 avant J.-C. : autour de la tombe de Saint-Romain-de-Jalionas, Isère (Grenoble 1990) 35-37.

Brun *et al.* 2009: P. Brun/B. Chaume/L. Dhennequin/B. Quilliec, Le passage de l'âge du Bronze à l'âge du Fer… au fil de l'épée. In: M.-J. Roulière-Lambert/A. Daubigney/P.-Y. Milcent (eds.), De l'âge du Bronze à l'âge du Fer en France et en Europe occidentale. Xe-VIIe siècle av. J.-C. La moyenne vallée du Rhône aux âges du Fer. Supplément à la Revue archéologique de l'Est 27 (Dijon 2009) 477-485.

Castan 1879: A. Castan, La tombelle gauloise d'Apremont (Haute-Saône). Revue Archéologique XXVIII, 1879, 380-383.

Chaume/Feugère 1990: B. Chaume/M. Feugère, Les sépultures tumulaires aristocatiques du Hallstatt ancien de Poiseul-la-Ville (Côte d'Or). Supplément à la Revue archéologique de l'Est 10 (Dijon 1990).

Fontijn/Van der Vaart-Verschoof 2016: D. Fontijn/S. Van der Vaart-Verschoof, Local elites globalized in death: A practice approach to Early Iron Age Hallstatt C/D chieftains' burials in northwest Europe. In: T. Hodos (ed.), The Routledge Handbook of Archaeology and Globalization (London 2016) 522-536.

Graells i Fabregat 2009: R. Graells i Fabregat, Banquet funerari i elements de banquet en tombes del nord-est de la Península Ibèrica entre la primera edat del ferro i l'ibèric antic. In: J. Diloli Fons/S. Sardà Seuma (ed.), Ideologia, pràctiques rituals i banquet al nord-est de la Península Ibèrica durant la Protohistòria. Citerior 5 (Tarragona 2009), 189-218.

Gruat 1993: P. Gruat, Une sépulture caussenarde particulière du début du premier Âge du fer: le tumulus 1 de Roumagnac à Sévérac-le-Château (Aveyron). Documents d'archéologie méridionale 16, 1993, 203-219.

Janin *et al.* 2002: T. Janin/O. Taffanel/J. Taffanel/H. Boisson/N. Chardenon/A. Gardeisen/F. Herubel/G. Marchand/A. Montecinos/J. Rouquet, La nécropole protohistorique du Grand Bassin II à Mailhac, Aude (VIᵉ – Vᵉ s. av. n. è.). Documents d'archéologie méridionale 25, 2002, 65-122.

Médard 2015: F. Médard, 150 ans après la fouille, l'épée hallstattienne de Rixheim-Hünerhubel (Haut-Rhin) réexaminée à l'initiative du Musée historique de Mulhouse. Annuaire historique de Mulhouse 26, 2015, 77-88.

Milcent 2004: P.-Y. Milcent, Le premier âge du Fer en France centrale. Mémoire de la Société Préhistorique Française XXXIV (Paris 2004).

Milcent 2009: P.-Y. Milcent, À l'Est rien de nouveau. Chronologie des armes de poing du premier âge du Fer médio-atlantique et genèse des standards matériels élitaires hallstattiens et laténiens. In: A. Lehoërff (ed.), Construire le temps. Histoire et méthodes des chronologies et calendriers des derniers millénaires avant notre ère en Europe occidentale. Bibracte 16 (Glux-en-Glenne 2009) 231-250.

Milcent 2012: P.-Y. Milcent, Le temps des élites en Gaule atlantique: chronologie des mobiliers et rythmes de constitution des dépôts métalliques dans le contexte européen, XIIIᵉ – VIIᵉ av. J.-C. Archéologie & culture (Rennes 2012).

Milcent 2015: P.-Y. Milcent, Bronze objects for Atlantic elites in France and beyond (thirteenth to eighth century BC). In: F. Hunter/I. Ralston (ed.), Scotland in Later Prehistoric Europe (Edinburgh 2015) 19-46.

Millotte 1965: J.-P. Millotte, Carte archéologique de la Lorraine: âges du Bronze et du Fer. Annales littéraires de l'Université de Besançon 73 (Paris 1965).

Mohen 1980: J.-P. Mohen, L'âge du Fer en Aquitaine du VIIIe au IIIe siècle avant Jésus-Christ. Mémoire de la Société Préhistorique Française XIV (Paris 1980).

Musée départemental de Gap 1991: Musée départemental de Gap, Archéologie dans les Hautes-Alpes (Gap 1991).

Pare 1991: C. Pare, Swords, Wagon-Graves, and the Beginning of the Early Iron Age in Central Europe. Kleine Schriften aus dem Vorgeschichtlichen Seminar der Philipps-Universität Marburg 37 (Marburg 1991).

Pare 1992: C. Pare, Wagons and Wagons-Graves of the Early Iron Age in Central Europe. Oxford University Committee for Archaeology, Monographs 35 (Oxford 1992).

Pare 1996: C. Pare, Chronology in Central Europe at the End of the Bronze Age. In: K. Randsborg (ed.), Absolute Chronology: Archaeological Europe 2500-500 BC. Acta Archaeologica Supplementum 1 (København 1996) 99-120.

Pare 2003: C. Pare, Tumulus Burial and the Question of the Start of the Hallstatt Culture. In: J. Bourgeois/I. Bourgeois/B. Cherretté (eds.), Bronze Age and Iron Age Communities in North-Western Europe (Brussels 2003).

Regione Valle d'Aosta 2016: Aosta, scavi ampliamento Ospedale. In: Sito ufficiale della Regione Autonoma Valle d'Aosta [http://www.regione.vda.it/cultura/patrimonio/siti_archeologici/news/ospedale_2014_i.aspx] (page viewed on 2016 April 21th).

Thévenin 1981: A. Thévenin, Informations archéologiques, Lorraine – Pont-à-Mousson. Gallia Préhistoire 24,2, 1981, 484-486.

Tremblay Cormier 2016: L. Tremblay Cormier, Identités culturelles et échanges entre Rhin et Rhône du Xe au Ve siècle avant notre ère. Art, Archéologie et Patrimoine (Dijon 2016).

Warmenbol 1993: E. Warmenbol, Les nécropoles à tombelles de Gedinne et Louette-Saint-Pierre (Namur) et le groupe "mosan" des nécropoles à épée hallstattiennes. Archaeologia mosellana 2, 1993, 83-144.

Author

Laurie Tremblay Cormier
UMR 7044 Archimède
Strasbourg
France
laurietcormier@gmail.com

List of French elite burials of the Early Iron Age

The following list includes all French elite burials based on several criteria discussed in the text. After the site and possibly the number of the barrow and the grave and the region, all known grave goods of the burials are mentioned. The list is based on information mainly derived from Beylier 2012; Bichet/Millotte 1992; Blanchet 1984; Gruat 1993; Milcent 2004; Mohen 1980; Tremblay Cormier 2016.

1   Amiens/Picquigny, Picardie; bronze sword

2   Amondans – Le Décret, Barrow 2, Jura; bronze sword, pottery

3   Aosta – Ospedale, Alps; iron sword, chape, brooche

4   Appenwihr, Barrow 1, Upper Rhine; pyxides, large rim cup, ladle, sieve, pottery

5   Appenwihr, Barrow 3, Upper Rhine; iron sword

6   Apremont, La Motte, Jura; iron sword

7   Argancy – Clos des Prés, Lorraine; bronze sword, chape, arm ring, pottery, 2 lignite rings

8   Aspremont – Coteau des Génévriers, Alps; bronze sword

9   Auberive – Grands Marais, Burgundy; iron sword, razor

10   Auberive – La Ferme de la Salle; Burgundy; iron sword, arm rings

11   Aubigny-la-Ronce – Chaumes d'Auvenay, Burgundy; iron sword, razor

12   Avançon – Chavignères, Alps; bronze jug, basin with pellets-decorated rim, knife, ring

13   Avançon – Les Santons, Alps; bronze sword, chape

14   Bagnols-sur-Cèze, Rhône valley; bronze sword

15   Baigneux-les-Juifs – La Corvée, Burgundy; iron sword, razor, arm ring

16   Barésia – Les Vouaites, Barrow 2, Jura; iron sword

17   Barésia – Les Vouaites, Barrow 2 (Group 3), Jura; bronze sword, chape

18   Barésia – Les Vouaites, Barrow 3, Jura; bronze sword

19   Barésia – Les Vouaites, Barrow 3, Jura; bronze sword

20   Barésia – Plaine de Vers, Barrow 3, Jura; bronze sword

21   Barésia – Plaine de Vers, unknown barrow, Jura; bronze sword

22   Barsac – Le Château, Rhône valley; iron sword

23   Beurey-Bauguay, Burgundy; iron sword

24   Boissia – La Vère, Clerc & Lemire Barrow, Jura; bronze sword

25   Boissia – La Vère, Unknown barrow, Jura; bronze sword

26   Boissia – La Vère, Unknown barrow, Jura; bronze sword

27   Boissia – La Vère, Unknown barrow, Jura; bronze sword

28   Bourges – Asnières, Berry; bronze sword, chape

29   Bourges – Lazenay, Berry; iron sword

30   Bouzemont – Haut des Fols/Faux, Barrow 1822 north, Lorraine; iron sword, razor, pottery, undetermined object

31   Bouzonville – Le Stockholz, Lorraine; bronze sword, rings

32   Brion – Grandes Chapelles, Unknown barrow, Berry; bronze sword, chape

33   Brion – Grandes Chapelles, Unknown barrow, Berry; bronze sword

34   Bucey-les-Gy – Plateau de Fresse, Barrow 1, Jura; iron sword, arm ring, pottery

35   Bucey-les-Gy – Plateau de Fresse, Barrow 2, Jura; iron sword, pottery

36   Buchères, Burgundy; cauldron

37   Carennac – Noutari, Barrow 17, Upper Quercy; bronze sword, chape

38   Causse Comtal, Génévrier Dolmen, Grands Causses; iron sword, bronze cup, pottery, undetermined object

39   Cazevieille, Barrow B4, Languedoc; iron sword, chape, razor, pottery, spindle whorl

40   Cazevieille, Barrow D14, Languedoc; iron sword, pottery, pin

41   Cazevieille, Barrow I Grave 1, Languedoc; bronze sword, chape, pottery, scalptorium, ring

42   Chaffois – La Censure, Barrow 3, Jura; iron sword, arm rings, pottery, gold ring

43   Charcier – Sur Glacé/La Vie des Salines, Barrow 3, Jura; iron sword

44   Charcier – Sur Glacé/La Vie des Salines, Unknown barrow, Jura; iron sword

45   Charmes-sur-Rhône, Rhône valley; bronze sword

46   Château-Gaillard – Cormoz, Saône-Rhône; bronze sword

47   Château-Gaillard – Cormoz, Saône-Rhône; iron sword

48   Châteauneuf-de-Bordette, Rhône valley; bronze sword

49   Châteauneuf-sur-Cher – Font James, Barrow 2, Berry; iron sword

50   Chavannes – Les Geneviève, Barrow 1 Grave 1, Berry; bronze sword

51   Chavéria – Les Massettes, Barrow II, Jura; bronze sword, chape

52   Chavéria – Les Massettes, Barrow III, Jura; iron sword, chape, pottery

53   Chavéria – Les Massettes, Barrow IV, Jura; bronze sword, chape, pottery

54   Chavéria – Les Massettes, Barrow IX, Jura; bronze sword, chape, horse-bits, basins with pellets-decorated rim, pottery, knife, pin

55   Chavéria – Les Massettes, Barrow XI, Jura; iron sword

56   Chavéria – Les Massettes, Barrow XVI, Jura; bronze sword, chape, horse-bits, phalerae, bone arm ring

57   Chavéria – Les Massettes, Barrow XVII, Jura; bronze sword

58   Clayeures – La Naguée, Barrow 27, Lorraine; iron sword, razor, 2 arm rings, rings, undetermined iron object

59   Clayeures – La Naguée, Barrow 38, Lorraine; iron sword

60   Clayeures – La Naguée, Barrow 49, Lorraine; iron sword

61   Clayeures – Petit Fays, Barrow 2, Lorraine; iron sword, razor

62   Clayeures – Petit Fays, Barrow 6, Lorraine; iron sword

63   Concoeur-Corboin – Derrière Cours, Olivier II, Burgundy; iron sword

64   Corent – Puy-de-Corent, Auvergne; bronze sword

65   Coust – Cortel, Barrow 1 Grave 1, Berry; iron sword, dagger, arm ring, pottery

66   Cras, Upper Quercy; iron sword

67   Cravant, Burgundy; cauldron

68   Créancey – Murots Bleus, Barrow D, Burgundy; iron sword, razor

69   Créancey – Murots Bleus, Barrow E, Burgundy; iron sword

70   Crémieu/La Tour-du-Pin, Saône-Rhône; bronze sword

71   Cusey – Sur Vesvres, Barrow 1, Jura; iron sword, pottery

72   Cusey – Sur Vesvres, Barrow 2, Jura; iron sword, finger ring

73   Darcey – La Combe Barre, Barrow 1, Burgundy; iron sword

74   Darcey – La Combe Barre, Barrow 2, Burgundy; iron sword, arm ring

75   Déols, Berry; bronze sword

76   Diarville – Devant Giblot, Barrow 1, Lorraine; iron sword

77   Diarville – Devant Giblot, Barrow 2, Lorraine; iron sword

78   Diarville – Devant Giblot, Barrow 3, Lorraine; iron sword, razor, arm ring

79   Diarville – Devant Giblot, Barrow 5, Lorraine; iron sword, 2 rings

80   Diarville – Devant Giblot, Barrow 6, Lorraine; iron sword

81   Dompierre-les-Tilleuls – Planquecet, Barrow 4, Jura; bronze sword, chape

82   Doucier – Moraine, Jura; bronze sword

83   Dun-sur-Auron – Tureau de la Girounée, Grave 1, Berry; iron sword

84   Eckwersheim, Grave 8001, Upper Rhine; Kurd situla, pottery

85   Épeugney – À Mortier, Jura; iron sword, razor, 2arm rings

86   Erondelle, Picardie; bronze sword, 2 arm rings

87   Esclanèdes, Roche Rousse, Grands Causses; bronze sword, chape, pottery

88   Flaysoc, Alps; bronze sword

89   Fleurey-sur-Ouche – Les Roches, Barrow 1, Burgundy; iron sword, lignite bead

90   Fleurey-sur-Ouche – Les Roches, Barrow 10 Grave A, Burgundy; iron sword

91   Fleurey-sur-Ouche – Les Roches, Barrow 10 Grave B, Burgundy; iron sword

92   Fleurey-sur-Ouche – Les Roches, Barrow 10 Grave C, Burgundy; iron sword

93   Fleurey-sur-Ouche – Les Roches, Barrow 14, Burgundy; iron sword

94   Fleurey-sur-Ouche – Les Roches, Barrow 14, Burgundy; iron sword

95   Floyrac, Barrow 3, Upper Quercy; bronze sword, pottery

96   Gramat, Barrow 1, Upper Quercy; bronze sword, chape, stud helmet?, ring, pottery

97   Gramat, Barrow 3, Upper Quercy; bronze sword, pottery, rings

98   Haroué – Bois de la Voivre, Barrow 20, Lorraine; iron sword

99   Haroué – Bois de la Voivre, Barrow 24, Lorraine; iron sword

100   Haroué – Bois de la Voivre, Barrow 27, Lorraine; iron sword, pin?

101   Hilsenheim, Barrow A, Upper Rhine; iron sword

102   Hures-la-Parade, Aven Armand, Grands Causses; iron sword, bronze cup, pottery

103 Igé – Saint-Germain, Barrow 2, Saône-Rhône; iron sword, razor, ring

104 Ispagnac, Freyssinel VIII, Grands Causses; iron sword, knife, pottery

105 Ispagnac, Freyssinel XII, Grands Causses; iron sword, pottery

106 Ivry-en-Montagne – Bois de la Pérouse, Barrow north Burgundy; iron sword, razor

107 Ivry-en-Montagne – Bois de la Pérouse, Barrow south, Burgundy; iron sword, razor

108 Jonquières, Rhône valley; bronze sword, chape

109 Kalhausen, Lorraine; bronze sword

110 La-Côte-Saint-André, Saône-Rhône; wagon, Kurd situla

111 Labruguière – Le Causse Languedoc; bronze sword, pottery

112 Lagnes-sur-Rhône, Rhône valley; bronze sword

113 Lamotte-sur-Rhône, Rhône valley; bronze sword

114 Lanuejols, Rasiguette, Grands Causses; iron sword, chape, bronze cup, pottery

115 La Laupie, Rhône valley; bronze sword, chape, pottery

116 Lect – Gros Molard, Jura; iron sword

117 Lect – Hameau de Vouglans, Jura; iron sword

118 Leuglay – Forêt de Lugny, Les Montagnottes, Burgundy; iron sword

119 Liniez – Moulin Barie, Berry; bronze sword

120 Lizine – Gros Buisson, Barrow 1, Jura; iron sword

121 Longvic-lès-Dijon – Champ à l'Ail/Romelet, Burgundy; bronze sword, chape

122 Lunery – Chanteloup, Grave 1, Berry; iron sword, razor, arm ring

123 Lyon Vaise – Rue du Mont d'Or, Saône-Rhône; iron sword

124 Magny-Lambert – Bois de la Chapelle, Burgundy; iron sword

125 Magny-Lambert – Champ Rocheux, Burgundy; iron sword, finger ring

126 Magny-Lambert – Combe à la Boîteuse, Burgundy; iron sword, razor

127 Magny-Lambert – Combe Bernard, Burgundy; iron sword

128 Magny-Lambert – La Meusse, Grave A, Burgundy; iron sword, razor

129 Magny-Lambert – Le Trembloi, Burgundy; iron sword, razor, arm ring, 2 amber beads, helmet?

130 Magny-Lambert – Les Fourches, Burgundy; iron sword, razor

131 Magny-Lambert – Monceau Laurent, Burgundy; iron sword, cist, bronze cup, ladle, razor

132 Magny-Lambert – Monceau Milon, Burgundy; iron sword, razor

133 Magny-Lambert – Rivanet, Burgundy; iron sword, arm ring, brooche

134 Magny-Lambert – Vie de Baigneux, Burgundy; iron sword, razor, 3? arm rings, pottery

135 Mailhac – Grand Bassin, Grave 14, Languedoc; basin with pellets-decorated rim

136 Mailhac – Grand Bassin, Grave 68, Languedoc; horse-bits, simpulum, pottery, brooche, scalptorium, 2 knives, hone

137 Mailhac – Grand Bassin, Grave 99, Languedoc; harness, pottery, brooche, shell

138 Marcillac-Vallon, Puech Basset Dolmen, Upper Quercy; iron sword

139 Marigny/Villard sur l'Ain, Lemire Barrow 1, Jura; iron sword

140 Marigny/Villard sur l'Ain, Berlier unknown Barrow, Jura; bronze sword

141 Mas de la Bastide, Barrow 1, Grands Causses; bronze sword, pottery

142 Mauriac – Aymons, Barrow 1 Grave 1, Auvergne; iron sword, chape, knife

143 Mauvilly – Bois de la Genevroi, Charmes, Burgundy; iron sword, razor, arm ring, clay bead

144 Meloisey – Montagne du Single/Murées d'Église, Barrow A, Burgundy; iron sword, chape

145 Meloisey – Montagne du Single/Murées d'Église, Barrow B, Burgundy; iron sword, razor

146 Meloisey – Montagne du Single/Murées d'Église, Barrow F, Burgundy; iron sword

147 Messein – Bois de Grève, Lorraine; iron sword

148 Mestes, Auvergne; iron sword

149 Miers – Les Barrières, Upper Quercy; bronze sword, chape, arm ring

150 Mignaloux-Beauvoir – Champ de Carthage, Berry; iron sword

151 Minot – Champ Vivant, Crais de Charmes Grave 5, Burgundy; iron sword

152 Minot – Crais de Vauchebaux/Vendues de Verroilles, Barrow 1, Burgundy; iron sword, tweezers

153 Minot – Crais de Vauchebaux/Vendues de Verroilles, Barrow 3 Grave A, Burgundy; iron sword

154 Minot – Crais de Vauchebaux/Vendues de Verroilles, Barrow 4, Burgundy; iron sword

155 Mirabel-aux-Baronnies, Rhône valley; bronze sword

156 Moncel-sur-Seille – Rosebois, Grave 1, Lorraine; iron sword

157 Moncel-sur-Seille – Rosebois, Grave 2, Lorraine; iron sword

158 Morey-Saint-Denis – Combe Aubin, Burgundy; iron sword

159 Nermier – Aux Combes, Barrow 1, Jura; iron sword, pottery

160 Noailles, Grave 1, Upper Quercy; bronze sword, pottery

161 Obenheim, Barrow 3, Upper Rhine; iron sword, razor, pottery, pin

162 Obenheim, Barrow 6, Upper Rhine; iron sword, pottery

163 Ohnenheim, Barrow 9, Upper Rhine; iron sword, wagon, horse-bits, pottery

164 Pardailhan, Languedoc; iron sword

165 Pierrefitte-sur-Sauldre – Les tombelles, Barrow 1 Grave 1, Sologne; iron sword, pottery

166 Poiseul-la-Ville, Barrow 1, Burgundy; iron sword, cauldron, razor, arm ring, ring

167 Poiseul-la-Ville, Barrow 2, Burgundy; iron sword, phalerae, razor, arm ring, undetermined object

168 Poiseul-la-Ville, Barrow 3, Burgundy; iron sword, Kurd situla, bronze ribbed cup, 2 razors, arm ring, clay bead

169 Poiseul-la-Ville, Barrow 4, Burgundy; iron sword, arm ring

170 Polignac, Auvergne; bronze sword

171 Pont-à-Mousson – Bois du Juré, Barrow VI, Lorraine; iron sword, arm ring, pottery

172 Pont-Sainte-Maxence, Picardie; bronze sword

173 Pontarlier – Sur le Mont, Jura; iron sword

174 Prusly-sur-Ource – Bois de Langres, Burgundy; iron sword, chape, razor, pottery

175 Quemigny-sur-Seine – Cosnes/La Brosse, Barrow IV, Burgundy; iron sword, razor

176 Quemigny-sur-Seine – Cosnes/Les Levaux, Barrow I, Burgundy; iron sword, razor

177 Quemigny-sur-Seine – Cosnes/Les Levaux, Barrow II, Burgundy; iron sword, chape

178 Richardménil – Bois de Grève, Lorraine; iron sword

179 Rixheim, Hünerhübel, Upper Rhine; iron sword

180 La Rochepot – La Chaume, Burgundy; iron sword, razor, pottery

181 La Rochette-du-Buis, Alps; iron sword

182 Saint-Aoustrille – Villement, Barrow 4 Grave 1, Berry; bronze sword, chape, arm ring?, pottery

183 Saint-Aoustrille – Villement, Barrow 6 Grave 1, Berry; bronze sword, chape

184 Saint-Aoustrille – Villement, Barrow 7 Grave 1, Berry; bronze sword

185 Saint-Aubin-sur-Gaillon, Picardie; bronze sword

186 Saint-Étienne-de-Carlat – Trin, Auvergne; iron sword

187 Saint-Étienne-du-Valdonnez – Les Bondons, Barrow 2, Grands Causses; iron sword, razor

188 Saint-Georges – Mons, Barrow 1 Grave 1, Auvergne; iron sword

189 Saint-Georges – Mons, Barrow 1 Grave 2, Auvergne; iron sword

190 Saint-Georges – Mons, Barrow 5 Grave 1, Auvergne; iron sword, chape, bronze cup

191 Saint-Georges – Mons, Bergeron Grave 1, Auvergne; iron sword, pottery

192 Saint-Jean-Saint-Paul, La Vialette, Grands Causses; 2 bronze cups, arm ring, pottery

193 Saint-Laurent-de-Trèves, La Can d'Artigues, Grands Causses; iron sword?, bronze cup, pottery

194 Saint-Louis, Lisbühl, Upper Rhine; wagon, horse-bits, pottery

195 Saint-Martin-Labouval – Nougayrac, Dolmen, Upper Quercy; iron sword, chape

196 Saint-Rémy-de-Provence, Rhône valley; bronze sword, chape

197 Sainte-Cécile-les-Vignes, Barrow Saint-Martin, Rhône valley; bronze sword, arm ring, pottery

198 Sainte-Montaine, Barrow 1 Grave 1, Sologne; iron sword, arm ring, spearhead?, ring

199 Sainte-Montaine, Barrow 2 Grave 1, Sologne; iron sword

200 Saulces-Champenoise – Le fond de Bernois, Enclos B, Champagne; iron sword, phalerae, yoke, pottery

201 Sauliac-sur-Célé – Le Cayrou de la Justice, Grands Causses; bronze sword, 4 arm rings, dagger

202 Sausheim, Barrow 2, Upper Rhine; iron sword

203 Semoutiers – Le Champ du Pré, Burgundy; bronze sword, chape

204 Serres, Barrow 1 Grave 3, Alps; bronze basin with pellets-decorated rim, razor, pottery, brooche, ring

205 Serres, Barrow 1 Grave 4, Alps; bronze basin with pellets-decorated rim

206 Servières-le-Château, Auvergne; iron sword

207 Séverac-le-Château – Roumagnac, Barrow 1, Grands Causses; iron sword, bronze cup, 2 arm rings, pottery

208 Solterre – La Gravière, Individual 1, Sologne; bronze sword

209 Soucia – Champ du Chat, Jura; iron sword

210 Soyons, Rhône valley; bronze sword

211 Sundhoffen, Upper Rhine; bronze sword, chape, razor

212 Vescles – Creux des Fossés/Sous Rametain, Barrow 1, Jura; iron sword

213 Veze – Croix de Baptiste, Barrow 1 Grave 2, Auvergne; iron sword, chape, arm ring, pottery

214 Viala-du-Pas-de-Jaux, Plo de las Faysses Barrow, Grands Causses; iron sword, bronze cup, razor, glas beads

215 Viala-du-Pas-de-Jaux, Les Fournélades Barrow, Grands Causses; iron sword

216 Villers-les-Nancy – Clairlieu, Lorraine; iron sword, 3 arm rings, pottery

217 Vitry-les-Nogent – Le Châtelet, Barrow 1, Burgundy; iron sword, razor, ring, ear ring?

218 Vornay – La Barrière Blanche, Barrow 1 Grave 1, Berry; iron sword, razor

219 Vornay, Barrow north, Berry; iron sword, bronze cup, pottery

A practice perspective

Understanding Early Iron Age elite burials in the southern Netherlands through event-based analysis

Quentin Bourgeois and Sasja van der Vaart-Verschoof

Abstract

In this paper we advocate a practice-based approach to funerary archaeology and demonstrate the value of this perspective using Early Iron Age elite burials in the southern Netherlands as an example. There is a clear, preconceived notion among archaeologists of how elite graves in this region 'should' look, and they have long since been defined by the types of objects they contain: weaponry, horse-gear, wagons and bronze vessels. The discovery in 2010 of an Early Iron Age inhumation burial containing an extraordinary ornament set in an urnfield on the Slabroekse Heide in the southern Netherlands rekindled a debate in the Netherlands as to what makes a grave a princely or chieftain's burial. The Uden-Slabroek grave was deemed not to 'fit' our understanding of rich Early Iron Age burials as it contained very different objects than the traditional princely or chieftains' burials. In this article, we advocate broadening research from solely focusing on the object types interred to include the actions taken, i.e. the burial practice. When considered from such an approach the Uden-Slabroek burial fits far better into the spectrum of Early Iron Age elite burials. This kind of switch of perspective results in very different understandings of past funerary practices and is relevant to all fields of mortuary archaeology. While we do not advocate abandoning an object-based approach to burial studies, we do argue that by including study of actions and practices we can expand, redirect and improve the approaches currently employed in funerary archaeology.

Zusammenfassung

In diesem Beitrag wird anhand ältereisenzeitlicher Elitegräber in den südlichen Niederlanden für eine auf Praktiken basierte Auswertung von Grabbefunden plädiert. Über die Frage, wie ein Elitegrab in dieser Region auszusehen hat, besteht seit langem unter Archäologen Einigkeit. Entsprechende Gräber sind über die Objekte, die in ihnen enthalten sind, definiert: Waffen, Pferdegeschirr, Wagen und Bronzegeschirr. Die verebbte Diskussion darüber, was ein Elitegrab zu einem solchen macht, wurde durch die Entdeckung eines außergewöhnlichen Grabes aus dem Urnenfeld auf der Slabroeker Heide in den südlichen Niederlanden wiederbelebt. Hier wurde 2010 eine Körperbestattung ausgegraben, in der sich ein herausragendes Schmuckensemble fand. Das Grab von Uden-Slabroek passt somit nach traditioneller Sichtweise nicht zu den bekannten Prunkgräbern in den Niederlanden, da weite Teile der üblichen Grabausstattung fehlen. In diesem Beitrag möchten wir allerdings durch eine Betrachtung der im Rahmen der Bestattung stattgefundenen Handlungen diese Sichtweise hinterfragen und somit die Auswertung und Einordnung dieses Grabes über die reinen Objekte hinaus thematisieren. Hieraus ergibt sich eine deutlich veränderte Sichtweise auf das Grab von Slabroek, da dieses Grab durch die im Rahmen des Bestattungsrituals durchgeführten Praktiken den traditionellen Elitegräbern durchaus an die Seite zu stellen ist. Dieser Perspektivenwechsel führt zu unterschiedlichen Wahrnehmungen prähistorischer Bestattungspraktiken weit über das hier behandelte Fallbeispiel hinaus. Durch die Betrachtung der Handlungen und Praktiken im Rahmen des Bestattungsrituals können die derzeit primär objektbasierten Herangehensweisen an die Gräberarchäologie deutlich erweitert und verbessert werden und ein umfassenderes Bild prähistorischer Bestattungen nachgezeichnet werden.

Introduction

A persistent problem in the study of burials is that archaeologists have a tendency to focus (almost exclusively) upon the objects recovered from these closed contexts. Burials have been invaluable in determining the co-occurrence of specific objects and have formed the basis of typochronologies all around the world. However, while this object-centeredness is characteristic of and significant to archaeology, objects are but a very small part of a burial ritual.

In recent years it has been argued on several occasions that we should view burials as structured events (Holst 2013, 109) aimed at re-negotiating and transforming the existing social order (*e.g.* Oestigaard/Goldhahn 2006; Robb 2013). Adopting such a perspective allows us to characterize burials in a very different fashion (Bourgeois 2013, 198; Holst 2013, 110-112).

In this paper, we argue that adopting such a practice perspective – viewing burials as events and sequences of activities – has the potential to radically alter our perception of burials, particularly of ones that initially might appear to deviate. We will do so by focusing upon a recently discovered inhumation burial dating to the Early Iron Age and containing an elaborate set of ornaments. It was discovered during the excavation of a ploughed-out urnfield on the Slabroekse Heide near Uden in the southern Netherlands (Fig. 1). The artifacts interred as well as the manner of burial were considered out of the norm for this region and period and the burial has been presented as highly unusual on multiple occasions (Jansen 2011; Jansen *et al.* 2011; Roymans 2011). The supposed deviation of the Uden-Slabroek burial in the context of other Early Iron Age elite burials has led some authors to classify this burial as that of an import-bride (for example Roymans 2011; *cf.* Jockenhövel 1991).

In contrast to this view we argue that the Uden-Slabroek burial does not deviate as strongly from the norm when the actions involved in the burial ritual are considered as well (see also Jansen/Van der Vaart-Verschoof in this volume). In fact it conforms in many ways to the other Early Iron Age elite burials and elite burial customs of the southern Netherlands. In this article we use the Uden-Slabroek grave and the other elite burials from this area to demonstrate the interpretive value of adopting such a perspective. An approach that we argue is not only relevant to the identification and interpretation of Early Iron Age elite burials, but rather to the study of burial ritual and funerary archaeology in general.

The inhumation grave of Uden-Slabroek

In this section we introduce the supposed unusual elite burial of Uden-Slabroek, before turning to the other more 'traditional' elite burials of the southern Netherlands. The inhumation grave of Uden-Slabroek (Fig. 2) was discovered in an open area bordered by several ring ditches in the northern part of a large ploughed-out urnfield predominantly dating to the Early Iron Age (Jansen forthcoming; Jansen *et al.* 2011; see also Jansen/Van der Vaart-Verschoof in this

Fig. 1. Map showing the location of Uden-Slabroek and chieftains' burials in the southern Netherlands. 1: Ede-Bennekom. – 2: Haps. – 3: Horst-Hegelsom. – 4: Meerlo. – 5: Oss-Vorstengraf. – 6: Oss-Zevenbergen. – 7: Rhenen-Koerheuvel. – 8: Someren. – 9: Uden-Slabroek. – 10: Wijchen (figure by Q. Bourgeois).

O Early Iron Age Elite Burial

0   25   50   100
Km

volume). The absence of a ring ditch around the burial pit indicates it was likely a flat grave, although the lack of overcutting suggests that the burial was marked above ground.

The deceased was buried in a deep pit (at least 1.5-2 m deep) in a small burial chamber (3 by 1.10 m) made with oak blocks and planks that had been intentionally charred in a controlled manner prior to being used to construct the small burial chamber (as shown by the presence of thin bands of charcoal outlining the edges of the oak blocks and the planks and the absence of fire-remains or burnt soil within the burial chamber and the good preservation of textile discovered directly underneath the planks). The lower half of the burial pit was filled with soil and the top half with large quantities of partially burnt oak branches. Again the lack of burnt soil or other fire-remains suggests that they were burned elsewhere.

The deceased was short (ca. 1.60 m as measured in the field). The few surviving skeletal elements do not allow for a sex or age determination. His or her arms and legs were adorned with bronze bracelets and anklets (Fig. 4). A set of two bracelets worn around the left wrist is decorated on the outside with a hatched, triangular

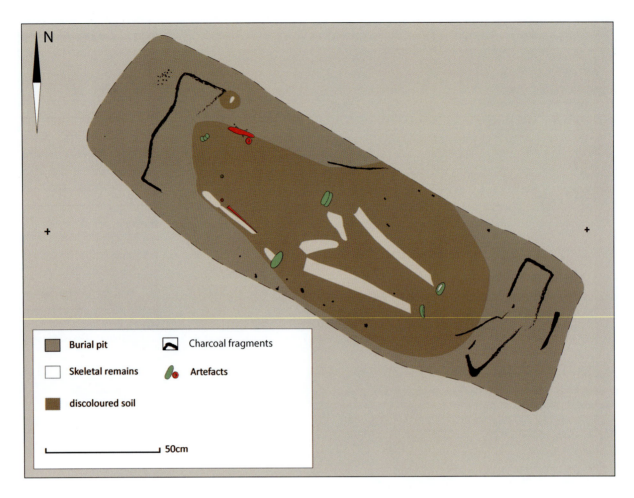

Burial pit

Skeletal remains

discoloured soil

Charcoal fragments

Artefacts

50cm

Fig. 2. Schematic plan of the inhumation grave of Slabroek. The figure is a simplified composition of two excavation levels (level 12 and 13; figure by Q. Bourgeois and J. van Donkersgoed).

design. They had been worn as a set for so long that they display heavy use-wear where they touched. On top of the right arm lay an iron pin with a twisted decoration and slightly higher towards the shoulder lay a small bronze ring. By the left shoulder lay a toilet set: an iron nail cutter (with twisted decoration similar to the iron pin) and iron tweezers that likely dangled from an iron ring (which still has a piece of leather knotted around it). Similar contemporary toilet sets have been found buried in leather pouches. In the *Fürstengrab* of Frankfurt-Stadtwald a leather pouch containing a toilet set had an amber bead used as a closing (Willms 2002, 49; see also Van der Vaart-Verschoof/Schumann in this volume). A similar amber bead lay by the Uden-Slabroek toilet set as well, and use-wear traces on this bead are consistent with use as a closing for some kind of pouch (Verschoof, pers. comm. 2013). A bronze pin was found next to this pouch and was recovered in seven fragments. The fragments were found in two distinct groupings, located apart from each other and at different depths (Fig. 3). This is the only object recovered broken in this manner. Considering the depth of the burial pit (outside of the reach of most burrowing animals and roots), the distribution of the fragments indicates that the pin was not fragmented post-depositionally. Rather, the position and distribution of the pin fragments suggest that it was broken deliberately prior to placement in the grave. Metal, probably bronze, spiraled rings found at the height of the head likely were worn in the hair, with a single ring made from the same wire (found at the height of the

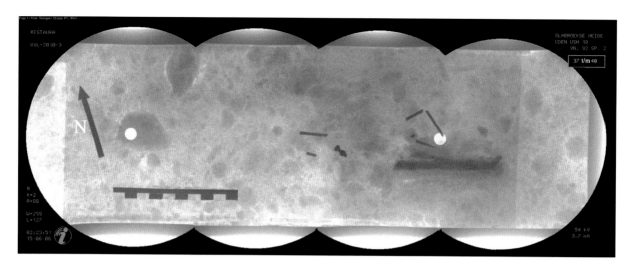

Fig. 3. X-ray of the bronze pin and iron toilet set in situ, taken from above (figure by Restauratieatelier Restaura, Haelen).

neck) perhaps decorating the end of a long braid. The rings probably are made of bronze, but the metal is so degraded that this cannot be confirmed. To the left of the head a small (burnt) fragment of human or animal bone was discovered. The purple discoloration of the soil surrounding the fragment suggests that it was placed within an organic pouch of some kind.

Another special feature of this burial, besides the general richness of the objects buried with the deceased, is the preservation of textile (see also Grömer in this volume). Fragments of woolen cloth survived in the bronze corrosion around the anklets and bracelets, as well as a small piece underneath a fragment of the bronze pin. The textile evidence suggests that the deceased was buried in a garment with long flowing sleeves, with the bracelets worn over the sleeves. The garment also covered the legs, as evidenced by the same textile being found on the bronze anklets. A shroud then covered the body of the deceased. Two fragments of animal hide were found with the bracelet set worn on the left wrist, though exactly in what relation to the bracelets is unclear, perhaps decorating the cuffs of a garment or the remains of another pouch.

A total of six charcoal samples from the grave have been radiocarbon dated, all of which were taken from outer tree-rings in order to minimize the own age of the samples. Unfortunately all six dates fall within the Hallstatt-plateau of the calibration curve. Therefore, a more precise dating than Early Iron Age, approximately 780-430 cal BC, cannot be given based on radiocarbon dating alone. The typochronology of the anklets, bracelets and toilet set suggest that the Uden-Slabroek inhumation is more likely to date to the beginning of the Early Iron Age, rather than the end. Particularly the bracelets date the grave to the beginning of the Early Iron Age. They have a hatched decoration that is frequently found on Early Iron Age Hallstatt C ornaments, such as found, for example, on a bracelet from the Neerharen-Rekem urnfield (Fontijn 2002, 200 fig. 9.5). The radiocarbon dates obtained from the burial pit and the typochronological evidence date the construction of this burial to the Early Iron Age, making it contemporaneous with the overall dating of the urnfield.

Chieftains' graves: the object-centered image of the 'ideal' elite burial

Since its discovery six years ago, the inhumation burial of Uden-Slabroek introduced above has been perceived (and published) as unusual (see Jansen *et al.* 2011). It does not fit the generally accepted perception of an elite burial in the Dutch Early Iron Age (Fontijn/Fokkens 2007). An image that is based on the rich burials from this period that predominantly take the shape of so-called Hallstatt C chieftains' graves.

The chieftain's grave, as an archaeological type of burial in the Netherlands, derives its name and image from the first scientifically excavated burial of this kind in the area: the Chieftain's grave of Oss. Found in the 1930s, it consists of a bronze situla used as an urn for a man's cremated remains and his (mainly imported) grave goods: a unique Mindelheim sword with gold-decorated hilt, dismantled yoke components, horse-gear, tools and personal items (see Fig. 3 in Van der Vaart-Verschoof/Schumann in this volume). This situla-urn was buried in a Bronze Age barrow and subsequently covered with a massive barrow 53 m in diameter (Fokkens/Jansen 2004, 133-135; see also Van der-Vaart-Verschoof/ Schumann in this volume and Jansen/Van der Vaart-Verschoof in this volume). As the first of its kind to be recognized and one of the richest Early Iron Age burials in the southern Netherlands, this grave in a way has become the 'ideal' chieftain's grave. It is through the objects found within this grave that we now define an elite (burial) for this period and area (see also Van der Vaart-Verschoof forthcoming).

Any Early Iron Age burial found in the Netherlands containing a bronze situla, a sword, horse-gear or wagon components, or any combination thereof, is compared to the Oss burial and our image of the Oss Chieftain as a wagon-riding, feasting elite warrior (see for example Braat 1935 in his discussion of a bronze vessel found at Baarlo; Kam 1956 in his discussion of a grave containing a bent sword found near Someren; Van Heeringen 1998 in his discussion of a grave with a bronze vessel and wagon components found at Rhenen; or Verwers 1968 in his discussion of a grave with bent sword and horse-bits found at Meerlo). For a newly found grave to be labeled a chieftain's grave, it must fit the image we have of such a burial and the people buried in them. It 'should' contain (a) similar (set of) items as those found in the Oss burial. In many cases graves with a 'partial' set are still referred to as chieftains' graves, yet their supposed incompleteness is emphasized. For example the "*Vorstengraf* of Meerlo", which contains a sword and two horse-bits (though no bronze vessel; Verwers 1968), or the "Chieftain's grave of Rhenen", which contains a bronze vessel and wagon components (but no sword; Van Heeringen 1998).

In turn, the Oss burial often is considered heavily influenced by and compared to the contemporaneous and even more elaborate princely burials in the Central European Hallstatt area, such as the *Fürstengräber* of Hochdorf or Frankfurt-Stadtwald (see for example Fokkens/Jansen 2004; Roymans 1991; though note that P.-Y. Milcent (2004, 108-112) recently argued that the elite burials are an Atlantic development which in turn influenced the burial customs of the Hallstatt culture in Central Europe). The *Fürstengräber* contain many of the same objects, such as bronze vessels, (components of) wagons and weaponry. Oss is seen as part of the periphery and as resembling these Central European burials, but as less 'complete' (Fokkens/Jansen 2004, 78-79; Verhart/Spies 1993, 80-82). This

Fig. 4. The objects from the burial of Slabroek. Note that the bronze pin (second from below) has been made whole during the restoration (photograph by J. van Donkersgoed).

comparison is two-sided. Not only do scholars working in the Low Countries compare the Dutch and Belgian burials to the burials in the Hallstatt culture area, scholars working on the Hallstatt culture burials often mention the Dutch and Belgian burials to show the extent of the distribution of certain types of objects (for example Koch 2006; Pare 1992).

While comparing burials that resemble each other is not necessarily a problem, the often superficial nature of the comparison is. Such comparisons often solely use the presence or absence of certain items – when compared to that image of an ideal grave – to make statements about the presumed social status reflected in these burials (Hessing/Kooi 2005; Van Heeringen 1998). Often only the checklist of objects is compared, rather than the burials as a whole.

It is in this manner that the Uden-Slabroek burial has been compared to the chieftains' burials. And indeed a comparison of the object types does suggest significant differences (Fig. 4; for example fig. 3 in Van der Vaart-Verschoof/ Schumann in this volume). Uden-Slabroek does not contain weapons, nor does it contain horse-gear or a bronze vessel. Instead it contains bracelets and anklets, which the chieftains' graves do not. The only objects found in both are toilet articles and pins. To many the objects found in the Uden-Slabroek burial indicate that a richly ornamented, elite woman was buried here, which is an image completely opposite to the feasting, wagon-riding warriors that we perceive the dead in the chieftains' graves to be, based on the objects that they contain.

So at first glance, when we judge solely on the base of object types, the Uden-Slabroek inhumation grave is indeed very different than what we have come to expect a rich Early Iron Age burial in the southern Netherlands to be.

How to bury a chieftain: examining graves through objects, choices made and actions taken during burial rituals

Including Uden-Slabroek, there are eleven rich Early Iron Age burials with relatively reliable context information known in the southern Netherlands (see Fig. 1). The identification of object types and definition of object categories found in them reveal only a small element of the burial rituals. Detailed analyses of the objects deposited and of the excavation records reveal strong similarities in how the burials were composed (see also fig. 5). By focusing on the actions taken during the burial rituals rather than fixating solely on this list of grave good types that special Early Iron Age burials supposedly should contain, a better rounded, balanced and more comprehensive understanding emerges (Fontijn *et al.* 2013; Van der Vaart 2011; Van der Vaart-Verschoof forthcoming).

The application of this approach to the chieftains' graves and other rich or special burials, like Mound 7 at Oss-Zevenbergen (see Fontijn *et al.* 2013), reveals a shared cultural concept regarding what the mourners considered the proper way of burying a specific group of people. This cultural concept is reflected in the eleven rich Early Iron Age burials in the southern Netherlands, and ongoing research indicates this is likely true for all such burials in the Low Countries. The graves are all the result of the same kind of actions taken during the burial rituals that created them, i.e. of similar burial practices. Below we have summarized several observations based upon published excavation results (Fokkens/Jansen 2004; Fokkens *et al.* 2009; Fontijn *et al.* 2013; Van der Vaart 2011; Van Heeringen 1998; Verwers 1968; 1972; Kam 1956; Pare 1992; Pleyte 1877-1903; Willems/ Groenman-van Waateringe 1988) as well as our own – still ongoing – research (Van der Vaart-Verschoof forthcoming).

The burial rituals all appear to have incorporated (as far as we can reconstruct from the archaeological record) a large fire and in most cases the dead were cremated. In some (some of) the grave goods show signs of burning and likely accompanied the decedents on the pyre (for example Wijchen). The use of fire seems to have been important, and in fact not only the fire itself but also the resultant charred wood and pyre remains. At Mound 7 of Oss-Zevenbergen, for example, the burnt out pyre was incorporated deliberately and carefully into the burial mound (Fontijn *et al.* 2013), while at Mound 3 of the same site a charred oak plank cut from a massive, ancient tree was deposited under the barrow (Fokkens *et al.* 2009).

Whether burnt or unburnt, larger grave goods were dismantled, and both large and small ones were manipulated and fragmented prior to deposition in the grave. Wagons and horse tack were dismantled and taken apart (Oss-Vorstengraf, Oss-Zevenbergen Mound 7, Rhenen, Wijchen). The manipulation of objects ranges from the bending of a sword (Horst-Hegelsom, Meerlo, Someren, Oss-Vorstengraf, Wijchen) or horse-gear (Meerlo, Rhenen), folding wagon components (Rhenen, Wijchen), to actually breaking and fragmenting pins, pendants and other objects (Haps, Oss-Zevenbergen Mound 3 and Mound 7, Rhenen, Wijchen).

All burial deposits, in their own ways, involve *pars pro toto* depositions. A pair of horse-bits for example representing a pair of draught horses (Meerlo, Oss-Vorstengraf), or a few bronze wagon decorations or wheel components representing the wagon (Oss-Zevenbergen Mound 7, Oss-Vorstengraf, Rhenen,

Wijchen). Not only the grave goods, but also the human remains sometimes were deposited partially and to varying degrees. While, for example, at Oss-Vorstengraf the entire skeleton is represented in the cremation remains, at Mound 7 a part of the cremation remains was deposited while the remainder was kept out of the burial (Lemmers, pers. comm. 2013; Smits 2013).

In rare cases textile has been preserved in the corrosion of bronze and iron objects (Oss-Vorstengraf, Rhenen). In these graves objects were wrapped either individually or in sets. This practice likely was more widespread, though evidence for this is elusive due to the degradable nature of textile and the thorough 'cleaning' that (chance) finds unfortunately frequently received.

The last (archaeologically visible) stage of the burial choreography was the construction of a barrow over the burial deposit, which invariably are located in or adjacent to urnfields (all graves). These burial mounds tend to be significantly larger than other barrows.

The actual creation of the burial deposit itself displays considerable variation. There are graves where everything was deposited in a ceramic (Horst-Hegelsom, Meerlo, Wijchen and probably Someren) or bronze (Ede-Bennekom, Oss-Vorstengraf, Rhenen) urn, while in others the cremated remains were deposited in a ceramic urn but the grave goods were placed alongside or left among the pyre remains (Mound 7 of Oss-Zevenbergen) or where everything simply was placed on the old surface (for example Mound 3 of Oss-Zevenbergen (Fokkens *et al.* 2009) and Haps (Verwers 1972)).

In short, all the graves were created using fire, the dismantling of objects, the manipulation and fragmenting of objects and people and *pars pro toto* depositions. In two cases (Oss-Vorstengraf, Rhenen) favorable conditions even preserved evidence of the wrapping of objects in textile. If we now take these observations, and examine Uden-Slabroek in a similar way, this supposedly deviating grave becomes far less different.

Not the odd one out

While an object-based comparison between Uden-Slabroek and the other more commonly accepted elite Early Iron Age burials highlights considerable differences between them, an analysis of the actions taken during the burial ritual reveals the opposite. It is important to stress that we do not want to only single out the similarities – we acknowledge that there are differences. Certainly, the choice of inhumation as opposed to cremation must have been significant (see also Jansen/Van der Vaart-Verschoof in this volume). The choice of objects deposited in the burial must be seen as relevant as well. Yet as we argue below, the actions taken during the burial ritual are comparable to a greater extent with the chieftains' burials than previously realized.

Like most rich Early Iron Age burials of which we know the original find context, the Uden-Slabroek inhumation was found in an urnfield. Inhumation, however, is unusual in this period. There is a cluster of Early Iron Age/Middle Iron Age inhumations in the Nijmegen area, but these contain only a few simple grave goods and do not compare directly to Uden-Slabroek (Van den Broeke 2002; Van den Broeke *et al.* 2011). In all other rich Early Iron Age burials the dead were cremated, making Uden-Slabroek stand out. However, if we look at what was burned in the fires that cremated all the other dead, the lack of cremation at Uden-

Figure 5 table — columns (left to right): Ede-Bennekom | Haps | Horst-Hegelsom | Meerlo | Oss-Vorstengraf | Oss-zevenbergen M.3 | Oss-zevenbergen M.7 | Rhenen-Koerheuvel | Someren-Kraayenstark | Uden-Slabroek | Wijchen

Legend

- ◗○— Barrow/ring ditch/flat grave
- Exposed to fire
- (Probably) wrapped in textile
- Bent and/or broken
- Wood in grave
- Unknown sex/male
- Pottery
- Bronze vessel
- Weaponry
- Horse-gear, yoke and/or wagon
- Tools
- Personal appearance
- Other

Fig. 5. A graphic representation of the choices made during the burial ritual. Note that when objects have been burnt it is unlikely that any textile present would have survived and that an absence of signs of burning does not necessarily mean that something was not exposed to fire (figure by S. van der Vaart-Verschoof).

Slabroek becomes somewhat less strange. At Wijchen everything was placed on the pyre, the dead and all grave goods. At Mound 7 of Zevenbergen, the deceased was cremated with a few grave goods. At the chieftains' graves of Meerlo, Oss and Rhenen and the weaponry burials of Horst-Hegelsom and Someren the dead were burned and fire may have been used to bend and fold the swords and some of the horse-gear while their other grave goods were untouched by fire. At Haps and Ede-Bennekom only the dead were burned. The decedent of Uden-Slabroek and his/her grave goods all may have been buried unburnt, but he/she was laid to rest in a burial chamber built of intentionally charred oak beams and planks. The burials form a spectrum, with at one end everything being exposed to fire prior to deposition (Wijchen), to graves where only a selection (Horst-Hegelsom, Meerlo, Oss-Vorstengraf, Oss-Zevenbergen Mounds 3 and 7, Someren-Kraayenstark) or only the dead were burned (Haps, Rhenen), to graves where only wood was charred (Uden-Slabroek). This spectrum is depicted schematically in figure 5. The point is that fire and burnt wood played a central role in all these burials (note also that objects, especially iron ones but also bronzes, can have been exposed to fire and show no signs of this).

The objects buried with this lady or man of Uden-Slabroek at first glance appear very different from the objects deposited in chieftains' graves. (S)he was buried with elaborate ornaments and a toilet set. No weapons, no tools, no elaborate drinking vessels. However, chieftains' burials usually also contain objects related to physical appearance, such as razors (Oss), tweezers (Rhenen), pins (Oss, Rhenen, Wijchen), hair rings and so on (as do some urnfield burials).

Another recurring and characteristic feature of the chieftains' burials is the deliberate manipulation and fragmentation of the objects accompanying the dead (and often also of the dead themselves; Van der Vaart-Verschoof forthcoming). This same feature is found in the Uden-Slabroek grave. A bronze pin was broken deliberately into many pieces prior to placement in the grave. Intentional fragmentation played a role in all rich burials.

A last feature common to the rich burials and Uden-Slabroek is the use of textile. For example, objects and human remains were wrapped carefully in precious textiles prior to deposition both in Oss and Rhenen (Van der Vaart-Verschoof forthcoming). At Uden-Slabroek a shroud covered the body. This wrapping the dead and their belongings in cloth was likely a common practice.

In short, when we look at the actions taken and the treatments of objects and people during elite Early Iron Age burial rituals, rather than solely focusing on the types of objects interred, we find that the choreography executed at Uden-Slabroek displays strong similarities to those of Haps, Horst-Hegelsom, Meerlo, Oss-Vorstengraf, Oss-Zevenbergen Mounds 3 and 7, Rhenen, Someren and Wijchen, but with nuanced variations. The rituals appear to be governed by the same cultural concepts, just with different emphases. The result being a spectrum of burials created through similar practices, but with many variations at the same time (Fig. 5). In a sense, no two burials are exactly alike, but at the same time they are all similar.

Conclusion

Above we have shown that while the inhumation grave of Uden-Slabroek initially was viewed by archaeologists as strange and completely deviating from the Early Iron Age burial norm for special people, in fact it appears to be the result of similar practices as the traditional chieftains' graves and other elite burials. There seems to have been a cultural concept that required specific actions to be part of these burial rituals. Variations in the burial choreographies are the result of different actions emphasized by different people. The result is a spectrum of burials with similarities and variations. The burials considered in this study were all discovered in or near urnfields and are the results of rituals that involved fire and wood, fragmentation, textile and emphasizing the physical appearance of the dead. At the same time the burial deposits take different forms and the degree of body treatment and the presence or absence of object types vary.

We wish to emphasize that we are not advocating switching out a check list of required objects for a similar list of required actions. We also are not claiming that objects were unimportant or not meaningful, on the contrary. Instead, this example serves as a thought exercise to illustrate that letting go of preconceptions and switching perspective can provide new and very different insights. With regard to the Uden-Slabroek inhumation, our point is that the actions taken during the burial ritual conform in many respects to what we see in contemporaneous elite burials and its otherness therefore can be questioned. Both in Uden-Slabroek and the 'traditional' elite burials we are seeing the results of the same burial custom, even though some different choices were made, such as the decision not to cremate the deceased or mark his/her burial with a barrow.

In conclusion, we have argued that solely studying object types found in archaeological burials limits our understanding of past mortuary rituals. It is our view that we need to expand our studies of objects in graves to also include studies of the actions and practices involved in creating those graves. As we have demonstrated for the Early Iron Age elite burials, this switch of perspective allows us to develop a more nuanced and better understanding of burial ritual and the people who took part in them.

Acknowledgements

This article was made possible by a NWO grant (no. 275-60-008) awarded by The Netherlands Organization for Scientific Research (NWO) to the first author and the project "Constructing powerful identities. The conception and meaning of 'rich' Hallstatt burials in the Low Countries (800-500 BC)" funded by an NWO "PhDs in the Humanities" grant (no. 322-60-004) awarded to the second author.

We would like to thank Richard Jansen for making the primary data of Uden-Slabroek available to us and David Fontijn and Maikel Kuijpers for commenting on earlier drafts.

Bibliography

Bourgeois 2013: Q. Bourgeois, Monuments on the horizon. The formation of the barrow landscape throughout the 3rd and 2nd millennium BCE (Leiden 2013).

Braat 1935: W. Braat, Een bronzen Hallstatt situla in het Rijksmuseum van Oudheden. Oudheidkundige Mededeelingen uit het Rijksmuseum van Oudheden te Leiden 16, 1935, 6-7.

Fokkens/Jansen 2004: H. Fokkens/R. Jansen, Het vorstengraf van Oss: een archeologische speurtocht naar een prehistorisch grafveld (Utrecht 2004).

Fokkens et al. 2009: H. Fokkens/R. Jansen/I. van Wijk, Het grafveld Oss-Zevenbergen. Een prehistorisch grafveld ontleed (Leiden 2009).

Fontijn 2002: D. Fontijn, Sacrificial landscapes. The cultural biographies of persons, objects and natural places in the Bronze Age of the Southern Netherlands, c. 2300-600 BC. Analecta Praehistorica Leidensia 33/34 (Leiden 2002).

Fontijn/Fokkens 2007: D. Fontijn/H. Fokkens, The emergence of Early Iron Age 'chieftain's graves' in the southern Netherlands: reconsidering transformations in burial and depositional practices. In: C. Haselgrove/R. Pope (eds.), The earlier Iron Age in Britain and the near continent (Oxford 2007) 354-373.

Fontijn et al. 2013: D. Fontijn/S. van der Vaart/R. Jansen, Transformation through destruction. A monumental and extraordinary Early Iron Age Hallstatt C barrow from the ritual landscape of Oss-Zevenbergen (Leiden 2013).

Hessing/Kooi 2005: W. Hessing/P. Kooi, Urnfields and cinerary barrows. Funerary and burial ritual in the Late Bronze and Iron Ages. In: L. P. Louwe Kooijmans/P. W. Van den Broeke/H. Fokkens/A. Van Gijn (eds.), The prehistory of the Netherlands (Amsterdam 2005) 631-654.

Holst 2013: M. Holst, Burials. In: H. Fokkens/A. Harding (eds.), The Oxford Handbook of the European Bronze Age (Oxford 2013) 102-120.

Jansen 2011: R. Jansen, Vorstengraf of graf van een lokale leider? What's in a name. Archeobrief 15, 2011, 37-38.

Jansen forthcoming: R. Jansen Heuvels op de heide. Een urnenveld met inhumatiegraf uit de vroege ijzertijd en grafveld uit de Romeinse tijd op de Maashorst.

Jansen *et al.* 2011: R. Jansen/Q. Bourgeois/A. Louwen/C. Van der Linde/I. van Wijk, Opgraving van het grafveld Slabroekse Heide. In: R. Jansen/K. Van der Laan (eds.), Verleden van een bewogen landschap – Landschaps en bewoningsgeschiedenis van de Maashorst (Utrecht 2011).

Jockenhövel 1991: A. Jockenhövel, Räumliche Mobilität von Personen in der mittleren Bronzezeit des westlichen Mitteleuropa. Germania 69, 1991, 49-62.

Kam 1956: H. Kam, Vondstmelding van urnen, ontdekt nabij het ven "Kraayenstark" Gem. Someren, Noord-Brabant. Berichten van de Rijksdienst voor het Oudheidkundig Bodemonderzoek 7, 1956, 13-14.

Koch 2006: J. Koch, Hochdorf VI. Der Wagen und das Pferdegeschirr aus dem späthallstattzeitlichen Fürstengrab von Eberdingen-Hochdorf (Kr. Ludwigsburg). Forschungen und Berichte zur Vor- und Frühgeschichte Baden-Württembergs 89 (Stuttgart 2006).

Milcent 2004: P.-Y. Milcent, Le premier âge du Fer en France centrale. Société Préhistorique Française, mémoire XXXIV (Paris 2004).

Oestigaard/Goldhahn 2006: T. Oestigaard/J. Goldhahn, From the dead to the living: Death as transactions and re-negotiations. Norwegian Archaeological Review 39, 2006, 27-48.

Pare 1992: C. Pare, Wagons and wagon-graves of the Early Iron Age in Central Europe. Oxford University, Committee for Archaeology Monograph 35 (Oxford 1992).

Pleyte 1877-1903: W. Pleyte, Nederlandsche oudheden van de vroegste tijden tot Karel de Groote (Leiden 1877-1903).

Robb 2013: J. Robb, Creating death: An archaeology of dying. In: L. N. Stutz/S. Tarlow (eds.), The Oxford Handbook of the archaeology of death and burial (Oxford 2013) 441-457.

Roymans 1991: N. Roymans, Late urnfield societies in the northwest European plain and the expanding networks of central European Hallstatt groups. In: N. Roymans/F. Theuws (eds.), Images of the past: Studies on ancient societies in northwestern Europe (Amsterdam 1991) 9-89.

Roymans 2011: N. Roymans, Een nieuw graf van een ijzertijdvorst of – vorstin in Zuid Nederland? Over ethische grenzen in de publieksvoorlichting. Archeobrief 15, 2011, 36-37.

Smits 2013: L. Smits, Analysis of the cremated bone from mound 7. In: D. R. Fontijn/S. A. Van der Vaart/R. Jansen (eds.), Transformation through destruction. A monumental and extraordinary Early Iron Age Hallstatt C barrow from the ritual landscape of Oss-Zevenbergen (Leiden 2013) 257-262.

Van den Broeke 2002: P. Van den Broeke, Vindplaatsen in Vogelvlucht. Beknopt overzicht van het archeologische onderzoek in de Waalsprong 1996-2001 (Nijmegen 2002).

Van den Broeke *et al.* 2011: P. Van den Broeke/J. den Braven/A. Daniël, Een ijzertijdgrafveld en een erf uit de Ottoonse tijd in het Lentseveld (Nijmegen 2011).

Van der Vaart-Verschoof forthcoming: S. van der Vaart-Verschoof, Fragmenting the chieftain. A practice-based study of Early Iron Age Hallstatt C elite burials of the Low Countries and their relation to the Hallstatt Culture of Central Europe (forthcoming).

Van der Vaart 2011: S. van der Vaart, Hail to the chieftain. A detailed examination of grave goods from Dutch chiefly burials and their role in funerary rituals during the Hallstatt period. Unpublished Master Thesis (Leiden 2011).

Van Heeringen 1998: R. Van Heeringen, Burial with Rhine view: the Hallstatt situla grave on the Koerheuvel at Rhenen. Berichten van de Rijksdienst voor het Oudheidkundig Bodemonderzoek 43, 1998, 69-92.

Verhart/Spies 1993: L. Verhart/P. Spies, De prehistorie van Nederland (Amsterdam 1993).

Verwers 1968: G. Verwers, Het vorstengraf van Meerlo (Maastricht 1968).

Verwers 1972: G. Verwers, Das Kamps Veld in Haps in Neolithicum, Bronzezeit und Eisenzeit. Analecta Praehistorica Leidensia V, 1972, 1-176.

Willems/Groenman-van Waateringe 1988: W. Willems/W. Groenman-van Waateringe, Een rijk graf uit de Vroege Ijzertijd te Horst-Hegelsom. In: P. Geurts/T. van Rensch/J. Schatorjé/G. Verheijen (eds.), Horster historiën 2: Van heren en gemeentenaren (Horst 1988) 13-29.

Willms 2002: C. Willms, Der Keltenfürst aus Frankfurt. Macht und Totenkult um 700 v. Chr. Frankfurt am Main. Archäologische Reihe 19 (Frankfurt am Main 2002).

Authors

Quentin P.J. Bourgeois
Faculty of Archaeology
Leiden University
Einsteinweg 2
P.O. Box 9515
2300 RA Leiden
The Netherlands
q.p.j.bourgeois@arch.leidenuniv.nl

Sasja van der Vaart-Verschoof
Faculty of Archaeology
Leiden University
Einsteinweg 2
P.O. Box 9515
2300 RA Leiden
The Netherlands
s.a.van.der.vaart@arch.leidenuniv.nl

New research on sword graves of the Hallstatt C period in Hesse

Sword graves of phase Ha C in Hesse are common finds and have been studied extensively. Most of the grave finds were excavated with outdated methods and were not or insufficiently documented. As a result the composition and exact location of the finds is often unclear. Furthermore, many objects were destroyed in the Second World War in the Museums of Hanau, Frankfurt, Darmstadt and Gießen and are no longer available for re-examination. Studies concerning the chronology of Early Iron Age in Hesse have had to stay quite rough due to the lack of trustworthy ensembles. Two new features from Nidderau provide a rare opportunity to examine sword graves of phase Ha C in detail and to consider new aspects of chronology and distribution of the finds.

Résumé

Les tombes avec des épées de la période Ha C en Hesse sont très fréquentes et ont déjà souvent été discutées. La plupart du matériel cependant ont été trouvés lors de fouilles anciennes dont on n'a pas exactement ou pas du tout documenté les résultats. C'est pourquoi on ne connaît ni la composition ni la position des objets funéraires. En plus, maints objets des musées de Hanau, Francfort, Darmstadt et Gießen ont été détruits pendant la Seconde Guerre mondiale et par conséquent une nouvelle étude n'est plus réalisable. De même, les recherches chronologiques de la période du Hallstatt en Hesse sont restées assez sommaires, faute de découvertes suffisantes et homogènes. Ces deux nouveaux faits de Nidderau présentent une rare occasion d'examiner en détail les tombes à épée du Ha C et d'envisager de nouveaux aspects à propos de la chronologie et la répartition du matériel trouvé.

Introduction

The sword graves of the early Hallstatt period in Hesse are located on the northern border of the core area of the western Hallstatt culture. There we have a dense concentration of such graves in a relatively small region, which extends from Darmstadt in the South and Muschenheim in the North. Swords are equally common in urn graves and in inhumations. Gerdsen listed 35 sites with over 60 swords in total (Gerdsen 1986, 21-22). Since then some new finds were made in this region, for example an inhumation from Frankfurt-Harheim which contains an iron sword (Flügen/Willms 2009, 63-66), or a bronze sword from Langenselbold (Bergmann 2011, 78-80). The number of iron swords found is ten times higher than the number of bronze swords. Usually the swords are covered with several layers of textile, among which in some cases may be a sheath made of wood (Trachsel 2005, 70-71). Recently examined swords had no wooden remains under the textile layer (Flügen/Willms 2009; Martins/Willms 2005; Riedel 2012). In inhumations the swords were placed on the right side of the dead with the point near the head, as is common in the region east of the river Rhine. In cremations the swords always are located in or near the remains or the urn (Gerdsen 1986, 23).

The main part of the grave goods consists of pottery, but there are also quite a few finds of metal objects in the swords burials. The average number of vessels is between four and 14 (Reinhard 2003, 43 fig. 24), consisting of bigger or smaller vessels, bowls and small pots with a pointed bottom. These cone cups are characteristic of the southern part of Hesse, where the local culture group is called *Koberstadter Kultur* (Schumacher 1974, 106-107). Arm rings of very different types were worn on the left wrist, as far as we can deduce from the circumstances of the finds. Sometimes pins of different types were found in the Hessian sword graves. They are relatively rare west of the Rhine, but very common in the sword graves of Bavaria (Reinhard 2003, 43 fig. 24). Knives are frequently present in connection with the pottery and probably indicate the existence of meat offerings (Gerdsen 1986, 20-24).

Toilet utensil sets made of iron or bronze often are found on or near the chest. They are composed of tweezers, nail cleaners, ear scoops and simple sticks. In parts of Bavaria the presence of two toilet sets in one grave is said to be characteristic for the Ha C period (Torbrügge 1979, 192), and this was observed in some Hessian graves as well. Razors are common in western sword graves, while in the eastern ones tweezers are predominant. Southern Hesse and Baden-Württemberg form a zone of transition between these two grave goods practices (Reinhard 2003, 41-45).

Parts of horse-gear or wagons are very rare and were found only in two burials in Hesse (Gerdsen 1986, 23). Swords are the only weapons found in this area.

The main part of the published material comes from old excavations of burial mounds. Therefore, the composition and arrangement of the finds, as well as the context of their discovery, is often unknown. The circumstances of the finds of Hallstatt graves in southern Hesse in general are poorly known and insufficiently studied and published (Torbrügge 1991, 402). This is why the results of modern excavations are so important, as for example the cemetery of Nidderau. The town is situated in the north-east of the Rhine-Main-area in the Main-Kinzig-Kreis (Hesse) and was already known for excavations of several Ha C burial mounds in the districts of Eichen and Windecken in the late 19th and early 20th century (Wolfram 1994a; 1994b). At least ten Hallstatt swords made of iron were found there.

The new cemetery was found approximately 4 km from the old mounds during the construction of a residential area and its affiliated road, and it was excavated from 2008 to 2011 (Hassler/Lasch 2009; Piffko 2011). Most of the approximately 115 graves date to the Ha C and Ha D periods, but there are also late Neolithic and La Tène period burials. In the following two graves with swords from Nidderau (Features 28 and 197), which were excavated and documented very well, will be presented. These graves show no traces of burial mounds, stone constructions or wooden chambers as some of the other burials, but only simple grave pits (250 x 170 and 300 x 205 cm). The lack of burial mounds in the northern part of the necropolis could be explained by the intensive agriculture. The anthropological determination of the skeletons from Nidderau is for the most part not possible due to the bad conservation of the bones, which is a general problem in this region.

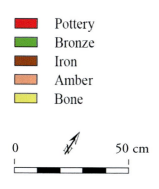

Pottery
Bronze
Iron
Amber
Bone

0   50 cm

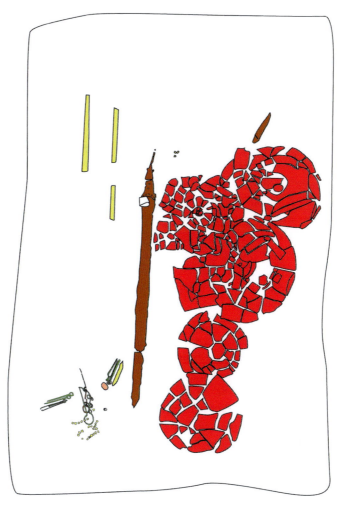

Fig. 1. Excavation plan of sword grave 1 (feature 28).

Fig. 2. The second toilet utensil set from grave 1 (feature 28) (photo W. Ney).

Sword Grave 1 (Feature 28)

This grave (Fig. 1) contained an iron sword of type Mindelheim, which was found on the right side of the dead with the point near the head (direction south). With a length of 119.5 cm it is one of the longest Mindelheim swords ever found. The handle shows traces of wood and at least ten rivets. Most of them are small round bronze platelets or false rivets, which are only for decoration. A small whetstone was placed on the handle. On the 97 cm long blade there were three oblique wrapped layers of varying woven textiles (wool). There were no traces of a wooden or metal sheath.

On each side of the chest there was a toilet utensil set made of bronze. Around them were dark organic traces, which indicate they were in leather or textile bags. One set consists of tweezers with two vertical grooves, two sticks with eyelet heads and twisted shaft and one stick with rolled up head and twisted shaft. The latter was used as a nail cleaner due to its slotted end, one of the others probably as an ear scoop, but the bottom end was not preserved complete. The second toilet utensil set (Fig. 2) was in very good condition. It consists of tweezers, nail cleaner, ear scoop and a stick made of organic material. It imitates the first set and traces of metal working (hammer, file, chisel) suggest that it was never used, but made especially for the burial (Riedel 2012, 177). Near both sets were tapered round iron bolts, and in one case a fragment of a bronze ring, which kept the pieces together. Two additional iron rings (diam. 1.2 and 1.8 cm) with tapered bolt were found close to one of the toilet utensil sets. At the upper end of one set there was a big ovoid amber bead (3 x 4 cm) with perforation. It might have been worn around the neck with an organic string, closing the bag that was containing the toilet utensils.

Below the jaw there were two objects made of metal which were covered in textile. One iron pin with a figure eight-shaped head and a remarkable bronze fibula (length 9.5 cm) whose arch consists of four loops in form of an eight. On the right side of the deceased were three big vessels, two bowls, two small cups with pointed bottom and an iron knife with a curved blade.

Sword grave 2 (Feature 197)

This grave (Fig. 3) contained a long iron sword (Fig. 4) of 112.5 cm, also type Mindelheim (Lasch 2012). The orientation of the skeleton and the sword is identical with sword grave 1. The handle shows traces of animal bone fixed with four iron rivets. The blade was wrapped in three layers of textile made of plant fiber, one fine and one coarse variant.

What is remarkable is the presence of an iron antenna dagger or knife (Fig. 5; length 42 cm) with one cutting edge, whose hollow ends are made of two compound hemispheres (Lasch 2011, 77 fig. 5). It belongs to the group of iron antenna weapons with multipart handles (Sievers 1982, 18-21), dated end of the Ha C period and the transition to Ha D. To this group also belongs a similar dagger from grave 755 from the Hallstatt necropolis, which also has only one cutting edge (Kromer 1959, pl. 140,2). The combination of Hallstatt swords and antenna weapons has never been found before in Germany, and only rarely in Western Europe (Gerdsen 1986, 54; 94. Belgium: Court-Saint-Etienne La Ferme Rouge, Tombelle 3 (short antenna sword; see contributions of De Mulder and Warmenbol in this volume); Austria: Hallstatt, grave 789 (antenna dagger);

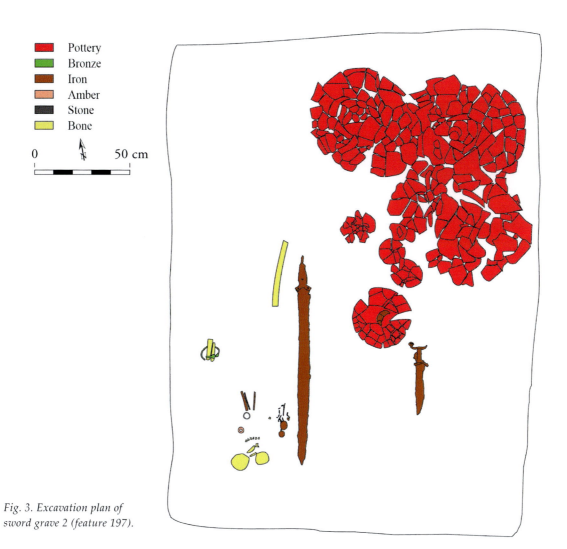

Pottery
Bronze
Iron
Amber
Stone
Bone

0   50 cm

Fig. 3. Excavation plan of
sword grave 2 (feature 197).

Fig. 4 Iron sword from grave 2
(Feature 197) after restoration
(photo M. Stotz).

Fig. 5. Antenna knife from
grave 2 (feature 197) after
restoration (after Lasch 2011,
77 fig. 5).

France: Concoeur-et-Corboin, mound Olivier II, central grave (antenna dagger)).
It is possible, that the antenna knife was used for cutting meat or as a hunting
knife and not as a ceremonial or representative weapon. It was placed parallel to
the sword at approximately 50 cm. Between those two items there was a bowl with
an crescent-shaped razor made of iron. On the chest of the deceased there was a
three-pieced toilet utensil set made of iron, including tweezers and two sticks with
enrolled head and a broken bottom end. Similarly to the first sword grave, amber
was in direct connection with the set (Hassler 2010). In front of the set lay two
small rings, one made of amber, the other made of stone, which were probably
worn with an organic string around the neck together with the toilet utensils.
Those amber rings were sometimes used as fastening for toilet utensil sets (for
example Gorszewice grave 2: Gedl 1988, 91; Stahl 2006, 348 fig. 15b). Such a use
is also possible for the rings of the grave from Nidderau.

Four poorly preserved iron pins were found near the right shoulder of the
skeleton, with a bent quadrangular shaft, which was fixed in the pins head. X-rays
showed that the head consists of two hemispheres, which were soldered together.
These pins are sometimes called *Kugelkopfnadeln* (Gerdsen 1986, 59-60; Reinhard
2003; 2004, 40-41), sometimes *Zweischalennadeln* (Baitinger 1999, 31; Schmidt
2013, 71). They were found in graves in Saarland, Hunsrück and Bavaria (Nakoinz
2005, 139). In the necropolis of Rubenheim seven of those pins were found, some
of them in Ha C sword graves (Reinhard 2003, 349-371; 2004, 32; 40-41). They
also originate from the necropolis of Impfingen, Tauberbischofsheim-Dittigheim
or Großeibstadt in Bavaria, where pins with straight and with bent shafts were
found (Nakoinz 2005, 139). In the Netherlands we have the three iron examples
with bronze heads from the princely tumulus of Oss (Mound from 1933; Fokkens/
Jansen 2004, 60; 65; see also Jansen/Van der Vaart-Verschoof in this volume) and
in Saint-Vincent in Belgium we have two pins made of iron (Mariën 1964, 152).
In inhumations one pin usually was placed on the shoulder or the chest, on the
other hand four pins in the Nidderau sword grave 2 were found. In Bavaria they
were found mostly in women's graves, where they were placed on both shoulders
or on the chest (Wamser 1981, 233; 241; Baitinger 1999, 31). In Großeibstadt
grave 1 five "biconical iron buttons with bent shafts" were found on the hip
and near the knee. Their interpretation is not really clear, Kossack suggested a
link with the sword point, were they were placed, as it was the case in Nidderau
too (Kossack 1970, 47; 55 pl. 32,124). Maybe these buttons are also strongly
corroded iron pins of the type described above.

The last object of sword grave 2 that should be noted is an open arm ring
made of bronze on the left wrist (Lasch 2011, 76 fig. 4). It has an oval pointed
cross section with lengthwise grooves and hemispherical ends. Such a ring was
also found on the left wrist of a swordsman from a grave in the necropolis of
Rubenheim (Reinhard 2003, 346-348). The practice of wearing one single ring
on the left wrist was often observed in men's graves, so one can assume that this
was a traditional costume for men (Polenz 1973, 129; Reinhard 2003, 37). With
eleven vessels, the pottery set in sword grave 2 was the largest in the necropolis
of Nidderau. It includes three large vessels, two smaller pots, four bowls and two
small cups with a pointed bottom.

Summary and outlook

These two sword graves are part of the relatively large Hallstatt and Early La Tène cemetery of Nidderau, which the author is currently analyzing as part his PhD thesis. Due to the long use of the cemetery, it should be possible to increase our knowledge of chronology and chorology of Iron Age material in Hesse and the surrounding regions. Especially the chronology of Ha C and Ha D is not as well developed as in southern Germany. Particularly sword grave two is interesting because it contained one of the rare late Ha C antenna weapons together with a Mindelheim sword. The good conservation of textile on some iron objects in both sword graves also allows further research on weaving technology and its utilization in the funerary context. But also some new simple conclusions can be made, for example the link between toilet utensils and amber beads or rings, which seems to be confirmed in more and more graves. In the end the final analysis should help us to study transitions, transformations and continuities between the Early Iron Age phases on the northern border of the western Hallstatt culture.

Bibliography

Baitinger 1999: H. Baitinger, Die Hallstattzeit im Nordosten Baden-Württembergs. Materialhefte zur Archäologie Baden-Württembergs 46 (Stuttgart 1999).

Bergmann 2011: C. Bergmann, Schwertträger – Untersuchung eines Grabhügels der frühen Eisenzeit in Langenselbold. HessenArchäologie 2011, 78-80.

Burmeister 2000: S. Burmeister, Geschlecht, Alter und Herrschaft in der Späthallstattzeit Württembergs. Tübinger Schriften zur ur- und frühgeschichtlichen Archäologie 4 (Münster 2000).

Flügen/Willms 2009: T. Flügen/C. Willms, Ein Schwertgrab der Hallstattzeit aus Frankfurt a. M.-Harheim. HessenArchäologie 2009, 63-66.

Fokkens/Jansen 2004: H. Fokkens/R. Jansen, Het vorstengraf van Oss. Een archeologische speurtocht naar een prehistorisch grafveld (Utrecht 2004).

Gedl 1988: M. Gedl, Die Toilettegeräte in Polen. Prähistorische Bronzefunde XV,1 (München 1988).

Gerdsen 1986: H. Gerdsen, Studien zu den Schwertgräbern der älteren Hallstattzeit (Mainz 1986).

Hassler 2010: D. Hassler, Interessante Neufunde aus dem hallstattzeitlichen Gräberfeld in Nidderau-Windecken. HessenArchäologie 2010, 46-49.

Hassler 2012: D. Hassler, Der hallstattzeitliche Bernsteinschmuck aus dem Gräberfeld Nidderau-Windecken „Allee Süd IV" (Main-Kinzig-Kreis). In: B. Ramminger,/H. Lasch (eds.), Hunde – Menschen – Artefakte. Gedenkschrift für Gretel Gallay. Internationale Archäologie, Studia honoraria 32 = Schriften des Vereins für Vor- und Frühgeschichte im unteren Niddertal 2 (Rahden/Westf. 2012) 147-170.

Hassler/Lasch 2009: D. Hassler/H. Lasch, „Elite und gemeines Volk" – Ein hallstattzeitliches Gräberfeld im Neubaugebiet „Allee Süd IV" von Nidderau. HessenArchäologie 2009, 59-63.

Kossack 1970: G. Kossack, Gräberfelder der Hallstattzeit an Main und fränkischer Saale. Materialhefte zur bayerischen Vorgeschichte 24 (Kallmünz/Opf. 1970).

Kromer 1959: K. Kromer, Das Gräberfeld von Hallstatt (Firenze 1959).

Lasch 2011: H. Lasch, Außergewöhnliche Beigaben eines zweiten Schwertträgers in Nidderau-Windecken. HessenArchäologie 2011, 74-77.

Mariën 1964: M.-E. Mariën, La nécropole à tombelles de Saint-Vincent. Monographies d'Archéologie Nationale 3 (Bruxelles 1964).

Martins/Willms 2005: S. Martins/C. Willms, Unter die Lupe genommen: ein Eisenschwert der Hallstattzeit aus Frankfurt a. M. HessenArchäologie 2005, 42-44.

Nakoinz 2005: O. Nakoinz, Studien zur räumlichen Abgrenzung und Strukturierung der älteren Hunsrück-Eifel-Kultur. Universitätsforschungen zur prähistorischen Archäologie 118 (Bonn 2005).

Piffko, 2011: S. Piffko, Einblick in ein ausgedehntes Gräberfeld der Eisenzeit in Nidderau-Heldenbergen. HessenArchäologie 2011, 71-74.

Polenz 1973: H. Polenz, Zu den Grabfunden der Späthallstattzeit im Rhein-Main-Gebiet. Berichte der Römisch-Germanischen Kommission 54, 1973, 107-202.

Reinhard 2003: W. Reinhard, Studien zur Hallstatt- und Frühlatènezeit im südöstlichen Saarland. Blesa 4 (Bliesbruck-Reinheim 2003).

Reinhard 2004: W. Reinhard, Die keltische Fürstin von Reinheim (Blieskastel 2004).

Riedel 2012: C. Riedel, Ein Schwertträger aus Nidderau-Windecken, Neubaugebiet „Allee Süd IV" – Bericht der Fundrestaurierung eines hallstattzeitlichen Grabinventars. In: B. Ramminger/H. Lasch (eds.), Hunde – Menschen – Artefakte. Gedenkschrift für Gretel Gallay. Internationale Archäologie, Studia honoraria 32 = Schriften des Vereins für Vor- und Frühgeschichte im unteren Niddertal 2 (Rahden/Westf. 2012) 171-180.

Schmidt 2013: M. Schmidt, Nadeln als Kopfschmuck in der Späthallstattzeit. Universitätsforschungen zur prähistorischen Archäologie 242 (Bonn 2013).

Schumacher 1974: A. Schumacher, Die Hallstattzeit im südlichen Hessen. Bonner Hefte zur Vorgeschichte 5-6 (Bonn 1974).

Sievers 1982: S. Sievers, Die mitteleuropäischen Hallstattdolche. Prähistorische Bronzefunde VI,6 (München 1982).

Stahl 2006: C. Stahl, Mitteleuropäische Bernsteinfunde von der Frühbronze- bis Frühlatènezeit: Ihre Verbreitung, Formgebung, Zeitstellung und Herkunft. Würzburger Studien zur Sprache und Kultur 9 (Dettelbach 2006).

Trachsel 2005: M. Trachsel, Kriegergräber? Schwertbeigabe und Praktiken ritueller Bannung in Gräbern der frühen Eisenzeit. In: R. Karl/J. Leskovar (eds.), Interpretierte Eisenzeiten. Fallstudien, Methoden, Theorie. Tagungsbeiträge der 1. Linzer Gespräche zur interpretativen Eisenzeitarchäologie. Studien zur Kulturgeschichte von Oberösterreich 18 (Linz 2005) 53-82.

Torbrügge 1979: W. Torbrügge, Die Hallstattzeit in der Oberpfalz. Materialhefte zur bayerischen Vorgeschichte Reihe A39 (Kallmünz/Opf 1979).

Torbrügge 1991: W. Torbrügge, Die frühe Hallstattzeit (Ha C) in chronologischen Ansichten und notwendige Randbemerkungen 1. Bayern und der „westliche Hallstattkreis". Jahrbuch des Römisch-Germanischen Zentralmuseums 38, 1991 (1995) 223-463.

Wamser 1981: L. Wamser, Wagengräber der Hallstattzeit in Franken. Frankenland, Zeitschrift für Fränkische Landeskunde und Kulturpflege NF 33, 1981, 225-261.

Wolfram, 1994a: S. Wolfram, Nidderau-Eichen. Grabhügel im Eichener Gemeindewald. In: S. Wolfram/P. Jüngling/O.-H. Schmitt (eds.), Hanau und der Main-Kinzig-Kreis. Führer zu archäologischen Denkmälern in Deutschland 27 (Stuttgart 1994) 219-221.

Wolfram 1994b: S. Wolfram, Nidderau-Ostheim. Grabhügelfelder im Windecker Gemeindewald. In: S. Wolfram/P. Jüngling/O.-H. Schmitt (eds.): Hanau und der Main-Kinzig-Kreis. Führer zu archäologischen Denkmälern in Deutschland 27 (Stuttgart 1994) 226-229.

Author
Wolfram Ney
Johannes Gutenberg-Universität Mainz
Institut für Altertumswissenschaften
Arbeitsbereich vor- und frühgeschichtliche Archäologie
Schillerstraße 11
55116 Mainz
Germany
wolney@students.uni-mainz.de

The early Hallstatt elite burials in Belgium

An analysis of the funerary ritual

Guy De Mulder

Abstract

The earliest Belgian elite Hallstatt burials were already discovered in the late 18th century. Most of them were excavated in the late 19th – early 20th centuries. Although these burials are known all over Belgium, the Dyle and Haine valleys stand out with a clear concentration of this specific burial rite. Within the ritual there is a certain variability. Cremation is dominant, but there are different ways to deposit the cremated bone. Most numerous is the habit of erecting a barrow directly on top of the pyre. Flatgraves are less prominent among the Hallstatt elite burials, but they are well present in the contemporary Early Iron Age urnfields. Another tendency are the larger dimensions of elite barrows in comparison with contemporary ring ditches. 21 weapon graves are recorded in Belgium which contain a bronze or iron sword. These can be accompanied by other prestige items such as razors, horse-gear etc. A few rich graves without a sword are also ascertained. The location of elite burials in the funerary landscape can be very different. At Hofstade and Neerharen-Rekem a single weapon grave was found within a larger cremation cemetery. By contrast, at Court-Saint-Etienne, Harchies and Gedinne these rich graves are concentrated in small groups. Within the group of Belgian elite Hallstatt burials different influences are discernible. Some graves show elite burial sets which have clearly Atlantic origins and represent the beginning of this tradition. On other sites Central European contacts and influence are also present.

Zusammenfassung

Die frühesten Entdeckungen hallstattzeitlicher Elitegräber in Belgien reichen bis in das späte 18. Jahrhundert zurück, der größte Teil wurde im späten 19. und frühen 20. Jahrhundert ausgegraben. Auch wenn entsprechende Bestattungen aus ganz Belgien bekannt sind, zeigen sich in den Tälern von Dyle und Haine klare Konzentrationen. Die Kremation überwiegt in diesen Bestattungen, aber es gibt unterschiedliche Arten, den Leichenbrand niederzulegen. Am häufigsten ist dabei die Sitte, einen Grabhügel direkt über dem Scheiterhaufen zu errichten. Flachgräber sind unter den ältereisenzeitlichen Elitegräbern deutlich seltener, in den zeitgleichen Urnenfeldern aber gut belegt. Eine weitere Tendenz zeichnet sich in den Dimensionen der Grabhügel entsprechender Gräber ab, die im Vergleich zu zeitgleichen Kreisgräben herausstechen. Insgesamt sind aus Belgien 21 Waffengräber bekannt, in denen bronzene oder eiserne Schwerter gefunden wurden. Diese können durch andere Prestigegüter wie Rasiermesser, Pferdegeschirr und anderes ergänzt werden. Einige wenige reich ausgestattete Gräber ohne Schwerter sind ebenso belegt. Die Lage der Elitegräber in der Funerärlandschaft kann sehr unterschiedlich sein. In Hofstade und Neerharen-Rekem wurde ein einzelnes Waffengrab in einem größeren Urnenfeld entdeckt. Im Gegensatz dazu konzentrieren sich diese Gräber in Court-Saint-Etienne, Harchies und Gedinne in kleinen Gruppen. In den hallstättischen Elitegräbern aus Belgien zeigen sich verschiedene Einflüsse. Einige Bestattungen weisen Beigabensets auf, die klare atlantische Bezüge zeigen. Diese Bestattungen repräsentieren den Beginn dieser Tradition. In anderen Fundstellen wiederum zeigen sich ebenso mitteleuropäische Einflüsse und Kontakte.

Introduction

Research of early Hallstatt elite burials started in Belgium in the late 18th century with the first discoveries at Court-Saint-Etienne. The late 19th and early 20th centuries saw a series of excavations in the southern part of Belgium. The presence of visible burial mounds in the landscape attracted the archaeological interest of different researchers. In the 1950s M.-E. Mariën again focused archaeological attention on these sites through his study of the excavated objects of these cemeteries which had been deposited and preserved in the Royal Museum for Art and History in Brussels (Mariën 1958). In the following decades new information on this type of burial has only been discovered in two new sites: Neerharen-Rekem and Hofstade, the last mentioned cemetery is currently under excavation and study. Field prospection suggests that a new cemetery with elite burials has been found at Marche-en-Famenne, but there has been no excavation to test this (Lecarme/Warmenbol 2015). New prospection techniques, such as Lidar, have shown that there is still an archaeological potential to develop new excavations on this type of cemeteries.

Overview of the sites

The bases of this overview are the sites which have been excavated before (Fig. 1). The potential site of Marche-en-Famenne is not integrated in this study but is discussed in this volume by E. Warmenbol.

Hofstade/Kasteelstraat (East-Flanders)(1)

This site has only recently been discovered during trial trenching and is being excavated (2016) (Beke *et al.* 2016). One of the cremation graves, discovered during the trial trenching, was an urn grave which contained broken and bent

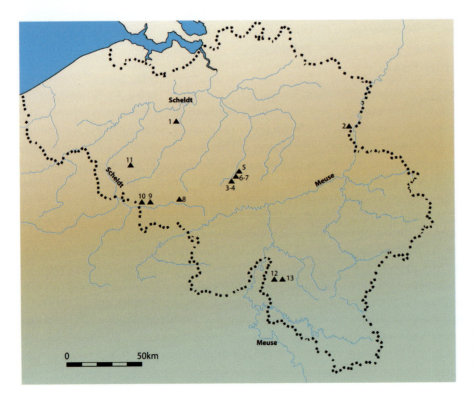

Fig. 1. Overview of the early Hallstatt elite burials in Belgium (drawing J. Angenon, UGent).

fragments from a bronze sword and a chape (Fig. 2). Based on the present available information this elite burial can be considered a flat grave since there are no indications for the presence of a burial mound on top of the cremation deposit (De Mulder/Laloo 2016).

Neerharen-Rekem/Hangveld (Limbourg)(2)

The urnfield cemetery of Neerharen-Rekem was known already in the late 19th century. It was excavated between 1978 and 1986 by the Belgian archaeological service (*Nationale Dienst voor Opgravingen*) and yielded a total of 236 cremations (De Boe *et al.* 1992; Temmerman 2007). One cremation grave stood out. In burial 72 the remains of three persons were deposited together with three bronze swords, three bronze spearheads and two chapes (De Boe *et al.* 1992; Warmenbol 1988; 2009).

Court-Saint-Etienne/La Quenique-Ferme Rouge (Brabant Wallon)(3)

The archaeological research from the site covers a long period from the late 18th century until 1914. A uniform reconstruction of the funerary occupation on the plateau is difficult due to the different excavators and the differences in the archaeological quality of the registration and documentation. From these sources it is at least possible to deduce that both barrows and flat graves were present in different areas of the site. In the late 19th century a series of flat graves were destroyed in a pine forest (Cloquet 1882). Other flat graves were ascertained at the area of Bettrémont and La Quenique. Preserved urns of these areas in the Royal Museum for Art and History prove that these mostly belong to the Late Bronze Age (De Loë 1913; Goblet d'Alviella 1908). Information on the Early Iron Age burials is available for the five barrows at La Ferme Rouge and some barrows at La Quenique. Unfortunately, reliable dates for La Quenique are limited to some barrows while according to the sources a few dozen of these monuments seem to have been destroyed during this period. The known Early Iron Age burials are concentrated on the southern border of the plateau which descends abruptly to the Orne brook (Guillaume 2003; Mariën 1958).

Court-Saint-Etienne/La Plantée des Dames (Brabant Wallon)(4)

This site is located on the border with the neighboring community of Bousval in a forest. The barrows were constructed on a plateau between the rivers Dyle and Thyle. Four barrows, grouped together produced evidence of burials. Ten other barrows were dispersed on the plateau. They covered layers of charcoal but no funerary goods were found. So their interpretation as funerary monuments is dubious, as well as an attribution to the Early Iron Age (Dens 1903; Mariën 1958).

Wavre/Bruyère-Saint-Job (Brabant Wallon)(5)

In 1882 and 1883 different persons excavated a series of barrows. They were located on the southern slope of a plateau. Two of these could be attributed to the Early Iron Age (Comhaire 1894/95; Mariën 1958).

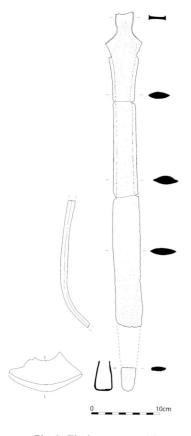

Fig. 2. The bronze sword (type Villement or Wehringen) and chape of Hofstade (drawing J. Angenon, UGent).

Limal/Morimoine (Brabant Wallon)(6)

In 1902 a series of barrows was excavated by C. Dens (Dens 1903). Only two of the four excavated monuments could be attributed to the Early Iron Age (Mariën 1958).

Limal/Stoquoy (Brabant Wallon)(7)

At another site in the village five barrows had been erected along the southern site of a steep plateau orientated towards the river Dyle. They were also excavated in 1902 by C. Dens (1903). One monument could be dated to the Early Iron Age (Mariën 1958).

Harchies/Maison Cauchies (Hainault)(8)

The finds from this site were unearthed between 1913 and 1955. The graves were discovered in the Rue Calvaire in the center of the village. Only two small excavations were undertaken in 1913 and 1955 by the Royal Museum for Art and History. Four graves have come to light. They are supposedly flat graves although M.-E. Mariën did not exclude the hypothesis of barrows assuming that these had disappeared due to the building activity in the village centre (Mariën 1975). Recent prospection with a metal detector has shown that there is still a potential for archaeological research on the site (Leblois 2010).

Havré/ Bois de la Taille des Vignes (Hainault)(9)

This cemetery was discovered in 1930 during the extension of a stone quarry and four barrows were recorded. The next year a limited excavation campaign was conducted by the Royal Museum for Art and History during which 17 more barrows were excavated. The barrows were implanted on the southern slope of a plateau oriented towards the river Haine (Mariën 1999).

Bernissart (Hainault)(10)

An isolated grave was found at the site during road works in 1851 (Toilliez 1857). Only the razor has been preserved. The ceramic finds are now lost.

Flobecq/Pottelberg (Hainault)(11)

A few barrows were excavated in 1837 at this site. Afterwards a local found different fragments of an Early Iron Age bronze sword in the spoil heaps of the excavation by (Joly De Laet 1982; Delvaux 1888/89). Unfortunately, no fragments are preserved in a known archaeological collection, so the attribution to an Early Iron Age burial cannot be proven.

Louette-Saint-Pierre/La fosse aux Morts (Namur)(12)

The site was excavated in 1865-66. 17 barrows were discovered. The exact location of the barrows is unknown, but they seem to have been erected on the southern slope close to a small river. Not all the graves seem to have an elite status (Dujardin/Gravet 1865/66; Warmenbol 1993).

Gedinne/Chevaudos (Namur)(13)

This burial place was excavated in the same years (1865-66) as the neighboring Louette-Saint-Pierre, which is located 1 km further. The barrows were constructed close to the top of the plateau. Twenty graves were excavated in this first phase (Dujardin/Gravet 1865/66). A new campaign in 1881 delivered evidence of 24 more barrows (De Radiguès 1881; Guillaume 2003; Warmenbol 1993).

Burial rites

Burial rites can be a complex and elaborated phenomenon. Unfortunately, from an archaeological point of view we can only capture a glimpse of this ritual through the potential preservation of the pyre, the deposition of the deceased's remains and funerary goods. After the cremation different options are possible through which to bury the remains of the deceased. Two main choices can be made: the remains are buried together with the pyre or the cremated bones are collected and buried at another location. Even during the collection of the cremains different choices can be made. In a lot of cases not all the bones, sometimes only some token fragments, were collected and deposited in the grave. Based on these actions a typology for the deposition of the cremated bones has been constructed which reflects the manipulation of the deceased's remains after the cremation and the manner in which they were deposited. (De Laet *et al.* 1986; De Mulder 2011).

Burial mounds and flat graves

Early Iron Age elite burials in Europe are traditionally covered by a burial mound. Nevertheless, in Belgium some of these burials seem rather to be so-called flat graves. The four cremation graves from Harchies and both weapon burials at Hofstade and Neerharen-Rekem can be catalogued in this group. There is no information available for the old find from Bernissart but an allocation to the group of flat graves cannot be excluded. It is important to take into account that these graves could have been covered by a monument which has left no archaeological traces in the subsoil. Although the recently excavated burials from Neerharen-Rekem and Hofstade have not delivered any indication for the presence of a burial mound according to the observation of the subsoil.

The majority of the elite burials are covered by a mound. The dimensions of these mounds are variable. Due to the early excavations of the monuments in the 19th and early 20th centuries we are missing a lot of information about the possible surrounding structures of the monuments. Excavation was focused on the center of the burial mound. There are no indications of peripheral structures such as ring ditches around these monuments. However, the excavation of the Late Bronze Age – Early Iron Age cemetery of Saint-Vincent in the 1950s showed that no peripheral structures were present around the burial mounds at this site (Guillaume 2003). At Louette-Saint-Pierre (barrow 2) and Gedinne (barrow 14) two mounds were probably surrounded by a stone circle according to the description by the excavator (De Radiguès 1881).

Concerning the size of these monuments we are relatively well informed about the cemeteries in the Dyle valley (Court-Saint-Etienne, Limal, Wavre) and some information for Louette-Saint-Pierre and Gedinne. For the other sites this information is less well documented. The majority of these barrows belong to the group between 10 and 20 m in diameter (Fig. 3). There are 20 examples known. Two monuments in the Dyle valley have a smaller dimension and measure respectively 8 and 9 m in diameter. One small barrow at the cemetery of Louette-Saint-Pierre measured only 2 m, although there is no indication that this could be an elite burial. Three barrows at Gedinne are also quite small and measure between 1.4 and 3 m in diameter (De Radiguès 1881). Five monuments are larger and measure between 20 to 25 m in diameter (De Mulder 2011). There is no information available for each separate burial mound at Louette-Saint-Pierre. Only four barrows were well documented concerning their dimension, one of them was a very small one (see above), but for the other monuments their size is estimated to vary between 7 and 18 m in diameter (Warmenbol 1993). The size of these monuments is larger than the contemporary ring ditches in the Early Iron Age urnfields of northern Belgium. Their dimensions are mostly less than 10 m in diameter (De Laet 1982; De Mulder 2011).

It is important to mention one enigmatic structure in this chapter. At Edegem/ Buizegem in northern Belgium two thirds of a circular structure were excavated (Fig. 4). The total dimension of the ditch was calculated at 53-54 m. In the center of this structure a Final-Neolithic ring ditch surrounded by postholes was located. The large ditch contained some ceramics that could be dated to the Iron Age. Due to erosion and bioturbation no indication of a central grave was ascertained. The layout of this monument and also its dimensions are exactly the same as the princely grave of Oss-Vorstengraf in the Netherlands (Fokkens/Jansen 2004). Due to the resemblance with the burial monument at Oss a hypothesis as a potential high status funerary monument was formulated, although there is no proof of a central burial (Vandevelde *et al.* 2008).

Cremation grave types

Among the early Hallstatt elite burial cemeteries different types of deposition of the cremated bones are ascertained (Fig. 5). Especially for the older excavations it is not always possible to determine the exact way of deposition due to a lack of attention to recording this in the late 19th and early 20th centuries. According to the descriptions by the excavators at five sites the burial mound covered the remains of the pyre. These are the cemeteries of Court-Saint-Etienne/La Ferme Rouge-Le Quenique, Gedinne/Chevaudos, Havré, Limal/Morimoine and Louette-Saint-Pierre. They describe in their reports layers of ashes and charcoal which they interpret as being the remnants of pyres. These layers can be 5 to 10 cm thick. Their size is sometimes more than 2 m wide (De Radiguès 1881). This specific ritual appears in the study region during the beginning of the Early Iron Age. It is necessary to be careful with this interpretation because until now no new excavations on this type of deposition have been conducted, which would confirm the old descriptions.

Two different treatments of the cremated bones are assessed. The bones were collected from the pyre, put into an urn which was then buried in the pyre (type H). In the other case (type I) there has been no selection of cremated bone at all and the pyre and associated grave goods were simply buried under the mound (Fig. 6) (De Mulder 2011). According to the descriptions of Gedinne and Louette-Saint-Pierre all the burials in both cemeteries can be attributed to both types of deposition (H and I) (Dujardin/Gravet 1865/66; De Radiguès 1881). In Gedinne

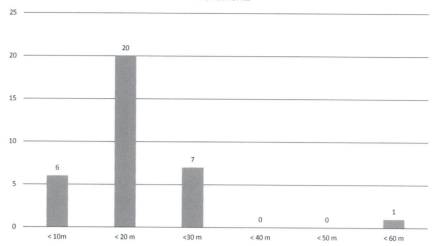

Fig. 3. The dimensions of the elite burials.

Fig. 4. The circular structure at Edegem-Buizegem plotted on an aerial photograph (photo Dienst Erfgoed, provincie Antwerpen).

there seems to be an exception and one grave could potentially be interpreted as an urn grave (type A) if we interpret the text correct (De Radiguès 1881). But it is not always possible to determine exactly which way of deposition was chosen due to erosion and/or disturbances of the burial mounds and negligent recording of the excavations. At Court-Saint-Etienne five cremation burials were attributed to the type H with selection of the cremated bone while two others are according to the description belonging to the type I (Mariën 1958). Both cremation graves at Limal/Morimoine seem to be the type I (Mariën 1958). The cemetery of Havré contains a lot of variety in depositing the cremated remains but two types H and one type I cremation burials are present on the site (Mariën 1999).

Secondary deposition of the cremated bones is attested for the so-called flat graves at Harchies, Hofstade and Neerharen-Rekem and also for the burials mounds at Havré. The first three mentioned consist of flat graves that contained sword fragments. At Harchies and Hofstade the human remains were put into an urn (Mariën 1975; De Mulder/Laloo 2016). The grave of Neerharen-Rekem is more complex since the bones of three individuals were deposited in three packets in the burial pit (Temmerman 2007; Warmenbol 2015). At Havré the only weapon burial was a type H cremation grave. The other grave types were urn graves with only cremated bone (type A) and urn graves mixed up with remnants from the pyre (type B). Next to urn graves there were also some urnless depositions as a cremation grave type Destelbergen (type D) and a so-called *Brandschüttungsgrab* which consists of a token deposition from pyre remains and some cremated bone in a pit (type E). It is interesting to note that the metal objects deposited in these cremation graves are all associated with body adornment as razors and tweezers (Mariën 1999).

Grave goods

The elite grave good par excellence is the bronze or iron sword in association with a chape. The number of sword graves is quite variable from one cemetery to another. Other elite graves contain mostly metal objects which are associated with bodily adornment. Nevertheless, in these cemeteries there are also barrows present which contain no funerary gifts at all.

Not all cemeteries with rich burials contain cremation graves with a sword deposition. There is an old isolated find of a razor at Bernissart and in the burial mounds of Louette-Saint-Pierre only razors were discovered. Both bronze and iron swords received a specific treatment and had been in contact with fire. The bronze swords were intentionally broken in different fragments before deposition (Fig. 7). The iron swords were bent and sometimes fixed into the soil. An exceptional artifact in this group of burials is the so-called antenna sword in barrow 3 at Court-Saint-Etienne (see fig. 7 in Warmenbol in this volume) (Mariën 1958). The dispersion of sword graves shows a strong concentration in

Fig. 5. Overview of the different types of cremation graves in the early Hallstatt cemeteries.

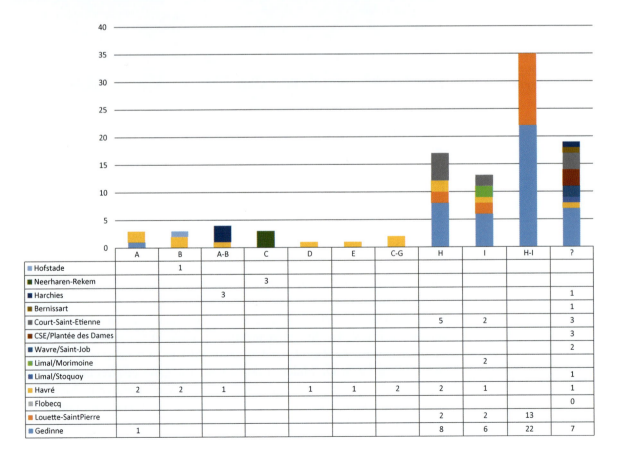

	A	B	A-B	C	D	E	C-G	H	I	H-I	?
Hofstade		1									
Neerharen-Rekem				3							
Harchies			3								1
Bernissart											1
Court-Saint-Etienne								5	2		3
CSE/Plantée des Dames											3
Wavre/Saint-Job											2
Limal/Morimoine									2		
Limal/Stoquoy											1
Havré	2	2	1		1	1	2	2	1		1
Flobecq											0
Louette-SaintPierre								2	2	13	
Gedinne	1							8	6	22	7

the Dyle valley, especially in the cemetery at Court-Saint-Etienne. Six burials with a sword have been recorded, but other fragments of bronze and iron swords from this site (though without any reference to their burial context) are preserved in the collection of the Royal Museum for Art and History. A total of 17 swords have been found on this site (Mariën 1958). Another group is visible in the southern Haine valley with an accent on the site of Harchies (De Mulder/Bourgeois 2011). Finally, there is a strong representation of this type of elite burial in the cemetery of Gedinne/Chevaudos, not so far from the site of Louette-Saint-Pierre (Guillaume 2003; Warmenbol 1993). Remarkable is the concentration of three bronze swords in the cremation grave at Neerharen-Rekem which contains the remains of three different individuals, probably two men and a woman (Temmerman 2007).

The swords can be accompanied by different objects which further confirm the status of the deceased. Some objects, deposited in the burial pit, form an elite funerary set. The chape from the scabbard is only ascertained in a few contexts (see Table 1). Fragments of horse-gear are present in two burial mounds at Court-Saint-Etienne and Limal/Morimoine. Although in the same region there are examples of deposition of elements of horse-gear only. At Court-Saint-Etienne barrow Z and barrow 4 fragments of horse-gear in bronze and iron were discovered, in the first mentioned burial accompanied also by some unidentifiable bronze elements. The site of Court-Sainte-Etienne/La Plantée des Dames is also present in this category with a bronze fragment in barrow 4 (Mariën 1958).

Other artifacts are less associated with the classical sword graves, but appear in a few cremation graves. The three bronze swords at the multiple burial at Neerharen-Rekem were accompanied by three bronze spearheads (Warmenbol 1998). An iron spearhead was also given to the deceased in barrow 3 Ferme Rouge at Court-Saint-Etienne, which was equipped with a rich set of other artifacts (Mariën 1958). Finally, at Gedinne/Chevaudos was a lone bronze spearhead deposited in burial 16. In the Dutch urnfield cemetery of Weert/Boshoverheide were also two spearheads discovered next to three bronze swords and a chape in the late 19th century. However, the spearheads were not found together with the swords (Hissel/Theunissen 2012; Ubaghs 1890).

In the deposited funerary set of the Ferme Rouge barrow 3 at Court-Saint-Etienne was also another remarkable artifact added, namely a bronze socketed axe (see figure 7 in Warmenbol in this volume) (Mariën 1958). This practice was

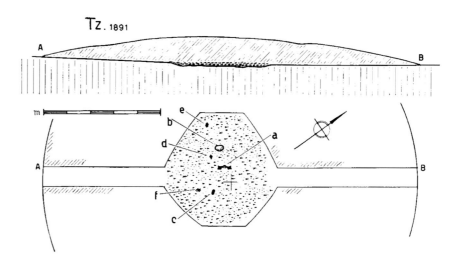

Fig. 6. Drawing of a type I cremation grave at Court-Saint-Etienne (after Mariën 1958, 85 fig. 12).

also attested at the Oss-Vorstengraf in the Netherlands. An iron axe formed part of a rich cremation burial in a situla which contained an iron Mindelheim sword, horse-gear and a set of other metal artifacts (Fokkens/Jansen 2004; Fokkens *et al.* 2012; see also Jansen/Van der Vaart-Verschoof this volume). A second example was discovered at Rhenen in the center of the Netherlands. Among the funerary set of a cremation in a bronze situla was a fragment of a socketed axe of the Wesseling type, as well as elements of horse-gear and a four-wheeled wagon (Van Heeringen 1998/99). The presence of these socketed axes is an interesting new phenomenon because during the Late Bronze Age axes were deposited in wet contexts such as valley streams and marshes and in the final stage of the Late Bronze Age also in large hoards of the so-called Plainseau culture (Fontijn 2002/03; Fontijn/Fokkens 2007). The inclusion of these axes among the funerary set of some elite burials suggests that they acquired a new specific value.

Among the numerous deposited artifacts of barrow 3 at Court-Saint-Etienne is also a hook that has been interpreted as a meat hook. One iron knife was also present in this richly provided burial (Mariën 1958).

Barrow 5 at Wavre/Bruyère is the only known example of the association of a sword and a razor (Mariën 1958). Toilet articles are an important item of the elite culture and bodily appearance during this period but most of these artifacts are found in different burial contexts. Next to razors appear also tweezers and small toilet kits. Among the oldest finds of attention for the care of the body are the loose find of a Late Bronze Age razor at Court-Saint-Etienne (Mariën 1958) and bronze tweezers in a 'bonepackgrave' at the urnfield of Herk-de-Stad/Donk (De Mulder *et al.* 2014; Van Impe 1980). In the early Hallstatt cemeteries bronze and iron razors are found at Bernissart, Court-Saint-Etienne (barrow 5 Ferme

Cemetery	Sword	Chape	Spearhead	Horse-gear	Razor	Other
Hofstade	1 (Br)	1				
Neerharen-Rekem	3 (Br)	2	3			
CSE/barrow A	1 (Fe)			3		
CSE/barrow K	1 (Br)					
CSE/barrow L	1 (Fe)					
CSE/barrow M	1 (Fe)					
CSE/barrow 1	1 (Fe)					1
CSE/barrow 3	1 (Fe)		1	1		1
Wavre/Bruyère barrow 5	1 (Br)				1	
Limal/Stoqouy barrow 5	1 (Fe)					
Limal/Morimoine barrow 1	1 (Fe)			1		2
Harchies/cremation 1	1 (Br)					
Harchies/cremation 2	1 (Br)					
Harchies/cremation 3	1 (Br)	1				
Harchies/cremation 4	1 (Br)					
Havré/barrow E	1 (Fe)					
Flobecq	1 (?)					
Gedinne/barrow 1	1 (Br)	1				2
Gedinne/barrow 2	1 (Fe)					
Gedinne/barrow 13	1 (Fe)					
Gedinne/barrow 14	1 (Fe)					

Table 1. Overview of the sword graves in Belgium and associated deposited bronze and iron artifacts.

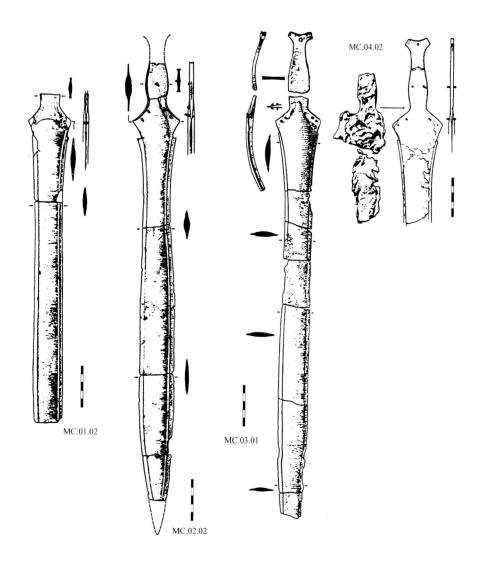

MC.04.02

MC.01.02

MC.03.01

MC.02.02

Fig. 7. The broken bronze Gündlingen swords from Harchies (after Guillaume 2003, 109 fig. 50).

Rouge), Court-Sainte-Etienne/La Plantée des Dames (barrow 2), Havré (barrows 9, 10 and 16), Limal/Morimoine (barrow 2) and Louette-Saint-Pierre (barrows I and III). At barrow 2 in Limal/Morimoine the razor was accompanied by tweezers (Mariën 1958). The cemetery of Havré contained the largest number of cremation graves with toilet articles. Both mentioned barrows 9 and 10 had also a toilet kit as part of the funerary goods. Another toilet kit was discovered in barrow 2. Finally, iron tweezers had been deposited in barrow A (Mariën 1999).

Elite burials in the funerary landscape

There are differences in the relationship between the described elite graves and other burials and cemeteries. The sites of Hofstade and Neerharen are located in an area where there is also a strong presence of excavated urnfields of the Late Bronze Age and Early Iron Age. The other sites in southern Belgium were found early in the archaeological history of Belgium and also in regions with less archaeological activity through the centuries.

Both weapon graves at Hofstade and Neerharen/Rekem are the only indication of people buried with a higher social status in a 'classic' urnfield with principally simple cremations. Both burials are also so-called flat graves. At this moment the urnfield of Hofstade counts 400 cremations but only one cremation with a sword and chape (De Mulder/Laloo 2016). Although the study is still going on there are no more explicit indications of outing of a higher social status. It is important to remark that the site is not that far away from the Scheldt river between Wichelen and Schoonaarde, an area known for its rich deposits of bronze artifacts during the Late Bronze Age (De Mulder/Bourgeois 2011; Verlaeckt 1996). The estimated walking time from Hofstade to the banks of the Scheldt is about 1.30 to 2 hours. The cemetery of Neerharen-Rekem counts 235 cremations although it is not completely excavated. Grave 72 is exceptional because it is made up of three different bronze swords and three different individuals were deposited in it, but it is also the only grave with an explicit social status (Temmerman 2007).

The Dyle valley stands out for its concentration of early Hallstatt burials. Five cemeteries at a short distance from each other were found in the southern region of this river valley. Among these cemeteries Court-Saint Etienne attracts attention by the numerous barrows from this period and their lavish funerary sets. In the archaeological literature different areas are mentioned at Court-Saint-Etienne but they probably belong to one large funerary zone (Fig. 8). The oldest finds come from the eastern part of the site at a place called Bettremont. The finds testify to the presence of flat graves from the Late Bronze Age and also the Early Iron Age in this area. The Late Bronze Age razor suggests the first indications of social status in the funerary ritual during the Late Bronze Age. In the transition to the Early Iron Age a new funerary ritual appears: the construction of burial mounds on top of the pyre. These funerary monuments are recorded in two areas, La Quenique and La Ferme Rouge, west of the urnfield cemetery. Due to the nature of the 19th-early 20th century excavations we have no detailed information of the location of other destroyed burials between these three recorded areas (De Mulder 2011; Mariën 1958). Another exceptional character of Court-Saint-Etienne is the high number of recorded sword graves both excavated and preserved without find context. This shows the importance of the site as a place for elite burial. This is further proven by the richness of other artifacts associated with social status. Concerning the other sites in the Dyle valley, the elite burials are located within groups of other barrows but these could not be dated due to limited information.

Another group of elite burials is ascertained in the southern Haine-valley. Bernissart is an old isolated find of a burial with a razor. The four burials at Harchies seem to be flat graves. Due to the limited excavation there is no information available on other funerary structures (Leblois 2010; Mariën 1975). Havré is a larger cemetery with 21 documented burial mounds (Fig. 9). There has only one sword grave been found, but five barrows contained artifacts associated with body care. In four other burials were bronze or iron fragments discovered that could not be identified anymore (Mariën 1999).

Finally, Louette-Saint-Pierre and Gedinne are also located a short distance from each other in the valley of the Houille, a tributary of the Meuse. The cemetery of Gedinne counts ca. 44 excavated burial mounds. Three were sword graves and one grave contained a bronze spearhead. Five other cremations yielded small bronze or iron fragments which were difficult to identify (Guillaume 2003). Regarding Louette-Saint-Pierre 17 monuments were excavated. In two of these razors were discovered. Furthermore, there exists also a loose find from a razor fragment from this site and also a fragment from a bracelet (Guillaume 2003; Warmenbol 1993).

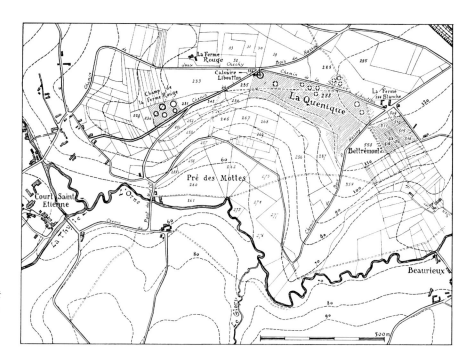

Fig. 8. Location of the different excavated cemeteries at Court-Saint-Etienne (after Mariën 1958, 15 fig. 2).

Other cremation graves contained only ceramics. Only a minority of the graves in both cemeteries reflect a certain social status.

Early Hallstatt burials and radiocarbon dating

Since the beginning of the 3rd millennium cremated bone can be dated using the carbon preserved in the bioapatite for the bone. To obtain a reliable radiocarbon date the bone has to be well cremated (800 C°) and be completely white in appearance (Van Strydonck *et al.* 2005; 2009; 2010). Since then radiocarbon dating cremated bone has become a standard practice in the study of cremation cemeteries, especially the urnfields of the Late Bronze Age and the Early Iron Age, resulting in new insights of the occupation history of these cemeteries (De Mulder *et al.* 2007). Nevertheless, for a detailed study of the early Hallstatt period burials we are confronted with some limitations. The 2σ certainty range of a radiocarbon date covers, depending on the calibration curve, one or two centuries. For the final phase of the Late Bronze Age and the transition to the Early Iron Age a good reliable calibrated radiocarbon date from one century (9th century) is possible. The largest problem is the so-called Hallstatt-plateau which covers the whole period of the Early Iron Age and so the appearance of the elite burials of this period. Due to solar activity around 800 BC the calibration curve covers a period of three to four centuries and cannot be refined at the moment. This limits the use of radiocarbon dating cremated bone for the chronological study of the early Hallstatt period. Another problem is the conservation of the cremated bone in museums. Since most cemeteries were excavated in the late 19th and early 20th centuries it is not always clear if the bone that has been preserved can be effectively associated with the objects in the museum collections.

Until now only a limited number of radiocarbon dates have been realized on elite burials in Belgium. There is one date for the grave at Neerharen-Rekem. The sword grave from Hofstade has to be dated in the near future. Finally, three

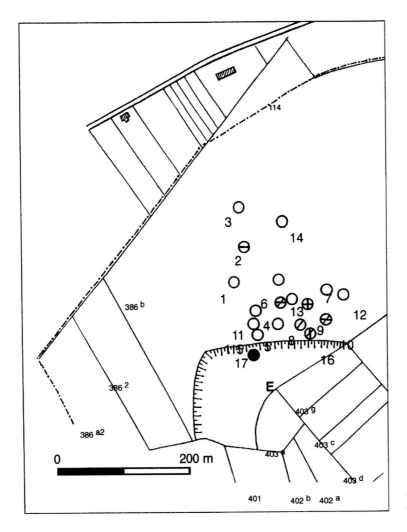

Fig. 9. The cemetery at Havré (after Mariën 1999, 229 fig. 4).

dates were obtained on cremated bone from Louette-Sainte-Pierre, but without an association with a grave context and grave goods (Warmenbol 2009).

The result for Neerharen-Rekem situates the grave between 905-796 cal BC, which covers the end of the Late Bronze Age and the transition to the Early Iron Age (Fig. 10). The three radiocarbon dates for Louette-Saint-Pierre cover, as expected, the whole period of the Early Iron Age until the 5th century BC. Although the oldest date (KIA-25593) tends to a greater probability at the beginning of the Early Iron Age (for further discussion see also Warmenbol this volume).

The international context of the early Hallstatt elite burials in Belgium

The discussed Belgian elite burials are part of a funerary tradition which covers the southern Netherlands and northeastern France (Warmenbol 1993). The Gündlingen bronze swords have their ancestors in the tradition of Atlantic Late Bronze Age swords (Milcent 2004; Warmenbol 1988). Some of the swords at Harchies can be described as proto-Hallstatt (see Warmenbol this volume). The chape in barrow 3 at Harchies was also an Atlantic Sion Reach type (Warmenbol 1988). The genesis of the Hallstatt funerary elite burial set seems to have its roots in the Atlantic region and influences the Central European elites (Milcent 2004). In the Dyle valley Central European

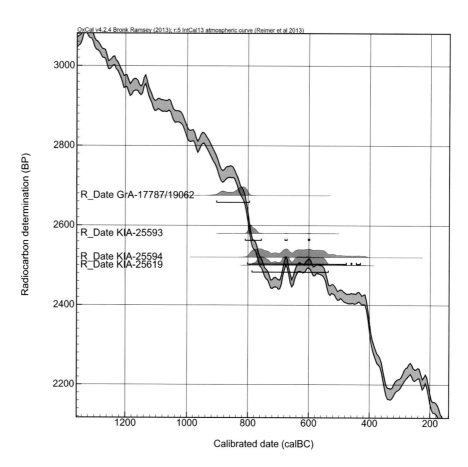

OxCal v4.2.4 Bronk Ramsey (2013); r:5 IntCal13 atmospheric curve (Reimer et al 2013)

Fig. 10. The radiocarbon dates of Belgium elite burials plotted on the calibration curve.

influences are also present. The iron horse-gear at Limal/Morimoine has rather Continental parallels (Mariën 1958). The barrows at Court-Saint-Etienne/la Ferme Rouge reflect influences from both cultural traditions. The presence of a socketed axe and elements of horse-gear in burial 3 represent the Atlantic tradition. On the other hand, the iron knife in the same barrow reminds of Continental European habits where knives are found back in association with swords (Brun *et al.* 2009). The appearance of the burial mounds that cover the remains of the pyre was a new element in the funerary traditions. Where it exactly originates is not clear but this tradition seems also to be recorded in the Hunsrück-Eifel culture (Krausse 1991).

Conclusion

In this overview we focused on the funerary ritual of elite burials in Belgium. Most of the finds can be considered relatively old since they have been excavated in the 19th and early 20th centuries, but it is still possible to extract a lot of information on the burial ritual. The elite burials in Belgium seem to be concentrated in small groups while both Flemish sites, Hofstade and Neerharen-Rekem are part of larger urnfield cemeteries. The recent discovery of Hofstade and Lidar images in Flanders and Wallonia show that there is still a great undiscovered potential.

Acknowledgments

I wish to thank colleague E. Warmenbol (Université Libre de Bruxelles) for sharing his information.

Bibliography

Beke *et al.* 2016: F. Beke/H. Hiddink/G. De Mulder, Vierhonderd urnen. Een uitzonderlijk groot grafveld uit de Metaaltijden in Hofstade. Ex Situ. Tijdschrift voor Vlaamse Archeologie 13, 2016, 22-23.

Brun *et al.* 2009: P. Brun/B. Chaume/L. Dhennequin/ B. Quiellec, Le passage de l'âge du bronze à l'âge du Fer...au fil d'épée. In : M.-J. Roulière-Lambert/A. Daubigney/P.-Y. Milcent/M. Talon/J. Vital (éds.), De l'âge du Bronze à l'âge du Fer en France et en Europe occidentale (Xe-VIIe siècle av. J.-C.). La moyenne vallée du Rhône aux âges du Fer. Actes du XXXe colloque internationale de l'AFEAF, co-organisé avec l'APRAB. Saint-Romain-en-Gal 26-28 mai 2006. Revue Archéologique de l'Est, Supplément 27 (Dijon 2009) 477-485.

Cloquet 1882: N. Cloquet, Tumulus du canton de Wavre et cimetière celtique du Court-Saint-Etienne. Annales de la Société Archéologique de l'Arrondissement de Nivelles II, 1882, 32-54.

Comhaire 1894/95: M. Comhaire, Les premiers âges du métal dans les bassins de la Meuse et de l'Escaut. Bulletin de la Société d'Anthropologie de Bruxelles XIII, 1894/95, 97-226.

Delvaux 1888/89: E. Delvaux, Notice explicative de la fouille de Flobecq. Bulletin de la Société d'Anthropologie de Bruxelles 7, 1888/89, 23-164.

Dens 1903: C. Dens, Sépultures à incinération du premier âge du Fer dans la région d'Ottignies. Annales de la Société d'Archéologie de Bruxelles 17, 1903, 140-162.

De Boe *et al.* 1992: G. De Boe/M. De Bie/L. Van Impe, Neerharen-Rekem. Een complexe bewoningsgeschiedenis gered van de grintbaggers. In : Speurwerk. Archeologische monumentenzorg in de Euregio-Maas-Rijn (Mainz 1992) 477-496.

De Laet 1982: S. De Laet, La Belgique d'avant les Romains (Wetteren 1982).

De Laet *et al.* 1986: S. De Laet/H. Thoen/J. Bourgeois, Les fouilles du Séminaire d'Archéologie de la Rijksuniversiteit te Gent à Destelbergen-Eenbeekeinde (1960-1984) et l'histoire la plus ancienne de la région de Gent (Gand). I. La période préhistorique. Dissertationes Archaeologicae Gandenses XXIII (Brugge 1986).

De Loë 1913: A. De Loë, Belgique ancienne. Bulletin des Musées Royaux du Cinquantenaire 13, 1913, 71.

De Mulder 2011: G. De Mulder, Funeraire rituelen in het Scheldebekken tijdens de late bronstijd en de vroege ijzertijd. De grafvelden in hun maatschappelijke en sociale context. Unpublished Doctoral Thesis (Gent 2011).

De Mulder/Bourgeois 2011: G. De Mulder/J. Bourgeois, Shifting centres of power and changing elite symbolism in the Scheldt fluvial basin during the Late Bronze Age and the Iron Age. In T. Moore/L. Armada (eds.), Western Europe in the first millennium BC. Crossing the divide (Oxford 2011) 302-318.

De Mulder/Laloo 2016: G. De Mulder/P. Laloo, Une tombe à épée à Hofstade (province de Flandre orientale, Belgique). Bulletin de l'Association pour la Promotion des Recherches sur l'Age du Bronze 14, 2016, 125-128.

De Mulder *et al.* 2007: G. De Mulder/M. Van Strydonck/M. Boudin/W. Leclercq/N. Paridaens/E. Warmenbol, Re-evaluation of the Late Bronze Age and Early Iron Age chronology of the western Belgian urnfields based on ^{14}C dating. Radiocarbon 49,2, 2007, 499-514.

De Mulder et al. 2014: G. De Mulder/L. Van Impe/M. Van Strydonck, ¹⁴C-dateringen op crematies uit het urnengrafveld van Donk (Herk-de-Stad, prov. Limburg, België). Lunula, Archaeologia Protohistorica XXII, 2014, 79-87.

De Radiguès 1881: F. De Radiguès, Continuation des fouilles des cimetières gallo-germains de Louette-Saint-Pierre été de Gedinne. Annales de la Société Archéologique de Namur XV, 1881, 249-261.

Dujardin/Gravet 1865/66: G. Dujardin/F. Gravet, Cimetières gallo-germains de Louette-Saint-Pierre et de Gedinne. Annales de la Société Archéologique de Namur IX, 1865/66, 39-59.

Fokkens/Jansen 2004: H. Fokkens/R. Jansen, Het vorstengraf van Oss. Een archeologische speurtocht naar een prehistorisch grafveld (Utrecht 2004).

Fokkens et al. 2012: H. Fokkens/S. van der Vaart/D. Fontijn/S. Lemmers/R. Jansen/I. van Wijk/P. Valentijn, Hallstatt burials of Oss in context. Analecta Praehistorica Leidensia 43/44, 2012, 183-204.

Fontijn 2001/02: D. Fontijn, Sacrificial landscapes. Cultural biographies of persons, objects and 'natural' places in the Bronze Age in the Southern Netherlands, c. 2300-600BC. Analecta Praehistorica Leidensia 33/34, 2001/02.

Fontijn/Fokkens 2007: D. Fontijn/H. Fokkens, The emergence of Early Iron Age 'chieftain graves' in the southern Netherlands: Reconsidering transformations in burial and depositional practices. In: C. Haselgrove/R. Pope (eds.), The earlier Iron Age in Britain and the near continent (Oxford 2007) 354-373.

Guillaume 2003: A. Guillaume, 150 années de recherches hallstattiennes en Wallonie. Les rites funéraires. Bulletin du Cercle Archéologique Hesbaye-Condroz XXVII (Amay 2003).

Goblet d'Alviella 1908: E. Goblet d'Alviella, Antiquités protohistoriques de Court-Saint-Etienne. Bulletin de l'Académie royale de Belgique. Classe des Sciences 1, 1908, 18-55.

Hissel/Theunissen 2012: M. Hissel/L. Theunissen, Cold case in het stuifzand. Het prehistorische grafveld op Boshoverheide ontsloten (prov. Limburg, Nederland). Lunula, Archaeologia Protohistorica XX, 2012, 75-80.

Krausse 1991: E.-B. Krausse, Brandgräber Type Laufeld. Scheiterhaufenbestattungen der frühen Eisenzeit an Mittelrhein und Mosel. In : A. Haffner/A. Miron (ed.), Studien zur Eisenzeit im Hunsrück-Nahe-Raum. Trierer Zeitschrift, Beiheft 13 (Trier 1991) 35-52.

Leblois 2010: E. Leblois. La nécropole hallstattienne d'Harchies "Maison Cauchies": Un bilan et des perspectives (province de Hainaut, Belgique). Lunula, Archaeologia Protohistorica XVIII, 2010, 107-111.

Lecarme/Warmenbol 2015: M. Lecarme/E. Warmenbol, Nouveaux objets métalliques de l'âge du Bronze final en provenance de Marche-en-Famenne 'La Campagnette' (prov. de Luxembourg, Belgique). Lunula, Archaeologia Protohistorica XXIII, 2015, 75-79.

Mariën 1958: M.-E. Mariën, Trouvailles du Champs d'Urnes et des Tombelles hallstattiennes de Court-Saint-Etienne. Monographies d'Archéologie Nationale 1 (Bruxelles 1958).

Mariën 1975: M.-E. Mariën, Epées de bronze « proto-hallstattiennes » et hallstattiennes découvertes en Belgique. Helinium 15/1, 1975, 14-37.

Mariën 1999: M.-E. Mariën, Nécropole hallstattienne à tombelles dans le « Bois de la Taille des Vignes » à Havré (Hainaut, Belgique). In : B. Chaume/J.-P. Mohen/P. Perin (eds.), Archéologie des Celtes. Mélanges à la mémoire de René Joffroy. Protohistoire Européenne 3 (Montagnac) 227-242.

Milcent 2004: P.-Y. Milcent, Le premier âge du Fer en France centrale. Mémoire de la Société Préhistorique Française XXXIV (Paris 2004).

Temmerman 2007: B. Temmerman, Het urnenveld van Neerharen-Rekem. Reconstructie en betekenis van grafrituelen in de late bronstijd-vroege ijzertijd. Unpublished Doctoral Thesis (Brussel 2007).

Toilliez 1857: A. Toilliez, Notice sur des antiquités Gallo-Romaines et Franques trouvées dans le Hainaut. Annales du Cercle Archéologique de Mons 1, 1857, 74-93.

Ubaghs 1890: C. Ubaghs, De voorromeinsche begraafplaatsen tusschen Weert en Budel en Nederweert-Leveroy. De Wetenschappelijke Nederlanden IV/7, 1890, 207-216.

Vandevelde et al. 2008: J. Vandevelde/R. Annaert/A. Lentacker/A. Ervynck/M. Vandenbruaene, Vierduizend jaar bewoning en begraving in Edegem-Buizegem (prov. Antwerpen). Relicta. Archeologie, Monumenten en Landschapsonderzoek in Vlaanderen 3, 2008, 9-68.

Van Heeringen 1998/99: R. Van Heeringen, Burial with Rhine view: the Hallstatt situla grave on the Koerheuvel at Rhenen. Berichten van de Rijksdienst voor het Oudheidkundig Bodemonderzoek 43, 1998/99, 69-97.

Van Impe 1980: L. Van Impe, Urnenveld uit de late Bronstijd en de vroege IJzertijd te Donk I. Beschrijvende inventaris. Archaeologia Belgica 224 (Brussel 1980).

Van Strydonck et al. 2005: M. Van Strydonck/M. Boudin/M. Hoefkens/G. De Mulder, ^{14}C-dating of cremated bones, why does it work? Lunula, Archaeologia protohistorica XIII, 2005, 61-63.

Van Strydonck et al. 2009: M. Van Strydonck/M. Boudin/G. De Mulder, ^{14}C dating of cremated bones: the issue of sample contamination. Radiocarbon 51/2, 2009, 553-568.

Van Strydonck et al. 2010: M. Van Strydonck/M. Boudin/G. De Mulder, Een status quaestionis van ^{14}C-dateringen op gecremeerd bot. Lunula, Archaeologia protohistorica XVIII, 2010, 5-12.

Verlaeckt 1996: K. Verlaeckt, Between river and barrow. A reappraisal of Bronze Age metalwork found in the province of East-Flanders (Belgium). British Archaeological Report, International Series 632 (Oxford 1996).

Warmenbol 1988: E. Warmenbol, Broken bronzes and burned bones. The transition from Bronze to Iron Age in the Low Countries. Helinium 28,2, 1988, 244-270.

Warmenbol 1993: E. Warmenbol, Les nécropoles à tombelles de Gedinne et Louette-Saint-Pierre (Namur) et le groupe « mosan » des nécropoles à épées hallstattiennes. In : F. Boura/J. Metzler/A. Miron (eds.), Actes du XIe colloque de l'Association Française pour l'Etude des Ages du Fer en France non Méditerranéenne. Sarreguemines (Moselle) 1-3 mai 1987. Archaeologia Mosellana 2 (Metz et al. 1993) 83-114.

Warmenbol 2009: E. Warmenbol, Les débuts de l'âge du Fer en Belgique. Chronologie relative, chronologie absolue. In: M.-J. Roulière-Lambert/A. Daubigney/P.-Y. Milcent/M. Talon/J. Vital (éds.), De l'âge du Bronze à l'âge du Fer en France et en

Europe occidentale (Xe-VIIe siècle av. J.-C.). La moyenne vallée du Rhône aux âges du Fer. Actes du XXXe colloque international de l'AFEAF, co-organisé avec l'APRAB. Saint-Romain-en-Gal 26-28 mai 2006. Revue Archéologique de l'Est, Supplément 27 (Dijon 2009) 373-384.

Warmenbol 2015: E. Warmenbol, The later Bronze Age and Early Iron Age in the southern Low Countries: Where east meets west. In: F. Hunter/I. Ralston (eds.), Scotland in later prehistoric Europe (Edinburgh 2015) 47-82.

Author

Guy de Mulder
Department of Archaeology
Ghent University
Campus UFO
Sint-Pietersnieuwstraat 35
B-9000 Ghent
Belgium
guy.demulder@ugent.be

At the crossroads of the Hallstatt East

Carola Metzner-Nebelsick

Abstract

The article gives an overview of the current state of research in those regions of the so-called eastern Hallstatt culture ('Osthallstattkreis') which have from a Western or Central European research perspective not been in the focus of attention in recent years: western Hungary and northern Croatia. Starting from previous own research in southeastern Pannonia (in geographical terms south-eastern Transdanubia in western Hungary and eastern Slavonia in northeastern Croatia) the author illustrates chronological parameters with focus on the Ha C period and cultural contacts between the members of various groups of regional identity between the east Alpine piedmont zone, the Drava-Sava interfluve and the bend of the Danube. An overview of social and ritual practices with special focus on burial customs and settlement structures is given, as well as an account of characteristic features of the material culture. The article stresses the important role the eastern fringe zone of the eastern Hallstatt culture played next to Italy in the formation processes of what should be labeled as Hallstatt culture. The immediate geographic vicinity to culturally distinct pastoral groups in the eastern Carpathian Basin and beyond as well as to others in the Lower Danube area was decisive for transmitting innovations like new bridling techniques, depending warfare and social role models as well as aesthetic principles to the west by various levels of social interaction as early as the 9th century BC. Some of these technical as well as aesthetic principles should become characteristic in the Ha C period. With regard to behavioral patterns of social distinction as well as expressions of material culture communities at the eastern fringe zones of the eastern Hallstatt culture formed an integral part of this cultural unit during the Ha C period.

Zusammenfassung

Der Artikel gibt einen Überblick über den Stand der Forschung zur älteren Hallstattzeit in jenen Regionen des Osthallstattkreises bzw. der östlichen Hallstattkultur, die aus mittel- und westeuropäischer Forschungsperspektive in den letzten Jahren nicht im Fokus standen. Dies gilt insbesondere für das westliche Ungarn und Nordkroatien. Ausgehend von eigenen Forschungen in Südostpannonien, worunter in geographischer Hinsicht das südöstliche Transdanubien in Westungarn sowie das östliche Slawonien in Kroatien verstanden werden, bietet der Artikel einen Einblick in chronologische Parameter mit Schwerpunkt in der Periode Ha C und schildert kulturelle Kontakte der einzelnen Identitätsgemeinschaften ('Kulturgruppen') zwischen östlichem Alpenfuß, Drau-Save-Zwischenstromland und Donauknie. Es werden vornehmlich auf die gesellschaftlichen Eliten bezogene Praktiken des Bestattungsbrauchtums und des Siedlungswesens sowie Spezifika der materiellen Kultur vorgestellt. Zudem wird betont, dass es gerade jene am östlichsten gelegenen Regionen der Hallstattkultur waren, die neben Italien maßgeblich Impulse für die Herausbildung der älteren Hallstattkultur insgesamt geliefert haben. Durch die direkte geographische Nähe zu den Lebensräumen kulturell divergenter Gruppen mit pastoralnomadischer Prägung im östlichen Karpatenbecken und angrenzenden Regionen sowie zu Bevölkerungsgruppen an der Unteren Donau wurden u. a. technische Innovationen im Reitwesen und damit einhergehend auch der Kriegsführung oder neue ästhetische Prinzipien durch verschiedene Interaktionsformen vermittelt und schließlich in den Gestaltungskanons der östlichen Hallstattkultur integriert. Darstellungsformen sozialer Distinktion einer älterhallstattzeitlichen Elite werden an den östlichen Rändern der östlichen Hallstattkultur mit jenen in westlich gelegenen Regionen geteilt.

Introduction

Even for some Hallstatt scholars the eastern fringe zone of the so-called eastern Hallstatt culture, the *"Osthallstattkultur"* (Jerem/Lippert 1996), also labeled as *"Osthallstattkreis"* (Müller-Scheeßel 2000), or in geographical term the areas east of the Vienna Basin and Burgenland in eastern Austria in the north or Styria and the Slovenian Dolenjska region in the south Alpine piedmont zone are still somewhat obscure. From a Central or Western European (Hallstatt) perspective various micro regions in Transdanubia, western Slovakia or northeast Croatia seem very remote and thus strange and unfamiliar. Finds from single sites are certainly found on various distribution maps; the cultural context and the significance of such contexts however are rarely fully recognized. This gap of knowledge of western Hallstatt scholars cannot only be explained by language obstacles alone, but is possibly also the result of diverging research traditions.

In this article I will therefore try to shed some light on these seemingly less illuminated areas of the Hallstatt culture's eastern fringe zones by giving an overview of recent as well as well-established research. Therefore the core areas of the eastern Hallstatt culture such as the Kalenderberg group in eastern Austria and western Slovakia, the Sulmtal or Kleinklein group in Styria or the Dolenjska in Slovenia (Fig. 1) are not in the focus, but rather Transdanubia i.e. western Hungary and north-eastern Croatia. As I have previously described in detail (Metzner-Nebelsick 1996; 1997; 2002) the southeastern part of Transdanubia, that is County of Baranya, and eastern Slavonia in northeast Croatia form a cultural unit, particularly during the Ha C period. In order to avoid modern political connotations I have called this cultural unit the Southeast Pannonian group of the Urnfield and Hallstatt period. Although I had thoroughly discussed the evidence, and had mainly argued on stylistic grounds of a distinct pottery style, the term did not gain wider recognition (Egg/Kramer 2005, 3 fig. 2; Šimić 2004). Partly because of a biased perspective from the south Alpine fringe zone like Styria and its rich grave inventories, but also because of the rather strong impetus the name *Dalj group* for the Iron Age in Slavonia already had.[1] The flat grave cemetery of Dalj-Busija had long been the largest Hallstatt period cemetery in the area although practically no grave contents had been published (Hoffiller 1938). This situation could partly be improved when I published comprehensive evidence of all Urnfield as well as Hallstatt period materials from burials which had been collected in various museums in present Croatia, Serbia, Hungary, Austria and Germany (Metzner-Nebelsick 2002) on which I based my evaluation of the Urnfield and Hallstatt period in southeast Pannonia i.a. southeast Transdanubia and eastern Slavonia in Croatia.

These areas are – again if seen from a mind-map of a western Hallstatt culture perspective – located at the very fringes of the Hallstatt world. However, those areas in particular played a decisive role in the formation processes of the early Hallstatt or Ha C period.

In absolute chronological terms the following sequence and terminology is used: Ha B3 = 9th century BC; early Ha C1 or Ha C1a = 1st half 8th century BC; younger Ha C1 or Ha C1b and later or developed Ha C or Ha C2 = 2nd half of the 8th and first half of the 7th century BC (Fig. 2). The Southeast Pannonian group of the Urnfield and Hallstatt culture during the Ha C period equals horizons IIIa and IIIb of my classification (Metzner-Nebelsick 2002, 178 fig. 78).

---

1   In some cases difficult access to literature may have been another reason.

Fig. 1. Cultural groups of the eastern Hallstatt culture (map C. Metzner-Nebelsick).

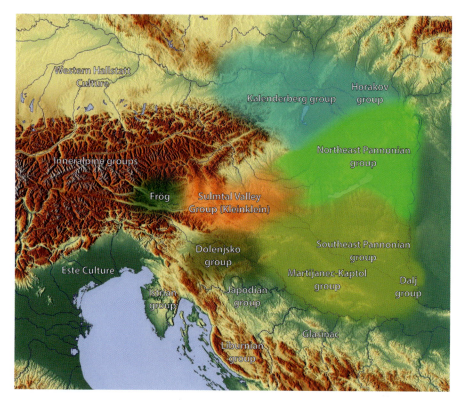

Fig. 2. Chronological chart of the eastern Hallstatt culture and adjacent areas (graphic C. Metzner-Nebelsick).

absolute dates B.C.	phases	equivalent horizons in Southeast Pannonia	indicative graves in Southeast Pannonia (HU & HR)	in the Zala-Rába-Marcal region (western Hungary)	in the Southeast alpine region	in the Northeast alpine region	Drava-Sava-Inverfluve & Požega Mountains	in the Lower Danube region
1000	Ha B1	I	Vukovar-Lijeva bara 39		i.e. Ruše group	Sopron-Krautacker 127		
920				Szombathely-Zanat 17/29		Stillfried 2		
	Ha B3	II	Vukovar-Lijeva bara 16; 75	Szombathely-Zanaz 8/18	i.e. Ruše group	Stillfried 38		Gomolava-collective buria (YU)
780			Dalj Busija, Postić 1909/47					
			Pécs-Jakabhegy Tum.1		Ormož 14	Stillfried 6 Sopron-Burgstall 81/1978		Balta Verde mound 2 (RO)
750	Ha C1a	IIIa	Batina Rajnić		Frög T. 70 (K)			
			Pécs-Jakabhegy 75		Poštela, Lepa ravna			Bujoru (RO)
730/20	Ha C1b	IIIb	Doroslovo 130; 151	Doba I Somlóvásárhely 1	Kleinklein, Hartner-michelkogel 1	Gemeinlebarn Tum. 1 Nové Košariská T. 1	Budinjak 139/6	Vajuga-Pesak (YU) Basarabi (RO) Sofronievo (BL)
			Dalj Busija, Kraus 1911	Vaszar-P. V Doba II			Martijanec-„Gamulica"	Gura Padinei (RO)
650	Ha C2			Vaskeresztes 1	Kleinklein, Kürbischhansl	Sütto (1983) Maiersch 61	Goričan XII/1 Kaptol IV/1	
			Doroslovo 58					
620	Ha D1	IV		Vaskeresztes 2 Boba	Kleinklein, Wiesenkaiser 4			Fergile (RO)
580			Batina, Matej 1972					
				Hegyfalu-OMV filling station	Kleinklein, Kröllkogel		Kaptol X/1	
540	Ha D late	V	Beremend			Sopron-Krautacker 22		
450								

Cultural setting in the 9th to the 8th centuries BC: becoming 'Hallstatt'

I will begin with briefly discussing the cultural setup at the end of the Bronze Age and the formation period of what we call the early Hallstatt or Ha C1a in the 8th century BC (Fig. 3). As figure 2 shows, various cultural groups are located within the Carpathian Basin and adjacent areas in the first half of the 9th century BC. Next to the Middle Danubian Urnfield Culture with various local pottery traditions as well as variations in burial ritual (Lochner 2013) other cultural groups or units can be identified who are direct neighbors of the Middledanubian Urnfield culture: first those using incised and stamped pottery – i.e. the Kalakača phase of the Bosut Culture (Hänsel/Medović 1991), located in the Balkans and the Lower Danube region, and secondly the so-called Mezőcsát group (Metzner-Nebelsick 1998; 2000) of mobile pastoralists in the eastern Carpathian Basin. The vicinity of the Middle Danubian Urnfield Culture – which evolves into the eastern Hallstatt culture in the late 8th century BC – to culturally distinct groups is crucial in order to understand the formation process of the Hallstatt culture as a whole.

Therefore it is likewise important to look at those neighboring regions east of the bend of the Danube and the transformations process which came to pass here around the time of 1000 BC.

As I have argued previously (Metzner-Nebelsick 2002; 2010), due to various factors of supposedly overexploitation of the natural resources in the eastern Carpathian Basin and the impact of an incoming group of eastern mobile pastoralists who also intermarried with women of local residents, parts of the Hungarian Plain (hung. Alföld) underwent substantial social and economic as well as ideological changes during the 9th century BC. Profound anthropogenic changes of the environment led to situations of crisis and a subsequent immigration of newcomers from eastern Europe led to a change of subsistence strategy with a pastoral economy, since for the time between 900/950 and 700/650 BC no indications of lowland settlements structures can be named. Secondly the burial custom of cremation or the custom of not burying larger parts of the population in an archaeologically detectable way as it is attested for the Gáva culture was abandoned. Instead members of this so-called Mezőcsát or Füzesabony-Mezőcsát group practiced inhumation as the exclusive rite, thus creating a distinctive cultural boundary to the traditional Middle Danubian Urnfield culture groups.

As I have argued it was either members of those Carpathian Basin Urnfield groups or the Mezőcsát people themselves who developed great creative potential in translating the prototypes of a new way of bridling technique – very appropriate for military purposes – into something genuinely 'Carpathian' (Fig. 4; Metzner-Nebelsick 1998; 2002). It is still unclear where the new horse-gear types were produced, since so far no workshops could be located, neither within the activity zone of the Mezőcsát people nor indeed in the hillforts and settlements of the sedentary Urnfield communities. Nonetheless, these Carpathian Basin hybrids of types of horse-gear and various forms of richly ornamented reign trappings, originating in the northern Caucasus and the north Pontic steppe belt, were those which lay the foundation of the emergence of the typically Ha C Mindelheim type horse-gear. G. Kossack was the first who observed those eastern connections of Ha C and the Hallstatt culture as a whole (Kossack 1954). His observations were then supplemented and put onto a wider material basis by incorporating a

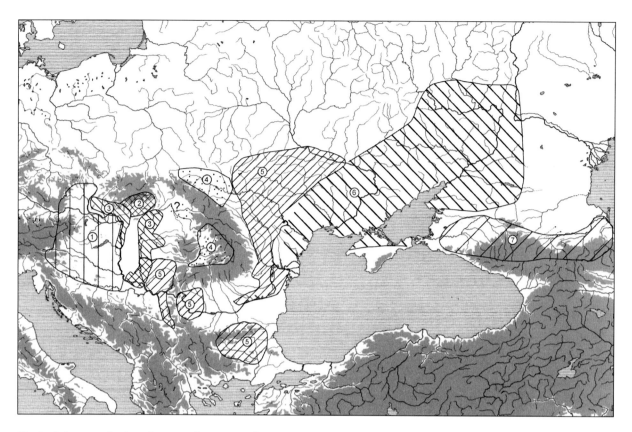

Fig. 3. Cultures and cultural
groups in the first half of the
9th century BC in Central
and eastern Europe. 1: Middle
Danubian Urnfield culture.
– 2: Kyjatice Urnfield group. –
3: Mezőcsat Group. – 4: Gáva
Culture. – 5: different groups
using stamped and incised
pottery (Gornea -Kalakača;
Ostrov-Insula Banului;
Babadag; Pšeničevo, Cozia
-Sacharna, Černoles). –
6: Černogorovka cultural
group. – 7: Koban culture
(after Metzner -Nebelsick
2010, 139 fig. 5a).

wider array of the so-called 'Cimmerian' that is eastern finds and their contexts (Metzner-Nebelsick 2002).

The various stages of translation of an initial steppe impact in the early 9th century BC into something specifically 'Hallstatt' in style was a manifold process, and did not only mean the adaptation of a technological innovation and the attended improvement of riding techniques, but also very likely the influx of larger horse breeds. Imports of superior horse breeds and new bridling techniques triggered the hybridization of those prototypes into new types, but most importantly so, the emergence of new forms of social behavior, including the role model of the mounted warrior as a new prestigious habitus concept of portraying powerful male members of society as a rider, instead of the traditional Central European wagon-driving image of the early Urnfield period (Pare 1987). Whether these images of the self, apparent in the context of death, reflect real-life scenarios can only by assumed.

I am dwelling on this aspect once again, because the process of a multi-stage adaptation and subsequent appropriation of eastern contacts became indicative for the eastern Hallstatt culture and beyond in the Ha C period. The fundamental changes happening after ca. 1000 BC were however geographically limited and had the strongest impact in regions immediately adjacent to the Mezőcsát group's living space – that is in southeast Pannonia (including areas of both southwest Hungary and northeast Croatia) and in eastern Austria (Lower Austria and Burgenland). Here the contact with the Mezőcsát people was direct and probably often antagonistic, triggering a quick adaptation of novelties in warfare.

It is one of the fundamental characteristics for the transition period between (Fig. 2) the late Urnfield and the early Hallstatt period that concepts social roles among the male elites of the eastern Hallstatt culture were not yet normative. Whereas in the west the funeral concept of the driver of the traditional four-wheeled wagon is again taken up in the Ha C period, after a gap in the younger Urnfield period (Ha B1) and with only a few exceptional wagon graves in the Ha B3 (Deicke 2011; Metzner-Nebelsick 2005), in contrast a remarkable dichotomy between two diverging contemporaneous concepts of status representation in a funeral concept can be observed in the Hallstatt east. In the eastern Hallstatt culture the emerging male elites either portray themselves as mounted warriors, clearly a progressive role model which is inspired by eastern contacts, or on the other hand according to the traditional model of the wagon driving warrior with all its depending ideological background.

In absolute dates this process must have happened sometimes during the 8th century BC. In some cases like in Pécs-Jakabhegy, tumulus Török 1 (Fig. 5A; Metzner-Nebelsick 2002, 129 pl. 121A) which is one of the founder's graves in the Hallstatt necropolis on the Jacabhegy in southeast Transdanubia (Southeastern Pannonia according to my terminology), the deceased is portrayed as a north Caucasian mounted warrior, in a rare case of a combination with a Caucasian weapon set of an iron axe, a bimetallic dagger of Gamów-Pjatigorsk type and an iron spearhead, but clearly in combination with local elements such as the cremation rite and local type pottery. The burial is one of the oldest within a larger cemetery (Bertok/Gáti 2014, fig. IV,3; Maráz 1978) of still vastly unpublished burials (Maráz 1996).

A contemporaneous example of the incorporation of eastern type horse-gear is Stillfried at the March River in northeast Austria (Kaus 1988/89; Lochner 2013). Here we observe quite a different context. Although also in this elite late Urnfield period grave the eastern style horse-gear is present, but in contrast to Pécs the ideological package of a steppe bound highly mobile warrior is missing. Instead we find the eastern hybrids and possibly Alföld imports of horse-gear within a cremation cemetery with an already then longer occupation period. The bits and bridles in addition are doubled, thus indicating a bridle of a wagon and not for a rider. The traditional early Urnfield period image of the deceased driving into the netherworld on a wagon is maintained or rather reinvigorated accounting for a process of appropriation of new impulses into existing forms of social behavior.

As could be demonstrated before, either ways or concepts should become iconic in the proper Ha C period of the late 8th and 7th century BC in the eastern Hallstatt culture. In certain parts of the eastern Hallstatt world the social role of the rider proved to be more successful. Riders in prominent graves of the Ha C period are for example found in Slovenian Dolenjska in Novo Mesto, Kapiteljska nijeva barrow I, grave 16 (Knez 1993, pl. 16-20)[2] or in barrow 136, grave 6 of the tumulus cemetery of Budinjak, in the Žumberak Mountains northwest of Zagreb (Fig. 5B; Egg et al. 1998). This classic early Hallstatt (Ha C) inhumation burial of a man and a sacrificed woman shows the paraphernalia of a member of the Ha C elite in the region. The disc helmet (Schüsselhelm) stands in a local tradition, not only in neighboring Dolenjska, but also in southeast Pannonia, where disc or

Fig. 4. A pair of bronze side pieces of type Metzner-Nebelsick B X of late Bronze Age date (9th century BC) from the cemetery of Dalj-Busija, eastern Slavonia, Croatia. Scale 1:2 (Prähistorische Abteilung, Naturhistorisches Museum Wien, photo C. Metzner-Nebelsick).

2 Here again in a combination of eastern and Hallstatt elements: two multi-headed pins ('*Mehrkopfnadeln*'), the disc helmet ('*Schüsselhelm*') and a socketed axe of Hallstatt type are reflecting the east Hallstatt world, whereas in addition to the broken bit, the sheathed Macheira with Balkanic spiral ornaments; a trunyan axe and bronze beads as part of the *balteus* or baldric stand for eastern inspirations and even imports.

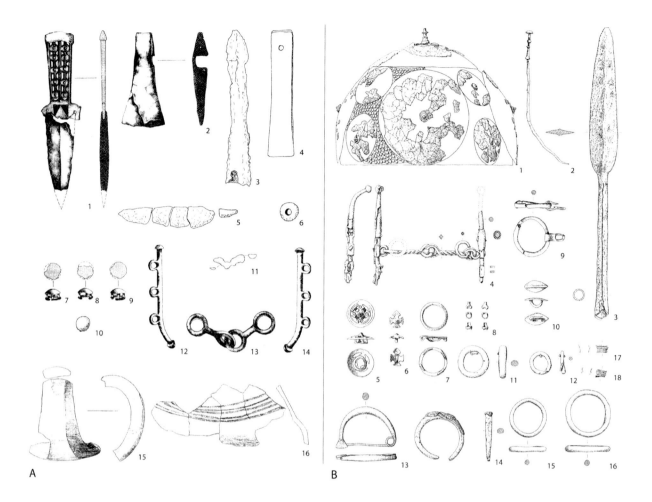

A

B

Fig. 5. A: Grave goods of a cremation burial in the central burial chamber of mound Török 1 from Pécs-Jakabhegy, County Baranya, southwest Hungary. – B: Finds from barrow 139/grave 6 of Budinjak, northwest Croatia. Scale 1:6. A1: bronze and iron; A2.3.5: iron; A4 stone; A6-14 bronze; A15-16 pottery; B3: iron, B1-2.4-16: bronze (after Metzner-Nebelsick 2001; Egg et al. 1998, 440 fig. 5).

composite helmets as well as bell helmets are more frequent. Two are known from Batina (Fig. 6)[3], another helmet was found in the flat grave cemetery of Sotin in eastern Slavonia within a cremation burial (Ložnjak-Dizdar, pers. comm.). The warrior from Budinjak barrow 136 was probably clad in a cloak that was fastened with the iconic Ha C dress pin for men: the *Mehrkopfnadel* or multi headed pin (Fig. 5B,2). Without going into detail of his other cultural affiliations it is vital in our context that the horse-gear is one of those Ha C Mindelheim type variations which originated from a Carpathian prototype (Metzner-Nebelsick 1994; 2002, 277-287) and again was a hybrid form of eastern role models.[4] The horse trappings type B of my classification (Metzner-Nebelsick 2002, 304 fig. 139; 306 fig. 141; 354 fig. 163) are even more closely modeled after those Carpathian types with Pontic-Caucasian prototypes. They continued to be used well into the Hallstatt period and were in contrast to the functional horse-gear itself only very rarely used or imported further west than Transdanubia and Dolenjska (Metzner-Nebelsick 2002, 320 fig. 147). Different stages of identification with eastern aesthetical concepts and role models, but probably also the actual vicinity

---

3   For a detailed description of the contexts see Metzner-Nebelsick 2002,

4   Kossack type I and types II and III of my classification (Metzner-Nebelsick 1994; 2002, 215 fig. 97-here with a wrong caption: it should read: '*Typengliederung der spätbronze- und früheisenzeitlichen Bronzeknebel pontisch-kaukasischer Prägung im Karpatenbecken und in Mitteleuropa*').

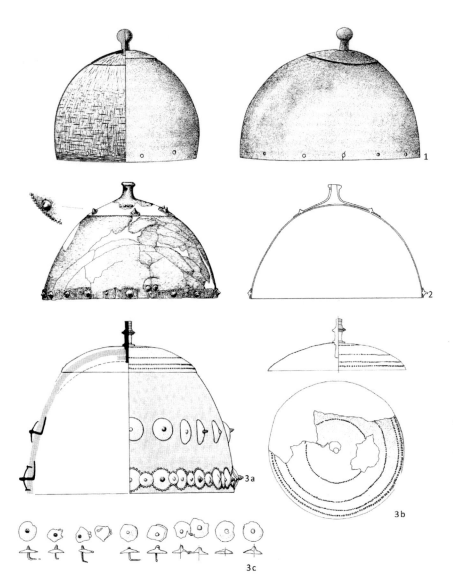

Fig. 6. Bell and disc helmets from Batina (1; 3); iron bell helmet from barrow 1 from Csönge, Vas County, southwest Hungary (2). Scale: ca. 1:4; not all pieces of the disc helmet from Batina are shown. 1.3: bronze; 2: iron (after Schauer 1988, 183 fig. 3; Metzner-Nebelsick 2002, 393 fig. 176; pl. 10; Patek 1993, 108 fig. 87).

to certain workshops as well as direct contacts and the exchange of fully harnessed horses is mirrored here.

Second to a steppe impact another form of eastern culture contact is crucial for understanding the formation of the Hallstatt culture and the Ha C period in the Hallstatt east: that is the impact of the Basarabi Culture Complex (Gumă 1993; 1996), sometimes referred to as Basarabi Culture (Vulpe 1986). The specific pottery style of the Basarabi complex (Fig. 7) has its core distribution in the Banat as well as in Muntenia and Oltenia south of the Danube. In the Banat and around the Iron Gate the specific pottery style can be connected to a cultural group, the Basarabi cultural group within the Basarabi cultural complex (Metzner-Nebelsick 2004, 283-286), since the distinctive incised and stamped pottery has a longer tradition here (Fig. 3). Next to settlements (Hänsel/Medović 1991) the pottery is regularly found in inhumation burials, sometimes in tumuli with several burials, with a distinctive set of gender specific grave goods and dress accessories in the

Ha C period[5]. During the early Ha C period (i.e. Ha C1a) or horizon IIIa of my periodization of the Southeast Pannonian Late Bronze and Iron Age (Fig. 2) as well as in Ha C1b Basarabi pottery was widely distributed (Eibner 2001; Metzner-Nebelsick 1992). In particular at the eastern fringe of the eastern Alps Basarabi style pottery or local transformations of typical motives like the stamped S-spirals, the Maltese cross or more complex designs of 'running' spirals were obviously highly attractive to Hallstatt potters. They copied those motives thus also creating new patterns (also Nebelsick 1997, 73-74 fig. 25-26; Brosseder 2004, 295 fig. 188; 309-316). The stamped and then incised pottery represents a very different stylistic approach to ornament pottery than the painted typical eastern Hallstatt pottery (Brosseder 2004; Schappelwein 1999), secondly the most iconic Basarabi motifs, the large Spiral bands or the hatched (filled in with light coloured lime paste to create a black and white effect) triangle groups were sometimes attached to specific Balkan vessel forms like the cantharos (Fig. 8). Cantharoi form also a distinctive part of the funeral vessel set in the southeast Pannonian or Dalj group in the eastern part of southwest Transdanubia (= "Southeast Pannonia") (Metzner-Nebelsick 2002, esp. 122-128) and the area immediately across the Danube opposite Batina in northern Serbia (Trajković 2008). Other distribution areas of cantharoi are the Adriatic coastal areas (Liburnian group of the Iron Age) or the southeast alpine region with Carinthia, here in the necropolis of Frög (Metzner-Nebelsick 1992; Tomedi 2002, pl. 52,1)[6], Slovenia, with cemeteries like in Molnik near Ljubjana (Puš 1985; 1991) or Ormož near Maribor (Tomanič-Jevremov 1988/89, pl. 18; pl. 19,1-4; 2001) as well as in Dolenjska Toplice (Teržan 1976, pl. 46,1) or Podzemlj, Skrile (Barth 1969, pl. 42,4) in Dolenjska. Ha C examples from Transdanubia are rare (Patek 1968, pl. 76,9).[7] In southeast Transdanubia cantharoi only occur in the Late Hallstatt period and are then continuously used until the La Tène period. In the areas mentioned the presence and integration of cantharoi into the ceramic pottery set in graves attests the cultural contact with the Balkan areas such as Bosnia (i.e. Gavranović 2011), in particular the Sava River valley with the Hallstatt cemeteries of Sanski Most and Donja Dolina (Ćović 1987; Truhelka 1904), but also with the mentioned Basarabi Cultural Complex in Romania and northern Bulgaria. One can only assume that Dionysiac believes which are intrinsically connected with the vessel form of the cantharos were adopted as well.

Becoming 'Hallstatt': the evidence from hillforts

One major characteristic of the Ha C period of the eastern Hallstatt culture is the occupation of hillforts with fortifications which were already erected in the Late Bronze Age but in contrast to the western Hallstatt period continued to be

---

5 See: Berciu/Comşa 1956; Dumitrescu 1968; Gumă 1993; Popović/Vukmanović 1992; 1998; Vulpe 1990; Ciocea Safta 1996: warriors are usually equipped with an iron spear, very rarely with a Machaira type short sword and also very rarely with horse-gear of Carpathian type of Pontic-Caucasian inspiration; further accessories are whetstones or a single bow fibula as dress fastener. Women always wear double fibulae, mostly various types of bow fibulae, neck rings, ankle rings and various ornaments for a headdress (see also Metzner-Nebelsick 2004, esp. 283-286).

6 The eastern – i.e. Pontic-Caucasian as well as Balkanic impact in the barrow cemetery of Frög in Carinthia is particularily prominent, not only as far as Basarabi-style pottery is concerned, but also in regard to the metal finds of weapons and horse-gear (Tomedi 2002; esp. pl. 84).

7 I interpret the handle from tumulus Török 1 from Pécs-Jakabhegy as one from a cantharos.

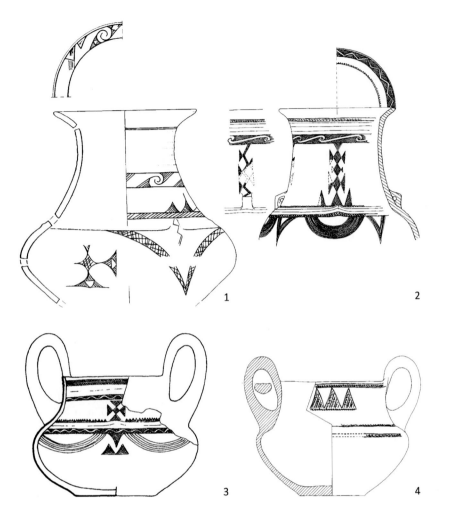

Fig. 7. Basarabi pottery with stamped and incised ornamentation formerly filled with light paste, from east alpine locations (1.4) and from Basarabi contexts (2.3). – 1: Poštela, Slovenian Styria, from a burial mound. – 2: Vajuga-Pesak, Iron Gate, Serbia, from an inhumation cemetery. – 3: Conteşti, Jud. Teleorman, southern Romania, from a settlement. – 4: Frög, tum. 75, Carinthia, Austria. Scale 1:6 (after Teržan 1990, pl. 65,1; Popović/Vukmanović 1998, pl. 12,5; Vulpe 1986, 75 fig. 4,13; Tomedi 2002, pl. 52,1).

used well into the Iron Age (Jerem/Urban 2000; Metzner-Nebelsick 2012). Two different models of transition in regard of hillfort occupation existed:

There are those prominent hill sites which were occupied already in the Late Urnfield period of the 9th century BC (Ha B3) or an early Ha C in the first half of the 8th century BC. If we translate that into a rhythm of cultural dynamics a noticeable break does not happen in Ha C proper (Ha C1b), but in fact earlier. According to this model new centers of power were being founded with a new kind of ancestor cult by burying the dead in widely visible tumuli in the forefront of the hillforts. Those hillforts functioned as focus of identity of the ruling elites, possibly combining the effort of several rural formerly lowland communities to build them. Their inhabitants decided to live together and mark their prominent and possibly newly acquired status visibly for visitors accessing the site not only by massive earthworks – preserved until the present day – but also by impressive sites for the veneration of their ancestors (i. e. see Sauer 2015) and thus also creating some kind of symbolically charged significant past which is crucial for the justification of the social standing of a ruling group. Visitors had to pass through the necropolis, the city of the dead or rather the heroic founders of the fort, before entering the settlement. This model can be compared with the Etruscan city states which were formed at the same time.

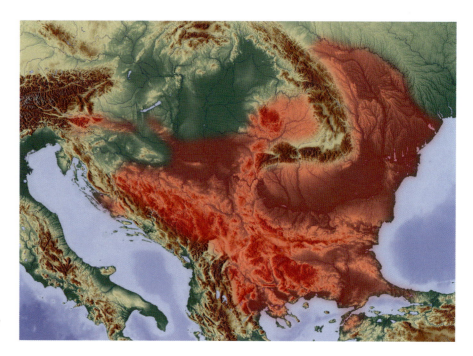

Fig. 8. Distribution map of Cantharoi in Late Bronze Age and Iron Age contexts. Parts of Greece are not mapped (map C. Metzner-Nebelsick).

Prominent places with such a pattern are Sopron-Burgstall (Patek 1982a; 1982b); Poštela near Maribor in Slovenian Styria (Teržan 1990, 256-325; Mlekuž/ Črešnar 2014); Pécs-Jakabhey in southeast Transdanubia (= southwestern Hungary) (i.e. Maráz 1996; Metzner-Nebelsick 2002, 182-184), Purbach Burgstall at the Neusiedler See in eastern Austria, or Burg at the Pinkaschlinge (Nebelsick 1997, 110 fig. 42); Batina in Baranja county northeast Croatia (Metzner-Nebelsick 2002, 187-189) or even Stična in Dolenjska (Gabrovec *et al.* 2006, 270 fig. 72).[8] In Kleinklein in Styria (Dobiat 1980; Smolnik 1994; Egg/Kramer 2005) or Burg at the Pinkaschlinke in Burgenland, eastern Austria (hillfort) and Schandorf (barrow necropolis) the spatial setup is slightly different (Sauer 2015, 54-63).

The second model of Urnfield-Hallstatt transition is represented by sites such as Stillfried in Lower Austria (Felgenhauer 1990-92 [1996]; Hellerschmid 2006; Kaus 1988/89) or Ormož at the Drava River in Slovenia (Tomanič-Jevremov 1988/89) where the earliest Hallstatt pottery forms such as larger vessels with a conical neck ('*Kegelhalsgefäße*'), cantharoi (Ormož)[9] or other features such as larger burial chambers in the case of Stillfried (Kaus 1988/89; Lochner 2013, 27 fig. 8) already occur in traditional flat cremation cemeteries which like the associated fortified settlement was already founded in the HaB1 period i.e. the younger Urnfield period, and continued to be in use well into the Ha C period. In the case of Stillfried as well as Ormož however, so far no Ha C period barrows have been identified.

8   In the family barrow 48, one of the tumuli in the vicinity of the hillfort of Stična, the oldest graves 100 and 101 – the only cremation burials – date to the early 8th century BC (Gabrovec *et al.* 2006, 76-77 pl. 58-59). The fibula in grave 100 is a double looped bow fibula with a hourglass shaped foot of type Gabrovec 2c (Gabrovec 1970) which is indicative for the earliest Hallstatt period equalling Ha C1a or horizon IIIa of my classification for southeast Pannonia. The fibula type shows strong affiliations to the Sava-Drava interfluves and the western Balkans (Vasić 1999) which is typical for the early Hallstatt period in the east alpine piedmont zone in general.

9   Next to the cantharoi these Urnfield period cremation burials from Ormož also contain iron objects and show patterns and ornamentation techniques which clearly underline the transitional position of the cemetery (Tomanič-Jevremov 1988/89; 2001).

Settlement and cemetery structure and organization

cemeteries in Transdanubia

It cannot be the aim of this article to describe the burial custom of the areas in question in detail. A comprehensive account of Ha C period burials or rather single mounds within larger barrow cemeteries in Transdanubia (Hungary west of the Danube) has been given by E. Patek in 1993, based on previously published material. As in eastern Austria with the Kalenderberg group or in the southeast Alpine fringe zone in Styria, Carinthia or Dolenjska large tumulus cemeteries are the rule in Transdanubia in the Raba-Marcal Basin north of Lake Balaton or in southern Transdanubia south and west of Lake Balaton between the Zala, Mur, Drava and Kapos Rivers. Only some of which have been excavated and published. The most prominent barrow cemeteries are Doba, Somlóhegy, Somlóvásárhely, Csönge, Kismező, Vaszar-Pörösrét, Nagyberki-Szalacska, Győrbarát-Nagybarát, Vaskeresztes-Diófás dűlő, Százhalombatta (with 122 identified tumuli), Zalaszántó-Várrét, Mesteri and Süttö[10], all having revealed Ha C period grave inventories.

Since E. Patek's compilation in 1993 new excavations and surveys of burial mounds and barrow cemeteries have been undertaken. In Százhalombatta barrow 115 a huge wooden chamber and a cremation burial is open to the public in the Archaeological Park of Százhalombatta (*százhalom* meaning a hundred mounds) (Jerem *et al.* 2014). Excavations at the barrow cemetery of Féhervár-Csurgo, Fejér county north of Lake Velencei still remain largely unpublished[11].

In regard to the spatial arrangement of those barrow cemeteries, and in addition to what had long been known, more detailed recording techniques such as aerial photography and remote sensing via Lidar Scans give a more accurate picture of their setting within the landscape (i.e. Czajlik 2008; Czajlik *et al.* 2012; Czajlik/ Holl 2015). Hallstatt flat grave cemeteries also exist, i.e. in Halimba-Cseres, Veszprém County (Patek 1993, 88-93) or in Süttö (publication in preparation by K. Novinszki-Groma).

It has been stressed that in contrast to the Ha C period in the western Hallstatt culture wagon burials are very rare in the Hallstatt east. The Ha C2 wagon burial under barrow I of Somlóvásárhely in Veszprém County is an exception (Egg 1996; Patek 1993, 74-84 fig. 54-64). Next to the iron tires of a wagon and the horse-gear and reign trappings a weapon set with an iron sword – beside Doba the most southeastern iron Hallstatt sword so far – six different spears and three different axe types (a trunyan axe, a battle axe and a socketed axe) – all made of iron, as well as a bronze shield boss make this burial unique in Transdanubia and indeed in the Ha C period as a whole. The pottery indicates a date in the later Ha C

---

10 For Vaskeresztes see Fekete (1985); for Zalaszánto (Patek 1974/75), Nagyberki-Salacska (Kemenczei 1974), all others with references to previous publications (Patek 1993). For the region around Lake Balaton see also Horváth 2014.

11 In one of the nine mounds of this little cemetery a wooden chamber with an angled roof and a stone mantel on top and rich Ha C material has been revealed. Very likely the hill site of Kisvárhegy represents the settlement belonging to this barrow group which are separated from each other by a brook (Jungbert 1993, 194 fig. 2; Raszky *et al.* 2001).

period[12]. Somlóvásárhely and Doba are both located at the foot of the prominent hill Somlóhegy in the County of Veszprém. This landmark revealed a number of important Ha C finds, unfortunately all from old excavations (Patek 1993, 64-72). Nonetheless the importance of the location in the early Hallstatt period must have been immense. There are indications that in fact western newcomers or at least men with strong links to western Hallstatt culture communities were buried around the Somló Hill. A high number of bronze vessels from the area also point at close contacts to Styria. In the destroyed barrow I, grave 1 from Doba a remarkable burial was discovered in the late 19th century (Gallus/Horváth 1939, 47; pl. 61,2-4). According to the reports an iron Hallstatt sword was found next to an inhumation in a burial chamber with stone construction. Next to the man a horse was buried there as well together with a Mindelheim type harness (Fig. 9A). In contrast to the west or Dolenjska inhumations are the absolute exception in Transdanubia and the whole eastern Hallstatt culture during Ha C; so besides western or southeast alpine artifact types a burial rite practiced either in the west or in Dolenjska is present. Horse burials are likewise unusual in the Ha C or Ha C2/D1 period in general, as they are in the Alföld or even further to the east as it was recently stressed by P. Kmeťová (Kmeťová 2013, 250 fig. 1; 251-252). In addition the double bridle in Doba I/1 clearly stands for a symbolically present wagon. A significant cultural contact with the west is also apparent in barrow II, grave 2 in which the hilt of a Mindelheim sword was found (Fig. 9B) (Gallus/Horváth 1939, 47; pl. 62; Patek 1993, 70-71 fig. 51). Although the original context of all finds allegedly found in this grave must remain unclear, other noteworthy artifacts found in barrow II of Doba include a bronze cup, a fragment of a 'Breitrandschale', and a ladle with a long twisted handle like in grave 22 in barrow III from Novo mesto, Kapiteljska njiva in Slovenia (Križ 1997, pl. 51,11) or in the Kröllkogel in Kleinklein (Egg/Munier 2013, 256 fig. 106).[13]

Another unfortunately destroyed wagon burial has been identified in Lengyeltóti, Somogy County south of Lake Balaton (Metzner-Nebelsick forthcoming). As mentioned before, the indicative status item of the western Hallstatt warrior in the Ha C period next to a four-wheeled wagon is the sword; both are reflecting an Urnfield tradition. In the Hallstatt east iron swords and also bronze swords are very rare (Egg 1996, 347 fig. 13). In contrast, the typical eastern custom to equip the warrior with parts of defensive armor and here most prominently with a helmet[14] is also attested in Transdanubia: in Csönge, mound 1 in Vas County with an iron bell helmet (Fig. 6,2; Patek 1993, 108 fig. 87,10; 115 fig. 93) and in Vaskeresztes-Diófás, tumulus 1 (Fekete 1985, 46 fig. 12). This exceptional tumulus dates to the very end of the Ha C or Ha C2/D1 period as the two multi-headed pins with needle stopper indicate (Fekete 1985, 45 fig. 11). The helmet with "zusammengesetzter Kalotte" is a type mainly distributed in the southeast alpine area with some specimen in northern Italy (Egg 1988a, 236 fig. 15), the one from Vaskeresztes being the most north-eastern one so far. It represents a chronologically progressive feature in this ensemble, i.e. dating

---

12 Teržan 1990, 163-165 proposed a date in a horizon Ha C2/D1,M. Egg (1996, 352) in contrast suggests a date in Ha C1.

13 Gallus and Horváth mention several other weapons, two ankle and other objects; see also Patay 1990 68; Patek 1993, 70-71 fig. 51.

14 Most often practiced in Dolenjska during the whole Hallstatt period. For references see Schumann 2015, 212-213.

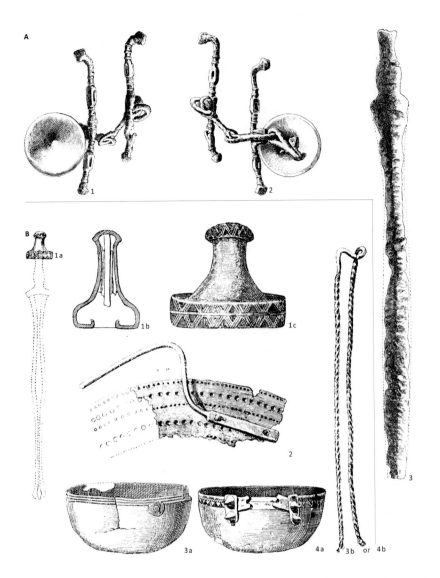

Fig. 9. Inventories from barrow I (A) and barrow II (B) from Doba, Veszprém County, western Hungary. A1-2, B1-4: bronze; A3: iron. It is unclear to which bowl the twisted handle of a ladle belonged. A1-2: Scale 1:4; A3: Scale 1:8; B1-2.4: Scale ca. 1:2; B3a/b: Scale 1:3 (after Gallus/Horváth 1939, pl. 61,2-4; 62).

the grave rather into a Ha C2/Ha D1 horizon. Among other items the warrior grave contained horse-gear, a flash hook and a luxurious pottery set. In fact several vessel were ornamented with meander ornaments in tin-foil application, others were adorned with bull-head protomes, one of the most characteristic features of the eastern Hallstatt culture. This set was supplemented by a large bronze situla (Fekete 1985; Patay 1990, 74-75; pl. 48) and a fragmented bronze *'Breitrandschale'*, a bowl with a broad ornamented rim (Fekete 1985, 45 fig. 11,3; Patay 1990, 79; pl. 63,143).

Larger sets of metal vessels are not a common feature of the Hallstatt period elite burials in Transdanubia or in northeastern Croatia (see below); the combination of two bronze vessels in addition to the exceptional clay vessel set underlines the prominent character of the Vaskeresztes-Diófás cemetery. Both excavated and published barrows represent a later stage of the early Hallstatt period which is – according to certain dress accessories and also horse-gear types – often dated to a Ha C2 period. The mentioned burials do however represent a horizon of rich burials at the eastern fringe of the Hallstatt world as well as in the east alpine area in general which is unsatisfactorily described by a phase – Ha C2 – which has been defined on the grounds of burials from southern Bavaria (Kossack 1959). With regard to features like the helmet in tumulus 1 of Vaskeresztes or the massive stone lined chamber with a dromos in mound 2 (Fekete 1985, 50 fig. 15) with comparisons in cemeteries like Kleinklein in Styria (Kröllkogel) (Dobiat 1980; Egg/Kramer 2013) one should rather date those burials into the Ha D1 period or the late 7th or early 6th century BC.

In Ha C the almost exclusive burial rite in the mentioned barrow cemeteries is cremation. Sometimes several individuals are buried within one burial like in Süttö (Vadász 1983) or Vaskeresztes (Fekete 1985). Weapons and horse-gear for a symbolic wagon with two horses is a regular feature, although it seems that due to the burial rite of cremation and the burning of personal belongings on the pyre together with the deceased a lot of information is being lost by deliberate destruction. Although prestigious items like helmets or multiple weapon sets are present, typical markers of a warrior identity according to the western Ha C ideology of the sword fighting wagon driver are missing. Most prominently the lack of sword graves needs to be mentioned. If this can be seen as an expression of a specific fighting technique in real life with a phalanx or formation fighting with axes and spears (Stary 1981) as shown on Situla Art images can only be assumed. In addition, this interpretation might entail that in the western Hallstatt culture the Urnfield ideal of the heroic warrior, fighting in man-to-man-combat is a traditional image of the past. This traditional and partly surely symbolic value of swords in the eastern Hallstatt culture is expressed by the presence of older sword types in younger graves like in the Sulmtal group elite burials in Kleinklein (Egg/Munir 2013, 109-114) or other sites (Tomedi 1996).

One of the most characteristic features of the eastern Hallstatt culture is the splendor of the funerary pottery.

Characteristic Pottery of the eastern Hallstatt culture

The Vaskeresztes barrow inventories as well as several others belong to a most indicative group of elite burials of the Ha C as well as Ha D1 period of the eastern Hallstatt culture: burials with a lavish pottery set with various characteristic features such as: bull-head-protomes (Metzner-Nebelsick forthcoming; Siegfried-Weiß 1980; Teržan 1990, 232 map 27) which adorned a large variety of vessel types and represent a specific symbolically charged pottery category with a ritual purpose in the burial ceremony (Nebelsick 2016): cherry-red engobe or slip, sheet bronze or tin-foil appliques (on pottery) (Dobiat 1980; Metzner-Nebelsick 2002, 95 fig. 29; forthcoming; Preinfalk 2003, 51) or clay rhyta or ladles (Metzner-Nebelsick 2002, 151-153; forthcoming) (Fig. 10) are other characteristic features of eastern Hallstatt pottery.

Cemeteries in northeast Croatia

As I have briefly mentioned in the introduction the term 'Dalj group' is most common to describe the Hallstatt period in northeastern Croatia, in the region of Slavonia as well as in the landscape Baranja. Stylistic conformity in the larger cemeteries in Batina (HR), Dalj (HR), and Vukovar Lijeva bara (HR) seems closest (Metzner-Nebelsick 2002), whereas the micro region around Pécs in the Hungarian County of Baranya and the areas in southern Hungary along the left bank of the

Drava River, or indeed pottery from sites in the immediate vicinity of the left bank of the Danube in the region Bačka in modern Serbia with the cemetery of Doroslovo-Đepfeld (Trajković 2008) displays slight variations in styles. We may thus suppose that this is the case due to an intensified transfer of aesthetic concepts via the exchange of goods, possibly at meeting points such as markets or animal fairs, or as a reflection of contacts between people by means of institutionalized marriage traditions between certain villages/settlements. Behavioral patterns could thus be transferred and shared. If we however compare burial customs, the cemeteries of Batina[15] and Doroslovo-Đepfeld (Trajković 2008), the so far unpublished flat grave cemetery of Sotin[16] and possibly also Dalj-Busija (Metzner-Nebelsick 2002) all share the same grave construction, grave good assemblages as well as the burial rituals. The exclusive burial rite is cremation. The cremated remains of the deceased were either placed in large vessels and covered with a bowl – sometimes more than one vessel contains cremated bone (i.e. Ložnjak Dizdar/ Hutinec 2012, 13) – or scattered within the pit or burial chamber. In Batina a pyre, an *ustrina*, was discovered (Hršak *et al.* 2015). Next to oval pits rectangular burial chambers were dug into the subsoil. As new excavations in Doroslovo, Batina and Sotin have shown, the arrangements of the pots hint at the existence of formerly square wooden chamber constructions, although no traces of wood survived in the loess. Both types of graves contained larger amounts of various vessel types of the horizons IIIa and IIIb (Ha C) of my classification. In one case in Batina up to 17 different vessels are attested (Hršak *et al.* 2014, 17). Smaller vessels are grouped around larger pots, being often urns, or are grouped within the larger rectangular burial chambers. In some cases smaller vessels and grave goods were placed within a large vessel or urn (Trajković 2008, 15).

The pottery spectrum comprises of large conical neck vessels ('*Kegelhalsgefäße*') or other large pots which are accompanied by smaller types such as cantharoi, simple and more complex bowls, sometimes cups or handled bowls as well as special forms like footed bowls, clay pyxides or bird shaped clay vessels (Fig. 11; Metzner-Nebelsick 2002; Trajković 2008). In some graves meat offerings are present.

Metal finds consist of various types of personal attire such as bow fibulae, armlets and neckrings as well as pendants for women and dress pins, horse-gear and reign ornaments, whetstones and iron and bronze beads for the baltric or sometimes helmets for the men (Fig. 6; Metzner-Nebelsick 2002). Weapons seem to have been rare grave goods – in Doroslovo not a single weapons grave is recorded. This may however mirror the difference between the burial ground of a rural community such as Doroslovo and a center of power like in neighboring Batina across the Danube with a prominent hillfort and the adjacent barrows as well as flat graves of the residing elite. The Batina community controlled one of the most crucial geographical as well as cultural border situations of the Hallstatt culture.[17] From the old unscientific excavations of the early 20th century two helmets, an early Hallstatt bimetallic sword, trunyan axes, an axe of Ha C type as well as iron spearheads are known (Metzner-Nebelsick 2002, pl. 10; pl. 14,1;

---

15 Bojčić *et al.* 2011; Hršak *et al.* 2013; Hršak *et al.* 2014; Hršak *et al.* 2015; Hršak *et al.* 2016; Metzner-Nebelsick 2002, pl. 46-47.

16 Until 2015 70 cremation burials were excavated (Ložnjak Dizdar *et al.* 2009; Ložnjak Dizdar/ Hutinec 2010; 2011; 2012; 2014; Ložnjak Dizdar/Dizdar 2015).

17 The Batina hillfort has a very favorable strategic position and overlooks the vast plains of the Great Hungarian Plain which extends to present day northern Serbia (Vojvodina). During World War 2 a decisive battle was fought here.

Fig. 10. Red coated clay rhyta and ladles with zoomorphic handles from a grave context (vineyard Kraus 1911) in Dalj-Busija, eastern Slavonia, Croatia. Scale 1:4; the two red ladles carry meander ornaments in tin-foil applications; the animals of the rhyta are painted black (after Metzner-Nebelsick 2002, pl. 72; after Hoffiller 1938).

pl. 15,11.13; pl. 19,1-2; pl. 20,15-16).[18] Horse-gear of Ha C type in contrast to earlier examples (Fig. 4) is likewise rare. Iron bridles and bits of Ha C type have been found in Batina, Dalj-Busija and in the cemetery of Erdut close by (Fig. 12; Metzner-Nebelsick 2002, pl. 14,5; 83,16; 94,1-2; 107,1). Interestingly in the case of Dalj, vineyard Pavošević 1910, grave 11 a double bridle for a (symbolic) wagon represents this typical Hallstatt culture feature (Pare 1992, 197 fig. 135).

Iron knives are frequent; women's burials often contain one or more spindle whorls. From the new excavations in Batina also glass beads in women's graves have been reported (Hršak *et al.* 2016). In the flat grave cemetery of Sotin loom weights were found in one woman's burial (Ložnjak Dizdar/Hutinec 2012, 13). Loom weights in graves are a characteristic feature of the eastern Hallstatt culture, the central eastern Alps and Italy as B. Teržan pointed out. They are signifying women of highest social standing (Metzner-Nebelsick 2007; Teržan 1996). The yet unpublished grave from Sotin thus exemplifies that the Southeast Pannonian group and here especially the Dalj group forms a fully integrated part of the eastern Hallstatt culture.

In chamber burial 93 from Batina a Basarabi pottery import was found among a larger set of 16 other vessels of local type, attesting the contacts to areas across the Danube as well as to the south to communities of the Basarabi cultural group (Hršak *et al.* 2014, 17 fig. 4-5; 19) which have been a constant feature since the formation of the Hallstatt period in the area.

barrows

The most eastern Hallstatt burial mounds have been discovered in Batina by L. Nebelsick and me during a field survey in 1988 (Metzner-Nebelsick 2002, 187-198; fig. 85; 87). In the meantime this could be verified by modern excavations (esp. Bojčić 2011; Hršak *et al.* 2015; 2016) in the course of which Ha C burials underneath burial mounds have been excavated. So far two mounds from Batina have been published in a preliminary report. Both revealed central rectangular chambers with timber construction with 4.5 x 4.5 meter in the case of barrow 1.

---

18   The sword has been reproduced several times i.e. in Harding 1995.

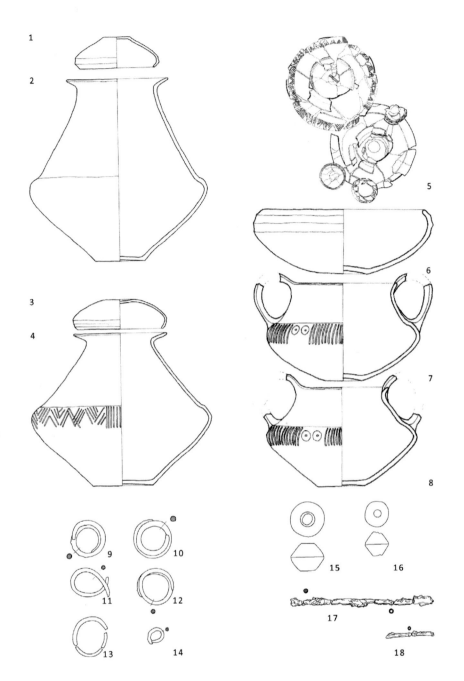

Fig. 11. Doroslovo-Đepfeld, near Sombor, northern Serbia: cremation burial 151; 5: grave plan; 1-4.6-8.15-16: pottery; 9-14: bronze; 17-18: iron. 9-18: scale 1:2; 1-4: scale 1:5; 6-8: scale 1:3 (after Trajković 2008, 170; 320-321).

The outline of the mounds was marked by a fence of densely set wooden posts (Hršak *et al.* 2016, 15 fig. 1). Tumulus 2, grave 1 was a woman's burial containing glass and gold beads, other dress accessories, spindle whorls and lavish red coated pottery with tin-foil application (Hršak *et al.* 2016, 18).

It is interesting that in Batina contemporary burial mounds and flat graves were located in direct vicinity to each other, a feature which has only recently been discovered in the western Hallstatt culture as well (Schumann 2015, esp. 45-49).

The situation for the cemetery of Dalj-Busija in eastern Slavonija remains yet unclear, although the existence of some of the most prestigious clay drinking sets of the eastern Hallstatt culture (Fig. 10; Hoffiller 1938; Metzner-Nebelsick 2002, pl. 72,9-12; pl. 74,8-9; forthcoming) and multiple bronze and iron objects,

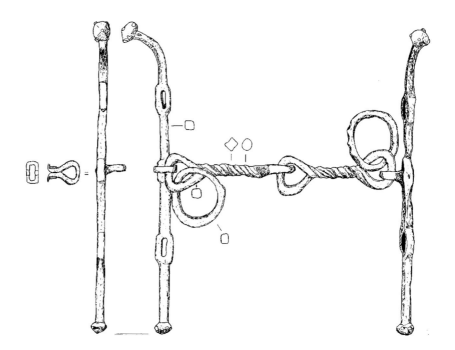

Fig. 12. Iron bridle from Erdut, Veliki Varad (Museum für Vor- und Frühgeschichte SMPK Berlin). Scale 1:4 (after Metzner-Nebelsick 2002, pl. 107,1).

however mostly without a secure context other than 'from a grave', suggest that also here burial mounds or at least larger well equipped burial chambers in a flat grave cemetery must have existed. Those specific drinking vessels are characteristic for the Drava River valley (Metzner-Nebelsick 2002, 152 fig. 59; forthcoming) and link Dalj with a couple of barrow cemeteries upstream the Drava River.

Only single barrows from this region have so far been published, like from a cemetery in Martijanec (Vinski-Gasparini 1961; Catalogue Zagreb 2010, 107; Metzner-Nebelsick forthcoming). Others as Goričan near Čakovec (Vidović 1983; Vinki-Gasparini 1987) and Dvoršće (Vidović 1989), also located in the Međimurje that is the Sava-Drava interfluve, remain largely unpublished, except for some grave inventories.[19] All are cremations burials. In Martijanec, the giant 'Gamulica' tumulus revealed a central rectangular burial chamber and a stone construction. The pottery set was numerous and next to a clay rhyton with a zoomorphic handle and two ladles, several other types are presents. The meander ornaments in tin-foil appliqué technique on a cherry red coated large vessel with a conical neck connects this set with many areas of the eastern Hallstatt culture. The rhyta and ladles from Dalj-Busija and a newly published vessel from in a rich rider's burial in mound 1 from Batina (Hršak *et al.* 2013, 14 fig. 5) are so far the most eastern examples for this specific prestigious Hallstatt pottery style. Metal finds are rare in Martijanec tumulus 1. A wooden bucket or situla with sheet bronze ornamentation and some iron objects being the only ones. This is a seemingly strange contrast between a tremendous input in constructing the barrow and a noticeable restriction in the equipment of the deceased. All mentioned burials date to the developed Ha C period (= Ha C2 or horizon IIIb).

Within this article I cannot dwell in detail on other cultural affiliations of the Southeast Pannonian group. A micro region of central importance in this context of the eastern fringes of the Hallstatt world is Kaptol in the Požega

19   In Dvoršće tumulus 1, grave 1 a bronze vessel and horse-gear was found, as well as a clay vessel with bird protomes on its shoulder (Vidović 1989, 85-86 fig. 8-9; Šimek 2004).

Mountains in central Croatia. This Hallstatt center of power with a prominent hillfort and two adjacent barrow cemeteries has gained wide attention, mainly because of the abundant evident of defensive armor such as helmets and greaves from several burials in the barrow cemetery Čemernica dating to a developed Ha C i.e. Ha C2/Ha D1 period or to horizon IIIb, but also younger Ha D1 period burials with defensive armor have been discovered (Vejvoda/Mirnik 1971; 1973; Šimek 2004). More recent excavations in the second barrow cemetery 'Gradac' have been undertaken by H. Potrebica (Catalogue Zagreb 2010; Potrebica 2004; 2008; 2013). Like in Batina, Pécs-Jakabhegy, Martijanec or others the mounds have a central grave chamber, mostly with dry-stone walling. The burial rite is again cremation. Pottery sets in the graves fit into the eastern Hallstatt spectrum of sumptuous ornamentations with tin-foil applications, graphite coating and bullhead protomes.

Settlements

Some of the prominent hillforts of the fringe zone of the eastern Hallstatt culture have already been mentioned. The state of research or rather the publication record is unfortunately rather poor. With the exception of at least some results of more recent excavations in the case of Sopron-Burgstall (Patek 1982a; 1982b), other excavations in western Hungary as well as in northeast Croatia remain – apart from minor preliminary excavation reports – unpublished. There have been excavations on the hillforts of Nagyberki-Szalacska, Somogy County south of Lake Balaton with a vast tumulus cemetery close by (Czajlik 2008; Czajlik *et al.* 2012; Czajlik/Holl 2015), on Pécs-Jalabhegy in County Baranya in southwest Hungary (Maráz 1996), in Batina Gradac in the Slavonian part of the landscape Baranja in Croatia with a barrow cemetery outside the main fortification discovered by L. Nebelsick and me in 1988[20] or in Kisvárhegy near Fehérvárcsurgó in Central western Hungary (Jungbert 1993) to name a selection. For some as Pécs-Jakabhegy, Sopron-Burgstall or Nagyberki-Szalacska aerial prospections have been undertaken recently and a new international EU-funded research project will follow that line of research. More substantial work has been done for the micro region of Kaptol in the Požega Mountains (Potrebica 2013).

In contrast to the hillforts work in so-called open settlements has been much more intensive, mostly in the course of rescue excavations. A full assessment cannot be given in this article.

Ritual deposits

As in many areas of Europe the formerly so prominent bronze hoarding practice is no longer performed during the Ha C period in the northeast as well as southeast alpine fringe zone. Only in Ha D1 religiously motivated hoarding practice sets in again. The majority of those hoard finds either comprise of female dress accessories like fibulae in the hoard of Ravazd-Kisravazd (Fekete 1973), bronze vessels as in Kurd (Patay 1990, 76-78; pl. 51-63) or a combination of personal attire, bronze

---

20 Excavated by S. Foltiny and K. Vinski-Gasparini and the Muzej Slavonije in Osijek in the 1970s (for reference see Metzner-Nebelsick 2002, 185-187; 186 fig. 84) remain unpublished.

vessels and other objects.[21] So far only five bronze hoards of the Ha D1 period have been found in Transdanubia.

Conclusion

Although previous studies and the publication of comprehensive work on hitherto available information have enhanced our knowledge about the Hallstatt period at the southeastern fringe of the Hallstatt culture immensely, there are still obvious voids. This is mainly true for information concerning grave constructions, anthropological analyses or even modern restoration of grave contents are lacking; some excavated burials or even larger parts of cemeteries are so far only published as preliminary reports. I have tried to give an overview of important sites and their close relation to those cultural groups of the eastern Hallstatt culture which are more in the focus of western research like the Kalenderberg group, the Sulmtal group or the Hallstatt period in Slovenian Dolenjska. Sites such as Dalj, Batina or Sotin in northeast Croatia and even Doroslovo across the Danube in northwestern Serbia formed an integral part of what one might call an eastern Hallstatt ideology – at least as far burial customs or aesthetical concepts such as in the production of pottery are concerned (i.e. the existence of red-coated pottery, bull-head protomes, tin-foil applications, same variety of pottery ornaments).

It is always difficult if not impossible to define the borders of so-called cultural groups, although it is often done (including the author of this article) as a useful tool to make far more complex scenarios more easily to grasp. We have however to bear in mind that maps such as figures 1 and 3 represent various layers of different interchanging levels of behavior and social practices resulting in a multitude of identities preserved in the archaeological record. Some are gender-biased, as specific types of dress accessories or pottery styles (Brosseder 2004), others are indicative for ritual practices and beliefs such as burial rites or status representation within the grave (see Nebelsick 1997; 2016).

The rhythms of stylistic concepts vary; culture contacts and affiliations can change. Even in the case of the Southeast Pannonian group of the Urnfield and Hallstatt period the picture is not consistent over the course of time. Only in the Ha C period does the Hallstatt outpost of the cemetery of Doroslovo for instance becomes an integral part of this group or its regional variation, the Dalj group, and then shares at least parts of an eastern Hallstatt ideology as far as burial practices are concerned. Whereas in the Kalenderberg group (Nebelsick 1997); or in Dolenjska (Gabrovec et al. 2006; Schumann 2015) 'Hallstatt' ideology and life style strive uninterruptedly into the late Hallstatt period – Ha D period, after Ha D1 the picture of homogeneity dissolves at the fringes of the eastern Hallstatt culture. Although even for the core areas of the eastern Hallstatt culture major disruptions

---

21 This composition pattern is represented in the remarkable ensemble of ritually deposited objects at the edge of a pit within the settlement of Ikervár, Vas County in southern Transdanubua. The hoard consisted of nearly 300 objects and weighed 5 kg. The so far published items are a fragment of a funnelled bronze sieve, several fibulae dating the hoard the Ha D1 period – among them a navicella fibula, a serpentine fibula S 4 and a horse fibula -, a belt plaque, two whetstones, a bronze anvil and several fragmented pottery vessels, the jaw bone of a pig and several plant remains (i.e. einkorn and millet). According to the pollen evidence the hoard was deposited in the summer. The find is interpreted by M. Nagy as the remains of a sanctuary for a goddess resembling Demeter or Persephone (Nagy et al. 2012).

at certain places can be observed after Ha D1 (Egg/Kramer 2013; Teržan 1998), the situation there cannot be compared with areas further to the east.

Here the geographical vicinity to the Alföld/Great Hungarian Plain with its population groups with a then 'Scythian' life style and a steppe bound identity of pastoralists on one hand and to western Balkanic groups on the other now had a greater impact. As E. Jerem has shown some time ago for southeast Transdanubia (Jerem 1968; 1973), also in northeast Croatia and northwest Serbia a new cultural orientation towards the southeast is noticeable (also Bertok/Gáti 2014; Metzner-Nebelsick 2002; Trajković 2008). New pottery forms, but also burial customs, including horse burials (in Doroslovo or Vukovar) like in the Vekerzug group in the Alföld with its Scythian appeal, or prestigious dress accessories of 'Balkanic' style are now dominating, whereas western contacts are diminished. The former strong integration into the eastern Hallstatt culture during the Ha C/Ha D1 is no longer maintained. To evaluate the character of the process in detail is an interesting aspect of future research.

Bibliography

Barth 1969: F. Barth, Die hallstattzeitlichen Grabhügel im Bereich des Kutscher bei Podsemel (Slowenien). Antiquitas 3,5 (Bonn 1969).

Berciu/Comşa 1956: D. Berciu/E. Comşa, Săpăturile archeologice de la Balta Verde şi Cogoşu (1949 şi 1950). Materiale şi Cercetări Arheologice 2, 1956, 252-489.

Bertok/Gáti 2014: G. Bertok/Cs. Gáti, Old Times – New Methods. Non-Invasive Archaeology in Baranya County (Hungary) 2005-2013 (Budapest 2014).

Bojčić et al. 2011: Z. Bojčić/M. Dizdar/T. Hršak/T. Leleković, Rezultati probnih istraživanja nalazišta Batina-Sredno 2010. Godine. Results of the 2010 Trial Excavations of the Batina-Sredno Site. Annales Instituti Archaeologici (Zagreb) 7, 2011, 13-19.

Brosseder 2004: U. Brosseder, Studien zur Ornamentik hallstattzeitlicher Keramik zwischen Rhônetal und Karpatenbecken. Universitätsforschungen zur Prähistorischen Archäologie 106 (Bonn 2004).

Catalogue Zagreb 2010: Guide to the Prehistoric Collection. Archaeological Museum in Zagreb (Zagreb 2010).

Ciocea Safta 1996: E. Ciocea Safta, Necropola tumulară de pe Ostruvu Mare. Studii şi Cercetări Istorie Veche şi Arheologie 47, 1996, 159-190.

Covié 1987: B. Covié, Grupa Donja Dolina-Sanski Most. In: Praistorija Jugoslavenskih zemalja 5 željezno doba (Sarajevo 1987) 232-286.

Czajlik 2008: Z. Czajlik, Aerial Archaeology in the research of Burial Tumuli in Hungary. Communicationes Archaeologicae Hungariae 2008, 94-107.

Czajlik/Holl 2015: Z. Czajlik/B. Holl, Zur topographischen Forschung der Hügelgräberfelder in Ungarn. Ein Vergleich der Angaben von Compte-rendu mit den Ergebnissen der Luftbildarchäologie. In: Dissertationes Archaeologicae ex Instituto Archaeologico Universitatis de Rolando Eötvös nominatae 3,3 (Budapest 2015) 59-70.

Czajlik *et al.* 2012: Z. Czajlik/G. Király/A. Czövek/B. Holl/G. Brolly, The Application of Remote Sensing Technology and Geophysical Methods in the Topographic Survey of Early Iron Age Burial Tumuli in Transdanubia. In: S. Berecki, (ed), Iron Age Rites and Rituals in the Carpathian Basin. Proceedings of the International Colloquium from Târgu Mureş, October 2011 (Cluj 2012) 65-76.

Deicke 2011: A. Deicke, Studien zu reich ausgestatteten Gräbern aus dem urnenfelderzeitlichen Gräberfeld von Künzing (Lkr. Deggendorf, Niederbayern). Jahrbuch des Römisch-Germanischen Zentralmuseums Mainz 58, 2011, 1-188.

Dobiat 1980: C. Dobiat, Dobiat, Das hallstattzeitliche Gräberfeld von Kleinklein und seine Keramik. Schild von Steier Beih. 1 (Graz 1980).

Dumitrescu 1968: V. Dumitrescu, La nécropole tumulaire du premier âge du fer de Basarabi (Dép. de Dolj, Olténie). Dacia N. S. 12, 1968, 177-260.

Egg 1988a: M. Egg, Italische Helme mit Krempe. In: Antike Helme. Sammlung Lipperheide und andere Bestände des Antikenmuseums Berlin. Monographien des Römisch-Germanischen Zentralmuseums Mainz (Mainz 1988) 222-271.

Egg 1988b: M. Egg, Die ältesten Helme der Hallstattzeit. In: Antike Helme. Sammlung Lipperheide und andere Bestände des Antikenmuseums Berlin. Monographien des Römisch-Germanischen Zentralmuseums Mainz (Mainz 1988) 212-221.

Egg 1996: M. Egg, Einige Bemerkungen zum hallstattzeitlichen Wagengrab von Somlóvásárhely, Kom. Veszprém in Westungarn. Jahrbuch des Römisch-Germanischen Zentralmuseums Mainz 43, 1996, 327-353.

Egg/Kramer 2005: M. Egg/D. Kramer, Krieger, Feste, Totenopfer. Der lette Hallstattfürst von Kleinklein in der Steiermark. Mosaiksteine Forschungen am Römisch-Germanischen Zentralmuseum 1 (Mainz 2005).

Egg/Kramer 2013: M. Egg/D. Kramer (eds.), Die hallstattzeitlichen Fürstengräber von Kleinklein in der Steiermark: der Kröllkogel. Monographien des Römisch-Germanischen Zentralmuseums 110 (Mainz 2013).

Egg/Munir 2013: M. Egg/J. Munir, Metallfunde, Pferdegeschirr, Trachtschmuck, Bronzemaske und Bronzehände, Bronzegefäße, Herdegeräte, unbestimmbare Metallobjekte. In: M. Egg/D. Kramer (eds.), Die hallstattzeitlichen Fürstengräber von Kleinklein in der Steiermark: der Kröllkogel. Monographien des Römisch-Germanischen Zentralmuseums 110 (Mainz 2013) 75-279.

Egg *et al.* 1998: M. Egg/U. Neuhäuser/Ž. Škoberne, Ein Grab mit Schüsselhelm aus Budinjak in Kroatien. Jahrbuch des Römisch-Germanischen Zentralmuseums Mainz 45, 1998, 435-472.

Eibner 2001: A. Eibner, Der Donau – Drave- Save – Raum im Spiegel gegenseitiger Einflußnahme und Kommunikation in der frühen Eisenzeit. Zentralorte entlang der „Argonautenstraße". The Danube – Drava – Save – region in the light of the reciprocal exertion of influence and communication in the Early Iron Age. Central places along the "Route of the Argonauts". In: A. Lippert (ed.), Die Drau – Mur- und Raab-Region im 1. vorchristlichen Jahrtausend. Akten des internationalen interdisziplinären Symposiums vom 26. bis 29. April 2000 in Bad Radkersburg. Universitätsforschungen zur Prähistorischen Archäologie 78 (Bonn 2001) 181-190.

Felgenhauer 1990-1992 [1996]: F. Felgenhauer, Stillfried. Lebensraum des Menschen seit 30 000 Jahren. Archäologischer Fundplatz von internationaler Bedeutung, Objekt interdisziplinärer Forschung von bedeutendem Rang. Ergebnisse der Ausgrabungen und Forschungen 1969-1989. Forschungen in Stillfried 9/10, 1990-1992 (1996) 9-29.

Fekete 1973: M. Fekete, Der Hortfund von Kisravazd. Acta Archaeologica Academiae Scientiarum Hungaricae 25, 1973, 341-358.

Fekete 1985: M. Fekete, Rettungsgrabung früheisenzeitlicher Hügelgräber in Vaskeresztes (Vorbericht): Acta Archaeologica Academiae Scientiarum Hungaricae 37, 1985, 33-78.

Gabrovec 1970: S. Gabrovec, Dvozankaste ločne fibule. Godišnjak (Sarajevo) 8, 1970, 5-44.

Gabrovec et al. 2006: S. Gabrovec/A. Kruh/I. Murgelj/B. Teržan, Stična II/1 Katalog. Gomile starejše železne dobe. Grabhügel aus der älteren Eisenzeit. Catalogi et Monographiae 37 (Ljubljana 2006).

Gallus/Horváth 1939: S. Gallus/T. Horváth, Un Peuple Cavalier Préscythique en Hongrie. Dissertationes Pannonicae II,9 (Budapest 1939).

Gavranoić 2011: M. Gavranović, Die Spätbronze- und Früheisenzeit in Bosnien. Universitätsforschungen zur Prähistorischen Archäologie 195 (Bonn 2011).

Gumă 1993: M. Gumă, Civilizaţia primei epoci a fierului în sud-vestul României. Bibliotheca Thracologica 4 (Bucureşti 1993).

Gumă 1996: M. Gumă, Der Basarabi-Komplex in Mittel- und Südosteuropa: Kolloquium in Dobreta-Turnu Severin (7.-9. November 1996) (Bukareşti 1996).

Hänsel/Medović 1991: B. Hänsel/P. Medović, Vorbericht über die jugoslawisch-deutschen Ausgrabungen in der Siedlung von Feudvar bei Mošorin (Gem. Titel, Vojvodina) von 1986-1990. Bronzezeit – Vorrömische Eisenzeit. Bericht der Römisch-Germanischen Kommission 72, 1991, 45-203.

Harding 1995: A. Harding, Die Schwerter im ehemaligen Jugoslawien. Prähistorische Bronzefunde IV,14 (Stuttgart 1995).

Hellerschmid 2006: I. Hellerschmid, Die urnenfelder-/hallstattzeitliche Wallanlage von Stillfried an der March. Ergebnisse der Ausgrabungen 1969-1989 unter besonderer Berücksichtigung des Kulturwandels an der Epochengrenze Urnenfelder-/Hallstattkultur. Mitteilungen der Prähistorischen Kommission 63 (Wien 2006).

Hoffiller 1938: V. Hoffiller, Corpus Vasorum Antiquorum Yougoslavie Fasc. 2. – Zagreb Museé National, Fasc. 2 (Zagreb 1938).

Horváth 2014: L. Horváth, Early Iron Age graves from Keszthely and its environs (Data publication). In: O. Heinrich-Tamáska/P. Straub (eds.), Mensch, Siedlung und Landschaft im Wechsel der Jahrtausende am Balaton, Castellum Pannonicum Pelsonense 4, 2014, 63-97.

Hršak et al. 2013: T. Hršak/T. Leleković/M. Dizdar, Resultati istraživanja nalazišta Batina-Sredno 2012. Godine. The results of the excavations of the Batina – Sredno site in 2012. Annales Instituti Archaeologici – Godišnjak Instituta za arheologiju (Zagreb) 9, 2013, 12-19.

Hršak *et al.* 2014: T. Hršak/T. Leleković/M. Dizdar, Resultati istraživanja nalazišta Batina-Sredno 2013. godine. The results of the excavations of the Batina – Sredno site in 2013. Annales Instituti Archaeologici – Godišnjak Instituta za arheologiju (Zagreb) 10, 2014, 14-20.

Hršak *et al.* 2015: T. Hršak/T. Leleković/M. Dizdar, Resultati istraživanja nalazišta Batina-Sredno 2014. Godine. Research results for the Batina – Stredno site in 2014. Annales Instituti Archaeologici – Godišnjak Instituta za arheologiju (Zagreb) 11, 2015, 18-22.

Hršak *et al.* 2016: T. Hršak/T. Leleković/M. Dizdar, Resultati istraživanja nalazišta Batina-Sredno 2015. Godine. Research results for the Batina – Stredno site in 2015. Annales Instituti Archaeologici – Godišnjak Instituta za arheologiju (Zagreb) 12, 2016, 14-18.

Jerem 1968: E. Jerem, The late Iron Age cemetery of Szent-Lőrinc. Acta Archaeologica Acadaemiae Scientiarum Hungaricae 20, 1968, 159-208.

Jerem 1973: E. Jerem, Zur Geschichte der späten Eisenzeit in Transdanubien. Späteisenzeitliche Grabfunde von Beremend (Komitat Baranya). Acta Archaeologica Acadaemiae Scientiarum Hungaricae 25, 1973, 65-86.

Jerem/Lippert 1996: E. Jerem/A. Lippert (eds.), Die Osthallstattkultur. Akten des Internationalen Symposiums, Sopron, 10.-14. Mai 1994. Archaeolingua 7 (Budapest 1996).

Jerem/Urban 2000: E. Jerem/O. Urban, Höhensiedlungen – Befestigungen – Zentralsiedlungen. Prozesse der Urbanisierung im Donau-Karpaten-Raum. In: V. Guichard/S. Sievers/O. H. Urban (eds.), Les processus d'urbanisation à l'âge du fer. Eisenzeitliche Urbanisationsprozesse. Tagung Glux-en-Glenne 1998. Collection Bibracte 4 (Glux-en-Glenne 2000) 157-164.

Jerem *et al.* 2014: E. Jerem/Zs. Vasáros/M. Vicze, Guide to the Archeological Park at Százhalombatta (Budapest 2014).

Jungbert 1993: B. Jungbert, Early Iron Age (Ha C2) Settlement Centre at Fehérvárcsurgó. Actes du XIIe Congrès International des Sciences Prehistoriques et Protohistoriques Bratislava 1991 volume 3 (Bratislava 1993) 191-197.

Kaus 1988/89: M. Kaus, Kimmerischer Pferdeschmuck im Karpatenbecken – das Stillfrieder Depot aus neuer Sicht. Mitteilungen der Anthropologischen Gesellschaft Wien 118/119, 1988/89, 247-257.

Kemenczei 1974: T. Kemeczei, Újabb leletek a Nagyberki Szalacskai koravaskori halomsírokról. Archaeologiai Értesitő 101, 1974, 3-16.

Király *et al.* 2013: Á. Király/K. Sebők/Z. Zoffmann/G. Kovács, Early Iron Age 'mass graves' in the Middle Tisza Region: Investigation and interpretation. In: N. Müller-Scheeßel (ed.), ‚Irreguläre‘ Bestattungen in der Urgeschichte: Norm, Ritual, Strafe? Akten der Internationalen Tagung in Frankfurt a.M. vom 3. bis. 5. Februar 2012. Kolloquien zur Vor- und Frühgeschichte 19 (Bonn 2013) 307-326.

Kmeťová 2013: P. Kmeťová, „Maters of horses" in the west, „horse breeders" in the east? On the significance and position of the horse in the Early Iron Age communities of the Pannonian Basin. In. R. Karl/J. Leskovar (eds.), Interpretierte Eisenzeiten. Fallstudien, Methoden, Theorien. Tagungsbeiträge der 5. Linzer Gespräche zur interpretativen Eisenzeitarchäologie. Studien zur Kulturgeschichte von Oberösterreich 37 (Linz 2013) 247-258.

Knez 1993: T. Knez, Novo mesto III. Knežja gomila. Fürstengrabhügel. Carniola Archaeologica 2 (Novo mesto 1993).

Kossack 1954: G. Kossack, Pferdegeschirr aus Gräbern der älteren Hallstattzeit Bayerns. Jahrbuch des Römisch-Germanischen Zentralmuseums Mainz 1, 1954, 111-178.

Kossack 1959: G. Kossack, Südbayern während der Hallstattzeit. Römisch-Germanische Forschungen 24 (Berlin 1959).

Križ 1997: B. Križ, B. Križ, Novo mesto IV. Kapiteljska njiva. Gomila II in gomila III. Carniola Archaeologica 4 (Novo mesto 1997).

Lochner 2013: M. Lochner, Bestattungssitten auf Gräberfeldern der mitteldonauländischen Urnenfelderkultur. In: M. Lochner/F. Ruppenstein (eds.), Brandbestattungen von der mittleren Donau bis zur Ägäis zwischen 1300 und 750 v. Chr. Cremation burials in the region between the Middle Danube and the Aegean, 1300-750 BC. Proceedings of the international symposium held at the Austrian Academy of Sciences at Vienna, February 11th-12th, 2010 (Wien 2013) 11-31.

Ložnjak Dizdar/Dizdar 2015: D. Ložnjak Dizdar/M. Dizdar, Sotin, arheološka istraživanja starije željeznodobnog groblja u Podunavlju 2014. Godine. Sotin, archaeological research of an Early Iron Age cemetery in Danube region, 2014. Annales Instituti Archaeologici – Godišnjak Instituta za arheologiju (Zagreb) 11, 2015, 14-17.

Ložnjak Dizdar/Hutinec 2010: D. Ložnjak Dizdar/M. Hutinec, Sotin-Jaroši, probna arheološka istraživanja 2009. Sotin-Jaroši, Archaeological Trial Excavations in 2009. Annales Instituti Archaeologici – Godišnjak Instituta za arheologiju (Zagreb) 6, 2010, 7-10.

Ložnjak Dizdar/Hutinec 2011: D. Ložnjak Dizdar/M. Hutinec, Sotin, probna arheološka istraživanja 2010. Godine. Sotin, Archaeological Trial Excavation 2010. Annales Instituti Archaeologici – Godišnjak Instituta za arheologiju (Zagreb) 8, 2012, 9-12.

Ložnjak Dizdar/Hutinec 2012: D. Ložnjak Dizdar/M. Hutinec, Sotin, probna arheološka istraživanja 2011. Godine. Sotin, trial archaeological excavation 2011. Annales Instituti Archaeologici – Godišnjak Instituta za arheologiju (Zagreb) 8, 2012, 9-13.

Ložnjak Dizdar/Hutinec 2014: D. Ložnjak Dizdar/M. Hutinec, Sotin – rezultati istraživanja 2013. godine. Sotin – the results of research in 2013. Annales Instituti Archaeologici – Godišnjak Instituta za arheologiju (Zagreb) 10, 2014, 9-13.

Ložnjak Dizdar et al. 2009: D. Ložnjak Dizdar/M. Ilkić/M. Hutinec, Sotin – Srednje polje, probna arheološka istraživanja 2008. g. Sotin – Srednje polje, Archaeological Trial Excavations in 2008. Annales Instituti Archaeologici – Godišnjak Instituta za arheologiju (Zagreb) 5, 2009, 12-14.

Maráz 1978: B. Maráz, Zur Frühhallstattzeit in Süd-Pannonien. Janus Pannonius Múzeum Évkönyve 23, 1978, 145-164.

Maráz 1996: B. Maráz, Pécs-Jakabhegy – Ausgrabungsergebnisse und die Fragen der Frühhallstattkultur in Südostpannonien. In: E. Jerem/A. Lippert (ed.), Die Osthallstattkultur. Akten des Internationalen Symposiums, Sopron, 10.-14. Mai 1994. Archaeolingua 7 (Budapest 1996) 255-265.

Metzner-Nebelsick 1992: C. Metzner-Nebelsick, Gefäße mit basaraboider Ornamentik aus Frög. In: A. Lippert/K. Spindler (ed.), Festschrift zum 50jährigen Bestehen des Instituts für Ur- u. Frühgeschichte der Leopold-Franzens-Universität Innsbruck. Universitätsforschungen zur prähistorischen Archäologie 8 (Innsbruck 1992) 349-383.

Metzner-Nebelsick 1994: C. Metzner-Nebelsick, Die früheisenzeitliche Trensenentwicklung zwischen Kaukasus und Mitteleuropa. In: P. Schauer (ed.), Archäologische Untersuchungen zum Übergang von der Bronze- zur Eisenzeit zwischen Nordsee und Jenissei. Tagung der Universität Regensburg Lehrstuhl für Vor-

und Frühgeschichte in Verbindung mit dem Römisch-Germanischen Zentralmuseum 28. – 30. Oktober 1992. Regensburger Beiträge zur Prähistorischen Archäologie 1 (Regensburg 1994) 383-447.

Metzner-Nebelsick 1996: C. Metzner-Nebelsick, Urnenfelder- und Hallstattzeit in Südostpannonien. In: E. Jerem/A. Lippert (eds.), Die Osthallstattkultur. Akten des Internationalen Symposiums, Sopron, 10.-14. Mai 1994. Archaeolingua 7 (Budapest 1996) 285-314.

Metzner-Nebelsick 1997: C. Metzner-Nebelsick, Hallstattzeitliche Zentren in Südostpannonien. In: Chronologische Fragen der Eisenzeit. Konferenz Keszthely 1994. Zalai Múzeum 8 (Zalaegerszeg 1997) 9-26.

Metzner-Nebelsick 1998: C. Metzner-Nebelsick, Abschied von den "Thrako-Kimmeriern"? – Neue Aspekte der Interaktion zwischen karpatenländischen Kulturgruppe der späten Bronze- und frühen Eisenzeit mit der osteuropäischen Steppenkoine. In: B. Hänsel/J. Machnik (eds.), Das Karpatenbecken und die osteuropäische Steppe. Nomadenbewegungen und Kulturaustausch in den vorchristlichen Metallzeiten (4000-500 v. Chr.). Prähistorische Archäologie in Südosteuropa 12 (München, Rahden/Westf. 1998) 361-422.

Metzner-Nebelsick 2000: C. Metzner-Nebelsick, Early Iron Age nomadism in the Great Hungarian Plain – Migration or assimilation? The Thraco-Cimmerian problem revisited. In: J. Davis-Kimball/E. Murphy/L. Koryakova/L. T. Yablonsky (eds.), Kurgans, ritual sites, and settlements: Eurasian Bronze and Iron Age. British Archaeological Reports International Series 890 (Oxford 2000) 160-184.

Metzner-Nebelsick 2002: C. Metzner-Nebelsick, Der „Thrako-Kimmerische Formenkreis" aus der Sicht der Urnenfelder- und Hallstattzeit Südostpannoniens. Vorgeschichtliche Forschungen 23 (Rahden/Westf. 2002).

Metzner-Nebelsick 2004: C. Metzner-Nebelsick, Wo sind die Frauen der Kimmerier? Ein Beitrag zum Kulturkontakt zwischen Kaukasus, nordpontischen Steppen und Karpatenbecken am Beispiel der Frauentrachten des 9. und 8. Jahrhunderts v. Chr. In: J. Chochorowski (ed.), Kimmerowie Scytowie Sarmaci. Księga poświęcona pamięci Professora Tadeusza Sulimirskiego. Cimmerians Scythians Sarmatians. In memory of Professor Tadeusz Sulimirski (Kraków 2004) 271-297.

Metzner-Nebelsick 2005: C. Metzner-Nebelsick, Das Wagengrab von Künzing im Licht seiner östlichen Beziehungen. In. K. Schmotz (ed.), Vorträge des 23. Niederbayerischen Archäologentages (Rahden/Westf. 2005) 105-137.

Metzner-Nebelsick 2007: C. Metzner-Nebelsick, Pferdchenfibeln – Zur Deutung einer frauenspezifischen Schmuckform der Hallstatt- und Frühlatènezeit. In: M. Blečić/M. Črešnar/B. Hänsel/A. Hellmuth/E. Kaiser/C. Metzner-Nebelsick (eds.), Scripta praehistorica in honorem Biba Teržan. Situla 44 (Ljubljana 2007) 707-735.

Metzner-Nebelsick 2010: C. Metzner-Nebelsick, Aspects of mobility and migration in the eastern Carpathian Basin and adjacent areas in the early Iron Age (10th-7th centuries BC). In: K. Dzięgielewski/M. S: Przybyła/A. Gawlik (eds.), Migration in Bronze and Early Iron Age Europe. Prace Archeologiczne 63 (Kraków 2010) 121-151.

Metzner-Nebelsick 2012: C. Metzner-Nebelsick, Social transition and spatial organisation: The problem of the Early Iron Age occupation of the strongholds in Northeast Hungary. In: P. Anreiter/E. Bánffy/L. Bartosiewicz/W. Meid/C. Metzner-nebelsick (eds.), Archeological, Cultural and Linguistic Heritage. Festschrift for Erzsébet Jerem in Honour of her 70th Birthday. Archaeolingua 25 (Budapest 2012) 425-448.

Metzner-Nebelsick forthcoming: C. Metzner-Nebelsick, Sumptuous vessels and animal protomes. New finds of the early Hallstatt Period in Southeast Pannonia. In: S. Stegmann-Rajtár (ed.), Das nördliche Karpatenbecken in der Hallstattzeit. Internationale Tagung Košice 9.-12. Dezember 2014. Archaeolingua (Budapest 2017/2018).

Mlekuž/Črešnar 2014: D. Mlekuž/M. Črešnar, Landscape and Identity Politics of the Poštela Hillfort. Pokrajina in Politika Identitet Utrjene Naselbine na Pošteli. In: S. Tecco Hvala (ed.), Studia praehistorica in honorem Janez Dular. Opera Instituti Sloveniae 30 (Ljubljana 2014) 197-211.

Müller-Scheeßel 2000: N. Müller-Scheeßel, Die Hallstattkultur und ihre räumliche Differenzierung. Der West- und Osthallstattkreis aus forschungsgeschichtlich-methodologischer Sicht. Tübinger Texte 3 (Rahden/Westf. 2000).

Nagy et al. 2012: M. Nagy/P. Sümegi/G Persaitis/S. Gulyás/T. Töröcsik, The Irone Age Hoard Found at Ikervár (Vas County, Hungary) in the western Region of the Carpathian Basin. A study in the reconstruction of the cultic life of the Hallstatt period in the light of archaeological and scientific analyses. In: S. Berecki (ed.), Iron Age rites and rituals in the Carpathian Basin. Proceedings of the international colloquium from Târgu Mureş 7-9 October 2011 (Târgu Mureş 2012) 31-64.

Nebelsick 1997: L. Nebelsick, Die Kalenderberggruppe der Hallstattzeit am Nordostalpenrand. In: L. D. Nebelsick/A. Eibner/E. Lauermann/J.-W. Neugebauer, Hallstattkultur im Osten Österreichs. Wissenschaftliche Schriftenreihe Niederösterreich 106/107/108/109 (St. Pölten 1997) 9-128.

Nebelsick 2016: L. Nebelsick, Drinking against death: Studies on the materiality and iconography of ritual, sacrifice and transcendence in later prehistoric Europe (Warszawa 2016).

Pare 1987: C. Pare, Der Zeremonialwagen der Hallstattzeit – Untersuchungen zu Konstruktion, Typologie und Kulturbeziehungen. In: Vierrädrige Wagen der Hallstattzeit. Monographien des Römisch-Germanischen Zentralmuseums 12 (Mainz 1987) 189-248.

Pare 1992: C. Pare, Wagons and wagon-graves of the Early Iron Age in Central Europe. Oxford University Committee for Archaeology, Monographs 35 (Oxford 1992).

Patay 1990: P. Patay, Die Bronzegefäße in Ungarn. Prähistorische Bronzefunde II,10 (Stuttgart 1990).

Patek 1968: E. Patek, Die Urnenfelderkultur in Transdanubien. Archaeologica Hungarica 44 (Budapest 1968).

Patek 1974/75: E. Patek, Zalaszántó, Várrét (Komitat Veszprém, Kreis Keszthely). Mitteilungen des Archäologischen Instituts Budapest 5, 1974/1975, 206-207.

Patek 1982a: E. Patek, Recent excavations at the Hallstatt and LaTène hillfort of Sopron-Várhegy (Burgstall) and the predecessors of the Hallstatt Culture in Hungary. In: Studies in the Iron Age of Hungary. British Archaeological Reports, International Series 144 (Oxford 1982) 1-56.

Patek 1982b: E. Patek, Neue Untersuchungen auf dem Burgstall bei Sopron. Bericht der Römisch-Germanischen Kommission 63, 1982, 105-177.

Patek 1993: E. Patek, Westungarn in der Hallstattzeit. Acta humaniora 7 (Weinheim 1993).

Popović/Vukmanović 1992: P. Popović/M. Vukmanović, Some remarks on the Early Iron Age Cemetery at Vajuga-Pesak. Balcanica 23, 1992, 359-366.

Popović/Vukmanović 1998: P. Popović/M. Vukmanović, Vajuga-Pesak. Nekropola starijeg gvozdenog doba. Early Iron Age cemetery Vajuga Pesak (Beograd 1998).

Potrebica 2004: H. Potrebica, Tumuli in the Hallstatt landscape. Continuity and transformation. In: L. Šmejda/J. Turek (eds.), Spatial analysis of funerary areas (Plzeň 2004) 115-128.

Potrebica 2008: H. Potrebica, Kaptol-Gradci, iztraživanjje 2007. Annales Instituti Archaeologici – Godišnjak Instituta za arheologiju (Zagreb) 6, 2010,109-112.

Potrebica 2013: H. Potrebica, Kneževi željeznoga doba (Zagreb 2013).

Preinfalk 2003: F. Preinfalk, Die hallstattzeitlichen Hügelgräber von Langenlebern, Niederösterreich. Fundberichte aus Österreich Materialhefte A 12 (Horn 2003).

Puš 1985: I. Puš Molnik pri Ljubljani. Grobišče starejse železne dobe. Arheološki Pregled 26, 1985, 74-75.

Puš 1991: I. Puš, Molnik. Sedež prazgodovinskih knezov (Ljubljana 1991).

Raczky *et al.* 2001: P. Raczky/M. Szabó/T. Kovács/J. Laszlovsky, Significant archaeological excavations in Hungary 1975-2000. Exhibition catalogue Budapest (Budapest 2001).

Sauer 2015: F. Sauer, Eisen – Gräber – Trinkgelage. Die Hallstattkultur und das Burgenland. Fundberichte aus Österreich, Sonderheft 24 (Wien 2015).

Schappelwein 1999: C. Schappelwein, Vom Dreieck zum Mäander: Untersuchungen zum Motivschatz der Kalenderbergkultur und angrenzender Regionen. Universitätsforschungen zur Prähistorischen Archäologie 61 (Bonn 1999).

Schauer 1988: P. Schauer, Die Kegel- und Glockenförmigen Helme mit gegossenem Scheitelknauf der jüngeren Bronzezeit Alteuropas. In: Antike Helme. Sammlung Lipperheide und andere Bestände des Antikenmuseums Berlin. Monographien des Römisch-Germansichen Zentralmuseums Mainz (Mainz 1988) 181-194.

Schumann 2015: R. Schumann, Status und Prestige in der Hallstattkultur. Münchner Archäologische Forschungen 3 (Rahden/Westf. 2015).

Siegfried-Weiß 1980: A. Siegfried-Weiß, Der Ostalpenraum in der Hallstattzeit und seine Beziehungen zum Mittelmeer. Hamburger Beiträge zur Archäologie 6 (Hamburg 1980).

Šimek 2004: M. Šimek, Grupa Martijanec-Kaptol, Martijanec-Kaptol Group, Martijanec-Kaptol-Gruppe. In: Ratnici na razmeđu istoka i zapada starije Željezno Doba u kontinentalnoj Hrvatskoj. Warriors at the crossroads of east and west. Krieger am Scheideweg zwischen Ost und West (Zagreb 2004) 79-129.

Šimić 2004: J. Šimić, Grupa Dalj, Dalj Group, Dalj-Gruppe. In: Ratnici na razmeđu istoka i zapada starije Željezno Doba u kontinentalnoj Hrvatskoj. Warriors at the crossroads of east and west. Krieger am Scheideweg zwischen Ost und West (Zagreb 2004) 36-77.

Smolnik 1994: R. Smolnik, Der Burgstallkogel bei Kleinklein II. Die Keramik der vorgeschichtlichen Siedlung (Marburg 1994).

Stary 1981: P. Stary, Zur eisenzeitlichen Bewaffnung und Kampfesweise in Mittelitalien: ca. 9. bis 6. Jh. v. Chr. Marburger Studien zur Vor- und Frühgeschichte 3 (Mainz 1981).

Teržan 1976: B. Teržan, Certoška fibula. Arheološki Vestnik 27, 1976, 317-536.

Teržan 1990: B. Teržan Starejša železna doba na Slovenskem Štajerskem. The Early Iron Age in Slovenian Styria. Katalogi in Monografije 25 (Ljubljana 1990).

Teržan 1996: B. Teržan Weben und Zeitmessen im südostalpinen und westpannonischen Gebiet. In: E. Jerem/A. Lippert (eds.), Die Osthallstattkultur. Akten des internationalen Symposiums, Sopron, 10.-14. Mai 1994. Archaeolingua 7 (Budapest 1996) 507-536.

Teržan 1998: B. Teržan, Auswirkungen des skythisch geprägten Kulturkreises auf die hallstattzeitlichen Kulturgruppen Pannoniens und des Ostalpenraumes. In: B. Hänsel/J. Machnik (eds.), Das Karpatenbecken und die osteuropäische Steppe. Nomadenbewegungen und Kulturaustausch in den vorchristlichen Metallzeiten (4000-500 v. Chr.). Symposium Mogilany 1995 (München, Rahden 1998) 511-560

Tomanič-Jevremov 1988/1989: M. Tomanič-Jevremov, Žarno grobišče v Ormožu. Arheološki Vestnik 39/40, 1988/89, 277-304.

Tomanič-Jevremov 2001: M. Tomanič-Jevremov, The 'urbanisation' of Ormož and the cemeteries. In: A. Lippert (ed.), Die Drau – Mur- und Raab-Region im 1. vorchristlichen Jahrtausend. Akten des internationalen interdisziplinären Symposiums vom 26. bis 29. April 2000 in Bad Radkersburg. Universitätsforschungen zur Prähistorischen Archäologie 78 (Bonn 2001) 191-205.

Tomedi 1996: G. Tomedi, Nochmals zur „Fabel von den Traditonsschwertern". Weitere Randbemerkungen zu den Schwertgräbern des Südostalpenraumes und zur „Schwertgrabchronologie". In: Th. Stöllner (ed.), Europa celtica. Veröffentlichungen des Vorgeschichtlichen Seminars Marburg, Sonderband 10 (Marburg 1996) 167-188.

Tomedi 2002: G. Tomedi, Das hallstattzeitliche Gräberfeld von Frög (Kärnten). Die Altgrabungen von 1883-1892. Archaeolingua 14 (Budapest 2002).

Trajković 2008: D. Trajković, Đepfeld – Nekropola starijeg gvozdenog doba kod Doroslova. Đepfeld – Early Iron Age necropolis at Doroslovo (Sombor 2008).

Truhelka 1904: Ć. Truhelka, Der vorgeschichtliche Pfahlbau im Savebett bei Donja Dolina. Wissenschaftliche Mitteilungen aus Bosnien und der Herzegowina 9, 1904, 3-170.

Vadász 1983: E. Vadász, Előzetes jelentés egy koravaskori halomsír feltárásáról Süttőn. Vorbericht über die Erschließung eines früheisenzeitlichen Hügels bei Süttő. Communicationes Archaeologiae Hungariae 1983, 19-54.

Vasić 1999: R. Vasić, Die Fibeln im Zentralbalkan (Vojvodina, Serbien, Kosovo und Makedonien). Prähistorische Bronzefunde XIV,12 (Stuttgart 1999).

Vejvoda/Mirnik 1971: V. Vejvoda/I. Mirnik, Istraživanja prethistorijskih tumula u Kaptolu kraj Slavonski Požege. Vjesnik Arheološki Muzej Zagreb 5, 197, 183-210.

Vejvoda/Mirnik 1973: V. Vejvoda/I. Mirnik, Halštatski kneževski grobovi iz Kaptola kod Slavonski Požege. Arheološki Vestnik 24, 1973, 592-610.

Vidović 1983: J. Vidović, Nastavak istraživanja perioda starijeg železnog doba na lokalitetu – Goričan '82. Muzejski Vjesnik (Zagreb) 7, 1984, 93-97.

Vidovic 1989: J. Vidović, Nekropola tumula kraj sela Dvorišća kod Turčišća u Međimurju. In: Arheološka istraživanja u Podravina i Kalničko-Bilogorskoj regija. Conference Kovprivnica 1986 (Zagreb 1990) 77-88.

Vinski-Gasparini 1961: K. Vinski-Gasparini, Iskopavanje kneževskog tumulske kod Martijanca u Podravini. Vjesnik Arheološki Muzej Zagreb 2, 1961, 39-66.

Vinki-Gasparini 1987: K. Vinski-Gasparini, Grupa Martijanec-Kaptol. In: Praistorija Jugoslovenskih zemalja 5 željezno doba (Sarajevo 1987) 182-231.

Vulpe 1986: A. Vulpe, Zur Entstehung der geto-dakischen Zivilisation. Die Basarabi-Kultur. Dacia N.S. 30, 1986, 49-89.

Vulpe 1990: A. Vulpe, Die Kurzschwerter, Dolche und Streitmesser der Hallstattzeit in Rumänien. Prähistorische Bronzefunde VI,9 (München 1990).

Author

Carola Metzner-Nebelsick
Ludwig-Maximilians-Universität
Institut für Vor- und Frühgeschichtliche Archäologie und Provinzialrömische Archäologie
Geschwister-Scholl-Platz 1
80539 München
Germany
metzner-nebelsick@vfpa.fak12.uni-muenchen.de